PERSPECTIVES
ON ORGANIZATION
DESIGN AND BEHAVIOR

Wiley Series On
ORGANIZATIONAL ASSESSMENT AND CHANGE

Series Editors:
**Edward E. Lawler III and
Stanley E. Seashore**

**Assessing Organizational Change:
The Rushton Quality
of Work Experiment**
by Paul S. Goodman and Associates

Measuring and Assessing Organizations
by Andrew H. Van de Ven and Diane L. Ferry

**Organizational Assessment: Perspectives on the Measurement of
Organizational Behavior and Quality of Working Life**
edited by Edward E. Lawler III, David A. Nadler and Cortlandt Cammann

Perspectives on Organization Design and Behavior
edited by Andrew H. Van de Ven and William F. Joyce

Work and Health
by Robert L. Kahn

SCHEDULED BOOKS

**The Quality of Worklife Approach To Management:
An Assessment of Its Use in New Plants**
by Veronica F. Nieva, Dennis N. T. Perkins, and Edward E. Lawler III

Employee Productivity and the Quality of Work Life
by Richard E. Walton and Leonard Schlesinger

**Observing and Measuring Organizational Change:
A Guide to Field Practice**
edited by Stanley E. Seashore, Edward E. Lawler III, Philip H. Mirvis,
and Cortlandt Cammann

The Bolivar Quality of Work Experiment: 1972–1978
by Barry A. Macy, Edward E. Lawler III, and Gerald E. Ledford, Jr.

Group Relations and Organizational Diagnosis
by Clayton P. Alderfer, L. Dave Brown, Robert E. Kaplan and Ken K.
Smith

Managing Strategic Change
by Noel Tichy

PERSPECTIVES ON ORGANIZATION DESIGN AND BEHAVIOR

Edited by

ANDREW H. VAN DE VEN
School of Management
University of Minnesota

and

WILLIAM F. JOYCE
The Wharton School
University of Pennsylvania

A WILEY-INTERSCIENCE PUBLICATION

JOHN WILEY & SONS
New York   Chichester   Brisbane   Toronto   Singapore

Library of Congress Cataloging in Publication Data:

Main entry under title:
  Perspectives on organization design and behavior.

  (Wiley series on organizational assessment and
change, ISSN 0194-0120)
  "A Wiley-Interscience publication."
  Includes indexes.
  1. Organizational behavior—Addresses, essays,
lectures. I. Van de Ven, Andrew H. II. Joyce,
William F. III. Series.

HD58.7.P48   658.4   81-11550
ISBN 0-471-09358-0   AACR2

Printed in the United States of America

10 9 8 7 6 5 4 3 2

To Martha and Jim,
Linda and Jeff

About the Contributors

W. GRAHAM ASTLEY is Assistant Professor of Management at The Wharton School, University of Pennsylvania. He obtained his Ph.D. in Administrative Theory and Organization Behavior from the University of Washington in 1978. From 1978 to 1979 he held a research fellowship at the University of Bradford Management Centre (England), where he served as a member of a team conducting a comparative empirical study of the strategic decision-making process in a wide variety of organizations.

Professor Astley is currently researching and writing on organization design, strategic decision making, and power relations within and between organizations.

CORTLANDT CAMMANN is Assistant Professor of Psychology at the University of Michigan in Ann Arbor. He also serves as an Associate Research Scientist at the Institute for Social Research, a position he has held since 1977. Professor Cammann received his Ph.D. in Administrative Sciences from Yale University in 1974, and he has worked at the University of Michigan since that time. His recent publications have included *Organizational Perspectives on the Measurement of Organizational Behavior and the Quality of Work Life* (New York: Wiley-Interscience, 1980), co-edited with Professors Edward Lawler and David Nadler.

ALFRED D. CHANDLER, JR., is Straus Professor of Business History at Harvard University. Since obtaining his Ph.D. from Harvard in 1952, Professor Chandler has had a distinguished career. His posts have included professorships at the Massachusetts Institute of Technology (1950–1963), Johns Hopkins University (1963–1970), and Harvard University (1970–present). He has also served as a Visiting Fellow at All Souls College, Oxford (1975), Visiting Professor at the European Institute for Studies in Advanced Management, Brussels (1979), Guggenheim Fellow (1958–1959), and Editor of the *Harvard Studies in Business History* (1971–present). He has served on numerous professional and advisory committees.

In addition, Professor Chandler has written many books and articles, including his recent Newcomen-, Bancroft-, and Pulitzer-Prize winning *The Visible Hand—The Managerial Revolution in American Business* (Cambridge, MA: Harvard University Press, 1977). He continues to do writing and research on the history of business in America.

J. RICHARD HACKMAN is Professor of Organization and Management and Professor of Psychology at Yale University. He obtained his Ph.D. in Social Psychology from the University of Illinois at Urbana. He has been teaching at Yale since 1966, and in the 1980–1981 academic year he served as Visiting Professor of Psychology at the University of Michigan in Ann Arbor and Visiting Research Scientist at the Institute for Social Research. His most recent book is a collaboration with Greg Oldham entitled *Work Redesign* (Reading, MA: Addison-Wesley, 1980).

LAWRENCE G. HREBINIAK is Associate Professor of Management at The Wharton School, University of Pennsylvania. He received his Ph.D. in Organization Theory and Management from the State University of New York at Buffalo in 1971. Professor Hrebiniak has taught at SUNY at Buffalo (1968–1970), Pennsylvania State University (1971–1976), and the University of Pennsylvania (1976–present).

Professor Hrebiniak has served on the Editorial Board of *Administrative Science Quarterly* since 1978. He has published numerous journal articles and is author of *Complex Organizations* (St. Paul: West Publishing Co., 1978). Professor Hrebiniak is currently working on another book (with William F. Joyce), which is an attempt to integrate and relate the areas of organizational strategy, design, and change. It is titled *Implementing Strategy,* and it is scheduled for publication in January, 1982 (New York: Macmillan).

WILLIAM F. JOYCE is Assistant Professor of Management at The Wharton School, University of Pennsylvania. He has taught at The Wharton School since obtaining his Ph.D. in Organizational Behavior from Pennsylvania State University in 1978. Before coming to the University of Pennsylvania, Professor Joyce served as an Instructor at Penn State and Bucknell University.

Professor Joyce has published several articles dealing with organizational climates, organization design, and research methodology. His current interests are in the area of organization design and strategy implementation. He is co-author of two forthcoming books: *Implementing Strategy* (with Lawrence Hrebiniak, New York: Macmillan) and *Organization Design* (with Jay Galbraith, 2nd ed., Reading, MA: Addison-Wesley).

JOHN R. KIMBERLY is an Associate Professor in the Schools of Organization and Management and the Center for Health Studies at Yale

University. He received his Ph.D. in Organization Behavior from Cornell University in 1970. From 1970 through 1975, Professor Kimberly taught at the University of Illinois, where he worked in both the Department of Sociology and the Institute of Labor and Industrial Relations. In the 1975–1976 academic year, he was a Visiting Professor at the Centre de Recherche en Gestion (Ecole Polytechnique) in Paris. Since 1977, Professor Kimberly has taught at Yale University. His most recent publication includes *The Organizational Life Cycle* (co-edited with Robert H. Miles, San Francisco: Jossey-Bass, 1980).

PAUL R. LAWRENCE is the Wallace Brett Donham Professor of Organizational Behavior at Harvard University. He received his M.B.A. (1947) and D.C.S. (1950) from the Harvard Business School, where he has taught since 1947. In addition, he serves as Chairman of the Organizational Behavior program at Harvard. He is also Director for the Millipore Corporation, a position he has held since 1975.

Professor Lawrence is the author of a number of well-known books and articles, including *Organization and Environment: Managing Differentiation and Integration* (written with Professor Jay Lorsch and published by Richard D. Irwin, Homewood, IL, 1969). His latest book is entitled *Managing Large Research and Development Programs* (written with Henry Lane and Rodney Beddows and to be published by SUNY Press). His current research concentrates on organizational structures and environmental influences.

CHARLES E. LINDBLOM is Sterling Professor of Economics and Political Science and William Clyde DeVane Professor at Yale University. He is a member and former director of the Yale University Institution for Social and Policy Studies. Professor Lindblom obtained his Ph.D. in Economics from the University of Chicago in 1945. In addition to serving on the faculties of the University of Minnesota (1939–1946) and Yale University, Professor Lindblom has held a wide variety of professional and political posts, including Fellow of the Center for Advanced Studies in Behavioral Sciences (1954–1955), Guggenheim Fellow (1960–1961), and Economic Advisor to the American Ambassador and to the Director of the U.S. AID Mission to India (1963–1965). His publications include a number of well-known books, such as his recent *Usable Knowledge: Social Science and Social Problem Solving* (with David K. Cohen, New Haven: Yale University Press, 1979).

JAMES G. MARCH is the Fred H. Merrill Professor of Management at Stanford University and a Senior Fellow at the Hoover Institution. He also has appointments to the Political Science, Sociology, and Education departments of Stanford University. Professor March received his Ph.D. from Yale University in 1953. Since that time he has taught at the Carnegie Institute of Technology (1953–1964) and served as Dean of the

School of Social Sciences at the University of California, Irvine (1964–1970). He is the author of numerous publications, including the classic *Organizations* (co-authored with Herbert Simon, New York: Wiley, 1958).

WILLIAM G. OUCHI obtained his Ph.D. in Business Administration from the University of Chicago in 1972. Since that time he has taught at Stanford University (1972–1979) and the University of California at Los Angeles, where he is now Professor of Management. His recent work includes research on the organization and management of Japanese business, and he has collaborated with Oliver Williamson on a number of articles concerning the Markets and Hierarchies research program. Professor Ouchi's latest book is entitled *Theory Z: How American Business Can Meet the Japanese Challenge* (Reading, Mass: Addison-Wesley, 1981).

CHARLES PERROW is Professor at the Behavior Science Center, Stanford, California. Prior to that he was Professor of Sociology at the State University of New York, Stony Brook. He received his Ph.D. in sociology from the University of California, Berkeley in 1960. Since that time Professor Perrow has served on the faculties of the University of Michigan (1960–1963), the University of Pittsburgh (1963–1968), the University of Wisconsin at Madison (1968–1970), and SUNY Stony Brook (1970–present). He has also been a Visiting Professor at the University of California, Berkeley (1968–1969) and the London Graduate School of Business (1972–1973).

Professor Perrow has written numerous books including a recent revision of his widely used *Complex Organizations: A Critical Essay* (Glenview, IL: Scott, Foresman, and Company, 1979). He is working on two new books: *A Society of Organizations,* dealing with the development and spread of industrial bureaucracy in the United States, and *Normal Accidents,* examining the occurrence of synergistic accidents in complex, tightly coupled high-risk systems.

JEFFREY PFEFFER is Professor of Organizational Behavior and Sociology at Stanford University, where he has taught since 1979. Professor Pfeffer obtained his Ph.D. from Stanford in 1972. Since that time, he has taught at the University of Illinois (1971–1973) and the University of California, Berkeley (1973–1979). His most recent book is titled *Power in Organizations* (Marshfield, MA: Pitman Publishers, 1981). He is also co-author with Gerald Salancik of *The External Control of Organizations: A Resource Dependence Perspective* (New York: Harper and Row, 1978).

DEREK S. PUGH is Professor of Organizational Behaviour at the London Graduate School of Business Studies. He graduated in psychology and industrial sociology at the University of Edinburgh and was awarded a

Doctor of Science degree in Organizational Behaviour from the University of Aston in Birmingham.

In the 1960s he was the senior member of the Industrial Administration Research Group at the University of Aston, which inaugurated the Aston program. In the 1970s, since going to the London Business School, he has led a program of developments from that work. He is currently concerned with longitudinal studies of organizational processes of stability and change.

Professor Pugh is the joint author and editor of the first three books in the Aston series: *Organizational Structure in Its Context* (1976, with D.J. Hickson), *Organizational Structure: Extensions and Replications* (1976, with C.R. Hinings), and *Organizational Behaviour in Its Context* (1977, with R.L. Payne)—all published by Saxon House (Gower Press in Britain and D.C. Heath [Lexington Books] in the United States). He is currently working on the fifth volume in the series, provisionally entitled *The Aston Approach: Developments and Critiques*. In addition, he is the joint author or editor of six books and many articles on aspects of organizational behavior and management education.

STANLEY SEASHORE is Professor of Psychology at the University of Michigan in Ann Arbor. He also serves as the Program Director of the Institute for Social Research and as Coordinator of research on organizational behavior at that institute. He received his Ph.D. in Social Psychology from the University of Michigan (1954) and has been teaching there from 1955 to the present. His latest book is *Observing and Measuring Organizational Change: A Guide to Field Practice* (New York: Wiley-Interscience, 1982).

WILLIAM H. STARBUCK is the Evan and Marion Helfaer Professor of Business Administration at the University of Wisconsin, Milwaukee. He received his doctorate from Carnegie-Mellon University, and he has served on the faculties of Purdue University (1960–1967), Cornell University (1967–1971), and the University of Wisconsin (1974–present). He has also been a visiting professor at Johns Hopkins University (1966–1967), the London Graduate School of Business Studies (1970–1971), the Norwegian School of Economics and Business Administration (1977–78), the Stockholm School of Economics (1977–1978), and the University of Gothenberg (1977–1978). From 1971 to 1974 he served as a Senior Research Fellow at the International Institute of Management in Berlin.

He has published numerous articles on a wide range of topics, and he has edited four books, including the *Handbook of Organizational Design* (co-edited with Paul C. Nystrom, London: Oxford University Press, 1981).

ERIC L. TRIST is Professor of Environmental Studies at York University in Ontario, Canada, and Emeritus Professor of Organizational Behavior and Ecology at The Wharton School, University of Pennsylvania. He is also the Chairman of The Wharton School's Management and Behavioral Science Research Center. He obtained his degree in Psychology from Cambridge University in 1933.

After World War II, Professor Trist became a founding member of the Tavistock Institute of Human Relations in London. He served with the Tavistock for over twenty years, the last eight of which he was chairman of the Institute.

From 1960 to 1961, Professor Trist was a Fellow at the Center for Advanced Studies in the Behavioral Sciences. While there, he wrote one of his best-known books, *Organizational Choice* (co-authored with G.W. Higgin, H. Murray, and A.B. Pollock, London: Tavistock, 1963). In 1966 he joined the faculty of the School of Management at UCLA, where he helped develop the first graduate program in sociotechnical systems. In 1969, Professor Trist left UCLA and moved to The Wharton School. After his retirement there, Professor Trist went on to York University, where he is still active.

In addition to having published numerous articles and books, Professor Trist serves as co-ordinating editor of the journal *Human Relations*.

ANDREW H. VAN DE VEN recently joined the School of Management at the University of Minnesota. From 1975 to 1981 he was Professor of Management and Director of the Doctoral Program in Organization and Management at The Wharton School of the University of Pennsylvania. He was also Associate Director of the Center for the Study of Organizational Innovation, which sponsored the conference at which the papers presented in this book were originally presented (in April 1980 at the University of Pennsylvania). He received his Ph.D. in Interdisciplinary Program Administration from the University of Wisconsin at Madison in 1972, and he was a faculty member at Kent State University from 1972 to 1975. Professor Van de Ven's research has focused on assessing alternative organizational designs; organizational planning, coordination, and innovation; and group processes for problem solving and decision making. He has published numerous articles and is the author of *Group Decision Making and Effectiveness* (Kent State University Press, 1974), co-author (with Andre Delbecq and David Gustafson) of *Group Techniques for Program Planning* (Addison-Wesley, 1975), and co-author (with Diane Ferry) of *Measuring and Assessing Organizations* (Wiley-Interscience, 1980). He is now preparing a book, *Organizing Collective Action,* which is based on a longitudinal study of planning, implementing, and coordinating fourteen new Texas child care organizations from 1972 to 1981.

OLIVER E. WILLIAMSON is the Charles and William L. Day Professor of Economics and Social Science at the University of Pennsylvania. He is also the director of the Center for the Study of Organizational Innovation, and his secondary appointments include professorships in the University of Pennsylvania's School of Law, the School of Public and Urban Policy, and Decision Sciences Department. Professor Williamson received his Ph.D. in Economics from Carnegie-Mellon University in 1963. Before coming to the University of Pennsylvania, he taught at the University of California, Berkeley (1963–1965). He was a Guggenheim Fellow and a Fellow at the Center for Advanced Studies in the Behavioral Sciences in 1977–1978. Professor Williamson served as Editor of the *Bell Journal of Economics* from 1975 to 1981. He is author of *Markets and Hierarchies: Analysis and Antitrust Implications* (New York: Free Press, 1975).

Series Preface

The ORGANIZATIONAL ASSESSMENT AND CHANGE SERIES is concerned with informing and furthering contemporary debate on the effectiveness of work organizations and the quality of life they provide for their members. Of particular relevance is the adaptation of work organizations to changing social aspirations and economic constraints. There has been a phenomenal growth of interest in the quality of work life and productivity in recent years. Issues that not long ago were the quiet concern of a few academics and a few leaders in unions and management have become issues of broader public interest. They have intruded upon broadcast media prime time, lead newspaper and magazine columns, the houses of Congress, and the board rooms of both firms and unions.

A thorough discussion of what organizations should be like and how they can be improved must comprehend many issues. Some are concerned with basic moral and ethical questions—What is the responsibility of an organization to its employees?—What, after all, is a "good job"?—How should it be decided that some might benefit from and others pay for gains in the quality of work life?—Should there be a public policy on the matter? Yet others are concerned with the strategies and tactics of bringing about changes in organizational life, the advocates of alternative approaches being numerous, vocal, and controversial; and still others are concerned with the task of measurement and assessment on grounds that the choices to be made by leaders, the assessment of consequences, and the bargaining of equities must be informed by reliable, comprehensive, and relevant information of kinds not now readily available.

The WILEY SERIES ON ORGANIZATIONAL ASSESSMENT AND CHANGE is concerned with all aspects of the debate on how organizations should be managed, changed, and controlled. It includes books on organizational effectiveness, and the study of organizational changes that represent new approaches to organization design and process. The volumes in the series have in common a concern with work organizations, a focus on change and the dynamics of change, an assumption that diverse social and personal interests need to be taken into account in discussions of organizational effectiveness, and a view that concrete cases and quantitative data are essential ingredients in a lucid debate. As such, these books consider a broad but integrated set of issues and ideas. They are intended to be read by managers, union officials, researchers, consultants, policy makers, students, and others seriously concerned with organizational assessment and change.

This volume, *Perspectives on Organizational Design and Behavior,* is central to the purpose of the series. It brings together, in a way that accentuates their differences and complementarities, the leading contemporary approaches to the understanding of work organizations. Each of the approaches selected for inclusion stems from theoretical and empirical inquiry extending over many years and conducted by teams of researchers and practitioners. Each has been subjected to field application to the end of explaining or influencing the effectiveness of "live" organizations engaged in their usual work activities. The extent to which the several approaches are supported, or brought into question, by such demanding tests is variable as the text shows, and is a matter for constructive debate. This debate is enlivened in critical analyses by invited commentators who are themselves notable contributors to organizational theory and who enter the debate from nonpartisan, or from their own unique perspectives. Overview chapters attempt to consolidate and integrate the conclusions to be drawn from this comparison of approaches, and to suggest main themes for future work.

EDWARD E. LAWLER III
STANLEY E. SEASHORE

Ann Arbor, Michigan
August 1981

Preface

This book presents original essays by leading researchers that describe and evaluate the major perspectives on organization design and behavior. The objective of this book is to advance theory and practice in this area. The research programs undertaken by these investigators have had a significant influence on our thinking about organization design and behavior, and many are being assimilated into what might be called "mainstream" organization theory and practice. However, as the commentaries, rejoinders, and debates in this book will indicate, each perspective is not without its limitations, and each is far from representing a completed product. Furthermore, the research programs examined in this book are not all-inclusive of the eclectic domain called organization design and behavior. A number of additional fresh "new" perspectives on organizations are beginning to surface and command attention. We believe that a careful evaluation of the "mainstream" perspectives and an appreciation of "new" perspectives on organization design and behavior are fundamental for injecting and redirecting theory and practice. This is an agenda that is both exciting and challenging for the future.

Two growing concerns led to the development of this book: a need to make sense of varying perspectives in the literature on organization design and a need for a novel and broader conception of organization design and behavior than now is available in any single perspective.

Several trends are causing us to extend our perspectives on organization design and behavior. Many practitioners and theorists believe that organizations are operating in more complex environments than ever before. This complexity is reflected throughout public and private organizational life. Consider, for example, the multiple and conflicting goals of most organizations; the growing environmental constraints, regulations, and opportunities confronting organizations; the increasing sophistication of technology and the tasks to which it is put; and the many partisan groups involved in the strategic issues that confront top managers of today's complex organizations.

Under these conditions, many of the axioms of classical organization theory seem less useful. Psychologists, sociologists, economists, political scientists, anthropologists, and management theorists began actively searching for alternative perspectives on organization design and behavior around 1950. The literature thus engendered has gone a long way to increase our breadth and depth of understanding, but it has also added complexity and confusion to the subject. It is no longer correct to say that there is one dominant or correct approach to structuring organizations and to managing the behavior of individuals within them. There are now many perspectives on organization design and behavior, as well as numerous instances of convergent and divergent research findings. To further understanding of this area, we believe it is timely to take stock of what has been learned and to explore what new directions can further theory and practice.

In order to do this, the Center for the Study of Organizational Innovation at the University of Pennsylvania sponsored a conference in April 1980. The leading contributors from some of the major research programs on organization design and behavior were invited to present original papers. In each paper, contributors were asked to: (1) develop the conceptual foundations of their research program, (2) summarize the major findings that have emerged from their investigations, and (3) discuss the directions and implications of their work for future research and practice on organizational design and behavior. These perspectives are the central subject of this book.

To critically assess the strengths and weaknesses of each of these major research programs, as well as to draw out the connections among them, highly respected authorities in the field also prepared original commentaries. In their papers, commentators were asked to: (1) constructively critique the strengths and weaknesses of their assigned research program, (2) indicate the role and contributions of the perspective to our larger understanding of organization design and behavior, and (3) discuss promising future directions for research and practice that are stimulated by the research program. These commentaries are presented immediately after the major papers.

Following the conference, all contributing authors and commentors revised their papers based on suggestions provided at the conference and by the editors. In addition, each contributing author was given the opportunity to prepare a written rejoinder to the commentaries, and several took this opportunity to clarify their views. In one instance, the paper prepared by Oliver Williamson and William Ouchi and the commentary by Charles Perrow (in Chapter 8) stimulated rejoinders and a constructive debate by the contributing authors as well as by Alfred Chandler (upon the editors' request).

Finally, two panelists and the editors prepared original papers which took a broader view of these "schools" of organization design. These integrative papers, presented in Chapters 9 to 11, attempt to evaluate and synthesize our state of knowledge on organization design and performance and suggest some alternative views for mapping the field for future research and practice.

The preparation, editing, and revision of original papers by many busy contributing authors represented a major coordination task. Fortunately, we were ably assisted by Mr. Robert Freeland. He was instrumental in preparing the Notes about Contributing Authors and in carefully reading several drafts of each chapter—suggesting many ways to improve their readability and to detect errors in them. Furthermore, Mr. Freeland—along with Ms. Melinda Brunger—provided much administrative assistance in organizing and conducting the conference on which this book is based. Finally, we appreciate the support of the Center for the Study of Organizational Innovation at the University of Pennsylvania, which made the conference and this book possible.

ANDREW H. VAN DE VEN
WILLIAM F. JOYCE

Minneapolis
Philadelphia
September 1981

Contents

xxii   CONTENTS

Rejoinder to Starbuck   199
Derek S. Pugh

Chapter 5   Decision Making Perspective   205
Decisions in Organizations and Theories of Choice
James G. March, Stanford University
Comments on Decisions in Organizations   245
Charles E. Lindblom, Yale University

Chapter 6   The Organization Assessment Perspective   249
The Organization Assessment Research Program
Andrew H. Van de Ven, University of Minnesota
Comments on the Organization Assessment Research Program   299
Cortlandt Cammann, University of Michigan

Chapter 7   Organization and Environment Perspective   311
The Harvard Organization and Environment Research Program
Paul R. Lawrence, Harvard University
The Organization and Environment Research Program: and
Overview and Critique   338
Lawrence G. Hrebiniak, University of Pennsylvania

Chapter 8   The Markets and Hierarchies and Visible
             Hand Perspectives   347
The Markets and Hierarchies Program of Research: Origins,
Implications, Prospects
Oliver E. Williamson, University of Pennsylvania
William G. Ouchi, University of California, Los Angeles
Markets, Hierarchies and Hegemony   371
Charles Perrow, State University of New York, Stony
Brook
A Rejoinder   387
Oliver E. Williamson and William G. Ouchi
Historical Determinants of Managerial Hierarchies: A
Response to Perrow   391
Alfred D. Chandler, Jr., Harvard University
Postscript   403
Charles Perrow
A Final Response   405
Alfred D. Chandler, Jr.

PERSPECTIVES
ON ORGANIZATION
DESIGN AND BEHAVIOR

CHAPTER ONE

Overview of Perspectives on Organization Design and Behavior

ANDREW H. VAN DE VEN
University of Minnesota

WILLIAM F. JOYCE
University of Pennsylvania

This book describes, evaluates, and integrates some of the major perspectives on organization design and behavior in order to advance theory and practice. Two growing concerns led to the development of this book: a need to make sense of varying perspectives in the literature on organization design and a need for a novel and broader conception of organization design and behavior than is presently available in any single perspective.

A number of trends are causing us to extend our perspectives on organization design and behavior. Many practitioners and theorists believe that organizations are operating in more complex environments than ever before. This complexity is reflected throughout public and private organizational life. Consider, for example, the multiple and conflicting goals of most organizations; the growing environmental constraints, regulations, and opportunities confronting organizations; the increasing sophistication of technology and the tasks to which it is put; and the many partisan groups involved in the strategic issues that confront top managers of today's complex organizations.

Under these conditions many of the axioms of classical organization theory seem less useful. The past 30 years have witnessed an active search for alternative perspectives on organization design and behavior by psychologists, sociologists, economists, political scientists, anthropologists, and management theorists. This literature has gone a long way to increase our breadth and depth of understanding, but it has also added complexity and confusion to the subject. It is no longer correct to say that there is one dominant, rational approach to structuring organizations and to managing the behavior of individuals within them. There are now many perspectives on organization design and behavior, as well as numerous instances of convergent and divergent research findings. In order to further our understanding, we believe it is time to take stock of what has been learned and to explore new directions that can further theory and practice.

In order to do this, the Center for the Study of Organizational Innovation at the University of Pennsylvania sponsored a conference in April 1980. The leading contributors from some of the major research programs on organization design and behavior were invited to present original papers. In each paper contributors were asked to: (1) develop the conceptual foundations of their research program; (2) summarize the major findings that have followed from their investigations; and (3) discuss the directions and implications of their work for future research and practice on organizational design and performance. These perspectives are the subject of the next seven chapters of this book.

In order to critically assess the strengths and weakness of each of these major research programs, as well as to draw out the connections among them, highly respected authorities in the field were also invited to prepare commentaries. These commentators were asked to: (1) constructively criticize the strengths and weaknesses of their assigned research program; (2) indicate the role and contributions of the program to our larger understanding of organization design and behavior; and (3) discuss promising future directions for research and practice that are stimulated by the program. These commentaries are presented immediately after the major papers in each of the next seven chapters.

Finally, two panelists and the editors prepared original papers that took a broader view of these "schools" of organization design. These integrative papers, presented in Chapters 9 to 11, attempt to evaluate and synthesize the state of our knowledge on organization design and performance and suggest some alternative views for mapping the field for future research and practice.

Following the conference, all contributing authors and commentators revised their papers based upon suggestions provided at the conference and by the editors. In addition, each contributing author was given the opportunity to prepare a written rejoinder to the commentaries, which two authors accepted. In one instance, the paper prepared by Oliver Williamson and William Ouchi and the commentary by Charles Perrow (in Chapter 8) stimulated rejoinders and constructive debate by the contributing authors as well as Alfred Chandler, upon the editors' request.

SELECTION OF PERSPECTIVES ON ORGANIZATION DESIGN AND BEHAVIOR

In selecting programs of research to be represented at the conference and in this book, one important question was which of many significant perspectives on organization design and behavior should be included. Beyond practical constraints of length and cost, the selection of research programs was based on a set of criteria flowing from a definition of organization design.

The design of an organization is the structural arrangement of resources (land, labor, and capital) of an organization in order to achieve desired ends. The structural arrangements are usually the products of decisions about: (1) how to divide the labor (vertical and horizontal differentiation); (2) what forms of departmental structures to adopt (functional, program, geographic, and matrix arrangements); (3) what forms of programs should be used to organize the work of units and positions (systematized, discretionary, and developmental); (4) how power and authority are to be distributed within and among organizational units; and (5) what systems of coordination, control, and incentives are appropriate for achieving collective ends. Beyond these standard notions of what organization design "is," two themes influenced the selection of the research programs to be included here.

First, organization design requires more than making decisions about the internal structure of an organization. Organizations do not exist in a vacuum. Their internal designs are often a significant reflection of: (1) strategic choices elaborated over many years; (2) the shifting complexity, uncertainty, and restrictiveness of the environment or industry in which they operate; and (3) cultural prescriptions concerning performance norms, power, interpersonal behavior, trust, and ethical conduct, which are enforced by society and variously adopted by individuals both within and outside the organization. An appreciation of organization design and behavior requires a multidisciplinary perspective across many levels of analysis: the individual, group, organization, industry or population of organizations, and macrosocial movements. Artificial barriers that now separate strategy, micro and macroorganization behavior, institutional economics, decision sciences, and political sciences are not germane to the development of new perspectives on organization design.

Second, organization design is not just a noun or a "thing"; it is also a verb that emphasizes the *processes* by which structural arrangements are created and changed. Generally the process aspects of organization design have been overlooked in favor of the development of general organizational alternatives and the linking of these alternatives to situational factors. Issues of diagnosis, intervention, and evaluation have received less attention than they deserve. Value judgments underlying definitions of organizational goals, performance criteria, and issues of power, subordination, and views of human beings inherent in any perspective of organization design tend to remain ignored and unrecognized. Organization design is not simply a technocratic process of adjusting means to ends; it is also a social and political series of engagements among partisan individuals and interest groups who enter and leave the decision process as their volition and commitments dictate. An understanding of collective processes of choice behavior and their normative implications needs to be incorporated in a perspective on organization design.

Seven research programs were chosen for presentation here because each has taken a position on these broader issues of organization design. Some have emphasized one aspect more than another, but each has adopted a perspective that has significantly influenced our thinking about organization design and behavior. As the commentaries, rejoinders, and debates will indicate, each research program is not without its limitations and is far from representing a complete product. However, the seven programs have achieved the following criteria of distinction:

1. They are each firmly grounded on a conceptual base, and research has been conducted in a number of organizations over the years to assess their underlying theories.

2. Each program represents a significant commitment of time and resources by groups of researchers toward the development and evaluation of a basic set of ideas, rather than simply being short-term efforts at theory building and research.

3. Each program has established a track record of followers over the years, indicating that they not only have made significant contributions in the past, but also that they will likely continue to have impact and set a standard for theory and practice in the foreseeable future.

Based on these considerations, the following research programs on organization design and behavior were chosen as the focus of this book.

THE SEVEN RESEARCH PROGRAMS

The Sociotechnical Systems Program of Research

A major and influential program of research on organization design and performance was initiated by the Tavistock Institute of Human Relations in London. One of the principal founders of the Institute is Eric Trist, who has maintained contact with the Institute since he came to the United

States in 1966. The Institute was founded in 1946 with the aid of a grant from the Rockefeller Foundation to undertake action research in the broader social field outside the mental health area with which the Tavistock Clinic was concerned. As Trist describes in Chapter 2, a main thrust of the Institute's research program has expanded into a number of other organizations and countries since then, and has become known as the sociotechnical perspective on organizations.

Sociotechnical theory relies on two essential premises. First, in a purposive organization in which people are required to perform functions, there is a joint system operating: a social and a technical system. The performance of an organization is a function of the fit between these two systems. Second, every sociotechnical system is embedded in an environment that is influenced by a culture and its values and sets of generally accepted practices, and the environment permits certain roles for organizations, groups, and people. To understand a work system, one must understand the environmental forces that are operating on it.

Based on these two premises, in Chapter 2 Trist sets forth the sociotechnical dimensions and principles of work design and focuses on the importance of the "primary work system" as the fundamental building block for applying these principles. Furthermore, Trist provides a rich historical description of the numerous studies that have been conducted over the years on the sociotechnical perspective at the job, work group, organization, and macrosocial levels, as well as principles for process intervention to create change in organizations at these levels.

In his commentary on Trist's paper, Richard Hackman raises and discusses six questions on the sociotechnical perspective:

1. What is being learned from sociotechnical work, and who is learning it?

2. Should one always opt for the autonomous work team as the basic performing unit in work systems?

3. What is to be done with individuals in highly interdependent work systems?

4. How much mileage can be gained from the sociotechnical notion of "key variances" in thinking about organization design?

5. What are the implications for scholarship and for action of approaching organizational design and change with the idea of merely attempting to create conditions for effective performance rather than trying to directly manage employee attitudes and behaviors?

6. What are the circumstances under which it is in fact feasible to create and maintain innovative organizational systems of the sociotechnical variety?

These questions are important not only to the further development of sociotechnical systems but to perspectives on organizational design and behavior in general. Hackman's observations provide a complementary perspective on sociotechnical propositions from one whose training has not been in this tradition, providing a useful point of departure for further research and practice.

The ISR Quality of Work Life Research Program

The Institute for Social Research at the University of Michigan was begun in 1947. It grew out of Rensis Likert's Division of Program Surveys, which was housed in the U.S. Department of Agriculture during World War II. Under the direction of Daniel Katz, Robert Kahn, Rensis Likert, Floyd Mann, Stanley Seashore, and Arnold Tannenbaum, the Michigan researchers have made important contributions to conceptualizing and measuring characteristics of organization design and behavior, as well as factors related to organization change and diffusion of innovations. Within the general theme of organization design and change, a large variety of research projects have been conducted at the ISR.

One of the most significant recent efforts has been the quality of work life program, which Seashore describes in Chapter 3. In response to requests by the National Commission on Productivity in 1973, the QWL program was organized. Its purposes were to develop measurement approaches for the evaluation of six demonstration-research experiments in planning organization change efforts with joint labor and management direction. In order to conduct the evaluation studies, the QWL researchers, under the direction of Stanley Seashore and Edward Lawler, developed the ISR Organizational Assessment Measurement Package. It includes a set of instruments to measure job and task characteristics, individual attitudes and perceptions, leader behavior, work group process, pay and performance evaluation, intergroup relations, and individual differences. In addition, the package contains a set of procedures for providing survey-based feedback to organizational participants involved in the planned change efforts. The ISR researchers have employed these instruments to evaluate the quality of work experiments and are now preparing a book, *Observing and Measuring Organizational Change* (Seashore et al., 1982), which will present the major findings obtained to date from their longitudinal evaluations. Seashore's chapter for this volume describes the methodology and assumptions utilized by the Michigan researchers in this assessment. Because of the scope and prominence of these investigations, Seashore's paper is important to all researchers and practitioners conducting field research in organizations.

In his commentary, William Joyce analyzes the methodological assumptions made by the Michigan researchers by reconstructing two models of organization assessment from Seashore's discussion. These models of assessment are utilized to illustrate implicit assumptions concerning the type of meaning to be emphasized in the Michigan research, the appropriate mode of inquiry in organization assessments, and the usefulness of eclectic approaches to organizational behavior. These implicit assumptions are shown to be consistent in encouraging the development of local understanding concerning the inducement of results judged important to organizational members but less consistent in furthering theory development.

The Aston Program of Research

In 1961 the Industrial Administration Research Unit of what is now known as the University of Aston in Birmingham, England, was formed with a grant obtained by Tom Lupton (then head of the Department of Industrial Administration) from the Department of Scientific and Industrial Research. The group began with four people, Derek Pugh, David Hickson, Bob Hinings, and Graham Harding, "in the basement of a condemned office block several hundred yards from the main college buildings. Its members sat with their desks touching one another, cramped in a small room with skylight lighting on to the pavement outside through which the wheels of Birmingham's city buses could be seen rolling by" (Pugh and Hickson, 1976: ix).

Through intensive internal discussions lasting over a year in this setting, the group developed one of the most comprehensive frameworks available for measuring and assessing the structure and process of organizations, work groups, and individual jobs. As Pugh describes in Chapter 4, the unit conducted research in hundreds of organizations in Europe, Canada, the United States, and Japan during the 1960s and 1970s. The findings from these studies were published in a long series of journal articles that have now been compiled in three volumes (Pugh and Hickson, 1976; Pugh and Hinings, 1976; Pugh and Payne, 1977). Since most of the publications centered on the context and bureaucratic dimensions of organizational structure, the Aston research program became identified with a "structuralist" approach to organization design, although an examination of organizational processes was and still remains a part of the Aston framework.

Since 1961 three "generations" of researchers contributed to the development of the Aston program. Pugh and Hickson (1976) include in the second generation Keith Macdonald, Christopher Turner, and Theo Nickols, while the third generation consisted of Kerr Inkson, Roy Payne, Diana Pheysey, and John Child. In 1973 the Industrial Administration Department of the University of Aston evolved into the Management Centre, and the official life of the unit came to an end. However, now the Aston researchers are independently continuing to test and elaborate on the original comprehensive scheme for assessing organizations, work groups, and individual jobs. In particular, Derek Pugh, David Hickson, and John Child are examining the processes of decision making, change, and power in organizations.

William Starbuck provides a penetrating assessment of the Aston studies in his commentary. He points out that "a critic of the Aston studies faces a mushy obstacle: it is not clear what the Aston studies are." Despite this problem, Starbuck argues that many of the findings of the Aston research may be due to erroneous conceptualization and statistical confusion. Three problems to which he devotes attention concern errors stemming from: (1) prior beliefs concerning what relationships should be studied from among all possible choices; (2) collinearities due to definitional similarities or spuriousness; (3) the constraints on allowable statistical inferences due to statistical methodology itself. Starbuck makes the appropriate data available in such a way to invite systematic assessment of the Aston research program. Derek Pugh concludes Chapter 4 with a stimulating rejoinder to Starbuck's commentary.

Decision Making under Conditions of Uncertainty

Herbert Simon, the 1978 Nobel Memorial Prize winner in economic sciences, set out his view of the manager in *Administrative Behavior* (1947). He viewed the individual as both intendedly and adaptively rational. The individual "satisfices" rather than "maximizes" in decision making because he or she possesses imperfect information and limited capabilities. In their acclaimed book *Organizations* (1958), James March and Herbert Simon further explored the implications of this view of human beings. Their typology of routinized, discretionary, and developmental programs is particularly important to organization design, and is basic to understanding how organizations function under ordinary as well as novel circumstances. A program is a sequence of activities and is evoked by some stimulus. If the stimulus is one that keeps recurring, a routine is developed to handle the situation efficiently whenever it occurs. Organization behavior is directed and controlled by these programs. Furthermore, decision-making processes and results can be made predictable by programming the premises of decision making.

This concept of programming organizational behavior and decision premises stimulated additional work dealing with choice behavior and structural variations within and between organizations. In particular, James March has continued and extended the work on rational and non-rational decision behavior under conditions of uncertainty.

In Chapter 5, March presents an illuminating survey of developments in perspectives on organizational choice behavior. He asks the pragmatic question, "How can we understand and improve human information processing, thinking, problem solving, and consciousness?" In reviewing the approaches that have been taken to study this question, March concludes that a cluster of assumptions and ideas have developed over time that represent alternatives to three assumptions of classical theories of choice: the irrelevance of the way decisions are made, the importance of decision results, and willfulness or the purposive nature of decision makers.

Charles Lindblom proposes in his commentary that the alternative conceptions of decision making advanced by March are a consequence of our recovery from the "mistake of regarding decision making as a technology." He proposes that organizational decision making is neither a technology nor a craft but rather an indeterminate practice. An indeterminate practice is one that is "at least partly skilled (and within which) it is not clear what accounts for such success as they (managers) achieve." There are two implications of this view: first, the need to test whether such a proposition actually holds, and second, to realize that if this is truly descriptive, then decision theory can only contribute marginally to organizational effectiveness. This is a challenging proposition to organization designers who traditionally embrace rational, or at least intendedly rational, approaches to organizational problems.

The Organization Assessment Research Program

A more recent program of longitudinal research is being conducted by Andrew Van de Ven and his colleagues. They are developing a program called Organization Assessment (OA), which consists of an evolving conceptual framework, a process, and a set of measurement instruments designed to predict and explain the performance of complex organizations on the bases of how they are organized and the environments in which they operate. The OA framework and measurement instruments examine various dimensions of the context, structure, and process of an organization at four levels of analyses: the overall organization, work units or groups, individual jobs, and relationships between units within and between organizations. Longitudinal research is in progress to test the OA framework in state government organizations in Wisconsin, Texas, and California. The program was begun in 1972, and Van de Ven and Ferry have extensively reported the findings of this research in a recent book, *Measuring and Assessing Organizations* (1980). The OA framework and instruments have generated considerable interest and are being used by a number of researchers to conduct studies in a variety of industrial, human service, and governmental organizations in the United States, Canada, England, Japan, and South Africa.

In Chapter 6 Van de Ven summarizes the OA framework and major research findings. He reports that the OA dimensions at each level of organizational analysis have been found to empirically explain about 55

percent of the variation in various indicators of organizational performance. However, he states that one can quickly become overwhelmed with
the complexity of problems, dimensions, and levels of analyses that are
involved in an in-depth assessment of organizations. To make sense of
this complexity, Van de Ven proposes a conceptual strategy for identifying
nine qualitatively different kinds of subsystems that tend to exist in
complex organizations. These subsystems are based upon three kinds of
performance programs that March and Simon (1958) have identified (systematized, discretionary, and developmental programs), and three qualitatively different functions that different levels of organizations tend to
perform (technical, managerial, and institutional), as Parsons and Smelser (1956) have suggested.

Van de Ven concludes by proposing a process model for conducting
assessments of organizations. He challenges the traditional approaches
by which organizational studies are conducted by management consultants as well as researchers. He proposes six phases to the assessment
process, which require the analyst to: respond to multiple partisan users
of the study, make explicit the multiple and conflicting values underlying
any definition of organization effectiveness, and facilitate learning among
users by having them involved in the assessment process.

In his commentary, Cortlandt Cammann notes that the OA research
program meets important scientific criteria concerning integration with
the field of organizational behavior, theoretical clarity, and empirical
orientation. Despite the comprehensiveness of the program, Cammann
believes that the major weaknesses of the OA framework "involve areas
that are not measured, rather than areas that are." He proposes that the
program has neglected informal rather than formal groups, the quality
of relationships, and the uses—as opposed to the nature—of organizational structures. Finally, he concludes that the OA researchers will soon
have to face squarely the somewhat natural antagonism between theory
and practice, research and use, or in the language of OA researchers,
antagonism between the OA framework and the OA process. This is a
problem that Cammann himself has faced during the Michigan QWL
experiments described above, and if we are to believe Joyce's earlier
commentary, one for which there is no ready solution.

The Organization and Environment
Research Program

In *Organization and Environment* (1967), Paul Lawrence and Jay Lorsch
at Harvard University proposed that if a firm is to be successful, its design
should be contingent upon the characteristics of the environment in which
it operates. They further suggested the importance of the psychological
correlates of structural differentiation and the attendant problems for
achieving integration of activities. Lawrence and Lorsch were among the

first to introduce "contingency theory" to organizations by showing that organizational performance was related to the degree to which organizational divisions were successful in developing management structures and processes that fit the levels of uncertainty encountered in the environments of organizations.

Since this early work, Paul Lawrence, Jay Lorsch, and their associates at Harvard have continued to extend this perspective. Lawrence has recently completed a longitudinal comparison of the structural adaptation of two research and development organizations, Bell Laboratories and the National Institute of Health. This work has been followed by the formation of the Organization Adaptation Research Group to expand and further study the subject. Robert Miles, Paul Lawrence, Michael Beer, Jack Sonnenfield, and Leonard Schleisinger are members of this group; they will shortly begin large-scale studies of adaptation in the insurance, airline, and public utility industries.

In Chapter 7 Lawrence begins with an assessment of his early work on organization and environment. He responds to six main arguments and criticisms that have been leveled at the O&E model. He then outlines the directions being taken to extend the original O&E formulation into a more dynamic view, with ideas from recent perspectives in the literature on enacted environments, markets and hierarchies, organizational life cycles, organizational paradigms, strategic choice, organizational ecology, and loose coupling. Lawrence concludes by proposing a nine-cell adaptation model that is based on two dimensions: a more expanded view of environmental uncertainty than the one earlier used, and resource scarcity. He uses the nine-cell scheme of organizational adaptation to speculate about (1) new firm start-ups and organizational life cycles, (2) the process of organizational learning and selection, (3) Thompson's (1967) three types of technology, and (4) organizational effectiveness criteria.

In his commentary, Lawrence Hrebiniak agrees with Lawrence in suggesting that a number of criticisms of the O&E program have been misplaced. Some problems remain, but they remain problems for the field of organizational behavior in general rather than the O&E program in particular. One such problem, of both practical and theoretical interest, is the problem of "fit." Hrebiniak proposes a number of alternative conceptions of this elusive variable, each with distinctive implications for organization design. Finally, he incorporates some of the recent findings from the strategy literature into the revised O&E framework proposed by Lawrence.

The Markets and Hierarchies Perspective

There has been a growing recognition of the contributions made by institutional economists to understanding organization design and behavior. In particular, the markets and hierarchies perspective developed by

Oliver Williamson at the University of Pennsylvania provides significant insight for integrating microeconomic theory with organization theory. This perspective views the organization (hierarchy) in a broader vein; that is, as but one of several alternative forms for executing transactions. Williamson challenges the classical economic assumptions of a market economy in which transactions are cost free and in which prices convey all the information that is necessary for the efficient allocation of goods and services. Under conditions of "market failures" (i.e., high uncertainty, opportunism, and small numbers of competitors), prices fail to accurately convey the necessary information, and transactions become increasingly costly to execute. In this case "hierarchy," or formal organizations, may be a superior mode for executing transactions. Hierarchy is a more efficient mode because the contracting parties have greater control and surveillance over uncertainties associated with a transaction and over personal opportunism of the parties involved.

Williamson initially set forth this comparative institutional transactions cost orientation in "The Vertical Integration of Production: Market Failure Considerations" (1971). The transactions costs ramifications of this perspective were traced out in *Markets and Hierarchies* (1975), which generated much interest among organization theorists and practitioners. In particular, Ouchi and Van de Ven (1980) adopted the perspective as a framework for suggesting alternative organizational arrangements for executing transactions that are intermediate to markets and hierarchies. Ouchi (1980) has also suggested conditions in which organizations fail and a new form of executing transactions—clans—replaces hierarchies. In addition, the markets and hierarchies perspective has been the organizing theme for several major recent professional conferences: (1) on antitrust law and economics, in Philadelphia, October 1978; (2) the European Group for Organization Studies in London, January 1980; (3) the European Consortium for Political Research in Florence, March 1980; (4) on marketing in Copenhagen, June 1980; and (5) the Academy of Management conference in San Diego, August 1981. Williamson, David Teece, and others are continuing a number of historical research investigations to test and extend the markets and hierarchies perspective. Ouchi, along with Professor Jay Barney and a team at UCLA, has embarked on a series of studies that will empirically test the transactions cost approach in a study of electronics companies in the United States and Japan.

In Chapter 8 Williamson and Ouchi summarize and extend the markets and hierarchies perspective as it applies to organization design and behavior. They argue that organization theory is seriously underdeveloped with respect to its economic content; more attention needs to be given to the importance of efficiency as a criterion for assessing organizational forms and designs. They offer four basic principles for determining efficient organizational forms: (1) make the transaction the basic unit of analysis; (2) identify alternative modes of contracting transactions; (3)

identify the dimensions by which these transactions differ; and (4) trace out the transactions costs ramifications of these alternative modes of contracting. To Williamson and Ouchi, the basic organization design problem is organizing transactions in such a way as to economize on bounded rationality, while simultaneously safeguarding against the hazards of opportunism.

In his commentary, Charles Perrow deviates from his assignment to comment on the Williamson and Ouchi paper. Instead he centers his remarks on Williamson's *Markets and Hierarchies* (1975) as well as Alfred Chandler's *The Visible Hand* (1977). Perrow attacks the efficiency criterion underlying Williamson's concept of transactions costs and Chandler's concept of administrative coordination in explaining the shift over the years from markets to hierarchies or from functional to multidivisional organizational structures. Perrow's argument is that initially hierarchy and vertical integration were designed to obtain market control and oligopolistic advantages, not the advantages of efficiency. Then, as a result of technological changes, hierarchy and vertical integration became inefficient, and less hierarchical structures were quickly adopted. However, the dominant firms moved back to more oligopolistic positions because, as Perrow argues in Chapter 8, the key issue is power and control, not efficiency.

Both Williamson and Chandler accepted our invitation to respond to Perrow's commentary, and their rejoinders and subsequent debate are presented in Chapter 8. We believe the debate makes an important and constructive contribution to the literature, because it is often only through such argumentation that the value judgments and ideological positions underlying any perspective on organizations become exposed and clarified. Furthermore, Alfred Chandler has used this opportunity to present an excellent summary of his definition of administrative coordination and his basic argument in *The Visible Hand* (1977).

ASSESSING AND EXTENDING
THE SEVEN RESEARCH PROGRAMS

Chapters 9 to 11 assess the contributions of the seven research programs and propose an integrative perspective to further the development of theory and practice on organization design and behavior.

In Chapter 9, Jeffrey Pfeffer distills four laws from his review of the seven research programs and commentaries. They are the laws of unresolvable ignorance, requisite simplicity, unrequited effort, and of no effect. Through these four laws Pfeffer politely focuses on the limitations of the seven diverse research programs. He states that organizational analysts, including himself, have all: (1) been too interested in building instead of pruning theories and ideas; (2) become so committed to our perspectives that disconfirming evidence only leads to making our perspectives more complex, instead of searching for a fundamental alternative; (3) become unaware of how much our research methods govern the organizational sites selected for study and what knowledge people at these organizational sites permit us to obtain; and (4) become too entrenched in the rational, proactive, strategic choice view of organizational action, and too quick to dismiss nonrational, externally controlled, and natural selection views of organization design and behavior. In conclusion, Pfeffer calls for a critical organization behavior, just as there has emerged a critical sociology.

In Chapter 10, John Kimberly indicates that three common themes struck him in the seven research programs: an emphasis on enhancing productive efficiency, an interest in describing and understanding *patterns* in organizational activity, and a concern for creating more humane work systems. Kimberly believes that the seven programs collectively embody a number of tensions, including the tensions between intuition and measurement, ideographic and nomothetic efforts, rational and nonrational models, and between theory and practice. In looking to the future development of organization design and behavior, Kimberly asks, "What forces propel ideas forward at particular points in time, and what forces explain their demise?" In answering this question, Kimberly pursues three lines of inquiry: the development of individual careers, dialectics in theory and research, and fluctuations in markets of ideas. Kimberly concludes by discussing the implications of his prediction that in the 1980s we are likely to see research on assessment, organization design, and performance as having an increasingly applied focus—much more applied than is represented in the seven research programs.

Finally, in Chapter 11, Andrew Van de Ven and W. Graham Astley call for a broader and more dynamic perspective on organization design and behavior than is available in any one of the seven research programs. They begin with a review of the extant organizational literature (including that in this book), and classify it into four basic perspectives: system-structural, strategic choice, natural selection, and collective action views of organizations. These four views represent different perspectives on organization structure, behavior, change, and managerial roles. Van de Ven and Astley then focus on the contradictions and complementarities between the seven research programs that are classified into the four perspectives. By examining these complementarities and contradictions, they develop a framework for examining change in organization design and behavior.

CONCLUSION

This chapter has introduced seven major research programs that have significantly influenced our current thinking about organization design and behavior. To varying degrees, each of the seven programs takes a broad view by examining organization design as both a noun and a verb across individual and collective levels of analysis, and gives due respect to the influences of environmental situations and individual differences. Further, each program is grounded in a sound but unique conceptual base, has been developed and tested over many years as the result of major commitments of time and resources by groups of investigators in studying many organizations, and has established a distinguished track record of followers over the years. Indeed the perspectives and findings flowing from the seven research programs have been and are being assimilated into what might be called "mainstream" organization theory.

These seven research programs have been juxtaposed in this book for the purposes of highlighting their similarities and differences and assessing what has been learned from them. As the commentaries, rejoinders, and appraisals will indicate, each program has both strengths and weaknesses. By making these explicit, we hope this book helps the reader take stock of what we know and don't know about mainstream organization design and behavior. By identifying the "unfinished business" in each of these programs, we hope the book makes clear what new directions need to be explored for future theory and practice.

While the seven research programs represent mainstream perspectives, they do not include the entire eclectic conceptual domain of organization design and behavior. As the commentaries and the last chapter indicate, a number of fresh new perspectives are beginning to surface and command attention among organizational analysts. They include: (1) the natural selection or population ecology models of organizations being developed by Hannan and Freeman (1977), Campbell (1969), Aldrich (1979), and McKelvey (1981); (2) symbolic and phenomenological views of organizational reality as proposed by Berger and Luckmann (1966), Silverman (1970), Weick (1969), and Pondy and Boje (1980); and (3) political economy and Marxian views of social conflict, dialectics, and change being advocated by Benson (1977), Burrell and Morgan (1979), Gouldner (1980), and Habermas (1976).

To the readers who advocate these perspectives, the editors can only plead "mea culpa!" While becoming increasingly important, these perspectives have not yet established as extensive a track record of theorizing and research among students of organization design as the seven programs set out here. However, as the concluding chapter argues, an appreciation of these new perspectives is fundamental for injecting and redirecting mainstream perspectives on organization design and behavior with an agenda that is both exciting and challenging for the future.

REFERENCES

Aldrich, H. (1979). *Organizations and Environments,* Englewood Cliffs, NJ: Prentice-Hall.

Benson, J. K. (1977). "Organizations: A Dialectical View," *Administrative Science Quarterly* **22**:1–21.

Berger, P. L., and T. Luckmann (1966). *The Social Construction of Reality,* Garden City, NY: Doubleday.

Burrell, G., and G. Morgan (1979). *Sociological Paradigms and Organizational Analysis,* London: Heinemann Educational Books.

Campbell, D. (1969). "Variation and Selective Retention in Socio-Cultural Evolution," General Systems **16**:69–85.

Chandler, A. (1977). *The Visible Hand,* Cambridge, MA: Harvard University Press.

Gouldner, A. (1980). *The Two Marxisms: Contradictions and Anomalies in the Development of Theory,* New York: The Seabury Press.

Habermas, J. (1976). *The Legitimation Crisis,* Boston, MA: Beacon Press.

Hannan, M., and J. Freeman (1977). "Obstacles to Comparative Studies," in P. S. Goodman, J. M. Pennings, and Associates, Eds., *New Perspectives on Organizational Effectiveness,* San Francisco, CA: Jossey-Bass.

Lawrence, P. R., and J. W. Lorsch (1967). *Organizations and Environments,* Cambridge, MA: Harvard Business School.

March, J. G., and H. A. Simon (1958). *Organizations,* New York: Wiley.

McKelvey, W. (1981). *Organizational Systematics: Taxonomy, Evolution, Classification,* in press.

Ouchi, W. (1980). "Markets, Bureaucracies, and Clans," *Administrative Science Quarterly* **25**:129–140.

Ouchi, W., and A. H. Van de Ven (1980). "Antitrust and Organization Theory," in O. E. Williamson, Ed., *Antitrust Law and Economics,* Houston, TX: Dame Publications, pp. 291–311.

Parsons, T., and N. Smelser (1956). *Economy and Society,* Glencoe, IL: Free Press.

Pondy, L., and D. Boje (1980). "Bringing Mind Back In," in William M. Evan, Ed., *Frontiers in Organization and Management,* New York: Praeger.

Pugh, D., and D. J. Hickson (1976). *Organizational Structure in its Context,* Westmead, England: Saxon House.

Pugh, D., and C. R. Hinings (1976). *Organizational Structure: Extensions and Replications,* Westmead, England: Saxon House.

Pugh, D., and Payne, R. L. (1977). *Organizational Behaviour in Its Context,* Westmead, England: Saxon House.

Seashore, S., and Associates (1982). *Observing and Measuring Organizational Change: A Guide to Field Practice,* New York: Wiley.

Silverman, D. (1970). *The Theory of Organisations,* New York: Basic Books.

Simon, H. A. (1947). *Administrative Behavior,* New York: Macmillan.

Van de Ven, A. H., and D. L. Ferry (1980). *Measuring and Assessing Organizations,* New York: Wiley.

Weick, K. E. (1979). *The Social Psychology of Organizing,* 2nd ed., Reading, MA: Addison-Wesley.

Williamson, O. E. (1971). "The Vertical Integration of Production: Market Failure Considerations," *American Economic Review* **61**:112–123.

Williamson, O. E. (1975). *Markets and Hierarchies,* New York: Free Press.

PART ONE

ALTERNATIVE
PERSPECTIVES

CHAPTER TWO

The Sociotechnical Perspective

The Evolution of Sociotechnical Systems as a Conceptual Framework and as an Action Research Program

ERIC L. TRIST
The Wharton School
University of Pennsylvania
and
Faculty of Environmental Studies
York University, Toronto

INTRODUCTION

This chapter reviews the evolution of the sociotechnical concept from its original formulation in conjunction with the early Tavistock mining studies in 1950 to the present time. When the relations between the technological and social aspects of organizations were instituted as a distinct field of study, there was a search for the conditions that would permit the best match to be made between technical and social systems. The concept was developed in terms of open system theory. Empirical studies were undertaken in an action-research mode.

Sociotechnical analysis is made at three levels: the primary work system, the whole organization, and macrosocial phenomena. The relations between these levels are examined in a historical context, which influenced the type and scope of the projects that could be carried out. Though important pioneer work, mainly in Britain, was done in the 1950s, there was little understanding of, and much resistance to, the new paradigm of work and organization that was identified. During the 1960s a large-scale action research project at the national level was undertaken in Norway, which led to substantial conceptual and methodological advances. During the 1970s sociotechnical projects were initiated in almost all Western countries, in North America as well as in Europe, and the approach became linked to a wider movement that concerned the quality of working life.

At the level of the primary work system, principles of work design and a method of work analysis become important. The question of motivation is related to individual differences and changing social values. The phenomenon of autonomous work groups, together with matrices and networks, afford a structural basis for self-regulating primary work systems, which constitute a new building block for organizational design.

The organization as a whole exists in relation to its changing environment. The new levels of complexity, interdependence, and uncertainty reached in this environment are rendering conventional technocratic and bureaucratic organizations more dysfunctional. New plants designed on sociotechnical principles and exemplifying the new paradigm perform at a higher level and yield more work satisfaction.

As for the future, the microprocessor revolution has many implications for the meaning of work, alternatives to paid employment, decentralization, and technological choice. Under conditions of environmental turbulence, single organizations are ill-equipped to go it alone, and sociotechnical projects at the industry level and in communities may be advisable.

THE HISTORICAL BACKGROUND (1950–1970)

Origin of the Concept

The sociotechnical concept arose in conjunction with the first of several field projects undertaken by the Tavistock Institute in the British coal mining industry. The time (1949) was that of the postwar reconstruction of industry in relation to which the Institute had two action research projects.* One was concerned with group relations in depth at all levels (including the management-labor interface) in a single organization, an engineering company in the private sector. The other project focused on the diffusion of innovative work practices and organizational arrangements that did not require major capital expenditure but gave promise of raising productivity. The former project represented the first comprehensive application in an industrial setting of the socioclinical ideas concerning groups being developed at the Tavistock. For this purpose a novel

---

*Through the Human Factors Panel of the then Government's Productivity Committee on funds administered by the Medical Research Council.

action research methodology was introduced. The book describing the project became a classic (Jaques, 1951). Nevertheless, it approached the organization exclusively as a social system. The second project was led, through circumstances described below, to include the technical as well as the social system in the factors to be considered and to postulate that the relations between them should constitute *a new field of inquiry*.

Coal being then the chief source of power, a plentiful and cheap supply of it was important for industrial reconstruction. But the newly nationalized industry was not doing well. Productivity failed to increase in step with increases in mechanization. Men were leaving the mines in large numbers for better opportunities in factories. Among those who remained, absenteeism averaged 20 percent. Labor disputes were frequent despite improved conditions of employment. Some time earlier the National Coal Board had asked the Institute to make a comparative study of a high-producing, high-morale mine and a low-producing, low-morale but otherwise equivalent mine. Despite nationalization, however, our research team was not welcome at the coal face under the auspices of the Board.

There were at the Institute at that time six postgraduate fellows being trained for industrial field work. Among these, three had a trade union background and one, the late Ken Bamforth, had been a miner. After a year, the fellows were encouraged to revisit their former industries and report any new perceptions. Bamforth returned with news of an innovation in work practice and organization taking place in a new seam in the colliery where he used to work in the South Yorkshire coal field. The seam, the Haighmoor, had become possible to mine "shortwall" because of improved roof control. I can recall now the excitement with which I listened to him. I lost no time in going up to visit this colliery where, since we were introduced by him, the local management and union readily agreed to our researching their innovation with a view to its diffusion to other mines. The Area General Manager, who managed some 20 mines, welcomed the idea. The technical conception of the new scheme was his, though the men, with union support, had proposed the actual working arrangements.

The work organization of the new seam was to us a novel phenomenon consisting of a set of relatively autonomous groups interchanging roles and shifts and regulating their affairs with a minimum of supervision. Cooperation between task groups was everywhere in evidence; personal commitment was obvious, absenteeism low, accidents infrequent, productivity high. The contrast was large between the atmosphere and arrangements on these faces and those in the conventional areas of the pit, where the negative features characteristic of the industry were glaringly apparent. The men told us that in order to adapt with best advantage to the technical conditions in the new seam, they had evolved a form of work organization based on practices common in unmechanized days when small groups, who took responsibility for the entire cycle, had worked autonomously. These practices had disappeared as the pits became progressively more mechanized when "longwall" working had been introduced. This had enlarged the scale of operations and led to aggregates of men of considerable size having their jobs broken down into one-man-one-task roles, while coordination and control had been externalized in supervision, which had become coercive. Now they had found a way at a higher level of mechanization of recovering the group cohesion and self-regulation they had lost and of advancing their power to participate in decisions concerning their work arrangements. For this reason, the book that surveyed the Tavistock mining studies was subtitled "The Loss, Rediscovery and Transformation of a Work Tradition" (Trist et al., 1963).

The transformation represented a change of direction in organizational design. For several decades the prevailing direction had been to increase bureaucratization with each increase in scale and level of mechanization. The organizational model that fused Weber's description of bureaucracy with Frederick Taylor's concept of scientific management had become pervasive. The Haighmoor innovation showed that there was an alternative.

Those concerned with it had made an *organizational choice* (Trist et al., 1963). They could, with minor modifications, have extended the prevailing mode of working. They chose instead to elaborate a major design alternative. It was not true that the only way of designing work organizations was to conform to Tayloristic and bureaucratic principles. There were other ways, which represented a discontinuity with the prevailing mode. The technological imperative could be disobeyed with positive economic as well as human results. As became clearer later, what happened in the Haighmoor seam gave to Bamforth and me a first glimpse of "the emergence of a new paradigm of work" (Emery, 1978a) in which the best match would be sought between the requirements of the social and technical systems.

Some of the principles involved were:

1. The *work system,* which comprised a set of activities that made up a functioning whole, now became the basic unit rather than the single jobs into which it was decomposable.

2. Correspondingly, the *work group* became central rather than the individual jobholder.

3. *Internal regulation* of the system by the group was thus rendered possible rather than the external regulation of individuals by supervisors.

4. A design principle based on the *redundancy of functions* rather than the redundancy of parts (Emery, 1967) characterized the underlying organizational philosophy, which tended to develop multiple skills in the individual and immensely increase the response repertoire of the group.

5. This principle valued the *discretionary* rather than the prescribed part of work roles (Jaques, 1956).

6. It treated the individual as *complementary* to the machine rather than as an extension of it (Jordan, 1963).

7. It was *variety-increasing* for both the individual and the organization rather than variety-decreasing in the bureaucratic mode.

Conceptually the new paradigm entailed a shift in the way work organizations were envisaged. Engineers, following the technological imperative, would design whatever organization the technology seemed to require. This was a rule accepted by all concerned (Davis et al., 1955). The "people cost" of proceeding in this way was not considered. Any people cost, it was presumed, could be compensated for first by improving the socioeconomic conditions of employment, next by improving "human relations." The movement under this latter title arose during the interwar period when the model of the technocratic bureaucracy was becoming entrenched. It failed to arrest the spread of work alienation after World War II (Baldamus, 1951, 1961; Walker and Guest, 1952). At the Glacier Metal Company where Jaques (1951) carried out his research, it was observed that, despite the progressive personnel policies adopted and the far-reaching changes made in the character of management-labor relations, there was no reduction in "the split at the bottom of the executive chain." Nothing had happened to change the structure of jobs. There was no change in the nature of immediate work experience.

The idea of separate approaches to the social and the technical systems in an organization could no longer suffice for one who had experienced, as I had, the profound consequences of a change in social-technical relations such as had occurred in the Haighmoor development. Work organizations exist to do work—which involves people using technological artifacts (whether hard or soft) to carry out sets of tasks related to specified overall purposes. Accordingly, a conceptual reframing was proposed in which work organizations were envisaged as sociotechnical rather than simply as social systems (Trist, 1950a). The social and technical systems were the substantive factors, that is, the people and the equipment. Economic performance and job satisfaction were outcomes, the level of which depended on the "goodness of fit" between the substantive factors. The following research tasks emerged in the Tavistock program:

1. The theoretical development of the core concept.

2. Methods for the analytical study of the relations of technologies and organizational forms in different settings.

3. A search for criteria to obtain the best match between the technological and social components.

4. Action research to improve the match.

5. Ways to measure and evaluate outcomes through comparative and longitudinal studies.

6. Ways to diffuse sociotechnical improvements.

These tasks could not be carried out in a preplanned sequence. The research team had first to make an extensive reconnaissance of the field to locate relevant opportunities. It then had to become actively linked to them in ways that would sanction their study in a collaborative mode. The idiom of inquiry was action research (Trist, 1976b).

Sociotechnical studies needed to be carried out at three broad levels, from micro to macro, each of which was interrelated.

1. *Primary Work Systems.* These are the systems that carry out the set of activities involved in an identifiable and bounded subsystem of a whole organization, such as a line department or service unit (see Miller, 1959). They may consist of a single face-to-face group or a number of such groups together with support and specialist personnel and representatives of management plus the relevant equipment and other resources. They have a recognized purpose, which unifies the people and the activities.

2. *Whole Organization Systems.* At one limit these would be plants or equivalent self-standing work places. At the other they would be entire corporations or public agencies. They persist by maintaining a steady state with their environment.

3. *Macrosocial Systems.* These include systems in communities and industrial sectors and institutions operating at the overall level of a society. They constitute what I have called "domains" (Trist, 1976a, 1979a). One may regard media as sociotechnical systems. McLuhan (1964) has shown that the technical character of different media has far-reaching effects on users. The same applies to architectural forms and the infrastructure of the built environment. Although these are not organizations, they are sociotechnical phenomena. They are media in Heider's (1942) as well as McLuhan's sense.

As the historical process of a society unfolds, individuals change their values and expectations concerning work roles, which in turn changes the parameters of organizational design. Conversely, changes in technology bring about changes in values, cognitive structures, lifestyles, habitats, and communication that profoundly alter a society and its chances of survival. Sociotechnical phenomena are contextual as well as organizational.

Not all social systems are sociotechnical. Emery (1959), following Nadel (1951), distinguished between "operative" and "regulative" institutions and proposed to restrict the term "sociotechnical" to the former. Regulative organizations are concerned directly with the psychosocial ends of their members and with instilling, maintaining, or changing cultural values and norms, the power and the position of interest groups, or the social structure itself. Many such organizations employ technologies as adjuncts and have secondary instrumental systems that are sociotechnical. By contrast, organizations that are primarily sociotechnical are directly dependent on their material means and resources for their output. Their core interface consists of the relations between a nonhuman system and a human system.

There are mixed forms typified by the copresence of psychosocial and sociotechnical ends that may be congruent or conflicting. An example of the latter would be a prison with both an electronic surveillance system and a therapeutic community. Hospitals are inherently sociotechnical as well as psychosocial, which accounts for the complexity of some of their dilemmas.

From the beginning the sociotechnical concept has developed in terms of systems, since it is concerned with interdependencies. It has also developed in terms of open system theory, since it is concerned with the environment in which an organization has to actively maintain a steady state. Von Bertalanffy's (1950) paper on "Open Systems in Physics and Biology" became available at the time that the sociotechnical concept was being formulated. It influenced both theory building and field projects, compelling attention alike to self-regulation and environmental relations. As regards the special role of technology, Emery (1959) put it as follows:

> The *technological component*, in converting inputs into outputs, *plays a major role in determining the self-regulating properties of an enterprise.* It functions as one of the major boundary conditions of the social system in mediating between the ends of an enterprise and the external environment. Because of this, the materials, machines and territory that go to making up the technological component are usually defined, in any modern society, as "belonging" to an enterprise, or are excluded from similar control by other enterprises. They represent as it were, an "internal environment." This being the case, it is not possible to define the conditions under which such an open system achieves a steady state unless the mediating boundary conditions are in some way represented amongst "the system constants" (cf. Von Bertalanffy, 1950). The technological component has been found to play this mediating role and hence it follows that the open system concept, as applied to the enterprise, ought to be referred to the socio-technical system, not simply to the social system.

Source Influences

An interest in social and technical relations arose in my own thinking first at the macrosocial level, next at the whole organization level, and then at the level of primary work systems. This last became the crucial level as regards the initiation of field projects that provided the concrete route through which the broader levels could again be reached.

Mumford (1934) in *Technics and Civilization* had introduced me to the idea of linking the two. Anthropology and cultural history suggested that, if the material and symbolic cultures of a society were not connected by any simple principle of linear causality, as some interpreters of Marx have implied, they were nevertheless intertwined in a complex web of mutual causality (Trist, 1950b). In the language of E. A. Singer (1959), they were coproducers of each other. The technological choices made by a society are critical expressions of its world view. As new technologies develop, new societal possibilities may or may not be taken up. The mode of their elaboration may be constructive or destructive. There are unanticipated consequences. In the period following World War II the information technologies of the second industrial revolution were already beginning to make themselves felt. It seemed likely that there would be as big a cultural shift associated with them as with the energy technologies of the first Industrial Revolution.

As regards the whole organization level, the first industrial project in which I was involved made it impossible not to look at the relations between technical and social systems. This encounter was with the jute industry in Dundee, Scotland, where in the late 1930s I was a member of an interdisciplinary research team studying unemployment. The spinning section of the industry was being "rationalized," causing not only more unemployment but a deskilling of the remaining workers, along with an extension of managerial controls. As to alienation, workers in the interview sample would say that they might as well be unemployed, while the appearance of time-study men provoked a bitter reaction in the trade unions. In the changes taking place, the technical and social aspects were interactive. A new sociotechnical system emerged—that of a more controlling "technocratic bureaucracy" with very different properties from the earlier system in terms of which jute spinning had been, and jute weaving still was, organized. Then came World War II. A new military sociotechnical system appeared in the form of the German Panzer Divisions, formidably competent in the way they linked men and machines to fit their purposes. The French army had failed to develop an equivalent, despite De Gaulle's proposals.

As the war proceeded, military technology gave increasing scope for, and prominence to, small group formations, recognizing their power to make flexible decisions and to remain cohesive under rapidly changing conditions. This led to a recasting of the role of junior officers and the kind of relations—more open and more democratic—best maintained between them and their men. In Britain the War Office Selection Boards, to which I was attached, were created to choose officers capable of behaving in this way. The Boards made extensive use of W. R. Bion's (1946) method of leaderless groups, which allowed leadership to emerge and rotate in a variety of group settings. All this opened up new areas of group dynamics—extended after the war when Bion (1950, 1961) introduced therapy groups at the Tavistock Clinic. A parallel influence was that of Lewin's (1939, 1951) experiments on group climates and group decision making, together with the beginnings of the National Training Laboratories. These traditions became fused at the Tavistock. Bion focused on the unconscious factors obstructing the attainment of group purposes and on group creativeness, Lewin on the commitment to action consequent on participation and on the performance superiority of the democratic mode. Both emphasized the capacity of the small group for self-regulation, an aspect of systems theory that received increasing attention as cybernetics developed (Weiner, 1950).

Going Against the Grain of the Fifties

To a number of us at this time, and certainly to me, it seemed that the small self-regulating group held the clue to a great deal that might be improved in work organizations. Knowledge about such groups had made considerable advances during and immediately after World War II. Yet experiences in industry in the reconstruction period had shown that sociotechnical relations were patterned on the breakdown of work into externally controlled one-man-one-job units, and that top-down management hierarchies were being even more rigidly maintained than in the prewar period. The pattern of technocratic bureaucracy was increasing in strength.

Hence the interest of the Haighmoor development, which pointed to the existence of an alternative pattern going in the opposite direction to the prevailing mode. The Divisional Board, however, did not wish attention drawn to it. They feared the power change that would be consequent on allowing groups to become more autonomous at a time when they themselves were intent on intensifying managerial controls in order to accelerate the full mechanization of the mines. They refused to allow the research to continue, and balked when Bamforth and I referred to it in the paper that we published (1951) on conventional longwall working. It would lead, they said, to expectations that could not be fulfilled; for, while autonomous groups might be successful on the Haighmoor shortwalls, they would not be feasible on the longwall layouts that represented the prevailing method of mining. Later this opinion was found to be false, though widely believed. The Divisional Board's reaction suggested that any attempt to reverse the prevailing mode would be met with very serious resistance. To move in the opposite direction meant going against the grain of a macrosocial trend of institution-building in terms of the model of the technocratic bureaucracy, which had yet to reach its peak or disclose its dysfunctionality.

Several major pioneer studies were carried out during the decade. They established a number of research findings of key importance. Their effect on industrial practice was negligible. Neither what happened nor what failed to happen is widely known. These studies are reviewed here to provide a short account of what turned out to be the latency decade of the sociotechnical approach.

The Continuation of the Mining Studies

If the Haighmoor development had general meaning, it was reasonable to assume that similar developments would occur elsewhere. In fact, a parallel development in a more advanced form and on a larger scale emerged in another division of the National Coal Board (East Midlands), where one of the area managers, W. V. Sheppard (1949, 1951), was developing a method of continuous mining—a radical innovation designed on what appeared to be sociotechnical principles. There were two versions: the semimechanized (Wilson and Trist, 1951) and the fully mechanized (Trist, 1953a). The second was delayed because of teething troubles in an ingenious but somewhat underpowered cutter-loader invented by Sheppard. Faces were 100 yards in length, alternating advance with retreat and concentrated in one district so that only one main road needed to be maintained. Autonomous groups of 20 to 25 conducted all operations on one shift. There were three production shifts every 24 hours instead of one; previously the other two shifts had been concerned with coal face preparation and equipment shifting, which were now done simultaneously with coal getting. All members were multiskilled and were paid the same day wage, which was judged more appropriate for continuous mining than a bonus. Productivity and work satisfaction were unusually and consistently high. A beginning was made in spreading the new system to six pits. Emery (1952), who was over at the Tavistock on sabbatical from Australia, made a study of this process, paying special attention to required changes in the supervisor's role. After area-wide appreciation conferences had been held for managers and undermanagers, an Area Training School was designed (Trist, 1953b) to which groups of eight (operators, foremen and mechanics) from each pit scheduled to go over to the new system came for a week, during which they visited the original mine. Members of these groups began to meet weekly to compare experiences. A kind of sociotechnical development center was created. This model was not picked up again for another 12 years, when something like it emerged both in the Norwegian Industrial Democracy project (Emery and Thorsrud, 1976) and the Shell Philosophy project (Hill, 1971). It was a forerunner of "the deep slice" used by Emery (1976) in his method of participant design.

A study of overall area organization was made (Trist, 1953c). The incoming technology in association with autonomous work groups reduced by one the number of management levels underground. Group centers between collieries and the area office were obviously redundant. Divisional boards between operating areas and the national headquarters in London also seemed unnecessary. These superfluous levels of management were based on narrow spans of control that implied detailed supervision of subordinates at all levels rather than the sociotechnical concept of boundary management, which was congruent with maximizing the degree of self-regulation throughout an entire organizational system. In time, these levels were in fact eliminated. This showed how the sociotechnical concept could affect the organization as a whole and reduce the administrative overhead that has become so excessive in large technocratic and bureaucratic organizations.

Having reached the whole organization system level, our research efforts, though on independent funds, were again stopped when a new divisional chairman took over. What had happened was seen in an entirely technological perspective, that of the recently introduced cutterloader. Since this was judged not as good a prospect for further mechanization, the whole project was regarded as not meriting continuation. Besides, granting more autonomy was not popular. The union regionally negotiated special pay for operators of new equipment. This broke up the unity of the face groups, which were further decimated when bonuses were introduced for various classes of workers. Within a year or two, the conventional system reinstated itself.

Sociologically, this setback and the earlier one over the Haighmoor may be seen as examples of what Schon (1971) has called the "dynamic conservatism" of organizations. Psychologically, at the unconscious level, these setbacks may be seen as stemming from "envious attacks" on the innovations and the innovators. In psychoanalytic object relations theory (Klein, 1958) a good object—that one cannot bear because it is not one's own—may for that reason be turned into something undesirable, which then becomes a threat through having one's hostility projected on to it. Creativeness is apt to stir up jealous hatred of this kind, and the creators all too often become the targets of destructive spite. I have encountered a number of cases of this in studies of innovation with which I have been associated.

A search of other coal fields produced only one, Durham, where the divisional board and the regional organization of the National Union of Mineworkers said they would like to proceed with social research into mining methods. Virtually all extant methods were available in the same low seam in a single area in the older part of the coal field, where customs were uniform and traditions common. Here the research team found what the conventional wisdom had held to be impossible: the working of the conventional, semimechanized, three-shift longwall cycle by a set of autonomous work groups, locally known as composite. Groups of 40 to 50 men interchanged the various jobs required while alternating shifts in ways they felt best and evolving an innovative pay system that seemed equitable to them. Output was 25 percent higher with lower costs than on a comparison face similar in every respect (conditions, equipment, personnel) except that of work organization. Accidents, sickness, and absenteeism were cut in half (Trist et al., 1963). Only one man left the composite faces in two years. Over the four-year period of the project, the conversion of an entire colliery with three seams from conventional to composite working was followed in detail. Much was learned about the conditions under which autonomous groups prosper and under which they fail. The potential of self-regulating groups in fully mechanized installations was studied, and the research team began to collaborate in the design of sociotechnical systems for the most advanced technology then available. A meticulous study of a single face team was made by Herbst (1962), exploring the mathematical relations between a number of key variables.

A report was submitted to the National Coal Board (Trist and Murray, 1958). The results were not disputed. But the board's priorities were elsewhere—on the closing of uneconomic pits in the older coal fields and carrying the union with it in implementing the National Power-Loading agreement, deemed critical for full mechanization. It was not willing to encourage anything new that might disturb the delicately balanced situation as the industry contracted in face of the greater use of oil. On the union side, the Durham Miners' Association sent the report to the National executive. No reply was received at the Tavistock Institute.

Dr. Hugh Murray has since* made an archival study of composite agreements in the various British coal fields. There were quite a few of these in the mid-fifties, but they were regarded simply as wage settlements. There was no understanding that they might have implications for work organization.

In the late 1960s Murray carried out an action-research study of layouts using very advanced technology. He found that the coincidence of specialized work roles and high absentee rates was giving rise to wide-scale disruption of production processes. Men were posted to places in their specialty all over the mine through a "pit market." There was little cohesion in work teams. Efforts to introduce multiskilling, which would have afforded the basis for greater team cohesion, met with little success (Murray et al., 1969).

During the 1970s an experimental section based on autonomous groups was tried out in a mine in the American coal industry with its room-and-pillar layouts and very different technology of roof bolting, continuous

*Personal communication, 1977.

miners, and shuttle cars. Positive results were obtained comparable to those obtained earlier in Britain, not only as regards productivity but as regards safety, which was the reason for union collaboration. Although a second autonomous section was started, an attempt to diffuse this form of work organization to the mine as a whole encountered insuperable difficulties that were not foreseen by members of the Labor-Management Steering Committee or the research team (Trist, Brown, and Susman, 1979). This project has been independently evaluated by Goodman (1979).

The difficulties centered on the resentment of those not included in the experiment towards the privileges of those who were. This resentment would not have become acute had not expansion of the mine led to some inexperienced new recruits winning places on the second autonomous section (and hence the top rate) when experienced men withdrew their bids at the last moment in order to stay with a foreman, who then deserted them. There was no infringement of seniority rules, but the issue split the union.

The project showed in great detail how unanticipated and uncontrollable events in the broader as well as the immediate context can influence outcome in the later stages of an action research undertaking. It also showed how the encapsulation of an innovation can prevent its diffusion and the dangers of applying classical experimental research design in the "moving ground" of a real-life field situation—even though this was a condition of receiving initial support at the mine and from the sponsors of the national program of which it was a part.

Studies in Other Industries

Meanwhile, at the Tavistock, opportunities were sought in other industries. The first to arise was not only in another industry, textiles, but in another culture—India. In 1953 the late A. K. Rice (1958, 1963) paid his first visit to the Calico Mills in Ahmedabad, in which an automatic loomshed was converted from conventional to autonomous group working, with results that surpassed expectations. Later the change was diffused throughout the nonautomatic weaving sheds in this very large organization, which employed 9000 people. Rice did no more than mention through an interpreter the idea of a group of workers becoming responsible for a group of looms. The loomshed employees took up the idea themselves, coming back next day with a scheme that they asked management's permission to implement. Terms of a progressive payment scheme were negotiated, and the first trials of the new system began. As with the mines, major initiatives were taken by the workers themselves. The depth of their commitment became apparent later, when the Communist Party of India (orthodox) took offense at the "Ahmedabad Experiment" and drafted a number of their members from various parts of the country into the city, swollen with refugees from West Pakistan, to agitate against it. Though their families were threatened and attempts were made to set Hindu and Muslim workers against each other, the Calico's employees stood by an innovation that was largely their own creation.

Yet the group method, as it was called, did not spread to other mills as originally expected. I asked Shankalal Banker, the venerable leader of the Ahmedabad Textiles Union, about this when I was in Ahmedabad in 1976. He replied that the other owners did not want to share power. Also, as Miller (1975) reports, the nonautomatic loomsheds gradually regressed to conventional ways of working. Training was not kept up. New middle managers took over who knew little of what had originally taken place. Senior management became preoccupied with marketing and diversification. The automatic loomsheds, however, have retained the group method and their high level of performance and satisfaction with it.

During the early 1950s also, Seymour Melman (1958), who had come over from Columbia to Oxford, made an in-depth study of work practices in the Standard Motor Company at Coventry. This company, which made both tractors and automobiles (and some airplane engines), employed 12,000 workers who, through their unions, largely controlled work arrangements and practices on the shop floor. There were only 70 foremen in the entire organization. Only 16 people were in the personnel department. There were only eight time-study specialists. The ratio of administrative to production workers was far lower than in the rest of the industry and had been held steady while it increased elsewhere. At the automobile plant, the workers formed themselves into 15 large, internally differentiated groups varying from 50 to 500, each of which comprised a worker constituency that negotiated its detailed conditions of work and operating rules within a plant-wide union agreement, itself separate from the rest of the industry. The large groups were known as "gangs." They controlled upgrading and deployment among eight broad classes of jobs, reduced to these few from a very large number. They negotiated the bonus for the number of products turned out in a given time. These products constituted a major subsystem of the automobile. The bonus was large and induced component groups in the gangs to cooperate. The primary work systems, which contained many component groups, represented a sophisticated adaptation of earlier gang systems that were disappearing, and constituted a complementary decision system to that of management. The foremen controlled the boundaries of productive activities, not the people.

The company increased its market share during the five years in question beyond that of other automobile companies in Britain, introduced automated equipment at a much earlier date, paid very much higher wages yet had lower unit costs, remained attractively profitable, and increased its assets by a third. In later years—the company was eventually taken over by British Leyland—this pattern of work organization met with severe management opposition. Too much power was being shared. Yet where the prevailing mode of a highly controlling technocratic bureaucracy has been imposed, there have been substantial increases in administrative costs and huge labor trouble.*

The Tavistock workers sought to discover how far alternative organizational patterns existed in service industries. An instance was found in a large national retail chain consisting of small shops run by four to six employees with shared tasks and all-around skills; the "manager" was a working charge-hand (Pollock, 1954). When, however, this organization enlarged its shops and extended its lines of sale, specialized jobs with several different statuses and rewards appeared along with formal control mechanisms.

At roughly the same time, opportunity arose to explore the possibility of an alternative organizational mode in a large teaching hospital. Advances in medical technology had turned the hospital into a "high pressure" center for intensive treatment, while reducing the length of patient stay and extending the range of diseases treated. This had created quite severe problems in nurse training. The work system consisted of a set of tasks broken down into narrow jobs in a similar way to that in large-scale industry. An attempt to introduce, in an experimental ward, the concept of a group of nurses becoming responsible for a group of patients met with both medical and administrative resistance, though much was learned about the embodiment in social structure and professional culture of psychological defenses against anxiety (Menzies, 1960). Integrated ward teams have since been developed in Australia by Stoelwinder (1978; Stoelwinder and Clayton, 1978).

As the last years of the postwar period came to a close in the early 1950s, the mood of the society changed from collaboration, which had fostered local innovation, to competition and an adversarial climate in management-labor relations, which discouraged it. No further instances of an alternative pattern were identified. Nevertheless the mining, textile, and automotive studies had suggested that continuous production industries that were advancing in automation might develop requirements that could eventually lead in a direction counter to the prevailing mode. Accordingly, analytic sociotechnical studies were instituted in chemical plants and power stations (Murray, 1960; Emery and Marek, 1962). These studies disclosed a basic change in the core shop-floor tasks: workers were now outside the technology, adjusting, interpreting, monitoring, and so on; they had become managers of a work system, needing conceptual and perceptual skills rather than manipulative and physical

---

*Melman's work was not known to the Tavistock at the time, nor the Tavistock work to him. An account of subsequent developments in shop floor control in the automobile and other industries is given in Coates and Topham (1980), "Workers' Control and Self-Management in Great Britain."

skills. They usually worked interdependently with others because their essential task was to keep a complex system in a steady state. The opportunity to go over to an alternative pattern, however, did not seem to be under any "hot pursuit," though Bell (1956) had pointed to the possibility and Woodward (1958) noted the presence of fewer supervisors in continuous process than in mass production plants.

For a moment it looked as though a major action research opportunity would be forthcoming in Britain. Richard Thomas and Baldwin (RTB), the largest complex in the British Steel industry, was preparing to build the most modern steelworks in Europe. They wanted to break with many constraining precedents in management and work practices that would inhibit taking full advantage of the most advanced equipment. The director of education and training invited the Tavistock to collaborate with him in evolving a new set of roles and decision rules, indeed a whole organizational structure, that would be a better match to the new technology. The method proposed was a series of participative workshops to be held in the RTB Staff College, which would be attended by the different levels and functions of management, like supervisors, key operators, and shop stewards. But there were delays in site construction—the ground proved more marshy than expected—and huge additional expenditures were incurred. The participative workshops were never held. In the end, an organizational structure and the various associated appointees were crash programmed, and all the old roles and practices were reinstated with negative consequences (as time showed) of a severe kind (Miller and Rice, 1967).

There was a rising interest in sociotechnical relations among several social scientists concerned with industry in the British setting. In Scotland, Burns and Stalker (1961) observed a new management pattern that they called "organismic," as contrasted with "mechanistic," in more technologically advanced industry. Woodward (1958) related changes in organizational structure to broad types of technology. Fensham and Hooper (1964) showed the increasing mismatch between conventional management and the requirements of a rationalized rayon industry. Such studies, however, were widely interpreted (not necessarily by their authors) as supporting a theory of technological determinism. There could be no organizational choice, as had been suggested by the Tavistock researchers.

In the United States, attention had been drawn to the counterproductive consequences of extreme job fractionalization (Walker and Guest, 1952). But concepts of job enlargement and rotation and later of job enrichment (Herzberg et al., 1959), though concerned with sociotechnical relations, focused on the individual job rather than the work system. In its orthodox form, job enrichment did not countenance participation but relied on experts brought in by management.

In Continental Europe there were occasional signs of a concern with alternative organizational modes. Westerlund (1952) reported the introduction of small groups on the Stockholm telephone exchange. Indeed a similar transformation had been carried out in Glasgow by a telecommunications engineer (Smith, 1952). King (1964), from a training approach, had introduced groups with a good deal of scope for self-regulation in small textile firms in Norway. Van Beinum (1963) had completed his studies in the Dutch telecommunications industry. In the United States, Davis (1957) introduced the concept of job design, which constituted a basic critique of industrial engineering and opened the way for systems change that could involve groups and encourage participation. A working relationship between him and the Tavistock group was established.

An opportunity for stock taking occurred at an International Conference on Workers' Participation in Management in Vienna (Trist, 1958). Interest centered on codetermination in Germany and the Yugoslav Workers' Councils. The idea of involving workers directly in decisions about what should best be done at their own level seemed strange to those concerned with industrial democracy. Only marginal attention was paid to the idea that an alternative pattern of work organization to that prevailing might be on the horizon; in the end, however, it was not entirely ignored (Clegg, 1960).

Confusion regarding the forms and meaning of industrial democracy has persisted and has still not been entirely cleared up. Four different forms may be distinguished, all of which represent modes of participation and the sharing of power. They are:

1. *Interest group democracy,* that is, collective bargaining, through which organized labor gains power to take an independent role vis-à-vis management.

2. *Representative democracy,* whereby those at the lower levels of an organization influence policies decided at higher levels (workers on boards, work councils).

3. *Owner democracy,* as in employee-owned firms and cooperative establishments where there is participation in the equity.

4. *Work-linked democracy,* meaning the participation of those directly involved in decisions about how work shall be done at their own level.

These four forms may be found independently or together, in consonance or contradiction and in different degrees in various contemporary industrial societies. The work-linked form has been the last to appear historically and is that with which sociotechnical restructuring of work is associated (Trist, 1979c).

Increasing congruence may be hypothesized among the four factors in the longer run. Table 2-1 summarizes their current relations in selected countries. Organizational democracy would be a preferable term to industrial democracy.

Table 2-1   Distribution of Forms of Organizational Democracy in Selected Countries (1980) on a Scale of 0–4[a]

	Collective Bargaining	Representative	Owner	Work-Linked
Norway	4	$3\frac{1}{2}$	$1\frac{1}{2}$	$2\frac{1}{2}$
Sweden	4	$3\frac{1}{2}$	$1\frac{1}{2}$	$2\frac{1}{2}$
Holland	3	2	1	$1\frac{1}{2}$
Australia	$2\frac{1}{2}$	1	1	1
Germany	$2\frac{1}{2}$	4	−1	−1
France	$2\frac{1}{2}$	1	−1	−1
Britain	4	0	1	0+
United States	2	0+	1	$1\frac{1}{2}$
Canada	$2\frac{1}{2}$	0+	$1\frac{1}{2}$	−1
Yugoslavia	0	4	4	0+

Note: Norway and Sweden exemplify a congruent Scandinavian pattern which Holland and Australia approximate. The larger European countries show no consistency. The U.S. and Canada express a North American form. Yugoslavia is very different with no independent unions.

[a]The ratings are personal estimates of the author.

Conceptual Developments

A monograph by Emery (1959), who had returned to the Tavistock, put forward a first generalized model of the dimensions of social and technical systems, showing that, though they were multiple, they were not so numerous that analysis would become unmanageable. Eight were identified on the technical side, including level of mechanization-automation, unit operations, the temporospatial scale of the production process, and so on.* On the social side, rigorous attention had to be paid to occupational roles and their structure, methods of payment, the supervisory relationship, and the work culture, all of which belong to the "socio" rather than the "psyche" group (Jennings, 1947). The psyche group, concerned with interpersonal relations and Bion-type "basic assumptions" regarding group behavior, however important, was not the starting point. Appropriate structural settings had to be created before desirable social climates and positive interpersonal relations would have the conditions in which to develop.

The original formulation of social and technical relations had been in terms of obtaining the best match or "goodness of fit" between the two.

---

*The others were the natural characteristics of the material, the degree of centrality of the various productive operations, the character of the maintenance and supply operations, and that of the immediate physical work setting.

In conjunction with the Norwegian Industrial Democracy project (see the following section), Emery reformulated the matching process, in terms of the more advanced systems theory that had become available, as the *joint optimization of the social and technical systems*. The technical and social systems are *independent* of each other in the sense that the former follows the laws of the natural sciences while the latter follows the laws of the human sciences and is a purposeful system. Yet they are *correlative* in that one requires the other for the *transformation* of an input into an output, which comprises the functional task of a work system. Their relationship represents a *coupling* of dissimilars that can only be jointly optimized. Attempts to optimize for either the technical or social system alone will result in the suboptimization of the sociotechnical whole.

In the language of Sommerhoff (1950, 1969), a work system depends on the social and technical components becoming *directively correlated* to produce a given goal state. They are *coproducers* of the outcome (Ackoff and Emery, 1972). The distinctive characteristics of each must be respected or else their *contradictions* will intrude and their *complementarities* will remain unrealized.

This logic was held to underlie job and organizational design. Failure to build it into the primary work system would prevent it from becoming a property of the organization as a whole.

The conceptual advances were "directively correlated" with the involvement of the Tavistock research team in the action-research opportunities that occurred as the decade of the sixties unfolded. A further round of developments took place in 1965 (Davis, Emery, and Herbst, 1965), which are incorporated in the next section. *On Purposeful Systems* (Ackoff and Emery, 1972) has had far-reaching influence on subsequent work.

The Pathfinding Role of the Norwegian Industrial Democracy Project

It seemed that no further advances could be expected until changes occurred in "the extended social field" of forces at the macrosocial level. Any happening of this kind would change the opportunities for and meaning of the efforts at the primary work system and whole organization levels. While no one could foretell where and when this might occur, such a happening could be expected from the increasing impact of the new information-based technologies.

The science-based industries were "the leading part" of the Western industrial system. They functioned as the principal change generators and brought about many other changes, directly or indirectly (Emery and Trist, 1973). Western societies were beginning what is often referred to as the second industrial revolution.

The anticipated happening occurred in 1962 in Norway, where little modernization of industry had taken place in comparison with other Scandinavian countries. Economic growth had slowed down; the largest paper and pulp company went bankrupt; Norwegian firms were being taken over by multinationals. In many other respects this very small country began to feel that it had lost control of its own destiny. Its environment had become what Emery and I (1963) have called "turbulent."

A sudden demand for workers' control erupted in the left wing of the trade union movement. Neither the Confederation of Employers nor the Confederation of Trade Unions felt they understood what it was about. Having set up an Institute for Social Research at the Technical University of Norway, they asked it to conduct an inquiry into the matter. Given the political pressures, Einar Thorsrud, the director, who had close contacts with the Tavistock, felt the inquiry would be better undertaken in association with a group outside Norway, which had accumulated relevant experience. Accordingly he invited the Tavistock to collaborate. Very soon Emery and I became, with Thorsrud, part of a planning committee composed of representatives of the two confederations. The task was to work out a jointly evolved research design. Involvement of the key stake holders in each step was a basic principle of the design.

The first inquiry undertaken was into the role of the workers' directors, whose existence was mandated by law in both state-owned enterprises and those in which the state had some capital, former German capital given to Norway by the allies after World War II. Various members of the board were interviewed, including the workers' directors, the principal members of management, and of the trade union organization. It was found that whether the workers' directors were outstanding performers or not, their presence, though valued as enhancing democratic control, had no effect on the feelings of alienation on the shop floor or on performance (Emery and Thorsrud, 1964, 1969). Accordingly it was proposed that a complementary approach be tried, that of securing the direct participation of workers in decisions about what was done at their own level. These findings were widely discussed throughout the two confederations and in the press. A consensus was reached that the mode of direct participation should be tried. The committee chose two sectors of industry that were not doing well and that were of strategic importance for the future of the economy—paper and pulp and metal working. Criteria were established in terms of which plants might be selected to conduct sociotechnical field experiments to serve as demonstration projects. Joint committees within these sectors then chose likely plants, which the research team visited to test their suitability and to secure local participation.

The research team made a study of the culture and history of Norwegian society. Industrialization had been late and more benign than in those European countries, or the United States, where industrialization had occurred earlier. Industrial relations were stable at the national level at which the two confederations accepted their complementarity. Norway had not passed through a period during which patterns of deference to authority had become entrenched. Egalitarian traditions were deep and had been more continuously maintained than in most Western societies. This configuration appeared to be favorable for the development of direct participation in the work place. These favorable conditions were strengthened by the homogeneity of the society and by its small size. Members of key groups knew each other and overlapped. If they decided to move in a new direction, there were networks through which a wide support base could soon come into existence.

These contextual conditions permitted a series of four major sociotechnical field experiments involving work restructuring not only to be launched but in three cases to be sustained (Emery and Thorsrud, 1969, 1976). Yet the hypothesis that widespread diffusion into Norwegian industry would occur from high-profile field sites turned out to be wrong. Instead they became encapsulated (Herbst, 1976). The diffusion took place in Sweden at the end of the decade, when the Norwegian results created great interest in the Employers and Trade Union Associations. Thorsrud was invited to visit Sweden. By 1973 between 500 and 1000 work-improvement projects of various kinds, small and large, were going on in many different industries. A new generation of Swedes, better educated and more affluent, refused (by absenteeism and turnover) to do the dullest and most menial jobs. The importation of Southern Europeans created social problems. Something had to be done. Managers and unions took up the Norwegian approach and adapted it to their own purposes.

After that, shifts in the macrosocial field in Scandinavia recentered attention on the representation of workers on boards of management just when, in Germany, some interest appeared in direct participation. A number of laws have been passed in Norway and Sweden whose effects are still being assimilated. In both countries a third of the members of the boards have to be workers' representatives.

The Shell Philosophy Project

In Britain a large-scale sociotechnical project begun by the Tavistock with Shell (U.K.) in 1965 showed the need to develop a new management philosophy to establish values and principles that could be seen by all to guide work redesign, if commitment was to be secured not only from the various levels of management but also from the work force (Hill, 1971). This project led to a whole series of 2½-day, off-site, residential conferences to discuss the original draft philosophy document and to amend and ratify it. These conferences involved all levels of the organization from the board to the shop floor, and the outside trade union officials as well as the shop stewards in five refineries.

After some four years, the advances brought about by this project were arrested by an exceedingly complex situation within both the company and the industry. The ways in which the clock began to be turned back are described in Hill's (1971) book. The approach, however, was taken up by Shell in other countries—Australia, Holland, and more recently Canada. It appears to be characteristic of innovative processes that after a certain time particular implemental sites reach their limit. The burden of trailblazing is then taken up by others where favorable conditions emerge.

Meanwhile, what had happened regarding work restructuring and participation, especially in Sweden, created interest in the United States. Though one or two pioneer sociotechnical projects had been under way for some time in the United States, it was not until 1973 that wider public interest was awakened. Notions of work alienation were popularized by the media and associated with the threat of declining productivity in the face of Japanese and West German competition.

At an international conference held at Arden House in 1972, the term "quality of working life" (QWL) was introduced by Dr. Louis Davis. Along with *Work in America* (O'Toole, 1972), which extended consideration to the mental health aspects of the work place and the work-family interface, this conference has set the tone for further developments. In Bateson's (1972) sense, it repunctuated the field. The two volumes of papers emanating from it (Davis and Cherns, 1975) have become its standard reference work. Since then, sociotechnical concepts and methods have become one input into a wider field concerned with changing social values and studying the effects of values on organizations and their individual members. The age of resource scarcity has coincided with increasing recognition that advanced industrial societies are producing conditions that are impoverishing the overall quality of life. The quality of life in the work place is increasingly seen as a critical part of this overall quality. It is now less accepted that boredom and alienation are inherently a part of work life for the many, or that they must perforce accept authoritarian control in narrow jobs. Examples in almost any industry of alternative forms of sociotechnical relations show that these negative features do not have to be endured. For individuals and organizations alike, there is a choice.

In the 1950s, the societal climate was negative toward sociotechnical innovation. Thirty years later, in the 1980s, the societal climate is becoming positive (Walton, 1979), though in most Western countries the support base remains limited in face of the persisting power of the technocratic and bureaucratic mode. Yet this mode is being experienced as increasingly dysfunctional in the more complex and uncertain conditions of the wider environment. Emergent values are moving in the direction of regarding personal growth as a human right. All who wish it should have the opportunity to cultivate it. The work place constitutes a key setting for this purpose. A Norwegian law of 1976 gives workers the right to demand jobs conforming to the six psychological principles described in the next section of this paper. These are the principles that shaped the original sociotechnical experiments of the Norwegian Industrial Democracy project.

DEVELOPMENTS AT THE LEVEL OF THE PRIMARY WORK SYSTEM

In reviewing the developments that have taken place since the sociotechnical concept was established, it is appropriate to begin with the primary work system, since this has been made the organizational building block.

The advent of the Norwegian Industrial Democracy project faced the research team with the task of intervening in the design of work systems. The situation was different from that of the 1950s, when the key innovations had appeared spontaneously. In the development of sociotechnical studies concepts and methods have evolved in relation to the demands of the field situation.

The Principles of Work Design

A set of principles was needed to improve work design so that the ideal of joint optimization could be approached. Basic to this was some knowledge of the psychological requirements individuals have of their work beyond what is usually included in an employment contract. Herzberg et al. (1959) seemed to be right in separating the extrinsic from the intrinsic dimensions of job satisfaction, whatever the statistical arguments about "dissatisfiers" and "motivators." What the trade unions had fought for had to be sustained, or to be won where it did not exist —adequate and fair pay, job security, benefits, safety, health, due process. These constituted the conditions of employment. What also had to be considered was the extent to which jobs satisfied other, intrinsic requirements that could only arise from the character of the jobs themselves and of the work organization in which they were embedded.

Drawing on Lewin's (1935) Berlin experiments on person-task relations, as well as on his and Bion's later work with groups, Emery (1964, 1976) identified six intrinsic characteristics (listed in Table 2-2, where they are compared with extrinsic characteristics). The intrinsic characteristics may be spelled out as follows:

1. The need for the content of a job to be reasonably demanding in terms other than sheer endurance, and to provide some variety—not necessarily novelty.

Table 2-2   Properties of Jobs

Extrinsic	Intrinsic
Fair and adequate pay	Variety and challenge
Job security	Continuous learning
Benefits	Discretion, autonomy
Safety	Recognition and support
Health	Meaningful social contribution
Due process	Desirable future
Conditions of employment: socioeconomic	The job itself: psychosocial

2. The need to be able to learn on the job and go on learning. Again it is a question of neither too much nor too little.

3. The need for an area of decision making that the individual can call his or her own.

4. The need for a certain degree of social support and recognition in the work place for the value of what he or she does.

5. The need to be able to relate the work and what is produced to his or her social life, so that it has meaning and affords dignity.

6. The need to feel that the job leads to some sort of desirable future—not necessarily promotion.

These intrinsic requirements are not confined to any one level of employment. It is not possible to meet them in the same way in all work settings or for all kinds of people. They cannot always be judged from conscious expression. When there is no expectation that any of the jobs open to a worker will offer much chance of learning, he or she will soon learn to forget such a requirement.

The requirements are too general to serve as principles for work redesign. For this purpose they need to be linked to the objective characteristics of industrial jobs (Davis, 1957). Table 2-3 (see Emery, 1978a) summarizes the linkage.

The redesigning of work leads beyond individual jobs to the organization of groups of workers, and beyond that to the organization of support services, such as maintenance. The wider implications affect organization design more generally. A congruent set of principles of work design and of "core dimensions" of jobs has been identified by other writers (Hackman and Lawler, 1971; Hackman, Oldham, et al., 1975; Herrick and Maccoby, 1975; Walton, 1975a; Hackman and Suttle, 1977). This degree of agree-

Table 2-3 Principles of Work Design

At the Level of the Individual	At Group Level, Interlocking Where
Optimum variety of tasks within the job	There is a necessary interdependence of jobs (for technical or psychological reasons)
A meaningful pattern of tasks that gives to each job a semblance of a single, overall task	Individual jobs entail a relatively high degree of stress
Optimum length of the work cycle	Individual jobs do not make a perceivable contribution to the utility of the end product
Some scope for setting standards of quantity and quality of production and a suitable feedback of knowledge of results	The linkages create some semblance of an overall task
The inclusion in the job of some of the auxiliary and prepatory tasks	There is some scope for setting standards and receiving knowledge of results
The inclusion of some degree of care, skill, knowledge, or effort that is worthy of respect in the community	Some control can be exercised over the "boundary tasks"
The inclusion of some perceivable contribution to the utility of the product for the consumer	Channels of communication are such that the minimum requirements of the workers can be fed into the design of new jobs at an early stage
	Channels of promotion to supervisor rank exist that are sanctioned by the workers

ment is exceptional in so new a field and has placed work redesign on a firmer foundation than is commonly realized.

Individual Differences in Motivation

A wide range of individual differences has been found in work force motivation. All workers do not want "enriched" jobs or to take on more responsibility. This was investigated by Hackman and Lawler (1971), whose findings indicate that employees with some need for "higher order" satisfaction perform better and feel more positive when their jobs rate high on the four core dimensions, which are similar to those identified by Emery. Those whose motivational pattern is not particularly oriented to higher need satisfaction do not show so strong a pattern of association, though most of the correlations are in the same direction.

Much of the literature on job satisfaction has attached too much importance to responses given at only one point in time, especially to questionnaires. People change over time and learn through experience. Many workers do not know what their real feelings will turn out to be until they have had actual experience of redesigned jobs. They need to know also whether such jobs are likely to be an enduring feature of their work lives or whether they represent merely a temporary change.

It makes a difference whether one is considering solely individual attitudes or also social change involving norms and values. Employees who are convinced that their organization has committed itself—long term—to joint optimization are more likely to commit themselves than those who are not. This is especially so if they sense that the norms and values of the wider society are also changing in the direction of the new paradigm.

A work group offers scope for a range of abilities and preferences. There is more room for individual differences in work groups than in standardized individual work stations.

Motivation in the work place has been reconceptualized by Susman (1976) in terms of a theory of directed action, which draws on the object relations tradition in psychoanalysis (Klein, 1932, 1959) and on the work, deriving from Lewin and gestalt psychology, of Chein (1954, 1972). Directed action is transactional. It is concerned with the completion of an object relationship. It is a molar concept coproduced by the characteristics of the object and the meaning that the subject imparts to the situation. The individual and the work place become directively correlated. This view enables Susman to spell out the conditions under which directed action can be incorporated into work design so that the individual experiences self-enhancement. These conditions are consistent with the principles summarized earlier and provide the enabling context in which commitment can develop.

Work Analysis

Also needed was a method for analyzing work systems. This had not only to be academically defensible but communicable to workers, managers, and staff specialists who could, after some practice, become able to use it for themselves. The following nine-step model derives from the second field experiment of the Norwegian Industrial Democracy project at the Hunsfoss Paper and Pulp Mill, which began in 1964 (Emery and Thorsrud, 1969, 1976) and where for the first time an "action group" of workers, technicians, and supervisors was created in order to diagnose the malfunctioning of the particular system they were concerned with. Emery was again the initiator. The condensed version, quoted below from Trist (1971), has been put in systems terms to make it as general as possible.

1. An initial scanning is made of all the main aspects, technical and social, of the *selected target system,* that is, the department or plant to be studied.

2. The *unit operations*—that is, the transformations (changes of state) of the material or product that take place in the target system—are then identified, whether carried out by people or machines.

3. An attempt is made to discover the *key variances* and their interrelations. A variance is key if it significantly affects (a) either the quantity or quality of production, and (b) either the operating or social costs of production.

4. A table of variance control is then drawn up to ascertain *how far the key variances are controlled by the social system*—the workers, supervisors, and managers concerned. Investigation is made of what variances are imported or exported across the social-system boundary.

5. A separate inquiry is made into *social-system members' perception* of their roles and of role possibilities as well as constraining factors.

6. Attention then shifts to *neighboring systems,* beginning with the support or maintenance system.

7. Attention continues to the *boundary-crossing systems* on the input and output side, that is, supplier and user systems.

8. The target system and its immediate neighbors are then considered in the context of the *general management system* of the organization as regards the effects of policies or development plans of either a technical or social nature.

9. Recycling occurs at any stage, eventually culminating in *design proposals* for the target or neighboring systems.

This procedure was first used as a training method for departmental managers in the Shell Management Philosophy project in the United Kingdom (Hill, 1971). It has since been incorporated by Davis in the UCLA Short Course on QWL.

The model was originally tailored to the requirements of continuous process industries. A variant for office units was then introduced. While a number of alternatives are likely to be required for different technologies, the logic of relating any target system to the set of its surrounding systems would appear to be general.

Autonomous Groups and Primary Work Systems

No one group in any organization can be completely autonomous. It can only be conditionally or semiautonomous. There are, nevertheless, several dimensions and degrees of autonomy. The most systematic analysis of these has been made by Susman (1976), who, building on an earlier paper by Gulowsen (1972), approaches this question by distinguishing three classes of decision: those concerning independence, those concerning self-governance, and those concerning types of self-regulatory activity. He separates boundary-transaction uncertainty from conversion uncertainty and proceeds to introduce categories of technically required cooperation, type of interdependence, and type of coordination. These concepts provide a framework for the analysis of autonomy more rigorous than that previously available.

A sociotechnical theory of the efficacy of autonomous work groups is based on the cybernetic concept of self-regulation. The more the key variances can be controlled by the group, the better the results and the higher the member satisfaction. Over a large array of situations, the range of variances controllable by a group is greater than that controllable by individuals separately linked to an external supervisor. The difference in the underlying design principle is summarized in Emery's concept of "participant design" (1974, 1976). The function of supervision is to manage the boundary conditions in the group's environment so that the group itself may be freed to manage its own activities. This is a very different concept from the bureaucratic theory of control.

Autonomous groups are learning systems. As their capabilities increase, they extend their decision space. In production units they tend to absorb certain maintenance and control functions. They become able to set their own machines. Their problem-solving capacity increases on day-to-day issues.* They negotiate for their special needs with their supply and user departments. As time goes on, more of their members acquire more of the relevant skills. Yet most such groups allow a considerable range of preferences as regards multiskilling and job interchange. The less venturesome and more modestly endowed can find suitable niches. The overall gain in flexibility can become very considerable, and this can be used to enhance performance and also to accommodate personal needs as regards time off, shifts, vacations, and so on.

Autonomous groups do not always succeed. A good deal is known about the conditions affecting their success or failure. These will not be reviewed here, except to note that one of the most common reasons for failure is lack of support in the surrounding organizational milieu. A year or two ago, my research center at the University of Pennsylvania carried out a study of "work teams" in a very large organization. Of the 90 that had existed at some time during a 10-year period, only two were extant when the study was made. In addition to the effects of the mid-seventies recession in disrupting work teams through layoffs, a principal reason for failure was lack of support in the wider organization. When the initiator departed, "fade-out" occurred (MBSC, 1978), no matter how successful the project was economically.

---

*Some of these features are found in the Japanese Quality Control Circles.

Autonomous groups of the face-to-face kind are not the only type of nonhierarchical social formation that has appeared at the level of the primary work system. Herbst (1976) points to matrix-type groups in which there is limited overlap between member skills that are too complex for all to learn. In such groups, there may be considerable spatial and temporal scattering. Herbst also mentions clusters of network roles that "boundary span" across primary work systems and also connect subgroups within such systems. Matrix groups and network clusters are becoming prominent as organizational interdependencies increase. This is apt to happen to a greater extent in advanced technologies and in organizations with large and varied clienteles.

There has been disagreement about the number of individuals suitable for inclusion in autonomous work groups. Small group theory supports an upper limit in the 8 to 12 range. The Tavistock mining studies, however, showed that "composite groups" tended to be much larger. A number of other studies have reported groups beyond the limit of the face-to-face range. These all tend to be complex groups with several subsets.

Another unit of analysis is required, namely the *primary work system,* which may include more than one face-to-face group along with others in matrix and network clusters. The primary work system is a functional system with a semi-independent operational identity, whether as a production or service unit. In the Saab 99 engine plant, all the assembly teams of three formed part of the same primary work system.

In a primary work system an individual is apt to have several group memberships. In the mining studies a miner considered himself as belonging basically to a "seam society" in which he had established rights and privileges regarding employment and deployment. Within the seam he belonged to a face or cycle group, and beyond that to a task group. This latter was more temporary than the former, which, though focal, was less enduring than belonging to the seam. These multiple but congruent memberships gave the miner considerable "space of free movement" within a seam population of more than 100 people, which still comprised a personal world. The seam group contained ancillary personnel, a district management system, and a complete territory, as well as all the equipment necessary for mining (see Miller, 1959, regarding the relations between territory, technology, and time). It constituted a *polity,* being a recognized worker constituency with representatives who conducted detailed negotiations for the seam within the overall union agreement for the colliery.

This was the type of group that Rice found in the automatic loomshed in Ahmedabad (though the overall number was smaller), which Melman found in the Standard Motor Company in Coventry (though the overall number was larger), and which Burden (1975) described in the microwax plant in Shell's Stanlow refinery in Cheshire. In my own work I have found such groups in a number of situations, including Alcan's Reduction

Division at Arvida, where the quite large divisional work force served as a reference community for the on-shift task groups of six. It functioned as their polity, making all decisions concerning self-governance, including the decision to accept the proposal (which its representatives took part in shaping) to try out autonomous work groups. The task groups made decisions concerning the self-regulation of their own activities.

Primary work systems of this scale and this complexity are the type of sociotechnical unit that is emerging at the present time in a number of new plants in North America. Cummins Engines' diesel plant in Jamestown, New York (Pava, 1979), and Shell's petrochemical plants in Sarnia, Ontario (Davis and Sullivan, 1980), are examples. In the latter the workers have the possibility of learning not only all the process jobs, but also a coordinating or service job in instrumentation, the lab, quality control, maintenance, and so on. An advantage from their point of view is that they can maximize their time on days (over 50 percent), a cherished improvement as regards the work-home interface.

Such arrangements increase the competencies that may be acquired, the number of deployment patterns available, and the career paths open. For the individual they create *roles* rather than mere jobs. For the organization they bring into being a *variety-increasing system* directively correlated with the complexities and interdependencies of the technology. Emery (1980) has described an elaborate system of this kind in a new metal mine in Australia, where there is a paramount need to share information and for all to have a cognitive map of the entire process. This cognitive map is the essential system control that has now become a new "dissipative structure" (Prigogine, 1968) in the workers themselves. It represents a "morphogenetic" change. The penalties of not evolving sociotechnical systems of this kind have been suffered in more than one nuclear power plant. Complex primary work systems will increase as computer-aided continuous process technology advances. Group or cellular technology offers a parallel opportunity in batch production (Williamson, 1972). These areas need an intensification of research efforts.

Multiple memberships in a larger group that comprises a *social aggregate* may be postulated as lessening the dangers of overinvestment that can easily occur if the individual is bound too exclusively in one face-to-face group. These dangers have been investigated by Miller and Rice (1967) in their work on the relations between task and "sentient" group boundaries. The benefit in greater cohesion consequent on the coincidence of these boundaries tends to be offset by a greater propensity to self-sealing. The presence of a social aggregate introduces properties into a primary work system different from those of the constituent task groups (see Churchman and Emery, 1966). It constitutes the ground on which they are the figures. To have some ground of its own on which to stand increases the power of a group in a wider organizational setting to relate to other groups having similar standing. This enables the members of a primary work system to become a polity. The ability of the system group to become a polity or worker constituency relates it directly to the trade-union organization. This may undo many fears that union people have concerning autonomous groups—that even though the consequence may be unintended, their effect will be to undermine the union by bringing into being a competing loyalty.

The development of self-standing primary work systems containing mixes of groups with commonly shared skills, matrices whose members have partly overlapping skills, and networks of mainly specialist skills constitutes a new basis for the effectiveness of sociotechnical organizations. They create organizational units of considerable robustness, which compose microsocieties having intragroup, intergroup, and aggregate relations with a whole operational task. These microsocieties provide considerable space of free movement to the individual and are open to the interorganizational environment.

Self-standing primary work systems exemplify a holographic principle of organization in which the whole is represented in the part (Pribram, 1977). The forms through which holographic primary work systems may best become linked to the overall organization constitute an area requiring further research. The question is not so much that of small being beautiful as of finding ways of retaining small in large so that the advantages of both may be realized. Open systems planning as developed by Clarke, Krone, and McWhinney (Jayaram, 1976; McWhinney, 1980) would seem to offer a promising new approach to this problem.

DEVELOPMENTS IN WHOLE ORGANIZATION SYSTEMS

Very early on in sociotechnical studies it became evident that innovations in work organization based on principles different from those on which conventional bureaucratic organizations were founded were not likely to survive for long unless the organization as a whole changed in the new direction. Joint optimization involves a different principle from that of following the technical imperative. The group-centered primary work systems that are evolving in relation to it are radically different from the one-person-one-job units upon which conventional organizations have built their top-down hierarchies.

The basic difference constitutes what Emery and Trist (1973; Emery, 1967) have called a *design principle*. There are two basic organizational design principles, both of which display "redundancy" in the systems theoretical sense. In the first, the redundancy is of parts and is mechanistic. The parts are broken down so that the ultimate elements are as simple and inexpensive as possible, as with the unskilled worker in a narrow job who is cheap to replace and who takes little time to train. The technocratic bureaucracy is founded on this type of design. In the second design principle, the redundancy is of functions and is organic. Any component system has a repertoire that can be put to many uses, so that increased adaptive flexibility is acquired. While this is true at the biological level, as for example in the human body, it becomes far greater at the organizational level where the components—individual humans and groups of humans—are themselves purposeful systems. Humans have the capacity for self-regulation so that control may become internal rather than external. Only organizations based on the redundancy of functions have the flexibility and innovative potential to give the possibility of adaptation to a rapid change rate, increasing complexity, and environmental uncertainty.

Rational choice between the two design principles must take the state of the wider social field into account. The increasingly disturbed state of this macrosocial level came to the attention of Emery and me (1963). In our action research projects at that time, we and our organizational clients were baffled by the extent to which the wider societal environment was moving in on their more immediate concerns, upsetting plans, preventing the achievement of operational goals, and causing additional stress and severe internal conflict. The magnitude of this impact was recognized by those concerned as greater than any previously experienced. The difference seemed to us to hold theoretical significance. Accordingly, we separated this wider environment, which we called the contextual, from the more immediate transactional environment and attempted a conceptual analysis of its characteristics.

Four types of contextual environment were isolated. The first two, called the random placid and the placid clustered, need not be discussed in the present context. The third environmental type, however, called the disturbed-reactive, reflects an accelerating change rate and became increasingly salient as the Industrial Revolution progressed. It peaked some time after World War II, when the science-based industries rose to prominence in the wake of the knowledge and information explosions. The best chances of survival in this world went to large-scale organizations with the capacity to make formidable competitive challenge through expertise and to maximize their independent power. The organizational form they perfected was the competitive and singular technocratic bureaucracy in which the ideas of Weber and Frederick Taylor are matched and operationalized to fit the requirements of the disturbed-reactive environment.

The very success of the technocratic bureaucracy has increased the salience of another type of environment, very different from the disturbed-reactive, which is mismatched with technocratic bureaucracy. The new environment is called the turbulent field, in which large competing organizations, all acting independently in diverse directions, produce unanticipated and dissonant consequences. These mount as the common field becomes more densely occupied. The result is a kind of contextual commotion that makes it seem as if "the ground" were moving as well as the organizational actors. This is what is meant by turbulence. Subjectively, it is experienced as "a loss of the stable state" (Schon, 1971).

As compared with the disturbed-reactive environment, the turbulent field is characterized by a higher level of interdependence among the "causal strands" (Chein, 1954) and a higher level of complexity as regards heterogeneity. Together these generate a much higher level of uncertainty. The turbulent field has the characteristics of a richly joined environment in Ashby's (1960) sense. He did not think the brain, as an ultrastable system, could cope with such an environment. While this may be true in other species, the human brain, through its unusual capacity for abstraction from the concrete (Goldstein, 1939), is able to think in terms of "possible worlds." This enables the human individual to be "ideal seeking," which Ackoff and Emery (1972) regard as the distinctively human attribute. The importance of ideals is that they can never be reached but provide continuous "guiding fictions" (Allport, 1937) in the pursuit of changing objectives and goals. Ideals are basic to value formation, and when common values are shared by large numbers of people, they become able to undertake congruent courses of action. They can move in the same direction on the basis of "shared appreciations" (Vickers, 1965). These are independent of particular social structures. The adaptability imparted would appear to be basic for the capacity to cope with environmental turbulence. The most recent analysis of this is by Emery (1976).

The higher levels of interdependence, complexity, and uncertainty now to be found in the world environment pass the limits within which technocratic bureaucracies were designed to operate. Given its solely independent purposes, its primarily competitive relations, its mechanistic authoritarian control structure, and its tendency to debase human resources, this organizational form cannot absorb environmental turbulence, much less reduce it. But such absorption and reduction are a necessary condition for opening the way to a viable human future.

In Sartre's sense, the technocratic bureaucracy has been "depassed" in the historical process. Though Galbraith (1967) has referred to it, and the disturbed-reactive environment to which it is linked, as the "new industrial state," these are both better seen, McLuhan-wise, through the rearview mirror, as the old industrial state. Once one has become freed from past fixations in this regard, one is able to proceed with the evolution of values, cognitive orientations, and organizational modalities capable of matching up to the precarious state of affairs now looming in the contextual environment.

Emergent organizational forms likely to have adaptive potential in this situation must be able to cope with the new levels of interdependence, complexity, and uncertainty.

New Plants

A major problem for sociotechnical research now arose: the identification of an organizational model that would offer an alternative to that of the conventional technocratic and bureaucratic types of organization. Theoretically one could expect to found it on the second design principle of the redundancy of functions. The most likely place to find examples of an emergent alternative seemed to be among new plants in the science-based industries. Accordingly, opportunities were sought for action-research engagements with companies bringing such plants on stream and willing to explore alternative designs with the help of social scientists.

In the latter part of the 1960s, a number of new plants of this kind came into existence in different countries. Projects in which social scientists were involved included a fertilizer plant in Norway, a refinery in the United Kingdom, an aluminum fabrication plant in Canada, and a consumer products plant and a pet food plant in the United States.*

Given well-developed primary work systems, these plants had fewer levels, functions, and numbers of management personnel than conventional plants. The numbers in the work force were also lower—often a third lower. Payment was for knowledge, not for what a person did at a particular time, so that individuals could evolve progressive work roles no longer confined by job classifications that rigidly defined wage differentials and statuses. Supervisors were either nonexistent or became facilitators, trainers, and forward planners. Information was shared for the purpose of problem-solving, which became the task of everyone, not only of management. This principle gave an underlying logic to management's adopting a participant style.

Performance levels were usually above those of conventional plants with which they could be compared. Moreover, these levels improved through time. The plants were learning systems. Employees, who tended to be volunteers and who were carefully selected, preferred them to conventional plants. A number of others preferred to stay where they were.

In the last two or three years, the number of new plants developed on these lines has increased very considerably, especially in the United States. In the latest versions, the social aspect has been considered much

*The firms were respectively: Norskhydro, Shell, Alcan, Proctor and Gamble, and General Foods. The social scientists concerned were part of an evolving sociotechnical network: Davis, Emery, Thorsrud, Trist, Walton. Trist collaborated with Emery and Thorsrud in the first phase of the Norwegian Industrial Democracy project which Davis and Walton visited later. Davis joined Emery and Trist for a while in the Tavistock's project with Shell. Davis and Trist both came to UCLA, where they held a seminar that began the work with Alcan and also with Proctor and Gamble (through Clarke). Walton spent a sabbatical year at UCLA. He later began the work with General Foods that Trist eventually became involved in. Hill (Shell), Cameron (Alcan), Krone (Proctor and Gamble), and Ketchum (General Foods) were key people involved on the companies' side.

earlier, so that the ideal of joint sociotechnical design is being more closely approached.

Another sociotechnical design principle that has begun to affect practice is "minimum critical specification" (Herbst, 1974). Only the essentials are decided a priori; as much as possible is left open to be decided at later stages, even when the plant is already in operation. The principle allows the progressive involvement of those concerned—at all levels. The barriers between planners and implementors are reduced. Design and operations are seen as a continuous process.

Sociotechnical design has now come to include a large number of factors of context, sanction, stake holder inclusion, and processes of implementation as well as joint optimization of the social and technical systems. A set of principles based on these factors has been put forward by Cherns (1976).

New and Old Organizational Paradigms

These plants exemplify the model that new installations are likely to emulate during the eighties. Beyond that, they may foreshadow a new organizational paradigm that, as time goes on, will displace the old paradigm of the technocratic bureaucracy. This displacement will come about because the new form has the flexibility and the resilience to cope with turbulent environmental fields, whereas the old form lacks these capabilities. It will use fewer resources in so doing; it will be efficient as well as effective (Trist, 1979b). Table 2-4 sets out the key features of the new organizational paradigm that can potentially lead to a high QWL for all

Table 2-4   Features of Old and New Paradigms

Old Paradigm	New Paradigm
The technological imperative	Joint optimization
People as extensions of machines	People as complementary to machines
People as expendable spare parts	People as a resource to be developed
Maximum task breakdown, simple narrow skills	Optimum task grouping, multiple broad skills
External controls (supervisors, specialist staffs, procedures)	Internal controls (self-regulating subsystems)
Tall organization chart, autocratic style	Flat organization chart, participative style
Competition, gamesmanship	Collaboration, collegiality
Organization's purposes only	Members' and society's purposes also
Alienation	Commitment
Low risk-taking	Innovation

members of the enterprise. They contrast strongly with those of the old organizational paradigm, set out on the left, which has been instrumental in constraining most employees to a low QWL.

Our traditional organizations follow the technological imperative, which regards people simply as extensions of the machine and therefore as expendable spare parts. By contrast, the emergent paradigm is founded on the principle of joint optimization, which regards people as complementary to the machine and values their unique capabilities for appreciative and evaluative judgment. People are a resource to be developed for their own sake rather than to be degraded and cast aside. As my former Tavistock colleague Phil Herbst (1975) has aptly observed, "the product of work is people," as well as goods or services. A society is no better than the quality of the people it produces.

Traditional organizations are also characterized by maximum work breakdown, which leads to circumscribed job descriptions and single skills—the narrower the better. Workers in such roles are often unable to manage the uncertainty, or variance, that characterizes their immediate environment. They therefore require strict external controls. Layer upon layer of supervision comes into existence supported by a wide variety of specialist staffs and formal procedures. A tall pyramidic organization results, which is autocratically managed throughout, even if the paternalism is benign. By contrast, the new paradigm is based on optimum task grouping, which encourages multiple broad skills. Workers in such a role system—as opposed to a job system—become capable of a much higher degree of internal control, having flexible group resources to meet a greater degree of environmental variance. This leads to a flat organization characterized by as much lateral as vertical communication. A participative management style emerges with the various levels mutually articulated (see Parsons, 1960) rather than arranged in a simple hierarchy.

In the traditional organization the members have first of all to compete with and defend themselves against everyone else, whether as an individual or as a member of a functional group—maintenance versus production, staff versus line. Rewards such as promotion and privilege go to those who, in the metaphor introduced by Michael Maccoby (1976), are "gamesmen"—those who excel in playing the political game of the organization. Cooperation, though formally required wherever tasks are interdependent, takes second place as a value. The new paradigm, by contrast, gives first place to coping with the manifold interdependencies that arise in complex organizations. It values collaboration between groups and collegiality within groups. It encourages the establishment of a negotiated order in which multiple and mutually agreed trade-offs are continuously arrived at.

Traditional organizations serve only their own ends. They are, and indeed are supposed to be, selfish. The new paradigm imposes the additional task on them of aligning their own purposes with the purposes of the wider society and also with the purposes of their members. By so doing, organizations become both "environmentalized" and "humanized" (Ackoff, 1974)—and thus more truly purposeful—rather than remaining impersonal and mindless forces that increase environmental turbulence.

A change in all these regards from the old paradigm to the new brings into being conditions that allow commitment to grow and alienation to decrease. Equally important is the replacement of a climate of low risk-taking with one of innovation. This implies high trust and openness in relations. All these qualities are mandatory if we are to transform traditional technocratic bureaucracies into continuous adaptive learning systems.

This transformation is imperative for survival in a fast-changing environment. It involves nothing less than the working out of a new organizational philosophy.

I use the term philosophy advisedly to indicate that far more is involved than methods or techniques. These or course have their place, but a philosophy involves questions of basic values and assumptions. Those of the new paradigm are radically different from those of the old. The old is based on technocratic and bureaucratic principles, the new on socioecological and participative principles. Each subsystem has a wide repertoire of response capability. It can thus better meet uncertainty and contain turbulence. This is one of the most important features of self-regulating systems—both autonomous work groups and open, mutually articulated organizational levels. The old is geared to the requirements and characteristics of industrial societies as these have been fashioned historically. The new is geared to the requirements and characteristics of the emerging postindustrial order. At present, we are in a transition channel between the two. A transition channel is always an uncomfortable place to be, full as it is of incompatibilities and mirages. Is there wonder that we have lost the stable state?

Innovative projects in new plants take advantage of privileged circumstances to demonstrate the reality of paths into the future that would otherwise remain no more than untested possibilities. They represent the fullest embodiment of the new model so far attained.

Established Work Organizations

In established plants one has to deal with the people already there, among whom are those who don't want to change or whose limitations of ability or forms of character prevent them from changing. The accumulated practices of the past exert their influence, as well as an array of vested interests. If the plant is unionized, management may fear to surrender prerogatives and workers may fear to compromise the union's independence. Yet there has to be some agreed-upon sharing of power if success is to be attained. Sharing of power is a basic principle of the new model.

In established plants, progress has been at best slow; at worst, the change effort has had to be abandoned. New methods of process consultation seem required. Ketchum (1975) has evolved a practice of uncovering what Argyris and Schon (1974) would call "theories in use" as distinct from "espoused theories." He attempts to draw away key participants from deep implicit attachments to the "traditional system" before anything new is proposed. But to cover a whole organizational population in this manner poses problems as yet unsolved in change efforts with social aggregates. Yet entire organizational populations are what one must deal with at this system level.

A dilemma now arises. The way forward would seem to lie in what is being developed in innovative work establishments. These innovations, however, are resisted in many if not most conventional establishments. Even where they are welcome, substantial change cannot be introduced across the board. Yet where such change is left in only one section of a plant or in only one plant in a corporation, more often than not it fades out or is actively stopped. In most of the plants mentioned earlier, so great were external pressures to conformity that sooner or later they underwent some regression toward the conventional mode (Hill, 1971; Walton, 1975b). For the most part, their example was rejected by other units in their own corporations, though they received large numbers of visitors from other organizations who not infrequently adapted some of what they saw to their own purposes. Whatever the course of diffusion, it is not linear.

Change Strategies

Given the increasingly turbulent environmental conditions likely in the 1980s, there is need to hasten the transformation of established organizations towards the new paradigm. To discover how this may be better attempted constitutes a priority for sociotechnical research.

What follows is a sketch of how far my own thinking has progressed in this matter. It is based on a theory of the appreciation-planning-implementation process that I am working out with my Wharton colleague, Howard Perlmutter, in a book we are at present struggling with.

The first step is to secure an appreciation (Vickers, 1965) of the issues at the highest level of the corporation or agency—the institutional level, as Parsons (1960) called it, the level of governance as distinct from "management", the level at which normative planning (Ozbekhan, 1969) takes place. At this level, critical choices are made about organizational values and philosophy. A methodology that has been evolved for working at this level is the "search conference" (Emery and Emery, 1978). The board, the president, and the vice-presidents (the overlap is important) go off-site for two or three days to scan the wider environment in a futures perspective, to review the present state of the organization in relation to this perspective, to discover how far they can create a shared image of a desirable organizational future, and finally to consider action steps towards that desired goal, keeping constraints in mind and looking for opportunities. The Tavistock project with Shell (United Kingdom) began in this way. A "philosophy document," based on a working draft jointly produced by the internal and external research teams, was sanctioned at a top management retreat and then discussed and modified at residential conferences, which were held at all levels, including the shop floor. An organizational population of 6000 employees was reached in this way. Many varieties of this type of procedure are likely to be tried.

The next step, at the strategic level of management, is concerned with a process that I have called "selective development" (Trist, 1979b). Since change cannot take place at all points at the same time, the plants or other self-standing establishments where sociotechnical change is most needed and most likely to be accepted have to be identified. This is a vice-presidential function, but the vice-presidents need to do it together with the president. If they have not participated in the normative meetings, they will not appreciate what is required.

A third step consists of selecting concrete project sites within plants or other self-standing work establishments. The plant manager would now consult with a cross-section of other managers at all levels. As early as possible the plant manager would include the union. If there is no union, some way has to be found of involving the work force. Procedures at this operational level tend to be more idiomatic, given the great variety of circumstances.

Ultimately, what Emery (1976) has called a "deep slice"—a task force of workers, line supervisors, specialists—may be selected to carry out an investigation and make recommendations on what might best be done at a given project site in consultation with those directly involved. Those persons would have to "own" the project or nothing much would happen.

At the operational level, joint labor-management steering committees have a key function in deciding on, assisting, and evaluating project sites. In the United States such committees have been developing in the sociotechnical field, though with many vicissitudes, since the beginning of the program of the then National Commission on Productivity and Work Quality in 1973.

One or two firms such as General Motors have now included the union in strategic and normative level conferences. This is a pointer to the future. The union may indeed initiate the whole process in its own interest as a union, as the United Auto Workers did with G.M. in introducing humanization of work clauses into the 1973 agreement.

The process described above derives from a theory of change based on the idea of stake holder participation. Those interest groups who have a stake in what is being decided are represented at every step, in overlapping sets much as in Likert's (1961) linking-pin theory, down, up, and across. There is scope for experimentation in involving the social aggregate in open meetings at shop-floor level: the microsocieties of primary work systems, combinations of such systems, even the entire plant population.* Line supervisors and junior staffs may require their own aggregate meetings. In the future, various levels within management are likely to formalize their own reference groups. They have already done so in several European countries. The kinds of people inside and outside the organization claiming stake holder status are likely to increase.

This type of process would not be embarked upon unless those concerned were convinced that sociotechnical change in the direction of the new paradigm was a long-term process contributing to enhanced organizational capability relevant to coping with rising contextual turbulence. The ultimate motivation is survival.

Change of this type, which involves the discontinuity of a paradigm shift, is an emotional as well as an intellectual experience for those undergoing it. Prolonged opportunities need to be given for "working through" the difficulties and issues that arise at many levels, conscious and unconscious. The structure and culture of organizations have evolved as an adaptation to the prevailing societal environment. People have learned to make this adaptation with considerable effort. Many of their ego defenses are projected into the existing structure and culture (Trist and Bamforth, 1951; Jaques, 1953; Menzies, 1960). They have formed their occupational identities in relation to them. They now find themselves faced with having to give up what it has taken a long time to learn and to become. Whatever its shortcomings, the status quo is familiar and has been internalized. Change involves loss (Marris, 1975). Room must be left for mourning in both its depressive and angry phases. To face the novel—which may not work—stirs up deep anxieties that easily lead to paranoid fantasies.

Such a situation of loss and threat may be expected to induce regressive behavior in the members of organizations undergoing radical change. This manifests itself at the group level by an increase in the frequency with which the primitive emotional cultures associated with what Bion

---

*At Bolsover colliery in Britain in 1953, the divisional chairman with the area general manager held a meeting with the entire colliery (1800 men) to decide whether or not to go ahead with a new method of continuous mining involving autonomous work groups, which would create 600 redundancies. Such meetings cannot be successful without intense preparation. In this case the union and management jointly interviewed every man and decided whether he was to stay or go. If he was to go, arrangements were made for his transfer to another mine (including housing), or job placement assistance was given in collaboration with the Ministry of Labour if he wished to leave the industry. Walton and Slesinger have been recently trying out town meetings in certain plants (personal communication).

(1961) has called "the basic assumption" group intrude into the behavior of what he has called the "sophisticated" group. These intrusions are unconscious. They obstruct the sophisticated group in carrying out its primary task, the work it was brought into existence to perform. Such a concept of work is wider than paid employment. It refers to the transactions that any group has to carry out to maintain a steady state in relation to its environment. These transactions are necessary because the group has only an incomplete control over this environment, whose resources it needs to achieve its ends. A transactional concept of work is analogous to the psychoanalytic concept of the ego as the institution in the personality mediating between the internal and external worlds.

Change that involves discontinuity, as a paradigm shift does, requires deutero-learning in Bateson's (1972) sense—that is, becoming aware of the context formed by one's basic assumptions and values, "learning to learn." This, as he says, is frustrating. The pain of this frustration causes the resistance that Bion has referred to as "the hatred of learning through experience." The new patterns can only be discovered by the individual and the group members when they undergo an experience through which they themselves can establish the validity of the patterns. Intellectual presentations are valuable in hindsight. They permit rational understanding of what has transpired, but they are of little use as reasons for undertaking the initial steps. The work of Bateson and Bion on these questions has recently been extended to the field of organizational change by Pava (1980).

A vision of a possible alternative mode is a necessary condition for bringing about substantial change. Hence the importance of articulating a new philosophy that embodies the vision. But the vision and the philosophy make little sense to most of those concerned until the process of enactment begins (Weick, 1979).

In the early Tavistock work in the sociotechnical field, the task and process orientations were unified. Later they became separated. This has led to negative results. Members of middle management have perhaps exhibited the most solid forms of resistance. This became apparent during the Norwegian Industrial Democracy project when an attempt was made to diffuse sociotechnical change throughout the largest enterprise in the country, Norskhydro. Some 500 middle managers, sensing all loss and no gain so far as they were concerned, said no. More thoroughgoing process intervention might have helped this group to work through their problems at an earlier stage. Massive retraining is required at the middle management and supervisory levels.

The recent trend in the United States to fuse the sociotechnical and organizational development traditions is welcome. The ecology-of-work meetings conducted by the National Training Laboratories are being attended by increasingly large numbers of people. Emphasis has been placed on process skills as well as work analysis skills in the national workshops conducted to train QWL facilitators sponsored by the Canadian Department of Labor.

The traditional skills of organizational development have had little success with organized labor. The trust level is usually too low and the political understanding of the facilitators too inconsequential. The conflicts between management and labor are of a different character than those within management and require different methods of conflict resolution. Facilitators tend to be ignorant of labor relations and trade union history. This ignorance is not forgiven.

The new fields opening up in organizational change are conveying the message that established notions of the change agent are outmoded. This agent of change needs to unlearn the role of being an expert and to learn the role of being a contributor to a process of colearning. In this process all stake holders make their resources available without claiming special privileges of role or status. This was learned many years ago in therapeutic communities by their originator, Maxwell Jones (1968, 1976), who has recently attempted to unify process theory for the clinical and nonclinical worlds.

The reunification of the task and process aspects of sociotechnical projects is a central task for future research and practice. It needs to be undertaken in terms of the emerging concept of a learning society. If the paradigm for alternative organizations—those capable of surviving environmental turbulence and eventually reducing it—requires their democratization, it also requires the democratization of the relations of those concerned with organizational change. This will entail breaking down the barriers between the changers and the to-be-changed. The ideal is pentecostal—that all parties speak with tongues.

DEVELOPMENTS AT THE MACROSOCIAL LEVEL

In the sociotechnical field as a whole, the knowledge base is unevenly distributed. Much is known about primary work systems and a good deal about modeling new plants. Far less is known about transforming existing work establishments, and even less about sociotechnical processes at the macrosocial level. The payoff from directing research attention to this level would be considerable.

The Microprocessor Revolution

As regards macrotechnological trends, the advent of the microprocessor and related electronic technologies may be regarded as an event of prime consequence. Many think that a fifth Krondradieff cycle has now started. A lead technology has been associated with each of these cycles since the beginning of the Industrial Revolution. Microprocessors are the lead technology of the new cycle (Emery, 1978b). The French have introduced the word "telematique" to denote the link with communications.

A number of questions and issues arise:

1. This family of technologies has applications in all industries, whether manufacturing or service. It is a universal with pervasive consequences. Its possible impact over the whole field has to be examined, choices made, and policies worked out. Otherwise the process will run blind.

2. Mass unemployment is likely unless offsetting measures are drawn up in advance. Simplifications and cost reduction are possible in some sections of the engineering industry in which layoffs have been estimated at 80 percent (Emery 1978b). Word processing is likely to cause similar personnel shrinkages in many white collar occupations, which will not be able to absorb those made redundant from manufacturing as they did during the first round of automation. Jenkins and Sherman (1979) forecast an overall reduction of 23.2% in the British labor force by the year 2000 and identify high risk job functions and sectors.*

3. The opportunities for decentralization are unprecedented, provided they are taken. But according to the value choices made, they could also lead in the opposite direction.

4. There are opportunities not only for decentralization but for democratization. Since a step-function increase in two-way communication is now becoming possible, large-scale dialogue will be feasible. Public learning systems, as imagined by Schon (1971), especially in relation to government, could be created—if people want them and are not stopped from developing them.

5. The sociotechnical systems involved are not confined to work organizations. They include the built environment—the urban scene, the home—and travel, leisure, and so on. Proactive consumer linkage with selling organizations represents another new field.

6. The designers of new technologies dependent on computers and telecommunications belong to engineering disciplines far removed from sociotechnical considerations. Unless educated to the contrary, they will follow the technological imperative and mortgage a good deal of the future. As with the industrial engineer, the

---

*They subtitle their book "The Collapsed Work." The senior author is a major trade union leader in Britain, being General Secretary of the Association of Scientific, Technical and Managerial Staffs (ASTMS). His would appear to be the most comprehensive statement on this issue from a trade union standpoint.

strategy of choice would be to open up collaborative projects with them. A colleague of mine formerly at York University, Toronto, himself a computer scientist, has begun a project with system builders on the hypothesis that if they will look at the quality of their own work life, this will be a step toward inducing them to look at that of users.*

Advanced Western societies are on the threshold of a profound change in the texture of their sociotechnical relations, a change not only in quantity but in quality. It represents a discontinuity, involving opportunities for scaling down rather than up, dispersal rather than concentration, and self-management rather than external control. For the first time since the Industrial Revolution, a major class of technological forces is supportive—potentially—of efforts to countervail some of the main negative impacts of that revolution on society.

The Meaning of Work and Alternatives to Employment. Simply to shorten the work week by a day or to propose some equivalent device is unlikely to provide a solution to unemployment on the scale anticipated in the 1980s and 90s, particularly when, in addition to microprocessors and industrial robots, further displacement of industry to the Third World is taken into account. The meaning of work itself will need reconsideration. Sachs (1978) has suggested that work in the sense of paid employment will have to be rationed, though it would presumably be possible for the work-addicted to purchase work stamps from the less addicted. In addition to their paid work, individuals would have an occupation in the "civil society," that is, the community. This concept is consonant with that of the dual economy (Robertson, 1978) in which gift and barter arrangements grow up in a "social economy" that exists in parallel with the market economy. The social economy includes activities that people undertake for themselves. These various activities comprise sociotechnical systems that merit research as well as those connected with what conventionally passes as the world of work. They may involve community workshops and may bring about new types of social arrangement. "Jobs" in this social economy would tend to be of high quality and to promote personal growth. They may, as a trade-off, increase the tolerance for restricted jobs in the market economy, or they may increase the demand for more interesting jobs. They may make the ordinary world of work less central and make ambition or status in it less preoccupying than it is at present—at least for some kinds of people. There will be more choices in lifestyles, more career paths open. Allied to these changes is a reassessment of the household as a work field that reflects the changing roles of men and women in the domestic sociotechnical system and the links of this system with outside employment. The divorce between home and

*R. Fabian, personal communication.

work, which has been so complete in industrial societies, may be less complete in the postindustrial order.

Decentralization. The logic of production since the Industrial Revolution has concentrated the employee in a large work place and the citizen in a large urban area. The new information technologies can radically offset this pattern. Several possibilities may be noted:

1. The scaling down of particular work establishments in large organizations—the attainment of small in large. These establishments will tend to take on the character of self-regulating primary work systems only loosely attached to the larger entity.

2. Increasing numbers of primary work systems will become independent businesses linked to others in a network rather than contained within an organizational boundary.

3. Much more work will be done at home rather than in a separate place of work. This trend is likely to be linked to life phases (as regards the presence of young children and the elderly), to serial careers, and to the greater plasticity of sex roles. Again, more diversity becomes possible.

4. The effect of these trends on urbanization, the types of houses built, schools, the journey to work, and so on, is likely to be far-reaching. Once again, more choices become possible than the mere continuation of current patterns.

Sociotechnical research needs to monitor emergent alternatives, establish criteria for making choices more explicit, and participate in action-research in selected projects.

Technological Choice

Appropriate Technology. The appearance of the appropriate technology movement has widened the scope of sociotechnical studies by bringing in the question of choice of technology in a new way. The appropriate technology is that which best fits the total circumstances of the case: those indirectly as well as those directly affected, the long term as well as the short term, and the physical in addition to the social environment. This movement began with an analysis of the "appropriateness" of what Schumacher (1973) called intermediate technology for the Third World. New arguments have since been raised concerning the elitism of high technology in the First and Second Worlds (Henderson, 1978). As long as only a few can understand a particular technology, there is danger of too great a concentration of expert power. If the technologies in question require very large capital inputs, there is the danger of too great a concentration of financial power, whether in the hands of corporations or governments. These are valid questions. To raise them, however, does not preclude the possibility of developing mechanisms of democratic control over high technology. This is an area of institution-building that sociotechnical studies should enter. Similarly, questions of hard versus soft energy paths (Lovins, 1976) or mixes of these should be investigated from a sociotechnical point of view.

End-Product Use.   This is another question whose appearance issues a new challenge to sociotechnical studies. A signal of social significance was given by the Lucas Aerospace Combined Shop Stewards Committee in Britain (Cooley, 1977), who proposed the manufacture of alternative product lines to those currently being produced by their management. The reasons were vintage union arguments—the stewards had concluded that the current lines were unlikely to survive in the marketplace and that their jobs were at risk. The alternatives proposed were of an appropriate technology type that provided an insight into the values of the work force. Though at first rejected by management, the committee sold several of its ideas to other companies, including Volkswagen. A recent report (Coates and Topham, 1980) gives an account of the feelings of joy experienced by workers who had designed and made an improved wheelchair for paraplegics. Worker initiatives of this kind have been taken in several companies following the Lucas example. One of the six criteria of psychological satisfaction at work is the worker's feelings concerning the end use of the product to which he or she contributes. If the worker perceives it as trivial, harmful, or a loser, he or she is likely to be negatively affected. These concerns will probably rise in the next two decades. Sachs (1978) has distinguished between pseudovalue and value in end use. Chevalier (1978) has elaborated this notion in his concept of demand innovation. Those organizations sensed by their members at all levels to have the capability of contributing to a desirable social future are the most likely to secure their commitment and to engage their effort. This is a break with the traditional market concept, which, as Chevalier says, has been promoted from the supply side. This break is likely to become wider in the decades ahead, and sociotechnical studies should monitor it.

Systems Larger than the Single Organization

The Industry Level.   I have argued elsewhere (Trist, 1976) that Western industrial societies are weak in the middle. Too little effective social structuring is available between institutions concerned with the management of the overall societal aggregate and the single organization. This deficiency puts excessive stress on both government and the corporation. The intermediate level consists of what I have called "domains," one example of which would be an industrial sector. Studies of this level are particularly important. One example is a collaborative project that Thorsrud and his colleagues have for some years been engaged in with the Norwegian Shipping Industry (Herbst, 1976), in which several critical conditions exist. An industry such as this comprises a system of "organizational ecology" (Trist, 1977a).* Though all the organizations belonging to the system are closely interdependent, no single one is in overall control. If the bureaucratic paradigm were followed, the danger is that a form of corporatism might emerge that would lead in a totalitarian direction. The new institution-building task is to discover an alternative route based on participative and democratic principles, which can secure interorganizational collaboration.

In the Norwegian shipping industry, an experiment was carried out in the design and trial of sophisticated bulk carriers. This has led to a further innovative step. For, though many technological alternatives were available, the chosen design was that which met most fully the needs of the small shipboard community that had to live together under isolated conditions 24 hours a day for considerable periods of time, while simultaneously undertaking all the work tasks. A common recreation room—as well as mess—was established where all ranks could socialize (and drink together rather than be isolated with a bottle in the cabin). Deck and engine room crews were integrated, and status differences between officers and men were reduced or even eliminated, through the development of open career lines on one or two "all officer" ships. Serial career structures also have been accepted, and training for a future job on shore can now be begun at sea.

Without these improvements, not enough Norwegians would have gone to sea to sustain the Norwegian Merchant Navy, which is critical for the balance of payments, even since the discovery of North Sea oil. Poorly educated and transient Southern European crews could not cope with technically sophisticated ships, and alcoholism, even among officers, was dangerously high. Such problems could not be effectively tackled at the level of the single company. Morevoer, competition was not so much between Norwegian companies as with foreign fleets. Several critical issues had to be taken up at the level of the industry concerning which types of decision were to be left to those at sea and which types should be brought ashore to headquarters and dockyard establishments. The

---

*The terms social and organizational ecology are not used in Aldrich's (1979) sense, which is close to biological usage and emphasizes determinism, but as in Emery and Trist (1973) in a systems sense, meaning that an ecological system is taken as a set of interdependencies in which no one entity can control the others, nor can it succeed apart from them. It constitutes a nonhierarchical field with open system characteristics in relation to its environment. It is composed of purposeful systems (organizations), which have to align their purposes with each other and with those of their members, since they are directively correlated with both (Sommerhoff, 1950, 1969).

technology was available to go either way. In the end, a great deal was left to those staffing the ships. The several seafaring unions, as well as the companies and various maritime regulatory organizations, took part in the discussions; these have produced a continuous learning process. The Norwegian experience was presented to the Maritime Commission of the Academy of Sciences (Davis, Trist, et al., 1972) when the question arose of re-expanding the U.S. Merchant Navy. To secure the collaboration of the many interest groups involved proved too difficult for much progress to be made. There are several industries and also social sectors in which pervasive problems in the sociotechnical and other fields would benefit by being treated at the domain level. Otherwise little reduction can be expected in their turbulence.

Community-Based Sociotechnical Endeavors. A distinctively American innovation above the level of the single organization has been the appearance of sociotechnical projects on a community-wide basis and in a framework of economic and social development (Trist, 1977b). The pioneer has been the Jamestown Area Labor-Management Committee created by the unions and management of a small manufacturing town in western New York State in 1972, when the largest local plant went bankrupt and unemployment rose above 10 percent. A young and able mayor, elected with bipartisan support, succeeded in getting labor and management, who had been in bitter dispute, to cooperate in arresting industrial decline and steering the community toward a viable future.

My own research team began work in Jamestown in 1973. An early study showed that the stock of key in-house skills in the dominant industries—sheet metal work and furniture making—was becoming seriously depleted. These skills were carried on by the older workers. There were no systematic training schemes in the small plants concerned, and many of the young workers were leaving the area. The committee sponsored a skills development program in which all members could share. They drew on the local community college, which had previously had little connection with local industries. Necessary courses (for blueprint reading, welding, etc.) were offered on any shift, including hoot owl, in the plants concerned. Some of the most skilled older workers were trained to be instructors.

Next, in-plant labor-management committees were formed in most of the member plants, where we helped to develop programs based on participation and job redesign. By 1976 there were more than 40 such projects (a number of them still ongoing) of 10 different kinds in 12 plants. Most of these plants are job shops. Worker-management teams have found new ways of winning contracts by bidding lower than the competition. Layouts have been jointly redesigned and product planning jointly undertaken. These activities saved a number of jobs during the recession. Joint sharing of productivity gains has been tried out with some success in plants that had become marginal and seemed too conflict-ridden to survive. While many of the individual projects have had a limited life, others have arisen to take their place—not so much in the same plant as in different plants. These projects have generated "themes" that have been taken up by various plants, often with no reference back to the research team (Keidel, 1978). A community-wide learning process in terms of this "theme set" has been sustained at the community level over a period of seven years (at the time of this writing), despite "casualties" at the level of particular organizations. This process cannot be seen if one is working exclusively at the organizational level. Keidel has referred to the coming into existence (through the emerging theme set) of an organizational community between individual organizations and the overall milieu of the city.

As the result of these developments, a major engineering company, Cummins Engines, has been attracted to the town. This will eventually employ 2000 to 3000 people. One or two small companies have followed, and a new hotel has been built in the city center.

Recently attention has been turned to the public sector, in which greater job security and higher wages had caused resentment in the industrial sector. Productivity was unacceptably low. Though faced with the difficulties inherent in civil service procedures, labor-management committees are beginning to make headway in one or two departments of the publicly owned electricity plant. The public school system and the local hospital have been successfully included. There are now multiple points of initiative. These become connected. There was a good deal of overlap among key individuals, and active networks were formed.

Networks. The study of networks, processes that are fluid and unbounded as contrasted to bounded and hierarchically arranged organizational systems, seems to offer one of the most promising ways of increasing our understanding of diffusion processes. During the last two years, my research center at the University of Pennsylvania has been involved in collaborative research into a network-building effort in labor management and work innovation in the public sector in 10 American cities (MBSC, 1980). This project is remarkable because the federal agency concerned, the National Center for Productivity and the Quality of Working Life, did not attempt to develop a central model but sought to elicit the ideas of the periphery and to encourage the various cities to learn from each other. It is also remarkable because the agency accepted a new methodology of evaluation based on developing learning capability at the sites through what has been called "thematic facilitation," rather than depending on a set of externally contrived, preprogrammed criteria. The research team worked in a participant mode with people at the sites, repeatedly feeding back material. The most advanced sites have certain common features. They proceed in terms of a programmatic theme as contrasted with single projects with a beginning, a middle, and an end;

the overall labor-management steering committee decentralizes responsibility for projects to an evolving set of subcommittees, which draw in an increasing number of people; these committees are empowered to implement and are not restricted to making recommendations; the overall committee is outward-oriented to the wider organization, whose general policies it seeks to influence; there is no attempt to interfere with the existing adversarial machinery, but rather an attempt to build a parallel organization in the collaborative mode.

Though this project was undertaken during the period when the Proposition 13 mentality was spreading throughout the country, all the committees have, with whatever vicissitudes, survived. This may be interpreted as a sign that an authentic collaborative process is beginning to emerge in the U.S. public sector. Analysis of the material has led to the first steps being taken towards formulating a theory of "normative incrementalism" (Pava, 1980) as a new strategy for organizational change and "continuous adaptive planning" when divergent factions are present.

In Canada, with several colleagues, I have been developing a nationwide sociotechnical network with nodes in almost all provinces.

The Canadian project began with the center-periphery model (Schon, 1971). Much was learned from the ensuing failure. The then Federal Minister of Labour included QWL in a wider political program of formal tripartism involving management, labor, and government. This program was rejected by the Canadian Labour Congress, which vetoed collaboration with government while price controls remained in force, and it was vetoed by the provinces because labor relations, apart from residual federal responsibilities, were a provincial jurisdiction. This attempt at "instant institutionalization" foundered. The setback provided an opportunity to foster network building in the periphery, and this has accelerated developments in the last three years. Rarely has the policy of a central department been so rapidly and effectively altered.

It may be asked what the criteria are for assuming that a nationwide process in favor of QWL is underway. In Canada, a number of signs may serve as pointers. The projects undertaken are not only numerous but constitute a series of multiple, independent initiatives. These initiatives are cross-sectoral—representing resource, manufacturing, and service industries—and cross-regional; almost all provinces are included. The Ontario government has set up a QWL Center with a joint labor-management advisory committee of prominent individuals. Dr. Hans van Beinum, formerly of the Tavistock Institute, gave up a university chair in Holland to come to Canada to direct it. It now has some 10 strategic projects in unionized companies. The business school in the French University in Montreal has taken a lead in stimulating developments in Quebec. Some Canadian projects are of an advanced kind and represent the state of the art in QWL. Some are enduring innovations and have been going on for several years in companies such as Alcan and Steinbergs. In the west, several large companies in the energy industry are seeking to design new installations along sociotechnical lines. In the public sector, the Treasury Board has initiated a series of experiments in the federal public service and has reached the point of no longer calling them experiments. At Dr. William Westley's QWL center at McGill University, projects have been undertaken in hospitals and schools. Meanwhile the Federal Department of Labour has held national workshops to identify and develop facilitators, made a set of five documentary films on QWL, arranged a large number of introductory presentations, and published a newsletter. Though these activities have suffered from severe budget cutbacks in Ottawa, they have survived when others have not.

A future research task will be to monitor and analyze such developments to discover what patterns may be in the early stages of moving towards a new paradigm for a country as a whole, and to clarify the principal obstacles, which in the Canadian scene are still numerous. Further research will also be required to establish the most effective ways of using available electronic technologies of communication for rapid and widespread diffusion to large organizational populations.

This section has touched on a few of the macrosocial processes relevant to sociotechnical studies. More attention needs to be paid to the domain level. Complex processes of interorganizational relations are involved, whether in industrial sectors or in communities. Collaboration at this level has not been encouraged by the competitive traditions of industrial societies, molded as these have been by the disturbed-reactive environment. Now that the salient environment is becoming that of a turbulent field, a greater emphasis on collaboration is mandatory, and relevant changes need to be fostered in large-scale social systems as well as within organizations.

The oncoming information technologies, especially those concerned with the microprocessor and telecommunication, give immense scope for solving many current problems—if the right value choices can be made.

The field has reached a stage at which a new attempt at repunctuation is required. To achieve this, an international conference on "The Quality of Work Life in the Eighties is being planned to take place (in Toronto) in the fall of 1981.

REFERENCES

Ackoff, R. L. (1974). *Redesigning the Future,* New York: Wiley.

Ackoff, R. L., and F. E. Emery (1972). *On Purposeful Systems,* Chicago: Aldine-Atherton.

Aldrich, H. E. (1979). *Organizations and Environments,* Englewood Cliffs, NJ: Prentice-Hall.

Allport, G. (1937). *Personality: A Psychological Interpretation,* New York: Henry Holt.

Argyris, C., and D. Schon (1974). *Theory in Practice,* San Francisco: Jossey-Bass.

Ashby, W. R. (1960). *Design for a Brain,* 2nd ed., New York: Wiley.

Baldamus, W. (1951). "Types of Work and Motivation," *British Journal of Sociology* **2**:44–58; (1961). *Efficiency and Effort,* London: Tavistock Publications.

Bateson, G. (1972). *Steps to an Ecology of Mind,* San Francisco: Chandler.

Bell, D. (1956). *Work and Its Discontents,* Boston: Beacon Press.

Bion, W. R. (1946). "The Leaderless Group Project," *Bulletin of the Menninger Clinic* **10**.

Bion, W. R. (1950). "Experiences in Groups V," *Human Relations* **3**:3–14.

Bion, W. R. (1961). *Experiences in Groups and Other Papers,* London: Tavistock.

Burden, D. W. F. (1975). "Participative Management as a Basis for Improved Quality of Jobs: The Case of Microwax Department, Shell U.K. Ltd.," in L. E. Davis and J. C. Taylor, Eds., *The Quality of Working Life,* Vol. II, New York: Free Press.

Burns, T., and G. Stalker (1961). *The Management of Innovation,* London: Tavistock.

Chein, I. (1954). "The Environment as a Determinant of Behavior," *Journal of Social Psychology* **39**.

Chein, I. (1972). *The Science of Behavior and the Image of Man,* New York: Basic Books.

Cherns, A. B. (1976). "The Principles of Organizational Design," *Human Relations* **29,8**:783–792.

Chevalier, M. (1978). *Potential for Industrial Development in a Conserver Society—Institutional Implications,* Montreal: Gamma.

Churchman, C. W., and Emery, F. E. (1966). "On Various Approaches to the Study of Organizations," in *Operational Research and the Social Sciences,* London: Tavistock.

Clegg, H. (1960). *Industrial Democracy,* Oxford: Blackwell.

Coates, K., and Topham, T. (1980). "Workers' Control and Self-Management in Great Britain," *Human Futures* **3**:127–141.

Cohen-Rosenthal, E. "The Involvement of U.S. Unions in Quality of Working Life Programs," *Quality of Working Life: The Canadian Scene* **3**(3):3–9.

Cooley, M. (1977). *Papers of the Lucas Aerospace Combined Shop Stewards Committee,* London: N.E. Polytechnic.

Davis, L. E. (1957). "Job Design Research," *Journal of Industrial Engineering,* November–December.

Davis, L. E., R. R. Canter, and J. Hoffman (1955). "Current Job Design Criteria," *Journal of Industrial Engineering* **6**:5–11.

Davis, L. E., and A. B. Cherns (1975). *The Quality of Work Life,* Vols. I and II, New York: Free Press.

Davis, L. E. "Evolving Alternative Organization Designs: Their Sociotechnical Bases," *Human Relations* **39**(3):261–273.

Davis, L. E., and C. S. Sullivan (1980). "A Labor Management Contract and Quality of Working Life," *Occupational Behavior* **1,1**.

Davis, L. E., E. L. Trist, et al. (1973). *Report to the Maritime Commission, Academy of Sciences,* Washington, D.C.

Emery, F. E. (1952). *The Deputy's Role in the Bolsover System of Continuous Mining,* London: Tavistock Document Series.

Emery, F. E. (1959). "Characteristics of Socio-Technical Systems," London: Tavistock Document #527. Abridged in F. E. Emery, *The Emergence of a New Paradigm of Work,* Canberra: Centre for Continuing Education.

Emery, F. E. (1964). *Report on the Hunsfoss Project,* London: Tavistock Documents Series.

Emery, F. E. (1967). "The Next Thirty Years: Concepts, Methods and Anticipations," *Human Relations* **20**:199–237.

Emery, F. E. (1974). "Participant Design," Canberra: Centre for Continuing Education, A.N.U., and in F. E. Emery and E. Thorsrud, *Democracy at Work,* Leiden: Martinus Nijhoff.

Emery, F. E. (1976). *Futures We Are In,* Leiden: Martinus Nijhoff.

Emery, F. E. (1978a). *The Emergence of a New Paradigm of Work,* Canberra: Centre for Continuing Education, A.N.U.

Emery, F. E. (1978b). *The Fifth Krondradieff Wave,* Canberra: Centre for Continuing Education, A.N.U.

Emery, F. E. (1980). "Designing Socio-Technical Systems for 'Green Field' Sites," *Occupational Behavior* **1,**1.

Emery, F. E., and J. Marek (1962). "Some Socio-Technical Aspects of Automation," *Human Relations* **15:**17–26.

Emery, F. E., and E. Thorsrud (1964). *Form and Content,* Oslo: Oslo University Press. English edition in *Industrial Democracy,* London: Tavistock, 1969.

Emery, F. E., and E. Thorsrud (1969). *New Forms of Work Organization,* Oslo: Tannum. English edition in *Democracy at Work,* Leiden: Martinus Nijhoff, 1976.

Emery, F. E., and E. L. Trist (1963). "The Causal Texture of Organizational Environments," paper presented to the *International Psychology Congress,* Washington, D.C. Reprinted in *La Sociologie Du Travail,* 1964, and in *Human Relations* **18:**21–32, 1965.

Emery, F. E., and E. L. Trist (1973). *Towards a Social Ecology,* London: Plenum Press.

Emery, M., and F. E. Emery (1978). "Searching for New Directions," in J. Sutherland, Ed., *A Management Handbook for Public Administrators,* New York: Van Nostrand Reinhold.

Fensham, F., and D. Hooper (1964). *Changes in the British Rayon Industry,* London: Tavistock.

Galbraith, J. K. (1967). *The New Industrial State,* New York: Houghton Mifflin.

Goldstein, K. (1939). *The Organism,* New York: American Book Company.

Goodman, P. S. (1979). *Assessing Organizational Change,* New York: Wiley.

Gulowsen, J. (1972). "A Measure of Work Group Autonomy," in L. E. Davis and J. C. Taylor, Eds., *Job Design,* Harmondsworth: Penguin Books.

Hackman, J., and E. Lawler (1971). "Employee Reactions to Job Characteristics," *Journal of Applied Psychology,* Monograph 55, 259–286.

Hackman, J. R., G. R. Oldham, R. Jansen, and K. Purdy (1975). "A New Strategy for Job Enrichment," *California Management Review,* Summer 1975.

Hackman, J. R., and J. L. Suttle (1977). *Improving Life at Work,* Santa Monica, CA: Goodyear.

Heider, F. (1942). "On Perception, Event Structure, and Psychological Environment," *Psychological Issues* **1,**2.

Heider, F. (1959). "Thing and Medium," *Psychological Issues,* Monograph 3 (originally published in German in 1926).

Henderson, H. (1978). *Creating Alternative Futures,* Berkeley, CA: Windhoven.

Herbst, P. G. (1962). *Autonomous Group Functioning,* London: Tavistock.

Herbst, P. G. (1975). "The Product of Work Is People," in L. E. Davis and A. B. Cherns, Eds., *The Quality of Working Life,* Vol. I, New York: Free Press.

Herbst, P. G. (1976). *Alternatives to Hierarchies,* Leiden: Martinus Nijhoff.

Herrick, N. Q., and M. Maccoby (1975). "Humanizing Work: A Priority Goal of the 1970s," in L. E. Davis and A. B. Cherns, Eds., *The Quality of Working Life,* Vol. I, New York: Free Press.

Herzberg, F., B. Mausner, and B. Snyderman (1959). *The Motivation to Work*, New York: Wiley.

Hill, C. P. (1971). *Towards a New Philosophy of Management*, London: Gower Press.

Jaques, E. (1951). *The Changing Culture of a Factory*, London: Tavistock.

Jaques, E. (1955). "Social Systems as a Defence against Persecutory and Depressive Anxiety," in *New Directions in Psycho-Analysis*, London: Tavistock (Reprinted in the United States by Basic Books).

Jaques, E. (1956). *Measurement of Responsibility: A Study of Work, Payment, and Individual Capacity*, New York: Dryden.

Jayaram, G. K. (1976). *Open Systems Planning*, in W. G. Bennis, K. D. Benne, R. Chin, and K. Corey, Eds., *The Planning of Change*, 3rd ed., New York: Holt, Rinehart and Winston.

Jenkins, C., and B. Sherman (1979). *The Collapse of Work*, London: Eyre Methuen.

Jennings, H. (1947). "Leadership and Sociometric Choice," *Sociometry* 10:32–49.

Jones, M. (1968). *Beyond the Therapeutic Community*, New Haven: Yale University Press.

Jones, M. (1976). *Maturation of the Therapeutic Community: An Organic Approach to Health and Mental Health*, New York: Human Sciences Press.

Jordan, N. (1963). "Allocation of Functions between Men and Machines in Automated Systems," *Journal of Applied Psychology* 47:161–165.

Keidel, R. (1978). "The Development of an Organizational Community through Theme Appreciation," unpublished Ph.D. dissertation, University of Pennsylvania, Philadelphia.

Ketchum, L. (1975). "A Case Study of Diffusion," in L. E. Davis and A. B. Cherns, Eds., *The Quality of Working Life*, Vol. II, New York: Free Press.

King, S. D. M. (1964). *Training within the Organization*, London: Tavistock.

Lewin, K. (1935). *The Dynamic Theory of Personality*, New York: McGraw-Hill.

Lewin, K. (1939). "Patterns of Aggressive Behavior in Experimentally Created Social Climates," *Journal of Social Psychology* 10:271–299.

Lewin, K. (1951). *Field Theory in Social Science*, New York: Harper and Row.

Likert, R. (1961). *New Patterns of Management*, New York: McGraw-Hill.

Lovins, A. (1976). "Energy Strategy: The Road Not Taken?" *Foreign Affairs*, October.

McLuhan, M. (1964). *Understanding Media*, New York: McGraw-Hill.

McWhinney, W. (1980). *The Resolution of Complex Issues*, unpublished draft monograph.

Maccoby, M. (1976). *The Gamesman*, New York: Simon and Schuster.

Management and Behavioral Science Center (1978). "The Dissolution of Work Teams in a Large Organization," Philadelphia: University of Pennsylvania, Management and Behavioral Science Center, The Wharton School.

Management and Behavioral Science Center (1980). "Improving Productivity and the Quality of Working Life in the Public Sector: Pioneering Initiatives in Labor/Management Cooperation," Philadelphia: University of Pennsylvania, Management and Behavioral Science Center, The Wharton School.

Marris, P. (1975). *Loss and Change*, Garden City, NY: Anchor Books.

Melman, S. (1958). *Decision Making and Productivity*, Oxford: Blackwell.

Menzies, I. E. P. (1960). "A Case Study in the Functioning of Social Systems as a Defence against Anxiety," *Human Relations* 13:95–121.

Miller, E. J. (1959). "Territory, Technology and Time: The Internal Differentiation of Complex Production Systems," *Human Relations* 22:3.

Miller, E. J. (1975). "Socio-Technical Systems in Weaving, 1953–1970: A Follow-up Study," *Human Relations* 28:349–386.

Miller, E. J., and A. K. Rice (1967). *Systems of Organization,* London: Tavistock.

Mumford, L. (1934). *Technics and Civilization,* New York: Harcourt.

Murray, H. (1960). *Studies in Automated Technologies,* London: Tavistock Documents Series.

Murray, H., and A. C. Trist (1969). *Work Organization in the Doncaster Coal District,* London: Tavistock Documents Series.

Nadel, S. F. (1951). *The Foundations of Social Anthropology,* London: Cohen and West.

O'Toole, J., Ed. (1972). *Work in America: A Report to the Secretary of State for Health, Education and Welfare,* Cambridge, MA: M.I.T. Press.

Ozbekhan, H. (1969). "Towards a General Theory of Planning," in E. Jantsch, Ed., *Perspectives in Planning,* Paris: O.E.C.D.

Parsons, T. (1960). *Structure and Process in Modern Societies,* Glencoe, IL: Free Press.

Pava, C. (1979). "State of the Art in American Autonomous Work Group Design," *Management and Behavioral Science Center/Wharton Applied Research Center,* Philadelphia: University of Pennsylvania, The Wharton School.

Pava, C. (1980). "Normative Incrementalism," unpublished Ph.D. Dissertation, University of Pennsylvania, Philadelphia.

Pollock, A. B. (1954). *Retail Shop Organization,* London: Tavistock Documents Series.

Pribram, K. (1977). "A New Perspective on Reality," special issue of *Mind-Brain Bulletin* **2,**16.

Prigogine, I. (1968). *Introduction à la Thermodynamique des Phénomènes Irréversibles,* Paris: Dunod.

Rice, A. K. (1958). *Productivity and Social Organization: The Ahmedabad Experiment,* London: Tavistock.

Robertson, J. (1978). *The Sane Alternative,* St. Paul: Riverbasin.

Sachs, I. (1978). "Development and Maldevelopment," Keynote Address, Annual Conference, *Canadian Institute for Public Affairs.* Also in *International Foundation for Development Alternatives,* Dossier 2.

Schon, D. (1971). *Beyond the Stable State,* New York: Basic Books.

Schumacher, E. F. (1973). *Small Is Beautiful,* New York: Harper and Row.

Sheppard, V. W. (1951). "Continuous Longwall Mining: Experiments at Bolsover Colliery," *Colliery Guardian* **182.**

Singer, E. A. (1959). *Experience and Reflection,* C. W. Churchman, Ed., Philadelphia: University of Pennsylvania Press.

Smith, F. (1952). *Switchboard Reorganization,* London: General Post Office (unpublished monograph).

Somerhoff, G. (1950). *Analytical Biology,* Oxford: Oxford University Press.

Somerhoff, G. (1969). "The Abstract Characteristics of Living Systems," in E. Emery, Ed., *Systems Thinking,* Harmondsworth: Penguin Books.

Stoelwinder, J. U. (1978). "Ward Team Management: Five Years Later," Philadelphia: University of Pennsylvania, Management and Behavior Science Center, The Wharton School.

Stoelwinder, J. U., and P. S. Clayton (1978). "Hospital Organization Development: Changing the Focus from 'Better Management' to 'Better Patient Care,' " *Journal of Applied Behavioral Science* **14,**3:400–414.

Susman, G. I. (1976). *Autonomy at Work,* New York: Praeger.

Trist, E. L. (1950a). "The Relations of Social and Technical Systems in Coal-Mining," paper presented to the *British Psychological Society,* Industrial Section.

Trist, E. L. (1950b). "Culture as a Psycho-Social Process," paper presented to the Anthropological Section, *British Association for the Advancement of Science.*

Trist, E. L. (1953a). *Some Observations on the Machine Face as a Socio-Technical System,* London: Tavistock Documents Series.

Trist, E. L. (1953b). *An Area Training School in the National Coal Board,* London: Tavistock Documents Series.

Trist, E. L. (1953c). *Area Organization in the National Coal Board,* London: Tavistock Documents Series.

Trist, E. L. (1958). "Human Relations in Industry," paper presented to the Seminar on Workers' Participation in Management, *Congress for Cultural Freedom,* Vienna.

Trist, E. L. (1971). "Critique of Scientific Management in Terms of Socio-Technical Theory," *Prakseologia* **39–40:**159–174.

Trist, E. L. (1974). "Work Improvement and Industrial Democracy," keynote paper for *E.E.C. Conference,* Brussels.

Trist, E. L. (1976a). "A Concept of Organizational Ecology," *Bulletin of National Labour Institute* (New Delhi) **12:**483–496, and Australian Journal of Management **2,2:**161–175.

Trist, E. L. (1976b). "Action Research and Adaptive Planning," in A. W. Clark, Ed., *Experimenting with Organizational Life,* London: Plenum.

Trist, E. L. (1977a). "Collaboration in Work Settings: A Personal Perspective," *Journal of Applied Behavioral Science* **13:**268–278.

Trist, E. L. (1977b). "A New Approach to Economic Development," *Human Futures* **1:**8–12 (with the collaboration of J. Eldred and R. Keidel).

Trist, E. L. (1979a). "Referent Organizations and the Development of Inter-Organizational Domains," Distinguished Lecture, Organization and Management Theory Division, 39th Annual Convention, *Academy of Management, Human Relations* (forthcoming).

Trist, E. L. (1979b). "New Concepts of Productivity," proceedings, *Ottawa Conference on Shaping Canada's Future in a Global Perspective,* August 1978.

Trist, E. L. (1979c). "Adapting to a Changing World," in G. Sanderson, Ed., *Industrial Democracy Today,* New York: McGraw-Hill-Ryerson.

Trist, E. L., and K. W. Bamforth (1951). "Some Social and Psychological Consequences of the Longwall Method of Coal Getting," *Human Relations* **4:**3–38.

Trist, E. L., G. W. Higgin, H. Murray, and A. B. Pollock (1963). *Organizational Choice,* London: Tavistock.

Trist, E. L., and H. Murray (1958). *Work Organization at the Coal Face: A Comparative Study of Mining Systems,* London: Tavistock Documents Series.

Trist, E. L., G. I. Susman, and G. R. Brown (1977). "An Experiment in Autonomous Working in an American Underground Coal Mine," *Human Relations* **30,3:**201–236.

Van Beinum, H. (1963). *Work Reorganization in the Telecommunications Industry,* unpublished Ph.D. dissertation, Erasmus University, Rotterdam.

Vickers, Sir Geoffrey (1965). *The Art of Judgment,* London: Chapman and Hall. Published in the United States by Basic Books.

Von Bertalanffy, L. (1950). "The Theory of Open Systems in Physics and Biology," *Science* **3:**23–29.

Walker, C. R., and H. Guest (1952). *The Man on the Assembly Line,* Cambridge: Harvard University Press.

Walton, R. E. (1975a). "Criteria for Quality of Working Life," in L. E. Davis and A. B. Cherns, Eds., *The Quality of Working Life,* Vol. I, New York: Free Press.

Walton, R. E. (1975b). "The Diffusion of New Work Structures: Explaining Why Success Didn't Take," *Organizational Dynamics,* Winter: 3–22.

Walton, R. E. (1979). "Work Innovations in the United States," *Harvard Business Review* **57**,4:88–98.

Weick, K. (1979). *The Social Psychology of Organizing,* Reading, MA: Addison-Wesley.

Weiner, N. (1950). *The Human Use of Human Beings,* New York: Houghton-Mifflin.

Westerlund, G. (1952). *Group Leadership,* Stockholm: Nordisk Rotogravyr.

Williamson, D. T. N. (1972). "The Anachronistic Factory," *Proceedings of the Royal Society of London,* **A331**:139–160.

Wilson, A. T. M., and E. L. Trist (1951). *The Bolsover System of Continuous Mining,* London: Tavistock Document #290.

Woodward, J. (1958). *Management and Techology,* London: H.M. Stationery Office.

SOCIOTECHNICAL SYSTEMS THEORY: A COMMENTARY

J. RICHARD HACKMAN
Yale University

When I was a college senior, my resolve to take up graduate study in psychology was strengthened by all my seemingly profound insights into various psychological phenomena. After entering graduate school, I discovered that William James had written about most of my insights years before.

As a graduate student in social psychology, I felt confirmed in my choice of careers as I came up with numerous fascinating theories about interpersonal relationships. My advisors were gentle in pointing out that Fritz Heider had written about most of them more than a decade earlier.

Now, being interested in the creation and diffusion of innovative work systems, I occasionally stumble onto an observation about organizations that strikes me as particularly interesting. Too often I discover later that Eric Trist already noted the same thing, wrote about it, and years ago incorporated it into his program of action research.

It is particularly humbling this time, because usually Trist first *said* it in the 1950s, I actually *read* it in the 1960s, and only now have I come to *understand* it. This delay of impact surely reflects my own limited powers of comprehension. But it may also say something about the character of sociotechnical systems theory as a scholarly enterprise.

While sociotechnical systems theory (STS theory for brevity) clearly is more right than wrong as a perspective on work and organizations, it can be frustratingly difficult to pin down. Part of the problem is the great scope and generality of the theory. The ideas just do not fit into small, neat packages. And part of the problem has to do with those elusive systems theory terms and concepts—notions such as "joint optimization" and "correlative systems" and "dissipative structures." What do these things mean, really? And how are they supposed to be pieced together to understand social systems? It may be that the only good way to comprehend sociotechnical message is to move from the library to the shop floor, to experience the phenomenon for one's self, to wrestle with various ways of making sense of it—and then finally to understand, "Ah ha! *That's* what it means."

This kind of learning process reflects what I believe to be an important feature of the theory. As frustrating as it may be to those of us who prefer to learn the easy way, by reading and thinking, the STS approach demands that a learning system itself wrestle with the problems and issues that confront it, come to its own resolution of the situation, and then decide how to accommodate the insights gained.

As we will see, this requirement that systems do their own learning is simultaneously one of the great truths of the STS approach and one of its great problems as a scientific paradigm and as a guide for planned organizational change.

Impact of the Sociotechnical Approach

Despite the elusiveness of some aspects of STS theory, the perspective has had great impact in changing how we think about work systems, how we study them, and how we attempt to change and improve them. Consider first the impact of STS theory on how we *understand* organizations and then on how we *deal with* them.

How We Construe Organizations. Organizations are systems. Most of us respond to such obvious assertions with a quick "of course" and move on to more interesting or controversial matters. Yet only occasionally do our research designs and change programs deal appropriately with this basic truth. Too often we stumble onto the systematic character of organizations only after discovering that the neat bivariate models we developed for our research, or the single-focus change techniques we generated for our organizational interventions, did not accomplish what they were supposed to. Those scholars and interventionists who have attended to the STS message and have comprehended it are less likely than the rest of us to make such mistakes.

The sociotechnical approach also requires that we deal with organizations as *multilevel* systems. Sociotechnical ideas have enriched our understanding of individuals in organizations, of groups and organizations as wholes, and of entire communities and societies. I expect we may even be treated to a full-scale intergalactic sociotechnical analysis one of these days. It turns out that what happens at one level of a system importantly affects, and is affected by, what happens at other levels. For this reason, understanding will be incomplete, and change may be seriously misguided, if one focuses only on micro or only on macrophenomena. Each of the levels is important in its own right, and the levels interact in ways that defy simplistic analysis. STS theory warns those of us who are comfortable operating only at a single level of analysis that we had better stop being that way if we aspire to excellence in scholarship and action. Increasing numbers of organizational researchers are hearing this warning and adjusting their research and change programs accordingly.

Finally, Trist and his collaborators have forced us to acknowledge that organizational systems are *sociotechnical* in character. Conclusions about organizations that are based solely on technological issues will be as far off the mark as those based only on data about the human and social aspects of organizational life. Only the hardest-headed industrial engineer will maintain, these days, that work organizations can be understood primarily in terms of technical efficiency and designed with only technological imperatives in mind. Sociotechnical research has shown us that technological imperatives are *not* sacrosanct: "Violations" of what the technology seems to require can sometimes improve rather than undermine work productivity. And these days only the softest-hearted human relations professional—or perhaps the most manipulative—will maintain that people can be made happy and productive ussing only social psychological principles and techniques. Sociotechnical theory suggests that human relations programs that do not also deal with the nature and structure of the work itself are likely to be limited both in impact and in longevity. Effective management of the human side of organizations, then, is *not* simply a matter of covering the social and emotional costs of technologies that do violence to people by improving the "human relations climate" of the enterprise. Thanks in part to the work of Trist and his collaborators, most thoughtful managers and scholars now understand this.

How We Deal with Organizations.   The preceding paragraphs summarize some of the ways that the STS approach has affected how people construe organizations. I will now review three sociotechnical lessons that have directly to do with the behavior of organizational researchers and interventionists.

First, sociotechnical researchers have taught us that we must deal with organizations as they are when we enter them, not as we wish they might be. What is important, and what is trivial, for a given organization is not under our control. Examining organizations through multifaceted sociotechnical glasses can help us see what is really of significance for the people and the organization being studied. And what we see, in many cases, will *not* have much to do with what we talked about in the discussion section of our last article. Our choice, then, may be between dealing with what is significant for the organization, even if that is not what we would most like to study, and dealing with what is significant for us, even if that is not much at issue in the organization being studied. STS theorists would have us tilt toward the former strategy. That they sometimes seem to ignore this imperative of their own approach, as will be seen below, does not detract from its significance for research on organizations.

Second, STS theory suggests that one of the best ways to discover what is important to organizational functioning is to try to help that organization change. As the examples in Trist's paper show, sociotechnical research is characterized by an interplay between description and action. At its best, the approach illustrates how describing social systems, intervening in them, and theorizing about them inform and support one another. It provides a model for research and action that those who aspire to scholarship that is useful as well as interesting must take seriously.

Finally, Trist and his colleagues help us understand that we must deal with both our own and organization members' values when we study organizations or attempt to change them. When we act as if organizational research or intervention is value free, it is just that: an act. It is not a coincidence that the pioneering book in the sociotechnical tradition was titled *Organizational Choice.* There *is* choice, sociotechnical researchers argue, in both research and action. And where there is choice there necessarily are values. Trist and his colleagues are not embarrassed about making their own explicit. Consider, for example, the following assertions from Trist's chapter in this book: "Personal growth [is] a human right. All who wish it should have the opportunity to cultivate it. The work place constitutes a key setting for this purpose" (pp. 39–40). Speaking of the fact that technology often is inherently neutral, providing choice about how to structure work: "The opportunities for decentralization [provided by innovations in microprocessing technology] are unprecedented, provided they are taken. But according to the value choices made, they could also lead in the opposite direction" (p. 61). A transformation to new organizational paradigms "is imperative for survival in a fast-changing environment. It involves nothing less than the working out of a new organizational philosophy" (p. 55). And the information technologies on the horizon "give immense scope for solving many current problems—if the right value choices can be made" (p. 69).

The sociotechnical insistence that we make our values explicit forces us to confront a number of comfortable assumptions we make about research and organizations, for example, that the study of organizations legitimately can focus on what *is* to the virtual exclusion of what *could be,* or that the imperatives of environment and technology, rather than the hopes and fears of human beings, determine what *must* be for formal organizational systems. Scholars and managers alike are confronted with the fact that we are creating and maintaining a certain kind of organizational world through the choices we make. Sociotechnical theorists offer a nontraditional vision for the design and management of organizations in the future—a vision that may or may not be realistic for our society and one that we may or may not seek to realize. But the choice, they remind us, is ours.

Some Problems and Unexploited Opportunities

The features of the sociotechnical approach reviewed thus far provide little cause for complaint; indeed I find them rather refreshing. Now comes the "but." In the remaining pages, I address some aspects of the theory and the approach that strike me as confusing, as difficult to deal with, or as wrong. And I identify some relatively undeveloped theoretical and practical issues in the STS tradition that seem to me worthy of increased attention in the years to come. My observations are couched as six questions.

1. *What is being learned from sociotechnical work, and who is learning it?* The principle of "minimum critical specification" for the design of work systems is applied by STS theorists with a vengeance—and to research and scholarship as well as to practical decisions about organizational design. This creates some problems, both conceptually and practically.

Sociotechnical theory, as theory, comes in many different suits of clothes and can be frustratingly nonspecific—about just what aspects of social systems are most critical to good design under what circumstances, and about the form of the interactions that proposed to occur among theory-specified variables and across the several levels of analysis subsumed by the theory.

Although some writers in the STS tradition, such as Albert Cherns (1976) and Thomas Cummings (1978) have recently presented STS ideas in a rather concrete and specific form, it remains exceedingly difficult to specify propositions of the theory that are empirically disconfirmable. This of course makes it difficult to assess the strengths and weaknesses of the theory using standard scientific tools and methods. As a result, sociotechnical systems theory is not as self-correcting as it could be; knowledge about organizations has not been moved forward by theory-based empirical work as much as it might have been; and the impact of the theory is less than one would hope and expect.

A similar difficulty is encountered in action projects that are guided by the STS approach. Presumably the criteria used in understanding and evaluating the results of sociotechnical change projects should include indicators at the individual, group, organizational, and environmental levels of analysis, in order to be congruent with the multilevel character of the theory itself. And while we do have in the literature numerous case reports of sociotechnical change projects, some of which do include data from several levels, there are few systematic, empirical assessments of the results of such projects. Worse, virtually none of the assessments allow readers to examine the interplays and trade-offs among results that emerge at the several levels of analysis. For a research and action program that is as oriented to change as this one is, the limited attention given to systematic, multilevel evaluation by STS theorists is both surprising and disappointing.

So: who learns from sociotechnical change projects, and what do they learn? The consultants to such projects and the managers and employees who participate in them learn, without question. The very nature of the change process ensures this. But *my* learning and, I venture, the learning of many others who themselves are not of a sociotechnical persuasion, is compromised. It is quite difficult for me to learn about the theory as a theory or about the effectiveness of sociotechnical changes from the kinds of data I am provided in sociotechnical case studies. It is therefore not surprising that the actors in such projects, that is, the consultants and the participants, tend to be far more excited about the theory and its uses than are young scholars in organizational behavior—not to mention those of us who are not so young any more.

2.   *Should one always opt for the autonomous work team as the basic performing unit in work systems?*   If one thing is predictable in a sociotechnical action project, it is that autonomous work teams *will* be created. They will most often be used as an organizational device for carrying out the work of the organization.

This is curious for two reasons. First, I can find in statements of the theory—including the paper Trist prepared for this book—no conceptualization of work systems that would inexorably have led to the development Trist correctly reports in recounting the history of the STS approach: "Correspondingly, the *work group* became central rather than the individual job-holder." Indeed in the specification of the basic principles for work redesign given by Trist himself (1971) and reproduced in his paper, the clear implication is that whether work is designed for individuals or for intact teams is a contingent matter and depends heavily on the nature of the work to be done. Why then are groups almost always used in sociotechnical redesign projects? I have not been able to come up with a satisfactory answer.

My curiosity grows—and becomes more a troubled than idle curiosity—when I reflect on what the research literature has to say about the *effectiveness* of work teams in performing work, solving problems, and making decisions. I've known for a long time that most of the groups of which I am a member—particularly decision-making committees in universities—are awful. It was reassuring, on studying the research literature on group effectiveness, to discover that I was not the causal agent—that groups, for many tasks, cannot be counted on to perform better than the most talented individual in the group. Or, for other tasks, better than the pooled products of a "group" of individuals who do not interact at all.

I do not dispute that groups are appropriate for some kinds of tasks and that, when well-designed and well-managed, they can perform these tasks very well indeed. But I can find neither in the research literature nor in my own experience justification for opting for groups as the design device of choice on an almost automatic basis, as seems to be done in a very large number of sociotechnical change projects. And my concern is reinforced by Trist's report that an organization that installed 90 work teams a decade ago now has only two remaining. *Something* is not going right if 98 percent of the work teams that are installed die. One would hope and expect instead that they would be so effective that they would multiply and diffuse across the organization. At least in this case they did not.

We need to know more about work teams in organizations. We need better understanding of the circumstances under which the use of work teams is and is not appropriate. We need more expertise in how best to design, install, and manage work teams. We need models that more clearly specify the factors that are most important in creating conditions for individual, social, and task effectiveness in work teams.

And we need to take more seriously what we already know. Sociotechnical practitioners too frequently seem not to be guided by knowledge they already have in hand, whether about how work teams should be designed and managed, or about the conditions under which it may not be a good idea to install them at all.

3. *What is to be done with individuals in highly interdependent work systems?* Sociotechnical theorists aspire to work systems in which individuals learn and grow. Indeed at least some of the STS persuasion see individual growth at work as a *right*. This right is to be protected and human growth is to be nurtured in the autonomous work groups that are created in sociotechnical systems. As Trist notes in his chapter "A work group offers scope for a range of abilities and preferences. There is more scope for individual differences in work groups than in standard individual work stations." He also notes that an especially important and valuable feature of the small work group is its capacity for self-regulation.

Yet, as numerous researchers have documented, highly cohesive groups also have considerable capacity to exploit individual members in the interest of collective goals. Or to suppress their personal aspirations and compromise their personal integrity. Or, at the other end of the continuum, to allow so much freedom as to invite anarchy. As Trist notes, individuals in work systems can "forget" to keep learning and growing if the matter is not kept in the forefront of their attention. To expect that small work teams will routinely excel in self-regulation and in fostering the learning of individual members is to expect a great deal.

The relationship between individuals and groups in work systems is one of the most important and interesting cross-level links in sociotechnical theory. It deserves more thought and attention than it has received.

4. *How much mileage can be obtained from the sociotechnical notion of "key variances" in thinking about organizational design?* The idea of "key variances" is central to sociotechnical analyses of work systems. As I understand it, key variances are those organizational features or operations that most strongly affect (a) the quantity or quality of production

or (b) the operating or social costs of production. They are the points of leverage that can make big differences in what is produced and what it costs.

The sociotechnical idea of key variances strikes me as a powerful concept, and it would be interesting to see how useful it could be if brought to bear on broader questions of organizational design and management. Consider, for example, the possibility of applying this kind of thinking to decision-making about how organizations are structured, for example, choices that are made between functional and product modes of organization and devices that are used to coordinate among organizational units.

Traditional wisdom suggests that environmental and technological considerations should be paramount in deciding about organizational structure and form. As an alternative to traditional approaches, one might begin not with technology and environment but with the points in the production process at which variances most powerfully affect the achievement of the strategic objectives of the enterprise. The organization would be structured to provide the greatest possible support for people in managing those key variances.

This approach would prompt inside-out, bottom-up design processes that contrast with traditional outside-in, top-down strategies for structuring organizations. Environment and technology would of course affect what are (and are not) key variances. But organization structures, coordination devices, and support mechanisms would be focused specifically on the variances rather than on these macroorganizational or external factors. And designers following this approach would circumvent a problem too often encountered using traditional approaches to organizational structure, namely, that most of the degrees of freedom available for making design decisions are already used up by the time planners get "down" to the points in the production process where the key variances in productivity and cost are actually located.

5. *What are the implications, for scholarship and for action, of approaching organizational design and change with the idea of merely attempting to create conditions for effective performance, rather than trying to directly manage employee attitudes and behaviors?* If one controls the appropriate stimuli and reinforcers, he or she can shape the behaviors and attitudes of individuals at work fairly powerfully. The success of various kinds of control procedures, attitude change and training programs, and behavior modification techniques attest to this fact.

Direct management of the norms and performance of work groups is quite a bit harder to carry off successfully, however. And it is well-nigh impossible to have direct and immediate managerial effects on the climate and productivity of whole organizations. Why? There are at least two reasons.

First, it is difficult and sometimes impossible to obtain and exercise direct control over the critical stimuli and reinforcers that affect what happens in performing units that are larger and more complex than individuals working more or less on their own. Second, groups and organizations routinely *enact their own environments* and *create their own internal realities.* Groups and organizations construct social definitions of reality and are powerful in communicating that reality to their members (see Hackman, 1976). And they often can take strong direct actions to alter the environments that impinge on them.

In sum, social systems change and develop at least partly because of what their members collectively decide about the nature of "reality" and how they want to deal with it. For this reason, it may be that the best way to deal with intact social systems, such as work teams and larger organizational units, is simply to *create conditions* that increase the chances that socially healthy and task effective patterns of behavior will emerge. Once the conditions are in place, which would include everything from how the system is staffed to how tasks are designed to how parts of the system are linked together, one might just step back and let unfold whatever does unfold within the context that has been created.

This of course is very close to the approach advocated by sociotechnical researchers and interventionists. Never is only one thing changed in an STS project; it's always a multiply-focused change effort that alters many aspects of the work and the context. And never is an attempt made to directly manage, on a minute by minute or even day by day basis, what transpires within the social system once it is set in motion or redirected. A great deal of "room" is left for the unfolding of the social system, and much is left unspecified for members to enact in their own ways. This of course is the idea of "minimal critical specification," and if taken seriously, it offers the possibility of significantly new and interesting ways to think about and execute organizational change and management.

While I find this way of thinking highly attractive, partly because it helps get us out of the rather manipulative "engineering" mentality that has crept into much recent thinking about the uses of organizational behavior, it is not easy to carry off. For one thing, those responsible for the creation of conditions for work unit effectiveness need to *know* some things. Certain kinds of structures are more likely to foster desired patterns of behavior than are other kinds of structures—and it would be pleasing to begin the design task knowing something about that. Moreover, anyone who takes this approach seriously will immediately confront what I call the "expertise dilemma." This is the tension between leaving all decision making about the design and management of the work system to system members versus telling members how they *should* design their enterprise, or doing it for them. The dilemma is frustrating: tilting too much one way can deprive system members of expertise that they may badly need to create the kind of organization they want to have; tilting too much the other can undermine members' feelings of ownership and commitment that may be critical to the eventual success of the venture.

How the dilemma should be resolved and which risk considered less dangerous will differ from organization to organization. But I hope we soon can be finished with the design strategy that simply turns the entire set of decisions over to a design team made up of system members who may not have much knowledge or expertise about organizational change, on the assumption that "the group will work things out." This approach often has been taken with labor-management committees, whose members may have a history of less than collaborative relationships but who are expected now to work together harmoniously to turn around the quality of life and productivity of an organization where things are going badly. That members may know little about what is required for organizational change or which factors may be most critical to productivity in the industry in which the changes are to take place is often ignored. That the group may be too large or otherwise composed in a way that undermines rather than fosters high-quality planning and decision making may be overlooked. That group members may neither have nor know how to get the expertise needed to carry out their design work competently may be considered unimportant: "The group will work it out." As noted earlier, it's not very likely. Some hard thinking about just what *is* required to create conditions for an organization that can be self-designing as well as self-managing is surely called for. The sociotechnical tradition would seem an excellent place from which to begin that kind of thinking.

6. *What are the circumstances under which it is in fact feasible to create and maintain innovative organizational systems of the sociotechnical variety?* If we have learned anything from the last decade of work in organization development—ranging from single-focused change strategies such as sensitivity training or job enrichment to multiply-focused interventions such as the "appreciation planning" implementation process described by Trist—it is that organizations are *hard* to change. Sometimes the intended changes are never installed at all; the level of inertia and resistance in the organization is just too great. Other times changes are made, but they fail to yield their intended effects or to persist over time. Still other times the effects "take" and persist, but they fail to diffuse to other parts of the organization as hoped. The rate of success for organizational interventions that are guided by behavioral science theory is not great, and the track record to date surely must call into question the feasibility of the kind of enterprise that the sociotechnical approach represents.

Part of the problem may be timing. As Trist notes, there was a long fallow period in the sociotechnical tradition, discussed under the heading "Going against the Grain of the Fifties." There was not great receptivity to sociotechnical ideas, or to any other approach to planned organizational change using behavioral science methods, in that decade. Now, Trist suggests, the times may have changed, and the decade ahead may be one in which the sociotechnical redesign of work systems will thrive and diffuse. The projects Trist cites in which new plants are designed from the ground up in accord with sociotechnical ideas are certainly encouraging. (For a more extended and equally optimistic account of the benefits of designing new organizational units using behavioral science knowledge and expertise, see the discussion by Lawler, 1978, of "the new plant revolution".)

Yet the chance to create a new organization or to wholly redesign an old one appears rarely. Sociotechnical principles also can be used to good effect on those more frequent occasions when the stable organizational systems that make planned change so difficult become temporarily *unstable*. During such periods of turbulence the defenses of an organization against change are less strong, and it may be possible to introduce substantial and multiply-focused changes in work systems before things settle down again.

Such "openings" for change may be provided by the advent of a new technology (e.g., word processing), by a significant reshuffling of line managers, by the introduction or elimination of a product or service, by rapid growth or shrinkage in an organizational unit, or by major changes in the market, the economy, the labor supply, or the legislative or regulatory context within which the organization operates.

The point is that organizations regularly move back and forth between periods of relative stability and periods of transition and instability. Rather than to try to change organizations when things are relatively stable, it may be better to wait for those times when an organization is, for whatever reasons, particularly open to the kinds of multilevel and multiply-focused innovations that typify sociotechnical interventions. In my view, the wait rarely will be a long one.

What then is required for sociotechnical changes that have a chance of "taking," persisting, and diffusing? For one thing, there needs to be a well-articulated and engaging *vision* of an alternative future—something that can guide the activities of system members and help pull them through the inevitably difficult times after the changes are made. There needs to be a real *opportunity* to make changes that will stay made and have a chance of diffusing. As noted above, this may depend both on the climate of the times and on the particular circumstances of the organization in which change is contemplated. There needs to be ample *expertise*—knowledge, skill, and experience—in designing, installing, and maintaining the innovations. It is now clear that changes managed by well-intentioned but poorly skilled amateur change agents have little chance of succeeding. Finally, there needs to be sufficient *power* to get the changes made and to protect and nurture them in the early stages of the project when they are particularly fragile and vulnerable.

The sociotechnical approach to intervention can provide the requisite vision in rich and exciting detail. If in the years to come sociotechnical theorists (and the rest of us) given increasing attention to the other three attributes listed—opportunity, expertise, and power—then I for one will applaud. My guess is that the proportion of sociotechnical change efforts that succeed in achieving their ambitious goals will increase dramatically.

REFERENCES

Cherns, A. (1976). "The Principles of Sociotechnical Design," *Human Relations* **29**:783–792.

Cummings, T. G. (1978). "Self-regulating Work Groups: A Sociotechnical Synthesis," *Academy of Management Review* **3**:625–634.

Hackman, J. R. (1976). "Group Influences on Individuals in Organizations," in M. D. Dunnette, Ed., *Handbook of Industrial and Organizational Psychology,* Chicago: Rand-McNally.

Lawler, E. E., III (1978). "The New Plant Revolution," *Organizational Dynamics* **6**:2–12.

CHAPTER THREE

Quality of Working Life Perspective

The Michigan Quality of Work Program: Issues in Measurement, Assessment, and Outcome Evaluation

STANLEY E. SEASHORE
Institute for Social Research
The University of Michigan

ORIGINS AND ORIENTATIONS

The research enterprise that is known as the "Michigan Quality of Work Program" has two facets. One is concerned with the assessment of a coordinated set of demonstration-experiments in the improvement of organizational life through joint labor-management collaborative structures. The second facet, and the subject matter of this paper, is the development and field testing of methods that may be employed for describing the structure and functioning of organizations and for detecting and documenting changes that may occur over time.

The assessment side of this program reflects the environment in which the program came into being. It has not been an autonomous intellectual exercise in theory building, although some contributions of that sort have emerged. It has not been directed toward the invention or perfection of novel methods for measurement, although a few side benefits of that kind

---

While this paper has singular authorship and responsibility, the work and ideas represented are an accumulative product of a team of researchers numbering over 25. The principal colleagues in this work include Cortlandt Cammann, Edward E. Lawler III, Barry Macy, and David A. Nadler.

have accrued. Instead the work aims to extract maximum knowledge and learning from complex social experiments and to provide credible information of sufficiently inclusive scope for the evaluation of their costs and benefits.

There are key words in the foregoing sentences. By "complex social experiments" we direct attention to multifaceted efforts for purposeful change in real-life settings, unprotected from the vagaries of environmental conditions. By "learning" we refer not to intellectual mastery on the part of the researcher, but to behavioral, attitudinal, and value changes on the part of individual actors, and to systemic changes on the part of organizations, which tend toward maximizing benefits and minimizing costs for all concerned. Campbell captures this theme in "Reforms as Experiments" (1969), as does Lawler in "Adaptive Experiments" (1977). By the words "credible information" we invoke aspirations to adduce information of such scope, cogency, and reliability as to command the attention of the disbeliever, the hostile critic, and the initially inattentive. The actual achievements of course are less grand than such aspirations suggest, but some progress can be reported.

An Historical Note

The Michigan program arose in the context of the quality of working life "movement" that was beginning to stir in the United States in the late 1960s. Some signal events occurred. A report issued by the U.S. Department of Health, Education and Welfare (1973) depicted a variety of ills associated with suboptimum working conditions and generated a good deal of controversy as well as public attention. In 1971 a conference on New Directions in the World of Work was held, stimulated by the Upjohn Institute and underwritten largely by the Ford Foundation; this brought together about 40 influential representatives of management, labor, government, and academia to debate the feasibility and means for achieving significant changes in the prevailing quality of working life. There followed the International Conference on the Quality of Working Life, again supported by the Ford Foundation and organized by Louis Davis of UCLA and Albert Cherns of Loughbrough University. Aside from the influential two-volume report of the proceedings, this event led to the formation of an international network of people concerned with the matter and the determination by the Ford Foundation and U.S. Department of Commerce jointly to stimulate some demonstration experiments of significant scale, high visibility, and ample assessment. The Institute of Social Research (ISR) was asked to take a leading role in planning the entire project and to itself address the task of developing and applying assessment procedures. Our original proposal to the supporting agencies was introduced as follows:

This proposal is submitted in response to a joint request from the Ford Foundation and the Quality of Work Program (QWP) of the U.S. National Commission on Productivity. The request stems from the commitment of the Commission (NCOP) to a program of experimental-demonstration efforts, to explore the efficacy of alternative approaches to improving the quality of work. An integral part of this program is an evaluation process that is broad in scope, intensive, and definitive, and that contributes maximally to increasing our understanding of organizations and of the means for assessing organizations. Since a major thrust of NCOP is dissemination and work place change, the evaluation must also be one that is credible to nonprofessionals and one which lends itself to easily communicated results.

This proposal further assumes the following conditions: (1) that the NCOP will undertake to develop access and cooperative relationships at research sites, and will fund the work of a change advisor at each site; we will have no obligation to aid or guide the change programs except in ways that may be jointly agreed at each site; (2) that the role of the Institute for Social Research shall be primarily that of implementing programs of description, measurement, evaluation, and results dissemination; (3) that the proposed work shall be initiated and funded early in 1974 and will continue for a period of about three years, unless extended by mutual consent; (4) that the number of research sites encompassed by this proposal shall not exceed a maximum of 20.

Objectives.   The formulation of our proposed activities has been guided by our concept of the objectives of the Quality of Work Program. These need to be stated in order to put our design into proper perspective. We conceive of the overall objectives of NCOP in their Quality of Work Program to be the public trial and demonstration of a variety of ways through which management and labor unions may apply social science knowledge to accomplish a significant improvement in the conditions of work within an organization.* In order to meet this objective, the changes need to be evaluated against the broadest possible range of considerations reflecting the interests of the employees, of the firm's management, of the employees' union, and of the public. We conceive of the more specific objectives of the evaluation phase of the program as follows:

1.   To describe the sites and their initial states and contexts in terms that are necessary for later interpretation of the changes that may occur and for evaluating factors contributing to or inhibiting changes of various kinds.

2.   To describe the nature of the interventions undertaken and the course of their development at each site.

3.   To measure as best as possible the kinds and degrees of changes that occur, or do not occur, at each site with special reference to:

Changes of an economic or operational nature concerning the firm—for example, changes relating to productivity, cost performance, quality of prod-

*For a characterization of the "variety of ways" see Drexler and Lawler (1977), Goodman (1979), Macy (1979), and Mills (1975).

uct or service, maintenance of facilities and effective staff, process innovation rates, and the like.

Changes in the attitudes, beliefs, and motivations of members of the firm (at all levels) as these may bear upon the effectiveness of the firm as an economic unit and its effectiveness in meeting the interests, needs, and preferences of its members—for example, satisfactions, willingness to remain with the enterprise, opportunities for career fulfillment, effectiveness of communications and coordination of activity, maintenance of health and safety, and the like.

Changes in the features of the relationship between management and the labor union that bear upon the effective resolution of issues which concern the union and its members.

Changes in any other features of the site organization, or its members, or its context that may in a particular case appear to be important, and feasible of measurement, as part of the intent to be inclusive in assessment. Examples of such "special" topics of measurement are: community relations, health and safety of members, rates of innovation and adaptation, problem-solving capabilities, communication effectiveness, and the like.

4.   To endeavor to understand the manner and degree to which the various changes arise from the activities of the intervention program.

5.   To endeavor to draw conclusions and suggested courses of action for those who may later wish to emulate one or another of the observed program plans.

6.   To assess in the context of these field trials the adequacy of concepts, procedures, and instruments used in evaluation and to suggest ways to make the instruments efficiently and effectively usable by others.

7.   To produce the basic data from these field trials in a form suitable for use by us or others who may need to pursue inquiries of a theoretical, methodological, or operational sort lying beyond the limits of this proposal, that is, to preserve and make usable the information from the trials.

8.   To produce data and materials from these projects that will help non-professionals understand the results of the projects and that will facilitate work place improvements elsewhere.

Conceptual and Theoretical Framework

In the foregoing history, the reader will not discern any commitment to a particular conceptual framework or theoretical approach. The task was defined with practical reference, not conceptual neatness. The value framework, while generally humanistic and oriented ultimately to the welfare of individuals, embraces the interests of workers, managers, union officers, the public, and others, whose individual interests are often divergent. The substantive orientation emphasizes topical breadth and inclusiveness rather than focus; the current roster of variables has over 1000 entries ranging alphabetically from the A's (attitudes, accident rates) through the G's and H's (groups and grievances, holidays and hand tools) through the P's (profit margins, piece rates) to the T's, V's, and Y's (technological changes, volume of output, yields), although there are no Z's yet. The entities for assessment span the hierarchy from individuals to groups to larger functional segments of organizations, to entire organizations, to surrounding communities.

The choice of concepts and operational variables for inclusion has not been random. Four principal guidelines have been employed in roughly the following order of priority: (1) preference for concepts representing results, that is, states or directions of change that are thought to be valued for their intrinsic worth by some segment of the interested parties; (2) inclusion of concepts and operational variables judged to be potentially relevant to the inducement of or understanding of such results; (3) preference for concepts and variables that exploit contemporary theoretical and empirical resources that might aid understanding of the results, their causation, and the contingencies associated with variance in the results; and (4) preference for concepts and operational variables thought to allow comparisons among the organizations studied and within each organization over time. There are some lesser considerations as well, but they will not be elaborated here. For example, some measures have been included simply because they are familiar to and expected among potential users of the resulting data; some because we aimed to invent an improved measurement method or test a novel hypothesis; some because the data could be collected without cost or risk and might prove useful to some analyst; some because they were requested by an interested party—perhaps the consultant-intervenor at a site. Also numerous concepts of importance have been omitted simply on grounds that we knew no way to obtain the information while still staying within bounds of ethics, validity, reliability, and cost.

Results have been conceived primarily as those results of interest to the organization's members and secondarily as those of interest to organizational researchers or the anonymous public. The original proposal to the sponsor (see preceding section) specified some of the gross categories of results. Some are primarily relevant at the individual level of analysis, such as security, health, or satisfaction, whereas others are primarily relevant at the level of organizational or institutional analysis, for example, systemic adaptability or economic viability. A "valued outcome," of course, and the priorities among such results, is a matter of opinion. The relevant opinion is, first of all, that of some organizational actor, and second, that of some analyst or interpreter. Thus, in a given organizational setting, a reduced rate of absences for reasons of illness might be regarded by some as an important intrinsically valued outcome, by others as an indicator of or causal contributor to organizational viability, or perhaps it might be regarded as merely a minor side effect of some technological change. Some results are positively valued by one segment of the organizational population and negatively by another. A rise in individual productivity may be valued by the management but not by employees if it is obtained at the cost of additional strain.

Explanatory and causal variables associated with outcome variables may enter into the assessment plan for a particular organization on theoretical or empirical grounds, or grounds of some plausible atheoretical, common-sense rationale. For example, the degree of change in work group cohesiveness might be assessed for any of several reasons: there might be an effort to increase group cohesiveness in the expectation that specified desirable results will then follow, or an intended outcome may be considered contingent upon the presence of group cohesiveness so that low cohesiveness might help explain a failure to achieve an intended outcome, or an increment in group cohesiveness might be regarded by some as an intrinsically valued condition. Similarly, there exists a prevalent view among production supervisors and managers that gains of some sort, for example, increased productivity, are often accompanied by offsetting costs or losses of some other kind, for example, in materials wastage or product quality. In such an instance the measurement of potential collateral conditions and changes may be undertaken in order to allow evaluation of the set of interdependent changes.

Theoretical preferences are prominent in the choice of concepts and measures to be employed. The measurement program here described is not dominated by any singular theoretical system but does incorporate, eclectically, a number of contemporary theories of proven or probable validity. The list of such incorporated ideas is quite extensive, including theories at the individual level relating to perceptions of equity, the role of expectations in motivation theory, the existence of a need hierarchy, the effects of participation, the differential effects of alternative forms of control, and so on. At the group level, theories are employed relating to cohesiveness, boundaries, size, and normative integration. Concepts at the level of complex organizational units include the traditional concepts arising from Weberian theory on organizational structures and, from other sources, theories concerning intergroup relations and the fit of formal structure to technological constraints. In these ways the approach to organizational assessment is richly imbued with theoretical orientations (plural), but not intentionally constrained by any one. Some other theories employed are the Hackman and Oldham (1980) theory of optimal job design, the theory of French (1963) concerning the sources of stress in work environments, and the theory of Tannenbaum (1968) concerning the distribution of control in hierarchical systems.

Comparability as a consideration in the choice of concepts and measures arises from two factors: first, the intended longitudinal and change orientation, which requires preference for measures that are likely to remain comparable over time; and second, preference for measures that are not unique to a given organization but that allow comparison of states and changes among organizations. The first consideration is not as self-evident as it may at first seem, for many commonly used measures of organizational characteristics are vulnerable to recalibration (Golem-biewsky, 1975) with changing circumstances, or are so embedded in a set of associated interacting variables that the meaning of any one may in time be altered or even reversed in its interpretive implication. The second consideration rests upon a belief that comparison among cases is just as important as understanding the uniqueness of a given case when search-ing for valid generalizations about organizational change and the suit-ability of alternative strategies and tactics for inducing desired changes.

There are of course severe limits to comparability among organizations. We conceived of a hierarchy of generality of concepts associated with a scale of comparability. The volume of shoes produced by one firm is hardly comparable with the volume of research reports produced by another, but more general concepts, for example, rate of change or direction of change in volume, may well be comparable. Similarly an index of "direct partic-ipation in day-to-day decisions" may well be comparable among organi-zations even though any single component of such an index may not be directly comparable; different organizations may elect alternative means for achieving the same degree of member participation. The assessment of the comparability of organizations is viewed as a matter that can be approached empirically. By attempting to achieve and validate compar-ability, we hope to contribute to some enhanced understanding of the degree and means through which interorganizational comparisons may be made.

Analytic and interpretive strategies of various kinds are implied by the foregoing description of the guidelines for inclusion of concepts and their operational variations. The main considerations are the "level" of anal-yses and the analytic role assigned to variables.

We have assumed that different purposes will require analyses at dif-ferent levels. To understand the impact of some QWL intervention upon individuals, analyses of individual-level data (treating each person as a "case") is highly desirable, even though valuable and valid clues or con-firming evidence may be found in aggregated population statistics or in cross-comparisons among work groups. Similarly, to ascertain whether a change in system productive output arises from system properties (e.g., increased rate of capital investment or reduction in available market) the analyses should be primarily at the level of the sociotechnical system as a whole, even though clues and confirming evidence may be sought at the levels of specific subunits (e.g., where the investments were concen-trated) or at the level of individuals (e.g., individual work motivations). Ideally, the data should be obtained in such a form that analyses may be multilevel in character without predetermining the level about which interpretations are to be made.

Similarly, we have avoided the constraints of relying upon any single conceptual model in which a variable is assigned some fixed role in analysis or interpretation. The discussion of "group cohesiveness," for example, affirms that the same variable may be treated, in different contexts, as an independent variable, a dependent variable, or in a contingent or moderating relationship to other variables. The analytic use of a variable is assumed to be independent of any inherent quality of the construct itself and indeed preference has been given to variables known or believed to have utility in several analytic roles.

Public controversy has been elicited by the foregoing approach to the assessment of organizations, and for valid reasons. The principal objections concern the basic theoretical assumptions, the uncertain fit to any particular case, and the impracticality of trying to assess "everything that is relevant." Some vocal critics have noted, correctly, that the approach is at odds with the contemporary thrust toward less reductionist, more "organic" and "molar" conceptions of organizational life; others have found that the approach does not encourage adaptation of assessment methods to the specific organizational change strategy that may be employed in a given case; some have observed that the approach involves factors of complexity, cost, and intrusiveness that are not supportable in the general practice of organizational and change assessment. Out of such controversy may emerge improved theory and practice.

METHODS

A report is in preparation that provides, in book-length detail, information on the methods that have been developed and field tested, as well as those still under development. Included are the interview and questionnaire forms and their statistical credentials—in instances which these can be established—together with procedural guidelines for field work, reporting, and alternative analytic strategies (Seashore, Cammann, Lawler, and Mirvis, 1981). The following pages will be limited to an overview of these methods and some comments on their utility.

Mapping of Content Coverage

In the course of the developmental work, a number of efforts were made to map the substantive territories to be included. Some of these maps are large-scale, that is, displaying in some detail a segment of the information domain to be represented with data, while others are "small-scale," intended to represent gross categories or classes of variables.

An example of the latter sort is shown as Figure 3-1. It shows a panel of outcome variables (organizational effectiveness and quality of work life) to be a product of the work-related behavior of individuals and groups, with these in turn partially determined by the prevailing attitudes, beliefs, and expectations of individuals and of individuals clustered in work

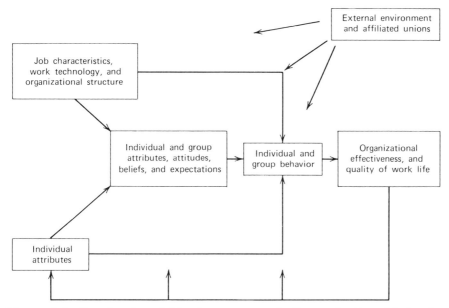

Figure 3-1 Panels of variables in assessment of organizational behavior (adapted from Lawler, Nadler, and Mirvis, 1980).

groups. Prior "causes" in this limited model include the attributes of individuals imported into the organization, as well as the attributes of the jobs and work subsystems and their surrounding organizational characteristics. The external environment, including attributes of the union(s), are given only token representation in this model.

This example of a modeling exercise displays only some features of the states and processes of an organization. Other models addressed stages of expected progress in the implementation of organizational or technological changes. Figure 3-2 provides an example; it shows gross stages of progress that, in principle, should be measured and documented in order to have an interpretable basis for understanding successes and failures in implementation of quality of work life initiatives.

Considerations in the Choice of Variables and Methods

A number of choices and dilemmas are encountered when planning a program for the assessment of organizations and of organizational change, and these are resolved with varying degrees of success. Among the prominent considerations are the following:

1. **Confirmatory Data.**   Certain variables are judged to be key variables in the sense that they are intrinsically important to some

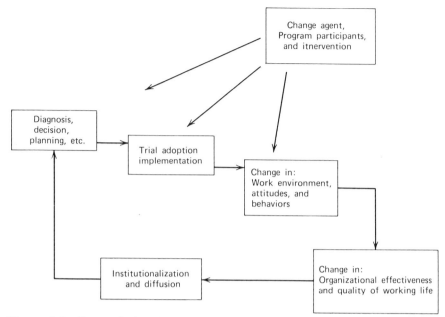

Figure 3-2   Stages in implementation of a quality of working life initiatives (adapted from Lawler, Nadler, and Mirvis, 1980).

interested party or have a role in more than one analytical and interpretive context. Where feasible, an attempt should be made to provide multiple measures of such variables using different methods. For example, an indicator of job variety can be obtained via questionnaire or interview with individual workers and also via direct observation by trained staff.

2. ***Adaptability to Different Site Conditions.*** For many variables, optimum measurement in the context of one organization may be incompatible with optimization in another and may indeed be irrelevant or impossible in another. This calls for standardized methods for some variables and for adaptive alternative methods for others. The decision may rest upon judgments of the feasibility of alternative methods and upon estimates of the range of conditions that may be encountered in different organizations.

3. ***An Open-Ended Measurement Plan.*** The preceding paragraph relates to the adaptability of the measurement plan to local opportunities and constraints at each site. A related consideration in the development of the plan has been to allow adaptation to emergent ideas about additional variables that merit attention. None of the instruments and procedures employed so far precludes the addition of new material.

4. *Measurement of Change over Time.*   Since an aim of the Michigan Quality of Work Program measures is the detection and documentation of changes, considerable emphasis is given to the measurement of variables that lend themselves to repeated or continuous measurement and thus to time series analysis. The aim of detecting change also forces comprehensiveness of topical coverage, as the nature of the changes cannot be known in advance. Included also is a questionnaire instrument designed for use a year or more after the initiation of a change program to assess the opinions of organization members concerning the progress and effectiveness of the program up to that time.

Instruments and Procedures

At the present time there are 11 distinguishable instruments or field procedures for collection of information. These vary as to the source of the information, the methods of collection, and the degree to which they are structured as to method and substantive content. Some are relatively complete as to development and field testing, whereas others are still in preliminary trial form. They are enumerated below with brief descriptions.

1. *Michigan   Organizational   Assessment   Questionnaire (MOAQ).*   This instrument is designed for use with organization members to obtain descriptive information on the respondent's job and work environment as well as the respondent's attitudes and perceptions in several domains. The instrument is composed of several modules, each relating to a different area of topical content. The modules presently in general use are: demographics, a "general attitudes" module, job rewards and reward contingencies, task and role characteristics, work group functioning, supervision, and compensation administration. Each module provides a number of discriminate scales so that the full instrument yields 67 multi-item indexes plus the demographic data. Many indexes have both short and long versions, the shorter being used when reduced reliability is acceptable given constraints on organizational and respondent time. The modular arrangement allows the preparation of a questionnaire tailored to the organization under study by selective omission of modules, indexes, or items. New items of special local interest may be added. The MOAQ is a "living" instrument, with additional indexes occasionally added and with additional modules under consideration.

2. *Interview: Organizational Structure and Environment.* A set of semistructured interview schedules is used to collect data about key aspects of organizational structure and environment.

The interviews are used with both line and staff personnel and serve also as a guide to the collection of relevant documents and data from archival sources.

3. *Technology and Technological Change.* Data about jobs and tasks are obtained primarily through questionnaires and direct observation (see 1 and 4). The detection, description, and assessment of change in larger technological systems has been resistant to approach through standardized methods. Observational and questionnaire methods have been used to examine dimensions of work processes, including material and informational flows, through fixed procedures and through technological adaptations and adjustments. These have been *ad hoc* instruments and procedures adapted to each site.

4. *Observations of Task Characteristics.* An instrument has been designed and field tested to guide the direct observation of jobs and reporting of aspects of task activities and job environment. Emphasis is upon job and task characteristics having psychological and behavioral implications. There are provisions for observer training and for scheduling of observation periods on a time-sampling basis.

5. *Union-Management Relations.* Semistructured interviews with key union and management informants are supplemented with questionnaire measures from union members. The main themes are concerned with union organization and activities, member involvement, and attitudes regarding union-management relationships.

6. *Behavioral-Financial Measures.* Standardized reporting forms and methods are provided for data collection or for abstracting information from archival sources, as well as for the analysis of such information. The focus is upon specific employee behavior in the work setting, such as absences, lateness, turnover, nonproductive behavior, accidents, and the like. The methods are oriented toward assessing the costs associated with such behavior in addition to the rates of their occurrence.

7. *Productivity Measures.* Semistandardized procedures and analytical guidelines are employed to measure output volumes, material utilization, machine time utilization, output quality, and the like. Measurements are sought, where feasible, at the individual, work group, departmental, and organizational levels.

8. *Intervention Observations.* Standardized recording forms and observer guidelines are used for assessing joint union-management committee meetings and similar meetings, and for reporting im-

plementation efforts in the target organization. These data can be used descriptively for producing narrative accounts of the course of events, or they can be quantified for purposes of documenting group interactions or the substantive content of discussions.

9. ***Change Implementation and Goal Attainment Questionnaire.*** A questionnaire is employed, perhaps on more than one occasion, to obtain employee views about the implementation of changes and about their impact. Topics include the activities of the joint labor-management committee, the effectiveness of actions taken, the clarity of the change program, receptivity to the program, and allied matters. Goal attainment measures assess the extent to which employees perceive improvements or other changes in their jobs, their rewards, their access to information, and other characteristics of their work environment that result from the change program.

10. ***Intervention Costs and Benefits.*** Standardized reporting and analysis guides are used for the collection of data about the costs of the change project, the benefits obtained that can be quantified, and the selective impact of costs and benefits in different parts of segments of the organization. The costs in question include, for example, the direct costs of consultants' time and expenses, lost productivity or productive time associated with the program, gains associated with productivity and "costly behaviors," and the like.

11. ***Naturalistic Observation.*** A log of events and on-site observations is maintained, together with tentative interpretations of their significance. From such records, and the recollections of the site observers, an interpretive history of the change program is derived.

Analysis and Evaluation

These diverse methods produce information of considerable scope and variety that plainly does not prescribe any singular analytical and evaluational process, nor was any intended. Further, the explicit intention from the start was to encourage evaluation of the consequences of the change programs from multiple value perspectives—changes and results that are valued highly by some might well be given small note by others. The interpretations of contingencies and dynamics of change processes were expected to remain indeterminate even though enhanced by a rich informational base. It was expected that the results would generate informed debate, that issues would be clarified but not settled.

The principal intended product from each demonstration site is a book-length, moderately technical report containing an account of the characteristics of the organization, the history of the flow of events during and following the initiation of the change programs, and chapters treating selected substantive topics or issues drawing on both quantitative data and observers' reports. Each report is also to have chapters of interpretation and evaluation representing the views of the principal researchers at each site.

The first such report from a coal mine site, for example (Goodman, 1979), aside from background material and a description of the events at the site, has chapters of evaluation results and interpretation titled as follows:

Beliefs and attitudes

Economic analysis

Safety

Job skills

Labor-management relations

Implicit goals and unintended consequences

Cost-Benefit analysis

Institutionalizing and sustaining change

Diffusion of the experiment within Rushton

Critical issues in designing QOW experiments

Critical issues in implementing QOW experiments

In addition to such summary reports, numerous analyses and publications have been and will be issued that deal with methodological topics, selected theoretical and interpretive issues, and speculative articles on the implications of these studies for future research and applications. Some reports of these kinds will appear in a forthcoming collection of papers on methodological topics, *Observing and Measuring Organizational Change: A Guide to Practice* (Seashore, Lawler, Mirvis, and Cammann, 1981). It includes, for example, a chapter on the application of network analysis to the explication of aspects of the informal structure of organizations, and a chapter detailing the procedures and validity tests associated with observers' reports on the characteristics of jobs and their microenvironments. The Rushton Mine site report mentioned above includes a chapter detailing the development of alternative production functions as an aid in assessing the increase or decrease in productivity at an experimental site, and a factory site report (Macy, Ledford, and Lawler, 1981) that contains a rare example of the application of time series analysis methods to behavioral data.

It is intended that the basic data from the several sites should be available for reanalysis by others, to the extent that adequate provisions can be made for protecting the privacy, confidentiality, and interests of the organizations and persons involved. Limited public sharing of the data has taken place up to this time, partly because of the difficulty and cost of "sanitizing" the data without excessive loss of meaning, and partly because the complexity of the data base makes it formidable for analysis by persons not familiar with both the data characteristics and the site characteristics.

APPLICATIONS

The Michigan Organizational Assessment program was conceived and designed expressly for the purpose of aiding the evaluation of a series of demonstration projects, as described in the opening pages of this paper. At the same time, it was part of the intention to develop an approach and methods and field procedures that would serve also for the evaluation of organizations and organizational change in other contexts. The program has in fact been applied to eight quality of work life (QWL) projects that were included in the original plan. These projects are listed in Table 3-1. Not all of these projects, however, received the same treatment, as some were in progress while the assessment plan and instruments were still in early development, and others required omission or modification of some parts of the overall assessment plan. In addition to these eight instances of application, various components of the assessment program have been employed in numerous other situations, by us and by others. Such applications include, for example, a tool and die factory, a metropolitan bank system, a ball bearing factory, a pharmaceutical factory, and a furniture factory. French and Spanish language versions of some instruments have been used in other countries.

From these experiences, some observations can be made concerning the suitability of the program for diverse field uses and concerning operational successes and failures that have been encountered:

1. *Scope of Assessments.* The full array of field procedures has been applied in only one project—a project characterized by ample funding, compliant and interested organization members, tolerance for observations at work and in meetings, and ready consent for access (with assurances as to privacy and confidentiality) to organizational records and information about identified individuals. Thus under near-ideal conditions the scale of the field work, intrusion into work settings and time, absorbed and unaccounted costs, and the risks of unauthorized revelations do not prohibit the application of the full range of methods and procedures. Nevertheless the full array of field activities is likely to be used only rarely, for three reasons. First, the program is plainly one of "overkill," justified on grounds of development and validation of

Table 3-1 Quality of Work Life Projects

Organization Name	Union(s)	Start Date	Study Team	Assessment Funding Source(s)
1. Rushton Coal Mine	United Mine Workers of America	1/73	P. Goodman[a] E. Lawler C. Cammann	NCPQOW; the Ford Foundation
2. Bolivar (Beatrice Foods; Harman Int'l Industries)	United Auto Workers	5/73	B. Macy[a] G. Ledford R. Mirris	The Ford Foundation; U. S. DOC
3. Tennessee Valley Authority	TVA Engineering Association (TVAEA) and Office and Professional Employees International Union (OPIEU)	1/74	B. Macy[a] A. Nurick M. Moch J. Feather J. Klesh M. Fichman	The Ford Foundation; U. S. DOC
4. ——— (Biscuit Division)	International Bakery, Confectionery, and Tobacco Workers Union	6/74	E. Lawler[a] M. Moch J. Bartunek	——— Inc.

5.	Hospital	6/75	E. Lawler[a] D. Nadler D. Gladstein M. Nanlon	NIMH
6.	The _____ Company	4/76	E. Lawler[a] J. Drexler B. Doyle B. Quayle C. O'Dell N. Bizony	The _____ Company
7.	Ann Arbor Transportation Authority	6/76	C. Cammann[a] D. Berg L. Laughlin J. Lapointe	NIMH
8.	City of San Diego	7/77	E. Lawler[a] J. Walsh D. Tracey	U. S. DOL

[a]Site coordinator

components of the program but not exceeding the assessment requirements in most cases. Second, some components may be inapplicable in certain organizations—for example, meetings cannot be observed in organizations in which meetings do not occur; the properties of work groups cannot be assessed where stable work groups do not exist; the organizational structure of a union cannot be described if there is no union. Third, there are reasonable economic, political, and ethical reasons for omitting some assessments in a given case, as the costs and risks must be compared with expected benefits. Selective use of the several program components is necessary.

2. *Confirming Evidence.*   One of the intentions has been to provide means for obtaining confirmatory information on topics that are either critical to the interpreters of the assessment data or else of uncertain significance in the absence of confirmatory data. On this point we can conclude without any hesitation that multiple measures and alternative information sources frequently prove their worth, sometimes by allowing strong interpretations of otherwise dubious data or by preventing overinterpretation of the data—and occasionally by adding credibility among diverse users who have unlike preferences and prejudices regarding "hard" data, observer's reports, and questionnaires.

3. *Comparison Units.*   In only four out of approximately 12 attempts have we been able to make effective use of the principle of interorganizational comparison in a quasi-experimental design for assessing change. In three of these instances the "controls" provided information of some significance for the interpretation of change processes or results, even though the controls were part of the same parent organization. While the principle remains sound, the practice is dubious except in those unusual instances in which comparable organizations exist, provide access for assessment, and can be assessed at moderate cost. In some promising instances, the comparison units proved to be contaminated by exposure to the change program or were easily shown to be noncomparable in ways that preclude confident comparison.

4. *"Loose" Organizations.*   Not surprisingly, the Michigan organizational assessment program proves to be more compatible with some organizational forms than with others. In general, the more "structured" components are more usable with organizational systems that are bounded, that are relatively independent of other related systems in the context, that have a relatively stable membership over the period of study, and that are relatively free of massive environmental disruptions during the period of study. All

but two of the many organizations studied have these properties in sufficient degree to sustain the use of questionnaires, record abstraction procedures, and semistandardized interview schedules. A notable and illustrative exception is a surgical ward of a large hospital in which the work of the unit is performed predominantly by "casuals" coming in from other functional departments, in which there is scheduled periodic reassignment of staff into and out of the unit, and in which much of the supervision is located elsewhere in the hospital. Under these conditions, who are the "members" of the unit, where are the records of attendance and performance to be found (if there are any at all), what can be done with "work groups" of ad hoc membership, and to what extent can any change be attributed to events, processes, and internal characteristics of the focal unit? This organization was amenable to the approaches of observation and unstructured interviewing, but only limited use of the more structured, preplanned procedures was warranted.

5. *Combined Use of Objective, Subjective, and Phenomenological Data.* The assessment program spans the scale of objectivity from readily confirmable "hard" data, through participants' somewhat discrepant reports about "objective" conditions and events, to data intended to capture the unique "reality" experienced by each participant or class of participants. These various kinds of information serve different analytic and interpretive purposes, and we are confirmed in the belief that all are important and all can be employed conjunctively. Some evaluators rely exclusively upon objective information, whereas others respond to the phenomenology of experienced quality of working life; they are entitled to their preferences. Some "hard" results are best understood analytically and theoretically by reference to the phenomenology of individual members of the organization. Given the interests of different constituencies with a stake in the organization and given the interests of different researchers with dissimilar theoretical or professional interests, the diversity of types of information collected is not only justified but required.

6. *The Independent Assessor's Role.* The original plan for the work of the Michigan group (see the first section of this chapter) provided an unusual arrangement under which the measurement, assessment, and evaluation of certain QWL projects would be conducted, to the extent feasible, independently of the planning and conduct of intervention and organizational change activities. There were three main reasons for this arrangement. First, it was envisioned that the measurement and assessment work would be very demanding and not to be conducted as a minor side concern of the site people or the site consultants. Second, there was a desire

to explore the feasibility and possible advantages (e.g., credibility bias) of separating the "action" responsibilities from the "evaluation" activity. Third, it was desirable to make the measurement and assessment activities comparable across the set of sites. It was anticipated that difficulties of various kinds would be encountered, some arising from the inherent incompatibilities of purposes and priorities among the site people, the consultants, and the evaluators; some from the sheer amount of intrusion implied by the planned measurement and observation work; and some from the relative absence of precedent and professional norms that could guide the parties. The clean separation of the intervention and assessment functions was not feasible in all cases; in some, ISR representatives had to take a fairly strong, active role in getting the project started before the consultants were chosen and began their work. In one, the fiscal sponsor required a strong ISR intrusion in order to continue a project that appeared to be in grave risk if defaulting consultants were not replaced by others. In another, a variation on the original plan was adopted in which both the consultant and the assessment teams were staffed by ISR members. The assessment activities occasionally were threatening to the consultants and may have impeded or altered their work, and there were occasions in which assessors' access to information was curtailed or temporarily withdrawn. Some account of these events is being made through papers in preparation or already in print (e.g., Mirvin and Seashore, 1979). The difficulties were worse than the reader probably imagines, but they were not defeating. In all locations, the assessment work was carried out more or less as intended, and usable information, although not always of prime quality, was obtained.

We conclude that the separation of intervention and assessment responsibilities is feasible and of significant advantage, but not without risks and costs that are difficult to evaluate. It is not timely to recommend the practice for general application. Certainly there should be further exploration of ways to do it with minimal strain, cost, and disturbing intrusion. The end to be sought is the development of professional norms that promote adequate and unbiased assessment practices selectively invoked to fit the purposes and requirements of the parties at interest. R&D need not always be the priority purpose.

7. *Research or Action?* In the initial pages of this chapter we mentioned the aims of enhancing "knowledge" about organizations and "learning" by the organization members. The crude distinction intended is that between generalized conclusions of a theoretical or empirical nature as against local, unique, and nongeneralizable

information of use primarily to the actors within the organization studied. The methods described are plainly oriented toward the former but do not exclude the latter. Others have addressed the differences between organic and rigorous research (Argyris, 1970) or clinical and nonclinical assessments (Alderfer, 1975) and the contrasting information requirements of each (Seashore, 1975). There is no need here to repeat the arguments. The priority aims of the Michigan Quality of Work Program have emphasized standardized procedures, comprehensive and theory based measures, comparison among the organizations studied, and insulation from the immediate demands of consultation, intervention, or participative action. The option for local modifications or additions to the procedures by the labor-management committee or by their consultants have rarely been exercised on any significant scale except at the sites where the Michigan team also undertook an active role as a participant in the change program.

LEARNING ABOUT ORGANIZATIONAL CHANGE

The principal applications of the Michigan Organizational Assessment program are in evaluating the progress and results of the eight projects itemized in Table 3-1. The utility of the assessment approach and program should be properly judged, in the long run, by the range and quality of its "product," that is, the contributions to basic knowledge about organizations and purposeful organizational change. These contributions potentially can range from the testing of theories and specific hypotheses to the generation of new or improved formulations of issues to the formulation of conclusions about optimal conditions and practices in initiating organizational change and the like. The approach is intended to provide information that can sustain a variety of uses. With respect to learning about organizational change through labor-management cooperative QWL committees, some illustrative areas of learning are itemized together below with citations of published material where available.

1. *Formation of Joint Committees.* Even when the parties are agreed in principle to form a joint labor-management QWL committee, there remain strong forces for and against the realization of the agreement. These forces can be estimated and steps taken to moderate their effects (Lawler and Drexler, 1978; Drexler and Lawler, 1977).

2. *Mixed Results.* The project results envisioned in the assessment program include potential side effects not intended by the actors on the scene and not necessarily beneficial. All projects for which

final data are available display a mixture of intended and unintended results and beneficial as well as adverse results. No project has been an unqualified success story for all classes of interested parties (Seashore et al., 1982; Goodman, 1979).

3. *Multiple Intervention.* The literature concerning purposeful organizational change strongly suggests that, in most instances, a single form of intervention or of change technique is dominant (e.g., Porras, 1979). In contrast, all of the projects assessed under the Michigan QWL Program, with the exception of two of short duration, involved a considerable range of types of actions. In all, there was at least one initial structural intervention (formation of the joint management-labor QWL Committee itself), and in most there were introduced a succession of others, including, for example, changes in reward and control systems; changes in technological and physical environment factors; alteration of work schedules; improvements in information and communication systems; skill training; intergroup problem solving; and autonomous work groups. Why should such various means and targets for change appear? One factor is the duration of activity and measurement, typically extending over a period of several years. Another is the initial structural intervention, which explicitly avoided defining in advance what activities the QWL committees might undertake. A third factor is the joint labor-management composition of the committees and their representational character, which broadened the range of concerns and assumptions brought to bear on the problem.

4. *Diffusion.* Five of the projects had a pair of characteristics in common, namely, an extended duration of activity *and also* a strategy of initiating change in some part of a larger organization with intention that site-wide diffusion would later occur. In only two of these does it appear that diffusion is occurring with some likelihood of being successful. The reasons for failure of diffusion are no doubt complex, but two stand out: first, in some cases the initially targeted unit was too unlike the others to serve as an acceptable or persuasive model. Second, in some cases issues of between-unit equity were exacerbated and became, at least in the short run, unresolvable. The strategic dilemma remains, given limited resources and commitment, of choosing between an intensive, focused effort in a demonstration or trial subunit as against a more diffused effort throughout the whole of an organization.

5. *The Critical Role of Environmental Events.* We think that those concerned with understanding purposeful organizational change and with assessing outcomes and their causation give too

little attention to the role of intrusive environmental events. In the few projects we have studied, major intrusions did occur, and they had both negative and positive consequences. In one, an event of succession in top management brought new persons and policies on the scene that were at odds with the QWL program assumptions. In another, an act of state legislation imposed upon the QWL site some fiscal requirements that almost wholly subverted the change program. In another, a deep industry recession appears to have had the effect of stimulating effective joint labor-management problem solving, thus providing a dramatic example of collaborative success. Available theories and assessment methods do not adequately treat such components of organizational change and adaptation.

6. *Consultant Selection.* In three projects in which the identification of the consultant(s) preceded initiation of the project, the project activities were substantially shaped by the consultants' previously known theoretical preferences and operational style; in all three a compatibility was achieved between the consultants and the principal site actors. At sites where the selection of consultant(s) was deferred to the QWL committee, mixed relationships emerged, ranging from highly successful and compatible to the opposite. Tentative observation: The presumed advantages of having an established QWL committee choose their own consultant may be offset by the advantages of having a consultant's assistance during the time leading up to the formation and initial activities of such a committee.

7. *Utility of Opinion-Attitude Survey Data.* In relatively large and complex organizations, measured changes in member attitudes and opinions regarding their work and organizational environments tend to be modest over a span of years. However, these changes are often statistically significant ones. Some are of kinds expected or intended from QWL improvement efforts, but many are not intended, and some arise from exogenous sources (e.g., an environmental event or change). Such results of attitude change for the organization as a whole serve to confirm the presence or absence of attitude shifts, but they are generally less interpretable and less convincing to evaluators than other kinds of evidence, because for the population as a whole the causes remain ambiguous and the change scores remain psychometrically problematic. On the other hand, the opinion and attitude data may reveal differential changes among subpopulations that are differentially exposed to QWL activities and their points of impact. For example, in one project such data confirmed dramatically a suspected negative impact among those excluded from certain work place "im-

provements." In another, the opinion and attitude data allowed an assessment of the relative effects of direct engagement versus indirect engagement in the planning and conduct of QWL activities (Nurick, 1978). The contribution of initial survey data to a committee's planning and priority setting is usually modest, but in two projects proved to be substantial and significant. In one of these, the people had prior experience in working with survey data and had little difficulty with its selective and expeditious interpretation. In the other, the ISR role included a participative, consultative component, and the QWL committee had an active part in planning and conducting the measurement activities.

PROBLEMS AND PROSPECTS

The Michigan Organizational Assessment program has both problems and promising prospects. The problems are mainly concerned with issues of operational feasibility, discussed earlier, and with the inadequacy of some of the conceptual schemes and methods attempted. The prospects relate to broader features of the task of assessing and evaluating organizational change, which are issues shared among all approaches and are not unique to this one.

Conceptual and Operational Issues

There are several domains of observation and measurement that remain recalcitrant and that should be addressed in the future. We mention a few that seem most problematic.

Technology and technological change figure substantially in virtually all approaches to the study of change in work organizations. Ideally, one wants the capability to describe technological systems, both informational and physical, along with their environmental requirements and constraints and their operational (cost and output) characteristics. One wants this capability not only for complex larger systems comprising many subsystems but also for specialized subunits of an organization, for work groups, and for individual jobs. One wants to be able to describe and assess the degree to which an existing technological system is an optimum one in comparison with available alternative systems that can produce a comparable array of outputs. One wants to be able to assess the extent to which the properties of the existing system(s) are in fact optimally exploited, misused, or underutilized. One wants to be able to detect and document changes in technological systems as well as locate the causal sources of the change and some of the consequences and side effects. One could say that such "wants" comprise about half of the information needed for the operationalization of design, diagnostic, and intervention strategies within the sociotechnical approach to organizational life.

Our mapping of this informational domain is displayed in Table 3-2 showing the conception of nested levels, three degrees of abstraction in measurement, and multiple data sources. Not shown in that table, although implied by some of the entries, are considerations of: (1) comparability across time and across situations, and (2) interpretability in terms of implications for persons and for social systems. In some parts of this domain, the available theory and practice are quite satisfactory. For example, at the level of the specific job or work group function there are readily applied procedures for measurement and observation of technology as well as conceptual resources for interpretations relating to psychological, social-psychological, and sociological correlates. The level of functional subsystems is more problematical, although given ample time and resources, an insightful observer can describe technological states and changes along with their consequences for the social system and for members. The feasibility of comparisons across subsystems is limited largely to higher-order abstractions. At the level of complex technological systems, the concrete measures often fail to allow comparisons even over time in the same organization, and the higher-order abstractions become of limited interest.

The reports coming from the Michigan Quality of Work Program will reflect these limitations in the capacity to represent technological factors. The report of a study of underground mining crews seems to most readers quite adequate in representing and interpreting the technological aspect of the setting (Goodman, 1979); the forthcoming report concerning a large engineering design organization deals successfully with certain selected aspects (e.g., underutilization of the available technology) of the technological system(s) and their implications (Hancock, Macy, and Peterson, 1981); the forthcoming report concerning a large factory with many different technologies and differentiated subsystems will succeed, at most, in merely hinting at the technological states and changes during the period of study except at the level of individuals and their jobs.

Union members' relationships to their union and the qualities of union-management relationships are underdeveloped regions of the Michigan assessment program. Semistructured interview schedules for use with union leaders and management representatives have been employed with success to obtain basic information about the formal structure of the union organization and its counterpart in the management organization. These interviews also yield information on key historical features, trends, and current relational practices. A questionnaire for union members has been developed to obtain members' descriptions and evaluations of union activities and also their own participation in union activity. A related questionnaire for use with union officers and representatives treats similar evaluative and descriptive topics from the viewpoint of active and

Table 3-2 The Technological Paradigm in Operation

Illustrative Measures, Three Levels of Abstraction

Sociotechnical System "Level"	A. Concrete	B. First-Order Abstraction	C. Higher-Order Abstractions	Data Sources	Dominant Conceptual Orientation
I. Job (Individual or group)	Task cycle time Number of tasks Output Down time Errors	Repetitiveness Skill level requirements Adequacy of tools, equipment, supplies	Automaticity Utilization of equipment capacity Adaptivity	Questionnaires Observation Records	Job Design Human Engineering/ Ergonomics
II. Functional Subsystem (e.g., production department, service unit)	Output Delay time Buffer inventory and backlog Reject, rework Number of discrete operations, or transactions	Coordination requirements Schedule and material adaptivity Interdependence with other units	Modernity Automaticity Skill time requirements Adequacy of feedback Adequacy of coordination	Questionnaire Observation Records Interviews	Operations Research Industrial Engineering
III. Total System (subsuming I and II)	Output Unit cost System capacity	Output variety Adequacy of subsystem buffering Budgetary requirements	Modernity Automaticity Adaptivity Range Time System type (unit, batch, continuous flow, etc.)	Records Interviews	Management Information Systems Operations Research Operational Accounting Production Engineering

influential union staff. However, these instruments and approaches have not yet been fully assessable for the reason that, at most sites, the use of the instruments has been vetoed by the union(s) or the management or the ISR representative. The limited information that is available suggests that member and officer views of their union can be obtained with much the same degree of consistency and content differentiation as can parallel information regarding the management and work environment. The encouraging evidence is in the form of scale reliabilities, patterns of correlation with independent variables, and changes over time that are consistent with data on other trends from other sources.

The methodology of measurement and observation is less problematic than conceptualizing the aspects of union-management relationships that are of interest to the actors involved and of interest to those who think about theories of interorganizational relationships. Existing methods for assessing relationships—for example, those of Biasatti (1979) and Martin (1976)—are of little help with respect to the treatment of such "political" issues as the definition of bargainable topics, the alternation between collaborative and adversarial postures of the parties, or the contrast between (potentially) democratic and autocratic agencies. In the context of quality of work life initiatives, such issues may be central, and measurement will have to follow, not precede, the formulation of models of relationships of change.

The *observation of jobs and job environments* has been conducted with technological success but with interpretational quandary. From the experience of comparing data from job occupants and from trained observers, we are impressed more with the differences in the meaning of the information obtained than with the numerical discrepancies. It appears that information of comparable reliability is obtained from the compared methods, but that there is highly variable agreement and disagreement across a range of topics; the data from the two sources cannot be assumed with confidence to be alternative measures of the same thing. This observation holds for both physical conditions or work environments (e.g., noise) and for the social conditions of work (e.g., closeness of supervision). There appears to be small correspondence between the actuality of jobs and working conditions and the experience of these by the employee. Improvements are needed in the way one can think about, evaluate, and interpret such information, and they are needed in the training of observers as well.

The *historical account* of events during the course of time as organizational changes occur and the imputation of meaning to these events remains an area of mysterious nature. Conferences with historians and with social anthropologists have not been of any help in working out either approaches or methods that go beyond the intuitive or, as they say, the "integrative." Impressive and persuasive accounts of events can be provided by independent observers, but as often as not they lead to incompatible or unrelated conclusions. The dilemma concerns not the identification of and characterization of events and changes but rather the attribution of meaning. Query: In the assessment of organizations and of organizational change, should the task of description be methodologically prescribed so that alternative interpretations by others are encouraged? Perhaps the intuitive, guided by incompatible theoretical postures, is best? Plainly an interpreter of distinctively different theoretical posture would need more, and different, information to work with than the distilled impressions and thoroughly crunched data tables of the typical case report. Ideally one would hope for the development of a meta-methodological discipline capable of specifying the historical and observational data required for diverse disciplinary interpretations. Alternatively, but perhaps not very feasibly, the field team can include persons of unlike conceptual persuasion, each to obtain his or her own data. At the least, there should be an exercise (analogous to that prevalent among historians and biographers) in which different analysts exploit the same documentary and field note resources in search of competing or complementary interpretations.

Basic Issues in Organizational Assessment

Three basic issues have been highlighted by our experience in attempting an exhaustive program of measurement, observation and interpretation of organizations over periods of change. These are: (1) the validity of the comparative method; (2) the explication of causes; and (3) the conversion of theory, research, and interpretation into dispersed practice.

The method of comparison is fundamental to the traditional canons of research on organizations. To understand the state of an organization, one must compare it with other organizations; to understand change, one must compare prior states with later states; to understand causation, one must compare potential causal factors and their links to different outcomes. This image or paradigm of organizational research is being challenged on grounds that each organization is unique in its input of energy, information, and purpose and correspondingly unique in its internal processes and outcomes. Such uniqueness can arise either from sheer complexity—meaning that combinations of inputs are so numerous as to preclude replication—or from conceptions of biological aberration, meaning that small variations in inputs may, in accommodating environments, be sustained rather than suppressed. The statistical view is not the same as the biological view. The approach of the Michigan organizational assessment program is based on the assumption that organizations are fundamentally the same as to identifiable and quantifiable inputs, organizational processes, and consequential outcomes. This is of course an hypothesis, not an immutable fact. The opposed view emphasizes the emergent new forms of organizational input, process, and outcome rather than the mere statistical range of variation that provides a semblance of uniqueness. Miller (1979) has addressed the issue of identity (as compared with analogy) of the structure and processes of living systems. Herbst (1970) has attempted to show that uniqueness in living systems may occur. Contributors too numerous to mention argue that an individual's purpose may intrude upon organizational processes and become an integral part of an organization.

The net of this is that the method of comparison in organizational studies is challenged, and nowhere is the challenge more evident than in the reductionist and decomposing strategy that has been emphasized, although not exclusively, in the assessment approach described in this paper. This is not a matter of dogma or philosophical belief but rather a matter of pressing to the limit the notion that understanding measurable components of organizational behavior will serve to explicate both the uniformities and the uniqueness of organizational phenomena.

The explication of causes and the potential for influencing results that may accompany such explications is surely the justification for efforts to describe, assess, and evaluate organizations as they change. The complexity of organizations makes it unlikely that significant insights into causal processes will occur from casual, unguided observation. There is a need for some model or theory of change processes. Some conception of organizational effectiveness is needed that can be regarded as defining the results desired from change. The approach to these matters exemplified by the Michigan organizational assessment program has two significant facets, both matters of choice in the presence of attractive alternatives.

As to *causation,* a slippery concept at best, the choice is to work with a large number of causal systems, each of manageable and therefore limited scope. The hope and expectation is that small theories, empirically validated, will in time become additive and connected. The imagery includes a network of variables hierarchically arranged so that each variable regarded as an outcome is supplied with multiple chains of potential causation; a large part of the outcome variance—but never all of it—can be predicted from a limited roster of prior descriptive variables. This is of course a linear model, and one that assumes some degree of indeterminacy; it is also a mechanistic model in the sense that there is no allowance for the possibility that "new" causal variables may come into being or that unprecedented, unique causal systems may emerge (Mitchell, 1979). There are alternative kinds of models of causation. It is likely that others will display, as ours does, features of dubious assumption, logical fallacy, and operational difficulty.

As to a model of effectiveness, we have again chosen scope over clarity. The valuing of results is left in the public domain, with each interested party entitled, even obligated, to choose the results of importance from his or her frame of reference and to weigh the results in their combinations. The domain of results is defined by three overlapping but distinguishable areas: (1) exportable outputs of the work system, including such factors as the volume, quality, timeliness, and cost of the goods or services; (2) systemic integrity of the organization with reference to its capacity to regulate its internal processes through the allocation of resources, provision of coordination, strain management, and the like; and (3) adaptive capacities of the organization as represented primarily in its means for information management and problem solving. An effective organization in this view is one that sustains its environment, maintains its own operational capacities, and regulates the relationships of the organization with its changing environment. Plainly this is a model of effectiveness that is appallingly complex. Other models exist that also serve the aims of understanding organizational states and changes.

As a terminal note to this paper, attention is drawn to a declared intention of the Michigan program for organizational assessment to make the product available to nonscientists and nonprofessionals for their autonomous use. This implies that the conceptual apparatus, the approach to assessment, and the operational methods should be transferable to people who manage or cope with organizational environments; it implies a goal of simplicity, clarity, and low-cost application. Such an aspiration is not commonly asserted in the context of developing methods in the social and behavioral sciences, but we think it should be. The expertise, such as it is, should be given away. Certainly one criterion for assessing an approach to organizational assessment is found in these questions: How widely can the approach be applied? Is it likely to help organization managers and members better to cope with their problems of effectiveness and of quality of working life?

REFERENCES

Alderfer, C. P., and L. D. Brown (1975). *Learning from Changing: Organizational Diagnosis and Development,* Beverly Hills: Sage.

Argyris, C. (1970). *Intervention Theory and Method,* New York: Addison-Wesley.

Biasatti, L. L., and J. E. Martin (1979). "A Measure of the Quality of Union-Management Relations," *Journal of Applied Psychology* **64,**4.

Campbell, D. T. (1969). "Reforms as Experiments," *American Psychologist* **24,**3: 409–429.

French, J. R. P. (1963). "The Social Environment and Mental Health," *Journal of Social Issues* **19,**4: 39–56.

Golembiewsky, R. T., K. Billingsly, and S. Yenger (1975). "Measuring Change and Persistence in Human Affairs: Types of Change Generated by OD Design," *Journal of Applied Behavioral Science* **12,**3:133–157.

Hackman, J. R., and G. Oldham (1980). *Work Redesign,* New York: Addison-Wesley.

Herbst, P. G. (1970). *Behavioural Worlds: The Study of Single Cases,* London: Tavistock Publications.

Martin, J. E. (1976). "Union-Management Problems in the Federal Government and Exploratory Analysis," *Public Personnel Management* **17:**353–362.

Miller, J. G. (1978). *Living Systems,* New York: McGraw-Hill.

Mitchell, T. R. (1979). "Organizational Behavior," in Rosenzweig and Porter, Eds., *Annual Review of Psychology,* Palo Alto, CA: Annual Reviews, Inc.

O'Toole, J, Ed. (1973). *Work in America,* Cambridge, MA: MIT Press.

Porras, J. I. (1979). "Comparative Impact of Different OD Techniques and Intervention Intensities," *Journal of Applied Behavioral Sciences* **15**,2:156–178.

Seashore, S. (1975). "The Design of Action Research," in A. W. Clark, Ed., *Experimenting with Organizational Life: The Action Research Approach,* New York: Plenum Press.

Seashore, S., E. E. Lawler, P. H. Miluis, and Cortland Commann (1982). *Observing and Measuring Organizational Change: A Guide to Field Practice,* New York: Wiley.

Tannenbaum, A. S. (1968). *Control in Organizations,* New York: McGraw-Hill.

SELECTED DOCUMENTS FROM THE MOA PROGRAM

Drexler, J. A., and E. E. Lawler III (1977). "A Union-Management Cooperative Project to Improve the Quality of Work Life," *Journal of Applied Behavioral Science* **13**,3:373–387.

Glick, W., P. H. Mirvis, and D. Harder (1977). "Union Satisfaction and Participation," *Industrial Relations* **16**,2:145–151.

Goodman, P. S. (1979). *Assessing Organizational Change: The Rushton Experiment,* New York: Wiley-Interscience.

Hancock, W. M., B. A. Macy, and S. Peterson (1981). "Assessment of Technologies and Their Utilization," in S. Seashore et al., Eds., *Observing and Measuring Organizational Change,* New York: Wiley-Interscience (1982).

Jenkins, G. D., Jr., D. A. Nadler, E. E. Lawler III, and C. Cammann (1975). "Standardized Observations: An Approach to Measuring the Nature of Jobs," *Journal of Applied Psychology* **60**,2:171–181.

Lawler, E. E. III (1974). "The Individualized Organization: Problems and Promise," *California Management REview* **27**,2:31–39.

Lawler, E. E. III (1977). "Adaptive Experiments: An Approach to Organizational Behavior Research," *Academy of Management Review* **2**(10), 576–585.

Lawler, E. E. III, and J. A. Drexler (1978). "Dynamics of Establishing Cooperative Quality-of-Worklife Projects," *Monthly Labor Review* **20**,3:23–28.

Macy, B. A. (1979). "Progress Report on the Bolivar Quality of Work Experiment," *Personnel Journal* **20**,8:527–559.

Macy, B. A., G. Ledford, and E. E. Lawler III (1981). *An Assessment of the Bolivar Quality of Work Experiment: 1972–1979,* New York: Wiley-Interscience (forthcoming).

Macy, B. A., and P. H. Mirvis (1976). "A Methodology for Assessment of Quality of Work and Organizational Effectiveness in Behavioral-Economic Terms," *Administrative Science Quarterly* **21**,6:212–229.

Macy, B. A., and J. P. Yaney (1978). "Union-Management Problem Solving for Quality of Working Life: Some Legal Issues," *Business Law Review* **2**,1:20–27.

Mills, T. (1975). "Human Resources: Why the New Concern?" *Harvard Business Review* **20**:121–134.

Mirvis, P. H., and E. E. Lawler III (1977). "Measuring the Financial Impact of Employee Attitudes," *Journal of Applied Psychology* **62**,1:1–8.

Mirvis, P. H., and B. A. Macy (1976). "Accounting for the Costs and Benefits of Human Resource Development Programs: An Interdisciplinary Approach," *Accounting, Organizations and Society* **1**,2–3:179–193.

Mirvis, P. H., and S. E. Seashore (1979). "Being Ethical in Organizational Research," *American Psychologist* **34**,9:766–780.

Moch, M. K. (1979). "Job Involvement, Internal Motivation, and Employees Integration into Networks of Work Relationships," *Organizational Behavior and Human Performance* **24**,12.

Moch, M. K., J. Bartunek, and D. J. Brass (1979). "Structure, Task Characteristics, and Experienced Role Stress in Organizations Employing Complex Technology," *Organizational Behavior and Human Performance* **24**,10.

Nadler, D. A. (1978). "Consulting with Labor and Management: Some Learnings from Quality-of-Work-Life Projects," in W. W. Burke, Ed., *The Cutting Edge: Current Theory and Practice in Organizational Development,* LaJolla, CA: University Associates.

Nadler, D. A. (1978). "Hospitals, Organized Labor and Quality of Work: An Intervention Case Study," *Journal of Applied Behavioral Science* **14**,3:366–381.

Nadler, D. A., M. Hanlon, and E. E. Lawler III (1980). "Factors Influencing the Success of Labor-Management Quality of Work Life Programs," *Journal of Occupational Behavior* **1**,1:53–67.

Nadler, D. A., P. H. Mirvis, and C. Cammann (1976). "The Ongoing Feedback System," *Organizational Dynamics* **20**:63–80.

Nieva, V. F., D. N. T. Perkins, and E. E. Lawler III (1980). "Improving the Quality of Work Life At Work: Assessment of a Collaborative Selection Process," *Journal of Occupational Behavior* **1**,1:43–52.

Nurick, A. J. (1978). "The Effects of Formal Participation in Organizational Change on Individual Perceptions and Attitudes: A Longitudinal Field Study," unpublished Ph.D. dissertation, University of Tennessee, Knoxville.

Seashore, S. E. (1976). "Assessing the Quality of Working Life: The U.S. Experience," *Labour and Society* **1**,2:69–79.

Seashore, S. E. (1980). "The Humanization of Work: Ethical Issues in the Conversion of Ideology to Practice," in *Business Ethics Report: Report on the Third National Conference on Business Ethics,* Waltham, MA: Bentley College.

Seashore, S. E., and T. D. Taber (1975). "Job Satisfaction Indicators and Their Correlates," *American Behavioral Scientists* **18**,3:333–368.

Walsh, J. T. (1978). *Technological and Structural Determinants of Perceived Job Characteristics,* unpublished Ph.D. Dissertation, University of Michigan, Ann Arbor.

Walsh, J. T., and D. S. Tracey (1981). "Implementing Quality of Work in the Public Sector: Results from a Major American City," Case Report in preparation.

THE MICHIGAN QUALITY OF WORK LIFE PROGRAM: AN ANALYSIS OF ASSUMPTIONS AND METHOD

WILLIAM F. JOYCE
The Wharton School
University of Pennsylvania

The purpose of this commentary is to provide a critical appraisal of the Michigan Assessment of Organizations (MAO) research program and its application in the evaluation of social experiments dealing with the quality of work life (QWL). Because of the size, visibility, and impact of the Michigan program, these comments are aimed not only at the specific efforts of the Michigan group but also at other researchers and practitioners in the field who may follow the lead set forward in Seashore's paper.

The title of Seashore's paper is important to the observations that follow, because it clearly states what his paper is and isn't about. It *is* concerned with problems of measurement, assessment, and outcome evaluation in complex social experiments; it *is not* concerned with specific theoretical developments following from the QWL research. I believe that this is both a strength and a weakness of Seashore's presentation. It is a weakness because the field could benefit from a unified, systematic discussion of the specific variables, laws, and perhaps theories that have been developed during these experiments. It is a strength because it allows us to focus on one set of important issues—perhaps the most important issues—contained in the research, with the hope that both the Michigan researchers and their students from other universities and organizations can learn something from the exchange.

Because of the topical restriction of Seashore's paper, I will also limit my analysis and comment to issues of primarily methodological content. The procedure of my assessment is as follows: I will attempt to synthesize the basic MAO process as set forth by Seashore in a single model, with two objectives: (1) to allow us to illuminate and comment on key explicit and implicit assumptions in the MAO approach, and then (2) to comment on specific shortcomings resulting from inconsistency between the implicit metatheoretical assumptions inherent in the methodology. The intention of this procedure is to shed light on problems of the organizational behavior field in general, as well as the usefulness of the MAO process as a basis for future organization assessments.

The Michigan Methodology

My first objective is to develop an integrated process perspective from which to assess the MAO methodology. The purpose of this development is to present the basic thrust of Seashore's prescriptions concerning the selection and measurement of variables in the MAO program, as well as my reconstruction of the theory-building functions implied in his discussions of the process. This unification has an important purpose: by condensing and integrating the "rules" adhered to in the MAO efforts, we gain insight into manifest elements of the process that are in agreement or contradiction, and we can more easily perceive areas of the process that are underdeveloped and require further consideration. At the metatheoretical level, a unified model is necessary to allow identification of the implicit assumptions upon which the process is based and without which a reasonably complete understanding of its nature is impossible.

The Process.   The MAO methodology is really a combination of two assessment processes that can be partially distinguished in terms of the frequency of measurement of key variables. The essential features and objectives of these methods are integrated and summarized in Figure 3-3. Method I has been termed classical-intermittent assessment, because it relies upon relatively infrequent measurement of explanatory and outcome variables and interpretations of these measures within classical field experimental designs. I am using the term "classical" loosely in this sense to refer to what others have called "quasi-experimental" as well as experimental designs (see Campbell and Stanley, 1963; Cook and Campbell, 1976). Method II has been termed a naturalistic-continuous assessment, because it emphasizes relatively continuous measurement of process *in situ,* relying primarily upon systematic observations or historical accounts taken with a minimum of measurement intrusion. The methods utilized by MAO to interpret these measures are not divulged by Seashore, but they are the subject of some speculation below, where differences between these methodologies are discussed.

What These Methods Have in Common.   The classical-intermittent and naturalistic-continuous approaches to organization assessment are similar in two important respects: their criteria for variable selection and their associated stance toward theory development. These issues are not separate, as we shall see, and they have implications for the refinement of the assumptions underlying MAO.

The choice of concepts within MAO is directly related to the objectives of the QWL experiments described by Seashore. I believe that we can reasonably ascribe such objectives to most other programs of research in planned change, so that the approach to variable selection taken in MAO becomes important to further research in this area in general. Seashore states the principal guidelines and their orders of priority. These guidelines apply equally to both the classical-intermittent (C-I) and natural-

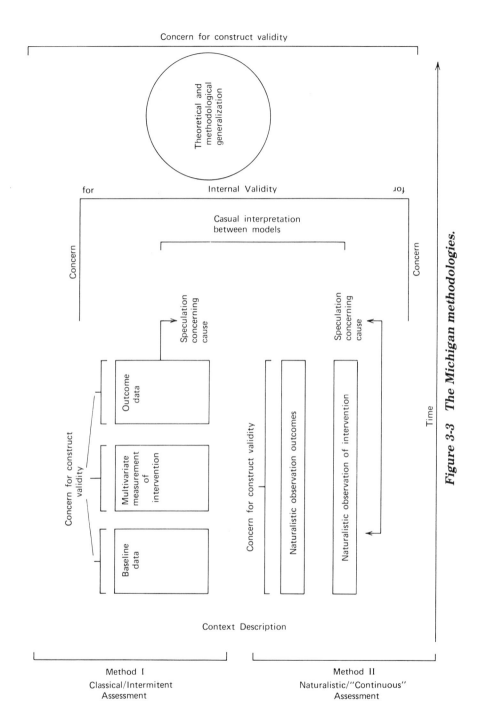

Figure 3-3 *The Michigan methodologies.*

istic-continuous (N-C) approaches. Taken together with the objectives of the QWL experiments, they imply a process of theory development that begins with a thorough description of the research setting and develops outcome measures that are "valued." A "valued outcome," of course, and the priorities among such results, is a matter of opinion. The relevant opinion is, *first of all,* that of some organizational actor, and *second,* that of some analyst or interpreter (Seashore, Chapter 3; emphasis mine). These results are then explained in terms of direct causal, moderating, and intervening variables. Preference is shown for those with previous theoretical referents in order that the researcher might be able ultimately to generalize to other settings.

These verbal descriptions of the MAO process are depicted in Figure 3-3, where I show the parallel paths of theory development within both the C-I and N-C methods. Following context description, both are initially concerned with variable measurement (issues of construct validity); later they are concerned with causal attribution within and between methods and within settings (issues of internal validity); and finally, they are concerned with the generalization of methods and theory to other settings (issues of external validity). At this point I will simply note that the MAO process attempts to explain results meaningful *to the participants* in the organization using concepts and theories constructed to be meaningful *to researchers* endeavoring to understand organizational behavior. These two positions represent very different types of meaning, and the assumption concerning the relevant types of meaning for outcome and explanatory variables is an important one to which I will return below.

How These Methods Differ.   Whereas the C-I and N-C methods are similar in terms of criteria for variable selection and theory construction, they differ in a number of important ways. Two that merit comment are: (1) the possibilities of discovering unintended explanatory variables; and (2) available methods for attributing cause.

The classical-intermittent method relies upon multivariate measurement of explanatory and outcome variables using a variety of methods. These include sophisticated questionnaires (MAOQ), structured interviews (union-management relations and organization structure), and formalized searches of archival data (behavioral-financial measures). The use of such a formalized battery of measures allows variables with previous theoretical connections to be included in MAO, but may restrict the potential emergence of unanticipated explanatory variables in the MAO process.

The naturalistic-continuous method guards against this possibility by including measures based upon participant observation (of intervention activities and labor management meetings) and naturalistic observation (event logs, historical accounts) that allow "new" variables to enter the analysis as necessary. The two methods are different but quite complementary in this respect; the C-I approach allows hypothesis testing to take place, while the N-C approach fuels this process by generating new propositions and variables. These two parallel theory-building processes correspond respectively to what Kaplan (1964) has called the "context of justification" and the "context of discovery," and they share the same relative emphasis in the MAO approach that these dual problems share in the general area of organizational studies: The MAO methodology emphasizes the C-I and underemphasizes the important contribution that the N-C method can make. By way of criticism, I believe that further expansion and development of the N-C approach would be very fruitful for the MAO process precisely because it would facilitate theory development as well as refinement, and it would contribute methodologically to a relatively unaddressed and certainly critical area of organizational inquiry. I also should say that I am leveling this criticism at a research program that actually is least deserving of it. Clearly the MAO researchers recognize both problems and are doing something about them.

A second difference between the N-C and C-I approaches concerns the experimental methodology and statistical techniques used to attribute causality. The C-I approach has been termed "classical," because these methods and techniques fall within a domain of methodology with which most researchers in organization are familiar and with which most would agree. That is, we attribute causality once an appropriately controlled experiment (or quasi-experiment) has been conducted in which levels of some criterion outcome are demonstrated to covary as a function of a manipulated explanatory variable. These topics are well developed in the literature (see Fisher, 1966; Campbell and Stanley, 1963; and Cook and Campbell, 1976) and include familiar techniques such as repeated measures analysis of variance and nonequivalent control group designs.

What Seashore does not discuss is how one goes about attributing causality in the N-C method. Statistical methods would remain relevant where quantitative measures could be employed, but the N-C method seems to require new techniques to aid in the interpretation of its data. For example, in the N-C approach, the intervention could usefully be viewed as a series of change episodes, which could be identified from change process narratives developed by participant observers from relevant portions of the organization. The MAO research does develop such measures from narrative accounts by change agents and through observation of key change events. What is not clear is how these are to be used practically and theoretically to explain observed changes in criterion levels. I believe the MAO process could profit from further development of appropriate methodology for the analysis of nontraditional field data, because without this development the large potential contributions of the N-C approach will remain an unfulfilled promise.

The Michigan Assumptions

The MAO program incorporates a number of assumptions that shape its methods and consequently the results of inquiry. These assumptions are both explicit and implicit in Seashore's discussion, and my reconstruction of them is likely to be somewhat at variance with what was actually intended by the Michigan researchers. This is only natural, however, because of a basic antagonism between the processes of theory construction and criticism. In theory construction one's assumptions give rise to methodological choices, whereas in criticism these processes are used to reconstruct the assumptions. The benefit of the critical process hopefully is illumination of these areas of disagreement and further development of the methods by both the critics and the architects of the approach.

There seem to be three key sets of assumptions in the MAO method: assumptions concerning how theories are constructed from simpler laws, assumptions concerning the type of meaning that should be primary in organization assessments, and assumptions concerning the usefulness of eclectic approaches to theory development. I believe that these assumptions are not entirely consistent with one another, and further, that the MAO process has been most productive in cases in which there has been some consonance among them.

Assumptions Concerning How Theories Are Built.   The purposes of an inquiry should shape its methods, and this is partially the case with the MAO. The MAO utilization of an approach that I shall call *Outcome-Centered Inquiry* (OCI) has serious limitations as these purposes move from determining the causes of local results deemed important in the QWL experiments to more general theoretical statements. Both purposes are objectives of MAO, and I believe that their assumptions favor the former to the detriment of the latter.

The path of theory development in MAO can be discerned in Seashore's discussion of the process for selecting variables for inclusion in the QWL experiments, mentioned above. In Figure 3-3, we can see that this process involves measurement of: relevant results, the variables that may cause or explain such results (giving preference to those with previous research histories), and finally, variables allowing interorganizational comparison. As the MAO attempts to develop laws and then theories relating these laws across organizations, results are usually the focus of their efforts. This process, which I call Outcome-Centered Inquiry (OCI), is fairly traditional in the organization sciences and follows nicely the path of development of theoretical laws.

The connection between OCI and the refinement of laws to develop theory is easily seen. Following Seashore's presentation of the criteria for variable selection and my Figure 3-3, the measurement of relevant results and potential causal variables corresponds to attempts to develop *simple generalizations* (Kaplan, 1964).

> A simple generalization is one which moves from a set of statements of the form xRy to a generalization $A(R)B$, where x and y are members of A and B respectively. . . . It is the product of a simple induction from some to all of an appropriately specified kind. A number of instances are known, and we generalize from them to all the instances of what we are prepared to call 'the same kind' (Kaplan, 1964: 105).

This type of rudimentary law is what Boring referred to in defining a law as a "relatively stable relationship between two variables."

The MAO process is not content with laws of this sort and attempts to also include in their theories variables "that might aid *understanding* of the outcomes . . . and *contingencies* associated with variance in the outcomes," (Seashore, 1980: 6; emphasis mine). I take this to mean that the MAO researchers also wish to explain simple generalizations relating independent and dependent (outcome) variables, and this requires development of laws of a more complex form than simple generalizations. These are called *intermediate generalizations*.

A quotation from Kaplan indicates the close relationship between the purposes of the MAO and development of intermediate generalizations. An intermediate generalization is one in which:

> we move from a statement of the form $A(R)C$ to two statements, $A(R')B$ and $B(R'')C$. An intermediary has been found between A and C, which resolves their relationship into two subsidiary ones. Such an intermediary is often said to account for the linkage between A and B; accordingly, we may say that intermediate generalizations are explanatory in the weak sense. Most familiar are the causes where the intermediate is a *missing causal link*. . . . Often, however, the intermediate generalization *selects a subclass* from the original one which has a stronger association with the second class than the original one did. (Kaplan, 1964: 151; emphasis mine)

The two types of variables emphasized in this quotation are intervening and moderating variables (see Zedeck, 1974)—the explanatory and "contingency" variables sought by Seashore. These variables "explain" the simple generalizations that are discovered in MAO to relate independent and dependent outcome variables.

Outcome-Centered Inquiry serves the purpose of discovering local causes of the results of organizational experiments. But there are other purposes to which such experiments can be put, and it is for these that OCI loses its appeal. A second strategy, which I will call *Law-Centered Inquiry* (LCI), is more appropriate when theory development, rather than outcome explanation, is the primary goal of the research. My point here is not that Law-Centered Inquiry is superior to Outcome-Centered Inquiry, but rather that they are different and serve different purposes. Since the MAO takes both outcome explanation and theory development as its purposes, yet relies primarily on OCI, we should not be surprised to find that it performs better with respect to the first objective than with the second.

Law-Centered Inquiry (LCI) differs from OCI in that it takes as its objective the explanation of laws (the "weak" explanation described by Kaplan above) rather than the explanation of results. Law-Centered Inquiry is therefore primarily concerned with the development of intermediate generalizations rather than simple generalizations, and it accomplishes this by introducing new moderating and intervening variables explaining simple generalizations. Unlike OCI, LCI does not seek to discover these simple generalizations and then explain them via intermediate generalization in the same research setting. Law-Centered Inquiry draws upon previous research to suggest simple laws and then conducts additional study in which these laws are linked through the introduction of new moderating and intervening variables. There is a critical difference between OCI and LCI, and this difference has important consequences. Because OCI focuses on outcome explanation as its primary purpose, it must discover the laws relating independent and outcome variables *before* it can explain them. Law-Centered Inquiry *begins* with such laws and occupies itself almost entirely with their explanation. Because these laws are believed known prior to further inquiry, more theoretical and empirical resources can be brought to bear on the problem of explaining them. In OCI, however, we must first determine the simple laws before we can explain them, and my point is that this will be more difficult to do than in LCI. This is so simply because it will always be difficult to anticipate and include in our analyses variables useful to the explanation of relationships that remain to be discovered. OCI is always preoccupied with first principles and generates a theoretical myopia that occasionally may be overcome by serendipity but rarely by the thoughtful inclusion of explanatory moderating and intervening variables.

Outcome-Centered Inquiry and Law-Centered Inquiry begin at different points and arrive at different destinations, though they traverse some of the same territory. Outcome-Centered Inquiry will never reach the plane of abstraction reached through LCI; neither will LCI deliver the unique appreciation of outcomes that OCI can when utilized in research such as the MAO QWL experiments. It is unlikely, however, that both outcome understanding and theoretical generalization can be achieved through exclusive reliance on either OCI or LCI.

Assumptions Concerning Meaning.   Earlier I noted that the MAO process attempted to explain results meaningful to organizational participants in terms of concepts and theories meaningful to researchers. It is time to return to that point now in order to indicate the extent to which these assumptions concerning meaning are consistent with the assumptions concerning theory development that I have discussed.

To return to this earlier point, I have noted that Seashore defines a valued outcome as one valued first of all by some organizational actor, with the theoretical preference of researchers given only secondary con-

sideration. This emphasis on results valued by organizational participants rather than those of theoretical interest to researchers represents
an assumption concerning the type of meaning to be given priority in the
course of the MAO research.

Social inquiry into the functioning of organizations differs from inquiry
in other disciplines such as physics and chemistry partially as a function
of its subject matter. Because we take other subjects as the objects of our
study, the possibility naturally exists that these subjects may assign
different meanings to organizational events and behavior than we do in
the process of constructing theories to explain such behavior. In this
connection, Kaplan distinguishes between *act* meaning, "what it signifies
to the actor or to those with whom he is interacting" (1964: 358), and
action meaning, related to the "significance [of these acts], not for the
actors, but for the scientists studying the actions. 'Action meaning' is that
provided by the perspectives of a particular theory or explanation of the
action" (1964: 358).

The assignment of meaning to an act is an explanation of the act. Act
meanings provide what Kaplan (1964) calls "semantic" explanations,
whereas the assignment of an action meaning provides a "scientific" explanation. The important point is not that one is more scientific than the
other in terms of susceptibility to empirical verification, but rather that
each type of meaning is appropriate for different purposes. Ultimately
the development of theories of organization design and change requires
some mechanism for the translation of act meanings to action meanings.
By giving primacy to act meanings in the development of its concepts,
the MAO process encourages the development of locally valid laws but
discourages the possibility of generalization to other settings. This is all
quite consistent with the objectives of Outcome-Centered Inquiry but less
so with respect to Law-Centered Inquiry. The MAO assumptions concerning meaning are consistent with their assumptions concerning theory
development. This consistency favors local explanation of results within
frames of reference meaningful to organizational participants but detrimental to broader explanations that are of interest to the theory of
organizations.

Assumptions Concerning Eclecticism.   The last assumption of the
MAO researchers that I will discuss is the stance taken toward eclecticism. The field of organizational science is often distinguished from other
areas of social science precisely on the basis of its eclectic nature (see, for
instance, the definitions of March and Simon, 1958; or Indik, 1968), so
it is not surprising that assumptions about eclecticism are found in the
MAO process. These assumptions are consistent with some of the objectives of the MAO studies but not with others. The largest resulting gains
are made in areas of consistency. Furthermore, eclecticism poses definite
threats to the progress of theory building in the organization sciences,

and such threats require a different orientation towards eclecticism than that taken by the MAO studies and the field in general.

An eclectic theory is one "composed of material gathered from various sources or systems," according to Webster's New World Dictionary. Within this definition the MAO program must surely be regarded as eclectic.

First of all, its methods are pluralistic, and this represents a type of eclecticism that Marx and Hillix (1973) have called metatheoretical eclecticism. It is represented by the use of many techniques of inquiry within a single study, and I have no quarrel with the importance of this type of eclecticism to organizational inquiry. In the context of previous discussions, metatheoretical eclecticism facilitates the theoretical objectives of the MAO process by encouraging the translation of act meanings to action meanings. As Kaplan notes, when such techniques yield equivalent results interpretation is facilitated, because "intersubjectivity is at least a mark of the objective" (1964: 362). But the MAO process is eclectic at the theoretical level as well. Seashore states that the MAO process "is not dominated by any singular theoretical system, but does incorporate, eclectically, a number of contemporary theories of proven or probable validity. . . . In these ways, the approach to organization assessment is richly imbued with theoretical orientations (plural) but not intentionally constrained by any one."

Now this quotation is very revealing because it points to the first of two problems with eclecticism that I will discuss—the problem of *premature eclecticism*. This problem occurs when, in attempting to explain some behavioral phenomena, we utilize a number of different theories, but in doing this we emphasize what these theories have in common rather than how they differ. In the MAO research this is exemplified by a choice of concepts useful to the understanding of how results are induced, but giving a lower priority to *why* these variables produce these results. This process emphasizes the similarities of these theories in terms of their relationships to valued results, but it deemphasizes the specific differences between these theories regarding how these relationships are understood. It is a single-minded eclecticism that asks questions about the relationship of potential explanatory variables with criteria but not with one another. It generates a "more variables are better" mentality (as evidenced by the MAO variable dictionary's inclusion of over 1000 variables, even without the Z's) by implying that the effects of these variables are independent and additive, as when Seashore speaks of *incorporating* theories rather than refining them.

Accompanying this additive assumption is a diminishing of theoretical differences in favor of similarities. This is what I think Seashore means when he says that the MAO process intends to include a number of theoretical perspectives but not to be constrained by any one. But theoretical developments proceed by making such differences (constraints) explicit and by conducting research to resolve these differences, often with the consequence of *new* theory. Because the MAO process emphasizes its eclecticism to the detriment of such differences, it compromises its possibility of discovering new theory. The limitations of a prematurely eclectic view are summarized by Henle (1957) as follows:

> The eclectics are, of course, right in maintaining that where a genuine controversy exists in psychology, and where evidence seems to support both sides, there is likely to be some truth to both positions. But they solve their problem too soon. Existing theories cannot be made more comprehensive by adding divergent ones together. They can be broadened to include all the relevant evidence only by looking more deeply into the phenomena with which they are concerned; and this means arriving at new theories.

The second problem of eclecticism in the MAO process is the problem of *implicit theoretical assumptions*. That the MAO process contains many implicit assumptions is implied (!) by Seashore's statement that we will not be able to "discern any commitment to a particular conceptual framework or theoretical approach." To be able to do so would require *explicit* statements concerning differences between these approaches. Eclecticism encourages a greater reliance on implicit theorizing, with several detrimental consequences. These are: (1) a lack of internal consistency; (2) a failure to test critical assumptions; and (3) a bias toward traditional theory and method.

When critical assumptions are implicit, the likelihood exists that some of these may be in conflict with others, leading to a situation in which actions taken in consonance with one set of assumptions produce unintended results that could have been predicted on the basis of a conflicting implicit set of assumptions. In short, the coherence of one's assumptions remains suspect as long as these assumptions remain implicit, and the presence of unanticipated results signals the possibility of such incoherence. This is precisely the case with the MAO researchers in which one of the principal "findings" is that, "All projects for which final data are available display a mixture of intended and unintended results, and of beneficial as well as adverse results" (Seashore, Chapter 3). My point is that this is not so much a finding of the research as a consequence of its assumptions regarding eclecticism.

A second consequence of implicit theoretical assumptions is that critical aspects of the theory may go untested. This raises a question, because if "such theory is often implicit, and thus unexpressed and unexamined, is it adequate to lead to the discovery of new facts?" (Henle, 1957: 296). For example, I have suggested that one consequence of the implicit assumptions of the MAO program is a relative emphasis on establishing predictor-criterion relationships rather than detecting moderating and intervening variables that may explain such relationships in the form of what Kaplan termed "intermediate generalizations." The implicit predisposition of the MAO program toward what I have called Outcome-Centered Inquiry results in the "more is better" model of interaction between various predictors and criteria. In such a model we assume that if *A* causes *C* and *B* causes *C*, then we may induce larger changes in the criterion *C* by manipulating both *A* and *B* concurrently. This is seen when Seashore states that in the MAO research, "The hope and expectation is that small theories, empirically validated, will in time become *additive* and *connected*" [emphasis mine]. This additive model is one type of congruency between predictors, but it is only one type. Other, more complex types of relationships are possible, of course, but the validity of the simplifying assumptions of the MAO program cannot be assessed until they are made more explicit and put to empirical test.

The third consequence of implicit theoretical assumptions is a tendency toward traditional methods and theory. Methodologically, this is clearly seen in the MAO program's relative overemphasis on Classical-Intermittent Assessment and lack of development of the Naturalistic-Continuous methods discussed above. As Henle notes: "It seems plausible to think that when theory is not explicit, and thus not examined, it draws upon doctrines prevailing both [in the area being investigated] and in the culture in general, rather than upon the newer and less widely accepted theoretical currents." This tendency toward traditional theory has also been noted by Kohler (1953), who writes:

> It has been said with approval that psychology now tends to be eclectic. Again, we have been told that in psychology we had better stay in the middle of the road. I cannot agree with these prescriptions because, if they were followed, psychologists would have to look first of all backward. In an eclectic attitude, they would be too much concerned with ideas which are already available; and, in attempting to find the middle of the road in psychology, they would have to give too much attention to the tracks along which others have moved before them. Such attitudes could perhaps be recommended if, in research, security were an important issue. Actually there is no place for it in this field. In research, we have to look forward, and to take risks.

Despite the importance of eclectic methods and theory to organizational inquiry, the MAO process fails to go far beyond approaches that may be fairly called prematurely eclectic in the sense that they achieve unification of competing theories to the detriment of their distinctive competencies. As Henle notes, they "solve their problem too soon," resulting in a bias toward traditional methods, conflicting implicit assumptions, and a failure to test critical assumptions of the process.

Conclusion

Methods of measurement and analysis imply more fundamental assumptions that, at the minimum, concern how theories are developed, types of meaning, and eclecticism. I have argued that such assumptions should be consistent with one another in order to further the purposes of inquiry. In this analysis the MAO researchers were seen to favor a type of theory development that I called OCI (to emphasize act versus action meaning) and to rely heavily on a premature eclecticism. The joint consequence of the intersection of these assumptions is that we should expect the MAO researchers to produce results most useful to the understanding and inducement of "local" changes in organizational behavior; we should not expect construction of *new* theories of organization and organizational change. I believe that in fact this has been the case, at least in terms of the summary of results given to us by Seashore. But in fairness, this is not as dismal as a limited concern with a *particular type* of theory development might make it seem. The MAO researches were undertaken with complex objectives aimed at both theory and practice, and my analysis indicates that the assumptions and methods chosen favor some of these objectives to the detriment of others. As Seashore himself notes in discussing models of causation, "It is likely that each will display, as ours does, features of dubious assumption, logical fallacy, and operational difficulty." These problems come with the territory when we attempt to study complex organizations. The MAO research has overcome many such problems to produce a contribution to organization theory of considerable magnitude. To conclude, I believe that this contribution, as well as its limitations, is best put in context by the following quotation from Kaplan:

> In the conduct of inquiry we are continuously subjected to pulls in opposite directions: to search for data or to formulate hypotheses, to construct theories or to perform experiments, to focus on general laws or on individual cases, to conduct molar studies or molecular ones, to engage in synthesis or analysis. . . . We do not make a choice of the lesser of two evils and abide by the unhappy outcome. The problems which [these] dilemmas pose cannot be solved at all, but only coped with (1964: 30).

REFERENCES

Campbell, D. T., and J. C. Stanley (1963). *Experimental and Quasi-Experimental Designs for Research,* Chicago: Rand McNally.

Cook, T. D., and D. T. Campbell (1976). "The Design and Conduct of Quasi-Experiments and True Experiments in Field Settings," in Marvin D. Dunnette, Ed., *Handbook of Industrial and Organizational Psychology,* Chicago: Rand McNally.

Fisher, R. A. (1966). *The Design of Experiments,* 8th ed., Edinburgh, Scotland: Oliver and Boyd.

Henle, M. (1957). "Some Problems of Eclecticism," *Psychological Review* **64**:296–305.

Indik, B. P. (1968). "Toward an Effective Theory of Organizational Behavior," *Personnel Administration,* 51–59.

Kaplan, A. (1964). *The Conduct of Inquiry,* New York: Chandler.

Kohler, W. (1953). "The Scientists and Their New Environment," in W. R. Crawford, Ed., *The Cultural Migration,* Philadelphia: University of Pennsylvania Press.

March, J. G., and H. Simon (1958). *Organizations,* New York: Wiley.

Marx, M. H., and W. A. Hillix (1973). *Systems and Theories in Psychology,* New York: McGraw-Hill.

Zedeck, S. (1974). "Problems with the Use of "Moderator" Variables," *Psychological Bulletin* **76:**295–310.

CHAPTER FOUR

The Aston Program Perspective

The Aston Program of Research:
Retrospect and Prospect

DEREK S. PUGH
London Graduate School of Business

INTRODUCTION

In the early 1960s a group of researchers at the Industrial Administration Research Unit of the University of Aston in Birmingham, England, came together to develop the study of organization on an empirical basis (Pugh et al., 1963). Their work, which has been continued at Aston and elsewhere (London Business School, Bradford, Birmingham, Sheffield, etc.) as some of the members dispersed in the late 1960s, has developed a distinctive approach, which this paper tries to encapsulate and summarize. The studies form a particular strand in the development of organization theory, which is placed in the general context of British work in this field by Pugh et al. (1975).

THE GENERAL APPROACH

At that time there was a considerable amount of case study research describing the functioning of organizations and aspects of the behavior of organizational members, but little in the way of systematic comparisons across organizations to permit the evaluation of the representativeness of case studies with their specific data bases and consequent danger of overgeneralization. This was perceived to be an important inadequacy in the field, and a strategy was therefore developed to carry out comparative surveys across organizations to explore meaningful stable relationships. This method would place in perspective particular idiosyncrasies of case studies. These studies would begin on a cross-sectional basis and would then be developed longitudinally so that the process of stability and change could be investigated. The research group, containing sociologists and psychologists, was interdisciplinary in its orientation and therefore wished to study group and individual behavior in relation to organizational settings. Previously such settings had been neglected.

The research strategy adopted was based on five main assumptions:

1. In order to find which organizational problems are specific to particular kinds of organizations and which are common to all organizations, comparative studies need to include organizations of many types.

2. Meaningful comparisons can be made only when there is a common standard for comparison, preferably measurement.

3. The nature of an organization will be influenced by its objectives and environments, so these must be taken into account.

4. Study of the work behavior of individuals or groups should be related to study of the characteristics of the organization in which the behavior occurs.

5. Studies of organizational processes of stability and change should be undertaken in relation to a framework of significant variables and relationships established through comparative studies.

Here we are attempting to generalize and develop the study of work organization and behavior into a consideration of the interdependence of three conceptually distinct levels of analysis of behavior in organizations: (1) organizational structure and functioning, (2) group composition and interaction, and (3) individual personality and behavior. We are also concerned with the interrelationships of each of these levels. Thus, for example, we aim to study group composition and interaction in relation to particular organizational structures.

We wish to undertake a comparative analysis to establish the significant variables at each level and their relationships, and then to develop at each level a processual analysis within the framework thus established. Initially we were interested in conducting an analysis at the first level of organizational structure and functioning that could be used as an empirical research tool.

The study of the structure and activities of an organization must also be conducted in relation to its other characteristics and to the social and economic context in which it is found. We have thus developed a list of contextual and structural variables in order to relate them to the variables of organizational structure and functioning. Thus we identify the effects of various patterns of these independent variables on organizational structure and functioning.

At the next level of analysis, group composition and interaction, a new set of variables is investigated, which in these studies is related to the contextual and structural variables established earlier. Later we study individual behavior and personality in relation to context, structure, and group behavior. In this way we hope to establish systematic comparative relationships across organizations between these various levels of analysis.

As a first approximation for comparative study, we assume one-way causality from the larger to the smaller unit. But this is clearly a great oversimplification, and a full analysis will have to take account of two-way interactions and feedback loops. Studies of this type cannot be done on a cross-sectional basis; they must be longitudinal, taking account of dynamic processes over time. Only in this way will data on rival causal hypotheses be obtained (Pugh and Hickson, 1972). Such process studies will then be carried out within a framework of established meaningful stable relationships.

Thus the overall strategy of the Aston approach is to conduct nomothetic studies to produce generalizable concepts and relationships, and then to conduct idiographic studies moderated by and developed from a generalized framework that can give proper balance to the common and specific aspects of a particular organization's functioning.

Since 1961 many studies have been conducted within this framework, which has become known as the "Aston Approach" by many researchers including the original members of the Aston group and their successors. The availability of data-collecting instruments has meant that there have been many replications and extensions both to different organizations and to different countries. Most of the studies are collected and reprinted in an Aston series of Research Monographs, of which the first four volumes (Pugh and Hickson, 1976; Pugh and Hinings, 1976; Pugh and Payne, 1977; Hickson and Macmillan, 1980) are available. They form the most convenient source of material on the work of the program.

THE OVERALL CONCEPTUAL FRAMEWORK

Chronologically the overall conceptual approach may be considered from the point of view of the diagram, Figure 4-1. We began with organization-level studies. At the point at which the comparative organizational measures could be used to specify the appropriate aspects of the organization to use as context for the next level of analysis, the group studies were inaugurated. These would then run parallel with the organization-level studies. Similarly, when the group-level studies were sufficiently specified

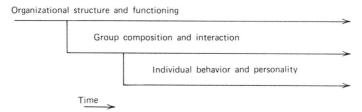

Figure 4-1   Chronological development of the Aston studies.

to be able to act as input variables for individual-level analysis, this final level of analysis would be undertaken and all three levels (organization, group, and individual) would be studied simultaneously. This was and still is the overall strategic thrust of the program.

One important objective in the studies of organizations at different levels of analysis was to obtain external validity by testing acceptable hypotheses about the relationships between, for example, characteristics of structure, context, performance, and behavior. Figure 4-2 gives a simple paradigm that we developed early on to relate an organization's structure to aspects of the behavior within it. The argument was that if we can postulate relationships between the four boxes shown and obtain data to support our hypotheses, then we have gone a considerable way toward demonstrating that our scales do measure those aspects of structure and behavior that are relevant to organizational functioning.

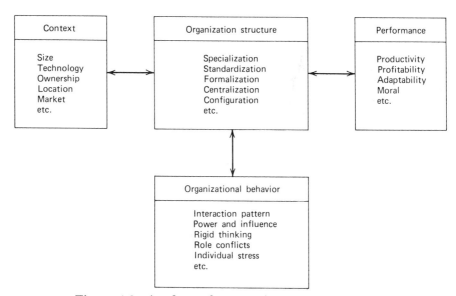

Figure 4-2   A scheme for organizational functioning.

Further, if we can predict to a considerable degree from a knowledge of an organization's context what its structural scores will be, we have evidence that its scores are meaningful. Again, if we can demonstrate that in given contexts an organization's structural scores will be directly related to its performance, we have that much more confidence in our conceptual framework. It is this concept of validity as a demonstrated link of data supporting conceptually defined hypothetical relationships that forms the epistemological basis of our endeavor.

The relatively simple diagram of Figure 4-2 has been elaborated, and Figure 4-3 presents a framework from a systems point of view, which outlines the current focus of the studies (from Pugh & Payne, 1977). The major units of analysis are the organization departments or major segments of organizations, small groups or teams, and the individual. In the diagram, the conversion process has been divided into "aims and resources" and "structure and processes" to emphasize that ensuing behavior and attitudes are a result of an interaction between these two aspects. The behavior and attitudes are a result of the attempt to achieve aims given the demands, opportunities, and constraints of the environment in which the unit of analysis (the system) is functioning. There are two-way arrows linking the boxes marked "aims and resources" and "structure and processes," since the resources available tend to determine the structure and processes that occur. There is a continual interaction between these processes and the aims, tasks, and uses to which the resources are put.

The lists of variables in the boxes are not meant to be exhaustive but to represent some of the major features that have been studied. Hopefully, Figure 4-3 also conveys the fact that individuals and groups are part of a larger system and that the larger system forms part of the environment of these subsystems. The dotted arrows down the left-hand side are intended to signify this. The research implication is highlighted by Katz and Kahn (1966): "The first step [in research] should always be to go to the next higher level of system organization to study the dependence of the system in question upon the supersystem of which it is a part, for the supersystem sets the limits of the variance of behavior of the dependent system."

The dotted arrows up the right side of the diagram indicate that lower-level systems also can have effects on the suprasystems. An individual, for example, a chief executive, can have considerable effects on the structure and processes of the organization as a whole. This illustrates nicely the interdependence between the various systems within organizations and allows us to stress the need for explanations that combine structural, group, and individual frameworks.

Using this overall conceptual framework with its reciprocal feedback loops underlines our view (Pugh et al., 1963) that an understanding of organizational operation cannot rest solely on the explication of structural characteristics and constraints or the constructions of the individual ac-

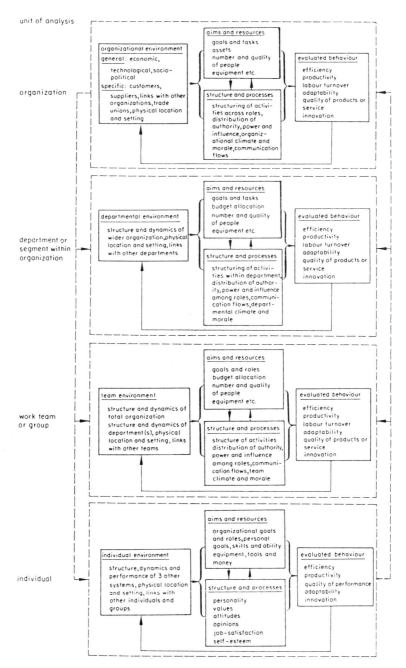

Figure 4-3 *Organizational functioning from a systems point of view (from Pugh and Payne, 1977).*

tors. Organizational theorists should concentrate on the interplays between them. Thus this approach deals with both system constraints and individual social action and attempts to bring them together in an overall framework (cf. Pugh and Hinings, 1976: 175–176).

ANALYSIS OF ORGANIZATIONAL STRUCTURE

Using the conceptual scheme of Table 4-1, our project (Pugh et al., 1963) initially sought to develop valid and reliable measures of organization structure and context. We utilized a sample of 52 extremely varied manufacturing and service organizations in the English Midlands, each of which employed at least 250 persons. We included manufacturing firms that made strip steel, toys, double decker buses, chocolate bars, injection systems, and beer, and service organizations such as chain stores, municipal departments, transport companies, insurance companies and a savings bank. Forty-six of these organizations comprised a stratified random sample by size (number of employees) and Standard Industrial Classification (type of product or service). Our tests for the internal scalability of measures utilized the entire sample; tests of relationships between structure variables used only the stratified sample. Although it was difficult to set up universally applicable methods, we wanted to assess organizations of as wide a range as possible. There were structured interview schedules for several main executives, containing objective questions such as: "Are there written operating instructions for direct workers?" We directed specific questions to executives who were responsible for particular areas and then received formal confirmations of their responses. For example, we may have asked the production manager about written operating instructions and then requested an actual set of instructions as evidence. Finally, we gathered information from public records and other sources to obtain measures such as an index of individuality of ownership.

We arranged individual item responses into a previously developed (Pugh et al., 1963) scheme and then into cumulative measures that characterized the organization. The following organizational variables were measured:

Contextual Variables
Origin and history: private versus public founding and the history of changes in ownership and location.

Ownership and control: public versus private ownership and the number and type of owners.

Size: number of employees, net assets, and market position.

Table 4-1 Conceptual Scheme for Empirical Study of Work Organizations

Contextual Variables	Activity Variables	Structural Variables	Performance Variables

Origin and history
Ownership and control
Size
Charter
Technology
Location
Resources
Dependence
	Identification
	  (charter, image)
	Perpetuation
	  (thoughtways, finance,
	  personnel services)
	Workflow
	  (production, distribution)
	Control
	  (direction, motivation,
	  evaluation, communication)
	Homeostasis
	  (fusion, leadership, problem
	  solving, legitimation)
		Specialization
		Standardization
		Formalization
		Centralization
		Configuration
			Efficiency
			  (profitability,
			  productivity, market
			  standing)
			Adaptability
			Morale

Charter: the nature and range of goods and services.

Technology: the degree of integration in work processes.

Interdependence: the extent of dependence on customers, suppliers, and trade unions.

Structural Variables

Specialization: the degree of division into specialized roles.

Standardization: the degree of standard rules and procedures.

Formalization: the degree of written instructions and procedures.

Centralization: the degree of decision-making authority at the top.

Configuration: long ve. us short chains of command and role structures, and percentage of "supportive" personnel.

These measures varied widely in number, type, complexity, and sophistication. For example, location was assessed by one relatively crude measure, number of operating sites; however, the main standardization scale had 128 dichotomous items that formed two subscales based on factor analysis. When possible, we used factor analysis within the main variables to confirm their existence as factors and to identify and make operational subsidiary factors. We also applied general dichotomous or Gutman procedures to relevant scales to confirm internal validity. Thus there were 132 fully operational measures for characterizing organizations, which ranged from simple dichotomies to large multi-item scales (Levy and Pugh, 1969).

We then examined interrelationships separately within the sets of contextual (Pugh et al., 1969a) and structural (Pugh et al., 1968) variables and also studied the relationships between contextual variables (treated as independent variables) and structural variables (treated as dependent variables).

A principal component factor analysis of structural interrelationships produced the factors listed in Table 4-2. We used the first three of these factors to create an empirical taxonomy of organization structures (Pugh et al., 1969b). Organizations were divided into those scoring high, medium, and low on Factor 1 (Structuring of Activities) and those scoring high and low on each of Factors 2 (Decision-Making Authority) and 3 (Means of Control), thereby yielding a 12-cell organizational taxonomy. Figure 4-4 shows that seven of the 12 possible cells contained one or more organizations, and these seven organizational types were designated, respectively, as: Full Bureaucracy, Nascent Full Bureaucracy, Workflow Bureaucracy, Nascent Workflow Bureaucracy, Pre-workflow Bureaucracy, Personnel Bureaucracy, and Implicitly Structured Organization.

We then examined the relationships between contextual and structural variables. Two major dimensions of context—organization size and technology—helped predict the "structuring of activities" dimension; large organizations that had complex but highly integrated production tech-

Table 4-2 Factors in Relation to Component Scales[a]

Factor	Component Scales
Structuring of activities: the degree of employee behavior that was defined by specialist jobs, routines, procedures, and formal written records	Specialization Standardization Formalization
Concentration of authority: the degree of decision-taking authority that was concentrated at the top or outside the organization, if it was part of a larger company	Centralization Degree of autonomy of chief executive
Line control of work flow: the degree of control that was exercised by line personnel versus impersonal procedures	Number of subordinates per supervisor (few versus many) Degree to which written records of role performance were collected (low versus high)
Relative size of supportive component: the relative number of nonproductive personnel or auxilliary support to main workflow	Percentage of clerks Percentage of non-workflow personnel

[a]From Payne & Pugh (1976).

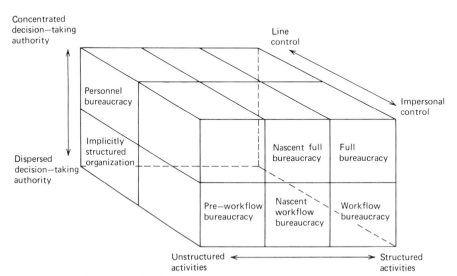

Figure 4-4 An empirical taxonomy of structures of work organizations (from Pugh and Payne, 1977).

nologies tended to structure and prescribe in detail the nature of people's work activities. Dependence predicted concentration of authority; organizations often concentrated decision-making authority at the top when they were dependent on or owned by some other organization. Thus decision making in organizational branches was more centralized than in autonomous organizations. The results are summarized in Table 4-3.

REPLICATIONS AND EXTENSIONS OF ORGANIZATIONAL LEVEL STUDIES

Pugh and Hinings (1976) collected a number of studies that were carried out in replication and extension of the original project (Hinings and Lee, 1971; Inkson et al., 1970; Child, 1972, 1973) on other manufacturing organizations in Britain. The approach was also applied to different types of organizations, including local government departments (Greenwood and Hinings, 1973), hospitals (Tauber, 1968), trade unions (Donaldson and Warner, 1974), churches (Hinings and Foster, 1973) and colleges (Holdaway et al., 1975).

How far do these new studies support the original framework? First, it is abundantly clear that the original measures of structure and context can be applied to a wide variety of diverse types of organizations with discriminating power and meaningful results. While it is true that in the studies of trade unions, local government departments, churches, and colleges, some detailed operational changes had to be made (i.e., in some of the specific items forming the scales), these changes were relatively minor. The Aston concepts forming the source variables can be readily applied in a rigorous manner. This is in itself an encouraging finding and a step forward in the development of organization theory.

A number of studies of particular types of organizations naturally developed contextual scales appropriate to the differences in the organizations examined, for example, political variables for local government, belief variables for churches. The methodological approach, however, remained the same, and this underlines the potential of such research for developing new concepts and variables that might then usefully be applied to other types of organizations such as work organizations.

Second, with regard to the patterns of structural variables, it is apparent that a considerable degree of similarity was found as well as many interesting differences. The dimension of structuring of activities demonstrated in the original study (i.e., the high intercorrelations of specialization, standardization, and formalization) was repeated in all the studies of work organizations and in the study of trade unions. Greenwood and Hinings found specialization to be related to standardization but not to formalization, which was linked to other aspects in local government departments. Holdaway et al. found that, while formalization and stand-

Table 4-3 Multiple Prediction Analysis of Structural Factors[a]

Contextual Predictors of Structural Factors	Single Correlation	Multiple Correlation	F Ratio	Degrees of Freedom	Level of Confidence
Structuring of activities					
Size	0.69	0.69	39.6	1:44	>99%
Workflow integration	0.34	0.75	8.2	1:43	>99%
Size of parent organization	0.39	0.76	1.9	1:42	NS
Concentration of authority					
Dependence	0.66	0.66	34.2	1:44	>99%
Location (number of operating sites)	0.39	0.75	12.5	1:43	>99%
Age of organization	−0.38	0.77	2.5	1:42	NS
Operating diversity	−0.30	0.78	3.0	1:41	NS
Workflow integration	−0.30	0.78	0.0	1:40	NS
Size of parent organization	0.39	0.79	0.4	1:39	NS
Line control of workflow					
Operating variability	−0.57	0.57	20.7	1:44	>99%
Workflow integration	−0.46	0.59	1.7	1:43	NS
Number of sites	0.39	0.59	0.1	1:42	NS

[a]From Pugh et al. (1969a).

ardization cluster, they are not related to other variables. This same separation was also found in the study of churches by Hinings et al., which suggests interesting comparisons. In general, though, the dimension of structuring of activities is seen to be a stable and discriminating one across a wide variety of organizations.

The relationship of this dimension to the second one of concentration of authority was found in the original Aston study to be moderately negative with manufacturing organizations, but to be much weaker over the whole sample, including public service organizations. Concentration of authority was thus considered to be independent of the structuring of activities dimension, particularly in view of its different conceptual basis (Pugh et al., 1968; Pugh and Hickson, 1976). The later studies appear to underline the differences between the business and public service organizations, as might have been expected, since their population and samples are more specifically delineated than in the original heterogeneous sample.

Thus all the studies of business organizations show a higher negative correlation between the structuring variables and centralization than did the original study. Child argues on the basis of these results that centralization, scored negatively, should be included in the same cluster as specialization, standardization, and so on, to form a Weberian dimension of bureaucratization, which, as he shows, included decentralization. It appears to us that this would be an unfortunate blurring of a useful distinction. For example, it would dilute the very high intercorrelations found between specialization, formalization, and standardization (of the order of 0.7 to 9.9) with a variable that correlated only -0.3 to -0.5 with them.

Underlining the point that Child's view is based on business organizations only is the finding by Holdaway et al. that in educational institutions centralization correlates quite strongly and *positively* with formalization and standardization, but not specialization. This supports the original Aston view that the patterns in personnel bureaucracies are different and that "bureaucracy takes different forms in different settings" (Pugh et al., 1969b). It would thus seem to be more useful to regard these two dimensions as conceptually separate and to determine empirically what their relationship is in different types of organizations.

With regard to the remaining two original dimensions—line control of workflow and relative size of supportive component—only two of the later studies collected and analyzed the appropriate data. In the national study, Child (1972) demonstrated that both these factors are shown in his factor analysis. Holdaway et al. also gave an analysis in which their dimension of administrative configuration corresponds closely with line control of workflow, with the addition in this case of functional specialization, whereas non-workflow proportion corresponds with relative size of supportive component. These results support the stability of these dimensions as discriminating across a range of different organizational types.

Third, consideration of the relationship of the contextual to the structural variables shows that the original Aston findings of the high relationship of size and structuring of activities is strongly supported in all the subsequent studies. Large size goes with high structuring across the whole extremely diverse range of organizations studied, with only one exception—churches. The relationship is an extremely stable and strong characteristic of organizations in general.

The relationship of size to the second dimension of concentration of authority follows, in the various studies, the patterns that would be expected, taking account of the different relationships found between structuring of activities and centralization. Thus the studies of business organizations and of trade unions showed a negative relationship of size and centralization, whereas the educational institutions showed a strong positive relationship. Size showed no relationship to concentration of authority in the local government departments nor, with regard to number of employees, in churches. But in the study of churches another aspect of size, namely number of members, related positively to centralization.

Consideration of the pervasive relationships of size to the structuring of activity variables has led Child to distinguish, on theoretical grounds, a concept of "complexity" (specialization of functions and roles, level of specialist qualifications) as being an intervening set of variables between size and "bureaucratic control" (standardization, formalization, and in this case, decentralization). This is an interesting conceptualization, with heuristic possibilities, and is used by Greenwood and Hinings. Child points out that the original Aston findings can be reorganized in this way and that the relationship of size with decentralization cannot be regarded as thus mediated. This is a limitation, since if size can be considered to have a direct effect on centralization, it is difficult to see why it would not affect formalization and standardization directly. But essentially this is a theory of the processes by which size affects structure, and it thus needs the support of longitudinal and dynamic studies.

The Aston finding of a strong relationship between the conceptual dimension of dependence (i.e., on owning group, customers and suppliers, etc.) and concentration of authority—that is, the greater the dependence of the organization on its environment, the greater the centralization of authority—is supported in both the Hinings and Lee and Inkson et al. studies. Child has not presented the data in this form but does state that greater concentration of ownership with control predicted greater centralization of decision making. Concentration of ownership with control is one of the variables included in the concept of dependence, and this result would thus appear to support this relationship. Studies of non-business organizations did not attempt to use this formulation of an organization's relationship to its environment, with the exception of Holdaway et al., who again found positive relationships among dependence, public ownership, and centralization.

CROSS-CULTURAL COMPARISONS OF ORGANIZATIONAL CONTEXT AND STRUCTURE

Hickson and Macmillan (1980) collected a number of studies of organizational structure and context carried out in a range of different countries, namely, Britain, Canada, the United States, Japan, Germany, Sweden, Jordan, India, and Poland.

The paradigm of relationships developed in the Aston approach (see Table 4-3) formed the framework used to collect data on business organizations in very different countries. Table 4-4 summarizes the relationships found.

Hickson et al. (1979) present the results as a series of causal hypotheses and explanations:

1. *Size.* In all countries, large organizations will be the most formalized and specialized in structure. Growth means reaping economies of scale and best use of expertise by dividing labor still further. More formalized documentation of action and intended action is required for control as the knowledge possessed by any one person of what is happening in the organization becomes a smaller part of the whole. Nonformalized custom is inadequate to control large numbers in organizations with a turnover of personnel.

2. *Size of Parent Organization.* In all countries, organizations in large parent groups will be the most formalized and specialized. This is because being part of a large group means having specialist sections as counterparts to head office specialisms and accepting

Table 4-4 The Relationships of Structure to Context in Cross-Cultural Comparisons[a]

Structure		Context
Formalization	Positive with	Size Parent size Dependence (usually)
Specialization	Positive with	Size and parent size
Centralization	Positive with, but sometimes negative with	Dependence Size

[a]From Hickson et al. (1979).

formalized documentation in standard forms common to the whole group. There is probably some difference here between specialization and formalization. Specialization correlates most closely with size, formalization equally with size and parent size. Thus being part of a large group may have greatest effects on formalization by imposing standard documentation.

An organization may therefore experience a double size effect, both from its own growth and from being or becoming part of a large parent group (e.g., through private takeover or public nationalization).

3. *Dependence.* In all countries, organizations dependent on others will take decisions centrally, and in addition decisions will be taken for them outside and above them—they lack autonomy. Ties of ownership or contract make relevant resource decisions so important that they are either centralized at the apex of the hierarchy or taken above the organization by a controlling board. For example, when a company purchases components from many different suppliers, decisions on each contract can be made within the buying department. But if it signs a contract for most of its needs with a single supplier, then relationships with that supplier become so important that the chief executive may attend to them, that is, centralization occurs. A similar situation results if a company is tied to sources within an owning group.

Dependence then largely repeats the relationship with formalization already noted with Size of Parent Organization; that is, firms dependent on other units, especially owning groups, have to take on the formalization of those to which they are linked.

To summarize and stretch the implications as far as they will go: It may be that all over the world the largest industrial units in the largest parent groups are the most bureaucratized in formalization and specialization of structure. If they are heavily dependent not only on that parent group but on large suppliers and customers, they are also centralized.

But this kind of kite flying is best done with careful attention to country-by-country variations. The magnitude of the correlation coefficients varies quite a lot and mostly accounts for much less than half the variance. It must be presumed that third variables are of major consequence. It is here that societal influences may be pursued, not only for their effects upon levels of scores but more so for their effects on relationships between variables. For instance, the relationship between size and specialization is positive in all countries, as has been said. That is, larger units break down what has to be done into more and more specialized sections. But whereas in Britain the correlation coefficients are all between 0.65 and 0.91, in Sweden the correlation coefficient is only 0.26. On a mere 11 Swedish units this is persuasive simply because it accords with all the other countries; on its own it has little meaning. Is there, then, something peculiarly Swedish affecting the magnitude of the relationship? On so little data, not even a guess is worthwhile.

There are many intricacies to be explored. Horvath et al. (1974) point to a possible difference between the Japanese and the Swedish responses to internal dependence (dependence on owning group) as against external dependence (dependence on suppliers and customers). In brief, with internal dependence the Japanese centralize while the Swedish formalize, but with external dependence it is the other way around. We also find that in the United States, Britain, and Germany, larger organizations may tend to decentralize (i.e., size and centralization are negatively related), whereas this tendency does not appear in the Canadian, Swedish, and Japanese results. Why not? It can be suggested that in the United States, Britain, and Germany, decentralization occurs once the structure of specialist offices is established under formalized control, whereupon decisions can be delegated to appropriate levels of specialist expertise (e.g., to quality-control specialists, to personnel specialists, etc.). Why not in Canada, Sweden, and Japan? Are the available samples so small as to be misleading, or is this an effect of some cultural factor common to the latter three countries?

Obviously there is still too little data to prompt further speculation. It may well be that culture, whatever that may be defined as, affects not only what organizations are like (i.e., levels of scores) but also the magnitudes of relationships between variables. Fortunately, the core of stable consistent relationships that stands out from our results offers something to hold on to while the great variations around it are explored.

RELATION OF ORGANIZATIONAL CONTEXT AND STRUCTURE TO PERFORMANCE

Child (1974) extended the examination of the original Aston conceptual scheme (Table 4-1) by presenting evidence on the relationship of organizational structure and context to performance in business firms. He found that some universalistic propositions received some support. Comparative youthfulness of management and a lower level of structuring of activities appear to be linked with more rapid growth. But a contingency analysis seems to hold more promise. This takes account of the context of the firm, particularly size and variability in the environment, and considers performance in relation to both context and structure. Successful companies (in terms of growth of sales) in variable environments had lower structuring of activities scores than less successful ones. No overall relationship with centralization was found, but there were some specific differences: production decisions were delegated to a greater extent in more successful companies in stable environments, while successful companies in variable environments had a greater tendency to centralize decisions concerned with finance and purchasing.

Child also found interesting differences in the slopes of the regression lines between structuring and decentralization on to size in higher and lower growth companies. The slopes were distinctly greater for the higher growth companies. Among the smaller companies there was little differences between the higher and lower performing groups, but as one moves to large companies the structural differences progressively widen, with the more successful large companies showing greater structuring of activities and dispersion of authority.

This would suggest that increasing size and coping with increasing environmental variability are contingencies that have opposite effects. Indeed the greatest differences in the rates of development by size are between higher and lower performers in stable environments, whereas the rates of the higher and lower performers in variable environments are much closer together.

The research reported by Child does not demonstrate very strong relationships comparable to the relationships between context and structure, but it does demonstrate the potential of a contingency approach to performance that needs to be explored further.

ORGANIZATIONAL BEHAVIOR IN RELATION TO STRUCTURE

Studies of group- and role-level variables in relation to organization structure have been carried out and are collected in Pugh and Payne (1977). The approach has again been to define a range of measurable dimensions based on the subjective feelings, expectations, and perceptions by managers of how their organizations function and what kind of role they play as managers. Table 4-5 gives examples of work role and behavioral variables, and Figure 4-5 gives the framework that we have used to relate these variables to structure and context.

The framework outlined in Figure 4-5 has been tested out in studies of top managers (i.e., the heads of major functions and others reporting directly to the chief executives) in over a hundred organizations. The argument goes that certain patterns of context are associated with particular structural profiles. The structure will in turn be associated with certain work role and behavioral variables. Thus, for example, large size and integrated technology will lead to high structuring of activities, which in turn will lead to greater role formalization and definition, which will be accompanied by less perceived conflict and less questioning authority and pressing for change. The thesis is that high structuring and cen-

Table 4-5   Examples of Measures of Work Role and Behavioral Variables

Work Role Variables	Perceived Behavior Variables
Role formalization: the extent to which the manager's role is formalized in official documents (five two-point items), e.g., is there a written job description or terms of reference for your job?	Questioning authority: the extent to which the manager perceives his or her colleagues as questioning formal authority and rules (three seven-point items of a semantic differential type), e.g., place a checkmark in one of the seven spaces that most accurately describes how on the whole managers carry out their tasks in the organization—a range of possible responses from "accepting authority" to "questioning authority."
Role definition: the extent to which the managers perceive their jobs and authority to be constrained within fixed limits (three five-point items), e.g., how precisely are your responsibilities laid down? (very precisely, fairly, not very, very imprecisely, not laid down at all.)	
Perceived authority: the scope of authority the managers perceive themselves as possessing (two eight-point items) e.g., I have complete authority on routine matters but refer the majority of unusual items to my superior for approval.	Conflict: the extent to which the manager perceives his or her colleagues as having difficulty in agreeing on aspects of decision making (four five-point items) e.g., How much difficulty do managers have in reaching agreement on the facts of a situation? (none, a little, some, quite a lot, a great deal.)

tralization are alternative strategies for the administrative reduction of variance in behavior and performance.

It should be noted that the indicated causal chains can be considered only as plausible hypotheses, since these studies are cross-sectional comparisons across organizations carried out at one point in time. Undoubtedly the directional arrows shown in Figure 4-5 can be only first simplifications, since many of them would be likely to be two-way interactions. The purpose of the present studies is to develop a comparative framework of the significant variables and their relationships at the group and individual levels of analysis corresponding to that established at the organizational level.

The proposed model has received partial support. The high structuring of activities at the organizational level was found to be strongly related to management work-role variables of role formalization and role definition as hypothesized, but this was *not* accompanied by less questioning of authority and was accompanied by *more*, not less, perceived conflict. Centralization of authority, on the other hand, was accompanied by less role formalization, less perceived authority, and less questioning of authority, as predicted by the model. Clearly the more formal effects on managerial authority and task of organization structures as strategies of control are as predicted by the model, but the interpersonal relationships are more complex and multidimensional.

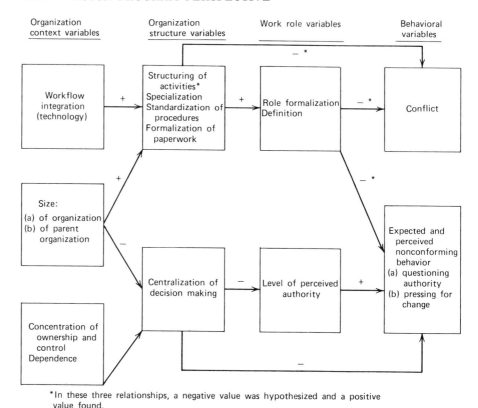

*In these three relationships, a negative value was hypothesized and a positive value found.

All other hypothesized relationships were supported in varying degrees of strength.

Figure 4-5   Strategies of control and organizational behavior: Main hypothesized relationships (from Pugh, 1976).

High structuring of activities was not accompanied by less questioning of authority and less perceived conflict of top managers; in fact, there is a clear trend in the opposite direction, suggesting that such managers may be likely to be above the organizational levels for which structuring of activities is a strategy for reducing the variance in behavior. The effects might be in the predicted direction at lower levels in the organization.

A more detailed study (Pheysey et al., 1971) of all the line managers and supervisors at every level of two organizations, similar in context (size and technology) but very different in structure (one high on structuring and centralization and one low on these characteristics), has been carried out using the dimensions of organizational climate illustrated in Table 4-6. As was predicted, relationships in the structured, centralized organization were more formal at all levels in the hierarchy, all groups saw themselves as having less autonomy, and the organizational climate was seen as being oriented towards rules and conventionality. On the

Table 4-6   Climate Index as a Variable in the Business Organization[a]

Rules orientation: the extent to which rules are revered and adhered to (six items), e.g., formal rules and regulations have a very important place here.

Conventionality: the extent to which correctness in clothing, appearance, and manner is characteristic (10 items), e.g., people here are always carefully dressed and neatly groomed.

Industriousness: the extent to which hard work is expected of people (14 items), e.g., it is fairly easy to keep up here without working too hard (scored *false*).

Readiness to innovate: the extent to which the organization encourages innovative activity (nine items), e.g., new ideas are always being tried out here.

---

[a]All items are of the true-false type.

other hand, and unexpectedly, it was in this organization that the managers showed a greater willingness to innovate and had a much more industrious work climate.

Thus, in general, the relationships between the contextual, structural, and work role variables in Figure 4-5 seem to hold up, but their relationships to the behavioral variables seem more complex, some supporting and some going against those hypothesized. One problem at the methodological level is that the behavioral data are all based on self-reporting techniques, which may have inherent limitations of validity. But insofar as the results are indicative, a contingency approach seems called for in which the interpersonal costs and benefits of the various structural strategies of control can be evaluated in a more comprehensive way.

LONGITUDINAL AND DYNAMIC STUDIES OF ORGANIZATIONAL PROCESSES

Since a formal authority structure is a construct derived from the activities of organizational members, it is sometimes considered a subject in its own right. However, a formal authority structure has also provided a framework for the study of members' attitudes and behaviors and of the processes behind organizational stability and change. Longitudinal and dynamic studies can help to develop convincing causal explanations; cross-sectional correlational studies can only infer causal hypotheses.

Thus Aldrich (1972) emphasized the use of causal models and path analyses to relate structural variables. He suggested that Pugh et al. unduly stressed size as a determinant of structure, and he argued that technology was more relevant. In a stimulating series of responses to Aldrich, Hilton (1972), Heise (1972), and Pugh and Hickson (1972) debated the value of path analysis as a tool for helping with causal analysis. All agreed that causal models required longitudinal data to reveal the processes by which organizations (a) remained relatively stable and (b) changed.

There have been few such longitudinal studies. Using the Pugh et al. measures (1968), Inkson, Pugh, and Hickson (1970) compared two samples at two points in time and found similar relationships between context (size, technology, dependence) and structure (structuring of activities, concentration of authority). Then they compared the structural and contextual features of 14 "workflow bureaucracies" (Pugh et al., 1969b) at two points with an intervening period of four to five years. Although technology and dependence measures remained the same over time, organizational size decreased 5 to 10 percent on the average. However, the structuring scores themselves usually showed a significant increase of about 10 percent, and concentration of authority scores significantly decreased about 33⅓ percent.

These results concurred with the developmental sequence implied by Pugh's taxonomy of structures (Pugh et al., 1969b). Inkson, Pugh, and Hickson hypothesized the operation of an organizational "ratchet mechanism"; here size increases would bring structuring increases, but size decreases would not result in structuring decreases—at least on a short-term basis. However, in the study of Pugh et al., decreased concentration of authority accompanied increased structuring.

Although the Inkson, Pugh, and Hickson study (1970) was longitudinal, it only implied the actual change processes of organizational structure. Pugh et al. (1976) forms the first preliminary report of a study of decision processes over time of the top management groups of three organizations.

Over periods of six to nine months all the members of the management committees of these organizations (i.e., the chief executive and the heads of the line and functional departments) were interviewed regularly for a period of one hour every two weeks. The interviews were primarily open-ended, directed towards asking managers what was currently on their "agenda" (what important problems they were facing, what decisions they were involved in, their aims for the coming weeks, and how they would set about achieving them, etc.), but some more systematic data will also have been collected, such as communication patterns (through the diary technique), and centralization of authority structure (through the Aston schedule).

The information from these interviews forms the data base for the study. They were basically nondirective, but inevitably over the period of the project many issues would recur, and in the later stages we would prompt for developments on these issues if they were not spontaneously mentioned.

CONTENT OF ISSUES

From the interviews we were able to identify 10 managerial issues, (a) which were sufficiently important to the managers concerned and to the organization to have generated decision processes within the top managerial group (i.e., decisions that could not or would not be taken by one manager alone or with consultation only within his or her own department), and (b) which recurred in more than one organization, to enable us to make a comparative study of the processes involved. All 10 issues occurred in at least two of the organizations, and seven of them in all three.

The issues were:

1. Product quality

2. Expansion and diversification

3. Variation in sales

4. Health and safety legislation

5. Budgeting

6. Management development

7. Pricing

8. Allocation of finished goods to customers

9. Reactions to trade union activity

10. Stock loss

On all of these issues, information on the "current debate" was obtained from the managers involved, and an attempt was made to construct an ongoing description of the processes taking place.

The conceptual framework being developed for the comparative analysis of organizational processes is given in Figure 4-6.

THE CONCEPTS DEFINED

The conceptual framework that has been developed represents a systematic set of concepts for the analysis of processes. Our aim is to avoid structural and static concepts and to concentrate on the "flow" nature of processes. The framework synthesizes the cybernetic approach of the Carnegie School with the concentration upon affective processes that is apparent in the work of Argyris. Hence it provides a melding of the instrumental and expressive factors involved in decision processes. It is congruent with our wider paradigm that organizational functioning is a

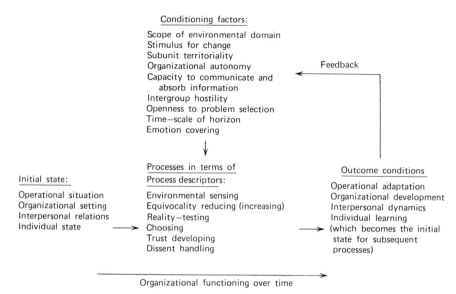

Figure 4-6 Conceptual framework for comparative analysis of organizational processes (from Pugh et al., 1976).

multilevel phenomenon in which specific organizational activities occur within a wider set of parameters that condition the internal processes. Hence the framework provides for 10 *conditioning factors* and six *process descriptors.*

The conditioning factors are the distinguishing characteristics of the organization and its top management groups. They capture the Chinese box of successive interlapping levels that make up the four levels: environment, organization, group, and individual. These conditioning factors delineate the crucial aspects of the setting that affect the processes of decision making. The processes themselves cover activities that enter directly into the organizational stream of consciousness: the cognitive decision trees that unfold in pulses down the pathways of the nerves of organizations, and those that describe these events at the level of interpersonal transactions. These levels constitute the symbol transformation and affective psychological base.

A further aspect of our framework is the process outcome analysis. This provides a way of posing the question: What are the consequences that the processes have for the wider organizational life? The impact, if any, made on the more permanent features of organizational structure, technical operations, interpersonal relations, and individual learning can be captured in this analysis. Hence the way in which each process contributes to subtly changing or reinforcing the existing organization can be noted. Just as the process analysis captures the flow aspects of organizational life, so the outcome analysis records the results of this flow in terms of the banks of the river.

The process outcomes are noted at each of four analytic levels by means of the comparison between initial state and outcome conditions. The comparisons are as follows:

Initial State	Outcome Conditions
Operational situation ⟶	Operational adaptation
Organizational setting ⟶	Organizational development
Interpersonal relations ⟶	Interpersonal dynamic
Individual state ⟶	Individual learning

At the end of each of the process analyses, an audit in these terms is made of the results of each process.

The Analytic Framework

This regards organizational processes as an ongoing stream of events, activities, interactions, interpersonal feelings, and individual reactions, conditioned by environmental, structural, and interpersonal relationships, to produce outcome conditions that may modify or reinforce the initial state of organizational functioning.

Using this framework of analysis, we consider the processes concerned with each decision issue on a comparative basis. Thus, for example, the processes involved in the issue of product quality in each of the three firms have been analyzed in these terms and comparisons made. Certain emerging patterns are beginning to develop that are characteristic of the three organizations. One organization, for example, on the quality issue, used a process that was congruent with its norm regarding cognitive openness and rationality. But this process was not combined with any attempt to resolve the increased interpersonal hostility that resulted from a rational analysis and solution of the problem. This hostility followed lines of antipathy within the organization and reflected the way in which the organization did not confront conflict but left interpersonal tensions unresolved.

The second firm dealt with product quality with its customary technique of passing decisions on up through the hierarchy, even though they themselves regarded this as inadequate management. Thus a product quality decision was delayed until it was necessary to exercise it in an ad hoc way hierarchically by a member of the main board.

In the third organization the product quality decision illustrated the continual negotiation for autonomy and power between the two levels that comprise the management board of the firm. The analysis has been able to chart three recent successful influence interactions of the technical director in relation to the managing director, but the managing director still intervenes considerably in the technical director's work.

The analysis of processes can thus illuminate prevailing structural, cultural, technical, and learning patterns within the organizations. By concentrating on actual processes, analysis can shed light on these features as revealingly as can approaches that proceed through questionnaire surveys of sets of employees. The dynamic aspect begins to illuminate the issues of how cultures reproduce themselves and how structures come to be as they are and are maintained through time.

It should be noted that our approach, by taking into the analysis the substantive content issues, points very firmly to processes as organizational events. This is an important distinction, which differentiates this work from that concerned only with the analysis of interpersonal processes in a content-free manner. Our intention is to produce a process analysis that places the primary emphasis on the functioning of the organization.

It is basic to the present approach that all processes and decision issues contribute to the ongoing stream of organizational functioning. Thus our strategy is not that of taking a major disjunctive change process and charting its ramifications, but rather that of building up a characterization of the ongoing organization through analysis of the considerable number of simultaneous processes in which it is engaged. The effects of any one of these processes on the outcome conditions compared with the initial state may be small or may reinforce the initial state, but the culmination of all such processes can realistically depict the degree of the development of the organization and its members.

OVERVIEW OF THE FINDINGS

The achievements of the Aston approach may be summarized in broad terms under the following points:

1. The development and application of a useful heuristic framework of stable, meaningful variables applied to organizational functioning and behavior. The framework enables reliable and valid comparative measures to be made, is publicly available for use by other researchers, and is applicable to a wide range of types of organization in a large number of countries.

    The existence and use of this framework is in itself a contribution to organization theory that develops by the interplay of nomothetic and idiographic approaches. The demonstration that a nomothetic comparative approach can be carried through rigorously with interesting results is important if we are to develop through a descriptive to an analytical discipline.

2. At the organizational level of studies, that is, organizational environment, context, structure, and performance, the relationships between context and structure have been sufficiently consistent to warrant a predictive approach (compare Figure 4-5). This approach has been viable when applied to industry, public services, nonwork organizations, and so on, and when applied to manufacturing organizations in a range of different countries.

    The stability of these relationships, which of course is considerable but by no means complete, provides an important orientation point for studies of variations, which will need to include additional predictor variables.

3. At the group level of analysis, relationships are less clear and well explicated (as Figure 4-5 shows). But dimensions of organizational climate have been established. The conceptual similarity between results based on objective structural measures and perceptual climate measures (first noted by Campbell et al., 1970) is very encouraging and has provided the basis of convergent validity of both types of measures.

    However, the percentage of variance predicted by subjective methods at the group level of analysis is considerably less than that at the organizational level, even when it is in the predicted direction. This is partially due to the probable lower reliability and validity of subjective measures, but it is also due to the fact that individual-level variables such as aspects of personality have not yet been sufficiently included in the framework and in the studies. Thus Ellis and Child (1973) have shown that a personality variable such as "preference for a varied working environment" predicts perceptions of role climate, so a start has been made on tracking down the factors that influence perceptions. Very much more needs to be done to find out what influences the way managers see their role.

4. The longitudinal and processual studies have begun to develop an eclectic approach, which attempts to combine the cognitive information processing concepts (as in Weick, 1979) with the affective cultural and interpersonal learning approach (as in Argyris, 1957). These studies will hopefully contribute to a generalizable empirical examination of organizational processes on a comparative basis.

FURTHER DEVELOPMENTS

Any attempt to summarize a research program immediately highlights its limitations and underlines how much more there is yet to be done. The studies reported here are being developed and the issues they raise are being examined, but on a somewhat diffuse basis, so that the effort would be better described as an "approach" rather than a "program." It is immediately clear that there are a number of issues that need to be tackled in the Aston approach if development is to be stimulated.

Improvement in Measures

There has been relatively little attempt to improve the operationalism and measures of the Aston concepts since they were first proposed (one is inclined to say promulgated). Greenwood and Hinings (1976) have reformulated centralization in regard to local government organizations but not in regard to manufacturing organizations, despite considerable discussion on this subject (Mansfield, 1973; Donaldson, 1974; Aldrich, 1975; Child, 1972). Similarly, Mindlin and Aldrich (1975) presented detailed criticism of the concept "dependence." In general, though, other items and measures of the Aston concepts since they were first proposed (one is In particular it is clear that the framework at the moment is necessarily of a very general and therefore relatively superficial kind. It would be of great interest to develop items measuring the established concepts for particular homogeneous groups of organizations, for example, all firms in a particular industry, or a particular range of service agencies. This has not yet been done.

Extension of the Concepts

There is clearly a need to extend the range of concepts to be included in the conceptual framework. One way to do this has been indicated by the development of particular variables in specific subgroups of organizations, for example, political variables in local government organizations, belief variables in the study of churches. These clearly apply not only to the specific groups on which they were developed but also more generally to a wider range of organizations. The extensions to individual-level studies within the Aston framework have hardly begun, and need to be put on a more substantial basis. Walton (1978) has attempted to relate perceptions of organizational structure by managers to their psychological characteristic of "cognitive complexity." Work relating managers' concepts of their role to personality variables and stress as proposed by Payne (1978) needs to be done. An important development here would be to go beyond data that might be called "attitudinal" (i.e., descriptions, perceptions, verbalized feelings, etc.) to observed behavior. This area still needs much more work in comparative organizational studies.

Cross-Cultural Research

In this field the organization-level work has been well established, and what is needed is an extension to group- and individual-level studies.

Seemingly it is at this level that differences between cultures can be established within a bureaucratic framework that appears to be stable across cultures.

Longitudinal Studies

The repetition of measurements at regular intervals over a period of time is a method much used in other disciplines. It is clearly possible within the Aston approach. Some research along these lines has taken place. For example, Inkson et al. (1970) looked at the structures of 14 organizations at two points in time; Dale et al. (1973) used the climate measures in a longitudinal evaluation of a change program in a manufacturing organization. The scales were administered at three points during a period of two years. In both these studies, the considerable stability over the time of the findings provides evidence for the reliability of the measures. Much more could be done in this field, however, particularly to monitor organization development intervention or the effects of environmental changes. It would also provide a conceptual opportunity to incorporate the "leads" and "lags" form of analysis, which is common in economics, into organization theory and thus come closer to causally based analysis.

Processual Studies of Organizational Functioning

The need here is to increase the richness of the analytical framework to take account of the greater richness of the data. It gives an opportunity for improving the complexity of the explanatory models used, as, for example, Pondy and Mitroff (1979) argue. It is indeed only with processual data analyzed at a systems level that the framework in Figure 4-3 can really be exploited. But these systems must be affective as well as cognitive if they are to capture much of the sense of the reality of organizational life.

CONCLUSIONS

The Aston program has been part of a development during the past two decades whose major impact on the study of organizational behavior has been the need to "take the structure seriously." A major component of the reaction against the traditional management theories on the part of the behavioral scientists, who established their particular approach to organizational functioning, was in fact to neglect or downgrade the organizational structure in favor of individual motivation, interpersonal relationships, group processes, and so on. This in effect gave less importance to the authority structure of an organization. One important impact for practice that the Aston studies have had is in helping to change this approach, in particular in the organizational development movement (see Strauss, 1976). Workers in that field are now much more aware of the importance of authority structures and power allocations within an organization and the way in which these may limit the possibilities of change via development of interpersonal relationships and revised attitudes. The movement itself is much more realistic in this way about what can be achieved.

The Aston program has also been part of the movement to establish a "contingency approach" to these issues. This movement supports the idea that there are organizational structures or methods of communication that are more appropriate to some situations and less appropriate to others. The concept that each particular situation will have its own more appropriate style sounds reasonable and sensible, but the actual working out of what is appropriate continues to be a necessary research activity to which the Aston approach has contributed.

Finally we must forge stronger links between the comparative and the processual approaches. Comparative cross-sectional studies are theoretically dry, since anything beyond statistical analysis is only inferential. However, different processual case studies often cannot be compared, are on a small scale, and overgeneralize greatly. An effective combination of these approaches is necessary if compelling theories of organizational behavior are to emerge.

REFERENCES

Aldrich, H. E. (1972). "Technology and Organizational Structure: A Re-examination of the Findings of the Aston Group," *Administrative Science Quarterly* **17**:26–43.

Aldrich, H. E. (1975). "Reaction to Donaldson's Note," *Administrative Science Quarterly* **20**:457–459.

Argyris, C. (1957). *Personality and Organization*, New York: Harper and Row.

Campbell, J. P., M. B. Dunnette, E. E. Lawler, and K. E. Weick (1970). *Managerial Behavior and Performance*, New York: McGraw-Hill.

Child, J. (1972). "Organization Structure and Strategies of Control: A Replication of the Aston Study," *Administrative Science Quarterly* **17**:163–177.

Child, J. (1973). "Strategies of Control and Organizational Behavior," *Administrative Science Quarterly* **18**:1–17.

Child, J. (1974). "Predictors of Variation in Managerial Roles," *Human Relations* **26**:227–250.

Dale, A. J., R. L. Payne, B. McMillan, and D. Pym (1973). "Evaluation of a 3-D Theory of Organizational Change," unpublished report, London Graduate School of Business Studies.

Donaldson, L., and M. Warner (1974). "Structure of Organization in Occupational Interest Associations," *Human Relations* **27**:721–738 (edited version in Pugh and Hinings, 1976).

Donaldson, L., and M. Warner (1975). "Organization Status and the Measurement of Centralization," *Administrative Science Quarterly* **20**:453–456.

Ellis, T., and J. Child (1973). "Placing the Stereotype of the Manager into Perspective," *Journal of Management Studies* **10**:233–255.

Greenwood, R., and C. R. Hinings (1973). "Research into Local Government Reorganization," *PAC Bulletin,* December.

Greenwood, R., and C. R. Hinings (1976). "Centralization Revisited: Further Discussion," *Administrative Science Quarterly* **21**. See also Pugh and Hinings, 1976, Chapter 10:162–177.

Heise, D. R. (1972). "How do I Know My Data? Let Me Count the Ways," *Administrative Science Quarterly* **17**:58–61.

Hickson, D. J., and C. J. McMillan (1980). *Organization and Nation: The International Aston Programme,* Farnborough: Saxon House/Lexington Books.

Hickson, D. J., C. J. McMillan, D. Azumi, and D. Howarth (1979). "Grounds for Comparative Theory: Quicksands and Hard Core," in C. J. Lammers and D. J. Hickson, Eds., *Organizations Alike and Unlike,* London: Routledge and Kegan Paul.

Hilton, G. (1972). "Causal Inference Analysis: A Seductive Process," *Administrative Science Quarterly* **17**:44–54.

Hinings, C. R., and B. D. Foster (1973). "The Organization Structure of Churches: A Preliminary Model," *Sociology* **7**:93–106.

Hinings, C. R., and G. L. Lee (1971). "Dimensions of Organization Structure and Their Context: A Replication," *Sociology* **5**:83–93.

Holdaway, E. A., J. F. Newberry, D. J. Hickson, and R. D. Heron (1975). "Dimensions of Organizations in Complex Societies: The Educational Sector," *Administrative Science Quarterly* **20**:37–58.

Horvath, D., K. Azumi, D. J. Hickson, and C. J. McMillan (1974). "The Cultural Context of Organizational Control: An International Comparison," *International Studies of Management and Organization* **15**:318–329.

Inkson, J. H. K., D. J. Hickson, and D. S. Pugh (1968). "Administrative Reduction of Variance in Organization and Behaviour: A Comparative Study," paper presented to the Annual Conference of the *British Psychological Society.* Reprinted in Pugh and Payne, 1977.

Inkson, J. H. K., D. S. Pugh, and D. J. Hickson (1970). "Organization Context and Structure: An Abbreviated Replication," *Administrative Science Quarterly* **15**:318–329.

Katz, D., and R. L. Kahn (1966). *The Social Psychology of Organizations,* New York: Wiley.

Levy, P., and D. S. Pugh (1969). "Scaling and Multivariate Analysis in the Study of Organizational Variables," *Sociology* **3**:193–213.

Mansfield, R. (1973). "Bureaucracy and Centralization: An Examination of Organizational Structure," *Administrative Science Quarterly* **18**:477–488.

Mindlin, S. E., and H. E. Aldrich (1975). "Interorganizational Dependence: A Review of the Aston Group," *Administrative Science Quarterly* **20**:382–392.

Payne, R. L. (1978). "Epistemology and the Study of Stress at Work," in C. L. Cooper and R. L. Payne, Eds., *Stress at Work,* New York: Wiley.

Payne, R. L., and D. S. Pugh (1976). "Organizational Structure and Climate," in M. Dunnette, Ed., *Handbook of Organizational Psychology,* Chicago: Rand McNally.

Pheysey, D. C., R. L. Payne, and D. S. Pugh (1971). "Influence of Structure at Organizational and Group Levels," *Administrative Science Quarterly* **16**:61–73.

Pondy, L. R., and I. I. Mitroff (1979). "Beyond Open System Models of Organization," in B. M. Staw, Ed., *Research in Organizational Behavior,* Vol. I, Greenwich, CT: JAI Press.

Pugh, D. S. (1976). "The 'Aston' Approach to the Study of Organizations," in Geert Hofstede and M. Sami Kassem, Eds., *European Contributions to Organization Theory,* Amsterdam: Van Gorcum.

Pugh, D. S., L. Donaldson, and P. Silver (1976). "A Comparative Study of Processes of Organisational Decision-Making: A Preliminary Report," London Business School Working Paper.

Pugh, D. S., and D. J. Hickson (1972). "Causal Inference in the Aston Studies," *Administrative Science Quarterly* **17**:273–275.

Pugh, D. S., and D. J. Hickson (1976). *Organizational Structure in Its Context: The Aston Programme I*, Farnborough, England: Saxon House/Lexington Books.

Pugh, D. S., D. J. Hickson, C. R. Hinings, K. M. Macdonald, C. Turner, and T. Lupton (1963). "A Conceptual Scheme for Organizational Analysis," *Administrative Science Quarterly* **8**:289–315.

Pugh, D. S., D. J. Hickson, C. R. Hinings, and C. Turner (1968). "Dimensions of Organization Structure," *Administrative Science Quarterly* **13**:65–105.

Pugh, D. S., D. J. Hickson, C. R. Hinings, and C. Turner (1969a). "The Context of Organization Structures," *Administrative Science Quarterly* **14**:91–114.

Pugh, D. S., D. J. Hickson, C. R. Hinings, and C. Turner (1969b). "An Empirical Taxonomy of Structures of Work Organization," *Administrative Science Quarterly* **14**:115–126.

Pugh, D. S., and C. R. Hinings (1976). *Organizational Structure: Extensions and Replications, The Aston Programme II*, Farnborough, England: Saxon House/Lexington Books.

Pugh, D. S., R. Mansfield, and M. Warner (1975). *Research in Organizational Behavior: A British Survey*, London: Heinemann.

Pugh, D. S., and R. J. Payne (1977). *Organizational Behaviour in its Context: The Aston Programme III*, Farnborough, England: Saxon House/Lexington Books.

Strauss, G. (1976). "Organization Development," in R. Dubin, Ed., *Handbook of Work, Organization and Society*, Chicago: Rand McNally.

Tauber, I. (1968). "A Yardstick of Hospital Organization," diploma thesis, University of Aston, Birmingham. See also Pugh and Hinings, 1976.

Walton, E. (1978). "An Empirical Investigation of Organizational Structure: The Relationships between Formal Structure and its Description by Members," unpublished Ph.D. dissertation, University of London.

Weick, K. (1979). *The Social Psychology of Organizing*, 2nd ed., Reading, MA: Addison-Wesley.

A TRIP TO VIEW THE ELEPHANTS AND RATTLESNAKES IN THE GARDEN OF ASTON

WILLIAM H. STARBUCK
University of Wisconsin-Milwaukee

Writing this critique was very difficult for me because I was caught between my love and admiration for the Aston researchers and my dislike for the type of research they did. Looking for guidance in this situation, I turned to a British philosopher of the Victorian period, Charles Lutwidge Dodgson. Dodgson was a professor of mathematics, but he is far better known for his philosophical poetry than he is for his mathematics. Professor Dodgson showed that he understood situations like mine when, in 1890, he published this verse:

> He thought he saw an Elephant
> That practised on a fife:
> He looked again, and found it was
> A letter from his wife.
> "At length I realise," he said,
> "The bitterness of Life!"

Several more verses from this poem express the feelings of sections of my critique.*

That I was asked to comment on the Aston studies should tell you a great deal about Derek Pugh, for he chose me. Derek knows that I once spoke enthusiastic praise of the Aston studies, that I subsequently lost this enthusiasm and now oppose this type of research. My esteem for Derek remains very high. One reason he elicits admiration is that he upholds the highest standards of inquiry: he encourages honest debates about ideas, and he does not mistake disagreement with his ideas for disrespect for himself. Indeed Derek has been one of the most perceptive critics of his own work. I am proud to call him friend.

The Aston studies comprise one of the most important clusters of organizational research during the last 20 years—possibly the most important cluster. The participants amount to a Who's Who of British organization theory: John Child, Lex Donaldson, David Hickson, Bob

*This critique was improved by reactions and suggestions offered by Mel Blumberg, Bill Joyce, Alan Meyer, Roy Payne, Derek Pugh, and Andy Van de Ven. I thank them.

Hinings, Kerr Inkson, Gloria Lee, Tom Lupton, Keith Macdonald, Theo Nichols, Roger Mansfield, Roy Payne, Diana Pheysey, Derek Pugh, Rodney Schneck, Christopher Turner, and Malcolm Warner. From the viewpoint of formal methodology, the Aston studies were better designed than any of their predecessors; the data were analyzed intelligently; and the researchers gave their findings sophisticated and unpretentious interpretations. Most of the research reports point out the studies' deficiencies or limitations, which Derek summarized on pages 161 to 163 of this chapter.

That Derek criticized his own work is fortunate for me: I would not want to anger so many influential people and friends by pointing out faults that they themselves did not see. Many of the Aston participants invested several years in these studies, and their reputations are inextricably bound to them. I count three of the Aston participants among my closest friends, and I like and respect several others. Moreover, since I was an early and sincere admirer of these studies, it would be hypocritical to imply that the Aston researchers might or should have predicted what I failed to predict.

It is also fortunate that the Aston studies were so carefully designed and so intelligently interpreted by such excellent researchers. The studies failed to find the kinds of phenomena they were intended to find. If the studies had been conducted poorly, one might wonder whether this failure resulted from errors, insensitivity, or incompetence. As it is, one can take the Aston studies as an ideal realization of a particular type of research, and then talk about what is wrong with this type of research. But first I had better explain the sense in which the Aston studies failed, and the concept of failure on which this judgment is based.

Adding up Confusion to get Ambiguity

> He thought he saw a Rattlesnake
> That questioned him in Greek:
> He looked again, and found it was
> The Middle of Next Week.
> "The one thing I regret," he said,
> "Is that it cannot speak!"

A critic of the Aston studies faces a mushy obstacle: it is not clear what the Aston studies are. They have this name because the key participants worked together at the University of Aston, where some were teachers and others students. With the brilliant leadership of Hickson and Pugh, this group jointly conceived a large-scale project, obtained a grant from the Social Science Research Council, and collected data on 52 organizations. Later these data were augmented by observations of 40 organizations and of nine organizations. When I speak of the Aston studies, I mean the initial analyses of those data by people at the University of Aston. The last of the original Aston studies were published in 1972.

But Derek Pugh does not use this definition. He sees the original Aston studies as the first steps in several endless chains of studies. His summary in this book includes work done at the Universities of Birmingham, Bradford, and Umeå, at London Business School, and in Japan by a professor from Rutgers University. Derek refers to statistics that have never been published, and he includes work by researchers who have never been associated with the University of Aston, work by researchers who have never collaborated with Hickson or Pugh, and even work that Derek himself undertook in order to complement the deficiencies he saw in the original Aston studies. One disadvantage of Derek's definition is that a criticism of the Aston studies involves the entire careers of many people.

The ambiguity of the Aston studies extends to the diverse portrayals of the studies' goals and methods. In some reports, the Aston researchers have said that their goal was to study relationships among variables, whereas in other reports they have said that their goal was to develop "reliable and valid comparative measures of stable, meaningful characteristics" (Pugh and Hickson, 1972; Pugh et al., 1969). When their project began, they said they intended to interrelate three levels of analysis: organizational structure and functioning, group composition and interaction, and individual personality and behavior; but out of perhaps 50 articles, only two address group composition and interaction, and it is debatable whether any deal with individual personality and behavior. In several reports, the Aston researchers have said their goal was to take organization theory beyond the limitations of case studies, but both of their studies of groups and their best study of organizational climate are case studies of three "organizations" (Payne and Pheysey, 1971a, 1971b; Pheysey, Payne, and Pugh, 1971). The Aston researchers have always portrayed their work as being concerned with organizations, but many of their "organizations" were actually organizational subunits such as branches and subsidiaries. Generally they have said they intended to study each organization at just one time; they gave no indication that they saw, in the early 1960s, a need to make longitudinal observations, and they never made longitudinal observations. However, Inkson, Pugh, and Hickson (1970) did go back to 14 organizations that had been observed earlier and obtained second observations.

Are the Variables Stable and Meaningful?   That 1970 study by Inkson, Pugh, and Hickson is very important because Pugh and Hickson (1972) have stated that the primary motive behind their research was their desire to measure, reliably and validly, the stable and meaningful characteristics of organizations. This seems a strange motive: since organizations are dynamic, I cannot imagine either why they wanted to observe stability or why they expected to observe it. They have not explained what kinds of measurements they would judge to be unreliable or to indicate instability. It is also strange that they have paid so little attention to their data on changes over time: Inkson, Pugh, and Hickson devoted only five paragraphs to these data. Yet this 1970 study is the only published study in which they observed any organizations more than once. Consequently, these data are the only evidence they have published about the reliability or stability of their variables. With only two observations made several years apart, however, there is no basis for distinguishing reliability from stability.

Table 4-7 gives a few statistics calculated from their data. These afford conclusive evidence that the Aston variables change over time: either these measures are not reliable, or organizations are not stable.

Most of the Aston variables also lack validity and meaning. Indeed it was my inability to make sense of these variables that first undermined my enthusiasm for the Aston studies.

The Aston researchers started out by creating many numerical scales and binary items that measure organizational characteristics. One can voice only mild disagreements with these basic scales and items; nearly all of them make sense, and some could be quite useful. For example, the Aston researchers identified 11 ways in which organizations record activities—including inspection records, time cards, and cash vouchers; they scored each organization from zero to 11 on "recording of role performance," depending on how many of these records the senior managers reported using.

At this level, the main deficiency of the Aston measures is that the data about contexts and structures were gathered mainly by interviewing senior managers. The 1962–1964 interviews were conducted with chief executives and department heads, and the 1967–1968 interviews were conducted with just one executive from each organization, usually the chief executive. Thus, these data represent managerial perceptions, and the numerical measures create a false impression of objectivity and concreteness. The measures may well be invalid in two senses. First, managers have different perceptions from other stakeholders: first-line workers see their organizations differently from their bosses; customers and suppliers have different viewpoints from organizational members; members of subunits focus on different phenomena than do members of headquarters units. Second, perceptions often deviate significantly from objectively measured phenomena (Downey, Hellriegel, and Slocum, 1975; Payne and Pugh, 1976; Tosi, Aldag, and Storey, 1973).

However, most organization theorists were less conscious of perceptual biases and perceptual diversity during the early 1960s than we are today. And the Aston data had more validity than many other data that were gathered during the 1960s. Most other studies asked organizational members for broad, Gestalt perceptions, whereas the Aston researchers asked

Table 4-7 Reliability and Stability of Five Aston Variables[a]

Variables	Numbers of Organizations Out of 14 in Which These Variables Had Different Values in 1967–1968 Than in 1962–1964	The Percentage Increases Which Would Equal the Root-Mean-Squares of, $\text{Log}\left(\dfrac{\text{Observation in 1967–1968}}{\text{Observation in 1962–1964}}\right)$	The Percentage Increases Which Would Equal The Mean-Absolute Value of, $\text{Log}\left(\dfrac{\text{Observation in 1967–1968}}{\text{Observation in 1962–1964}}\right)$
Size (employment)	14	26.7%	18.3%
Workflow integration	8	15.4%	10.8%
Dependence	7	30.0%	18.0%
Structuring of activities	13	28.4%	19.8%
Concentration of authority[b]	12	724.8%	352.4%

[a]Changes are measured with logarithms on the premise that they have lognormal distributions: for small changes, this means that percentage changes are normally distributed. The root-mean-square is analogous to a standard deviation, but it measures the deviations from no change, not the deviations from average change.

[b]Where concentration of authority was measured as zero, it has been treated as being .1.

171

managers whether they perceived specific phenomena: does someone work full-time recording financial transactions? or how often are workers' activities recorded?

Do Different Labels Really Signify Different Contents? The Aston researchers aggregated their basic scales twice. The first aggregation created variables that they labeled role specialization, standardization, formalization, and so on. For example, role specialization sums the scores on 15 scales, and standardization sums the scores on 68 scales, some of which are binary. When I contemplate these aggregate variables, I begin to wonder whether I understand what the variables denote.

I can illustrate my doubts in terms of the major finding of the Aston studies: that specialization, standardization, and formalization are strongly associated. Table 4-8 lists the correlations that have been reported. Functional specialization, role specialization, and standardization are highly intercorrelated, and formalization correlates highly with standardization; these correlations have been replicated by studies of different kinds of organizations. Ostensibly, this shows that four distinct characteristics of organizations go together.

But the distinctions among these four variables begin to blur when one looks beneath their labels and compares their constituents. The Aston measure of functional specialization seems to be merely an alternative way of aggregating the role-specialization scales. Each role-specialization scale counts the number of distinct jobs in a single functional specialty, such as accounting or sales; and role specialization sums these job counts across 15 functional specialties. The specialties are mainly administrative ones; the Aston researchers excluded from their specialties lathe operators, welders, carpenters, surgeons, teachers, telephone operators, receptionists, and (surprisingly) secretaries and typists. Suppose that each role-specialization scale is transformed into a binary scale: zero if no one performs a particular role, unity if one person or more performs it. Evidently, the sum of these transformed scales would be functional specialization, with just one exception: functional specialization encompasses a possible legal specialty, whereas role specializaton does not. Thus the two aggregates have to be positively correlated. High correlations, as reported by the Aston studies, basically say that the observed organizations possessed different numbers of these 15 specialties; some have none or few of them, others have most or all of them. One could obtain lower correlations by observing organizations that are more homogeneous in the sense that they have approximately equal numbers of specialties.

Standardization constitutes a similar case, for the basic standardization scales and items readily classify into 14 of the functional specialties, and many of these scales would take the value zero if no one performs these functions. For instance, if there is no inspection, all five of the standardization scales concerning inspection would equal zero; and con-

Table 4-8 Correlations among Specialization, Standardization, and Formalization

	Across 46 Diverse Organizations Observed by the Aston Researchers	Across 82 Business Firms Observed by Child	Across 9 Manufacturing Firms Observed by Hinings and Lee	Across 6 Unions and 1 Professional Association Observed by Donaldson and Warner	Across 23 Small Colleges Observed by Holdaway and Colleagues
Functioral specialization versus:					
Role specialization	.87	.87	.86	NM[a]	NM
Standardization	.76	.78	.98	.92	NM
Formalization	.57	.69	.86	.52	.26
Role specialization versus:					
Standardization	.80	.83	.90	NM	NM
Formalization	.68	.72	.91	NM	NM
Standardization versus:					
Formalization	.83	.87	.85	.74	NM

[a]NM denotes that a variable was not measured. Donaldson and Warner did not measure role specialization. Holdaway and colleagues did not measure role specialization or overall standardization.

173

versely, if these inspection scales all equal zero, no one specializes in inspection.

Table 4-9 classifies the standardization scales and items by functional specialties and by the kinds of phenomena these data report. Over half of the data merely observe whether various activities occur, without considering whether these activities follow standardized procedures. More than a quarter of the data report the existence of documents that could be produced through unstandardized activities; indeed many of these items also appear in the formalization scales. Another 16 percent of the data say that standardized procedures have been spelled out, but not that these procedures are followed. Only 3 percent of the data indicate that people adhere to standardized procedures.

All of the items measuring formalization indicate the existence of written documents, so formalization is an overly general label. In fact, John Child sometimes called this variable "documentation."

Can One Make Sense of Relations between Heterogeneous Agglomerations? The Aston researchers aggregated a second time to create macro variables. For example, they fabricated structuring of activities by adding up functional specialization, role specialization, standardization, and formalization. In view of the overlaps among these four variables, adding them makes some sense, but information is lost by adding the aggregates rather than the constituents. The contents of the constituent items imply that one should create at least two aggregate variables, specialization and documentation, by reallocating the standardization items. Whether specialization would correlate with documentation depends on: (1) the kinds of organizations observed, and (2) whether specialization emphasizes paperwork activities. The Aston specialties give great importance to paperwork.

Structuring of activities is a bad example, however, because it is a macro variable I can understand. Several other macro variables appear to be confusing hodgepodges. For instance, charter, dependence, and workflow integration all incorporate measures of lot sizes and product standardization; both charter and dependence take account of relations with customers; structuring of activities, concentration of authority, and line control of workflow all reflect personnel-management activities and documents. Confusion is bolstered by the Aston researchers' practice of including variables representing different levels of aggregation in a single calculation or table, and by the heterogeneity of the "organizations" they observed (Donaldson, Child, and Aldrich, 1975).

After several well-intentioned efforts to interpret correlations among the macro variables, I concluded in frustration that the correlations make little sense to me because the macro variables themselves lack meaning and validity. In order to interpret a correlation between two macro variables, I have to decompose the variables into their constituents. When

Table 4-9 Phenomena Observed in the Standardization Items

Functional Specialties	Equivalent Numbers of Binary Items				
	Existence of Activities	Existence of Documents	Existence of Standardized Procedures	Adherence to Standardized Procedures	Subtotals for Functional Specialties
Public relations	3	0	0	0	3
Sales and service	0	7	0	0	7
Transportation	0	0	0	0	0
Employment	9	10	12	0	31
Training	9	0	0	0	9
Welfare and security	8	5	2	2	17
Buying and stock control	10	1	4	0	15
Maintenance	2	0	2	0	4
Accounting, financial control	11	2	0	1	14
Workflow control	5	7	0	0	12
Inspection	12	0	1	0	13
Working methods	10	2	0	0	12
New products and processes	3	3	2	2	10
Administrative methods	0	3	2	0	5
Legal services	0	0	0	0	0
Market research	2	2	0	0	4
Column totals	84	42	25	5	156
Percentages	54	27	16	3	

I do this, (a) each macro variable appears to incorporate disparate items and scales, and (b) both macro variables include some identical or very similar items. Sometimes the stimulus correlation seems to have made a trivial point, and other times the stimulus correlation seems to have been a resultant of conflicting relationships. Almost always I end up with a different interpretation from the one I made originally when considering only the names of the macro variables.

For example, three studies have reported moderately large correlations between dependence and concentration of authority: .66 by Pugh and colleagues (1969); .66 by Inkson, Pugh, and Hickson (1970); and .68 by Hinings and Lee (1971). In the preceding section of this chapter, Derek states: "Dependence predicted concentration of authority; organizations often concentrated decision-taking authority at the top when they were dependent on or owned by some other organization."

To puzzle out what these words mean is not easy, because different reports have portrayed them differently, and because Inkson, Pugh, and Hickson (1970) used somewhat different measures from the original Aston study. Table 4-10 summarizes the ways the terms have been portrayed in three reports. A plain-language interpretation is: an organization has concentrated authority if it takes orders from a larger, owning organization; a dependent organization is one which constitutes a small branch of a larger, owning organization. Or if one inverts the scales: an organization with diffuse authority does not take orders from a larger, owning organization; and an independent organization is not a branch or subsidiary. Small wonder that these two variables correlate! The wonder is that this correlation has been discussed repeatedly and at length.

Only one study, the original Aston study, has reported on all of the macro variables. Two other studies have reported on most of the macro variables, and three studies have reported on some. Table 4-11 summarizes the reported correlations between the macro variables for context and those for structure. Because several studies could have computed macro variables but did not do so, Table 4-11 also gives correlations for five aggregate scales that constitute components of structuring of activities and concentration of authority.

Just two correlations between the Aston macro variables have been consistently large: (1) the correlation between dependence and concentration of authority, which was discussed just above; and (2) the correlation between size (employment) and structuring of activities. The latter indicates that large organizations use more documents and more full-time specialists than small organizations do; it is unclear whether an organization that is twice as large as another would use twice as many documents or specialists, because the measurements were not designed to support scalar comparisons. Neither correlation makes a surprising or profound point.

Table 4-10 Weights Given to Components When Computing Concentration of Authority and Dependence

	As Described by Pugh and colleagues (1968, 1969)	As Described by Mindlin and Aldrich (1975)	As Described by Inkson, Pugh, and Hickson (1970)
Components of Concentration of Authority			
Centralization[b]	+1	+1	0
Autonomy of the organization[a,b]	+1	−2	−1
Standardization of personnel procedures	+1	0	0
Components of Dependence			
Relative size, percent of owning organization	−1?[c]	−1	+1
Status: principal unit, subsidiary, or branch	−1?	−1	−1
Founded by organization or by person	+1?	0	+1
Owned by government, corporation, or untraded	+1?	0	+1
Representation in policy making	−1?	−1	0
Number of functional specialties contracted out	+1?	+1	0
Vertical integration	+1?	0	0
Recognition of trade unions	?	0	0

[a]Autonomy of the organization is a component of centralization. Various studies have reported that autonomy and centralization correlate from −.42 to −.85.

[b]Reported correlations between dependence and centralization range from .28 to .87. Reported correlations between dependence and autonomy range from −.33 to −.72.

[c]According to Pugh and colleagues, dependence incorporates four of these scales; but they did not say which four.

177

Table 4-11 Correlations among Macro Variables, Size, and Five Components

	Studies Using All of the Aston Macro Variables		Studies Using Most of the Aston Macro Variables	
Researchers	The Aston Researchers	The Aston Researchers	Inkson, Pugh, and Hickson	Hinings and Lee
Types of organizations	Diverse	Manufacturing Firms		Manufacturing Firms
Subunits of organizations	38	23?	26?	9
Autonomous organizations	8	8?	14?	0
Dates of observation	1962 to 1964	1962 to 1964	1967 and 1968	?
Dates of publication	1968 and 1969	1968 and 1969	1970	1971
Size (employment) versus				
Structuring of activities	.69	.77 or .78	.61	.89
Concentration of authority	-.10	-.20	.11	-.33
Line control of workflow	-.15 or .15	.13	NM*	
Workflow integration	.07, .08, or .15	.30	.23	
Dependence	-.17 or -.06		.15	-.6
Components of structuring of activities				
Functional specialization	.67	.75		.84
Standardization	.56	.65	NM	.84
Formalization	.55	.67		.83
Components of concentration of authority				
Lack of autonomy	-.09	-.23	.11	-.10
Centralization	-.39	-.47	NM	-.64
Dependence versus				
Structuring of activities	-.05 or -.04	.04	.17	-.64
Concentration of authority	.66	.63	.66	.68
Line control of workflow	.13		NM	
Workflow integration	-.05		-.31 or .23	
Components of structuring of activities				
Functional specialization		-.22		-.76
Standardization		.12	NM	-.76
Formalization		.09		-.57
Components of concentration of authority				
Lack of autonomy		.68	.66	.52
Centralization		.54	NM	.87
Workflow integration versus				
Structuring of activities	.34	.17	.51	.28
Concentration of authority	-.30	-.01 or .00	-.39	.47
Line control of workflow	-.46	-.05	NM	
Components of structuring of activities				
Functional specialization	.44	.19		.09
Standardization	.46	.19	NM	.00
Formalization	.17	.04		.41
Components of concentration of authority				
Lack of autonomy	-.22	-.02	-.39	.53
Centralization	-.16	-.05	NM	.36

*NM indicates that a variable was not measured in a particular study. A blank space indicates that a relationship has not been

Two more correlations between the macro variables have been consistently small—the correlations of workflow integration with size and with structuring of activities. The remaining eight correlations between macro variables have varied erratically across studies. I find it unrewarding to puzzle over such correlations because the macro variables themselves make so little sense. In this, I may not be alone: according to Table 4-11, the studies published after 1971 collected sufficient data to compute the Aston macro variables, but refrained from using these variables.

Is It Failure Not to Find the Holy Grail? When the Aston studies began I had great hopes for them because they represented a sophisticated

of Macro Variables

Studies Using Dependence or Workflow Integration, But Not the Macro Variables for Structure				Study Using No Macro Variables	
Child Business Firms	Child Manufacturing Firms	Payne and Mansfield Manufacturing Firms	Holdaway and Colleagues Small Colleges	Donaldson and Warner 6 Unions and 1 Professional Association	Ranges of Reported Correlations
3	3?	14	6	0	
79	37?	0	17	7	
1967 to 1969	1967 to 1969	1968	1971	1971 and 1972	
1972 and 1973	1972 and 1973	1973	1975	1974	
					.61 to .89
					.33 to .11
		NM		NM	.15 to .15
.24	.17	.39		NM	.07 to .39
		.35	.31		.6 to .35
.60 or .61	.65	.34	.43	.73	.34 to .84
.63	.76	NM	NM	.82	.56 to .84
.58	.69	.53	.43	.70	.43 to .83
−.18	−.10	−.63	.31	.43	.63 to .31
−.58	−.74	NM	.47	.62	.74 to .47
					.64 to .17
					.63 to .68
		NM		NM	.13
		.20		NM	.31 to .23
		.30	.06		.76 to .30
		NM	NM		.76 to .12
		.40	.37		.57 to .40
		.23	.33		.23 to .68
		NM	.28		.28 to .87
				NM	.17 to .51
				NM	.39 to .47
		NM		NM	.46 to .05
.39 or .41	.19	.68		NM	.09 to .68
.26	.15	NM	NM	NM	.00 to .46
.06 or .10	.12	.36		NM	.04 to .41
.14	.15	.17		NM	.39 to .53
.13	−.10	NM		NM	.16 to .36

reported even though the relevant measurements were made.

search for extremely general characteristics and relationships. Although Hall, Haas, and Johnson (1967b) had fruitlessly analyzed a very heterogeneous sample of organizations, the Aston researchers seemed to be using carefully thought-out methods. If anyone could find propositions that describe all kinds of organizations, these people could.

I still believe this. No one could assemble a better group of organization theorists, elicit greater cooperation from them, or hold them to higher ethical standards. Although hindsight shows that the Aston researchers made methodological mistakes, every research project incorporates methodological mistakes, and I do not think the methodological mistakes in the Aston studies affected the overall pattern of their findings.

But after reading almost all of the reports from these studies and looking carefully at their methods, I cannot point to interesting general propositions that these studies established beyond question. The Aston studies and their close successors do show: (1) that large organizations are usually more bureaucratic than small ones, but not necessarily proportionately so; and (2) that people who work in larger, more bureaucratic organizations espouse different values and describe different perceptions than do people who work in smaller, less bureaucratic organizations, but these differences are small and quite inconsistent (Child, 1973b; Ellis and Child, 1973; Payne and Mansfield, 1973; Payne and Pheysey, 1971a, 1971b; Pheysey, Payne, and Pugh, 1971). However, I believe that organization theorists already knew these things before 1960.

Does this lack of interesting results constitute failure? Of course it does if one takes seriously the hypothesis-testing ideology of classical statistics. This ideology implies that the results of the Aston studies should be evaluated in terms of the researchers' beliefs when they started the studies. What a silly idea that is! I do not believe today what I did in 1960, nor does Derek Pugh, nor do the other Aston researchers. The Aston researchers themselves have raised many of the objections about their work that I have voiced, and their ideas evolved over time. For example Table 4-11 makes it clear that many of the Aston researchers recognized the deficiencies of their macro variables after 1971 or 1972.

The Aston studies failed only in comparison to this one unrealistic criterion. By other, more realistic criteria, the Aston studies produced useful results. The next two sections argue that organization theorists should learn several lessons from the Aston studies, including lessons about research methods, about organizations, and about the behavioral norms of researchers.

Success Is Learning

> He thought he saw a Garden-Door
>   That opened with a key:
> He looked again, and found it was
>   A Double Rule of Three:
> "And all its mystery," he said,
>   "Is clear as day to me!"

Creating Randomness through Systematic Efforts. In simulations of stochastic processes, the computers produce what are called pseudorandom numbers. These numbers look random insofar as they satisfy various tests that random numbers would satisfy, yet the numbers are generated by totally systematic algorithms. Similarly, the Aston researchers proceeded very systematically and logically, yet inconsistent results like those in Table 4-11 look like the outputs of partly random processes.

Why did this happen? I am not sure, but I do have some ideas.

First, the Aston researchers relied on statistical analyses. This can be misleading because statistical analyses are not designed for drawing inferences from the kinds of data researchers ordinarily collect about organizations.

Organizations are complex entities with myriad measurable characteristics. One virtue of the Aston studies is that they measured many, many characteristics of each organization—at least 1000 measurements, perhaps 2000 measurements, not counting the measurements concerning work groups or managerial roles. The more measurements one makes, the better idea one has what any given organization looks like. But myriad measurements suggest myriad statistical calculations and myriad ways to aggregate measurements. When interpreting and choosing statistical calculations and aggregate variables, one encounters three issues: prior beliefs, collinearity, and identifiability.

Prior beliefs have to determine many of the relationships one analyzes. For example, some rough calculations indicate that the Aston researchers had so many opportunities to make decisions about aggregations that the number (one followed by 4000 zeros, give or take several hundred zeros) has no intuitive meaning. They evidently made approximately 5000 of these decisions, clustering their 1000–2000 measurements into about 50 aggregate variables. Although 5000 are quite a lot of decisions, they comprise an infinitesimal fraction of the opportunities for decisions. This infinitesimal fraction was chosen on the basis of prior beliefs. Moreover, $\frac{4}{5}$ of the 5000 decisions were based entirely on prior beliefs; the Aston researchers made only 1000 or so decisions about aggregation on the basis of statistical analyses of their data.

Potential examples of results determined by prior beliefs abound. For one thing, the Aston researchers decided to classify organizational size as a contextual variable instead of a structural one. As a consequence, they found high correlations between size and structuring of activities, and a high multiple correlation between structuring of activities and a linear combination of contextual variables (a combination of size and workflow integration). A similar example would be their decisions to classify dependence and the number of operating sites as contextual variables rather than structural variables: these classifications led to a high multiple correlation between concentration of authority and a linear combination of contextual variables. Pugh and colleagues (1969: 111) concluded that "The predictability of the structural dimensions from contextual elements serves as external validating evidence for the structural concepts themselves." But this validity arises from the researchers' prior beliefs, which determined their classifications of variables as contextual or structural.

Early in their project, Pugh and colleagues (1963: 295–298) observed that previous analysts treated bureaucracy as "a unitary concept," whereas the Aston researchers intended to "isolate the conceptually distinct elements that go into Weber's formulation of bureaucracy. Then the relationships between these elements become a subject for empirical investigation and not for a priori postulation. The insights of Weber can then be translated into a set of empirically testable hypotheses." In their 1968 report, they defined 16 aggregate variables measuring aspects of structure, and subjected the observed intercorrelations between these variables to factor analysis. They extracted four principal components, which they transformed into four orthogonal factors. They said:

> Since these are mutually independent, an organization's structure may display all these characteristics to a pronounced degree, or virtually none at all, or display some but not others. . . . It is demonstrated here that bureaucracy is *not* unitary, but that organizations may be bureaucratic in any of a number of ways (1968: 87–88).

The word demonstrated implies that this conclusion represents an inference from data, but such is not the case: it is solely a statement about the researchers' prior beliefs. In principle, the Aston researchers could have aggregated all of their structural measures into a single macro variable called bureaucratization. But they chose not to do this, deciding instead to aggregate their measures into 16 variables. With 16 variables, they could have extracted only one factor, which they could label bureaucratization. But they chose not to do this, deciding instead to extract four factors. They could have transformed these four factors so that the factors would be intercorrelated (oblique rotation): this would enable them to observe that different aspects of structure are interdependent. But they chose not to do this, deciding instead to create orthogonal factors. They could also have created four factors that shared the explained variance rather equally (varisim rotation), so that one would have to consider all four factors in order to characterize an organization's structure. But they implicitly chose not to do this, deciding instead to create a hierarchical array of factors.

In general, the Aston researchers lacked awareness of the effects of their prior beliefs upon their inferences. From their reports, a reader gets the impression that their studies were inductive ones—that they gathered objective data, used neutral schemata to analyze these data, and discovered previously unknown facts about the world. This impression is quite misleading. It would be equally accurate to say that their studies were deductive ones—that they selected certain phenomena to perceive and label as data, chose analytic schemata that matched their preconceptions, and merely translated their prior beliefs into the professionally legitimated language of data and statistical tests.

In this respect, the Aston researchers typify contemporary organizational research. Nearly all organization theorists understate the effects of their prior beliefs upon their inferences, and the least self-aware researchers seem to be those who claim to gather objective data and who use sophisticated statistical methods. The practical fact is that researchers can only weaken, not escape, the effects of their prior beliefs; and this weakening results from self-awareness and thorough analysis. When researchers rely on prescriptions by methodologists and adopt authorized analytic schemata, they bypass self-awareness and substitute ritual for analysis.

Collinearity means that variables covary, either because of definitional similarities such as the similarities between functional specialization, role specialization, and standardization, or because of empirical regularities such as the correlations of many variables with organizational size. Collinearities make it difficult or impossible to draw reliable inferences about the relative effects of different causes: statistical estimates involving collinear variables may be quite volatile, because changes in correlated variables produce similar effects.

The original Aston study involved very few problems with collinearity, fewer such problems than most organizational research. One reason is that the Aston researchers used contextual variables that generally had small intercorrelations, and another reason is that they aggregated most of the scales and items that were highly intercorrelated. For example, relative size, status, representation in policy making, and specializations contracted out were moderately intercorrelated (between .50 and .68). If two of these appeared simultaneously as independent variables in a single regression calculation, the two regression coefficients would have an arbitrary quality, because increasing the coefficients of either of these variables would produce similar effects. The Aston researchers avoided such ambiguities by combining all four of these variables into one macro variable, dependence.

Nevertheless, one can find collinearity problems in the Aston studies if one looks hard enough. On page 147 of this book, Derek Pugh says:

> Thus all the studies of business organizations show a higher negative correlation between the structuring variables and centralization than did the original study. Child argues on the basis of these results that centralization, scored negatively, should be included in the same cluster as specialization, standardization, and so on, to form a Weberian dimension of bureaucratization, which, he shows, included decentralization. It appears to us that this would be an unfortunate blurring of a useful distinction. For example, it would dilute the very high intercorrelations found between specialization, formalization, and standardization (of the order of 0.7 to 0.9) with a variable that only correlates -0.3 to -0.5 with them.
>
> Underlining the point that Child's view is based on business organizations only, is the finding by Holdaway et al. that in educational institutions centralization correlates quite strongly and *positively* with formalization and standardization, but not specialization.

Derek is quite likely right. However, he is not taking account of the correlations of all these variables with organizational size and with workflow integration. The zero-order correlations are summarized in Table 4-12. The four structural variables correlate moderately strongly with size and weakly but consistently with workflow integration. A multiple correlation computed by Pugh and colleagues (1969) suggests that the structural variables would correlate approximately .75 with linear combinations of size and workflow. Inconsistent correlations of centralization with workflow integration leave doubts, but centralization may correlate about − .6 with a linear combination of size and workflow. Thus, even if there are no direct causal links between centralization and structural variables, one would expect to observe correlations in the vicinity of − .45. The findings of Holdaway and colleagues (1975) might be explained either, as Derek proposes, or by different correlations of centralization with structural variables, or by different correlations of centralization with size and workflow integration.

The foregoing echoes some other debates evoked by the Aston studies. Pugh and colleagues (1969: 112) concluded "that size, dependence, and the charter-technology-location nexus largely determine structure." Howard Aldrich (1972) challenged this conclusion, arguing that size depends on structuring of activities, charter, and workflow integration, and that structuring of activities depends on charter and workflow integration, but not on size. Gordon Hilton (1972) showed that the Aston data are consistent with at least three causal models: one's conclusions depend strongly on one's assumptions. Hickson, Pugh, and Pheysey also challenged their own conclusion indirectly when they said: "operations technology did not relate to structure, or did so only secondarily to other variables" (1969: 395). Don Gerwin (1979a, 1979b) reinforced this latter opinion after he reviewed several studies, including the Aston ones. Gerwin (1979b: 71–72) observed: "The results of organizational level studies indicate that very few consistent relationships exist between structural and technological variables. Further, almost all of these are adversely affected [become inconsistent] when size is controlled."

The general point is that statistical calculations make undependable attributions of effects among possible causes when the causes covary. Organizational variables frequently covary, and organizations incorporate multiple causal paths, so statistical analyses of organizational data draw undependable inferences about cause-effect relations. The inferences are undependable in that they might shift dramatically if analyses start from different prior beliefs or if observations are chosen in ways that alter the intercorrelations between independent variables (Aldrich, 1972; Hilton, 1972).

The third statistical issue is identifiability. A study has identifiability insofar as it gathers enough data and the right kinds of data to support desired statistical inferences. Prior beliefs about causation determine what kinds of data and how many data are necessary. Organizational

Table 4-12 Root-Mean-Square Correlations[a]

	Workflow Integration	Functional Specialization	Role Specialization	Standardization	Formalization	Centralization omitting the observation by Holdaway et al.	Centralization as observed by Holdaway et al.
Size (employment)	.23	.61	.74	.63	.57	−.53	.47
Workflow integration		.44	.38	.33	.19	[b]	[c]
Functional specialization			.87	.80	.62	−.47	.14
Role specialization				.82	.72	−.49	NM
Standardization					.85	−.44	[d]
Formalization						−.45	.62

[a]Squared correlations have been averaged across studies, weighted in proportion to the numbers of organizations observed. The studies are those listed in Table 4-11.
[b]The original Aston study obtained a negative correlation (−.16), whereas Child and Hinings and Lee obtained positive correlations (.13 and .36).
[c]This correlation was not published.
[d]Pugh (1981) mentions that Holdaway et al. observed a large correlation between centralization and standardization. Holdaway et al. did not measure overall standardization, but they did measure standardization of personnel procedures, and they calculated a correlation of .52 between centralization and standardization of personnel procedures. The correlation between overall standardization and standardization of personnel procedures has been observed in three studies to be only .23, .32, and .44; and correlations of these two variables with other variables often have opposite signs.
NM denotes that a variable was not measured.

studies usually confront many identification problems, because sample sizes are small and causal paths multitude. Cross-sectional studies in particular have identification problems arising from two-way causation.

The implications of two-way causation warrant elaboration. Suppose that z actually depends upon x and y while x depends on z and w, as diagrammed in Figure 4-7. Such mutual dependence might arise because changes in x induce immediate changes in z, which gradually feed back and affect x: differences in speeds of reaction would not show up in a cross-sectional study or in a longitudinal study with large time intervals. Mutual dependence might also arise because changes in x and z emerge jointly from episodic interactions such as bargains, reorganizations, or planning exercises. Some algebra shows that one might obtain good fits for z (1) with a function of x and y, (2) with a function of w and y, or (3) with any of an infinite number of functions of x, y, and w. Which function emerges as the best fit from statistical analyses depends on the analytic methods, the criteria for fit, the accuracies of beliefs about functional forms, the sample size, sample variances, whether all relevant variables have been observed, and sheer luck.

Again the Aston studies were superior to the vast majority of organizational research. For one thing, the Aston researchers explicitly acknowledged the importance of two-way causation (Pugh and Hickson, 1972). For another thing, these researchers replicated their original study, and even their original study encompassed 52 organizations; 52 organizations constitute a very large sample in comparison with other organizational studies. One basic rule of thumb is that one can validly draw no more interdependent inferences than the number of observations; 52 inferences are a lot.

But every study has limited identifiability insofar as some causal paths are inaccessible to statistical inference with the data that have been gathered. The Aston researchers used the same 52 observations in several cascaded analyses: they used these observations to decide whether items could be scaled, to decide which scales should go into aggregate variables, to decide which aggregate variables should go into macro variables, and to estimate the correlations among macro variables and aggregate vari-

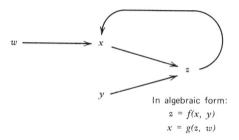

In algebraic form:
$$z = f(x, y)$$
$$x = g(z, w)$$

Figure 4-7   An example of two-way causation.

ables (Pugh and colleagues, 1968, 1969). These analyses were loosely linked, but they generally used up observations. Thus, when one looks at the multiple-regression calculation in which structuring of activities is portrayed as depending on organizational size and workflow integration, one is not seeing three parameters being estimated, but three more parameters; dozens of parameters were estimated in constructing structuring of activities, and dozens more in constructing workflow integration, and at least one parameter was used deciding whether size should be logarithmically transformed. Consequently some of the Aston researchers' calculations concerning the original 52 organizations involved many fewer degrees of freedom than their tables imply, and some of those calculations might have produced results that were grossly distorted by small random errors.

This is where replication comes to the rescue. If the Aston researchers had stopped after their original study, one would have no way of deciding which of their calculations to trust. But replications expanded the Aston samples considerably: Table 4-11 covers 196 organizations. One can draw much stronger conclusions from Table 4-11 than one could draw in 1969 from only the original Aston study. Unfortunately, this gain in conclusiveness was bought at the expense of conceptual progress. The later studies duplicated exactly the measurements of the earlier ones, and so amplified the costs of faulty initial decisions.

The Aston researchers did go beyond the limits of identifiability when they drew causal inferences. Their ambivalence about causal inferences is one striking characteristic of their reports (Aldrich, 1972: 27). On one hand, they talked about two-way causation and said that cross-sectional studies do not justify causal inferences. And on the other hand, they made inferences such as these:

> The second major gain from establishing dimensions is that it makes possible a multivariate approach to causality. If similar scales can be developed for aspects of an organization's context, then the relationships between dimensions of context and dimensions of structure can be examined using correlational and multivariate techniques. This obviates the need to select a particular aspect of context *a priori* as the determining variable for structure (Pugh and colleagues, 1968: 89, 91).

> It is tempting to argue that these clear relationships are causal. . . . It can be hypothesized that size causes structuring through its effect on intervening variables. . . . Dependence causes concentration of authority. . . . Integrated technology may be hypothesized to cause an organization to move towards the impersonal control end. . . . The causal argument need not run only one way. It can be suggested that a policy of specializing roles and standardizing procedures, that is, of structuring, would require more people, that is, growth in size. Concentration of decisions in the hands of an owning group is likely to result in . . . more dependence; while the production control, inspection, and work-study procedures of staff control might raise the level of workflow integration in the technology. But a cross-sectional study

such as this can only establish relationships. Causes should be inferred from a theory . . . about changes over time (Pugh and colleagues, 1969: 112).

With these measures, the sweeping "technological imperative" hypothesis on organizational level technology and structure is not supported. Broadly speaking, operations technology did not relate to structure, or did so only secondarily to other variables. . . . On these results, a general "technology-causes-structure" hypothesis could only be sustained by the argument that technology also assumes size, and that to operate a given technology, an organization must be of the requisite size. . . . Such a view would not be consistent with the approach taken here (Hickson, Pugh, and Pheysey, 1969: 395).

In many cases, the Aston researchers could have made strong causal inferences about the relations among their variables without even observing one organization. They had only to look at the scales and items comprising the variables. Two variables incorporating very similar items are causally related in the most direct way, as are two variables incorporating items dealing with associated phenomena, such as product standardization, lot sizes, personnel management, or documents (McKelvey, 1975).

Let me reiterate that the Aston studies are not unusual in raising issues like these. All organizational research confronts such issues, and the Aston researchers dealt with collinearity and identifiability far better than most organization theorists have. The issues remain quite intractable even against the efforts of a large, integrated team of excellent researchers. If anyone could draw reliable inferences while depending strongly on statistical analyses, these people could.

To deal more effectively with these issues, organization theorists should: (1) recognize the strong influences of their prior beliefs on their inferences, (2) analyze the causal relations among their variables before they gather any data, (3) recognize that statistical analyses afford undependable bases for inferences, (4) use simultaneous-equations methods for statistical analyses, and (5) collect genuinely longitudinal data at frequent intervals. However, the issues will still be there. For example, simultaneous-equations analyses state that some questions simply cannot be answered reliably.

Comparing Cross-sectional and Longitudinal Changes.   The Aston researchers have been quite conscientious about one kind of extrapolation from their studies: they have avoided drawing inferences about the development of one organization over time. For example, Pugh, Hickson, and Hinings (1969) proposed a developmental theory, not about changes in one organization but about changes in the entire population of organizations. Since they had no data on changes over time, they assumed that the average size of organizations increases over time and that size dominates technology, dependence, and so on.

Other organization theorists would do well to emulate the restraint of the Aston researchers in this regard. All too often, organization theorists have manufactured artificial developmental patterns from cross-sectional studies (Aldrich, 1972; Blau, 1970; Blau and Schoenherr, 1971; Child, 1973a). As a consequence, much of what organization theorists claim to know about organizational growth and development is pure fiction.

To some extent, even the concepts of organizational growth and development are fictional. Figure 4-8 shows some survival statistics for American corporations and governmental agencies: very few organizations survive long enough to change dramatically in size or structure. Only 9 percent of corporations and 15 percent of governmental agencies survive longer than 20 years (Starbuck and Nystrom, 1981). The small organization that grows to middle size is rare, as is the middle-sized organization that grows large. Most middle-sized organizations and many large organizations are quite young. Moreover, among organizations with more than 100 members, larger organizations do not survive noticeably longer. Older organizations do have higher probabilities of survival, but most of the increases in survival probabilities occur during the first 20 years of existence. Among the corporations and governmental agencies that are now 50 years old, which comprise just 3 percent of those created 50 years ago, approximately 85 percent will survive five years or more.

Insofar as developmental changes do occur, they are likely to deviate considerably from cross-sectional patterns (Freeman and Hannan, 1975; Holdaway and Blowers, 1971; Hummon, Doreian, and Teuter, 1975). Table 4-13 compares the correlations obtained by the Aston researchers with the correlations they would have gotten by correlating the changes in variables: seven of the ten correlations have inconsistent signs.

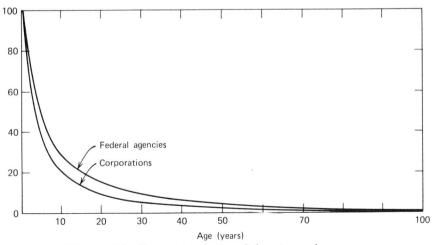

Figure 4-8 Percentages surviving to various ages.

Table 4-13 Correlations across Organizations as Functions of the Variables Observed and the Organizations Observed

	Correlations among Variables		Correlations among Logarithmic Changes in Variables between Two Times of Observation[a]		
	46 Organizations Observed 1962–1964	40 Organizations Observed 1967–1968	14 Organizations Observed 1962–1964 and also 1967–1968	3 Organizations that Grew and Gained More Autonomy	6 Organizations that Shrank and Gained More Autonomy
Structuring of activities versus:					
Size	.69	.61	–.39	.99	–.51
Workflow integration	.34	.51	.00	–.50	.27
Dependence	–.05 or –.04	.17	–.24	–.61	.43
Concentration of authority	–.16	–.24	–.37	–.57	–.17
Concentration of authority versus:					
Size	–.10	.11	.15	–.43	.77
Workflow integration	–.30	–.39	–.20	–.42	–.76
Dependence	.66	.66	.39	–.30	.44
Dependence versus:					
Size	–.17 or –.06	.15	–.28	–.73	.36
Workflow integration	–.05	.23	–.09	.99	–.21
Workflow integration versus size	.07, .08, or .15	.23	–.31	–.64	–.83

[a]The logarithmic changes are Log $\left(\dfrac{\text{Observation in 1967–1968}}{\text{Observation in 1962–1964}}\right)$; they resemble percentage changes.

190

Of course, one would need many more observations than two in order to sort out the effects of time.

Giving up Searching for the Holy Grail.   Suppose one were to study the relations between structure and technology across animals. One could define measures of structure such as the number of animals in a communal unit (pride, herd, hive, band, tribe, or city), the number of specialized roles (hunting, guarding, egg laying, nursing, wizardry, or teaching), and centralization of leadership (autocratic, polycentric, or dispersed and amorphous). One could also define measures of technology such as speed of movement, diet (herbivore, carnivore, or omnivore), use of tools (none, sticks and leaves, axes and knives, or airplanes and computers), and means of communication (alarm signals, singing, dancing, speech). Then one could go out and observe all kinds of animals; one would have to use stratified sampling to observe animals other than insects. The correlations one could compute would have great generality, since they would describe every animal on earth.

But these general correlations might say almost nothing about any animal. The measures chosen to characterize all animals might be quite uninformative when applied to a single species, say lions or ants, and might be completely irrelevant to a single communal unit such as a hive or a tribe. If variables assume different meanings at different levels of aggregation, the relations among variables will also differ. But relations among variables may be different at different levels of aggregation even if variables have similar meanings—as would the number of animals in a communal unit or the speed of movement.

The foregoing analogy says a great deal about the Aston studies, for the Aston studies set out to encompass all kinds of organizations except very small ones. All of the organizations employed more than 250 people in 1962–1964, although at least one shrank to 159 employees by 1967–1968. Otherwise, the 52 organizations included manufacturing entities, service entities, distribution entities, business firms, governmental agencies engaged in people processing and public services, internal departments from both governments and business firms, branches, subsidiaries, autonomous organizations, proprietorships, corporations, and a cooperative; some covered local territories and others national ones. Not only was this sample intended to represent the full range of work organizations, but so were the measures. According to Pugh and colleagues: "It is the strength and the weakness of this project that no items were used unless they are applicable to *all* work organizations, whatever they did; several possible items of information had to be sacrificed to this end. Since the research strategy was to undertake a wide survey to set the guidelines, the result was superficiality and generality in the data" (1968: 69).

One consequence has been endless debates concerning the interactions between sample characteristics and the meanings of variables (Aldrich,

1972; Child, 1972; Child and Mansfield, 1972; Donaldson, Child, and Aldrich, 1975; Gerwin, 1979b; Greenwood and Hinings, 1976; Holdaway and colleagues, 1975; McKelvey, 1975; Mansfield, 1973; Mindlin and Aldrich, 1975; Pugh, 1981). For example, Aldrich (1972: 28–29) pointed out that workflow integration acted as a surrogate for the dichotomy between service and manufacturing: workflow integration has a different meaning when applied to a mixed sample of service and manufacturing entities than when applied to manufacturing entities alone. One can take Aldrich's argument further, in that workflow integration would have a different meaning when applied to a homogeneous sample of manufacturing entities than when applied to a heterogeneous sample of manufacturing entities.

A second consequence is that the Aston measures contravene some of the original goals of the Aston project. At the outset, the Aston researchers wanted to find ways to distinguish among types of organizations because they intended to relate group composition and interaction to organizational contexts. But the properties that are common to all organizations discriminate poorly among types of organizations, just as the properties that are common to all animals afford poor discrimination among species or genera. One can obtain sharper discriminations among animals by considering properties that some animals do not share, such as breathing air or having wings. By excluding distinctive properties, such as manufacturing versus service, or welding versus surgery, the Aston researchers fabricated a false appearance of homogeneity and added equivocality to their variables. For example, manufacturing entities differ from service entities even if no measures explicitly draw this distinction, and the manufacturing-service distinction muddles the meaning of workflow integration.

Consider the three right-hand columns in Table 4-13: the two subcategories differ strikingly from each other and from the overall sample of 14 organizations. One cannot extrapolate statements about the entire population to homogeneous clusters within the population, just as one cannot extrapolate statements about all animals to one species. Suppose that a relationship is positive for an entire population, as dependence correlates positively with concentration of authority across all 14 organizations. This same relationship might be negative for any single homogeneous cluster, as dependence correlates negatively with concentration of authority across the three organizations that grew and gained more autonomy. More disconcertingly yet, this same relationship might be negative for every single homogeneous cluster (Thorndike, 1939). There is no logical basis for saying that true general statements about all organizations are true statements about some organizations or about any organization.

One realistic way to characterize the Aston studies is to say they set out to study the characteristics that generalize across all organizations, and to find relations among these characteristics. And one realistic way to characterize the results of the Aston studies is to say they show that there are few interesting, strong relations among the completely general characteristics of organizations. The Aston researchers set out to find the Holy Grail, and they came back with a broken teacup.

This is a very important finding. For one thing, when the Aston project began, belief in the Holy Grail was widespread. There were several contemporaneous studies of heterogeneous samples of organizations (Fouraker and Stopford, 1968; Friedlander and Pickle, 1968; Hall, 1962; Hall, Haas, and Johnson, 1967a, 1967b; McNulty, 1962; Pondy, 1969; Udy, 1970). Organization theorists often spoke of "the organization" when they meant some insurance companies, or many schools, or even a small group of strangers in a laboratory. In fact, reports have been published in which a reader finds it difficult or impossible to identify the kinds of organizations studied. Many reports create the impression that inferences drawn from data about, say, welfare agencies or hospitals ought to generalize to all organizations; and several heroic theories purport to describe "the organization." But it takes more than a uniform term to produce uniformity.

For another thing, the lack of interesting, strong relations reflects the interrelations among organizations. All kinds of organizations exist, and they perform quite diverse functions. In fact, most organizations have characteristics that compensate for the characteristics of other organizations. Small job shops serve customers who would not be satisfied with the standardized outputs from large bureaucracies; governmental agencies provide services in which there is no profit; professional associations counteract some of the demands made by employers (Schriesheim and colleagues, 1977; Starbuck and Dutton, 1973). Furthermore, organizational survival depends on comparative criteria: an organization must have comparative advantages in order to persist, and an organization that looks like other organizations lacks comparative advantages. Thus, to some extent, the completely general characteristics of organizations are the characteristics that cause organizations to fail. Of course, one of the truly general characteristics of organizations is that the overwhelming majority have short lives.

Finally, the lack of interesting, strong relations suggests that organizational structures may have little to do with organizational behaviors; structures may be only superficial facades in front of behavioral processes. Meyer and Rowan (1977) have argued that structures perform useful services for schools by creating the impression that the schools are conforming to societal expectations, while leaving classroom behaviors autonomous. This idea has some generality. Organizational structures, especially the general characteristics of structures, provide threads of consistency that enable interorganizational flows of information, money, and people. Outsiders think, often erroneously, that they know who should send or receive messages. Lenders assume, usually wrongly, that conventional structures signal responsible management. New personnel believe, but not for long, that their past experiences with people having the same job titles extrapolate to new associates. But that says little about the messages organizations exchange or the skills personnel exhibit. Organizations with similar structures may be plotting mass destruction or humanitarian services, may be extracting teeth or inventing machines, may be going bankrupt or raking in large profits.

Criticizing and Learning from One's Own Research

> He thought he saw an Argument
> That proved he was the Pope:
> He looked again, and found it was
> A Bar of Mottled Soap.
> "A fact so dread," he faintly said,
> "Extinguishes all hope!"

Most of my criticisms of the Aston studies should not surprise Derek Pugh, for he has astutely criticized his own work and has consistently sought to improve what he does. For instance, by contrasting the so-called National study (Child, 1972) with the original Aston study, one can draw some inferences about Derek's own skepticism at the time he designed the National study. The Aston study surveyed all kinds of organizations including governmental agencies, whereas the National study concentrated solely on business firms in six industries. Only 17 percent of the entities in the Aston study were autonomous organizations, whereas 96 percent of the entities in the National study were autonomous organizations. The National study covered many more organizations than the Aston study. Also, as his report in this book indicates, Derek later undertook longitudinal case studies of decision processes in three organizations.

Indeed, other organization theorists ought to take the Aston researchers as an ethical prototype. Derek may be unusual, but he is not alone. Two outstanding characteristics of the Aston researchers have been their openness to criticism and their willingnes to attempt replications. Both testify that the Aston researchers are not mere opportunists seeking publications in academic journals and that they try not to become personally committed to specific empirical findings. It makes no sense to replicate unless one remains skeptical about what one has already observed. And replications invite criticism: critics with doubts about some initial data do not themselves have to go out and gather additional data.

One of the few domains in which the Aston researchers have shown rigidity is their adherence to the original items, scales, and aggregate variables such as standardization or formalization. The aggregate variables surely could have been improved, and experimental items could have been added to each study in order to test earlier conclusions.

The ethical standards of the Aston researchers appear even more impressive when one allows for the size of their project. Big projects involving many people elicit commitments to the projects' substantive outputs that are independent of the outputs' qualities; and investments of time and effort, struggles to get the projects funded and organized, career implications, or social relations among project staff can exert stronger influences than any intrinsic properties of the substantive outputs (Starbuck, 1975). Although one can see a few of these liabilities of large projects in the Aston studies, the liabilities are remarkably weak.

The Aston studies do illustrate one of their major findings: large organizations produce numerous documents. Table 4-14 summarizes other impressions of the Aston studies. If we pursue the virtues of these studies and avoid their vices, we will ask better questions and use better methods of answering them. But Table 4-14 implies that this is difficult; virtues and vices tend to go together in complementary pairs. We shall be doing well indeed if our answers are as perceptive as those offered by Professor Dodgson when he was masquerading as Lewis Carroll.

Table 4-14   The Virtues and Vices of the Aston Studies

Virtues	Vices
A large team of researchers	Group cohesion
Sincerity, idealism	A large investment in one project
Self-criticism	A project without an end
Replication	Many analyses based on a few initial decisions
Broad perspectives	Amorphous goals
Careful design of measures	Commitments to measures
Careful choices of analytic techniques	Commitments to results of analyses
Measures focus on concrete phenomena	Data obtained from senior managers
Many measures	Aggregation into macro variables
	Measures consider only completely general characteristics
Many organizations	Heterogeneous sample of organizations
	Static, cross-sectional study
Focus on inferences from data	Little consciousness of prior beliefs
	Identification problems because not enough organizations
A few high correlations	Correlations due to definitional relations among variables
Many small or inconsistent correlations	Disappointment? Rationalization?
Awareness of two-way causation	Some unjustified causal inferences
Unpretentious inferences	Unrealistically simple analytic techniques

REFERENCES

Aldrich, H. E. (1972). "Technology and Organizational Structure: A Reexamination of the Findings of the Aston Group," *Administrative Science Quarterly* **17:**16–43.

Blau, P. M. (1970). "A Formal Theory of Differentiation in Organizations," *American Sociological Review* **35:**201–218.

Blau, P. M., and R. A. Schoenherr (1971). *The Structure of Organizations,* New York: Basic Books.

Carroll, L. (Charles Lutwidge Dodgson) (1890). "The Mad Gardener's Song," from *Sylvie and Bruno,* London: Macmillan, Chapters 5 through 12.

Child, J. (1972). "Organization Structure and Strategies of Control: A Replication of the Aston Study," *Administrative Science Quarterly* **17:**163–177.

Child, J. (1973a). "Predicting and Understanding Organization Structure," *Administrative Science Quarterly* **18:**168–185.

Child, J. (1973b). "Strategies of Control and Organizational Behavior," *Administrative Science Quarterly* **18:**1–17.

Child, J., and R. Mansfield (1972). "Technology, Size, and Organization Structure," *Sociology* **6:**369–393.

Donaldson, L., J. Child, and H. E. Aldrich (1975). "The Aston Findings on Centralization: Further Discussion," *Administrative Science Quarterly* **20:**453–460.

Donaldson, L., and M. Warner (1974). "Structure of Organizations in Occupational Interest Associations," *Human Relations* **27:**721–738.

Downey, H. K., D. Hellriegel, and J. W. Slocum, Jr. (1975). "Environmental Uncertainty: The Construct and Its Application," *Administrative Science Quarterly* **20:**613–629.

Ellis, T., and J. Child (1973). "Placing Stereotypes of the Manager into Perspective," *Journal of Management Studies* **10:**233–255.

Fouraker, L. E., and J. M. Stopford (1968). "Organizational Structure and the Multinational Strategy," *Administrative Science Quarterly* **13:**47–64.

Freeman, J. H., and M. T. Hannan (1975). "Growth and Decline Processes in Organizations," *American Sociological Review* **40:**215–228.

Friedlander, F., and H. Pickle (1968). "Components of Effectiveness in Small Organizations," *Administrative Science Quarterly* **13:**289–304.

Gerwin, D. (1979a). "The Comparative Analysis of Structure and Technology: A Critical Appraisal," *Academy of Management Review* **4:**41–51.

Gerwin, D. (1979b). "Relationships between Structure and Technology at the Organizational and Job Levels," *Journal of Management Studies* **16:**70–79.

Greenwood, R., and C. R. Hinings (1976). "Centralization Revisited," *Administrative Science Quarterly* **21:**151–155.

Hall, R. H. (1962). "Intraorganizational Structural Variation: Application of the Bureaucratic Model," *Administrative Science Quarterly* **7:**295–308.

Hall, R. H., J. E. Haas, and N. J. Johnson (1967a). "An Examination of the Blau-Scott and Etzioni Typologies," *Administrative Science Quarterly* **12:**118–139.

Hall, R. H., J. E. Haas, and N. J. Johnson (1967b). "Organizational Size, Complexity, and Formalization," *American Sociological Review* **32:**903–912.

Hickson, D. J., D. S. Pugh, and D. C. Pheysey (1969). "Operations Technology and Organization Structure: An Empirical Reappraisal," *Administrative Science Quarterly* **14:**378–397.

Hilton, G. (1972). "Causal Inference Analysis: A Seductive Process," *Administrative Science Quarterly* **17:**44–54.

Hinings, C. R., and G. L. Lee (1971). "Dimensions of Organization Structure and Their Context: A Replication," *Sociology* **5**:83–93.

Holdaway, E. A., and T. A. Blowers (1971). "Administrative Ratios and Organization Size: A Longitudinal Examination," *American Sociological Review* **36**:278–286.

Holdaway, E. A., J. F. Newberry, D. J. Hickson, and R. P. Heron (1975). "Dimensions of Organizations in Complex Societies: The Educational Sector," *Administrative Science Quarterly* **20**:37–58.

Hummon, N. P., P. Doreian, and K. Teuter (1975). "A Structural Control Model of Organizational Change," *American Sociological Review* **40**:81–824.

Inkson, J. H. K., D. J. Hickson, and D. S. Pugh (1977). "Administrative Reduction of Variance in Organization and Behaviour: A Comparative Study," in D. S. Pugh and R. L. Payne, Eds., *Organizational Behaviour in Its Context,* Farnborough, England: Saxon House, pp. 14–20.

Inkson, J. H. K., D. S. Pugh, and D. J. Hickson (1970). "Organization Context and Structure: An Abbreviated Replication," *Administrative Science Quarterly* **15**:318–329.

Levy, P., and D. S. Pugh (1969). "Scaling and Multivariate Analyses in the Study of Organizational Variables," *Sociology* **3**:193–213.

McKelvey, W. (1975). "Guidelines for the Empirical Classification of Organizations," *Administrative Science Quarterly* **20**:509–525.

McNulty, J. E. (1962). "Organizational Change in Growing Enterprises," *Administrative Science Quarterly* **7**:1–21.

Mansfield, R. (1973). "Bureaucracy and Centralization: An Examination of Organizational Structure," *Administrative Science Quarterly* **18**:477–488.

Meyer, J. W., and B. Rowan (1977). "Institutionalized Organizations: Formal Structure as Myth and Ceremony," *American Journal of Sociology* **83**:340–363.

Mindlin, S. E., and H. E. Aldrich (1975). "Interorganizational Dependence: A Review of the Concept and a Re-examination of the Findings of the Aston Group," *Administrative Science Quarterly* **20**:382–392.

Payne, R. L., and R. Mansfield (1973). "Relationships of Perceptions of Organizational Climate to Organizational Structure, Context, and Hierarchical Position," *Administrative Science Quarterly* **18**:515–526.

Payne, R. L., and D. C. Pheysey (1971a). "Organization Structure and Sociometric Nominations amongst Line Managers in Three Contrasted Organizations," *European Journal of Social Psychology* **1**:261–284.

Payne, R. L., and D. C. Pheysey (1971b). "G. G. Stern's Organizational Climate Index: A Reconceptualization and Application to Business Organizations," *Organizational Behavior and Human Performance* **6**:77–98.

Payne, R. L., and D. S. Pugh (1976). "Organizational Structure and Climate," in M. D. Dunnette, Ed., *Handbook of Industrial and Organizational Psychology,* Chicago: Rand McNally, pp. 1125–1173.

Pheysey, D. C., R. L. Payne, and D. S. Pugh (1971). "Influence of Structure at Organizational and Group Levels," *Administrative Science Quarterly* **16**:61–73.

Pondy, L. R. (1969). "Effects of Size, Complexity, and Ownership on Administrative Intensity," *Administrative Science Quarterly* **14**:47–60.

Pugh, D. S. (1981). "The Aston Program of Research: Retrospect and Prospect," Chapter 4 of this volume.

Pugh, D. S., and D. J. Hickson (1972). "Causal Inference and the Aston Studies," *Administrative Science Quarterly* **17**:273–276.

Pugh, D. S., D. J. Hickson, and C. R. Hinings (1969). "An Empirical Taxonomy of Structures of Work Organizations," *Administrative Science Quarterly* **14**:115–126.

Pugh, D. S., D. J. Hickson, C. R. Hinings, K. M. Macdonald, C. Turner, and T. Lupton (1963). "A Conceptual Scheme for Organizational Analysis," *Administrative Science Quarterly* **8**:289–315.

Pugh, D. S., D. J. Hickson, C. R. Hinings, and C. Turner (1968). "Dimensions of Organization Structure," *Administrative Science Quarterly* **13**:65–105.

Pugh, D. S., D. J. Hickson, C. R. Hinings, and C. Turner (1969). "The Context of Organization Structures," *Administrative Science Quarterly* **14**:91–114.

Reimann, B. C. (1973). "On the Dimensions of Bureaucratic Structure," *Administrative Science Quarterly* **18**:462–476.

Schriesheim, J., M. A. Von Glinow, and S. Kerr (1977). "Professionals in Bureaucracies: A Structural Alternative," in P. C. Nystrom and W. H. Starbuck, Eds., *Prescriptive Models of Organizations,* Amsterdam: North-Holland, pp. 55–69.

Starbuck, W. H. (1975). "Information Systems for Organizations of the Future," in E. Grochla and N. Szyperski, Eds., *Information Systems and Organizational Structure,* Berlin: de Gruyter, pp. 217–228.

Starbuck, W. H., and J. M. Dutton (1973). "Designing Adaptive Organizations," *Journal of Business Policy* **3**:21–28.

Starbuck, W. H., and P. C. Nystrom (1981). "Designing and Understanding Organizations," in P. C. Nystrom and W. H. Starbuck, Eds., *Handbook of Organizational Design,* Vol. 1, London: Oxford University Press, pp. ix–xxii.

Thorndike, E. L. (1939). "On the Fallacy of Imputing the Correlations Found for Groups to the Individuals or Smaller Groups Composing Them," *American Journal of Psychology* **52**:122–124.

Tosi, H., R. Aldag, and R. Storey (1973). "On the Measurement of the Environment: An Assessment of the Lawrence and Lorsch Environmental Uncertainty Subscale," *Administrative Science Quarterly* **18**:27–36.

Udy, S. H., Jr. (1970). *Work in Traditional and Modern Society,* Englewood Cliffs, NJ: Prentice-Hall.

REJOINDER TO STARBUCK

DEREK S. PUGH

To stay in Lewis Carroll's world for a moment: Bill Starbuck's description of the search for the Holy Grail sounds to me like the Hunting of the Snark. But in this case the Snark has *not* turned out to be a Boojum (or broken teacup) because the Aston approach has not faded away.

This is important because the need for replication and development (cf. Starbuck Table 8 "virtues") is as strong as ever and is being met. So, for example, currently Badran and Hinings (1981), Routamaa (1980), Kuc et al. (1980), and Wheeler et al. (1980) have replicated parts of the Aston framework and found supporting results in studies in Egypt, Finland, Poland, and Britain, respectively. Of course they have been critical of the limitations of the approach as it currently stands; of course they have added other aspects of organizational functioning to their analyses, but they have been able to use both the conceptual approach and the methodology and work from there.

This does mean that, as Starbuck points out, I do see "the original Aston studies as the first steps in several endless chains of studies." But I do not see this as a source of difficulty (except perhaps for the critics—and they will have to fend for themselves) but rather as a source of strength through virtues such as a large "team," self-criticism, replication, many measures, many organizations (cf. Starbuck, Table 8 again). The approach is delineated in the Pugh et al. (1963) paper which spelled out a conceptual framework I still see as the paradigm for the Aston Studies and am therefore grateful for all contributions to its working out from wherever they come.

The need for systematic comparative study which encourages replication is the first basic prior belief of those of us working in the Aston approach. Starbuck has correctly pointed out the importance of prior belief in the design and interpretation of research, and so I should like to outline some further beliefs that are important in understanding our work.

The second belief is a philosophical one. While I accept that what we normally call "data" (i.e., givens) should more appropriately be called "capta" (i.e., takens), I have a prior ontological belief that the organizational behavior universe is replete with regularities and our aim is to manipulate our concepts so that the relevant data/capta expose them. Thus if, for example, I accepted Starbuck's point that Table 5 in his paper is the result of random processes (which I most emphatically do not), then

199

I would draw the conclusion, not that the O.B. universe is random, but that we had not developed the appropriate analytical concepts to expose the regularities in it. It would be back to the drawing board to attempt to formulate other concepts.

The third prior belief is a substantive one concerned with the design of the investigation, and this clearly affects what range of possible results can be obtained. The Aston group are frequently written about as though we were "size theorists," that, contrary to, for example, Woodward and Perrow, we set out to demonstrate that size was the most important factor associated with formality of structure. This is not so. Our prior beliefs are obvious from the design; the wide range of contextual variables considered (cf. Table 4-1); the obtaining of a stratified random sample, leading to greatly reduced problems with collinearity as Starbuck notes; the analytical framework of multivariate prediction—all show that our prior belief was that a wide range of contextual factors affected organization structure. The demonstration that size had such enormous impact on structuring, for example, was a finding, not a prior belief.

The fourth belief is what Starbuck calls "the search for the Holy Grail"—that one can substantiate propositions that apply to all organizations. I consider that this is so and is worth doing, but I do not put the importance on it that Starbuck seems to. I see it as a tactical decision. Otherwise one is forced in principle to argue that only an idiographic (i.e., case study) approach is possible, since any subgrouping is logically bound to be inadequate, as Starbuck argues. While I accept that a dimension which discriminates insightfully across all organizations does not *necessarily* do so when considering only pharmaceutical manufacturers, for example, I would regard it as a tactical empirical question to see whether it does. If it does, as is the case with standardization, for example, and if it replicates the relationship with other variables (e.g., correlation of size with standardization in national study [total sample: 0.63; manufacturing firms: 0.76; pharmaceutical firms: 0.80 (Child, 1973)], then this is an empirical finding that is obtained more efficiently than having to start from the beginning with every new subgroup.

Thus for me the "search for the Holy Grail" amounts to saying: start with these generalized concepts and methods, apply them to your own particular group, and see how far they will get you. This is not of course to imply that newer, more specific concepts and methodologies for particular groups should not be developed. They very certainly should, and in my paper I call for these developments no less than Bill Starbuck.

Thus I see the basic prior beliefs of the Aston approach as valuing systematic, comparative, replicative, generalizable study, and as being concerned with ontological regularities and multiple causality. These will certainly affect the framework of the study as designed.

The examples Bill Starbuck gives of prior beliefs (apart from the Holy Grail) seem to be of much less importance than these. I also find his argument that they determine the results unconvincing. For example, Starbuck points out that it is the decision to classify size as a contextual variable which enables us to say that structure can be predicted from context. If we had not made the distinction between context and structure, then by definition we could not have made that statement and would have had to describe the observed set of intercorrelations in some other way. But would the *results* have been different—or just the same results subjected to a different interpretation.

The suggestion that it was our particular form of factor analysis which determined that bureaucracy was not a unitary concept is similar. Factor analysis is, as is known, quite a weak technique and our use of it for summarizing purposes is fully described in Levy and Pugh (1969), but it is not as weak as all that—and there is no way that one factor could adequately summarize all the variables in the original Aston correlation matrix. But the basic finding of variability of structure is based on interpretation of the correlation matrices. That is why I argue in my paper that, even with the National Study which consisted only of business organizations, the correlations would lead me to disagree with Child's formulation of the dimension of bureaucratization. Again my view is that we are not determining results but arguing about their interpretation.

Starbuck's Table 5 also raises these issues. Starbuck says the results there "look like the outputs of partly random processes." I assume he means by this something more than that the results contain error variance, which they surely do, and that they are in principle not interpretable. I disagree. I find the structure of results eminently interpretable and the variations within the range which pinpoints our ignorance and encourages us to proceed.

It is because I wish to proceed that I find Starbuck's prescriptions useful. As to the first, I have spelled out what I recognize as the impact of some prior beliefs in this paper. I am intrigued by the second suggestion of analyzing the logical relationships among the variables, and I intend to explore the specific data implications of this approach. But I would say immediately that for me many of the relationships are only hypotheses—if limited and plausible ones. Thus, for example, if there is a complete inspection of the final output, it may be likely, but it cannot be logically necessary that there must be specialist inspectors to carry it out. Indeed it is not difficult to point to situations where there are not, as in universities or job-enriched manufacturing plants. Thus the high correlation between standardization and specialization must, in major degree, be empirically and not logically determined.

I read the third prescription—recognition of the limitations of statistical inferences—as a spur to their improvement, and I am most grateful for Richard Hackman's drawing of my attention at the conference to the latest work on validity generalization. I intend to use the Hunter –Schmidt approach on the Aston data bank. The fourth prescription—use of simultaneous equation methods—encourages my own growing conviction that correlational methods have considerable limitations as a basis for analysis and that regression equations linking the variables would be more interesting. They would also enable predictions to be made and directly tested, because contrary to Starbuck's statement, the measures are designed to support scalar comparisons, hence all the work on scaleability using the general biserial correlation. This reworking of the data is, again, high on my research agenda. I can only echo the final prescription's call for more longitudinal studies.

Finally, the basic question that Starbuck asks is: Is it worth doing? He suggests not and points out that organization theorists already knew before 1960 the generalizations that the Aston program has laboriously been establishing. This is the fundamental difference between us. Of course, some theorists, some of the time, were thinking in terms of systematic variations in structure associated with systematic variations in size, for example, but they were also thinking a lot of other incompatible things at the same time—such as the overwhelming importance of technology, the preponderance of personal relationships over formal structure, conceived of as the organization chart (a favorite one this—I detect notes of it in Bill Starbuck's paper). Organization theorists, like the White Queen, are capable of believing six impossible things before breakfast.

In my view, this is an inevitable process in the development of a discipline. I find it useful here to make the distinction between wisdom and knowledge. Organization theorists have a particularly rich store of wisdom (mainly, as I have argued elsewhere, because of the large range of disciplines and approaches that fertilize the subject) some of which on systematic study analysis may turn out to be knowledge, but others of which will inevitably turn out to be superstition. Because that is the nature of wisdom—always richer and deeper than systematic knowledge, but also always shot through with complicating superstitions and incompatibilities. The Aston approach attempts a contribution to knowledge, therefore in terms of *some* wisdom will always be lagging far behind, but will make its contribution in characterizing *other* wisdom for the superstition it is.

It seems to me that at the Conference on which this book is based, there could be discerned exemplars of two basic approaches. I summarized above the Aston program's values as concerning systematic, comparative, replicative, generalizable study. These are, of course, the bureaucratic virtues and, as befits students of bureaucracy, the Aston group embraced them. Several programs that take a bureaucratic view of the nature of research are represented in this book. They contrast with another approach also represented here which I will call, using a term of one of its protagonists, a "garbage can model" of research, in which the world is a loosely coupled anarchy and research is about good ideas looking for something to explain, since trial and error is more important than system.

We had some difficulty in talking through this divide, and inevitably both sides went away feeling that the others were missing the point.

It is for his contributions to wisdom that we value Bill Starbuck. Bill is a truly wise man and the Aston group is most grateful to him for his energy and interest in our work over a long period! But he does not shake me from my view that knowledge comes from us bureaucrats.

REFERENCES

Badran, M., and C. R. Hinings (1981). "Strategies of Administrative Control and Contextual Constraints in a Less Developed Country. The Case of Egyptian Public Enterprise," *Organization Studies* **2**, 3–21.

Child, J. (1973). "Predicting and Understanding Organization Structure," *Administrative Science Quarterly* **18**, 168–185. (Reprinted in Pugh and Hinings, 1977)

Kuc, B., D. J. Hickson, and C. MacMillan (1980). "Centrally Planned Development: A Comparison of Polish Factories with Equivalents in Britain, Japan and Sweden," *Organization Studies* **1**, 253–270.

Levy, P., and D. S. Pugh (1969). "Scaling and Multivariate Analyses in the Study of Organizational Variables," *Sociology* **3**, 193–213. (Reprinted in Pugh and Hickson, 1976)

Pugh, D. S., D. J. Hickson, C. R. Hinings, K. M. Macdonald, C. Turner, and T. Lupton (1963). "A Conceptual Scheme for Organizational Analysis," *Administrative Science Quarterly* **8**, 289–315. (Reprinted in Pugh and Hickson, 1976)

Routamaa, V. (1980). "Organizational Structuring: An Empirical Analysis of the Relationships between Structure and Size in Form of the Finnish Shoe and Clothing Industry," *Acta Wasaensia*, No. 13, Vaasa School of Economics, Finland.

Wheeler, J., R. Marsfield, and D. Todd (1980). "Structural Duplications of Organizational Dependence upon Customers and Owners: Similarity and Differences," *Organization Studies* **1**, 327–348.

CHAPTER FIVE

Decision Making Perspective

Decisions in Organizations and Theories of Choice

JAMES G. MARCH
Stanford University

INTRODUCTION

This chapter examines some theories of organizational decision making. It is neither a proper history of their development nor a proper review of their content. It is limited in time, covering only the past 25 to 30 years. It is limited in scope, focusing primarily on a few streams of ideas among many. And it is limited in historical perspective, being less an attempt to examine the real confusions of intellectual history than to tidy those confusions into some coherence. The limitations are real; the story is incomplete. It underestimates the importance of Aristotle, ibn Khaldon, Mill, Bagehot, and Marx. It does not reflect adequately the extent to which the development of theories of organizational decision making has depended on the simultaneous development of broader ideas about organizations in general. And it conceals the real process of theoretical thinking. It is an essay on ideas as we present them, not as we discover them.

A serious effort in intellectual history would require much more attention to the ways in which the study of decision making in organizations has been part of a general enthusiasm for understanding and improving

This paper is based on work supported in part by grants from the Spencer Foundation, the National Institute of Education, and the Hoover Institution. I am grateful for the comments of Charles E. Lindblom and Allyn Romanow.

human information processing, thinking, problem solving, and consciousness. The behavioral and social sciences have become distinctively more cognitive over the past two decades, and the interest in organizational choice is part of a much broader interest in how individuals and institutions interpret information and act willfully in an uncertain world. Microeconomics, decision theory, statistics, operations research, cognitive psychology, linguistics, rational models of politics, social exchange, and power, information theory, population ecology, and cybernetics are all visions of how humans perceive, code, interpret, and respond to their environments in consciously rational ways. The development of theories of decision making in organizations is obviously linked to the parallel development of such ideas, as well as to the widespread acceptance of a social ideology that sees deliberate choice as self-evidently important for interpreting human existence.

Theories of organizational decision making have developed within a few broad traditions, but they are not the result of a program of research as that expression is normally used. There has been no single project, no project staff, no project locale. The work has been done by a group of independent investigators connected by mutual intellectual interests rather than a common employer or dominant figure. Whatever coherence we can find in the tradition is the result of an incremental process of development of a changing set of ideas among a loosely linked group of people drawn from different disciplines and traditions, and located in different countries. No plan; no grand scheme; no leader.

If it is useful to describe efforts to make key elements of the way we talk about organizational choice behavior more consistent with how we observe it, that usefulness lies partly in the special role that theories of organizational decision making have had among theories of choice. For the most part, organization theorists who have been interested in decision processes have been linked in spirit and style to decision theorists and microeconomists. They have also persistently been family scolds, questioning one assumption or another of received doctrine. As the ideas have developed, many key assumptions have been criticized. Most of the time the process has been gradual enough and the accommodation of other theories steady enough to make students of organizational choice only a little peculiar; not quite normal, but not quite crazy either.

Theories of organizational decision making are efforts to make some sense out of the naturally occurring events of organizational life. For the most part, the implicit strategy has not been to discover relatively subtle phenomena that demand refined experimental design and suitable sample sizes, but to explore the implications of relatively conspicuous phenomena. Many of the key observations are close to everyday knowledge. Often the problem is not so much to discover additional evidence for a phenomenon as to provide a plausible interpretation of it, or to see how organizational events fit together.

Although theories of organizational decision making draw data from experimental studies of choice behavior, from studies of large samples of organizations or organizational events, and from analyses of large collections of archival records, much of the work is close to that of a classical ethnographer, historian, or novelist. Many of the studies are of particular decision situations or specific decisions in which careful observation of ordinary organizational life is critical. If there are insights to be found in modern perspectives on organizational choice, they are borrowed from the fine detail of good field observations.

Because of such work, we know some things about the making of decisions in organizations. It is harder to argue that we have a single, coherent theory. Although there is fairly persistent use of some concepts, there is no simple structure for a theory. There is no agreement on a set of assumptions, no canonical form of analysis. Rather we have several clusters of ideas about organizations and decisions in them. The clusters are interrelated, but the relations are loose. To some extent they form alternative perspectives for interpreting events rather than alternative models susceptible to decisive test. In the main, the ideas are intended to describe behavior, and assume that at least some of the strange behavior that is described may also be intelligent.

The remainder of this essay identifies a few of those ideas and explores some of their implications. The selection is personal and makes no pretense of completeness or even representativeness. It is a brief review of some developments. One advantage of brevity is that it is easier to exhibit the simplicity of the ideas and their interrelations than in a more complete treatment.

THREE CLASSICAL PRESUMPTIONS

Theories of organizational choice have developed as counterpoint to three presumptions of classical theories of choice. These presumptions are sometimes explicit in the choice literature, sometimes implicit, and they can fairly be described as core assumptions of many standard treatments of choice. The presumptions are patently useful, but to many students of organizations they seem misleading.

Presumption 1. *Process Irrelevance.* Organizational actions are instantaneous and unique adaptations to an exogenous environment. Thus knowledge of the process of decision making is unnecessary to predict decision outcomes. Results are uniquely determined by constraints.

Presumption 2. *Willfulness.* Organizational decision making is willful. It results from intentional actions taken in the name of individual or collective purpose. It is derived from expectations about future consequences of current actions.

Presumption 3. *Outcome Primacy.* The results of decisions are important to individuals and groups in the organization. The salience of a decision process stems from decision outcomes.

These three presumptions guide much of the work that is done in studies of organizational choice. They form a basis for describing relations among environmental constraints, intentional actions, and decision processes with a certain clarity. Although it is easy to show that each of them is false in some ways, it is harder to develop powerful alternatives. Theories of organizational decision making involve efforts to find acceptable alternatives, but the search for alternatives should not obscure the durability and continuing utility of the presumptions.

ALTERNATIVES TO
PROCESS IRRELEVANCE

For the most part, classical theories of economic decision making assume that choice is dictated by the environment. In particular, the organizational process involved in decision making within a firm cannot affect decision results. Processes may vary from one firm to another, they may appear to differ substantially from the processes assumed in the theory, but decisions will be uniquely determined by environmental constraints, including competitive pressures. As a result, an understanding of decision process is unnecessary to an understanding of organizational decisions. A similar argument is made about noneconomic organizations. Since political and social systems are subject to economic, social class, and demographic constraints, it is argued that knowledge of the constraints alone will be adequate to predict most major features of society and politics. The idea that environmental constraints determine all significant characteristics of actions taken within that environment is a fundamental premise of much of social science.

Constraints make a difference; organizational decision making is embedded in an environmental context in numerous ways. In fact, theories of organizational decision making are theories of organizational response to environmental constraints and to information about events in the environment. Nevertheless organizational processes probably affect the relation between an organization and its environment. It seems plausible that organizational adaptation to environmental demands may sometimes violate a presumption of process irrelevance.

Environmental constraints may not impose *unique* solutions on organizations. If we wish to predict organizational decisions from properties of the environment, we require not only that the organization be responsive but also that there be only a single viable response to a particular set of environmental pressures. In most cases the single response is assumed to be one that optimizes the fit of the organization to the environment. Since Simon's early work, most studies of organizational decision making have elaborated ways in which organizations act on the basis of both incomplete knowledge and search rules that emphasize feasibility more than optimality. As a result, it is argued, decisions are not uniquely determined by external constraints. Rather they depend on the order in which alternatives are presented, on the (changing) aspiration levels of the organizations, and on the way in which organizational slack operates to dampen major swings in environmental stringency. In effect, such considerations suggest that somewhat sloppy organizations adapt to somewhat sloppy environments in ways that make general sense, without reaching a unique solution. Many students of decision making in organizations would suggest that sloppiness is a characteristic feature of the relation between organizations and their environments, and that environmental constraints do not uniquely determine organizational actions—at least in the short run.

Moreover, they would argue that understanding history involves understanding the short run, that knowledge about long-run equilibrium properties of a current process is often of little predictive utility. The argument reflects doubt about a second implicit basis for asserting process irrelevance, the assumption that organizations adjust to their environments *instantaneously,* or at least substantially faster than the environment itself changes. To many students of organizational behavior, statements about equilibrium relations between environments and organizations seem of modest interest, for it often seems that the processes by which such systems move toward equilibria are significantly slower than the processes by which an environment or organization changes exogenously. For example, it has been useful to show that under some conditions satisficing approaches optimizing as a limit, but that property, however satisfying to enthusiasts for the intelligence of satisficing, is not immediately relevant to understanding organizational choice in worlds that are changing rather rapidly. In general, the implicit argument of most efforts to develop theories of choice in organizations is that it is usually more fruitful to examine the time paths of organizational adjustments to a changing environment than to examine equilibrium choices within stable environmental constraints.

A third presumption underlying assertions of process irrelevance is that environment is *exogenous* to an organization, that organizations adapt to environments, but environments do not adapt to organizations. The modern cliché is the converse. Organizations affect their environments, even create them. Such a perspective is of course familiar not only in ecological ideas about organizations but also in theories of oligopoly and conceptions of the relations among political systems. Nonunique solutions to an environmental situation are fed back into the environment and change it. As a consequence, subsequent actions are based on an environment that is changing on the basis of current (process dependent) actions. Environmental constraints become in part dependent on organizational decision processes.

Although students of organizational choice rarely go so far as to assert that these problems make environments irrelevant, they clearly want to establish that environmental constraints do not completely determine organizational action, that the microbehavioral phenomena of choice are often important. There is a tendency to assume that existing organizational practices have evolved through a sensible and understandable process, but that existing practices do not represent unique solutions to the problems of environmental pressure. In that sense at least, behavioral theories of organizational choice lie somewhere between decision engineers, who tend to assume that strange organizational practices are pathologies, and natural selection economists, who tend to assume that strange organizational practices must be forms of optimization.

ALTERNATIVES TO WILLFULLNESS: BOUNDED RATIONALITY

Most theories of organizational choice use metaphors of willfulness. They maintain a basic prejudice that organizational behavior can be understood as intentional, consequential action. The presumptions of rationality provide a convenient theoretical core. The decision process of a rational organization has these characteristics:

1. A knowledge of alternatives. Organizations have a set of alternatives for action, which are defined by the situation and known unambiguously.

2. A knowledge of consequences. Organizations know the consequences of alternative actions, at least up to a probability distribution.

3. A consistent preference ordering. It is possible to specify an objective function by which alternative results of action can be associated with their subjective value.

4. A decision rule. Organizations have rules by which they select an alternative on the basis of its consequences for organizational preferences.

In the most familiar form of rational model, we assume that an organization knows all alternatives, the probability distribution of consequences conditional on each alternative, and the subjective value of each possible consequence; and we assume decisions are made by selecting the alternative with the highest expected value.

The durability of this simple structure has been impressive. It is also understandable. Rational models capture some truth. It is possible to predict important elements of human behavior within a willful paradigm. Demand curves for consumer products generally have negative slopes, and labor unions usually are more resistant to wage cuts than to wage increases. The core ideas are flexible. When the model seems not to fit, it is often possible to reinterpret preferences or knowledge and preserve the axioms. And rational models are linked to the ideologies of the Enlightenment—rationality is a faith as well as a theory.

The prevalence of rational models of behavior in economics, political science, psychology, sociology, linguistics, and anthropology attests to the attractiveness of rationality as a theory of human behavior. Nevertheless such models have been subject to two broad kinds of behavioral challenges. The first is that decision processes often appear to follow other kinds of logic; the second is that rational elements in decision making often appear to be more symbolic than real. Most of the remainder of this paper is devoted to describing the development of such ideas within the study of organizational decision making, but for most rational model enthusiasts the allegations are not so much wrong as irrelevant, although they are often described as both. The argument of irrelevance depends on two propositions—one effectively statistical, the other evolutionary.

The statistical argument is that any one decision maker is likely to have a small component of rationality among large elements of random irrationality. Alternatively, there are a few rational individuals among a large number of randomly irrational individuals. As we aggregate over a large number of decision makers, the random irrationalities essentially cancel each other, and the aggregate behavior, for example, in a market, is dominated by elements of rationality. The evolutionary argument is that the prima facie characteristics of the process of decision are irrelevant. Regardless of what individual actors appear to be doing or think they are doing, the procedures they follow will vary in their effectiveness. In the long run, competition will drive out those actors who use suboptimal procedures, and the remaining choices will be made *as if* the decision makers were rational actors. As a number of careful analyses have shown, both aggregation and selection have limits as devices for saving the core rational model, but they have become important justifications for its persistence.

In a grander sense, however, the most powerful testimony on behalf of the classical rational model is given by its critics. Behavioral students of decision making in organizations have organized their ideas around the assumptions of rationality. To be sure, their work has been dedicated to modifying each of the assumptions in significant ways, and in the end they have left only a barely recognizable shell, but the main logic is to improve the assumptions about preferences, knowledge, and decision rules, not to abandon the basic idea of choice. It is only within the last few years that the concept of decision itself as been seriously questioned.

The earliest developments in modern theories of organizational choice were modifications of the informational assumptions of rational theories.

They were built on some simple ideas of the limitations of human institutions in implementing intendedly rational behavior. Suppose we assume that decisions are made on the basis of estimates of the consequences of alternative actions. The argument, due originally to Simon, is that informational and computational limits on decision making in human institutions require a theory of organizational choice to be a theory of *limited* rationality. There are limits on the number of alternatives that will be considered, and limits on the amount and accuracy of information that will be used.

Because of such limits, the decision process that is used differs in some significant ways from the decision process anticipated by a more classical formulation. Decision making is seen as problem solving, search, and incremental trial and error. Described as "muddling through" by Lindblom, as "feedback-react" procedures by Cyert and March, and as "cybernetic" by Steinbruner, incremental, limited rationality is usually contrasted with long-run planning, forecasts, and commitments. The intelligence of organizational action is seen as lying not in the capability to know everything in advance but in the ability to make marginal improvements by monitoring problems and searching for solutions. Thus theories of limited rationality are essentially theories of search or attention: What alternatives are considered? What information is used?

The core ideas are elementary and by now familiar. Rather than all alternatives being known, alternatives have to be discovered through search; rather than all information about consequences being known, information has to be discovered by search. Search is seen as being stimulated by a failure to achieve a goal and continuing until it reveals an alternative that is good enough to satisfy existing goals. New alternatives are sought in the "neighborhood" of old ones, and new information is obtained. Failure focuses search on the problem of attaining goals that have been violated; success allows search resources to move to other domains. The key scarce resource is attention, and theories of limited rationality are for the most part theories of the allocation of attention.

Consider an organization with only one goal, for example, a sales target. As long as performance equals or exceeds the goal, the search for new alternatives is modest, organizational slack accumulates, and aspirations increase. When performance fails to meet the goal, search is stimulated, slack is decreased, and aspirations decrease. This classic control system does two things to keep performance and goals close. It adapts goals to performance. That is, organizations learn what they should expect. At the same time, it adapts performance to goals by increasing search and decreasing slack in the face of failure, decreasing search and increasing slack when faced with success. To the familiar pattern of fire alarm management are added the dynamics of changes in aspirations and slack buffers.

These ideas have seemed reasonably robust in exploring some features of organizational adaptation to a changing environment. For example, consider the role of organizational slack in absorbing fluctuations in the environment. Organizations appear often to meet external adversity by discovering new economies in their operations, despite having functioned in an apparently efficient way previously. If we assume that organizations optimize, it is not immediately obvious why new economies can be discovered under conditions of adversity if they could not be discovered during good times. The explanation is natural in the organizational slack version of organizational adaptation. During favorable times, slack (unexploited opportunities, undiscovered economies, waste, etc.) accumulates. Such slack becomes a reservoir of search opportunities during subsequent periods of trouble. As a result, environmental fluctuations are dampened by the organizational decision process. Such a description seems to provide at least a partial understanding of the resilience of organizations in the face of adversity.

Several studies indicate that organizations do search for new alternatives in the face of adversity. They discover more efficient refinements in technology; they economize. The simple search model, however, has not always been adequate. For example, it is clear that innovation, as a general phenomenon, cannot be explained simply in terms of problem-oriented search. Innovations are not always discovered and adopted by organizations that are failing to meet goals and ignored by organizations that are successful. Although the more complicated mechanisms involved are by no means well understood, it is possible to identify several themes in the literature. The first of these themes emphasizes *solution-driven* search. In the original formulation, search is driven by problems. Solutions are assumed to be discoverable through search; search is seen as stimulated by the existence of a problem. Solutions are effectively passive, and search is effectively prospecting. Such a conception does not fit many organizational situations. Solutions look for problems to which they might be imagined to be answers. Search is a form of mating, and the level of discovery through search depends not only on the activity of problems looking for solutions but also on solutions looking for problems. This becomes particularly important where the technological connection between a specific solution and a specific problem is ambiguous. Then decision making consists in the temporal linkage of active problems and active solutions, in what has come to be called a garbage can model of choice.

A second theme is one of *risk satisficing*. The basic theory draws a contrast between decision behavior under conditions of plenty and under conditions of adversity. There is some evidence, taken mostly from studies of individual behavior, that choices among alternative gambles with expected values greater than a target goal will tend to be risk avoiding. Conversely, when choices are made among alternative gambles with expected values less than the target, the choices tend to be risk seeking. Thus we would expect organizations to be risk avoiding under persistently improving environmental conditions, risk seeking under persistently declining conditions. The combination has the consequence of making organizations in both situations improve their prospects for meeting their goals at the same time as it shortens the life expectancy of those organizations that are failing.

The idea of an association between risk preference and success or failure fits the limited rationality paradigm, but it is qualified by the third theme of *slack search*. Organizations search in two ways. Under conditions of failure, search is focused on solving a particular problem; It is localized; it is intense. This kind of problem-directed search is the kind of search discussed in the original limited rationality formulations. Search is linked tightly to organizational goals. Under conditions of success, on the other hand, search occurs as a part of the slack activities of the organization. It reflects the professional instincts of highly qualified workers and the irrelevant wanderings of loosely controlled subunits. Search is not tightly linked to organizational goals. This slack search has a relatively low expected value for the organization, but a substantial variance. The distribution of results from problem-directed search has a higher expected value, but a lower variance. From the point of view of the goals of the organization, slack search is a form of foolishness, but it has a small chance of discovering something of considerable value. Problem-oriented search is more sensible, but it has less chance of discovering a major innovation. The distinction is drawn too sharply, but it reflects a recognition that the search phenomena of slack are vital to the limited rationality model.

A fourth theme emphasizes the *slack reservoir* of ideas. Under good conditions, slack search occurs. Ideas are accumulated, many of them too risky for adoption. When conditions change, central authorities become more inclined to look for risky alternatives and find them easily, stored in the slack of a formerly successful organization. A prolonged period of adversity depletes the reservoir. Consequently an organization is able to meet occasional brief periods of decline by drawing on discoveries and innovations generated but overlooked during better times. A sustained history of environmental difficulties, or of efficiency in reducing slack, leaves the organization vulnerable.

A fifth theme involves observations about *slack decisions*. Just as search is affected by slack, so also is decision making. Under conditions of plenty, organizational decisions tend to become more decentralized, more diffuse, less tightly linked to a coordinated organizational strategy. Consequently, although central decisions may tend to become risk avoiding during good times, slack decisions become (implicitly) risk seeking. Foolish experiments with possible innovations are produced not by decisions of central authorities but by autonomous actions of loosely coupled subunits or individuals. On average, these actions are inefficient from the point of view of the central goals, but they increase the level of risk taken. Thus fluctuations in slack move an organization from a situation (high slack) in which central authorities are relatively cautious but slack search and local decisions introduce significant levels of risk taking, to a situation (low slack) in which central decisions are more risk-seeking but slack search and local decisions are more constrained.

The result is a considerably more complicated understanding of the relation between success, search, slack, and organizational decisions. The complications have the usual costs of making it more difficult to unravel the net effects of changes in risk taking, changes in search, and changes in the level and character of slack search, solution-driven search, and decision making.

ALTERNATIVES TO WILLFULNESS: CONFLICT AND STRATEGIC ACTION

As long as we assume that organizations have goals and that those goals have some classical properties of stability, precision, and consistency, we can treat an organization as some kind of rational actor. But organizations do not have simple, consistent preference functions. They exhibit internal conflict over preferences. Once that conflict is noted, the language of problem solving shifts toward a more political vision. Suppose we consider organizations as conflict systems. That is, suppose an organization is composed of individuals or groups with independent (and well-behaved) preferences, and that there is scarcity. Not everyone can have everything desired. The level of conflict depends of course on the level of resources available to the organization, on the aspirations of participants, and on the complementarity of their demands. Scarce resources, high aspirations, and low complementarity make conflict more obvious; plentiful resources, low aspirations, and high complementarity reduce conflict.

There are numerous ways in which internal organizational conflict can be mediated in the making of decisions. Most conspicuously, classical theories of the firm assume that markets—particularly labor, capital, and product markets—convert conflicting demands into prices. In this perspective, entrepreneurs are imagined to impose their goals on the organization in exchange for mutually satisfactory wages paid to workers, rent paid to capital, and product quality paid to consumers. Such a process can be treated as yielding a series of contracts by which participants divide decision making into two stages. At the first stage, each individual negotiates the best possible terms for agreeing to pursue another's preferences, or for securing such an agreement from another. In the second stage, individuals execute the contracts. In more sophisticated versions the contracts are designed so that the terms negotiated at the first stage are self-enforcing at the second.

Such a view of agreements between participants with conflicting objectives and with mutual advantages to be gained through cooperation is a basic feature of political visions of organizational decision making. In those, however, the emphasis is less on designing a system of contracts between principals and agents, or partners, than it is on understanding a political process that allows decisions to be made without necessarily resolving conflict among the parties. Organizational versions of a political process therefore emphasize mechanisms for obtaining and exercising power, negotiating bilateral exchanges, and arranging coalitions.

Power is an enduring concept in social science, and a seductive one. It treats choice as being possible without agreement on collective goals; it links results to a (prior) distribution of resources among participants; it portrays collective results as a consequence of competition among self-interested participants. Thus a theory of power allows much of the apparatus of market theories of choice, substituting the exogenous distribution of resources for the familiar exogenous distribution of wealth, and it fits a sense of *realpolitik* by which we simultaneously affirm our consciousness of the world, our ability to function successfully in it, and our discomfort with its inequities. The disadvantages of the concept of power are also well-known. It tends to become a tautological summary of the (large) residual variance in studies of collective choice; it confounds a variety of quite different behavioral mechanisms; it has no consistent measure; and the models that underlie it seem often to be either clearly wrong or impossible to test.

Despite the problems, power is a label for an important collection of approaches to organizational decision making. Those approaches are political, although the language and analyses often borrow heavily from economics. The core idea is that individual participants enter an organization with preferences and resources; each individual uses personal resources to pursue personal gain. The usual metaphors are those of politics. First, a metaphor of combat. Disputes are settled by "force," that is, by reference to some measurable property by which individuals can be scaled. Organizational decisions are weighted averages of individual desires, where the weights reflect the power distribution among individuals. Second, a metaphor of exchange. Disputes are settled by offering or withholding resources and establishing a mutually acceptable structure of prices. Markets facilitate cross-sector trading, for example, bribery, blackmail, and encourage pursuit of resources with high exchange value, for example, the taking of hostages. Third, a metaphor of alliance. Disputes are settled by forming teams through exchange agreements and side payments and then engaging in combat. Results are (mostly) clear once the coalition structure is given. The coalition structure is problematic.

All such metaphors assume that collective choices are made without agreement on collective objectives—that organizational decisions are made and accepted even though they are different from the preferences of individual actors. In most cases they assume that choice is determined completely by a few things, each of which is thought to be exogenous. The results depend on the rules of the game. Rules include such things as the distribution of formal authority in the organization, procedures for determining a winning coalition, and the rules of evidence, argument, agenda, and so on. Although such rules may have been decided by some "metagame," they are taken as given. The results also depend on the resources or endowments of the participants. Those resources may include factors of immediate relevance to the particular decision; they may also include any resource that can be made important by exchange. Finally, the results depend on the distribution of preferences of the participants. It is possible for the rules of the game to make only a few coalitions feasible. In such a case, the "nondecisions" of the system may be of greater interest than the decisions. It is possible that any particular participant will be excluded from winning coalitions because of an inadequacy of resources or an extremity of preferences. There may be many possible winning coalitions and some indeterminacy in the result.

Such complications and ideas about decision making in organizations fit naturally into the tradition of rationality in organizations. They assume an organization of several rational actors, rather than one. Thus the rationality they presume is game rationality or market rationality. But the spirit is one of optimization. The theories become more behavioral when we consider how organizations of human actors try to function in a game of this general sort. An emphasis on the political character of organizational decision making is implicitly a focus on the strategic nature of organizational information, on the ways in which organizational alliances are formed and maintained, and on the complications introduced by the use of agents in organized action.

In a conflict system, information is an instrument of consciously strategic actors. Information may be false; it is always serving a purpose. Actors may provide accurate information about their preferences; normally they will not, except as a possible tactic. They may provide accurate information about the consequences of possible alternative decisions; normally they will not, except as a possible tactic. Thus information is itself a game. Except insofar as the structure of the game dictates honesty as a necessary tactic, all information is self-serving. Consequently meaning is imputed to messages on the basis of theories of intention that are themselves subject to strategic manipulation. The result is a complicated concatenation of maneuver in which information has considerably less value than it might be expected to have if strategic considerations were not so pervasive.

Alliances are formed and broken. They represent the heart of many political visions of organizations, yet the real world of organizational alliances is unlikely to be as simple as the world of the metaphor. Political alliances involve trades across time in the form of promises and implicit promises. Rarely can the terms of trade be specified with precision. The future occasions are unknown, as are the future sentiments with which individuals will confront them. It is not a world of contracts but of informal loose understandings and expectations.

Mobilization is important. In order to be active in forming and maintaining a coalition and monitoring agreements within a coalition, it is useful to be present. But attention is a scarce resource, and some potential power in one domain is sacrificed in the name of another. Allies have claims on their time also, and those claims may make their support unreliable at critical moments. To some extent the problems of attention can be managed by making threats of mobilization, or developing fears on the part of others about potential mobilization, or using agents as representatives. However, each of those introduces more uncertainties into the process. The difficulties of mobilization in fact are the basis for one of the classic anomalies of organizational behavior in the face of conflict—the sequential attention to goals. If all participants were activated fully all of the time, it would not be possible to attend to one problem at one time and another later. Since attention fluctuates, it is possible to sustain a coalition among members who have what appear to be strictly inconsistent objectives.

Effective alliances depend on logrolls, that is, on the support of individuals who are indifferent about a current issue but who trade their backing on it for subsequent support on another issue. Logrolls combine individuals with complementary interests into viable coalitions and make a political process feasible. But they are invitations to disappointment. Support that is strategic (as most support in a logroll is) tends to be narrow. It is possible to organize a coalition for a decision; it is less feasible to assure that all coalition members will be willing to invest equally in coping with postdecision complications that may arise. Perhaps for this reason, studies of coalition formation suggest that logrolls occur less frequently than would be expected. The most natural logroll is among individuals who are mutually indifferent about each other's concerns. Although such alliances certainly occur, they appear to be less common than alliances requiring more significant compromises between individuals with overlapping concerns.

Information is unreliable; inferences are difficult. Much of the structure of alliances and action depends on beliefs about who has power to do what, who might be activated when, and who will do what under what conditions. This dependence of the political process on beliefs makes much of what we call politics in organizations actually second-order politics. Knowing who has power is important in making judgments about actions and promises. As a result, politics emphasizes competition over reputations that might subsequently be used as scarce resources. In such competition, of course, individuals who have resources have an advantage, but possession of an advantage does not allow resource holders to ignore competitive challenges without consequence.

Organizations are systems of agents. A political vision of organizations emphasizes the problems of using self-interested individuals as agents for other self-interested individuals. It is a set of problems familiar to studies of legislators, lawyers, and bureaucrats. If we assume that agents act in their own self-interest, then we seem to require some ideas about how to ensure that the self-interest of agents coincides with the self-interest of principals. This has led to extensive discussions of incentive and contractual schemes designed to assure such a coincidence and to the development of theories of agency. It is clear, however, that organizations are often unsuccessful in assuring the reliability of agents. Agents are often bribed or coopted. Thus they ordinarily risk being suspected of bribery or cooptation, and they undertake (jointly with other agents with whom they deal) to produce a scenario of behavior that might persuade a suspicious audience of their innocence.

Organizational politics often emphasizes trust and loyalty along with a widespread belief that they are hard to find. It is difficult to construct firm agreements and enforce them easily. The temptations to revise contracts unilaterally are frequently substantial, and promises of uncertain future support are easily made worthless in the absence of some network of favor giving. A first principle of politics is that if everyone is rational, no one can be trusted. A second principle is that someone who never trusts anyone will usually lose, because although no rational person can be trusted, some people are innocent and can be trusted. Those who, by chance or insight, trust those who can be trusted will have an advantage over those who are unconditionally untrusting. A third principle is that all players will try to look trustworthy even though they are not, in order to be trusted by those people who might become winners (by virtue of being willing to trust some people). A fourth principle is that the only reliable way of appearing to be trustworthy is to be in fact trusthworthy. Thus all rational actors will be trustworthy most of the time. And so on. The principles of politics are not in general blessed with equilibrium solutions that are transparent. Political actions are based on ambivalent beliefs about others in an uncertain world.

Politics organizes those beliefs into a grand insurance scheme. Actions taken now are implicit investments in future favors. However, they are investments subject to severe limitations. The time discount on favors is quite heavy. "What have you done for me lately?" is viewed as a legitimate question. Future requirements for assistance are difficult to predict. There is a small probability that help will be needed from almost anyone, but the specific needs are hard to know in advance. There is no certainty that the insurance writer is reliable; past favors may be forgotten or ignored. So favors are done in loose expectation of a return, but on average many more favors are done than are requested. In effect, insurance against future adversity is purchased at very unfavorable terms. The system works, most people are protected reasonably well, and virtually all people receive far more favors than they request. In this sense politics is like politeness. As with politeness, not everyone is equally advantaged in such a scheme. Although it seems likely that almost all people receive more favors than they request, the powerful have a particularly favorable position only somewhat moderated by their consequent greater exposure.

Political complications extend to the problems of implementation and control. If organizations were simple administrative systems, then a theory of choice would be a theory of decisions taken by central authorities. But a theory of organizational choice must attend to the way so-called decisions are embedded in a system that can be expected to transform them. Conflict systems are driven by their control systems, their records of accounts, and the actions contingent on them. The fundamental complication in control is that the procedures developed to measure performance or compliance with directives involve some measures that can be manipulated. Once the rules for evaluation are set, conflict of interest between the rule setters and the rule followers assures that there will be some incentives for the latter to maximize the difference between their score and their effort. Such incentives produce new efficiencies, new technologies, and new procedures, but they also produce new devices for managing the accounts. Any system of accounts is a road map to cheating on them. As a result, control systems can be seen as an infinite game between the controllers and the controlled, in which the advantage lies with the relatively full-time player with a direct personal interest.

The problem of control is echoed in the problem of implementation. Decisions in organizations unfold through a series of interrelated actions. If all conflict of interest were settled by the employment contract, the unfolding would present only problems of information and coordination, but such problems are small compared to the complications of unresolved conflict. It makes little sense to develop a theory of decision making without attending to the ways in which policies as adopted differ from policies as implemented. Moreover, it is necessary to consider the ways in which variations in the tightness of implementation affect variations in the character of policies being developed. For example, formal decision making in a system in which there is considerable implementation flexibility is likely to reflect somewhat greater symbolic concerns than decision making where implementation is fairly rigid.

These relatively extensive political features of organizations arise from one very simple modification of the classical core ideas of rationality—seeing organizations as collections of individuals or groups with unreconciled preferences. It seems hard to avoid the obvious fact that such a description comes closer to the truth in most organizations than does one in which we impute a preference function to the organization. Somewhat more problematic is the second feature of much of the behavioral study of organizational politics: the tendency for the political aspects of decision making to be interminable. If it were possible to imagine a two-step decision process in which first we established, through side payments and formation of coalitions, a set of organizational preferences acceptable to a winning coalition and *then* we acted, we could treat the first stage as "politics" and the second stage as "economics." Such a division has often been tempting, for example, the distinction between policy making and administration, but it has rarely been satisfactory as a description of organizations. The organizations we observe seem to be infused with strategic actions and politics at every level and at every point in a long decision process. But even that does not exhaust the behavioral complications. Organizations develop cultures of beliefs about proper behavior. Some of those beliefs are restrictions on strategic, self-interested behavior on the part of individuals. Although it would be foolish to ignore the problems of control implicit in intraorganizational conflict and personal incentives, it would be equally foolish to assume that individuals in organizations always act in a consciously self-interested manner.

ALTERNATIVES TO WILLFULNESS: RULES AND OBLIGATORY ACTION

Much of the decision-making behavior observed in an organization reflects the routine way in which people do what they are supposed to do. Most of the time, most people follow organizational operating procedures. They follow rules even when it is not obviously in their self-interest to do so. The behavior can be viewed as contractual, an implicit agreement to act appropriately in return for being treated appropriately, and to some extent there certainly is such a "contract." But socialization into rules and their appropriateness is ordinarily not a case of willful entering into an explicit contract. It is composed of comprehension of the nature of things, of self-conceptions, and of organizational images.

The proposition that organizations follow rules, that much of the behavior in an organization is specified by standard operating procedures, is a common one in the bureaucratic and organizational literature. To describe behavior as driven by rules is to see action as a matching of behavior with a position or situation. The criterion is appropriateness rather than consequential optimality. The terminology is one of duties and roles rather than anticipatory decision making. Search involves an inquiry into the nature of a particular situation, and choice involves matching a situation with behavior that fits it. Rule following can be described as obligatory action, though the idea of obligation may suggest an overly narrow conception, as contrasted with consequential action.

The contrast can be characterized by comparing the conventional litanies for individual behavior:

Consequential Action

1. What are my alternatives?

2. What are my values?

3. What are the consequences of my alternatives for my values?

4. Choose the alternative that has the best consequences.

Obligatory Action

1. What kind of a situation is this?

2. What kind of a person am I?

3. What is appropriate for me in a situation like this?

4. Do it.

Research on obligatory action emphasizes understanding the kinds of rules that are evoked and used, the ways in which they fit together, and the processes by which they change.

It is possible of course to treat the word "rule" so broadly as to include any regularity in behavior, and sometimes that temptation is too great to be resisted. But for the most part, we mean something considerably narrower. We mean regular operating procedures, not necessarily written but certainly standardized, known, and understood with sufficient clarity to allow discourse about them and action based on them. The rules may be procedural rules specifying a process that is to be followed under certain circumstances. They may be decision rules specifying how inputs are to be converted into outputs. They may be evaluation rules specifying criteria for assessing results. They may regulate record-keeping, information gathering and handling, or the allocation of responsibility.

Rules are fundamental to understanding both the ways in which organizations maintain stability and the ways in which they change. On the one hand, the existence and persistence of rules, combined with their relative independence of idiosyncratic concerns of individual participants, makes it possible for organizations to function reasonably reliably and reasonanly consistently. At the same time, change in organizations is closely linked to mundane rules. Most organizations respond· to the environment most of the time easily and routinely on the basis of procedures that depend on environmental signals. Most organizational adaptation consists in monitoring the environment and the organization for familiar messages about the state of the world, and doing what is appropriate (according to the rules) given the situation. Rules are efficient and effective devices for allowing complex organizations to respond to variations in conditions. Moreover, organizations adapt to their environments by changing rules, though the processes of such change are slower than the routine adaptation to changing conditions within rules. Current rules store information generated by previous organizational experiences and analyses, even though the information cannot easily be retrieved in a form amenable to systematic current evaluation. Seeing rules as coded information invites questions of the long-run sensibility of rule following and its vulnerability to short-run anomalies. In this way studies of organizational decision making are connected to some classical puzzles of studies of culture and history, as well as population ecology.

Research on rules in organizations has examined the ways in which rules are learned, applied, and broken by individual actors, but the major efforts in studies of organizational decision making have been toward understanding some ways in which rules change. Within this tradition, three major processes are commonly considered.

Experiential Learning

We can imagine an organization as learning from its experience, modifying the rules for action incrementally on the basis of feedback from the environment. Choice depends on the response propensities associated with particular situations on the basis of past experiences. Ideas about experiential learning have been applied to learning with respect to three different components of the decision process. The first is learning with respect to organizational goals. Aspirations can be seen as changing over time in response to experience. In a typical form, they are represented as being an exponentially weighted moving average of past experience. Organizations learn what to expect. The second kind of experiential learning is learning competence. Organizations improve abilities through experience. They become more competent in the activities they have pursued, relatively less competent in the activities they have not pursued. The third kind of experiential learning is learning decision rules. Organizations change their propensities to use one rule or another as a result of experience, and certain rules become established as routine responses.

Most experiential learning models are adaptively rational. They allow an organization to find good, even optimal, rules for most of the choice situations they are likely to face. However, the process can produce some surprises. Learning can be superstitious. An organization may have a subjective sense of learning under conditions in which the real situation is substantially different from what is believed. In addition, learning can lead to local optima that are quite distant from the global optimum. If goals adapt rapidly to experience, learning what is likely may inhibit discovery of what is possible. If strategies are learned quickly relative to the development of competence, an organization will learn to use strategies that are intelligent given the existing level of competence, but it may fail to invest in enough experience with a suboptimal strategy to discover that it would become a dominant choice with additional competence. Although such anomalies are not likely to be frequent, they are important. They are important in practical terms because they are unanticipated by ordinary ideas of learning. They are important in theoretical terms because they make a useful link between sensible organizational learning and surprising results.

Evolutionary Selection

We can see organizational action as driven by an evolving collection of invariant rules. As in the case of experiential learning, choice is history dependent, but the mechanism is different. Although individual rules are invariant, the population of rules changes over time through differential survival and reproduction. The changes occur primarily through variations in the growth of organizational units that follow different rules in a particular environment. Most of the recent effort exploring selection models has gone into examining how differential survival and reproduction of organizational forms (rules in the case of decision making) might affect the distribution of forms in a population of organizations interacting in an ecology of competition and cooperation.

A key step in developing these perspectives was the speculation that if organizational behavior is rule-bound, it might be possible to treat rules as the approximate equivalent of organizational genes. The analogy is a rough one and requires considerable qualification, as does the use of growth as an analogue to a more conventional reproductive process. However, selection models yield some general qualitative results, mostly equilibrium properties, and some detailed time-paths associated with distinct assumptions about the environment and the detailed structure of the selection process. The general results are familiar to students of ecology. For example, it is possible to show that an organization can become so specialized to a particular environmental condition that small changes in the environment produce serious problems. More detailed results are more difficult to characterize in simple terms, but they are probably more important. For example, they permit examination of the relation between the rate of change in the environment and the rate of change in rules, one of the most critical relations in the study of organizational change.

Such evolutionary arguments about the development of decision rules were originally made as justification for assuming that organizations maximize expected utility. The argument was simple: Competition for scarce resources resulted in differential survival of organizations depending on whether the rules produced decisions that in fact maximized utility. Thus, it was argued, we could assume that surviving rules, whatever their apparent character, were optimal. Although the argument has a certain charm to it, most close students of selection models have suggested that derivation of the argument requires several dubious assumptions. Selection will not reliably guarantee that rules are optimal at any arbitrary point in time. Not all rules are necessarily good ones, least of all indefinitely. It has been pointed out, for example, that species that disappear were once survivors, and unless selection processes are instantaneous, some currently "surviving" rules are in the process of disappearing.

Contagion

Organizational adaptation can be seen as reflecting rules that spread through a group of organizations like fads or measles. The particular pattern of spread depends on interorganizational connections associated with product, locational or personnel similarities, technological and market linkages, and status hierarchies. The basic idea is that rules may change by the relatively slow processes of learning and selection, but rapid changes in rules come about through imitation. Organizations copy each other. Contagion is in fact much easier to observe than either learning or selection. If we want to account for the adoption of accounting conventions, for example, we normally would look to ways in which standard accounting procedures diffuse among organizations. We would observe that individual organizations adopt those rules of good practice that are certified by professional associations and implemented by organizational opinion leaders. If we try to understand the adoption of participative rules for making decisions, we probably err if we see them as a willful choice of an individual organization and fail to note the tendency for similar rules to be adopted by other organizations at the same time. The simultaneity may be due to independent adaptation to identical conditions, but it seems more often to reflect considerable elements of direct imitation.

Although imitation is a conspicuous process, its properties are not well understood. The spread of organizational rules seems to have many of the properties and perversities that are exhibited by the spread of agricultural innovations. We know that organizations copy other organizations sometimes, but we have difficulty specifying the details. It is not easy to predict which organizations will adopt new rules first, which rules will spread faster than others, and in what order different organizations will adopt a particular rule. It seems unlikely that simple epidemiological models will be adequate, but we have not yet specified a model that captures very much of this diffusion process.

Insofar as organizational action can be viewed as rule following, decision making is not willful in the normal sense. It does not stem from the pursuit of interests and the calculation of future consequences of current choices. Rather it comes from matching a changing set of contingent rules to a changing set of situations. The intelligence of the process arises from the way rules store information gained through learning, selection, and contagion, and from the reliability with which rules are followed. The broader intelligence of the adaptation of rules depends on a fairly subtle intermeshing of rates of change, consistency, and foolishness. Sensibility is not guaranteed. At the least, it seems to require occasional deviation from the rules, some general consistency between adaptation rates and environmental rates of change, and a reasonable likelihood that networks of imitation are organized in a manner that allows intelligent action to be diffused somewhat more rapidly and more extensively than silliness.

ALTERNATIVES TO WILLFULNESS: AMBIGUITY

Ideas of willful anticipatory action in organizations often emphasize the uncertainties associated with future consequences of current action. These uncertainties form the basis for much of statistical decision and game theoretic approaches to problems of decision. Two major uncertainties are discussed in that literature: (1) risks associated with the possibility that future consequences may be known only up to some probability distribution; (2) uncertainties associated with the extent to which future consequences depend on actions taken by other strategic actors. However, at least two other uncertainties are associated with organizational choice, which are important for behavioral theories of choice. There are ambiguities of history. When organizations try to learn from their experience, or try to retrieve a history, they interpret a past that may be difficult to recall and untangle. There are also ambiguities of preferences. When organizations try to act willfully, they try to deal with preferences that are changing, inconsistent, imprecise, and partly dependent on the actions that are taken in their name.

Ambiguities of History

The problems of interpreting the past are the classic ones of understanding relatively complicated, changing phenomena on the basis of small samples of observations without any experimental controls. When an organization learns from the past, it learns from a past that is ordinarily hard to interpret with precision. Several errors of interpretation are likely. Organizational participants seem likely to see history in a way that reflects favorably on themselves, to attribute favorable results to the intelligence of their own actions and unfavorable results to the actions of others. They write history with the usual human predilection to see what they want to see.

But these personal biases are only a part of the story. There are some broader human inclinations. Organizational participants seem to exaggerate the reliability of historical data. They construct a story of historical events, which resolves considerable potential subjective uncertainty about what happened. Once it is accepted, it becomes the effective history, as compelling to the actors involved as any other history. Organizational participants seem to exaggerate the intentionality of events. Because they are dedicated to the possibility of willful action, participants bias interpretations of organizational history to emphasize the role of intention in human affairs. Things that happen are seen as intentionally caused. Finally, organizational participants seem to exaggerate the necessity of historical events. They overestimate the likelihood of events that actually occur and underestimate the likelihood of events that do not occur but might very easily have occurred.

The ambiguities of history are important for understanding organizational learning. Suppose we imagine that an organization learns by acting, monitoring environmental response to the action, then modifying subsequent action. It is a process of considerable power for moving the organization in the direction of more intelligent action, *provided* the environmental response is clear, stable, and affected by the action of the organization. The confusions of history make it likely, however, that organizations will learn under conditions in which environmental responses are ambiguous, when they are only loosely linked to the actions taken in the organization and are hard to interpret. As a result, learning is likely to be superstitious. Organizations, and the individuals in them, will have learning experiences that are more powerful in reinforcing behavior than seems warranted by the ambiguities of the situation. Moreover, interpretations of experience tend to be developed jointly by individuals within the organization. Thus a theory of organizational learning is in part a theory of how organizations develop and communicate stories of history. Where history is ambiguous and collective interpretations are not easily subjected to direct assessment, the social construction of history becomes even more important than otherwise.

Ambiguities of Preferences

Theories of rationality assume that organizations have preferences. Theories of conflict assume that preferences are knowable and known by participants in an organization, but that their mutual inconsistency makes it impossible to talk about an organizational goal with the orderliness required of preference functions. In recent years these observations have been supplemented by comments on the ways in which preferences are ambiguous. Standard theories of choice indicate that preferences will drive action. Indeed in the revealed preference form of the theory, preferences are deduced from action. Preferences are expected to be stable.

We act now in the name of preferences under the assumption that they will be unchanged when the consequences of action are realized. Preferences are expected to be consistent. Any possible inconsistency is removed through the specification of trade-offs. Preferences are expected to be precise. Whether a particular outcome is consistent with a particular taste must be clear. Preferences are expected to be exogenous. In particular they are presumed to be unaffected by choices made in their name.

All of these features of preferences as they appear in the theory seem incongruent with observations of choice behavior by individuals and organizations. Preferences, even individual preferences, do not seem to have the properties assumed by a willful theory of action. Preferences are expressed but not followed. Preferences change; and they change as a result of choices. They are inconsistent and imprecise. From the point of view of standard decision theory, it seems clear that organizations routinely and habitually make decisions without the kind of preferences that would satisfy the axioms of rational choice.

Examination of organizational decision making under conditions of goal ambiguity has pursued two tacks. The first explores the ways in which organizations make decisions without having well-defined preferences. That tack has led students of organizational choice to an interest in rule-bound decision making and the adaptation of rules over time, to temporal linkages between problems and solutions, and to the symbolic and ritual aspects of choice in organizations. The second route explores the possibility that ambiguity in preferences is not only a common phenomenon but also a form of intelligence. The argument is that ambiguous preferences have sensibility that is obscured by the conventional model of consequential rationality. In particular, it is argued that ambiguity allows preferences to develop through action, that ambiguity reflects an intelligent modesty about the adequacy of guesses about future wants, that ambiguity is part of a sensible effort to manage the tendency for preferences to become inappropriate, and that ambiguity is a way of building protection from the political use of rational argument.

The ambiguities of history and preferences contribute to the attractiveness of forms of organizational action that are less willful than classical rational choice. For example, rules provide a way of acting when goals are ambiguous. In general, obligatory action has been seen as one of the ways organizations and individuals explore possible goals and evade the limitations of current information. But before we rush to see rule following as a clear response in an ambiguous world, it may be well to note that rules of behavior are subject to their own ambiguities. The history through which they have evolved or have been learned may be confusing; as a result the information coded into a rule may be erroneous. The match between behavior and a situation may be unclear; thus the application of rules may be as uncertain as the statement of preferences. The obvious speculation is that clear rules will dominate ambiguous preferences, and clear preferences will dominate ambiguous rules, but most situations probably involve a dialectic between somewhat ambiguous rules and somewhat ambiguous preferences.

ALTERNATIVES TO OUTCOME PRIMACY

Studies of organizational decisions and decision process usually assume that the primary results of a decision process are decisions, that decisions can be understood by an analysis of the process, and that the centrality of a particular decision for an observer assures its centrality for participants. This emphasis on substantive results is a part of the tradition of economics and politics. What matters is who gets what how. Some recent studies suggest that such an exclusive focus on results and the implicit projection of their theoretical importance onto a belief in their subjective centrality and unity may be misleading. Two modifications of this view have been suggested: (1) Any specific decision process involves a collection of individuals and groups who are simultaneously involved in other things. Therefore it is hard to understand the way decisions are made in one arena without understanding how those decisions fit into the lives of participants. (2) Decision processes are linked to important symbolic concerns of organizations and society. Therefore many of the phenomena within a decision process are better understood as part of a symbolic process than as a way to produce substantive decision results.

Decision Making as a Cross Section of Lives

Most studies of decision making interpret choice in terms of a decision process that is linked to an external environment that defines both constraints and the bargaining resources available to participants. A recent idea is that decision making occurs within an environmental context to include attention to the consequences of a highly textured, changing environment. Suppose we see a decision process as involving a number of potential participants. Each participant is involved in a life with a variety of changing demands. Thus the meaning, importance, and accessibility of any decision to any one participant depend on the mosaic of demands on that individual at that time. From this perspective, decision processes are cross-sections of the lives of individual participants and cannot easily be understood without embedding them within those lives. The context is a shifting intermeshing of the vagaries of demands on the lives of the whole array of actors. In this mosaic, any particular decision, however important to the observer, is likely to be substantially less important to many participants. Consequently it seems likely that theories of choice in organizations may err by separating the decision process from the complexities of ordinary lives.

The perspective takes two forms. The first tries to understand the course of a decision in full cross-sectional detail. We fit a decision into the life of each participant, displaying organizational action as the more or less fortuitous consequence of combining different moments of different lives. It is an old vision and can easily be trivialized into a treatment in which great events are interpreted as the result of indigestion, but it sometimes seems to be almost tractable. The requirements of scholarship are such, however, that it has rarely been attempted seriously.

The second form of a contextual perspective focuses specifically on the allocation of attention. The idea is simple. Each potential participant in a decision process is faced with a personal decision problem—how to allocate scarce attention across various demands for attention. Individual decisions are made in the context of the array of opportunities presented. Individuals attend to some things and thus do not attend to others. Individual decisions to participate determine the collection of individuals involved in any specific decision and thus the outcome of the process. There are structural constraints on attention. Some people are not allowed to participate in some things; some people are required to do so. But within those structural limits, attention is allocated to a particular decision in a way that depends not only on properties of that decision but also on the variety of other demands that face various possible actors.

The most powerful part of the idea is also the most elementary. The attention given to a particular decision will depend both on attributes of that decision and on alternative claims for the attention of possible decision participants. Since those claims are not homogeneous across participants and change over time, the attention that any particular decision will receive can be both quite unstable and remarkably independent of the properties of the decision. The same decision will attract much attention or little, depending on the other things that possible participants might be doing. Participation in the process can become quite difficult to understand within a narrow focus on a single decision arena.

The argument depends on the notion that attention is a scarce resource. In pure form, we can imagine each participant as having a fixed amount of time to allocate to organizational and other concerns, and that each unit of time is allocated to one and only one activity. Such a pure form is useful as a starting metaphor, but it clearly requires some modification. It is possible to conserve attention by simultaneously attending to more than one activity, and it is possible to augment attention through purchase, barter, representation, or threat. As a result of individual variations in capabilities for attention conservation and augmentation, some people have considerably more time to devote to their concerns than others. The assumption of attention scarcity does not depend on the simple metaphor, however. All we require to make decision results highly contextual is that results depend on who attends to the process, that attention is a scarce resource among individuals, and that changes in the array of demands on potential participants are neither homogeneous nor synchronous.

The perspective has been used to make some general predictions about decision making. For example, suppose that important decisions must be made by important decision makers, and suppose that important decision makers have many demands on their time. Then important decisions are likely to receive less attention per unit of elapsed time than somewhat less important decisions. As a result, they either will require a longer (calendar) time to complete or will be made with less total attention than their less important cousins. Alternatively, suppose access to important decisions is not restricted to important people, but important people have more demands on their time than do unimportant people. Then important decisions will be much influenced by unimportant people. It is a result that is familiar to discussions of participation in political decision making.

If we assume that attention is necessary for influence and that attention is a scarce resource, we can see a possibility for trade-offs between attention and position, or status. The influence of someone in a relatively weak position could balance the influence of someone in a relatively powerful position if the former is able to devote more attention than the latter to the issue. The result seems especially possible if there are substantial differences between the two people in the attention claims they face and in the importance they attach to the issue. In situations in which less powerful people have narrower concerns than more powerful people, the weak are able to exploit the scarce time and diffuse interests of the strong.

This potential trade-off between activation and position has been the basis for frequent proposals to increase the participation in decision making by individuals who appear to be relatively inactive. The proposals are common in formal organizations and in other social institutions, most notably communities. The usual argument is that results are affected by the *product* of power and activation and that the impact of an individual or group can be increased by a unilateral increase in activation. The argument is sensible and seems to reflect experience, but the result is not guaranteed. It is quite possible that a change in the activity level of some participants will mobilize others, with net effects on the results that depend on who is activated and for how long. Therefore it is possible that unilateral increases in participation will decrease rather than increase influence. In some cases, low participation rates reflect a sophisticated assessment of the indirect effects of activity on the activity of others as well as the direct effects on results.

Decision Making as Symbol and Ritual

To focus exclusively on the results of a decision process is also to risk overlooking one of the more obvious things about decisions in organizations: that they are of considerable symbolic importance. Decision processes are sacred rituals. The symbolic importance of decision making reflects two interrelated phenomena. At a simple instrumental level, organizations and the individuals in them need to communicate to their observers that the decisions they make are legitimate. Legitimacy is established by showing that the decisions accomplish appropriate objectives or by showing that they are made in appropriate ways. The first demonstration is often difficult. It is hard to show the linkage between decision and outcome. Thus legitimacy often depends on the appropriateness of the process as much as it does on the outcomes. Both for the organization and the observer, process measures are possible surrogates for outcome measures. It is a story familiar to students of organizational control and should not be surprising here.

Organizations establish that they are good decision makers by making decisions in a way that symbolizes the qualities that are valued. They consult relevant people, consider alternatives, gather information, and act decisively but prudently. Decision making is in part a performance designed to reassure decision makers and others that things are being done appropriately. Good decision makers are those who do what good decision makers do, and as organizations and decision makers compete for legitimacy and reputations, decision processes are ways in which they attempt to signal competence at decision making. Where decision quality is difficult to measure directly, as it often is, the competition for reputation is likely to lead to an emphasis on displaying process attributes. For example, we would expect a proliferation of plans, information gathering, analysis, consultation, and other observable features of normatively approved decision making.

The symbolism of decision process is not limited to the tactics of competition among organizations and decision makers. The idea of intelligent choice is a central idea of modern ideology, and organizations are institutions dedicated to that vision of life. Consequently, activities within organizations, and particularly decision activities, are part of a set of rituals by which a society assures itself that human existence is built around choice, and that human institutions are manifestations of the intelligent control of human destiny through rational action. The decision process is a ritual by which we recognize saints, socialize the young, reassure the old, recite scripture, and come to understand the nature of our existence.

Certain conspicuous features of organization decision making can be interpreted as stemming from the symbolic importance of the process. We observe that individuals will fight for the right to participate in decision making, then not exercise that right with any vigor. We observe that organizations ignore information they have, ask for more information, then ignore the new information when it is available. We observe that managers spend substantial amounts of time in activities that appear to have few consequences beyond acknowledging the importance of others, and themselves. We observe that organizational participants will contend vigorously and acrimoniously over adoption of a policy, but once the policy is adopted, the same contenders will appear to be largely indifferent to its implementation, or lack of it. Although each of these observations could be explained in other ways, it is hard to consider all of them without beginning to suspect that decision making may be an occasion for exercising problems and solutions more than connecting them, for displaying decision making more than profiting from it, and for exhibiting virtue more than using it.

To recognize the symbolic significance of decision making is not to denigrate it. Symbols and social ritual may be a way of concealing the reality of outcome perversities, and unquestionably symbols sometimes hide realities. However, the converse can also be true. Students of decision making probably have a systematic tendency to exaggerate the significance of the explicit substantive results of decisions and to underestimate the significance of the symbolic contributions that decision making gives to organizations and the society. For such students, symbols obfuscate outcomes. Yet it is hard to imagine a society with modern Western ideology that would not require a well-elaborated and reinforced myth of organizational choice, both to sustain a semblance of social orderliness and meaning and to facilitate change. We may quarrel with the ideology and seek a different set of symbols, but by most reasonable measures the symbolic consequences of organizational decision processes are at least as important as the substantive consequences. In many respects decision results are minor embellishments of a life of symbols rather than the other way around.

CONCLUSION

Every history of progress is a listing of unfinished business, and it is not hard to see the intellectual terrain of theories of organizational decision making as littered with unresolved issues and incompletely explored ideas. We began with a simple conception of organizations acting in the name of anticipations of uncertain future preferences and uncertain future consequences of current action. We complicated the assumptions of such a conception by noting the ways in which information was not provided automatically but had to be discovered, and by noting the ways in which goals may be in conflict within an organization. Then we observed the extent to which organizational action was based on rules and identified the ways in which rules can be viewed as developing through experiential learning, selection, and imitation. We complicated the picture by observing the ways in which ambiguity about preferences, history, and technology confound both rational action and learning. And finally we noted that organizational choice is part of a highly contextual and symbolic world in which organizations and the actors in them attribute a sense of meaning to life.

Each of the complications defines another domain of empirical and theoretical research, mostly underexplored. We need more work on shifting aspiration levels and their effects on search activities; on the dynamics of information and control under conflict of interest; on the ways in which the rationing of time affects decisions and decision processes; on organizational hill-climbing and learning; on responses of organizations to variations in environmental adversity; on the intertemporal comparison of fuzzy goals; on the symbolic content of decision making. None of those are minor things.

The theory of decision making in organizations has become an arena for several of the more interesting methodological and philosophical issues of contemporary social science. It is difficult to consider organizational choice without dealing with the relation between normative and descriptive theories of human life; with alternative conceptions of ways of establishing the credibility of ideas; with the relation between the methods of ethnography and history and the development of systematic theory; with the role of willfulness in behavior; with the place of conflict and instrumentalism in the good life; with the relation between simplicity and complexity in understanding human existence.

Among the more conspicuous features of this development, three may be particularly noteworthy. First, the theories have become increasingly contextual in character. In order to understand decision making in organizations, we are led to consider how any particular decision is embedded in a history, a set of alternative activities for various possible participants, and many other things that are happening simultaneously. Students of decision making are tempted to think that the world is organized around decisions simply because that is their own research focus. In many ways decisions and decision processes can be portrayed better as the incidental consequence of the confluence of numerous, relatively autonomous streams of history. The streams are sufficiently independent to make the short-run consequences of the process surprisingly dependent on largely arbitrary temporal connections among exogenous events.

Second, much of the work is interpretive. Ordinary participants in organizations know a good deal about what happens in them. Unfortunately, their theory of what happens in them is often rather distant from their experience. At the intellectual level, they are driven to viewing most of what they see in organizations as pathological, inappropriately remote from a theory of good decision making. At the pragmatic level, they have some ideas about how to make a real organization work. Those pragmatic ideas have little connection to the intellectual model of an organization that they accept. To a considerable extent, work on theories of organizational decision making is an effort to develop an interpretation of organizational life that is theoretical, yet consistent with pragmatic knowledge. As a result, it tends to be cautious about assuming that differences between observed behavior and theoretically proper behavior reflect mistakes in behavior. Students in this tradition are somewhat more likely than others to assume that peculiar organizational behavior reflects a theoretical misunderstanding of what is sensible. No one believes that organizations are always sensible. But the tradition tries to move the discrepancy between theories of decision making and organizational experience in decision making a bit further from the level of schizophrenia and a bit closer to intellectual tension.

Third, there are no clear universals in this business. Although organizations appear often to satisfice rather than maximize, some reasonably clear counter examples can be observed. Although individuals and groups in organizations often act strategically in the face of conflict of interest, they sometimes fail to do so. Although organizational actions are often incremental, they sometimes seem to reflect heroic leaps. Although organizations often learn from their experience, they sometimes appear to create rules as an organizational tour de force. Although many ideas and procedures spread through a community of organizations like chicken pox, other similar ones do not. Although organizations frequently have goals that are unclear and unstable, sometimes they seem to be acting in terms of precise, stable preferences. Although decisions and decision processes seem always to be part of a system of symbols and social drama, sometimes those symbols seem conspicuously more salient than at other times. The situation is familiar throughout the social sciences, and the conventional response is to attempt to specify the conditions under which one response or another is observed. It is impossible to quarrel with such a strategy in general, but it is not at all clear that it will be helpful here. The users of theories of organizational decision making need to profit from the theories in two ways. The obvious way is in using the theories to understand the decision behavior of organizations. The less obvious way is in coming to an appreciation of the nature of understanding itself.

It is easy to become overly fanciful about such things, but the problem of understanding is not remarkably different from the problem of decision in organization. It involves the complications of limited capacity, conflict, ambiguity, symbols, and the rest. It probably profits from a perspective that is relatively incremental, emphasizing alternative interpretations of past events as a guide to learning from those events rather than attempting to make a precise forecast of what will happen. Existing theories of organizational choice are not well constructed to stand alone. Rather they are implicitly designed to be used by someone of ordinary organizational sense and specific organizational experience to improve an understanding of what is going on. Such a perception of theory as contributing marginally to ordinary knowledge, rather than summarizing all knowledge, makes theoretical speculations analogous to the contributions of a good consultant. Or possibly a minor poet.

ACKNOWLEDGMENT

Although this essay has been written without explicit references, I would not want to be blamed for it all. A selected bibliography of relevant work is appended. In addition, I will attribute partial responsibility to a long list of friends and colleagues, some of whose contributions are not reflected directly by the bibliography. Specifically: Peter Abell, Susan Abramowitz, Flemming Agersnap, Torben Agersnap, Howard Aldrich, Graham Allison, Ib Andersen, David Anderson, Chris Argyris, Kenneth Arrow, Robert Axelrod, J. Victor Baldridge, Eugene Bardach, Chester Barnard, William Baumol, Alex Bavelas, Selwyn Becker, Guy Beneviste, Jonathon Bendor, Peter Blau, Joseph Bower, David Brereton, Michael Butler, Richard Carlson, Glenn Carroll, E. Eugene Carter, Dorwin Cartwright, Hanoria Casey, Ellen Chaffee, Alfred Chandler, Søren Christensen, Burton Clark, Stewart Clegg, Kalman Cohen, Michael Cohen, Michael Cole, James Coleman, Terry Connally, Ronald Corwin, J. Patrick Crecine, Michel Crozier, Larry Cuban, Richard Cyert, Richard Daft, Robert Dahl, R. H. Day, Terrance Deal, William Dill, Anthony Downs, George Downs, Robert Dubin, Vicki Eaton, Harry Eckstein, Murray Edelman, Carla Edlefson, George Ekker, Gunnar Eliasson, Omar El Sawy, Jon Elster, Harald Enderud, Lars Engwall, Carson Eoyang, Suzanne Estler, William Evan, Edward Feigenbaum, Julian Feldman, Martha Feldman, John Freeman, William Gamson, Alexander George, Donald Gerwin, David Gibson, James Glenn, Bohdan Glinski, Erving Goffman, Robert Golembiewski, Alvin Gouldner, Chris Gudnason, Harold Guetzkow, Chadwick Haberstroh, Ingemund Hägg, Mason Haire, Morton Halperin, Michael Hannan, Jane Hannaway, Elisabeth Hansot, Bo Hedberg, Gudmund Hernes, Helga Hernes, David Hickson, Albert Hirschman, Edwin Hollander, David Holmberg, George Homans, Pierre Huard, Alice Isen, Knut Jacobsen, Torben Beck Jørgensen, Robert Kahn, Daniel Kahneman, Mark Kamlet, Daniel Katz, Herbert Kaufman, Neil Kay, Harold Kelley, Peter Keen, Sara Kiesler, Michael Kirst, Kenneth Knight, Lena Kolarska, Charlotte Koo, Kristian Kreiner, Susan Krieger, Per Laegreid, Martin Landau, Pat Larkey, Charles Lave, Jean Lave, Paul Lawrence, Harold Leavitt, Daniel Levinthal, Raymond Levitt, Rensis Likert, Charles Lindblom, S. Martin Lipset, Norton Long, Jay Lorsch, William Lucas, Mary Ann Maguire, Curtis Manns, Edwin Mansfield, James C. March, Kathryn March, Rod March, Stephen Marglin, Robin Marris, Jacob Marschak, Andrew Marshall, Joanne Martin, Lewis Mayhew, Arnold Meltsner, Robert Merton, John Meyer, Anne Miner, Henry Mintzberg, Ian Mitroff, Lawrence Mohr, Chad Moore, Bertil Naslund, Richard Nelson, Richard Neustadt, Johan Olsen, William Ouchi, John Padgett, Andreas Papandreou, Elisabeth Paté, Edith Penrose, Charles Perrow, Vance Peterson, Andrew Pettigrew, Louis Pondy, William Pounds, Melanie Powers, Jeffrey Pfeffer, Derek Pugh, Roy Radner, Theodore Reed, Everett Rogers, Allyn Romanow, Pierre Romelaer, Kaare Rommetveit, Michael Rothschild, J. Rounds, Brian Rowan, Paul Sabatier, Harald Saetren, Gerald Salancik, Thomas Schelling, Joseph Schlesinger, Kaye Schoonhoven, W. Richard Scott, Philip Selznick, Guje Sevón, Zur Shapira, Ed Sherry, Martin Shubik, David Sills, Herbert Simon, Jitendra Singh, Paul Slovic, Peer Soelberg, A. Michael Spence, Lee Sproull, Per Stava, Barry Staw, Andrew Stedry, John Steinbruner, Shelby Stewman, Joseph Stiglitz, Arthur Stinchcombe, Nelly Stromquist, Robert Strotz, Steven Swerdlick, Serge Taylor, Judith Tendler, James Thompson, Eric Trist, Donald Trow, David Truman, David Tyack, Gordon Tullock, Nancy Tuma, Amos Tversky, Geoffrey Vickers, Victor Vroom, Eugene Webb, Karl Weick, Stephen Weiner, Andrew Whinston, Harrison White, William Whyte, Aaron Wildavsky, Matthew Willard, Oliver Williamson, James Wilson, Sidney Winter, Roberta Wohlstetter, David Wolf, Joan Woodward, Alice Young, Mayer Zald; and some others inadvertently overlooked and to be remembered with embarrassment tomorrow. If the essay seems an inadequate tribute to such an impressive roster of collaborators, I can only make the usual pleas of incompetence and reluctance to steal any more from them than I already have.

REFERENCES

Alchian, A. A. (1950). "Uncertainty, Evolution, and Economic Theory," *Journal of Political Economy* **58**:211–221.

Aldrich, H. E. (1979). *Organizations and Environments,* Englewood Cliffs, NJ: Prentice-Hall.

Alexis, M., and C. Z. Wilson (1967). *Organizational Decision Making,* Englewood Cliffs, NJ: Prentice-Hall.

Allison, G. T. (1972). *Essence of Decision,* Boston: Little, Brown.

Allison, G. T., and M. H. Halperin (1972). "Bureaucratic Politics: A Paradigm and Some Policy Implications," in R. Tantner and R. H. Ullman, Eds., *Theory and Policy in International Relations,* Princeton, NJ: Princeton University Press.

Arrow, K. J. (1974). *The Limits of Organization,* New York: W. W. Norton.

Baldridge, J. V. (1971). *Power and Conflict in the University,* New York: Wiley.

Bardach, E. (1977). *The Implementation Game,* Cambridge, MA: MIT Press.

Barnard, C. (1938). *Functions of the Executive,* Cambridge: Harvard University Press.

Baumol, W. J. (1959). *Business Behavior, Value, and Growth,* New York: Macmillan.

Blau, P. (1964). *Exchange and Power in Social Life,* New York: Wiley.

Bower, J. L. (1968). "Descriptive Decision Theory from the 'Administrative Viewpoint'," in R. A. Bauer and K. J. Gergen, Eds., *The Study of Policy Formation,* New York: Free Press.

Bower, J. L. (1970). *Managing the Resource Allocation Process: A Study of Corporate Planning and Investment,* Boston: Harvard University Graduate School of Business Administration.

Bower, J. L. (1965). "The Role of Conflict in Economic Decision Making Groups," *Quarterly Journal of Economics* **70:**253–277.

Braybrooke, D., and C. E. Lindblom (1963). *A Strategy of Decision: Policy Evaluation as a Social Process,* New York: Free Press.

Burns, T. J. (1970). *The Behavioral Aspects of Accounting Data for Performance Evaluation,* Columbus: Ohio State University College of Administrative Sciences.

Carter, E. E. (1971a). "The Behavioral Theory of the Firm and Top-Level Corporate Decisions," *Administrative Science Quarterly* **16:**412–428.

Carter, E. E. (1971b). "Project Evaluations and Firm Decisions," *Journal of Management Studies* **9:**253–279.

Castles, F. G., D. J. Murray, and D. C. Potter (1971). *Decisions, Organizations and Society,* Middlesex, England: Open University Press.

Clark, B. R. (1956). "Organizational Adaptation and Precarious Values: A Case Study," *American Sociological Review* **21:**327–336.

Clark, P. B., and J. Q. Wilson (1971). "Incentive Systems: A Theory of Organizations," *Administrative Science Quarterly* **6:**129–166.

Clegg, S. R. (1975). *Power, Rule and Domination,* London: Routledge and Kegan Paul.

Cohen, M. D., and J. G. March (1974). *Leadership and Ambiguity: The American College President,* New York: McGraw-Hill.

Cohen, M. D., J. G. March, and J. P. Olsen (1972). "A Garbage Can Model of Organizational Choice," *Administrative Science Quarterly* **17:**1–25.

Coleman, J. S. (1966). "Foundations of a Theory of Collective Decisions," *American Journal of Sociology* **71:**615–627.

Connolly, T. (1977). "Information Processing and Decision Making in Organizations," in B. M. Staw and G. R. Salancik, Eds., *New Directions in Organizational Behavior,* Chicago: St. Clair Press, pp. 205–234.

Crecine, J. P. (1967). *Governmental Problem Solving,* Chicago: Markham Publishing.

Crozier, M. (1964). *The Bureaucratic Phenomenon,* Chicago: The University of Chicago Press.

Crozier, M., and J-C Thoenig (1976). "The Regulation of Complex Organized Systems," *Administrative Science Quarterly* **21:**547–570.

Cyert, R. M., and J. G. March (1963). *A Behavioral Theory of the Firm,* Englewood Cliffs, NJ: Prentice-Hall.

Daft, R. L., and S. W. Becker (1978). *The Innovative Organization,* New York: Elsevier.

Dahl, R. L., and C. E. Lindblom (1953). *Politics, Economics, and Welfare,* New York: Harper and Row.

Davis, O., M. Dempster, and A. Wildavsky (1969). "A Theory of the Budgetary Process," *American Political Science Review* **60:**529–547.

Day, R. H. (1967). "Profits, Learning and the Convergence of Satisficing to Marginalism," *Quarterly Journal of Economics* **81:**302–311.

Day, R. H., and T. Groves (1975). *Adaptive Economic Models,* New York: Academic Press.

Devons, E. (1950). *Planning in Practice,* Cambridge, England: Cambridge University Press.

Dill, W. R. (1962). "Administrative Decision-Making," in S. Mailick and E. H. Van Ness,

Eds., *Concepts and Issues in Administrative Behavior,* Englewood Cliffs, NJ: Prentice-Hall.

Dill, W. R. (1958). "Environment as an Influence on Managerial Autonomy," *Administrative Science Quarterly* **2:**409–443.

Dornbusch, S. M., and W. R. Scott (1975). *Evaluation and the Exercise of Authority,* San Francisco: Jossey-Bass.

Downs, A. (1967). *Inside Bureaucracy,* Boston: Little, Brown.

Downs, G. W., Jr. (1976). *Bureaucracy, Innovation, and Public Policy,* Lexington, MA: D. C. Heath.

Downs, G. W., Jr., and L. B. Mohr (1976). "Conceptual Issues in Innovation," *Administrative Science Quarterly* **21:**700–714.

Dror, Y. (1968). *Public Policymaking Reexamined,* San Francisco: Chandler.

Edelman, M. (1960). *The Symbolic Uses of Politics,* Champaign: University of Illinois Press.

Eliasson, G. (1976). *Business Economic Planning,* New York: Wiley.

Elster, J. (1979). *Ulysses and the Sirens,* Cambridge, England: Cambridge University Press.

Feldman, J., and H. E. Kanter (1965). "Going to the Wall: School District Administrative Intensity and Environmental Constraint," *Administrative Science Quarterly* **24:**119–133.

Feldman, M. S. and J. G. March (1981). "Information in Organizations as Signal and Symbol," *Administrative Science Quarterly* **26:**171–186.

Freeman, J., and M. T. Hannan (1975). "Growth and Decline Processes in Organizations," *American Sociological Review* **40:**215–228.

Gamson, W. A. (1968). *Power and Discontent,* Homewood, IL: Dorsey Press.

George, A. (1980). *Presidential Decisionmaking in Foreign Policy: The Effective Use of Information and Advice,* Boulder, CO: Westview.

Gerwin, D. (1969). *Budgeting Public Funds: The Decision Process in an Urban School District,* Madison: University of Wisconsin Press.

Goldman, D. R. (1973). "Managerial Mobility Motivations and Central Life Interests," *American Sociological Review* **38:**119–126.

Goodman, P. S. (1977). "Social Comparison Processes in Organizations," in B. M. Staw and G. R. Salancik, Eds., *New Directions in Organizational Behavior,* Chicago: St. Clair Press, pp. 97–132.

Halperin, M. H. (1974). *Bureaucratic Politics and Foreign Policy,* Washington, DC: Brookings.

Hannan, M. T., and J. Freeman (1977). "The Population Ecology of Organizations," *American Journal of Sociology* **82:**929–966.

Harrison, E. F. (1975). *The Managerial Decision-Making Process,* Boston: Houghton Mifflin.

Hedberg, B. L. T, P. C. Nystrom, and W. H. Starbuck (1976). "Camping on Seesaws: Prescriptions for a Self-Designing Organization," *Administrative Science Quarterly* **21:**41–65.

Heller, F. A. (1976). "Decision Processes: An Analysis of Power-Sharing at Senior Organizational Levels," in R. Dubin, Ed., *Handbook of Work, Organization, and Society,* Chicago: Rand McNally.

Hernes, G. (1975). *Makt og Avmakt,* Oslo: Universitetsforlatet.

Hickson, D. J., C. R. Hinings, C. A. Lee, R. E. Schneck, and U. M. Pennings (1971). "Structural Conditions of Intraorganizational Power," *Administrative Science Quarterly* **19:**22–44.

Hirschleifer, J., and J. G. Riley (1979). "The Analytics of Uncertainty and Information—An Expository Survey," *Journal of Economic Literature* **17:**1375–1421.

Hirschman, A. O. (1967). *Development Projects Observed*, Washington, DC: Brookings.

Hirschman, A. O. (1970). *Exit, Voice and Loyalty*, Cambridge: Harvard University Press.

Jacobs, D. (1974). "Dependency and Vulnerability: An Exchange Approach to the Control of Organizations," *Administrative Science Quarterly* 19:45–59.

Janis, I. L., and L. Mann (1977). *Decision Making*, New York: Free Press.

Jones, W. M. (1973). "On Decision Making in Large Organizations," in M. H. Halperin and A. Kanter, Eds., *Readings in American Foreign Policy: A Bureaucratic Perspective*, Washington, DC: Brookings, pp. 138–154.

Kaufman, H. (1971). *The Limits of Organizational Change*, Birmingham: University of Alabama Press.

Kay, N. M. (1979). *The Innovating Firm: A Behavioral Theory of Corporate R&D*, New York: St. Martin's.

Keen, P. G. W. (1977). "The Evolving Concept of Optimality," *TIMS Studies in the Management Sciences* 6:31–57.

Knight, K. E. (1967). "A Descriptive Model of the Intra-Firm Innovation Process," *Journal of Business* 40:478–496.

Krieger, S. (1979). *Hip Capitalism*, Beverly Hills, CA: Sage.

Krause, C. G. (1972). "Complex Objectives, Decentralization, and the Decision Process of the Organization," *Administrative Science Quarterly* 17:544–554.

Laegreid, P., and J. P. Olsen (1978). *Byraakrati og Beslutninger*, Bergen, Norway: Universitetsforlaget.

Landau, M. (1973). "On the Concept of the Self-Correcting Organization," *Public Administration Review* 33:533–542.

Latham, E. (1959). "The Body Politic of the Corporation," in E. S. Mason, Ed., *The Corporation in Modern Society*, Cambridge: Harvard University Press.

Lawler, E. E. (1976). "Control Systems in Organizations," in M. D. Dunnette, Ed., *Handbook of Industrial and Organizational Psychology*, Chicago: Rand McNally, pp. 1247–1291.

Lawrence, P. R., and J. W. Lorsch (1967). *Organization and Environment*, Boston: Graduate School of Business Administration, Harvard University.

Lindblom, C. E. (1959). "The Science of 'Muddling Through'," *Public Administration Review* 19:78–88.

Lindblom, C. E. (1965). *The Intelligence of Democracy*, New York: Macmillan.

Lindblom, C. E. (1968). *The Policy-Making Process*, Englewood Cliffs, NJ: Prentice-Hall.

Lindblom, C. E. (1977). *Politics and Markets*, New York: Basic Books.

Long, N. E. (1958). "The Local Community as an Ecology of Games," *American Journal of Sociology* 44:251–261.

Long, N. E. (1962). "The Administrative Organization as a Political System," in S. Mailick and E. H. Van Ness, Eds., *Concepts and Issues in Administrative Behavior*, Englewood Cliffs, NJ: Prentice-Hall, pp. 110–121.

Lourenco, S. V., and J. C. Glidewell (1975). "A Dialectical Analysis of Organizational Conflict," *Administrative Science Quarterly* 20:489–508.

MacCrimmon, K. R., and D. N. Taylor (1976). "Decision Making and Problem Solving," in M. D. Dunnette, Ed., *Handbook of Industrial and Organizational Psychology*, Chicago: Rand-McNally, pp. 1397–1453.

Mack, R. P. (1971). *Planning on Uncertainty: Decision Making in Business and Government Administration*, New York: Wiley-Interscience.

Manns, C. J., and J. G. March (1978). "Financial Adversity, Internal Competition, and Curriculum Change in a University," *Administrative Science Quarterly* 23:541–552.

Mansfield, E. (1968). *The Economics of Technological Change*, New York: Norton.

March, J. G. (1962). "The Business Firm as a Political Coalition," *Journal of Politics* **24**:662–678.

March, J. G. (1966). "The Power of Power," in D. Easton, Ed., *Varieties of Political Theory,* Englewood Cliffs, NJ: Prentice-Hall, pp. 39–70.

March, J. G. (1969). "Politics and the City," in K. J. Arrow, J. G. March, J. S. Coleman, and A. Downs, *Urban Processes,* Washington, DC: The Urban Institute.

March, J. G. (1978a). "Bounded Rationality, Ambiguity, and the Engineering of Choice," *Bell Journal of Economics* **9**:587–608.

March, J. G. (1978b). "American Public School Administration: A Short Analysis," *School Review* **86**:217–250.

March, J. G., and J. P. Olson (1976). *Ambiguity and Choice in Organizations,* Bergen, Norway: Universitetsforlaget.

March, J. G., and J. P. Olson (1975). "The Uncertainty of the Past: Organizational Learning Under Ambiguity," *European Journal of Political Research,* **3**:147–171.

March, J. G., and H. A. Simon (1958). *Organizations,* New York: John Wiley & Sons.

Marris, R. (1964). *The Economic Theory of "Managerial" Capitalism,* New York: Free Press.

Marschak, J., and R. Radner (1972). *Economic Theory of Teams,* New Haven: Yale University Press.

McFarland, A. S. (1969). *Power and Leadership in Pluralist Systems,* Stanford, CA: Stanford University Press.

McGuire, C. B., and R. Radner, Eds. (1972). *Decision and Organization,* Amsterdam: North Holland.

McNeil, K., and J. D. Thompson (1971). "The Regeneration of Social Organizations," *American Sociological Review* **36**:624–637.

Meyer, J. W., and B. Rowan (1977). "Institutionalized Organizations: Formal Structures as Myth and Ceremony," *American Journal of Sociology* **83**:340–360.

Mintzberg, H. (1973). *The Nature of Managerial Work,* New York: Harper and Row.

Moch, M. K. (1976). "Structure and Organizational Resource Allocation," *Administrative Science Quarterly* **21**:661–674.

Moch, M. K., and E. V. Morse (1977). "Size, Centralization and Organizational Adoption of Innovations," *American Sociological Review* **42**:716–725.

Mohr, L. B. (1969). "Determinants of Innovation in Organizations," *American Political Science Review* **63**:111–126.

Mohr, L. B. (1973). "The Concept of Organizational Goal," *American Political Science Review* **67**:470–481.

Nelson, R. R., and S. G. Winter (1973). "Towards an Evolutionary Theory of Economic Capabilities," *American Economic Review* **63**:440–449.

Nelson, R. R., and S. G. Winter (1981). "Neoclassical versus Evolutionary Theories of Economic Growth," *Economic Journal,* forthcoming.

Neustadt, R. E. (1960). *Presidential Power,* New York: Wiley.

Nisbet, R., and L. Ross (1980). *Human Inference: Strategies and Shortcomings of Social Judgment,* Englewood Cliffs, NJ: Prentice-Hall.

Niskanen, W. A. (1971). *Bureaucracy and Representative Government,* Chicago: Rand-McNally.

Olsen, J. P. (1972a). "Voting, 'Sounding Out', and the Governance of Modern Organizations," *Acta Sociologica* **15**:267–283.

Olsen, J. P. (1972b). "Public Policy-Making and Theories of Organizational Choice," *Scandinavian Political Studies* **7**:45–62.

Olsen, J. P. (1978). *Politisk Organisering,* Bergen, Norway: Universitetsforlaget.

Olsen, J. P., and H. Saetren (1980). *Aksjoner og Demokrati,* Bergen, Norway: Universitetsforlaget.

Olsen, M. (1965). *The Logic of Collective Action,* New York: Schocken.

Ouchi, W. G., and M. A. Maguire (1975). "Organizational Control: Two Functions," *Administrative Science Quarterly* **20**:559–569.

Padgett, J. F. (1980). "Bounded Rationality in Budgetary Research," *American Political Science Review* **74**:354–372.

Penrose, E. T. (1959). *The Theory of the Growth of the Firm,* Oxford: Basil Blackwell.

Perrow, C. (1961). "The Analysis of Goals in Complex Organizations," *American Sociological Review* **26**:854–866.

Perrow, C. (1970). *Organizational Analysis: A Sociological View,* London: Tavistock.

Perrow, C. (1972). *Complex Organizations: A Critical Essay,* Glenview, IL: Scott, Foresman.

Peterson, P. E., and T. Williams (1972). "Models of Decision Making," in M. W. Kirst, Ed., *State, School and Politics,* Lexington, MA: D. C. Heath, pp. 149–168.

Pfeffer, J. (1977). "Power and Resource Allocation in Organizations," in B. M. Staw and G. R. Salancik, Eds., *New Directions in Organizational Behavior,* Chicago: St. Clair Press, pp. 235–266.

Pfeffer, J. (1980). "Power and Politics in Organizations," unpublished manuscript.

Pfeffer, J., and G. R. Salancik (1974). "Organizational Decision Making as a Political Process: The Case of a University Budget," *Administrative Science Quarterly* **19**:135–151.

Pfeffer, J., and G. R. Salancik (1978). *The External Control of Organizations,* New York: Harper and Row.

Pfeffer, J., G. R. Salancik, and H. Leblecici (1976). "The Effect of Uncertainty on the Use of Social Influence in Organizational Decision Making," *Administrative Science Quarterly* **21**:227–245.

Pondy, L. R. (1969). "Varieties of Organizational Conflict," *Administrative Science Quarterly* **14**:499–505.

Pondy, L. R. (1970). "Toward a Theory of Internal Resource Allocation," in M. Zald, Ed., *Power in Organizations,* Nashville, TN: Vanderbilt University Press, pp. 270–311.

Porat, A. M., and J. A. Haas (1969). "Information Effects on Decision Making," *Behavioral Science* **14**:98–104.

Radner, R. (1975a). "A Behavioral Model of Cost Reduction," *Bell Journal of Economics* **6**:196–215.

Radner, R. (1975b). "Satisficing," *Journal of Mathematical Economics* **2**:253–262.

Richman, B. M. (1965). *Soviet Management,* Englewood Cliffs, NJ: Prentice-Hall.

Riker, W. H. (1962). *The Theory of Political Coalition,* New Haven: Yale University Press.

Robinson, J. A., and R. R. Majak (1967). "The Theory of Decision-Making," in J. G. Charlesworth, Ed., *Contemporary Political Analysis,* New York: Free Press, pp. 175–188.

Rourke, F. (1969). *Bureaucracy, Politics, and Public Policy,* Boston: Little, Brown.

Salancik, G. R., and J. Pfeffer (1974). "The Bases and Use of Power in Organizational Decision Making: The Case of a University," *Administrative Science Quarterly* **19**:453–473.

Schelling, T. C. (1960). *The Strategy of Conflict,* Cambridge: Harvard University Press.

Schelling, T. C. (1971). "On the Ecology of Micro-Motives," *Public Interest* **25**:59–98.

Schelling, T. C. (1978). *Micromotives and Macrobehavior,* New York: Norton.

Selznick, P. (1949). *TVA and the Grass Roots,* Berkeley: University of California Press.

Shubik, M. (1970). "A Curmudgeon's Guide to Micro Economics," *Journal of Economic Literature* **8**:405–434.

Shull, F. A., Jr., A. L. Delbecq, and L. L. Cummings (1970). *Organizational Decision Making*, New York: McGraw-Hill.

Sills, D. L. (1957). *The Volunteers*, Glencoe, IL: Free Press.

Simon, H. A. (1953). "Birth of an Organization: The Economic Cooperation Administration," *Public Administration Review* **25**:31–37.

Simon, H. A. (1957a). *Administrative Behavior*, 2nd ed., New York: Macmillan.

Simon, H. A. (1957b). *Models of Man*, New York: Wiley.

Simon, H. A. (1959). "Theories of Decision Making in Economics and Political Science," *American Economic Review* **49**:253–283.

Simon, H. A. (1960). *The New Science of Management Decision*, New York: Harper.

Simon, H. A. (1964). "On the Concept of the Organizational Goal," *Administrative Science Quarterly* **9**:1–22.

Simon, H. A. (1965). "Administrative Decision Making," *Public Administration Review* **25**:31–37.

Simon, H. A. (1979). "Rational Decision Making in Business Organizations," *American Economic Review* **69**:493–513.

Simpson, R. L., and W. H. Gulley (1962). "Goals, Environmental Pressures, and Organizational Characteristics," *American Sociological Review* **27**:344–351.

Sproull, L. S., S. Weiner, and D. B. Wolf (1978). *Organizing an Anarchy*, Chicago: University of Chicago Press.

Stagner, R. (1969). "Corporate Decision Making: An Empirical Study," *Journal of Applied Psychology* **53**:1–13.

Starbuck, W. H. (1965). "Organizational Growth and Development," in J. G. March, Ed., *Handbook of Organizations*, Chicago: Rand-McNally, pp. 451–533.

Starbuck, W. H. (1976). "Organizations and Their Environments," in M. D. Dunnette, Ed., *Handbook of Industrial and Organizational Psychology*, Chicago: Rand-McNally, pp. 1069–1123.

Staw, B. M., and G. R. Salancik, Eds. (1977). *New Directions in Organizational Behavior*, Chicago: St. Clair Press.

Staw, B. M., and E. Szwajkowski (1975). "The Scarcity-Munificence Component of Organizational Environments and the Commission of Illegal Acts," *Administrative Science Quarterly* **20**:345–354.

Steinbruner, J. D. (1974). *The Cybernetic Theory of Decision*, Princeton, NJ: Princeton University Press.

Stinchcombe, A. L. (1974). *Creating Efficient Industrial Administration*, New York: Academic Press.

Swidler, A. (1979). *Organization Without Authority*, Cambridge: Harvard University Press.

Taylor, D. W. (1965). "Decision Making and Problem Solving," in J. G. March, Ed., *Handbook of Organizations*, Chicago: Rand-McNally, pp. 48–86.

Taylor, R. N. (1975). "Psychological Determinants of Bounded Rationality: Implications for Decision-making Strategies," *Decision Sciences* **6**:409–429.

Tendler, J. (1975). *Inside Foreign Aid*, Baltimore: Johns Hopkins University Press.

Thompson, J. D. (1967). *Organizations in Action*, New York: McGraw-Hill.

Thompson, J. D., and W. J. McEwen (1958). "Organizational Goals and Environment: Goal-setting as an Interacting Process," *American Sociological Review* **23**:23–31.

Thompson, J. D., and A. Tuden (1959). "Strategies, Structures, and Processes of Organizational Decision," in J. D. Thompson et al., Eds., *Comparative Studies in Administration*, Pittsburgh, PA: University of Pittsburgh Press.

Tversky, A., and D. Kahneman (1974). "Judgement under Uncertainty: Heuristics and Biases," *Science* **185**:1124–1131.

Vickers, G. (1965). *The Art of Judgment: A Study of Policy-Making,* New York: Basic Books.

Weick, K. E. (1976). "Educational Organizations as Loosely Coupled Systems," *Administrative Science Quarterly* **21**:1–19.

Weick, K. E. (1977). "Enactment Processes in Organizations," in B. M. Staw and G. R. Salancik, Eds., *New Directions in Organizational Behavior,* Chicago: St. Clair Press.

Weick, K. E. (1979). *The Social Psychology of Organizing,* 2nd ed., Reading, MA: Addison-Wesley.

White, P. E. (1974). "Resources as Determinants of Organizational Behavior," *Administrative Science Quarterly* **19**:366–379.

Wildavsky, A. B. (1964). *The Politics of the Budgetary Process,* Boston: Little, Brown.

Wildavsky, A. B. (1975). *Budgeting: A Comparative Theory of Budgetary Processes,* Boston: Little, Brown.

Wilensky, H. L. (1967). *Organizational Intelligence: Knowledge and Policy in Government,* New York: Basic Books.

Williamson, O. E. (1964). *The Economics of Discretionary Behavior: Managerial Objectives in a Theory of the Firm,* Englewood Cliffs, NJ: Prentice-Hall.

Williamson, O. E. (1970). *Corporate Control and Business Behavior,* Englewood Cliffs, NJ: Prentice-Hall.

Williamson, O. E. (1975). *Markets and Hierarchies,* New York: Free Press.

Wilson, J. Q. (1966). "Innovation in Organizations: Notes toward a Theory," in J. D. Thompson, Ed., *Approaches to Organizational Design,* Pittsburgh, PA: University of Pittsburgh Press.

Winter, S. G. (1964). "Economic 'Natural Selection' and the Theory of the Firm," *Yale Economic Essays* **4**:225–272.

Winter, S. G. (1971). "Satisficing, Selection, and the Innovating Remnant," *Quarterly Journal of Economics* **85**:237–261.

Winter, S. G. (1975). "Optimization and Evolution in the Theory of the Firm," in R. H. Day and T. Groves, Eds., *Adaptive Economic Models,* New York: Academic Press.

Wohlstetter, R. (1965). "Cuba and Pearl Harbor: Hindsight and Foresight," *Foreign Affairs* **44**:691–707.

Zald, M. V., Ed. (1970). *Power in Organizations,* Nashville, TN: Vanderbilt University Press.

COMMENTS ON DECISIONS IN ORGANIZATIONS

CHARLES E. LINDBLOM
Yale University

At the end of his illuminating survey of developments in the theory—if it can yet be called that—of organizational decision making, March comes to three significant conclusions that I would like to accept and take as the text for my comments. (But his comments would be even more illuminating if coupled with citations from the literature he canvasses.* His single footnote, perhaps modeled after the Social Register or the list of the honored dead on war memorials, is more playful than helpful.) They are:

1. Theories have become more contextual. They are the consequences of the confluence in time of numerous streams of events.

2. The theories are interpretive rather than causal, moving in the direction—though March does not use the word—of hermeneutics and away from the cause-and-effect propositions of conventional science. (I may be putting words in March's mouth to give his second conclusion the meaning I here give it. As March puts the conclusion, it seems to me to be a mixture of several points, of which I think mine is at least one.)

3. There are no clear universal propositions in the theory, for sometimes organizations behave as theory says they do, but often they do not.

I should like to offer what is at least a plausible explanation for these three shifts in the character of theory. It is that we are recovering from the mistake of regarding decision making in organizations as a technology.

Consider the varied circumstances in which people cope with practical tasks: practicing medicine or law, playing a violin, crafting pottery, carpentering a house, teaching school, fabricating an automobile or a part of one, or adjudicating a legal conflict, among countless others. All these tasks, activities, and accomplishments are practices. But as more or less successful practices they are strikingly different with respect to the degree to which successful practice can be described, codified, and made the

*Editor's note: March provided the citations on pp 237–244 after Lindblom wrote this commentary.

subject of systematic instruction. In these respects, I suggest that more
or less successful practices are of three kinds:*

1. *Technologies.* These are highly codified practices. To a great
   degree, good practice can be systematically described, and therefore
   taught. They are common in mechanized manufacturing processes
   in which relatively unskilled and inexperienced persons can be
   instructed to follow known rules for success. But practices of laboratory technicians, inventory clerks, bookkeepers, and paramed-
   icals are largely technologies; and they indicate that those practices
   that I am calling technologies are not limited to mechanized manufacturing.

2. *Crafts.* These skilled practices are in some significant degree
   teachable but for the most part through demonstration and ap-
   prenticeship. They cannot be reduced to a code of prescriptions
   derived from a systematic description of practice. Yet skill level
   varies greatly from one practitioner to another, implying that some
   practitioners know in some sense much more than others know.
   Pottery throwing, sculpting, some kinds of singing, playing a mus-
   ical instrument, cooking, bricklaying are all crafts; and craft elements are prominent, though not dominant, in the practice of medicine, as well as in some practices that are largely technologies.

3. *Indeterminate Practices.* These at least partly skilled practices
   are neither technologies nor crafts, and it is not clear what accounts
   for such success as they achieve. For that reason, I call them indeterminate. Successful teaching is such a practice. If a business
   executive wins success that is not attributable wholly to external
   circumstances or luck, his or her work is an example of an indeterminate practice. As a congressional leader, prior to his presi-
   dency, Lyndon Johnson appeared to be extraordinarily skilled as
   an indeterminate practitioner, as was Franklin D. Roosevelt as
   president.

I suggest that it is reasonably clear that good decision making in organizations is neither technology nor craft. Unless we can find a fourth
category into which it will fit, it appears to be an indeterminate practice.
As such, it defies description by theories of conventional causal variety.
It can be captured, to return to March's three points, only by theory that
is contextual, interpretive, and does not attempt universals.

The older and, I believe, inappropriate view of decision making in
organizations as a technology is still much alive. It is in this very con-

*The classification and much of the use to which I put it, I owe to David K. Cohen, Judith
Gruber, Richard Murnane, Carl Milofsky, Edward Pauly, and Janet Weiss, all participants
in a seminar in which practices were explored.

ference illustrated, for example, by the work of Van de Ven and his associates in the Organizational Assessment Research Program. Van de Ven, and perhaps his associates as well, hope to find in decision making the kind of regularities that characterize a technology.

An article by Almond and Genco of a few years ago illuminates the inappropriateness of the technological view of decision making. Commenting on new views of the scientific method, it argues that social scientists are frequently engaged in trying to explain not a cause-and-effect regularity but a specific event, like the outbreak of war, a downturn in employment, a riot, or a coup d'etat. Specific events, however, are not only unique but highly improbable—that is, they are the improbable resultants of a great combination of influences. For that reason they defy prediction or conventional scientific generalization (Almond and Genco, 1977). As March observes, if I interpret him correctly, the task of understanding a unique event, scientific or otherwise, is much like the task of making a successful decision. Indeed making a good decision requires understanding of the unique and improbable state of affairs in which the organization finds itself at the point of decision.

A good decision maker is consequently someone who responds appropriately to a unique and improbable situation. Good decision making cannot therefore be captured in a set of descriptive or prescriptive propositions suitable to a technology.

What then can research on organizational decision making hope to accomplish, if it cannot capture decision making as though it were a technology? A first recommendation is that researchers should examine the phenomena of organizational decision making to test such a proposition as I have just offered—that it is not a technology or a craft, that it is an indeterminate practice. No doubt careful examination will show that it contains elements of all three, even though I suspect it is largely an indeterminate practice. If it were found to be, say, a technology, Van de Ven's style of research would be appropriate. If it is found to be an indeterminate practice, other kinds would subsequently be called for.

A second plausible recommendation is that of March. Let theory aim to contribute only marginally to good organizational decision making. Let theorists acknowledge how much will necessarily escape any attempt at conventional theoretical formulation. Let them acknowledge that a more ordinary knowledge produces an interpretation by the decision maker of his or her unique circumstances. That interpretation is his or her major resource. A scientific theory of decision making can make a significant contribution only by not attempting wholly to displace the ordinary knowledge.

Many years ago Simon called our attention to a curious development: the literature of public administration had produced many highly persuasive prescriptions for good organization and good decision making. But they were mutually contradictory. Once he had called our attention to such an embarrassing state of affairs, it seemed clear to all of us that at most only one of any two contradictory prescriptions could be valid. And the scientific study of administration quickly plunged into an attempt to sort out the true from the false. I think, however, there is now some appreciation that conflicting academic prescriptions are acceptable in a complex world in which "it all depends" (Starbuck, Greve, and Hedberg, 1978). Each of the contrary prescriptions carries a message valid in the appropriate circumstance. If decision making were a technology, it would be possible for research to match circumstance to prescription. Since decision making is an indeterminate practice, the matching cannot be done through articulation of scientific propositions. But skilled decision makers, drawing on experience and ordinary knowledge to sort over a battery of mutually contradictory scholarly propositions—as well as aphorisms, conventions, and rules of thumb originating among practitioners—can achieve a better than random ad hoc match of circumstance to prescription. That gives research on organizational decision making a limited, modest, yet substantial role in improving the practice of organizational decision making.

Another way to see the limits of a theory of decision making is to recognize that decision making is a method of moving an organization from one unique situation to another. For any such move, countless possibilities are identifiable. They include—by one method of classification—moving by obtaining agreement on or effective consent to targets or goals, moving by agreement or effective consent to policies directly (despite disagreement on goals), and moving by agreement on or effective consent to *processes* for resolving disagreements. Classified in another way, moving from one unique situation to another can be accomplished through persuasion at one extreme, coercion at the other, or by many forms of control between the two extremes. A simple cross-classification of these two classifications begins to reveal countless varieties of ways by which decisions can move organizations through a succession of unique improbable points. That being so, it seems that scientific understanding of good organizational decision making has to take a different and more discriminating approach than the conventional scientific attempt to develop universal generalizations suitable for a technology. For any one of many possible decision procedures will be suitable, or sometimes even optimal, if conjoined appropriately with others; and none will be suitable or optimal taken by itself.

REFERENCES

Almond, G., and S. Genco (1977). "Clouds, Clocks, and the Study of Politics," *World Politics* **29**,4, July 1977.

Starbuck, W. H., A. Greve, and B. L. T. Hedberg (1978). "Responding to Crisis," Chapter 5 of C. F. Smart and W. T. Stanbury, Eds., *Studies on Crisis Management*, Montreal: Butterworth and Company, Ltd. (for the Institute for Research on Public Policy). See especially pp. 122–123.

CHAPTER SIX

The Organization
Assessment Perspective

**The Organization Assessment
Research Program**

ANDREW H. VAN DE VEN
School of Management
University of Minnesota

This paper provides an overview of the Organization Assessment (OA) research program in terms of: (1) the problems it attempts to address, (2) its historical evolution and major findings, and (3) its future directions and implications for assessing organization design and performance. Begun in 1972, the purpose of the OA research program is to develop a *framework,* a *process,* and a set of *measurement instruments* for assessing the performance of complex organizations in relation to how they are organized and the environments in which they operate.

PROBLEMS AND NEEDS IN
ASSESSING ORGANIZATIONS

Management theorists and practitioners generally agree that the ways in which organizations are designed and the environments in which they operate affect organizational performance. Given this general agreement, it is amazing that so little systematic effort has been made by theorists and practitioners to develop reliable and valid ways for measuring and assessing organizations.

Most organization theorists and researchers have dwelt upon trying to describe the functioning of an organization as a sociological entity and have generally ignored the criterion that apparently matters most to managers—the performance effectiveness or efficiency of alternative organizational designs. The absence of performance criteria by which organizational structures can be assessed under varying environmental conditions has been one of the major blocks to putting organization theory and research into practice.

On the other hand, in practice most organizations tend to dwell on their performance and ignore their sociological nature. That is, most organizations invest great sums of money and effort in management information systems that routinely measure and distribute data throughout the organization on the performance of various cost centers, departments, and individual jobs. Information and problems about the designs of jobs, work groups, and the organization are generally left for managers to figure out—after all, that is their job, isn't it?

Unfortunately, most of the information systems used in practice and those created by organizational researchers for their studies are not designed to provide a clue as to *why* or *how* a given level of performance was achieved. *What does a manager or consultant do when performance is unsatisfactory?* Equally important, but too often ignored: *How and why did a work group or the entire organization exceed its performance expectations?* These questions are basic if managers hope to improve the management of organizations. However, those who work with or observe managerial behavior quickly recognize that practitioners at all levels of organizations are hard pressed to provide logical and supportable answers to these questions. For that matter, if organizational consultants and analysts are honest with themselves, they too are unable to answer these questions adequately.

Although many explanations can be given, there are three basic reasons for this unfortunate state of affairs: (1) inadequate theories about how organization design affects performance under varying environmental conditions; (2) lack of reliable and valid measures of organization structure and behavior; and (3) incomplete management information systems used by organizations.

Many of the principles and prescriptions that either exist in management literature or are implicit in managerial explanations about how organizational and environmental characteristics influence performance lack sound theoretical and empirical support. More than 30 years ago, Herbert Simon (1946) recognized this predicament by pointing out that many of the principles of classical management literature are nothing more than proverbs. He suggested that if a science of administration was to develop, it was necessary to go beyond the superficial and oversimplified principles of management. A valid approach to the study of administration, Simon argued, requires that all relevant dimensions of organization structure and environment that may affect performance be identified, that each administrative situation be analyzed in terms of the entire set of dimensions, and that research be instituted to determine empirically how the organizational characteristics explain organizational performance. Simon concluded that until administrative description reaches this higher level of sophistication, and until analysts are willing to undertake the tiresome task of conducting the systematic research this entails, there is little reason to hope that rapid progress will be made in identifying and verifying valid administrative principles.

A second basic reasons why so little is known about how organization design and environment influence performance is that our capability to measure, and thereby investigate, some basic characteristics of the structure and behavior of organizations, work groups, and jobs has been very limited. As a consequence, little data are available on the relationships of organizational structure and function to performance or on the effectiveness of alternative organizational designs under varying environmental conditions. Without reliable and valid ways to measure the context and designs of organizations, work groups, and jobs, one cannot come to know in any objective sense how these factors interrelate and affect the efficiency, effectiveness, or quality of working life in organizations.

Finally, while most managers will assert that organizational and environmental factors are important for explaining performance, the fact is that organizations typically do not do much to obtain or provide periodic data on these factors with their management information systems. Indeed the so-called "management information systems" used by most organizations are more appropriately labeled "performance information systems," because they only tend to provide information on various indicators of performance outcomes: quantity, quality, cost of outputs, efficiency, and effectiveness. We believe one basic reason why most practitioners find their information systems of little or no help in making basic managerial decisions is that these systems only include the performance side of the equation and do not provide information on the organizational and environmental conditions that managers deal with on a direct and daily basis in efforts to influence performance.

Equally important, Pfeffer and Salancik (1978: 74) point out that the information collected in an information system focuses organizational energy, attention, and demand on that information. The distribution of that information in periodic reports and tables throughout the organization means not only that it can be used but also that it is more likely to be used in making decisions, because its existence and prominence conveys the impression that the information is important. Unless information is regularly available to managers about organizational and environmental factors, it is not likely they will consider or place much emphasis on these factors when attempting to explain, and thereby coming to understand, how and why a given level of organizational performance was achieved.

Summary of Organization Assessment Research Program

The purpose of the OA research program is to respond to these problems by developing a framework, a set of measurement instruments, and a process that are valid and useful from conceptual and empirical perspectives, for conducting in-depth assessments of complex organizations on an ongoing basis. Although much work lies ahead to achieve this ambitious goal, the detailed results presented in our recent book, *Measuring and Assessing Organizations* (Van de Ven and Ferry, 1980) demonstrate that much progress has been made. Only a brief summary of the major findings will be discussed here.

The OA framework attempts to follow Simon's (1946) advice by identifying the dimensions of context, structure, and behavior that are important for explaining the performance of organizations, work groups, individual jobs, and interunit relationships. This conceptual scheme is a synthesis of the extensive literature on organizations and represents an ongoing attempt to inventory the factors relevant for conducting an assessment of complex organizations at all levels of analyses. Van de Ven and Ferry (1980) include empirical tests of the main theories included in the OA framework. The results show substantial support for the theories underlying OA and suggest specific areas where extensions of the framework are needed. These will be discussed in the following section.

The *Organization Assessment Instruments* (OAI) consist of a set of questionnaires and survey procedures for measuring the dimensions included in the OA framework, that is, various characteristics of the context, structure, and behavior of the overall organization, work groups, jobs, and interunit relationships. In 1972 and 1973 two initial versions of the OAI were created and administered in employment security organizations, but they produced results that were not considered satisfactory for our purposes. In 1975 a third version of the OAI was developed and again administered in the employment security organizations as well as a sample of child care organizations. Van de Ven and Ferry (1980) show in detail that most of the measures in this version of the OAI have good indications of reliability and validity and explain large variations in the performance of different types of organizations, work units, jobs, and interunit relationships in the sample. The evaluation also found specific areas where improvements are needed, and these are incorporated in a fourth version of the OAI, which has been made available for use in other organizations to conduct basic and applied research. For basic research, the OAI provide a set of measures that can be used to examine how the contexts and designs of organizations, work groups, and jobs are interrelated and influence organizational performance. For applied purposes, the OAI provide a set of instruments for diagnosing strengths and weaknesses in organizational design and for examining the consequences of organizational changes over time.

The *process* component of the OA research program is concerned with developing ways to apply and use the OA framework and instruments in organizations. Although the OAI can be used to obtain a cross-sectional snapshot of organizational design and practices, their practical usefulness to an organization is greatly enhanced when OAI surveys are conducted periodically over time. Longitudinal assessments greatly facilitate learning and managerial development because they allow one to identify trends and examine how changes in organization, environment, and performance characteristics covary over time. This information stimulates one to take an experimental approach by using the survey feedback to develop and implement alternative interventions in areas where improvements are needed, and to evaluate the consequences of these interventions in subsequent surveys of the ongoing assessment process.

Thus, in practical terms, OA represents an attempt to develop an *organizational* information system that is analogous to the existing performance information system within most organizations. Once developed and implemented, data obtained periodically with the organizational and performance information systems can be linked together as an overall *OA Management Information System.* By examining data in such an OA MIS, one can learn what the relationships are between characteristics of organization context, structure, and performance. When incorporated as part of an ongoing management and organizational development program, we believe that managers and analysts can begin to obtain the benefits outlined above from longitudinal organizational assessments. In addition, they can learn to explain the performance of their organization on the bases of how it is structured and the environments in which it operates. This, then, is one of the practical objectives of the OA research program.

However, before these basic and applied uses of OA are realized, a further basic issue needs to be addressed. As organizations become more complex, so also do problems of organization design and assessment. *How can one cope with the complexity of structures, preferences, and technologies within many organizations?* Substantively, this question deals with the fact that one quickly becomes overwhelmed with the complexity of problems, dimensions, and levels of analyses involved in an in-depth organization assessment. What is needed is a strategy for reducing this complexity to manageable proportions. Procedurally, this question accepts the fact that a framework and set of measurement instruments are not enough to conduct an organization assessment and to use its information for practical purposes. Some process steps are also needed to guide analysts in designing and conducting these assessments and in managing complex problem solving and change in organizations. The development of substantive and procedural strategies for coping with these complexities constitutes the major current and future directions of the OA research program and will be discussed in later sections of this paper. However, first I will summarize the framework and major empirical findings.

ORGANIZATION ASSESSMENT FRAMEWORK AND MAJOR FINDINGS

Our starting premise is that an assessment of a complex organization requires an operational framework and method that cuts across and links the overall organization, work unit, and individual job levels of analyses. An organizational diagnosis is not obtained by focusing on just one particular level of analysis in terms of a narrow set of factors, particularly given our limited current knowledge about organizations. Instead what is needed is a systems perspective that:

1. Identifies the relevant properties of context, design, and performance at the macroorganization, unit, and job levels of analyses.

2. Examines the different structural patterns of units and jobs that are located in various levels and sections within the complex organization.

3. Determines how these different units and jobs are integrated and what functional contributions they make to the overall performance of the organization.

Specifically, we propose that an assessment of an organization focus on the different levels of analyses illustrated in Figure 6-1 in terms of the dimensions outlined in Table 6-1.

As Figure 6-1 illustrates, the OA framework examines a complex organization at four different levels: the overall organization, work groups or units, individual jobs, and relationships among jobs and units within the organization and with other organizations. At each of these four levels, Table 6-1 outlines the dimensions of context, design, and perform-

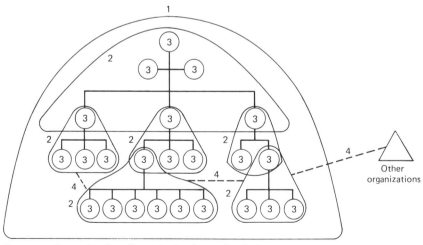

Key to numbers: 1 = Overall organization focus of analysis
                  2 = Organizational unit focus of analysis
                  3 = Individual job or position focus of analysis
                  4 = Relations within and between units focus of analysis

Figure 6-1   Illustration of levels of analyses involved in conducting an in-depth organization assessment.

Table 6-1 Dimensions Examined in Organization Assessment Framework

Macroorganization Focus of Analysis

Macroorganization Context	Macroorganization Design	Macroorganization Results
1. Organization demographics History, age, growth stage 2. Organization domain (strategy) Type, uncertainty, complexity, restrictiveness 3. Projected demand and supply for period Production/Service quota Resources (budget, personnel) available	1. Structural configuration Vertical, horizontal, and spatial differentiation Forms of departmentation (by function, program, geography, matrix) Administrative intensity 2. Distribution of power and authority among corporate decision makers	Value judgments on criteria used to evaluate the overall effectiveness of the organization. For example: 1. Attainment of goals in organization's domain 2. Market share in product lines 3. Profitability, return on investment

Organizational Unit or Group Focus of Analysis

Organizational Unit (Department) Context	Design of Organizational Units (Work Groups)	Organizational Unit Results
1. Macroorganization context and design Functional contribution of unit to organization Vertical and horizontal location of unit in organization chart 2. Nature of work performed by unit Task difficulty and variability 3. Size of unit (number of personnel)	1. Unit specialization Different tasks assigned unit Different job titles in unit 2. Personnel composition Heterogeneity of personnel skills Interchangeability of roles 3. Unit standardization Automation of work methods Number and detail of unit rules, procedures 4. Unit decision making Centralization of decisions in spv. Decision strategies used (computational judgmental, bargaining, heuristic) 5. Unit performance norms and standards Quality/quantity-control emphasis Group/individual-based incentives Group pressures to conform (soldiering)	Value judgments on criteria to evaluate effectiveness of organizational unit. For example: 1. Percent of unit performance goals attained 2. Unit efficiency Cost per unit of output 3. Unit morale Cohesiveness of work unit Turnover rate 4. Unit adaptiveness Responsiveness to changing demands

255

Table 6-1 *continued*

Individual Job or Position Focus of Analysis

Individual Jobs or Positions Context	Design of Individual Jobs or Positions	Individual Job or Position Results

1. Organization and unit context and design
  Functional role or contribution of job to unit and organization
2. Characteristics of person in job
  Education and job-related skills
  Job tenure and job career history
  Growth need strength
	1. Job specialization
	  Number of different tasks performed
	  Scope of tasks performed
	2. Job expertise
	  Education
	  Length of job-entry orientation
	  Time in on-the-job training
	3. Job standardization
	  Detail of job description
	  Number and detail of job rules, procedures
	4. Job discretion
	  Latitude in making job-related decisions
	  Closeness of supervision
	5. Job incentives
	  Feedback from work, supervisor, peers
	  Job contingent rewards and sanctions
		Value judgments on criteria used to evaluate effectiveness of individual jobs or positions. For example:
		1. Percentage of job performance goals attained (MBO)
		2. Quantity of individual output
		3. Quality of individual output
		4. Individual productivity: cost per unit of output
		5. Job satisfaction
		6. Work motivation

Relations within and between Units Focus of Analysis

Resource Flows (Work, Personnel, Money)	Information Flows (Impersonal, Personal, Group Communication Mechanisms)	Coordination and control results

1. Resource dependence pattern
  Directions and amounts of resource flows within and between organizational units, levels, and with other organizations
2. Routinization of resource flows
  Number of exceptions encountered in resource flows
	1. Integration pattern
	  Direction and frequency of information flows within and between organizational units, levels, and with other organizations
	2. Distribution of influence in relations
	  Amounts of say on relations by parties
	  Impact of parties in relationships
		Value judgments on criteria used to evaluate effectiveness of coordination and control between jobs, units, levels and with other organizations. For example:
		1. At interposition level, the perceived effectiveness of interpersonal relationships.

Table 6-1 *continued*

3. Perceived dependence among organizational units, levels, and positions	3. Conflict and quality of communications
	    Frequency of conflict
	    Modes of conflict resolution
		2. At interunit level, the degrees of suboptimization and competition among organizational units.
		3. At macroorganizational level, the costs of managing transactions across units within organization relative to across organizations or the market.

ance that are examined to conduct the assessment. These dimensions do not represent a comprehensive list of the factors that may be useful and important for organizational assessment and problem solving. Instead, they are a limited set of factors that: (1) have a conceptual foundation in the literature on organization theory; and (2) have been found in research to be important for diagnosing general areas of strengths and weaknesses in the context, design, and performance of organizations. Once general problem areas are detected with this OA framework and measurement instruments, then it is usually necessary to conduct further and more specific investigations into the problem areas by focusing on other organizational characteristics and methods directly relevant to those problems. Thus it should be recognized that the OA framework is neither comprehensive in breadth of organizational characteristics examined nor in depth of a given organizational aspect; it represents a limited attempt to apply a systems view to organizational diagnosis by examining the associations between jobs, work groups, interunit relations, and the overall organization on a selective number of dimensions.

This OA framework is summarized below by clarifying our position on organizational performance and then discussing the dimensions examined at each level of organization. Detailed discussions of the theories and empirical findings underlying the OA framework are available in Van de Ven and Ferry (1980).

Organizational Performance

Organizational performance is the ultimate criterion and starting point in an assessment of organizations. Performance is a normative concept that reflects the criteria and standards used by decision makers to assess the effectiveness of an organization. As this definition suggests, performance is a *value judgment* on the results desired from an organization. It is misleading to search for a set of universal and objective criteria of organizational performance because the external validity of any effectiveness criteria are very limited. Decision makers with unique values and frames of reference will use different criteria and standards for judging the effectiveness of an organization. As a result, decision makers representing different organizational positions and interest groups are likely to disagree on most any set of performance criteria for evaluating organizational effectiveness. However, a measurement of performance does not require that different people agree on effectiveness goals, criteria, and standards. Consensus may in fact be an unrealistic goal to attempt to achieve. An organization assessment simply requires that the unique and conflicting definitions of performance be made explicit, and that the organization analyst determine at the outset whose value judgments and criteria will be put into operation and measured.

The section entitled "A Process for Organization Assessment and Problem Solving" deals with these complexities of organizational performance by proposing a strategy for defining performance and putting it into operation, as well as for conducting all the phases involved in an organization assessment. The basic process begins by conducting a series of meetings with the people who commission an organization assessment, in order to (1) identify the partisan interest groups who will use the findings from such an OA, and (2) ask each user group through a series of meetings what goals, criteria, and standards they consider relevant for judging the effectiveness of the organizations, units, and jobs that will be investigated in the organization assessment. Subsequent steps in the OA process include involving user groups in developing specific performance measures, the overall design of the data collection process, and the methods for providing feedback on OAI survey data. The involvement of user groups throughout the assessment process is critical not only for making effectiveness operational, but also for finding practical and useful ways to implement OA on an ongoing basis in organizations.

The outcome dimensions listed in the right column of Table 6-1 are those that have frequently been used and discussed in the literature as effectiveness criteria for different levels of organizational analyses. They are listed in Table 6-1 simply to provide an example of the kinds of effectiveness criteria that are used in organizational assessments.

The Context and Design of the Overall Organization

At the macroorganizational level the OA framework incorporates the prevailing view that in varying degrees organizations are designed by choices and not simply by natural or deterministic conditions outside the organization. The basic premise underlying the OA macroorganizational dimensions in Table 6-1 is that in order for an organization to operate on an ongoing basis, decisions must be made about the organization's domain, the production function problem, and the organization design problem.

The *choice of a domain* refers to the specific goals an organization chooses to pursue in terms of the functions it performs, the products or services it delivers, and the target populations and markets it serves. Past choices and behavior constrain future choices and behavior. Therefore an historical assessment of the evolution of domain choices is necessary to avoid drawing the incorrect conclusion that organizations are not purposive or that goals are of little use for understanding organization behavior simply because goals and the meaning of actions are increasingly inferred retrospectively by organizational participants as organizations grow older.

The organization's *production function problem* is concerned on the one hand with making decisions about production or service quotas that a firm hopes to deliver to selected markets during an operating period, and on the other hand in securing and allocating the necessary resources; that is, money, personnel, and technologies. Although the economic production function problem has too often been overlooked in organizational studies, it is critical for understanding how an organization puts into operation its domain choices and goals. For a specific operating period the production function problem is solved by determining the quantity and mix of products or services to produce, the resources or budget needed to produce at this level, and the allocation of these resources among organizational units.

The *organization design problem* is concerned with (1) the division of labor and resources, (2) the interdependence and suboptimization thereby created among organizational units, and (3) the structure of authority and reporting relationships established to manage interdependence. At the macro level, the organization design problem consists of making decisions on how to divide the labor (vertical and horizontal differentiation), what form of departmentation to adopt (functional, program, geographical, and matrix arrangements), and how power and authority should be distributed among organizational units and levels.

Implied in the type of domain chosen by an organization are various degrees of uncertainty, complexity, and restrictiveness of environments that organizational decision makers choose to live with, which in turn significantly influence the alternatives available in solving the production function and organizational design problems.

Domain uncertainty refers to the level of agreement among organizational decision makers on the operating priorities of an organization, as well as the extent to which methods to achieve given ends are clearly understood or predictable. Defined in this way, domain uncertainty is the basic dimension underlying most conceptions of organizational *rationality*. March and Simon (1958) and Thompson (1967) point out that rational action is rooted on the one hand in *known or agreed-upon results or ends*, and on the other hand in *certainty about cause-effect* relationships. Specifically, with reference to the Thompson and Tuden (1959) types of decision strategies in Figure 6-2, it becomes clear that when people agree on the results desired of an organization, the production function and organization design problems can be solved rationally using either computational or judgmental decision strategies. However, when there is little or no agreement on the domain or goals of an organization, the rational model is replaced with partisan or anarchic models of choice (e.g., the garbage can model by Cohen et al., 1972). Here power, bargaining, and negotiation among partisan decision makers overshadow analytical approaches to solving the production function and organizational design problems.

Domain complexity is the diversity or heterogeneity of products, markets, and geographical territories that decision makers choose for the organization to operate in. It is the dimension that underlies much of the literature on how diversification strategies affect organizational structure (Chandler, 1962; Wrigley, 1970; Rumelt, 1974). Because humans have a limited capacity for retaining conscious information, as domains become more complex organizations carve up their production function and design problems into quasi-independent simpler problems and assign them to various loosely coupled divisions. However, personnel within these loosely coupled divisions managing different domain components develop different norms about interpersonal behavior, organizational goals, structuring of activities, and time span of attention (Lawrence and Lorsch, 1967). Thus with increasingly complex domains, there is likely to be decreasing interdivisional agreement on organizational goals, but increasing agree-

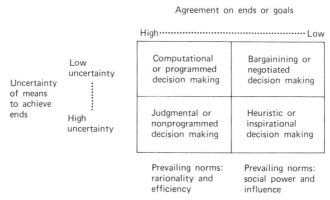

Figure 6-2 Thompson and Tuden (1959) typology of decision-making strategies under varying conditions of agreement on ends and uncertainty of means.

ment on subgoals within divisions. As overall domain complexity increases, macrodecisions about the production function and organization design problems become increasingly nonrational, while microdecisions within divisions tend to be more rational.

Domain restrictiveness refers to the market structure in which a firm chooses to operate, in terms of governmental regulation, economic competition, barriers to entry, and unionization of the labor force, as well as an organization's internal flexibility of technologies, surplus of resources, and specificity of domain statement (Williamson, 1975; Miles and Cameron, 1978; Khandwalla, 1977). Domain restrictiveness is a dimension central to addressing the current debate on the relative importance of externally versus internally driven models of organization structure and behavior (e.g., Aldrich, 1979; Van de Ven, 1979; McKelvey, 1979). At relatively low levels of domain restrictiveness, models emphasizing internal leadership and individual choice are instrumental in shaping organizations, while externally driven models, for example, the population ecology model, become increasingly salient when domains are highly restrictive.

Perhaps more productive and interesting than resolving this debate are the qualitatively different strategies organizations employ to solve their production function and organization design problems over the range from low to high domain restrictiveness. Three sets of strategies are summarized here and discussed in greater detail in Ouchi and Van de Ven (1980). One set of strategies is to obtain closure to the production function and organization design problems by limiting production quotas or operations to the amount of resources that an organization can control during an operating period through buffering, leveling, forecasting, and rationing techniques (Thompson, 1967). Second, an organization can decrease the criticality of any single restrictive source by initiating market transactions with a larger number of alternative suppliers, customers, and in more diverse product lines. This decreases a firm's domain restrictiveness by increasing its domain complexity and reducing uncertainty or risk. Third, an organization can set out to expand control over its domain by coopting, coventuring, or merging with other organizations that represent critical contingencies for the organization.

The second and third strategies are analogous to the markets and hierarchies framework proposed by Williamson (1975). He argues that the decision over whether resource transactions are executed across markets (strategy 2) or by hierarchy within a firm (strategy 3) depends on the degree of opportunism of decision makers and the perceived uncertainty and restrictiveness of an organization's domain. Holding opportunism constant, the greater the domain restrictiveness and uncertainty, the more strategy 3 is preferred to strategy 2. Of course combinations of these strategies are often employed by organizations simultaneously, particularly those with complex domains. Organizations facing heterogeneous environments will segment their markets and adopt unique strategies for coping with each (Thompson, 1967).

The Context and Design of Organizational Units

In addition to understanding the overall and structural configuration of an organization, an assessment of organizations requires an examination of the design of work units or departments. The organizational unit represents the basic and smallest source of collective behavior within organizations and is defined as consisting of a supervisor and all personnel reporting directly to that supervisor. As Figure 6-1 illustrates, Likert's (1967) concept of "linking pins" is used to identify work units at all supervisory levels in an organization.

A focus on organizational units is needed to examine the different patterns of structure and process that exist within organizations. Complex organizations divide their labor and resources among various units, and each deals with a different relevant environment and has different performance standards to meet. As a result, these units adopt different structures to perform their unique tasks and functions. Van de Ven and Ferry (1980) show empirically that attempts to examine these different units from a macroorganizational perspective inherently present a distorted view of organizations. Some units may be highly structured, others may be very organic, and any overall average profile of these different unit structures is an inaccurate summary of them all.

The logic underlying the development of the unit context and design dimensions outlined in Table 6-1 is that the difficulty and variability of the work performed by an organizational unit largely predicts how the unit will be organized. *Task variability,* or the number of exceptions encountered in the work, affects the degree to which work processes can be structured in a specialized and standardized way (Perrow, 1967; Hage and Aiken, 1969; Hall, 1962). *Task difficulty,* or the analyzability and predictability of the work, directly influences the personnel composition and expertise in the unit, the distribution of authority among unit personnel, and the mutual adjustments required to perform the tasks (Hage, 1965; Bell, 1967; Mohr, 1971).

Empirically, task difficulty and variability have been found to explain: (1) the different modes of unit design to be discussed in the following section (Van de Ven and Delbecq, 1974); (2) variations in unit specialization, standardization, and expertise among equally efficient organizational units (Van de Ven, 1976); (3) different methods of coordination and communication among unit personnel (Van de Ven, Delbecq, and Koenig, 1976); and (4) different patterns of supervisory, employee, and collegial authority over time (Van de Ven, 1977). Finally, in a comparison of the effects of various contextual factors at the overall organization and work unit levels, Van de Ven and Ferry (1980) found that task difficulty and task variability were consistently the strongest predictors of the structures and processes of units in employment security organizations. The correlations between macroorganizational factors and unit design were found to be near zero. From this we concluded that it is not correct to draw inferences about the designs of work units from the structure and context of the overall organization, and vice versa.

The design of an organizational unit focuses on its performance program. Programs are strategies for organizing the work of a unit into a predictable pattern of recurring activities (March and Simon, 1958). These programs are assessed in terms of the following OA dimensions: (1) *specialization,* the number of different tasks assigned to a unit; (2) *personnel composition,* the heterogeneity of personnel skills and the interchangeability of roles among personnel in the unit; (3) *standardization,* the procedures and pacing rules that are to be followed in task performance; (4) the *distribution of authority* on work-related decisions among the supervisor or unit employees; and (5) *the performance norms and incentives* that are provided to unit personnel to work as a group in achieving its goals. In addition, an assessment of the program used to structure an organizational unit also requires a consideration of the interdependence among unit personnel and the processes of coordination and control that are used to manage this interdependence. The *interdependence,* or tightness of couplings among role occupants, is reflected in the flows of work, clients, or resources among unit personnel and the extent to which they rely on each other to receive their work, perform their individual jobs, and send their completed work on to others to complete the total task. *Coordination* and *control* processes to manage this interdependence are accomplished with various forms of information flows among unit personnel and the methods used to resolve conflicts.

In summary, the structural referent of an organizational unit is its work program, and its dimensions are defined in terms of specialization, personnel composition, standardization, distribution of authority, and unit incentives. In addition, processes within the unit are assessed in terms of resources and information flows. "Knowledge of the program of an organization permits one to predict in considerable detail the behavior of members of the organization. This is such a common-sense fact that its importance has been overlooked" (March and Simon, 1958: 143).

Empirically, Van de Ven and Ferry (1980) found that not all these unit design dimensions were equally important in explaining the performance of the different types of units that exist in employment security (ES) organizations. However, each of the OA dimensions was found to be significantly associated with the efficiency, effectiveness, and job satisfaction of at least one of the kinds of units in ES organizations. Indeed, when regressing performance on the OA unit dimensions for each of the different kinds of ES units, on the average it was found that 52, 55, and 57 percent of the variances in unit efficiency, effectiveness, and job satisfaction were explained. These percentages of explained variance in unit performance are far higher than those reported in other research reports, and they demonstrate the predictive validity of the OA unit design dimensions. In contrast, when the regressions were conducted on all ES units combined, as has been done typically in other studies, only 8, 11, and 41 percent of the variances in unit efficiency, effectiveness, and job satisfaction, respectively, were explained. The reason for this much lower ability to explain performance is that the correlations of various dimensions of unit design with performance were often found to be positive for one kind of ES unit and negative for another; hence a washout effect.

These major findings underscore the need to carefully identify and discriminate among the different types of units within complex organizations if one desires to assess and improve performance. Indiscriminant inclusion of all kinds of organizational units (with each kind pursuing different tasks, functions, and performance criteria) in a regression analysis will produce little evidence that organizational design is important in explaining performance—an incorrect conclusion that is currently being drawn in the literature (e.g., Perrow, 1979). Furthermore, uniform strategies for designing organizational units will not serve to increase organizational performance. A uniform organizational intervention will in effect increase performance in some units and decrease performance in others—hence a stalemate. These results suggest that organizational analysts need to develop more operational frameworks and that practitioners should become more selective in managing and organizing different types of organizational units.

The Context and Design of Jobs

At the microlevel of analysis, the job or position that individuals occupy is the core element of any in-depth assessment of organizations. As Figure 6-1 illustrates, complex organizations consist of numerous units; a unit in turn is composed of identifiable jobs or positions.

The OA job design dimensions represent individual-level counterparts to the dimensions of work unit design. That is, the following five pairs of core job and unit design characteristics tap similar conceptual domains but from a different level of analysis: unit and job specialization, unit personnel composition and job expertise, unit and job standardization, unit centralization and job discretion, and unit and job incentives. Although these counterpart dimensions of units and jobs clearly have different meanings, reference points, and measurement procedures, their parallel construction is important for identifying what options or tradeoffs may exist between the design of jobs and units. For example, Hackman (1976) indicates that one important option in the design of autonomous work groups is to determine under what conditions heterogeneous skills should be structured within a job (by decreasing job specialization) or between jobs in a unit (by staffing a unit with experts from heterogeneous disciplines).

Another major consideration in selecting the five OA job dimensions is that they build and expand upon the major contributions of Hackman and Oldham (1975) and their foretrekkers. Whereas the Hackman and Oldham job dimensions focus heavily on the attitudinal aspects of jobs, the five OA job factors instead tend to emphasize their behavioral aspects. The reason we lean toward a behavioral description of jobs is because behavior is more objective and easier for analysts and practitioners to observe, control, and change than the subjective attitudes of people regarding their jobs.

Three basic propositions provide the rationale for linking these OA job dimensions to individual performance, that is, job satisfaction, work motivation, and productivity. Thus far only partial tests of the propositions have been made.

First, *job performance increases as the design of the job more closely matches (1) the skills and interests of the job incumbent, and (2) the technical and functional work requirements of the organization.* Part one of this proposition reflects the prevailing view that the background characteristics of individuals—their skills, job career experiences, and personal desires for growth and challenge—moderate the relationships between the design of a job and employee reactions to it (Hackman and Oldham, 1975; Brief and Aldag, 1975; Wanous, 1974; Oldham et al., 1976; Morgan, 1977). The second part of the proposition assumes sufficient flexibility on the technological side of almost any organization to suit social requirements of individuals for a high quality working life, an assumption central to sociotechnical theory and argued convincingly by Trist (1970). Within the limits of this assumption, Part two of the proposition is made operational by expecting systematic variations in job design to be a function of the difficulty and variability of tasks performed by a job incumbent as well as the location and role of the job in the organization's hierarchy.

Van de Ven and Ferry (1980) have developed the logic for this proposition and conducted a partial test of it by examining the correlations of task difficulty and variability, level in the hierarchy, and tenure of job incumbents with the job design factors for employees with low and high levels of job satisfaction. Support was found on the more formal characteristics of jobs, that is, job expertise, standardization, and authority, but not for the less formal dimensions of jobs such as work load pressure, job feedback, and expectations of rewards and sanctions for doing good or poor work. When combining these results with those of Oldham et al. (1976), we speculate that the less formal characteristics of jobs may be more strongly predicted by individual differences, particularly growth need strength, which was not measured in the 1975 OAI but subsequently included in OA. The more formal properties of jobs, on the other hand, may largely reflect the task and position requirements of a job by the organization. An interesting direction for future research is to examine further how individual differences and organizational task and position requirements interact to explain different job design characteristics and outcomes.

The second proposition is that *job performance increases when there is greater internal consistency in the pattern of relationships among the job design dimensions.* Van de Ven and Ferry (1980) show that a consistently stronger pattern of interrelationships among most of the job design characteristics distinguish ES employees with high versus low job satisfaction. In particular, the correlations among the more formal characteristics of jobs, that is, among job specialization, personnel expertise, job standardization, and job authority, were substantially larger and in the expected directions for highly satisfied employees than they were for those who reported low job satisfaction. These preliminary findings indicate that a potentially fruitful and interesting direction for further research is to examine job performance as a function not only of the fit between job design, individual background, and organization context but also of the pattern of congruence between the job design characteristics themselves.

Finally, we are not prepared to address a third crucial proposition underlying the OA job design dimensions, but simply state it to indicate our future directions: *Performance of organizational units and individual jobs increases when they reflect logical and internally consistent counterpart patterns in the dimensions of units and jobs imbedded in these units.* Clearly, much further theory building and research lies ahead to develop and test these three major propositions.

The Context and Design of Interunit Relationships

Critical to an assessment of organizations, units, and jobs is an understanding of how they link with their relevant environments in terms of patterns of differentiation, interdependence, and integration with other units and positions inside and outside of the organization. Most of the early studies on organization-environment relationships focused on the macro level and treated the environment abstractly as a set of constraints existing outside the organization (see review in Van de Ven et al., 1974). Conceptualizing the environment in this gross sense limits the potential for a systematic assessment, because different units in complex organizations have different relevant environments that consist of specific other parties and units (instead of an abstract set of constraints) that exist just as much inside the organization as outside (Starbuck, 1976). By definition, complex organizations have multiple domains, tasks, and functions that are assigned to different organizational units and levels. Thus the location and salience of the relevant environments for each unit depend on its specific tasks and its relative position in the organizational hierarchy.

A more penetrating assessment of the pluralistic nature of environmental relationships can be obtained if one (1) begins by treating each unit or position, rather than the total organization, as a focal unit; (2) identifies the specific other units or groups both inside and outside the organization that each focal unit is linked with; and (3) adopts a social network approach to measure the transactions that occur in these pairwise interunit relationships. The dyad is the basic building block for identifying clusters of tightly and loosely coupled units and for determining how these clusters are linked into larger organizational and interorganizational networks. With social network analysis interunit relationships can be analyzed from multiple perspectives to obtain an understanding of the emergent social structure in organizations as distinct from formal structures displayed in organization charts. Aldrich (1974) and Tichy, Tushman, and Fombrun (1979) discuss additional insights and uses of social network analysis for assessing organizations.

The transactions that occur in interunit relationships are principally assessed in OA in terms of the kind, direction, amount, and stability of resource and information flows. *Resource flows* include work, materials, money, and personnel services that are transferred between organizational units, while *information flows* are communications about the resource transactions transmitted through a variety of media, including signs, written reports and memos, personal discussions, and group meetings. The importance of resource and information flows in OA is that they: (1) appear to be the basic elements of process in organizations; (2) behaviorally indicate the forms and intensities of instrumental and maintenance activities between units; and (3) provide a different perspective of interdependence, coordination, and control among organizational components that complements the structural perspective described above to assess the designs of jobs, units, and the overall organization (Van de Ven and Ferry, 1980).

The starting assumption underlying the OA interunit dimensions in Table 6-1 is that interunit relationships are a consequence at the macro level of the need to manage interdependencies that emerge with the division of labor and scarce resources, and at the micro level of the perceived need by unit personnel for resources or help to achieve their goals or self-interests. Interunit relationships are usually mandated by administrative directives within organizations—and also often between organizations. However, administrative mandates are seldom sufficient to develop and maintain effective interunit relationships. Among the parties involved there must be awareness and consensus on the "law of the situation," that is, they must perceive the tasks, problems, or issues encountered as dictating coordination, as Mary Parker Follett (1926) discussed. The parties also must agree on the specific terms of their relationship. Once resource transactions occur, they are maintained by adopting structures and processes for coordination that are commensurate with the nature and amount of resource transactions among the parties involved. Those resource transactions that are stable and predictable can be coordinated by impersonal programming of rules, policies, procedures, and plans. It is in this sense that March and Simon (1958: 159) state that "The more repetitive and predictable the situation, the greater the tolerance for interdependence. Conversely, the greater the elements of variability and contingency, the greater is the burden of coordinating activities that are specialized by process." Thus the greater the variability and difficulty of the work and other resources transacted between units, the more personal discussions and group meetings will occur to make the necessary mutual adjustments among interdependent parties.

Over time, then, the creation and maintenance of interunit relationships are viewed as a result of macroorganizational differentiation and microorganizational needs for resources or support, interunit communications to spread awareness and consensus of the "law of the situation" and the terms of relations, resource transactions, and structural and process adaptations to maintain the relationships. What may start out as an interim solution to a problem or as an attempt to obtain a specific resource may eventually become a long-term set of commitments and resource transactions *if* previous cycles in the process are perceived by the parties involved to have been successful or effective encounters.

Van de Ven and Ferry (1980) present partial tests of this framework for assessing interunit relationships based on an assessment of external unit relationships in employment security (ES) organizations in Wisconsin and a study of pairwise relations among child care agencies in Texas. In both studies the cross-sectional correlations among the OA interunit dimensions were found to be largely consistent with the above framework, although longitudinal data, now being analyzed, are necessary to test it. Further, in the ES study the interunit dimensions explained large proportions of the variations in the performance of each of the major kinds of units in ES offices. On the average it was found that the OA interunit dimensions accounted for 49, 53, and 45 percent of the variations in unit efficiency, effectiveness, and job satisfaction, respectively, of different kinds of ES units. However, as found for unit design, when the external relationships of all kinds of ES units are combined in the regression analyses, only 7, 4, and 18 percent of the variations in overall organization efficiency, effectiveness, and job satisfaction were explained. This "washout" effect, which occurs when all units are combined in the analysis, again brings out the importance of discriminating between the different kinds of external unit relationships that exist in complex organizations and of the need to assess them separately if one desires to understand how the external affairs of organizational units are associated with their performance.

The need for a selective approach in the assessment of interunit relationships was again brought out in the Texas study, in which the OA dimensions were found to explain between 34 and 65 percent of the variations in different kinds of resource flows between pairs of child care organizations. Different interunit dimensions were found to be important in explaining the transactions of money, client referrals, technical assistance, and visibility or goodwill between these organizations. These major findings point out the importance of understanding the different reasons for interunit relationships. When organizational units are dependent upon one another for different types of resources, they adopt different patterns of coordination.

DESIGN VARIATIONS WITHIN ORGANIZATIONS

The preceding section has provided an overview of the OA framework and major research findings. In a sentence, we propose that a systematic assessment of complex organizations should focus on four different levels of analyses (organization, work unit, job, and interunit relationships) in terms of the dimensions of context, design, and performance outlined in Table 6-1.

The OA framework is admittedly complex, but so too are complex organizations. Indeed the complexity of organizations is one of our most consistent and dramatic empirical findings at each level of assessing organizations.

At the macro level it was found that people in different vertical and horizontal positions in the organization have significantly different views of the overall structure of authority in the organization.

At the unit level, large differences exist between organizational units at each hierarchical level in terms of task, structure, and process, and in patterns of correlations between unit context, design, and performance.

The contexts and designs of individual jobs were also found to differ systematically and affect employee responses to their jobs in different ways depending upon the kinds of tasks performed and the levels in the hierarchy of these jobs.

In terms of interunit relationships, different patterns of interdependence, coordination, and control exist for organizational units because they deal with different relevant environments.

These results have important implications for research and practice by suggesting that an assessment of organizations may require a greater level of conceptual and methodological sophistication than previously recognized. Although simple approaches are obviously preferred to complex ones, the major OA findings indicate that simple, quick, and neat approaches may not be adequate.

These findings also emphasize the need for a substantive strategy that can help one make sense of these complexities in organizations and reduce them to manageable proportions. This section attempts to develop such a strategy by classifying the different types of subsystems that tend to exist within most complex organizations. The classification represents an initial attempt to: (1) explain why and how organizations are complex; (2) motivate an appreciation of the broader set of issues and implications involved in assessing organizations; and (3) reduce the complexity of organization design and assessment by singling out the most salient OA dimensions for each organizational subsystem.

The classification is illustrated in Figure 6-3. It is obtained by cross-hatching technical, managerial, and institutional functions with systematized, discretionary, and developmental modes of structure. This nine-cell classification of subsystems is superimposed on an organization chart in order to illustrate the relative locations where these design variations tend to exist.

In practice of course there is considerable overlapping of functions and tasks among organizational units and positions. Seldom are they as clearly distinguished as Figure 6-3 and the following discussion implies. In addition, a given organizational unit or position may often operate in a number of different cells of Figure 6-3 at different points in time. This is particularly true when the unit or position performs a variety of functions in the organization or encounters tasks, problems, or issues that vary substantially in difficulty or variability.

The important point is that the nine cells in Figure 6-3 represent qualitatively different kinds of subsystems found in many complex organizations. Organizational units or positions operating in these nine subsystems: (1) strive to achieve different subgoals; (2) respond to different relevant environments to perform their unique tasks and functions; (3) adopt different structural programs for organizing their activities into predictable patterns of behavior; (4) tend to be evaluated on different criteria of performance; and (5) approach problems and organizational issues from different perspectives and value orientations. These qualitative differences among subsystems are elaborated below.

What makes organizations complex to manage and assess is not the sheer number of organizational units or positions but rather the problem of determining what kinds of designs are appropriate and feasible for organizing each subsystem and for integrating these qualitatively different subsystems into the overall organization. Those organizations that do not contain all nine subsystems in Figure 6-3 tend to be easier to manage than those that do. Indeed a count of the number of different

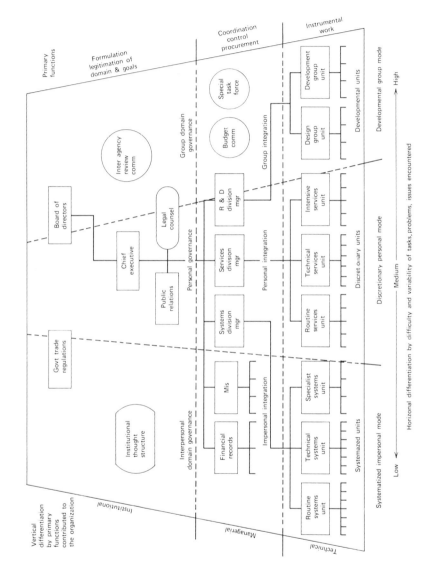

Figure 6-3 *A classification of design variations within complex organizations.*

271

Table 6-2 Hypothesized Patterns of Systematized, Discretionary, Developmental Modes on Institutional, Managerial, and Technical Subsystems within Organizations

Difficulty and Variability of Tasks, Problems, Issues Encountered by Subsystem	Systematized Impersonal Mode (Low)	Discretionary Personal Mode (Medium)	Developmental Group Mode (High)
Salient dimensions of institutional subsystem			
Organizational referent	Institutional thought structure	Top management unit	Board and stake holders
Domain restrictiveness	High	Medium	Low
Domain formalization (codification)	High	Medium	Low
Conflict on domain ends (goals)	Low	Medium	High
Uncertainty of domain means to ends	Low	Medium	High
Domain decision process	Computational	Judgmental	Bargaining
Locus of power and influence	Diffuse	Hierarchy	Interest groups
Salient dimensions of managerial subsystem			
Organizational referent	Central information systems	Hierarchy and staff	Coordination committees
Coordination and control by:	Rules, plans, schedules	Exceptions to hierarchy	Mutual group adjustments
Resource and information flows among organizational levels, units, and positions:			
a. Direction	Diffuse	Vertical	Horizontal
b. Amount	High	Medium	Low
c. Standardization and codification	High	Medium	Low
Perceived interdependence among components	Low	Medium	High
Frequency of conflict amont components	Low	Medium	High

Salient dimensions of technical subsystem

Organizational referent	Capital-intensive operations	Labor-intensive services	Team-intensive R&D projects
Unit specialization	High	Low	Medium-high
Heterogeneity of personnel skills	Medium	Low-medium	Medium-high
Interchangeability of roles	Low-medium	High	Low-medium
Standardization of work procedures	High	Medium	Low
Centralization of decision making	High	Medium	Low
Incentives based on performance of:	Individual or work system	Individual	Group

Typical design of jobs in all subsystems

Job specialization	High	Low	Medium-high
Required job expertise	Low-medium	Low-high	Medium-high
Job standardization	High	Medium	Low
Job discretion	Low-medium	Medium-high	High
Major source of feedback	Supervisor or controller	Supervisor and work	Peers and work

Results in all subsystems

Uniformity of product, service, or program	High	Medium	Low
Adaptability of product, service, program	Low	Medium	High
Quantity of outputs or services	High	Medium	Low
Cost per unit of output or service	Low	Medium	High
Personnel orientations	Universalistic	In between	Particularistic
	Neutrality	In between	Affective
	Specific	In between	Diffuse

cells in Figure 6-3 that are represented in a given organization provides a good measure of the structural complexity of that organization.

Differentiation of Functions in Complex Organizations

Parsons (1960) warned against undertaking an analysis of complex social systems without adequately clarifying the contexts and structural reference points that identify the functional subsystems in which behavior occurs. Parsons and Smelser (1956) and Katz and Kahn (1978) argue that to survive, organizations must perform: (1) *technical* functions of production to achieve task-instrumental goals; (2) *managerial* functions of coordinating, controlling, and procuring resources for the performance of technical functions; and (3) *institutional* functions, which include formulating, legitimating, and governing the domain and charter of the organization in relation to the larger social system of which the organization is a part. In small organizations participants will necessarily perform all these functions simultaneously. Given sufficient size, however, organizations divide the primary performance of these functions to different hierarchical levels. Obviously personnel at all levels in the hierarchy will perform all these functions to varying degrees; the point is that units at lower, middle, and upper levels in the hierarchy tend to be primarily responsible for technical, managerial, and institutional functions, respectively. Moreover, when certain personnel or units in an organization shift between technical, managerial, or institutional functions, different dimensions of context, design, and performance (listed in Table 6-2) become salient for assessing how these functions are performed.

1. *Technical Functions.* The appropriate referent for assessing the performance of technical functions is the nature of the work and the ways in which units and position are organized to do their work. Most of our understanding of technical functions in organizations has been contributed by the literature on the design of jobs (see reviews by Hulin and Blood, 1968; Pierce and Dunham, 1976; and Steers and Mowday, 1977), work groups or units (Grimes et al., 1972; Hrebiniak, 1974; Van de Ven and Delbecq, 1974; Hackman and Suttle, 1977) and more generally, sociotechnical theory (Emery and Trist, 1960; Trist, 1970). Most of the OA unit and job dimensions come from this literature. Although these dimensions have been used extensively for examining technical operations at the lowest levels of organizations, they are also very relevant for understanding how instrumental activities are organized into jobs at all organizational levels.

2. *Managerial Functions.* Stimulated by the Weberian model of bureaucracy, most organization theories and research to date have

focused upon structural configurations for coordination and control by examining differentiation, departmentation, and administrative overhead (Crozier, 1964; Blau and Schoenherr, 1971; Pugh et al., 1968; Galbraith, 1977). Recently, however, an increasing number of researchers are using social network analysis to focus on processes of resource and information flows and patterns of coordination and control (Tichy, 1973; Roberts and O'Reilly, 1974; Aldrich, 1979; Van de Ven et al., 1976; Tushman, 1977; Tichy et al., 1979). A combination of the structure and process perspectives is taken in OA to examine managerial functions of coordination, control, and procurement.

3. *Institutional Functions.* As suggested by the domain choice problem, institutional functions are principally concerned with: (1) selecting the charter of the organization in terms of its role in society, the products or services it delivers, and the target populations and markets it services; and (2) legitimating this corporate domain and the contributions of the organization to the larger social system of which it is a part. Generally the unit of analysis for assessing institutional functions includes the board of directors or trustees, the top management unit, and also influential stake holders and external interest groups who have control over critical organizational contingencies and resources.

The OA dimensions that are particularly relevant for assessing institutional functions are: domain uncertainty, complexity, and restrictiveness; organizational age and history; the distribution of power and authority among corporate decision makers; and group decision-making strategies and conflict. Much further work in OA is needed to understand the institutional subsystem in organizations. Fortunately the institutional function is receiving increasing attention in the recent "policy" literature on strategic choice (Child, 1972; Miles and Snow, 1978), corporate planning (Hofer and Schendel, 1978; Steiner and Miner, 1977; Mintzberg, 1977), and political behavior (Pfeffer, 1978; MacMillan, 1978).

Design Modes within Complex Organizations

As illustrated in Figure 6-3, systematic design variations should also be expected to the extent that organizational units performing these functions encounter tasks, problems, or issues that differ in difficulty and variability. Our previous research found that organizational units that undertake work at low, medium, and high levels of difficulty and variability adopt systematized, discretionary, and developmental programs or modes of structure, respectively (Van de Ven and Delbecq, 1974; Van de Ven, 1976). As March and Simon (1958) suggest, differences between the systematized, discretionary, and developmental modes are not simply variations on a theme; instead, they are qualitatively different logics for organizing patterns of behavior.

To make these qualitative differences clear, Table 6-2 hypothesizes the specific differences expected between the three design modes in terms of the dimensions most salient for assessing institutional, managerial, and technical functions in a complex organization. In other words, the dimensions in Table 6-2 make operational the classification in Figure 6-3, which focuses specifically on explaining design variations within an organization. These design variations are discussed in the following sections.

The Systematized Mode. The logic of a systematized mode is to create a program for efficiently organizing and managing tasks, problems, or issues that occur repetitively, are generally well understood, and exhibit the same basic characteristics each time they are encountered. A systematized program generally specifies: (1) a detailed blueprint of the sequence of steps and procedures to be followed in advance of their execution; (2) the standards to be attained at each step in terms of quantity (timing and pacing rules) and quality (specifications on tolerable ranges of behavior and output); and (3) built-in monitoring and control devices to detect departures from the blueprint so that corrections can be made. Once implemented, departures from the blueprint are immediately detected, and human discretion does not enter into the determination of what, where, when, and how roles are to be articulated to deal with the problem, task, or issue; rather roles and their articulation are formally prescribed in the impersonal blueprint for action. Since the coordination and control procedures are impersonally codified, their use requires minimal verbal communication between role occupants (Van de Ven et al., 1976: 323).

As Figure 6-3 illustrates, there are many examples of technical, managerial, and institutional functions in organizations that are structured according to the impersonal systematized mode. Mechanical or clerical assembly lines, technicians operating capital intensive systems, and intensive-care nursing units exemplify the kinds of organizational units found in the systematized mode for performing technical functions.

Impersonal integration of managerial functions is often accomplished by manualized or computerized management information systems and financial, bookkeeping, payroll, and purchasing units. From this perspective, we view the functional contributions of the disciplines of operations research, computer science, managerial finance, and accounting largely as that of developing systems for impersonally coordinating and controlling organizations. Indeed the rapid growth and demand for personnel trained in these disciplines is a reflection of the current trend in most complex organizations to increasingly systematize those managerial functions that are repetitive, simple, and nonvarying.

The systematized mode for institutional domain governance often is not supported or maintained with full-time personnel positions. Instead it is exhibited in organizational records and documents, verbal agreements, and "between the ears" of organizational members. *The Wall Street Journal* and other practitioners' newsletters provide daily examples of the growth and concerns over impersonalized and systematized ways that the domains of organizations are governed and legitimated. They include: trade, legal, and governmental regulations; contracts and agreements that organizations enter into with labor unions, governments, and other organizations; and also ethical values, standards, and norms regarding acceptable practices for personnel within the organization and in the larger trade, profession, or craft.

Although these examples have long been recognized as having significant influence on the structure and the behavior of organizations, they have not been incorporated into a systematic framework of organization design. Instead they have been viewed as largely exogenous to the organization and existing somewhere in its environment. Yet the fact remains that organizational decision makers either create many of these impersonal mechanisms for domain governance themselves, or choose to accept them as constraints and as consequences of the type of domain they choose for the organization. Furthermore, in this post-Watergate era, there is ample evidence that decision makers have the option to either abide by or violate regulations, contracts, and ethical standards governing organizational domains—and to suffer the personal and organizational consequences when violations are detected. Therefore we view organizations as having significant control over the institutional regulations, contracts, and standards of fair practice by which they choose to govern themselves.

When internalized and codified, these controls become a systematized mode for organizing what Roland Warren identified and labeled as the "institutionalized thought structure" of an organization. The institutionalized thought structure consists of the aggregate set of values, norms, and expectations of an organization in relation to its members and to other organizations. It "serves to reduce uncertainty and to insure organizational viability. . . . This institutionalized thought structure is reflected in the technological and administrative rationales of organizations, the source of their legitimation, and their relation to power configurations" in the industry or community (Warren, 1971: 67–68).

The Discretionary Mode. The logic of a discretionary mode is to create a program for organizing and managing tasks, problems, or issues that recur periodically but exhibit a sufficient number of variations each time they are encountered that different procedures and adjustments are required to handle them. A discretionary mode generally consists of: (1) a repertoire of alternative means or strategies for handling various issues; (2) guidelines for using discretion to diagnose and to respond to situations by selecting an appropriate strategy from the repertoire; and (3) standards on expected levels of output quantity and quality for which personnel are held accountable. Once trained and indoctrinated in the discretionary program through formal academic or craft schools, job-entry, and continuing on-the-job training programs (which themselves represent examples of discretionary modes) personnel are basically independent actors, and the output of one group member often does not affect the output of others. Increases in group output are achieved by increasing the number of personnel or the skills of individuals. Thus the discretionary mode is a labor-intensive structural design because the number of exceptions encountered in the work renders systematization either impractical or impossible to completely program in advance. Finally, the discretionary mode is a relatively flexible structure. Frequent alterations and substantial changes of strategies in the repertoire are less costly and time-consuming than in the systematized mode (Van de Ven and Delbecq, 1974).

Examples of routine, technical, and intensive discretionary modes of structure for the performance of task-instrumental functions include: watch guards, janitors, and secretaries; salespeople, butchers, bakers, and candlestick makers; and medical, legal, and professional consulting units. As predicted by the more difficult tasks performed by these three groups of discretionary units, they will have personnel with progressively higher levels of skills and expertise and will exercise increasing levels of discretion in task performance (Van de Ven and Delbecq, 1974: 187).

The discretionary mode for managerial coordination and control is exhibited in the forms of departmentation and in the flows of vertical and horizontal communications among departments and positions. Organizations will divide labor and resources into functional, geographic, program, and matrix arrangements to respond to critical contingencies in their product and factor markets and to minimize problems of coordination and control (Galbraith, 1977; Davis and Lawrence, 1977). Within and between these departmental arrangements, hierarchy serves as the basic mechanism for vertical integration (Thompson, 1967), and its basic function is to deal with exceptions (Dale, 1965). That is, repetitive and predictable integration issues are systematized through rules, plans, and schedules, whereas exceptions are referred to higher levels of authority.

As the number of exceptions and the interdependence among organizational units increase, more information exchange is required to make the necessary mutual adjustments. Two ways to "extend the arms of a manager" are to appoint assistant managers and add support staff to handle technical and administrative matters. In addition, horizontal channels of communication will emerge in which the integration function is assumed by organizational members who communicate directly with others on a one-to-one basis in a nonhierarchical relationship. If there is a continuing need for mutual adjustments through horizontal communications, these nonhierarchical mechanisms are often formalized by designating individuals to the roles of project expeditor, integrator, or coordinator (Lawrence and Lorsch, 1967). Ultimately the personal, discretionary mode of coordination at the managerial level may expand to the point at which coordination departments are established, as is frequently observed in matrix or program management organizations (Galbraith, 1971; Delbecq and Filley, 1974).

The positions and units that operate in a discretionary mode to perform institutional functions generally include the chief executive officer, vice-presidents, and headquarters staff (e.g., legal counsel, public relations, and corporate affairs). Although considerable variations in the design of these discretionary mode units and positions may exist, the common element is that their principal functions are to deal with the exceptions and problems encountered in formulating, legitimating, and governing the domain of an organization in relation to its members and external constituents.

The Developmental Mode.   The logic of a developmental mode is to create a program for handling tasks, problems, or issues that have not been encountered before or are sufficiently difficult and complex that they require group search, evaluation, and judgment. To varying degrees developmental programs consist of: (1) general goals or ends to be achieved in a specified amount of time, leaving unspecified the precise means to achieve them; (2) a set of norms and expectations regarding the nature of behavior and interactions among group members. There is an important distinction between the adaptive processes in discretionary and developmental programs. A discretionary program is adaptive insofar as it has procedures for selecting from a repertoire of strategies appropriate to the various tasks or problems encountered. With a developmental program, the repertoire of strategies does not exist, and the unit is adaptive insofar as trial and error processes are followed in the design of a strategy. As a result, during the period of task performance adaptation through problem-solving and learning is a distinctive feature of the developmental program (March and Simon, 1958). Typically tasks and issues undertaken by developmental-mode units are temporary and center on the solution to specific problems through a creative problem-solving process (Delbecq and Van de Ven, 1971; Van de Ven and Delbecq, 1974). Developmental modes are team intensive, and group members are highly interdependent because they contribute their complementary skills to group problem solving. Depending upon the degree of agreement among members on means or ends, decisions tend to follow either judgmental or bargaining strategies (Thompson and Tuden, 1959), and an individual's discretion is subject to guidelines set forth by the team.

Two variations in technical functions of developmental mode units are illustrated in Figure 6-3. In the *design group,* tasks center on analysis, revision, and modification of existing products or services; in the *development groups,* the tasks require conceptual reorientations (Normann, 1971). For example, industrial design groups may perform yearly product revisions, whereas development groups explore the creation of new products or services traditionally not considered germane to the organization's technology. Thus the distinction between design and development units is that the latter undertakes more difficult and open-ended tasks and problems.

As Figure 6-3 illustrates, a variety of temporary and standing committees, task forces, and study groups are commonly used to perform managerial and institutional functions. Classically, the developmental mode, with its group decision-making processes and committee structures, has been viewed as an aberration of formal organization. For example, Weber (1947: 402) states, "Collegiality unavoidably obstructs the promptness of decision, the consistency of policy, the clear responsibility of the individual, and the ruthlessness to outsiders in combination with the maintenance of discipline within the group." Weber did recognize, however, that collegial bodies may be necessary where thoroughness in weighing of the institutional and managerial decisions is more important than efficiency (Weber, 1947: 399). We should add that these developmental modes of structure and group decision processes for managerial and institutional functions provide a necessary and important forum for: (1) making strategic corporate decisions; (2) addressing conflicts and power contests among competing participants; and (3) creating and periodically reorganizing the discretionary and systematized modes of structures used by various organizational units and levels. An indication of the criticalness of these functions is that an entire industry of management consulting firms and professionals has grown up largely to assist organizations in creating temporary developmental modes and group processes to deal with these problems.

The institutional role of the board of directors is a subject that has received far too little attention in practice and management theory (Drucker, 1978). By law, the "managing organ" of every U.S. corporation is its board of directors, and currently the composition and responsibilities of corporate boards are being scrutinized and debated in the courts and federal regulatory agencies. For example, the Securities and Exchange Commission has recently proposed that the composition of corporate boards become totally independent of top management personnel, and the courts are increasingly demanding more responsibility and higher standards of accountability for boards of directors in stockholder suits. Clearly there is a need to systematically include an examination of the structure and process of the board of directors as an institutional decision making and governing unit in an assessment of organizations.

Summary

This section has presented a classification of nine different subsystems that often exist in complex organizations. The structural configurations that these subsystems are likely to adopt can largely be predicted from the different kinds of functions and tasks they perform. The classification helps to explain the significant design variations that exist within organizations. It also brings out the realistic complexity of an organization by highlighting that at least nine qualitatively different subsystems may need to be taken into account when managing and assessing organizations.

Of course any particular organization may not have all nine subsystems in the classification. From the view of a discretionary mode, Figure 6-3 represents a repertoire of nine key design strategies, and the analyst must use discretion, first in determining which particular subsystems exist in the specific organization being assessed, and second, in terms of judging what dimensions of context, design, and performance are relevant for evaluating and understanding each subsystem.

Hopefully, the descriptions and examples of each subsystem are useful in exercising this discretion. The classification reduces the complexity of the OA framework to manageable proportions by: (1) providing nine key reference points from which to diagnose a complex organization; (2) suggesting what specific dimensions in the OA framework are most relevant to focus upon when assessing each subsystem; and (3) hypothesizing the particular structural arrangement each subsystem is likely to have. Empirical support for the systematized, discretionary, and developmental modes has been provided by Van de Ven and Delbecq (1974). Research is now under way to test the entire classification scheme.

A PROCESS FOR ORGANIZATION ASSESSMENT AND PROBLEM SOLVING

The previous sections have presented the OA framework and major findings obtained with the OA instruments. A classification scheme was offered to synthesize the complexity of organizations by describing nine qualitatively different subsystems that typically exist in complex organizations. However, as any individual who actually conducts an organizational study quickly learns, a conceptual framework and set of measurement instruments are not enough to conduct an organization assessment and to use its information for practical purposes. Also needed are some process guidelines on what steps are involved in assessing organizations and in helping decision makers address complex problems that either stimulate or are identified by such assessments.

Unfortunately, prevailing research practice, as reflected in standard research methodology texts, provides little assistance in developing these process guidelines. Most research methodology texts advocate an objective, nonpartisan orientation on the part of the researcher and assume that he or she is the sole decision maker who has the competence and information necessary to reduce a complex problem into a clear-cut and definitive set of issues and criteria. Although traditional models of problem solving and assessment may apply when conducted *within* a given organizational subsystem, they clearly do not apply *across* these subsystems. Indeed assessments and problem-solving efforts that reach across these subsystems often occur in a context reflecting an organized anarchy, in which: (1) individual and collective needs, goals, and values are inconsistent and ill-defined; (2) technologies or means to achieve given ends are unclear, as are the consequences of collective action; and (3) there are multiple partisan groups—each controlling various amounts of power, competence, and information relevant to organization assessment and problem solving—who enter and leave the process at different points in time as their available energies and volitions dictate (Cohen, March, and Olsen, 1972). These turbulent or anarchic conditions have been found to be manifest in portions of most (but not all) complex organization endeavors, and organization assessment can be no exception (March and Olsen, 1976; Schon, 1971; Lindblom and Cohen, 1979; and Trist, 1979).

These conditions defy application of the traditional, centralized, and synoptic approach to organization assessment and problem solving for the following reasons. First, no single evaluation or decision-making unit commands sufficient competence and information about a complex organization to obtain an overview and make rational, comprehensive decisions. Whatever decisions it makes will therefore be arbitrary and partisan. Second, few if any commonly accepted criteria and models of organizational effectiveness are likely to exist among partisan groups. Therefore whatever results are obtained from an assessment will be used for partisan purposes, even if the assessment itself is conducted as objectively and disinterestedly as possible. Third, contrary to what one might incorrectly infer from the previous sections, it is highly doubtful that comprehensive organization design decisions should be made by a single decision-making unit in the first place. Instead the ambiguity of the problems being investigated and the great potential for decision failures point directly to the need for a multiplicity of decision makers reflecting variety of partisan interests, so that no line of adverse consequences fails to come to the attention of each decision maker. For this to happen, the assessment and problem-solving process will need to be decentralized and incremental; it will occur through partisan mutual adjustments (Lindblom, 1965; Lindblom and Cohen, 1979).

Given these conditions and consequences, people who are commissioned to conduct an organization assessment are confronted with three basic but often ignored problems: (1) Who should decide what effectiveness criteria to use for evaluating an organization? (2) Whose conceptual model or framework should be used to guide the assessment? (3) How can one facilitate learning and mutual adjustments among partisan users of the assessment results? A critical new thrust to the OA research program is the need to develop a process model for conducting organization assessments that addresses these questions instead of side-stepping them as conventional models of evaluation and choice do. Actually, the writings of Lindblom (1965), Suchman (1967), Argyris (1968), and March and Olsen (1976), as well as our work on planning and complex problem solving,* have greatly influenced and speeded the development of such a normative procedural model for organization assessment and problem solving. This section will outline the process model that is emerging to guide the conduct and use of the OA framework and instruments.

Outline of the OA Process Model

Figure 6-4 proposes six overlapping phases of activities for conducting an organization assessment. The overriding objective of the process model is to place the analyst or researcher into a larger intervention context than that which the narrow definition of research often implies, that is, to measure, analyze, and report results of a study designed on the basis of the researcher's own value judgments and conceptual model. The OA process model proposes that the analyst respond to the concerns of a greater number of users, only one of which is the researcher; make explicit the multiple and conflicting values underlying any definitions of organization effectiveness; and facilitate learning among partisan users by having them become a part of the organization assessment process. By following these process recommendations, it will become clear that the OA framework and instruments described in previous sections only rep-

---

*This work has focused on the development of the Nominal Group Technique (NGT) and the Program Planning Model (PPM) as proposed initially by Delbecq and Van de Ven (1971). The NGT is a structured group meeting format for generating ideas on a question or problem, and has been found to outperform conventional group meetings and delphi techniques (see Van de Ven, 1974; Delbecq, Van de Ven, and Gustafson, 1975). The PPM is a normative process model for complex problem solving that divides the process into a manageable series of task phases and proposes that different participants and decision-making strategies be used in each phase while planning an organizational program. Subsequent to its initial development, the PPM has been extended by Van de Ven and Koenig (1976), empirically tested and found largely supported by Van de Ven (1980a), and generalized as a normative theory of collective action for coping with complex problems (Van de Ven, 1980b).

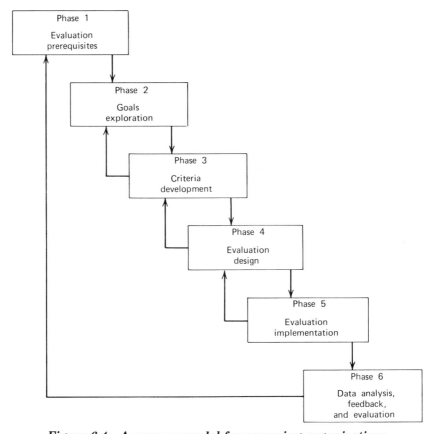

Figure 6-4   A process model for assessing organizations.

resent an initial point of departure, not a conclusion, for designing and conducting an OA. Activities in each phase of the process model are summarized below.

Phase 1, Evaluation Prerequisites.   At the outset, the analyst and the commissioners of the study establish their working contract and clarify their roles by answering the following questions:

1.   What are the reasons for conducting an organization assessment?

2.   How will the results of the study be used?

3.   What organizational components or issues are to be assessed?

4.   What individuals and groups will be the users of the study?

5.   Who should be involved in designing the assessment?

6. To what extent is there a commitment to using the methods and knowledge of science to design and conduct the study?

7. What amount of resources is available to conduct the assessment?

Answers to these questions are crucial for determining whether an OA is worthwhile, what the nature of the working relationships between the evaluators and the users will be, and how to tailor the process and content of the OA to specific user needs.

The decision to undertake an OA represents a significant commitment of resources and human energy on the part of the analysts and the users involved in the process as well as on the part of all the organizational employees affected by it. The involvement of users in the assessment process may heighten their expectations that the study itself will increase organization effectiveness in the ways they define it. Furthermore, individuals within complex organizations have multiple, partisan, and sometimes dishonest personal motives for implementing and using an evaluation study.

These realities imply that the negative side effects from naively undertaking an OA without establishing a clear understanding of its process and content can easily outweigh its positive and intended consequences. Thus the decision on whether or not to undertake an OA should not be made lightly. It has been our experience that most problems encountered in later phases of an OA are caused by either failing to ask the prerequisite questions or misunderstanding answers to these questions.

Phase 2, Exploration of Effectiveness Goals. Obviously organizations do not have goals; instead people have goals for an organization. As stated in the second section, organizational performance or effectiveness is a *value judgement* about the results desired from an organization by various decision makers. Therefore in Phase 2 the evaluators conduct a series of meetings with various groups of users to identify the effectiveness goals they have for the organizational components being assessed. Users are defined as people within and outside of the organization who have a stake in the organization assessment. If the dominant coalition of decision makers within an organization is chosen in the prerequisites phase as the only user of an OA, then it is quite likely that the effectiveness goals developed in Phase 2 will narrowly reflect internal managerial values and will tend to ignore issues of who benefits from the organization, whether the organization should exist at all, or what the contributions of the organization should be to society. These latter issues tend to be questioned only if the user groups involved in Phase 2 represent not only the organization's dominant coalition but also outside organizational clients or customers, funders, community interest groups, and employees within the organization. Including a wide cross section of users to identify effectiveness goals for an organization: (1) minimizes the tendency for assessments of organizations to be myopic; (2) brings out the different and often conflicting goals various stake holders expect of an organization; and as a consequence (3) tends to produce the information needed to stimulate conflict resolution and partisan mutual adjustments in choosing effectiveness goals that are responsive to the multiple expectations people have of an organization.

It is presumptuous to expect users to be able or willing to articulate completely the content and intensity of their effectiveness goals for an organization. That would be analogous to expecting an individual to verbalize completely the personal goals for his or her life. However, it is even more presumptuous for an analyst to impose his or her own value judgments on an organization by selecting the effectiveness goals and criteria on which an organization will be evaluated without consulting the people who are the principal users of the study. We simply assume and have found that users can and will articulate, in an operational form, *some* of their value judgments about effectiveness when asked to do so—particularly when users are provided a process to make repeated estimations of their value judgments in a nonthreatening manner. For example, we have found it useful to conduct a series of meetings over time, in which users perform different roles at each meeting and have repeated opportunities to second guess their prior judgments. First, nominal group meetings could be conducted to develop a preliminary list of effectiveness goals with each group of users. In subsequent meetings the preliminary goals can be classified, ranked, discussed, modified, and reranked to identify goal priorities.

The goal exploration phase concludes with a review session in which user representatives: (1) evaluate the unique sets and priority rankings of effectiveness from each user group; (2) confront disagreements; and (3) make the mutual adjustments necessary to proceed to the next phase. All of this occurs with an explicit awareness of the goals on which there is consensus and conflict among user groups.

Phase 3, Development of Effectiveness Criteria.   The evaluators obtain the value judgments of users concerning the criteria they will use to assess the extent to which each goal priority is attained. Whereas effectiveness goals are desired end states, criteria are operational dimensions representing the degree to which goals are met. The process of criteria development requires that users make three normative decisions: (1) select *concrete, observable characteristics or dimensions* that are to be measured and used as indicators of goal attainment; (2) specify *standards* or cut-off points on the dimensions above which users believe goals are attained and below which goal attainment is considered unsatisfactory; and (3) in the usual case of multiple criteria, determine the *weights of importance* to be assigned to the dimensions in order to understand hierarchical relations among the criteria and to develop an aggregate or composite measure of goal attainment (Scott, 1977; Campbell, 1977). The evaluators assist users in making these decisions incrementally through a series of group meetings, discussions, and workshops as in Phase 2.

Of course the raw data obtained in the criteria development workshops do not automatically become useful for developing operational measures of effectiveness. A necessary intermediate task between the generation of criteria and the development of effectiveness indicators is a content analysis of the qualitative data. A substantial proportion of bias that enters the content analysis of the data can be detected and corrected at the conclusion of the criteria development phase in a rigorous review session with users.

At this review session, the evaluators present the major effectiveness criteria developed by each user group and present their content analysis of the criteria. In addition, conflicting priorities among the effectiveness criteria of various user groups are outlined. User representatives at the evaluation session then review this material, are encouraged to confront disagreements, and are asked if the evaluators can proceed to the design phase with an explicit understanding of the varying degrees of consensus among users on effectiveness goals and criteria.

Phase 4, Evaluation Design.   Given the goals and criteria chosen by the user groups, the evaluators develop and pilot test a set of effectiveness measures. In addition, they conduct a workshop with user representatives to develop a specific experimental or field research design of the organizational and environmental characteristics that are likely to explain effectiveness in the organizational components being assessed. Such a workshop incorporates the in-depth knowledge of the organization that users have and facilitates their ultimate use of the OA results.

In conducting these workshops with user representatives, we have found it useful to begin with a nominal group meeting in which the effectiveness criteria selected in Phase 3 are presented, and users are asked, for example, "What situational or organizational factors predict or explain effectiveness (as defined)?" Such a nominal group will not result in an operational evaluation design, nor does it replace the result in an operational evaluation design, nor does it replace the need for the analyst to have a systematic framework of organization and effectiveness, as we attempted to describe in the second and third sections. Instead such a meeting gives evaluators the information needed to modify or include in such a framework the factors of concern to users, and to design comparative studies of alternative organizational strategies or designs. Indeed when there is a prevailing consensus among practitioners on the conventional wisdom for including or excluding factors in a study of their organization, how can a conscientious analyst justify ignoring them? John Campbell (1977: 18) aptly summarizes this point: "If the people won't use a particular kind of criterion, there is no sense in collecting it. Why build indicators of organizational health if these are going to be ignored? Why develop new measures of performance if no one trusts them?"

User involvement in developing the conceptual model is also important for identifying those factors and organizational units that influence effectiveness. Users can identify which organizational units and components are held accountable for each effectiveness measure; supraorganizational and environmental factors that are beyond the control of the organizational components being evaluated should be measured but controlled for when explaining organizational effectiveness.

Once the evaluators have identified operational effectiveness measures and obtained user input on an evaluation design, they proceed to develop the operational research design for assessing an organization. It is here where the evaluators modify and tailor a general OA framework and measurement instruments, as described in previous sections, to the particular needs of the organization(s) being assessed. In addition to developing the operational OA framework, activities in Phase 4 involve the technical tasks described in most research methodology texts; including selection procedures, sample size, measurement, and procedures for data collection, analysis, and feedback.

The work in this phase concludes with a review session with user representatives to evaluate the operational OA research design, to revise it where necessary, and to obtain a decision to proceed to Phase 5. Given the knowledge and resource constraints in constructing an ideal design, the evaluators present the limitations of the proposed OA design in terms of the desired information that cannot be provided and the factors threatening the internal and external validity of the research results (Campbell and Stanley, 1963). The users then judge whether to proceed with the assessment with a clear understanding of its limitations.

Phase 5, Evaluation Implementation. The data collection process is implemented in this phase by following the procedures outlined and approved in Phase 4. The principal concerns during this phase are: (1) maintaining integrity and controls on the uniformity of data collection procedures; (2) tracking of organizational units and respondents, particularly with a longitudinal study; (3) recording unanticipated events that may influence results of the experimental or quasi-experimental study; and (4) responding to feelings of threat and sensitivities of respondents and users.

Phase 6, Data Analysis and Feedback. The evaluators process the data to construct computer data files and analyze the data-following procedures set forth in the assessment design (Phase 4). The major process concerns during this phase are to provide users opportunities to participate in analyzing, interpreting, and learning from the results of the OA.

Although the most appropriate ways for doing this are unknown, we have relied upon a series of one- and two-day workshops with users in which preliminary findings on initial questions and problems are presented orally, in writing, and with illustrations.

These workshops begin with a review of the decisions made in Phases 1 to 5 and a presentation of the organizational scores obtained on the effectiveness criteria of each user group. These highlight the alternative results that are obtained given the conflicting criteria of different users. When these findings are presented, users quite naturally raise a host of questions and issues. They become embroiled in group discussions and debates as they review and evaluate the data—and learning has begun. Some of the questions can be answered by reanalyzing the data, and these become part of the agenda for the next workshop. Some of the questions raised can be clarified and answered directly with the data at hand and require that users make some decisions to change existing organizational patterns. Finally, some new issues and effectiveness goals are raised that cannot be addressed with the current OA data. These become the inputs for conducting the next assessment cycle of Phases 1 to 6.

Subsequent assessment cycles generally require less effort, because only marginal revisions are made in each phase from the preceding cycle. However, with each recycling of the phases, significant increases in information become available for learning about organization design and effectiveness by examining the data collected over time. Moreover, an ongoing OA process permits users to learn about the consequences of their decisions to implement changes in the organization based on problems identified in previous assessment cycles.

Discussion of OA Process Model

The process described here for assessing organizations may appear as requiring so much involvement of users in each assessment phase that it stretches out to be an endless series of conflict-ridden meetings and potential veto decisions. In addition, the process may appear to threaten the integrity of the overall OA framework described in previous sections. Admittedly, the OA process model will not provide speedy solutions, and it deviates considerably from conventional notions of what is involved in conducting an organizational study. This is because the OA process model attempts to avoid many of the unintended consequences that result from the ways organizational studies are traditionally conducted. It also admits to the limitations inherent in any attempt to develop and impose one's OA framework on an organization without the inputs of users.

Argyris (1968) points out that in efforts to achieve traditional criteria of "rigorous" research (establish experimental controls, minimize contamination, standardize observations, replicate procedures, etc.), the researcher places organizational participants—aptly called "subjects"—into a world in which their "behavior is defined, controlled, evaluated, and reported to a degree that is comparable to the behavior of workers in the most mechanized assembly-line conditions" (p. 186). Argyris goes on to argue that the unintended consequences of traditional field studies (which parallel those found in formal organizations) include not responding to questionnaires or physically withdrawing from interviews (absenteeism and turnover), fudging or lying in answers to questions (sabotage), second-guessing the research design and trying to circumvent it in some fashion (soldiering), participating in the study for a price (emphasis on monetary rewards), and ignoring or rejecting study findings (apathy and nonresponsibility).

We view the OA process model as a realistic attempt to: (1) avoid these unintended consequences of traditional research methods; (2) identify and confront the different and conflicting values held by various groups of users regarding any organizational assessment; and (3) cope with the lack of knowledge about what factors and issues are critical for investigating the specific questions and problems requiring solutions. In even moderately complex and changing organizations, these "crises of values and knowledge" (Friedmann, 1973) are beyond the cognitive and physical limits of any single central evaluation unit.

The proposed solution is to portray the OA process as a strategy for mutual adjustment and learning among various user groups and evaluators who interact to design and conduct a study that incorporates their value judgments and partisan perspectives. Lindblom (1965) has shown that such a strategy of partisan mutual adjustment imposes on no one the heroic demands for information, intellectual competence, and value judgments that are required of a centralized evaluation or decision-making unit. Instead rationality in assessing complex organizations is obtained from the participation of a multiplicity of decision makers pursuing their own interests and values in interaction with others. "Groups become watchdogs for values they fear will be neglected by other groups: each group consequently develops sensitivity to certain lines of consequences and becomes more competent to explore them than do other groups to whom these consequences are incidental" (Lindblom, 1965: 156). Multiple decision makers bring the energies, skills, and values that are needed to identify the relevant issues and consequences of alternative approaches to organization assessment and problem solving that would otherwise be neglected by a central evaluator.

Moreover, participation legitimates the undertaking; it builds support and use of an OA. There is ample evidence that active self-assessment and development of corrective adjustments by users facilitates their adoption of whatever solutions are reached (Bass, 1971; Bennis et al., 1962; Delbecq, et al., 1975; Filley et al., 1976). Applying the concept of participation to the design and conduct of an organizational study, Argyris (1968: 194) reports the following:

> In our experience the more subjects are involved directly (or through representatives) in planning and designing the research, the more we learn about the best ways to ask questions, the critical questions from the employees' views, the kinds of resistances each research method would generate, and the best way to gain genuine and long-range commitment to the research.

The six phases in the OA process model should be viewed as a continuous process of incremental action, review, and adaptation over time and not as a discreet, comprehensive leap in assessment and problem solving. Emphasis is placed on taking small, tentative, and consecutive steps in assessment with each step being subject to review, modification, and reiteration on the basis of experience and knowledge gained during the intervening period. In this way users can learn by second-guessing their initial value judgments; and tangible performance expectations and alternative organizational redesigns become apparent during the process. The design and use of an organization assessment thereby become fused during the course of the action itself.

The importance of partisan mutual adjustment and of incremental steps in assessment become clear when compared with alternative methods often used for organization assessment and redesign. Two widely espoused remedies for avoiding bureaucratic problems of obstruction, delay, and resistance are to go outside the organization by hiring consultants or to create new departments within old organizations as a means of developing reorganization plans. While these remedies may expedite the creation of reorganization proposals, they lead evaluation and problem-solving efforts astray because they circumvent the very organizational units and people that are subsequently needed to implement and administer the proposals for change. This is because outside consultants or independent planning units often tend to avoid contact with the very political forces that are necessary to preserve the thrust of their reorganization plans.

More basic is the recognition that exclusive reliance on outside consultants or internal planning departments are but two of many ways to separate planners from doers, or to divorce planning from implementation. *"Learning fails because events are caused and consequences are felt by different people"* (Pressman and Wildavsky, 1973: 135). Learning is a trial-and-error process, and its essential steps include idea generation, execution, evaluation, and adjustment. When assessment is divorced from operations, or when attempts are made to circumvent the bureaucracy, the learning process is short-circuited because different people experience these steps. Learning requires that design, implementation, and evaluation become fused in the assessment and problem-solving process, and that interaction occurs among the people principally concerned with design, implementation, and evaluation. For this to happen, organizational assessments will need to be incremental rather than comprehensive.

Alexander and his architectural colleagues (1975) stimulate the following critical orientations underlying incremental versus comprehensive approaches to organization assessment and problem solving. *Comprehensive* or "large lump" assessments are based on the fallacy that problems in complex organizations can be largely *isolated* and *separated,* and each can be addressed with *"once-and-for-all"* solutions by *replacement* of obsolete policies or structures with new ones. *Incremental* or "piecemeal" assessments are based on the more dynamic view that complex organizations represent systems of continually *changing* and *interdependent* problems for which there are no final solutions. Through trial and error, *temporary and relatively better* responses to problems are possible by *repair* of existing policies or programs, *addition* of small new components where necessary, and their *adjustment* to existing structures so as to achieve a new semistable equilibrium in the social system.

Learning Involves Mistakes

Comprehensive leaps in organization assessment and problem solving virtually eliminate opportunities for learning because of their scope and magnitude, and the hierarchical structure of thought and power on which they tend to be based. To maintain integrity of "the plan," central decision-making units (just as many outside consulting units) tend to avoid or deny error by minimizing open contact with other partisan groups, being secretive in their decision making, and acting as if they know what they are doing when they don't (Michael, 1973). As stated above, no central assessment or decision-making unit commands sufficient competence and information of many problems in complex organizations to obtain an overview and make rational decisions.

An incremental approach to assessment and problem solving, as proposed by the OA process model, is based on a pluralistic structure of thought and partisan influence. It views mistakes as inevitable when coping with the design and performance of complex organizations, and it facilitates learning by taking small and gradual steps among multiple partisan participants in conducting an OA. Each step permits ideas, arguments, and information from those who presumably will gain and lose from the unfolding of the process. Each step in the process is thereby subject to review and modification on the basis of what has been learned, and mistakes can be detected and prevented from becoming major errors.

For complex organizations to remain viable institutions they must not only adapt continuously to changing environmental conditions and values, but must also maintain an equilibrium or balance between their new and existing structural components. Organization assessment and problem solving, therefore, must be just as much concerned with *maintaining* and *repairing* the organization as with *creating* and *integrating* new social orders. This is facilitated when organization assessments occur within instead of outside of existing organizations, consist of an incremental series of steps as opposed to comprehensive leaps, and follow a process of decentralized partisan mutual adjustments rather than centralized and synoptic decision making.

CONCLUSION

This chapter has presented an overview of the Organization Assessment (OA) research program, which was begun in 1972. To assess complex organizations, the OA framework and instruments emphasize the need to:

1. Identify the relevant properties of context, design and performance at the macro-organization, unit, job, and interunit levels of analyses;

2. Examine the unique design patterns of jobs, units, and inter-unit relationships that are located vertically and horizontally within the complex organization; and

3. Determine how these different jobs, units, and inter-unit relations are integrated and what contributions they make to the overall performance of the organization.

Although ambitious, the major findings of OA to date indicate that continued theory building and research along the lines suggested in this chapter constitute a promising and important direction for the scientific study of organization design and performance.

We believe that application of the OA findings can help practitioners and analysts address the practical problems described in the first section. In this regard, it is important to conclude by clarifying what we believe is the proper role of the OA framework and instruments in practice. Our experiences suggest that the *processes* followed in designing and conducting organizational assessments are far more important in obtaining their acceptance and use than the specific framework or instruments that are used to conduct such assessments. Obviously we consider it important to have a good framework and a reliable set of measurement tools to conduct quality assessments of organizations. They are, after all, the technical core of any organization assessment. However, the OA framework and instruments are precisely that: they are *tools* that can be used constructively for organizational learning and problem solving or misused with destructive consequences. When used properly within the context of an overall process of assessment that is tailored to the needs of specific organizational users, as suggested by the OA process model in the fourth section, we believe that the OA framework and instruments can provide substantial opportunities for learning about and improving the design and performance of organizations, work groups, and jobs.

REFERENCES

Aldrich, H. (1974). "The Environment as a Network of Organizations," paper presented at the International Sociological Association Conference, Toronto (August).

Aldrich, H. (1979). *Organizations and Environments,* New York: Prentice-Hall.

Alexander, C., M. Silverstein, S. Angel, S. Ishikawa, and D. Abrams (1975). *The Oregon Experiment,* New York: Oxford.

Argyris, C. (1968). "Some Unintended Consequences of Rigorous Research," *Psychological Bulletin* **70,**3: 185–197.

Bass, B. (1971). "When Planning for Others," *Journal of Applied Behavioral Sciences* **6:**151–172 (April/June).

Bell, G. (1967). "Formality versus Flexibility in Complex Organizations," in *Organizations and Human Behavior: A Book of Readings,* Englewood Cliffs, NJ: Prentice-Hall, pp. 97–106.

Bennis, W. G., K. D. Benne, and R. Chin (1962). *The Planning of Change,* New York: Holt, Rinehart, and Winston.

Blau, P. M., and R. H. Schoenherr (1971). *The Structure of Organizations,* New York: Basic Books.

Brief, A. P., and R. J. Aldag (1975). "Employee Reactions to Job Characteristics: A Constructive Replication," *Journal of Applied Psychology* **60,**2:182–186 (April).

Campbell, D. T., and J. C. Stanley (1963). *Experimental and Quasi-Experimental Designs for Research,* Chicago: Rand-McNally.

Campbell, J. P. (1977). "On the Nature of Organizational Effectiveness," in P. S. Goodman, J. M. Pennings, and Associates, Eds., *New Perspectives on Organizational Effectiveness,* San Francisco: Jossey-Bass, pp. 13–15.

Chandler, A. (1962). *Strategy and Structure,* Garden City, NY: Anchor Books.

Child, J. (1972). "Organizational Structure, Environment and Performance: The Role of Strategic Choice," *Sociology* **6:**1–22.

Cohen, M. D., J. G. March, and J. P. Olsen (1972). "A Garbage Can Model of Organizational Choice," *Administrative Science Quarterly* **17,**1:1–25.

Crozier, M. (1964). *The Bureaucratic Phenomenon,* Chicago: University of Chicago Press.

Dale, E. (1965). *Management: Theory and Practice,* New York: McGraw-Hill.

Davis, S. M., and P. R. Lawrence (1977). *Matrix,* Reading, MA: Addison-Wesley.

Delbecq, A. L., and A. C. Filley (1974). "Program and Project Management in a Matrix Organization: A Case Study," Madison: Bureau of Business Research, Graduate School of Business, University of Wisconsin.

Delbecq, A. L., and A. H. Van de Ven (1971). "A Group Process Model for Problem Identification and Program Planning," *Journal of Applied Behavioral Sciences* **7:**466–492 (September).

Delbecq, A. L., A. H. Van de Ven, and D. H. Gustafson (1975). *Group Techniques for Program Planning,* Glenview, IL: Scott-Foresman.

Drucker, P. F. (1978). "The Real Duties of a Director," *The Wall Street Journal* (June 1).

Emery, F. E., and E. L. Trist (1960). "Socio-Technical System," in C. W. Churchman and

M. Verhulst, Eds., *Management Science, Models, and Techniques*, Vol. 2, Elmscord, NY: Pergamon, pp. 82–97.

Filley, A. C., R. J. House, and S. Kerr (1976). *Managerial Process and Organizational Behavior*, 2nd ed., Glenview, IL: Scott-Foresman.

Follett, M. P. (1926). "The Giving of Orders," in H. C. Metcalf, Ed., *Scientific Foundations of Business Administration*, Baltimore: Williams and Wilkins.

Friedmann, J. (1973). *Retracking America*, Garden City, NY: Doubleday.

Galbraith, J. R. (1971). "Matrix Organization Designs: How to Combine Functional and Project Forms," *Business Horizons* 14:29–40.

Galbraith, J. R. (1977). *Organization Design*, Reading, MA: Addison-Wesley.

Grimes,A. J., S. M. Klein, and F. A. Shull (1972). "Matrix Model: A Selective Empirical Test," *Academy of Management Journal* 15:9–31.

Hackman, J. R. (1976). "The Design of Self-Managing Work Groups," Technical Report No. 11, New Haven: Yale University School of Organization and Management.

Hackman, J. R., and G. R. Oldham (1975). "Development of the Job Diagnostic Survey," *Journal of Applied Psychology* 60,2:159–170 (April).

Hackman, J. R., and J. L. Suttle (1977). *Improving Life at Work: Behavioral Science Approaches to Organizational Change*, Santa Monica, CA: Goodyear.

Hage, J. (1965). "An Axiomatic Theory of Organizations," *Administrative Science Quarterly* 10:289–320 (December).

Hage, J., and M. Aiken (1969). "Routine Technology, Social Structure, and Organization Goals," *Administrative Science Quarterly* 14:366–376 (September).

Hall, R. H. (1962). "Intraorganizational Structural Variation: Application of the Bureaucratic Model," *Administrative Science Quarterly* 7:295–308 (December).

Hofer, C. W., and D. Schendel (1978). *Strategy Formulation: Analytical Concepts*, St. Paul, MN: West Publishing.

Hrebiniak, L. G. (1974). "Job Technology, Supervision, and Work-Group Structure," *Administrative Science Quarterly* 19,3:395–410 (September).

Hulin, C. L., and M. R. Blood (1968). "Job Enlargement, Individual Differences, and Worker Responses," *Psychological Bulletin* 69:41–55.

Katz, D., and R. L. Kahn (1978). *The Social Psychology of Organizations*, 2nd ed., New York: Wiley (first edition published 1966).

Khandwalla, P. N. (1977). *The Design of Organizations*, New York: Harcourt, Brace, Jovanovich.

Lawrence, P. R., and J. W. Lorsch (1967). "Differentiation and Integration in Complex Organizations," *Administrative Science Quarterly* 12:1–47 (June).

Likert, R. (1967). *The Human Organization: Its Management and Value*, New York: McGraw-Hill.

Lindblom, C. (1965). *The Intelligence of Democracy*, New York: Free Press.

Lindblom, C. E., and D. K. Cohen (1979). *Usable Knowledge: Social Science and Social Problem Solving*, New Haven: Yale University Press.

MacMillan, I. C. (1978). *Strategy Formulation: Political Concepts*, St. Paul, MN: West Publishing Co.

March, J. G., and J. P. Olsen (1976). *Ambiguity and Choice in Organizations*, Oslo, Norway: Universitetsforlaget.

March, J. G., and H. A. Simon (1958). *Organizations*, New York: Wiley.

McKelvey, W. (1979). "Comment on the Biological Analog in Organization Science on the Occasion of Van de Ven's Review of Aldrich," *Administrative Science Quarterly* 24,3:488–493 (September).

Michael, D. A. (1973). *On Learning to Plan, and Planning to Learn,* San Francisco: Jossey-Bass.

Miles, R. E., and C. C. Snow (1978). *Organizational Strategy, Structure, and Process,* New York: McGraw-Hill.

Miles, R. H., and K. S. Cameron (1978). "Coffin Nails and Corporate Strategies: A Quarter-Century View of Organizational Adaptation to Environment in the U.S. Tobacco Industry," New Haven: Yale University, School of Organization and Management, Working Paper No. 3 (Summer).

Mintzberg, H. (1977). "Patterns in Strategy Formation," Montreal: McGill University Faculty of Management, Working Paper (August).

Mohr, L. B. (1971). "Organizational Technology and Organizational Structure," *Administrative Science Quarterly* **16**,4:444–459 (December).

Morgan, M. A. (1977). "The Relative Impact of Job Histories on Career Outcome Variables," Unpublished Ph.D. dissertation, Northwestern University, Graduate School of Management, Evanston, IL.

Normann, R. (1971). "Organizational Innovativeness: Product Variation and Reorientation," *Administrative Science Quarterly* **16**:203–225.

Oldham, G. R., J. R. Hackman, and J. L. Pearce (1976). "Conditions under Which Employees Respond Positively to Enriched Work," *Journal of Applied Psychology* **61**:395–403 (August).

Ouchi, W. G., and A. H. Van de Ven (1980). "Antitrust and Organization Theory," in O. E. Williamson, Ed., *Antitrust Law and Economics,* Houston: Dame Publication Co., Chapter 8.

Parsons, T. (1960). *Structure and Process in Modern Societies,* New York: Free Press.

Parsons, T., and N. J. Smelser (1956). *Economy and Society,* Glencoe, IL: Free Press.

Perrow, C. B. (1967). "A Framework for the Comparative Analysis of Organizations," *American Sociological Review* **32**:194–208 (April).

Perrow, C. B. (1979). "Organization Theory in a Society of Organizations," paper presented at the 1979 Annual Meeting of the American Sociological Association.

Pfeffer, J. (1978). *Organizational Design,* Arlington Heights, IL: AHM Publishing.

Pfeffer, J., and G. R. Salancik (1978). *The External Control of Organizations: A Resource Dependence Perspective,* New York: Harper and Row.

Pierce, J. L., and R. B. Dunham (1976). "Task Design: A Literature Review," *Academy of Management Review* **1**:83–97 (October).

Pressman, J. L., and A. B. Wildavsky (1973). *Implementation,* Berkeley: University of California Press.

Pugh, D. S., D. J. Hickson, C. R. Hinings, and C. Turner (1968). "Dimensions of Organization Structure," *Administrative Science Quarterly* **13**:65–105.

Roberts, K. H., and C. A. O'Reilly III (1974). "Measuring Organizational Communication," *Journal of Applied Psychology* **59**,3:321–26 (June).

Rumelt, R. (1974). "Strategy, Structure and Economic Performance," Boston: Harvard Business School, Division of Research.

Schon, D. A. (1971). *Beyond the Stable State,* New York: Norton.

Scott, W. R. (1977). "Effectiveness of Organizational Effectiveness Studies," in P. S. Goodman, J. M. Pennings, and Associates, Eds., *New Perspectives on Organizational Effectiveness,* San Francisco: Jossey-Bass, pp. 63–95.

Simon, H. (1946). "The Proverbs of Administration," *Public Administration Review* **6**:53–67 (Winter).

Starbuck, W. H. (1976). "Organizations and Their Environments," in M. D. Dunnette, Ed.,

Handbook of Industiral and Organizational Psychology, Chicago: Rand-McNally, pp. 1069–1123.

Steers, R. M., and R. T. Mowday (1977). "The Motivational Properties of Tasks," *Academy of Management Review* **2**:645–658 (October).

Steiner, G. A., and J. B. Miner (1977). *Management Policy and Strategy: Text, Readings, and Cases,* New York: Macmillan.

Suchman, E. (1967). *Evaluation Research,* New York: Russell Sage.

Thompson, J. D. (1967). *Organizations in Action,* New York: McGraw-Hill.

Thompson, J. D., and A. Tuden (1959). "Strategies, Structures, and Processes of Organizational Decision," in J. D. Thompson et al., Eds., *Comparative Studies in Administration,* Pittsburgh, PA: University of Pittsburgh Press.

Tichy, N. M. (1973). "An Analysis of Clique Formation and Structure in Organizations," *Administrative Science Quarterly* **18**:194–208.

Tichy, N. M., M. L. Tushman, and C. Fombrun (1979). "Social Network Analysis for Organizations," *Academy of Management Review* **4**,4:507–519.

Trist, E. L. (1970). "A Socio-Technical Critique of Scientific Management," paper presented at the Edinburgh Conference on the Impact of Science and Technology, Edinburgh University (May 24–26).

Trist, E. L. (1979). "Referent Organizations and the Development of Inter-Organizational Domains," Distinguished Lecture presented at the 39th Annual Academy of Management Conference, Atlanta, Georgia (August 9).

Tushman, M. L. (1977). "Special Boundary Roles in the Innovation Process," *Administrative Science Quarterly* **22**:587–605.

Van de Ven, A. H. (1974). *Group Decision Making and Effectiveness,* Kent State, OH: Kent State University Press.

Van de Ven, A. H. (1976). "Equally Efficient Structural Variations within Organizations," in R. H. Kilmann, L. R. Pondy, and D. P. Sleven, Eds., *The Management of Organization Design: Research and Methodology,* Vol. 2, New York: North-Holland, Elsevier, pp. 155–170.

Van de Ven, A. H. (1977). "A Panel Study on the Effects of Task Uncertainty, Interdependence, and Size on Unit Decision Making," *Organization and Administrative Sciences* **8**,2:237–253.

Van de Ven, A. H. (1979). Book Review of "Organizations and Environments" by H. E. Aldrich, *Administrative Science Quarterly* **24**,2:320–326 (June).

Van de Ven, A. H. (1980a). "Problem Solving, Planning, and Innovation, Part I: Test of the Program Planning Model," *Human Relations,* forthcoming.

Van de Ven, A. H. (1980b). "Problem Solving, Planning and Innovation, Part II: Speculations for Theory and Practice," *Human Relations,* forthcoming.

Van de Ven, A. H., and A. L. Delbecq (1974). "A Task Contingent Model of Work Unit Structure," *Administrative Science Quarterly* **19**,2:183–197 (June).

Van de Ven, A. H., A. L. Delbecq, and R. Koenig, Jr. (1976). "Determinants of Coordination Modes within Organizations," *American Sociological Review* **41**:322–338 (April).

Van de Ven, A. H., D. Emmett, and R. Koenig, Jr. (1974). "Frameworks for Inter-organizational Analysis," *Organization and Administrative Sciences Journal* **5**,1:113–129 (Spring).

Van de Ven, A. H., and D. L. Ferry (1980). *Measuring and Assessing Organizations,* New York: Wiley-Interscience.

Van de Ven, A. H., and R. Koenig, Jr. (1976). "A Process Model for Program Planning and Evaluation," *Journal of Economics and Business* **28**,3:161–170.

Van de Ven, A. H., M. J. Treis, G. Esser, and D. L. Ferry (1976). "1975 Wisconsin Job Service Organization Assesment: Organization and Performance Efficiency of District Offices," Report prepared for Wisconsin Job Service Division of the Department of Industry, Labor and Human Relations, Madison.

Wanous, J. P. (1974). "Individual Differences and Reactions to Job Characteristics," *Journal of Applied Psychology* **59**:616–622 (October).

Warren, R. (1971). *Truth, Love and Social Change,* Chicago: Rand-McNally.

Weber, M. (1947). *The Theory of Social and Economic Organizations,* trans. by A. M. Henderson and T. M. Parsons, New York: Free Press.

Williamson, O. E. (1975). *Markets and Hierarchies,* New York: Free Press.

Wrigley, L. (1970). "Divisional Autonomy and Diversification," Unpublished Ph.D dissertation, Harvard Business School, Boston.

COMMENTS ON THE ORGANIZATION ASSESSMENT RESEARCH PROGRAM

CORTLANDT CAMMANN
University of Michigan

In approaching this commentary, I found myself pulled in a number of directions. The program is a complex and interesting one. Its theories integrate a variety of perspectives and models relevant for understanding the consequences of organizational designs. Its methods include a unique and innovative mix of approaches. Its purposes include, but extend beyond, the straightforward tasks of description and hypothesis testing, and some of its findings are significant and insightful.

I will limit my comments to three areas. First, the OA Program as a program of research, serves as a useful model for other research programs. Second, I will comment on the strengths and weaknesses of the OA framework as a basis for conducting organizational assessments. Finally, I will explore some dilemmas inherent in the dual OA objectives of research and use. The OA researchers clearly wish to develop a program that can contribute to both knowledge and practice of organizational design, and their program demonstrates some of the dilemmas that must be resolved if the science of organizational design is to produce practical results as well as theoretical advances.

The OA Program as a Program of Research

If someone were to describe the characteristics of a good research program, the following elements would probably be included:

1. *Integration with the Field.* A research program should be closely linked to the broader context of research and knowledge concerning the phenomena under investigation. It should integrate relevant existing knowledge, extend existing knowledge, and evolve as new knowledge is developed within the program or outside of it.

2. *Theoretical Clarity.* A research program should develop clear theoretical models for describing characteristics of the phenomena being studies, and should include a framework that describes the relationships between the theoretical models and the situations in which each of the models is appropriate.

3. **Empirical Orientation.** A research program should include empirical tests of the theories and frameworks being developed in order to ensure that they represent accurate descriptions of the phenomena and to identify areas where current theoretical models are inadequate.

4. **Methodological Attention.** A research program should attend to the relationships between the theories being developed and the methods being used to test them. Theories limit methods and vice versa, and unless researchers attend to underlying theories of methods, they may find that their theories become constrained by the methods they are using, or that their methods represent inappropriate tools for collecting information for testing their theories. Either outcome can reduce the value of a research program, particularly if the researchers have an inadequate theory of methodology to articulate their current methodological limitations.

5. **Perspective on Use.** A research program should have a clearly identified set of objectives about how the program's findings will be used. Ultimately, research programs are only useful if the results are used by some group. Since different potential consumers of research results are likely to have different interests, to assimilate information differently, and to employ different standards for judging results, researchers need to know the nature of their audience and adapt their theories, methods, and reports accordingly.

One of the impressive aspects of the OA research program is the extent to which it includes each of the aspects of a model program of research.

Integration with the Field. The purpose of the OA program is "to develop a *framework,* a *process,* and a set of *measurement instruments* for assessing the performance of complex organizations in relation to how they are organized and the environments in which they operate" (Van de Ven, 1980). Thus the domain of the program includes any research that bears on the functioning of complex organizations. This domain includes work from psychology, sociology, economics, administrative science, and related disciplines. Van de Ven and his colleagues have done a laudable job in drawing on work from all of these fields and attempting to include relevant knowledge from each in their research program. Further, as the fields have developed and produced new knowledge and methods, the OA researchers have attempted to integrate the developments into their approach, for example, by adding network theories and methods to their program. Finally, the OA researchers have contributed to the development of theories and methods in their field both by extending knowledge, for example, examining the theoretical level that is appropriate for analyzing the relationship between structure and performance (Van de Ven and Ferry, 1980), and developing new methods, for example, using nominal group techniques as part of the development of effectiveness criteria (Delbecq and Van de Ven, 1971; Van de Ven and Ferry, 1980). Thus the OA program appears to be closely linked to the many domains that are relevant for its programmatic direction and attempts to integrate relevant knowledge for a variety of fields.

Theoretical Clarity. The OA researchers have based their research on the assumption that organizational functioning is complex and that complex theories are required to describe it. They have developed theoretical models at four different levels of analysis: that of the overall organization, that of work groups or units, that of individual jobs, and that of relationships—both between jobs and units and between the organization and other organizations. Given the complexity of the theories they are working with, the OA researchers have done an impressive job in developing clearly articulated models and a framework for relating them. At each level of analysis, the theoretical models being employed are clearly stated, and hypotheses are generated for testing the validity of the theoretical approach. Further, at each level the concepts have been defined so that they can be related to the concepts used in the models at other levels, and the broader framework linking the models has been articulated. Clearly much work remains in order to fully develop the OA framework. Most of the models are as yet only partially tested; some of the links among models, such as those between job and unit characteristics, are more clearly specified than others, such as those between job and relationship characteristics; and the range of organizations in which the framework has been applied is limited. Yet the focus on developing a clear, integrated theory underlies all the OA research and represents one of the most valuable aspects of the overall program.

Empirical Orientation. All of the work done on the OA framework is closely tied to empirical tests of theoretical propositions. As theories are integrated into the framework, hypotheses are generated for testing their validity, and methods are developed for collecting information to test the hypotheses. The resulting information is examined to determine its implication for the theory and for the reality experienced by people familiar with the organization. Thus the evolution of the OA framework is closely linked with empirical results from functioning organizations, and theories and concepts are adopted or dropped if they cannot be validated. This close linkage of the OA theory and research results clearly represents one of the strengths of the program and ensures that the theory has internal validity, if not generalizability. As time goes on and the OA instruments are used in more organizations, it seems reasonable to expect that generalizability will be developed as well.

Methodological Attention. In developing their research instruments, the OA researchers have paid careful attention to the theory underlying their methodology and to the relationship between their theory and their methods. In deciding how to collect information, they have tried to specify the constraints facing assessors working in organizational settings, and to develop instruments that can be used to collect information in the face of these constraints. They have drawn on research knowledge concerning respondent behavior to try to develop instruments that will provide information that is as accurate as possible. The measures used are tested for psychometric properties whenever appropriate, and tests of instrumentation are made, using multiple methods and construct validation, whenever possible. The OA researchers have not fallen into the trap of using available methods when they are not appropriate given the underlying theory. In the case of assessing effectiveness, for example, the theory specifies that different constituencies may use different criteria, and that individuals may not be aware of the criteria they employ. To deal with this, methods were developed to involve different groups in defining the criteria that are relevant and to aid the individuals involved in clarifying the nature of the criteria they employ.

There is one area of methodo logical attention, however, that the OA researchers have not given sufficient attention. They have designed their methods so that they can be used over time in organizational settings. Among other things, this has meant designing their methods to be useful to organization members, because the data collection activities are intrusive and time consuming, and organization members cannot be expected to cooperate in providing information over time if they do not feel that they get a return for their effort. This type of design means the OAI will have effects on the organization. The methods for determining effectiveness criteria, for example, are likely to have a marked effect on the way organization members understand effectiveness and each other. It seems likely that this will result in changes in their behavior and the organization. Yet the OA researchers have not fully documented these effects, nor have they developed a theory for predicting what they will be. In my view, this area needs attention. I fully agree with their implicit position that intrusive methods are required in organizational assessments, but I feel that assessors should attend to the effects of the intrusions and integrate them into their theoretical perspectives.

Perspective on Use. The OA researchers have clearly specified two different audiences for their program results. The first audience is basic researchers interested in the effectiveness of different organizational designs for coping with variations in organizational environments. The second audience is organizational managers interested in using the OA theory and methods to improve the design of their organizations. In many ways this dual focus represents one of the major strengths of the program.

In trying to meet the needs of both these audiences, the OA researchers are building a number of useful attributes into their program. They are developing theories that can contribute to a scientific understanding of organizations and can also guide organizational change. They are using measures that are both scientifically valid and practical. They are establishing assessment processes that will allow them to conduct longitudinal research without destroying the willingness of organization members to provide them with valid data. In short, by trying to meet the needs of both researchers and practitioners, the OA researchers are developing assessment tools that can contribute to both the study of organizational design and the practice of developing effective organizations.

But trying to achieve dual objectives apparently creates some problems for the OA program. For example, Van de Ven and Ferry (1980) imply that organization members can have models and theories for describing organizational functioning that conflict with the OA framework. In such a case the research and practical objectives of the OA program may come into conflict. The research objectives would lead assessors to use standard measures, whereas the practical objectives would lead them to develop new constructs and measures more acceptable to users. This type of conflict, which has also been described by Alderfer and Brown (1972) is likely to create serious dilemmas for researchers interested in developing measures that are comparable across organizations while also developing ones that are acceptable to people within them.

The fact that the dual objectives lead to the use of measures and procedures that will affect organizational functioning will be troublesome to many members of the research audience. While I can only speculate, I would guess that many researchers would find the results of such an intrusive process unacceptable according to their criteria for good research. In my view, the problem here is that current conceptions of good research designs may not be applicable for organizational research (see Alderfer and Smith, 1980; and Argyris, 1968, for elaborations of this argument), but as long as current conceptions exist, the results of the OA program are likely to be problematic for many of the members of the research audience.

Conclusion.   Overall, I believe that the OA program represents a model for research work in this area. It has all the characteristics one would like to see in a program of research, and it is producing results that should help us better understand the effects of different organizational designs. There are some areas in which the program is underdeveloped, and some aspects of its theory and method have not been adequately tested. These issues should be dealt with if the progress of the program is to continue.

Strengths and Weaknesses of the OA Framework

As I view the OA program, it seems to me that its strengths and weaknesses reflect the orientation of the researchers and the problems they have been trying to solve. Most of the work to date has been done in the context of studies examining the effectiveness of different organizational designs for solving problems in social service agencies; this work had the purpose of helping agency decision makers develop new, more effective designs. This has led to a focus on a particular set of questions: (1) How should effectiveness be defined? (2) What dimensions of agency structure and technology should be measured to help organizational decision makers and researchers better understand the determinants of effectiveness and the policy decisions that can be made to improve it? (3) What dimensions of the agency's context (history and environment) should be described to help decision makers and researchers understand what is currently being done and what problems must be solved if it is to be done better?

These questions have led the OA researchers to develop theories and methods that can be used to assess the effectiveness of an organization, the "formal" structure* and technology inside the organization, and the external context within which the organization must operate. In each of these areas, the OA researchers have developed tools that can help researchers and decision makers assess an organization's functioning. While individual researchers might quarrel with specific hypotheses and measures, the overall framework and approach seems generally consistent with developments in the field.

In my view, the major weaknesses of the OA framework involve areas that are not measured, rather than areas that are. The OA program is trying to develop a set of comprehensive assessment tools to facilitate organizational research and change, and there are a number of theoretical areas that could be added to the framework to help it serve this purpose.

1. *Individual Differences.*   In the end, much organization action is the result of individual choice and activity. While individual-level behavior is clearly influenced by a variety of organizational factors, it is also the result of the individual's skills, needs, and perceptual sets. The OA measures currently include a number of relevant individual differences measures, for example, expertise and growth need strength; but others could also be incorporated, for example, need for achievement, authoritarianism, internal or external orientation. The problem of course is that valid measures of individual differences are frequently time consuming to administer and personally intrusive, and often without face validity to the respondents. Thus this area may be difficult to assess. Yet if these problems could be solved, adding more individual difference

---

*By "formal" structure I mean the aspects of organizational structure that can be immediately changed as a result of decisions by organizational policy makers. This will generally be reflected by up-to-date organizational charts.

measures would allow for a more systematic exploration of the effects of individual differences on organizational functioning than has been done to date.

2. **Perceptions, Attitudes, and Implicit Theories.** Underlying the OA framework is the assumption that measurement should focus on what people do rather than on what they think. Van de Ven and Ferry (1980) say, for example, "The reason we lean to a behavioral description of jobs is because behaviors are more objective and are easier for analysts and practitioners to observe, control and change than the more subjective attitudes of people regarding their jobs." Yet there are a number of reasons why it might be appropriate to include perceptions, attitudes, and implicit theories more explicitly in the OA theoretical framework. Organization members' beliefs about how their organizations function, that is, their implicit theories, may influence their perceptions and interpretations of events and then their reactions to them (Mitchell and Wood, 1980; Staw, 1975; Rosenthal and Rosnow, 1969; Lowin and Craig, 1968; Weick, 1979). Differences in perceptions held by organization members may create or escalate conflicts and coordination problems (Alderfer and Smith, 1980; Argyris and Schon, 1978; Sherif, 1966; Smith, 1977; Walton and McKersie, 1965). In addition, the use of symbols and theories may represent key tools for developing and changing organizations (Pettigrew, 1979; Argyris and Schon, 1978; Bowers and Franklin, 1977), serving as models that organization members first learn intellectually and then put into practice.

3. **Informal and Identity Groups.** The primary focus of the unit-level analysis in the OA program is on formal work units, since these represent the interpersonal systems most directly influenced by organizational designers. It is clear, however, that informal groups exist in organizations, that they create systemic boundaries, and that they can influence individual and organizational behavior (Roethlisberger and Dickson, 1939; Blau and Scott, 1962; Smith, 1977; Alderfer, 1977). Though these groups are harder to identify, assess, and change than formal work units, they clearly represent an important part of any organization's design. Developing assessment methods to measure the characteristics of these groups may require new and innovative methodologies (Alderfer and Smith, 1980), but this process has the potential for generating knowledge about the particular aspects of organizational structure that are probably the most difficult to affect in a planned way.

4. **Quality of Relationships.** A closely related issue involves increasing the attention paid to the quality of relationships within

the organization. Much of the focus in the current OA program is on mapping the structure of relationships that exist. Less attention is paid to the quality of the relationships when they exist. Again this is consistent with the general focus of the assessment package, since it is easier for designers to create a relationship than to specify its quality. Yet networks of relationships that are made up of links with different characteristics are different networks and can be expected to produce different effects. For example, supervisors whose relationships with subordinates can be characterized as autocratic and controlling are likely to produce different behavioral and affective results than supervisors whose relationships can be characterized as participative and problem oriented (McGregor, 1960; Likert, 1967). These differences are important to describe because they can influence consequences and because they may relate to other aspects of relationships such as whether or not information and resources flow freely. Future work on the OA program could usefully focus on measuring the quality of relationships in more detail, and could explore the effects of different relational qualities on the overall effects of structural configurations.

5. **Use of Structures.**   Finally, the OA program examines in detail the nature of the structures that exist, but devotes less attention to the way the structures are actually used. Different structures may be used by organization members for solving problems, and the enacted structure of the organization depends to a large extent on which structures are used to solve problems of different types (Ranson et al., 1980). Organizations with similar formal structures may operate quite differently depending on the predisposition of organization members to use the available formal and informal networks of relationships for solving problems. It would be useful to know how organization members make choices about the structures to use, and it would also be useful to examine the effects of different patterns of usage on overall organizational effectiveness.

Conclusion.   The purpose of the OA program is in part to help people understand what causes variations in performance. To date, the theory and measures have focused on aspects of organizations that are directly affected by decision makers, and the strength of the program lies in this area. Yet there are a variety of less accessible organizational characteristics that may have an important effect on performance and that are only touched on by the current OAI. I would like to see more attention paid to these areas in the future, because they could add significantly to the value of the Program's assessment tools.

In making this suggestion, I may be asking the OA researchers to do more than they intend. To some extent the measurement domains I have suggested represent areas I am personally interested in. Yet I think that most of my suggestions are consistent with the OA researchers' own experiences and results. Specifically, the design of the OA process for conducting assessments reflects concern with most of the areas I have suggested. The use of constituencies in defining effectiveness demonstrates the importance of informal groups and the salience of variations of perceptions. The process for developing effectiveness criteria illustrates the importance of differences in perceptions and of the process of interaction for producing effective results. The use of the OA process to facilitate learning illustrates the use of alternative structures for influencing the quality of organizational action. In short, the design and description of the way in which OA researchers interact with an organization suggests that most of the areas I have suggested are important determinants of organizational functioning. It therefore seems to me that they are logical areas for future development in the OA framework.

Design and Intervention

In terms of broad program design, there is one issue that OA researchers will probably have to resolve in the near future if their program is to continue to develop as an integrated approach to organizational assessment. The issue involves the type of research and theory that are to be included in the program, because of the apparent contradiction between the theoretical framework they have developed and the process that they use. The theoretical perspective is based primarily on accurate description, a traditional research value; and the models included in the OA framework have been drawn from research that has tried to describe how organizations function. In my view these models are more useful for describing the way organizations are than the way they change, and they are more useful in helping people recognize the current state of affairs than in deciding what they should do about it.

Taken alone, this poses no problem. The contradiction develops when the OA process is considered. The OA process is based on the work of action researchers, people interested in creating organizational change. The methods create change in organizations in order to generate information about them; they structure feedback processes designed to facilitate change so that organization members recognize the utility of the information being collected; they make the researchers actors in the organization in order to allow them to get better information about the way it functions. It is this contradiction between the process of the research and its theoretical content that is in my view, the source of the dilemma.

The OA program can develop in one of two directions. One is to emphasize descriptive research. If this choice is made, the researchers in the OA program will continue to develop descriptive theories and methods in much the say way that they have in the past. New models will be added to the OA framework, and a variety of important theoretical questions will be addressed. This type of research will require the development of some new approaches to the OA process, including, I suspect, an increased reliance on organizational records and the training of researchers to collect information from organization members in a minimally intrusive manner. If the OA program evolves in this direction, it should produce a stream of scientifically useful findings and an assessment program that organizations can use to give decision makers information in domains not covered by their current information systems. This approach, however, has two disadvantages. First, while the information may help them understand why organizational units are effective or ineffective, it may not help them learn how to use the information to increase effectiveness. As Argyris and Schon (1978) have argued, knowing what is wrong is not necessarily the same as learning how to do things right.

An alternative approach would be for the OA program to focus more explicitly on developing normative theories of design and assessment processes that facilitate change. Following this direction would not involve replacing existing models and methods, but it would require supplementing them. Theories and methods would have to be developed to help organization members complement existing processes for examining the way the organization is currently functioning. The OA process would need to develop new methods for teaching organization members to supplement existing ways of surfacing information. Research methods would have to be used that allow the examination of the effects of new organizational designs, to supplement existing methods that focus on predetermined design dimensions. Training programs would need to be developed to teach assessors to act as interventionists, to supplement existing programs that teach them to be researchers.

It seems to me that this second approach is more consistent with the underlying purposes of the OA program. If it is followed, it will significantly contribute to the development of organizational assessment and design. An intervention-oriented program of this sort would contribute to our understanding of the process of designing organizations and of the role of social scientists as designers and intervenors. Both of these areas are critically important for our field and need to be addressed if we are going to develop knowledge that can be applied in organizations in ways that make a difference to the people who live in them.

Conclusion

Overall, it seems to me that the Organizational Assessment program represents an impressive program of research. It has set difficult objectives to achieve and seems to be developing in ways that will result in their accomplishment. There is no question that the work to date contributes to an ability to assess organizations and that it will help us better understand problems in organizational design. The weaknesses of the program generally reflect things they have not yet done rather than things that have been worked on. This is not surprising, since the program is still evolving and developing.

Two primary areas deserve attention by OA researchers in the future. Their theoretical framework should be expanded to include more focus on individual and interaction variables that may influence organizational structure and functioning. The increasing importance of these areas is being demonstrated, and a complete assessment approach should include them. In addition, I think they need to more completely integrate the OA process and framework. The process seems oriented toward intervention and design, while the theory seems focused on description. If the direction of the program is toward intervention and change, the theory should be supplemented to include relevant models, and the process, should be developed further so that these purposes can be accomplished more effectively.

REFERENCES

Alderfer, C. P. (1977). "Group and Intergroup Relations," in J. R. Hackman and J. L. Suttle, Eds., *Improving Life at Work,* Santa Monica, CA: Goodyear, 227–296.

Alderfer, C. P., and L. D. Brown (1972). "Questionnaire Design in Organizational Research," *Journal of Applied Psychology,* **56:**456–460.

Alderfer, C. P., and K. Smith (1980). "Studying Intergroup Relations in Organizations," working paper, Yale University, School of Organization and Management.

Argyris, C. (1968). "Some Unintended Consequences of Rigorous Research," *Psychological Bulletin,* **70,**3:185–197.

Argyris, C. P., and D. A. Schon (1978). *Organizational Learning: A Theory of Action Perspective,* Reading, MA: Addision-Wesley.

Blau, P. M., and W. R. Scott (1962). *Formal Organizations: A Comparative Approach,* San Francisco: Chandler.

Bowers, D. G., and J. L. Franklin (1977). *Survey-Guided Development I: Data-Based Organizational Change.* La Jolla, CA: University Associates.

Delbecq, A. L., and A. H. Van de Ven (1971). "A Group Process Model for Problem Identification and Program Planning," *Journal of Applied Behavioral Sciences,* **7:**466–492.

Likert, R. (1967). *The Human Organization: Its Management and Value,* New York: McGraw-Hill.

Lowin, A., and J. R. Craig (1968). "The Influence of Level of Performance on Managerial Style: An Experimental Object-Lesson in the Ambiguity of Correlational Data," *Organizational Behavior and Human Performance,* **3:**440–458.

McGregor, D. (1960). *The Human Side of Enterprise.* New York: McGraw-Hill.

Mitchell, T. R., and R. E. Wood (1980). "Supervisor's Responses to Subordinate Poor Performance: A Test of an Attributional Model," *Organizational Behavior and Human Performance,* **25:**123–138.

Pettigrew, A. M. (1979). "On Studying Organizational Cultures," *Administrative Science Quarterly,* December, **24:**570–581.

Ranson, S., R. Hinings, and R. Greenwood (1980). "The Structuring of Organizational Structures," *Administrative Science Quarterly* (March), **25**:1–17.

Roethlisberger, F. J., and W. J. Dickson (1939). *Management and the Worker,* Cambridge, MA: Harvard University Press.

Rosenthal, R., and R. L. Rosnow (1969). *Artifact in Behavioral Research,* New York: Academic.

Sherif, M. (1966). *In Common Predicament,* Boston: Houghton Mifflin.

Smith, K. K. (1977). "An Intergroup Perspective on Individual Behavior," in J. R. Hackman, E. E. Lawler III, and L. W. Porter, Eds., *Perspectives on Behavior in Organizations,* New York: McGraw-Hill, 359–372.

Staw, B. M. (1975). "Attribution of the Causes of Performance: A General Alternative Interpretation of Cross-Sectional Research on Organizations," *Organizational Behavior and Human Performance,* **13**:414–432.

Van de Ven, A. H. (1980). "The Organization Assessment Research Program," Paper presented by the Center for the Study of Organizational Innovation on "Assessing Organization Design and Performance," Philadelphia.

Van de Ven, A. H., and D. L. Ferry (1980). *Measuring and Assessing Organizations,* New York: Wiley.

Walton, R. E., and R. B. McKersie (1965). *A Behavioral Theory of Labor Negotiations,* New York: McGraw-Hill.

Weick, K. E. (1979). *The Social Psychology of Organizing,* 2nd ed., Reading, MA: Addison-Wesley.

CHAPTER SEVEN

Organization and Environment Perspective

The Harvard Organization and Environment Research Program

PAUL R. LAWRENCE
Graduate School of Business
Harvard University

In this chapter I will focus on work done on the organization and environment (O&E) subject by my colleagues and myself at Harvard while fully recognizing the many other contributions that have been made to this broad subject. (I might add that I have never thought of the work at Harvard on this subject as a Program with a capital P.) I see the history of organization and environment work at Harvard as anchoring on and swinging around the book that Jay Lorsch and I published in 1967 by that title. Here I will sketch out both the prior works that were the major influences on our O&E study and the subsequent related research focused on the work done at Harvard. I will then review and respond to the major criticisms that have been raised about this line of work, in terms of both substance and method. This will set the stage for a restatement of the status of the theory and its current contribution as I see it. Finally, I will relate our approach to organization theory to several of the other approaches that have emerged in the past decade.

PRECURSOR WORK

It is no secret that all research efforts are indebted to many earlier works. The authors themselves cannot always see this at the time as clearly as others can. I believe Jay would agree with me that we were most influenced by Burns and Stalker (1961), and this is fairly well indicated in the text. We were not so clear about the extent we were influenced by some others like Dill (1958) with his comparative study of two Norwegian firms. Thompson's major work *(Organizations in Action,* 1967) was a simultaneous publication, but we knew of his work through personal contacts, and his thinking undoubtedly influenced us more than we were aware of at the time. My subsequent rereading of March and Simon (1958) and Barnard (1938) has highlighted for me some places where they use the differentiation and integration ideas more than we had realized.

In terms of my own prior work, I was highly aware that the research study I did with Arthur Turner (1965) affected the design of the O&E project. We had in rapid succession taken a fairly intensive look at a wide range of manufacturing operations, and I was strongly impressed with what a wide variety of management methods were succeeding in terms of both economic performance and employee satisfaction. As far as we could tell, these different management methods were associated with different kinds of tasks and different worker predispositions. This started me on the contingency idea. Only recently, however, on rereading the book I did with Harriet Ronken (*Administering Changes,* 1952), did it dawn on me that not only was my interest in differences in structure and orientation between functional groups a longstanding one, but so was the idea that task differences greatly complicate achieving the needed integration through conflict resolution. So my interest in intergroup differentiation and integration stems from my dissertation days.

O&E REVISITED

At this point I believe it would be useful to restate a few basic features of the O&E study—what it was and what it was not. It was an exploratory, theory-building study, not a hypothesis- or theory-testing study. It was a comparative cross-sectional study using a sample of 10 businesses as the primary unit of analysis. It was not a dynamic, longitudinal study of a single case or a statistical study with casts of hundreds. The sample was deliberately selected, not randomly, in order to see some extreme differences in business environment and in economic performance. Jay and I picked the container industry as a site because it was the most stable industry we could find.

We did this on the assumption that the phenomenon we wanted to study was somewhat elusive and very difficult to measure. We were interested in making a contribution to both theory and practice in addressing both the social scientist and manager. We designed a complex, multivariable, multimethod study in which the overall pattern of the findings would have to carry the message more than the rigor of any two variable associations. We believed that a crude preliminary test of our overall emerging theory was better than simply presenting either an interesting theory without any testing or a rigorous test of only a small piece of it. In this regard we may well not have been in the main track of American social science and its frequent preoccupation with measurement refinements on the one hand or with free-floating theory on the other.

SUBSEQUENT STUDIES

When, in writing this chapter, I made a list of the various studies that have come out of the organizational behavior group at Harvard Business School that pursue some aspect of the O&E theme, I frankly was surprised by its length. As I indicated above, we have never thought of this work as a Program. We have never had a program budget or a program director. There has never been a master plan. But given the range of publications, I can now see how those not involved can see it as a Program. Here I will list the follow-up studies and indicate their focus; some I will refer to again in the next section.

The one volume that best displays the nature of the follow-up research at Harvard is *Studies in Organization Design* (Lorsch and Lawrence, 1970). The chapters in this book moved the O&E ideas into a cross-cultural comparative study (Reudi and Lawrence), into a production function study (Walker and Lorsch), into a historical, preindustrial study (Udy), and into a more dynamic longitudinal study (Galbraith). In addition, the volume has four studies (Burns, Fisher, Hampden-Turner, and Athreya) that move the inquiry to a microlevel by examining differentiation and especially integration at the small group and interpersonal levels. Two of the studies that were first reported in this volume were later extended and appeared as books that retested the original findings and then applied the O&E ideas at the multidivisional level (Lorsch and Allen, 1973) and at the level of individual motivation (Lorsch and Morse, 1974). About this time Jay and I made a statement of these ideas addressed entirely to managers (Lawrence and Lorsch, 1969). Subsequently I have been involved with others in studies that used these ideas in modified form in three different organizational sectors: city government (Kotter and Lawrence, 1974), academic medical centers (Weisbord, Charns, and Lawrence, 1978), and large-scale government R&D projects (Lane, Beddows, and Lawrence, 1981). I see the matrix book (1978) I did with Davis as a practical application of the contingency framework.

Any such listing of follow-up studies tends to be rather tedious, but it does at least serve to indicate that there has been an extension and application of the original ideas in numerous directions: up into the multidivisional and interorganizational realm; down into the small group, interpersonal, and motivational realm; out into the cross-cultural in one direction and the cross-sectoral in the other; and finally back historically and forward longitudinally. The movement in all these directions is of

Table 7-1 Industry Economic Data from Original O&E
Study—Comparison of Population and Gross National Product
with Sales of Standardized Containers, Packaged Foods, and
Plastics Industry, 1964[a]
(1957–1959 = 100)

Population	106.1
Gross National Product	127.2
Standardized containers	130.0
Packaged foods	138.0
Plastic materials	260.4

[a]Census of Manufacturers: Annual Survey of Manufacturers: Annual McGraw-Hill Survey of Business Plans for New Plants and Equipment, 1965–1968, April 1965; and National Science Foundation, *Basic Research, Applied Research, and Development in Industry, 1961*.

course incomplete. It is no accident that in this brief review I have not mentioned any methodological follow-up that Jay and I had hoped would be stimulated by the original work. As I will indicate, there has been some follow-up on methods, but in my view the progress has been limited.

CRITICISMS, METHODOLOGICAL AND SUBSTANTIVE

In one respect we are fortunate—or at least we should feel that way—because the original book, and to a lesser extent its follow-up studies, have received a good deal of critical attention. In preparation for this paper I sat down for the first time to read together all the assorted reviews that I had been accumulating over the years. Along with some painful moments I found some cause for amusement; for instance, as regards writing style, the *American Journal of Sociology* reviewer commented that "This book is definitely written for managers," while the *Dun's Re-*

Table 7-2 Current Percent of Industry Sales Comprising
Products Introduced Commercially 5, 10, 20 Years Ago
(As of 1965)[a]

Industry	1960	1955	1945
Plastics[b]	15%	20%	65%
Packaged foods[c]	5	10	85
Standardized containers[d]	0	0	100

[a]**Organization and Environment** (1967), pg. 88.
[b]U.S. Tariff Commission Reports: Modern Plastics. Arthur D. Little, Inc.; Standard & Poors.
[c]Annual Survey of Manufacturers, Standard & Poors, and Progressive Grocer.
[d]Standard & Poors.

view writer said, "The book has one fault—a tendency to sound like a college thesis. . . . both authors are steeped in the scholarly tradition." I noticed also that the sociology reviews ignored our treatment of the process of conflict resolution and influence distribution, whereas the psychological reviews seemed to draw a blank on our handling of structural variables. The methodologists focused on the quality of our questionnaire numbers and essentially ignored our interview data and our objective archival data, while the opposite held for managerial journals. One reviewer summarized his negative comments on our methods by saying, "But a case is a case is a case." I wonder at times whether anyone wearing the HBS label will ever be able to produce research that is not perceived as "just another case study." In a more serious vein, we will first take a look at the methodological criticisms.

There have been several formal criticisms of the methodology of the original O&E study, and these have drawn some attention, judging by the frequency with which they are cited. I have in mind particularly Tosi, Aldag, and Storey (1973); Downey, Hellriegel, and Slocum (1975); and Pennings (1975). All three of these focus their criticism on the questionnaire instrument we used in O&E as one of three ways to measure environmental uncertainty.

Frankly, Jay and I have been somewhat puzzled by the amount of attention that has been given to this one instrument. As indicated above, we deliberately picked industries that were as different in terms of uncertainty as we could, *a priori*, find. At that time the specialized plastics industry was facing two primary sources of uncertainty: the rapidly changing field of polymer chemistry and a rapidly changing set of uses and preferences on the part of its industrial customers. These sources of uncertainty were partially generated by the plastics firms themselves. Other potential sources of uncertainty, such as capital markets or government regulation, simply were not a major factor at that time. In contrast, the container industry was then facing a set of customers with predictable needs and a set of relatively unchanging technical possibilities and no other important source of uncertainty. We found that our judgment in this regard was confirmed by all our interviews with experienced senior executives in these industries. We also collected some "hard" economic indicators, which I reproduce here in Tables 7-1 and 7-2 only because all the critics have failed to acknowledge their existence. No one to my knowledge has claimed that at the time of our study the specialized plastics industry did not face a great deal more uncertainty as we defined it than the container industry. If this point still holds, then all of the rest of our patterned data as regards formalization, orientations, functional differentiation, integration, conflict resolution, and performance are still unchallenged. The only point left in doubt is whether our questionnaire instrument is, without change, a strong tool to use by itself in other studies as a reliable measure of environmental uncertainty.

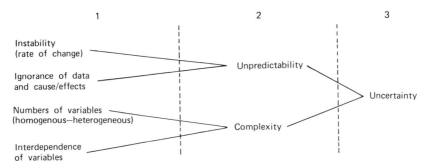

Figure 7-1   Factors and terms related to uncertainty.

It would surprise us if the answer was yes. We warned of the crudity of the tool and the slipperiness of the variable in our book. However, the way Tosi et al. and Pennings tested our scale still left the verdict in doubt. We have commented on our problems with the Tosi et al. article elsewhere (1972). My difficulty with Pennings' approach was that he tried to use it to find how the business environment varied among 40 units that were all in the very same business—brokerage branch offices. I wonder if any questionnaire instrument can be expected to make such fine distinctions. However, I find the Downey et al. study much more convincing, and its conclusion that this one instrument, by itself, should be used with considerable caution is a very reasonable one. So I reiterate the hope I have expressed before that someone with a greater interest in and aptitude for instrument development than I might undertake the difficult task of developing a better instrument. I am also thankful Jay and I did not rely heavily on this one instrument.

All of this methodological discussion does not deal with the separate question of whether there is a nonrandom gap between the perceived or enacted environment and the objective relevant environment or domain. In the original study Jay and I were trying entirely to get a handle on the objective domain, and our scale was intended as one way of verifying by a questionnaire what our archival and interview data revealed. I will address later the question of the usefulness of making the enacted-objective distinction and a possible way of accounting for a systematic difference between the two.

In order to address the substantive comments, I have found it convenient to group them into the six main arguments that I am aware of. The first of these is the criticism that contingency theory as we have presented it is only static, not dynamic. The closely related argument is that it presents a passive picture of organizations as only reacting to environmental conditions and never initiating change in their relevant environments. The cross-sectional nature of our research design undoubtedly contributed to a "static" feel in the study. We focused on what "fits" were most effective and not on the process by which these fits were achieved. I must confess, however, that we authors continue to have trouble taking this fairly consistent criticism seriously because we still see so very clearly the potential of the model for thinking about the dynamic interplay between an organization and its environment. Jay and I did one longitudinal study (1969), but more of course are needed. Kotter's recent book (*Organization Dynamics*, 1978) is one example of how the model can be explicated for managers in a dynamic manner.

The "only reactive" critique of the book seems much more relevant to me. Our book almost entirely ignored the impact of the organization on its domain, and certainly such impacts do occur even if, as I would argue, the flow is mostly the other way. In the book being completed with Lane and Beddows, we are making extensive use of the concept of "mutual adaptation" between the organization and its domain as a way to stay focused on this interdependence and the reality of initiatives from both directions. I say this even though the locus of initiative is very difficult to identify and sometimes is only in the eye of the observer. I would hope that all future organization and environment studies will be sensitive to this interactive process.

A second criticism is that we did not treat the concept of environmental uncertainty with conceptual clarity. There is considerable truth in this comment, and subsequent researchers have continued to have trouble finding a strong, persuasive way of defining this key idea. It remains both very useful and very elusive, a comment that I believe Plato made about the idea of citizenship a long time ago. I have thought a good deal about the problem and venture a few remarks that might help matters.

I think the notion of environment is the type of idea that we should be completely comfortable in defining in different ways, depending on the research purpose involved. For certain purposes the "environment" can usefully be treated as the "immediate relevant environment" of customers, competitors, and technological options. This was our O&E definition. For other purposes it is appropriate to extend this definition. I would advise that we accept these definitional variations as a normal state of affairs and be careful not to mix them up in comparative reviews.

The more sticky problem is conceptualizing and operationalizing the concept of uncertainty. This problem is a precursor to the methodological difficulties discussed above. Various researchers such as Galbraith (1973) and Duncan (1975) have addressed and contributed to this issue. The key problem is whether we can treat this idea as a unitary dimension of environment for the sake of simplicity, or whether we must treat it as a set of separate but related factors for the sake of accuracy. The factors and terms that have been discussed as related to uncertainty are complexity, number of variables, predictability, ignorance of relevant data and cause-and-effect relations, interdependence of variables, and rate of change. As a possible logical way of relating these factors I would now suggest we consider the chain of relationships in Figure 7-1. What I have in mind is the possibility of scaling each initial pair of factors and plotting isobars of their joint effects.

We would be assuming that, for instance, less instability would reduce the unpredictability of future events in the face of a constant amount of ignorance, and vice versa. Finally, we would assume that less complexity would reduce uncertainty in the face of a constant level of unpredictability. Perhaps such an approach can contribute to both conceptual clarity and the related measurement problems.* We will return to this formulation below.

Another criticism of the O&E book is that it started a trend that has gone too far in seeking a never-ending stream of contingent variables to account for organizational features. The fear is that we will reach the ridiculous extreme of saying that every item of organizational behavior is contingent on everything else. If that day comes, we will be in worse shape than when everyone seemed to be searching for the one universally right way to manage all organizations. At times I share this fear. But if we are aware of it we can, I believe, avoid it. We can focus our search for those few contingent factors that account for significant chunks of organizational variation and can be critical of undocumented proliferation of contingency variables.

A fourth criticism is that the O&E study did not offer an explanation for the observed uniformities. I agree that our book did not develop a clear and explicit explanatory argument. We left many clues to our implicit explanation, which Jay Galbraith (1973) later did an excellent job of articulating. In summary, the explanation is that improved performance flowed from the improved information processing and decision making, which in turn flowed from having the kind of differentiation and integration required to pick up and process the pertinent data from the relevant environment. This reasoning, we feel, provides the socioeconomic explanation. I believe the follow-up study by Lorsch and Morse (1974) provided a complementary psychological explanation. Their evidence indicates that a three-way fit between environmental uncertainty, organizational arrangements, and individual predispositions makes it possible for the individual at work to experience an inner feeling of competence. This feeling is a self-reinforcing reward that in turn energizes the organization and contributes to performance over and above the amount generated by anticipated extrinsic rewards. I believe these two levels of explanation complement and reinforce each other and provide a sound response to a gap in the original study. I would also add that the Lorsch and Morse study enriched the original model's performance criteria by explicitly adding a quality-of-work criterion.

---

*I am indebted to Thomas Clough for significant contributions to this formulation.

A closely related criticism has been that the study, with its normative emphasis on fit, does not encourage organizations to foster the potential that exists for individual development. I see so many "misfits" between individuals and organizations whose "cure" to a state of "fit" would release significant human development potential that it never occurred to me that the study could be read in a frozen, static way. For instance, three-way fit at one point of time could readily evolve to a misfit if nothing changed except that the people involved had moved further along the learning curve. Then an organizational and a domain shift to reestablish a fit would be indicated. For example, one reason organizations extend their domains and restructure is to keep the challenge to organization members at a high level. However, if we are ever able to calibrate the quality of fit with sufficient precision, I would recommend a deliberate small error toward a "growing fit," an additional increment of uncertainty and differentiation beyond what the people involved are comfortable with.

The final criticisms I am aware of are that the O&E approach, with its emphasis on the critical importance of environmental uncertainty, has not come to terms with works that emphasize the technological imperative or the effects of organization size. There is some merit in both of these arguments. All of the business units in our sample were comparatively large divisions, and we picked them that way as a control for size. It is well established that organization forms change with size. I believe more research that explores the compound effects of uncertainty and size would be very useful.

As for technology, let me first say that I have never thought in terms of any kind of an imperative that controls organizational form, be it technology, size, or uncertainty. Human choice is always involved; environments can be changed within limits; and there is probably more than one way to survive, even in the face of some immutable givens. Beyond that, I believe technology, while it may be more intractable than some other variables such as size, is seldom, if ever, unchangeable. There are, as we know, different ways to make even automobiles. Still, it has been very difficult to find a typology of technologies that seems to relate strongly to organization form. Woodward's (1965), while it has been rigorously questioned, still seems to stand up the best within the limited sphere of the manufacturing function. Thompson's (1967) typology is certainly more encompassing, but it has not been empirically tested or linked effectively to the variable of uncertainty as used in our original study. Later in this chapter I will suggest one possible way that this gap can be spanned.

Having come so far, the reader can be in little doubt about my own judgment on the status of the theory expressed in the O&E book. I see it as thriving and continuing to evolve. These are my present convictions, even though I know I must have some remaining bias that the critics have not yet helped me to see. I say this in full recognition that many,

many important questions remain unanswered. All I would assert is that our existing organizational contingency theory can be built upon further. As a step in that direction, I would now like to explore an extension of our original formulation that I believe can tie that existing theory together with some more recently developed, useful ideas such as enacted environments, organizational life cycles, organizational paradigms, strategic choice, organization ecology, loosely coupled organizations, and so on. It is this possibility that I would now like to consider at some length, starting with the organization selection approach.

ORGANIZATION SELECTION

One of the newer useful approaches to organization theory has been variously identified as the population ecology of organizations or as organization selection (Hannan and Freeman, 1978). This work draws upon and attempts to relate organization theory to the study of biological evolution. It focuses on the fact that existing organizations are the survivors that can be thought of as being "selected for" by having an initial set of resources and organizational features that did not exist among the organizational casualties. This perspective can serve to correct for the bias of seeing organizational change as entirely a process of adaptation by learning.

The selection process is most clearly seen when a considerable number of organizations occupy the same environmental niche or have the same set of resource dependencies. A large number of organizations is more apt to be present when a niche is newly opened up by a significant innovation with an "easy entry" technology. If a unit starts with a viable set of resources and features, it will survive. If not, it may well not have the reserves and differentiated learning capacity to adapt before it collapses. I would extend this "selection" reasoning into the "adaptation by learning" realm. If an organization survives this early stage and expands along any one of several lines (product mix, geographic, etc.), it may evolve a set of more differentiated subsystems and appropriate integrative mechanisms, enabling it to adapt to subsequent environmental changes that would have been fatal at an earlier stage.

The concepts of differentiation and integration are of course widely used in biology in ways that parallel this discussion in organizational terms. I am personally involved now in historical research of several industries around the theme of organizational adaptation by selection and by learning with a view to developing and testing these general ideas further. One of the tools I am finding useful in this inquiry is an analytical framework that I have developed by borrowing from the field of population biology (Grime, 1977) and learning theory (Schroder, Driver, and Streufert, 1968; Janis and Leventhal, 1968). Its simplicity is appealing, and

I introduce it here in an abbreviated form since, as a more dynamic version of the original O&E model, it does seem to help link our original study with a number of newer developments in organization theory, including the organization selection ideas. In explaining my adaptation model here, my intent is to test its utility in establishing a shared language without pushing through yet to a statement of propositions and implications. I see it now as a helpful way of describing general tendencies to be observed in organization-environment systems.

THE ADAPTATION MODEL AND INDUSTRIAL ORGANIZATION

My proposed adaptation model positions the familiar environmental dimension of uncertainty against the environmental dimension of resource scarcity. It thus makes a rough distinction between a focal institution's transactions with a domain of information and a domain of tangible resources—physical, human, and energy. The basics of this analytical framework are shown in Figure 7-2. As an introduction to the use of this framework, I will describe the start-up of a new firm and a new industry in terms that draw on both population biology terminology and theory and then on industrial organization concepts.

To start this process, imagine a product market (ecological niche) where, because of some new technical or market development, a producer initially faces a large untapped demand and low entry costs (low resource tension) and no competitors (low strategic uncertainty). This initial state of affairs could soon be expected to attract a considerable number and variety of organizational start-ups. Among these firms, the ones who initially dominate can be expected to be those with a set of traits that foster the fastest growth in this lush environment. Now imagine the highly probable development over time of a gradual tightening up on resources as this new market starts being filled. Under these new conditions biological theory suggests that the changed niche will start to select for traits that offer a competitive edge in securing resources. These traits are likely to involve both marketing skills and production efficiencies as well as product development strengths. This process will force some of the initial fast-growth stragegic types out of business (selected out). Finally, imagine this product market shifting its niche characteristics and becoming extremely tight on resources. These conditions, as suggested by biological theory, will select for stress toleration traits (likely to take the form of stringent cost reduction measures) in firms that will fill in the holes created by other types failing to meet their resource needs.

In biological terms, this entire three-stage process is constrained and influenced not only by the amount of resources available but also by the

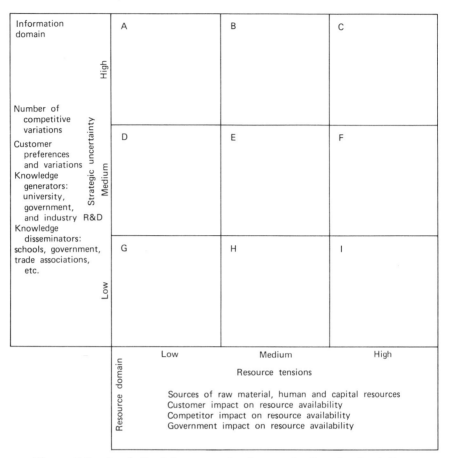

Figure 7-2   Analytical framework of organizational adaptation.

variety in the gene pool of all the species in the niche. The variety in the gene pool is the biological analogy to the number of *different* stragegic variations that exist in the organization's domain. Any given organization can then imitate or be stimulated by these strategic variations in seeking its own successful mutual adaptation. The concept of strategic uncertainty represents, I believe, a useful focusing on that subset of the more general environmental uncertainties that are of survival importance for focal institutions. *Strategic uncertainty* would roughly be determined in a two-step process. The first step would be to determine the number of discrete competitors that are each running different "trials" to find a successful mutual adaptation and to determine the number of other sources of new, relevant strategic ideas (from suppliers, customers, or university-government research, etc.) that could add to the "tech pool," as McKelvey (1978) calls it. This would be the number of strategic options or variables. The second step would access the other uncertainties in choosing among these strategic variables in terms of instability, ignorance, and interdependence.

The concept of *resource tension* reflects the obvious fact that organizations require resources and favorable resource exchanges. The degree of tension could be read by such indicators as gross margins and reserves in private firms and the reliability and level of funding in public ones.

Figure 7-3 draws on the language of industrial organization studies to show a possible, highly simplified, organization or industry life cycle trajectory. The starting point of such a trajectory represents, as we stated in the O&E book (p. 209), "the strategic choice, 'What business are we in?' Once that decision is made, whether explicitly or implicitly, the attributes of the chosen environment can be analyzed." The line of move-

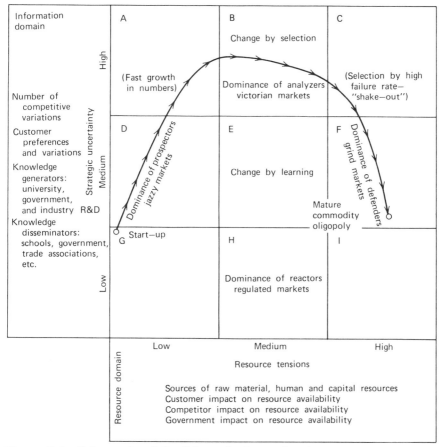

Figure 7-3   Schematic of the life cycle dynamic of easy entry industries from start-up to maturity.

ment can be visualized as representing the locus of the modal firm in the industry at various points in time. During the three development stages described above it would be expected that the amount of strategic uncertainty would tend to increase as shown, and then at some point of increased resource scarcity it would decrease. The course of such a trajectory can also be analyzed in an organization-life-cycle fashion, with key turning events identified where the dominant coalition can "steer" the system toward a temporary equilibrium in cells E or F, for instance. To help the reader translate between biological, organizational, and economic terms, I have indicated how I think the four strategic types identified in the research of Miles and Snow (1978) would fit into the model. Some—but due to historical inertia not all—organizations of each type, unlike biological organisms, will be able to learn and adapt, transform themselves from one strategic type to another as needed to avoid being selected out. This very real possibility of adaptation by learning clearly distinguishes social organizations from biological organisms (Buckley, 1967). Miles and Snow argue that some of all four of these strategic types are to be found in every industry. Without denying that finding, my diagram suggests in which cells each of these strategic types would tend to dominate. I have also added the corresponding terms used by White (1979) in his provocative typology of markets.

To further bridge to economic theory, Figure 7-4 has labeled the nine niches with some conventional economic categories to indicate where firms and even the clusters of firms that form an industry would tend to reach a point of temporary equilibrium.

The introduction of economic terms into this analytical framework suggests a bridge to the markets and hierarchies literature. This literature has already proved very useful in calling attention to the choice that exists in the means of carrying out transactions; this has rich implications for both economic and organizational theory as well as for public policy (Williamson, 1975). This line of inquiry was hinted at as a possible extension of the O&E model, when we pointed out (p. 239) that the consolidations referred to as vertical integration,

> for whatever reason they occur, have had the indirect effect of removing certain transactions of goods and services from the open marketplace and placing them within the purview of a single organization. The marketplace is, of course, one type of integrating device, and consolidations that convert marketplace transactions into intraorganizational transactions will not be viable over time unless the intraorganizational integrative devices prove more effective than the marketplace.

If we use my adaptation framework to highlight the markets versus hierarchies choice, I would suggest that market transactions as well as change by selection will, almost by definition, tend to dominate in the "northern" tier, while hierarchical transactions, as well as change by learning, will

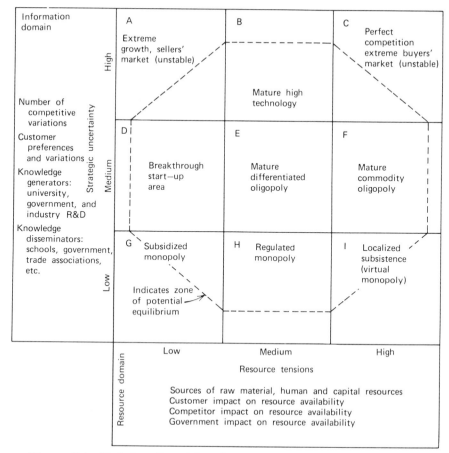

Figure 7-4 Defining the niches in conventional economic terms.

dominate the "middle" and "southern" tiers. The one exception is that I would expect markets to dominate in extreme cases such as firms in the lower corner of cell I.

Figure 7-5 represents an attempt, for illustrative purposes only, at locating some industry examples in the framework. This placement is obviously only based on my general perception and furthermore needs to be dated, because all of these industries are in movement.

In terms of the original O&E study, the adaptation model has hopefully focused the concept of uncertainty further and has added the concept of resource tension or resource dependency that has been both the historic concern of economists and also of considerable recent interest in organization theory (Pfeffer and Salancik, 1978). In fact, Aldrich (1979) organizes all of the current organization theory literature around either

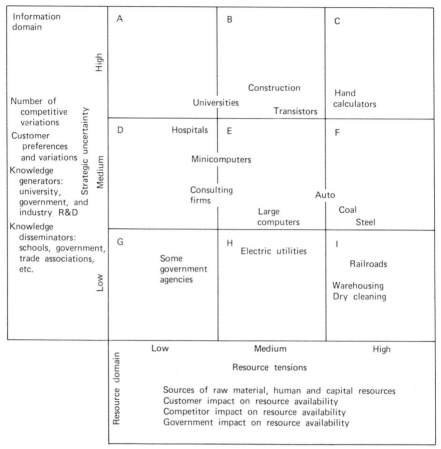

Figure 7-5 Approximate location of industry examples.

the environment as information flows approach or the environment as resource flows approach. He concludes, "I have not forced the two distinctions . . . into a dichotomy, thus permitting the inchoate nature of these competing conceptualizations to remain visible throughout" (p. 111). Our adoption model is clearly an effort to synthesize these two perspectives, and its capacity in this regard is explored next.

THE ADAPTATION MODEL AND
RECENT ORGANIZATION STUDIES

This analytical framework also seems helpful to me in defining some of the limits of the original O&E framework and in placing this work into perspective with other more recent organizational behavior studies. Figure 7-6 suggests a way to use the framework to analyze the specialty

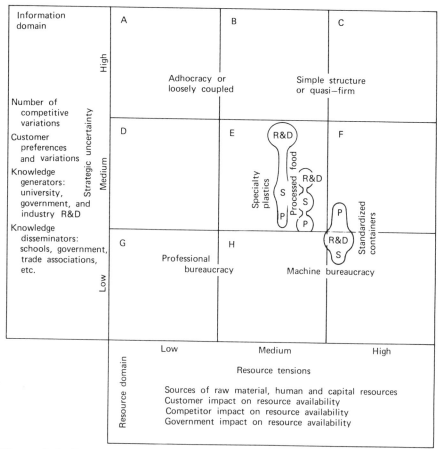

Figure 7-6   Location of organization types and of industries in original O and E studies.

plastics, processed food, and standardized container industries that were in the original studies. I have indicated the major differentiated subsystems of modal firms in these industries and the "distance" between the subsystems that calls for integration and a differential in organizational power. I have taken the liberty of suggesting how I would locate four of the forms of organization Mintzberg (1978) has written about, as well as the kind of "loosely coupled" organizations that use "garbage can" decision procedures in dealing with high levels of ambiguity such as the school systems that March and Olsen (1976) have written about. The fifth organization form of Mintzberg's, the divisionalized form, does not fit readily in the framework, which lends itself more readily to positioning single strategic business units. However, the multidivisional form can be visualized as operating in a number of different cells, and the nature of this spread can in itself be revealing in terms of portfolio analysis. I have also included in Figure 7-6 the term "quasi-firm" to signal a line of research that is exploring institutions representing middle points between hierarchies and markets. This term has been used by Eccles (1979) in his study of the home construction industry with its persistent use of a network of prime and subcontractors. Other examples that come to mind are the franchise systems we see in the fast food, bottling, and motel businesses.

Clearly the attempt to locate industries and types of firms in the framework represents an effort to link environmental and organizational attributes. In this regard it would be easy to say, based on the original O&E study, that increasing stragegic uncertainty would drive up differentiation within the firm and that increasing resource tension would drive up integration within the firm. This in turn would suggest that organic structures would dominate in the "northern" tier and mechanistic in the "southern," with tight control for integration in "eastern" regions and loose in the "western." Subsequent work, however, makes me uncomfortable with such a simple formulation. During the intervening decade, the work especially of Weick (1969) on such ideas as the enacted environment, Pfeffer (1980, in press) on organizational paradigms, and Duncan and Weiss (1978) on organizational learning has forced me to rethink this linkage between domain and organizations. There seems to be a lack of a tight and obvious linkage. What I propose now is a fresh way of thinking about the linkage that hopefully takes account of newer insights but still suggests a relatively simple, patterned relationship between the objective environment, the enacted environment, and organization attributes.

The O&E model tended to presume a rational decision maker who noted the amount of uncertainty in the selected domain by sector, then structured and oriented each subsystem to that reality, and then followed up by creating the integrating mechanisms indicated by the amount of subsystem differentiation. This model largely ignored the impact that resource scarcity has on perceptions and therefore on responses. My reading of the perception literature in psychology suggests that people tend not to perceive things that are not relevant to them, and that they also tend to simplify and tightly focus their perceptions on their surroundings when faced with a threatening situation. I am suggesting that this translates into the environmental enactment process I have depicted in Figures 7-7 and 7-8. Figure 7-7 shows that the objective increase in strategic uncertainty is modified by the side effect of resource tension into an overly simplified enacted environment in the "NE" and an overly complex enacted environment in the "SW." I have indicated in shorthand terms the kind of structure and orientations each quadrant would be hypothesized to induce, consistent with earlier findings of contingency research (Burns

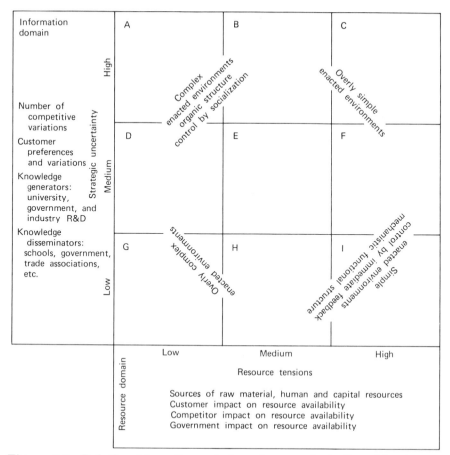

Figure 7-7 Relationships of enacted environments to the objective domains.

and Stalker, 1961; Hage, 1974). I should add, however, that I foresee continuing operational problems in relating objective and perceived environments; most managers, even top managers, have perceptions constrained to their own immediate experience. Many will judge uncertainty in terms of the history of their own industry rather than by comparison to other industries. It is in this way that I think history as a determinant of organizational form can be introduced (Stinchcombe, 1965).

Figure 7-8 looks at perceived survival threat and suggests the primary impact of resource tension and how it may be modified by the side effect of strategic uncertainty. Again I have indicated the kind of orientations that would be expected. The leader-oriented organization is suggested for the SW cell, because the environment is placing only the weakest

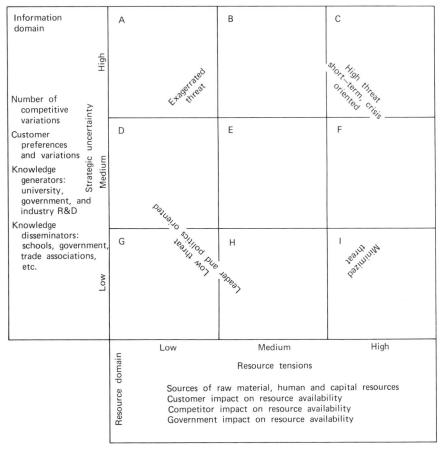

Figure 7-8 Relationship of the objective domain, perceived survival threat and organizational orientations.

demands on such organizations. We would expect them to be preoccupied with their own internal affairs and full of organizational politics (Petti-grew, 1973).

This framework, I believe, also holds out some promise of help in coping with four remaining thorny issues in organization theory. I refer to the issues of organization learning, the impact of technology, the problem of organizational effectiveness, and issues of institutional legitimacy.

Figures 7-7 and 7-8 indicate that Cell E in the center of the framework is an especially interesting one as regards organizational learning. It turns out to be the cell that is least likely to misread its environment. It is where several influences come to bear simultaneously. It could, according to these projections, wind up being organic or mechanistic, being controlled by socialization or by immediate feedback (Hage, 1974). It could be leader or crisis dominated. It represents a location that is full of paradoxes and competing forces. If any one of these forces comes to dominate, we would anticipate the firm developing a "misfit" with its domain and then either moving into another niche or failing. Staying in Cell E may always be problematical. How can the paradoxes be resolved other than in a win-lose manner? In the O&E study we explored this issue under the heading of conflict resolution. There we saw the difficulty of reconciling differentiation *and* integration. But such dichotomies are rife in complex organizations: short versus long term; efficiency versus innovation; control versus entrepreneurship. Matrix organizations could be expected to appear in Cell E as one way to handle these paradoxes. Our framework in no way answers the question of how such paradoxes are constructively resolved, but it does help focus the question.

One lead is coming from learning theory (Schroder, Driver, and Streufert, 1968). It seems to tell us that learning is curvilinear in relation to both tension (resources) and variety (uncertainty). One can have either too much or too little of either variable if one wants to learn. This curvilinear relation provides the reason why it is important to keep track of nine and not four niches. The center zone of niche E may be the spot that induces innovations. It is an area where an organization cannot afford complacency, but still has some slack resources to explore new possibilities. It has the stimulus of variety and uncertainty while perhaps avoiding information overload. It will take more work to follow up on this lead and care to avoid reifying the organization.

The question of technological effects on organization attributes has long been a thorny one. The use of Thompson's typology in relation to my analytical framework might, however, offer a new approach to the problem. Thompson's trichotomy of intensive, long-linked, and mediating technologies can roughly be thought of as one of several influences in determining the more probable equilibrium point of an industry on the adaptation framework. I suggest that intensive technologies as Thompson defines them share the quality of being pushed to locate near-the-end-users, being user-site bound. Here I am thinking of his examples of hospitals and schools. With my definition we could add restaurants, motels, consumer shops, and home construction. The "technological" feature of these industries tends to multiply the number of firms. As stated above, they tend to grow only in the form of quasi-firms, as franchise or contracting networks. The variety of firms and stragegic approaches that technology tends to generate would locate these industries in the "northern" tier of our model, and as we have seen, this tends to check out with the expected organization form, the heavy reliance on market mechanisms, and change by selection.

Thompson's second category (long-linked) is of course where he included the typical manufacturing firm whose principal added value comes from transforming raw or semifinished materials into states desired by some consumers. These transforming firms have more choice about their sites and therefore about their size. To put it in economic terms, their technology offers opportunities for economies of scale. To the extent this influence is felt, it would reduce the number of firms to an oligopoly condition and locate them in the middle tier of our model. Our projected organization forms in this tier would not seem to contradict this idea. It would be in this tier that we would expect to find the job shop, mass production, and process technologies stressed by Woodward.

In Thompson's third type, mediating or network, he drew on examples such as telephone systems, railroads, electric utilities, banks, and insurance companies. Some of these industries are what economists have called natural monopolies, and it is relatively easy to assign them to the lower end of our strategic uncertainty scale and place them in the "southern" tier. Others, such as banks and insurance companies, are usually regulated—but not as heavily, because they mediate information, not physical objects, and thus have greater degrees of freedom in regard to industry structure. This also seems to be true of extractive technologies. They are site bound to the sources of the raw materials, but how constraining this is, in fact, varies greatly depending on the distribution of the raw materials in nature.

So we have found a way to relate Thompson's typology to our model. It by no means suggests a technological "imperative" but something closer to a predisposition. Figure 7-9 displays these connections.

The third issue I wish to address briefly is that of organizational results or effectiveness. The general position of the O&E approach is that effectiveness is associated with a three-way fit between environmental uncertainty, organizational characteristics (structure and process), and human predispositions. I believe this still holds, but as I will indicate below, some fit combinations can be expected to emphasize some performance criteria at the expense of other criteria.

There are of course many potential criteria for judging organizational effectiveness. Without in any way claiming to have dealt with this vexing problem, let me simplify the issue for present purposes by focusing on just three outcome variables, efficiency (ratio of output to inputs), innovation (new processes, goods or services regularly employed), and quality of work life. Figures 7-10 and 7-11 represent a first pass at how I would expect these three results to array across the model. My reasons are, frankly, not completely thought out as yet. The issue of innovation was touched on in connection with the discussion of learning theory above. The distribution of efficiency would, I believe, be consistent with current economic theory. The quality of work life issue is not as clear. Jaques (1978) has argued quite persuasively why cells C, F, and I tend to induce either labor exploitation or, in conjunction with strong collective bargaining, alienation through boredom. I am also suggesting that alienation

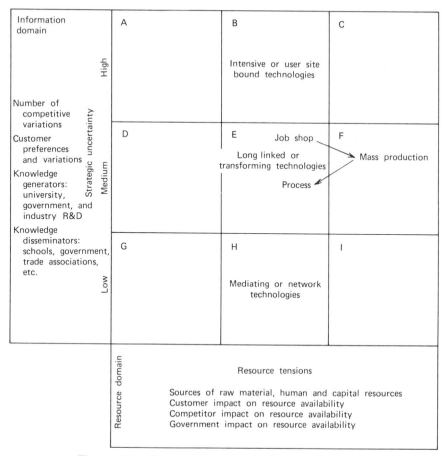

Figure 7-9   General locus of technological types.

by boredom is associated with the "SW" area, but this may be based on stereotype rather than on anything more substantial. The overstressed area has been documented to a limited extent, and my suggestion, I believe, would also be consistent with the findings of experimental psychology. This, by default, leaves Cell E unlabeled, which might suggest that this is the locus of high quality work life. Perhaps. But, as with mental health, one may best define the positive state only by the absence of identifiable negatives. In any event, I only desire to be provocative at this point with these speculations about organizational outcomes, especially quality of work life. If these ideas stand up to further analysis and empirical testing, they will of course have implications for management and public policy.

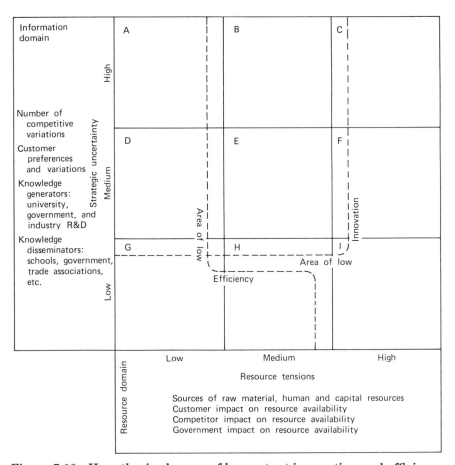

Figure 7-10   Hypothesized areas of low output innovation and efficiency.

So far we have not discussed the increasingly important subject of institutional issues involving broad social legitimacy. Instead we have focused on the managerial issues (to use Parsons' distinction) and to a lesser extent the operational, input-output issues. This whole realm of institutional affairs could much more be taken for granted in the early 1960s when the original research was done than it can today. To add this set of issues to the model could require adding an entire third dimension ranging from low to high in institutional legitimacy. Another approach would be to add institutional uncertainty to the dimension of strategic uncertainty on the assumption that they covary and place similar demands on organizations. These assumptions could be tested. Either approach adds complexity to the model that could best be avoided if such distinctions are not germane.

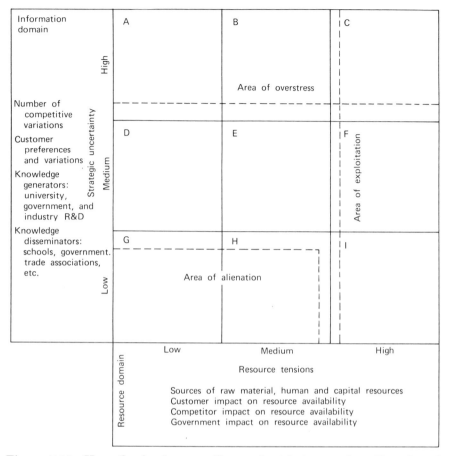

Figure 7-11   Hypothesized areas of low output in terms of quality of work life.

CONCLUSIONS

The adaptation model sketched out above represents at present a descriptive model designed to synthesize the earlier O&E contingency approach with more recent work in organizational behavior and, to a lesser extent, in industrial organization. It needs to be tested in multiple ways. Does it help reconcile findings that have appeared to be inconsistent? Does it stimulate some new propositions? Are such hypotheses supported by empirical evidence? Does it have any significant implications for action? I will be exploring these questions to see if it is a framework whose simplicity still encompasses much of the real world and whose utility goes beyond the development of just another set of terms.

REFERENCES

Aldrich, H. E. (1979). *Organizations and Environments,* Englewood Cliffs, NJ: Prentice-Hall.

Barnard, C. (1938). *The Functions of the Executive,* Cambridge, MA: Harvard University Press.

Buckley, W. (1967). *Sociology and Modern Systems Theory,* Englewood Cliffs, NJ: Prentice-Hall.

Burns, T., and G. M. Stalker (1961). *The Management of Innovation,* London: Tavistock Press.

Davis, S., and P. Lawrence (1977). *Matrix,* Reading, MA: Addison-Wesley.

Dill, W. (1958). "Environment as an Influence on Managerial Autonomy," *Administrative Science Quarterly* **2**:409–443.

Downey, K., D. Hellriegel, and J. Slocum, Jr. (1975). "Environmental Uncertainty: The Construct and its Application," *Administrative Science Quarterly* **20**:623–629.

Duncan, R. (1975). "Characteristics of Organizational Environment and Perceived Environmental Uncertainty," *Administrative Science Quarterly* **20**:313–327.

Duncan, R., and A. Weiss (1978). "Organizational Learning: Implications for Organizational Design," in B. Staw, Ed., *Research in Organizational Behavior,* Vol. I, Greenwich, CT: JAI Press.

Eccles, R. (1979). *Organization and Market Structure in the Construction Industry: A Study of Sub-Contracting,* Cambridge, MA: Harvard Business School.

Galbraith, J. (1973). *Designing Complex Organizations,* Reading, MA: Addison-Wesley.

Grime, J. P. (1974). "Vegetation Class by Reference to Strategies," *Nature* **250**,7:26–30.

Hage, J. (1974). *Community and Organizational Control: Cybernetics in Health and Welfare Settings,* New York: Wiley.

Hannan, M. T., and J. H. Freeman (1977). "The Population Ecology of Organizations," *American Journal of Sociology* **82**:929–964.

Janis, I., and H. Leventhal (1968). "Human Reaction to Stress," in R. Borgatta and J. Lamberts, Eds., *Handbook of Personality Theory,* Chicago: Rand-McNally, pp. 1041–1085.

Jaques, E. (1976). *A General Theory of Bureaucracy,* New York: Wiley.

Kotter, J. (1978). *Organizational Dynamics,* Reading, MA: Addison-Wesley.

Kotter, J., and P. Lawrence (1974). *Mayors in Action: Five Approaches to Urban Governance,* New York: Wiley.

Lane, H., R. Beddows, and P. Lawrence (1981). *Managing Large Research and Development Programs,* Albany, NY: State University of New York Press.

Lawrence, P., and J. Lorsch (1969). *Developing Organizations: Diagnosis and Action,* Reading, MA: Addison-Wesley.

Lawrence, P., and J. Lorsch (1967). *Organization and Environment,* Cambridge, MA: Harvard Business School.

Lawrence, P., and J. Lorsch (1973). "A Reply to Tosi, Aldag and Storey," *Administrative Science Quarterly* **18**:397–400.

Lorsch, J., and S. Allen (1973). *Managing Diversity and Interdependence: An Organizational Study of Multidivisional Firms,* Cambridge, MA: Harvard Business School.

Lorsch, J., and P. Lawrence (1969). "The Diagnosis of Organizational Problems," in W. Bennis, K. Benne, and Chin, Eds., *The Planning of Change,* 2nd ed., New York: Holt, Rinehart, and Winston.

Lorsch, J., and P. Lawrence (1970). *Studies in Organizational Design,* Homewood, IL: R. D. Irwin.

Lorsch, J., and J. Morse (1974). *Organizations and Their Members: A Contingency Approach,* New York: Harper and Row.

March, J., and J. Olsen (1976). *Ambiguity and Choice in Organizations,* Bergen: Universitetsforlaget.

March, J., and H. Simon (1958). *Organizations,* New York: Wiley.

McKelvey, B. (1978). "Organizational Systematics: Taxonomic Lessons from Biology," *Management Science* **24,**13:1428–1440.

Miles, R., and C. Snow (1978). *Organizational Strategy: Structures and Processes,* New York: McGraw-Hill.

Mintzberg, H. (1979). *The Structuring of Organizations,* Englewood Cliffs, NJ: Prentice-Hall.

Pennings, J. (1979). "The Relevance of the Structural Contingency Model for Organizational Effectiveness," *Administrative Science Quarterly* **20:**383–410.

Pettigrew, A. (1973). *The Politics of Organizational Decision-Making,* London: Tavistock.

Pfeffer, J. (1980). "Management as Symbolic Action: The Creation and Maintenance of Organizational Paradigms," in Larry L. Cummings and Barry M. Staw, Eds., *Research in Organizational Behavior,* Vol. 3, Greenwich, CT: JAI Press.

Pfeffer, J., and G. Salancik (1978). *The External Control of Organizations: A Resource Dependence Perspective,* New York: Harper and Row.

Ronken, H., and P. Lawrence (1952). *Administering Changes,* Cambridge, MA: Harvard Business School.

Schroder, H. M., M. Driver, and S. Streufert (1967). *Human Information Processing,* New York: Holt, Rinehart, and Winston.

Stinchcombe, A. (1965). "Social Structure and Organizations," in J. G. March, Ed., *Handbook of Organizations,* Chicago: Rand-McNally.

Thompson, J. (1967). *Organizations in Action,* New York: McGraw-Hill.

Tosi, H., R. Aldag, and R. Storey (1973). "On the Management of the Environment: An Assessment of the Lawrence and Lorsch Environmental Uncertainty Questionnaire," *Administrative Science Quarterly* **18:**27–36.

Turner, A., and P. Lawrence (1965). *Industrial Jobs and the Workers: An Investigation of Responses to Task Attributes,* Cambridge, MA: Harvard Business School.

Weick, K. (1969). *The Social Psychology of Organizing,* Reading, MA: Addison-Wesley.

Weisbord, M., M. Charns, and P. Lawrence (1978). "The Three Dilemmas of Academic Medical Centers," *Journal of Applied Behavioral Sciences* **14,**3.

White, H. (1979). "Markets as Social Structures," Talk for Plenary Session, *American Sociology Association,* August 28, 1979.

Williamson, O. (1975). *Markets and Hierarchies: Analysis and Antitrust Implications,* New York: Free Press.

Woodward, J. (1965). *Industrial Organizations: Theory and Practice,* London: Oxford University Press.

THE ORGANIZATION
AND ENVIRONMENT RESEARCH PROGRAM:
OVERVIEW AND CRITIQUE

LAWRENCE G. HREBINIAK
The Wharton School
University of Pennsylvania

The first section of this commentary provides an overview and critique of the pioneering research of Lawrence and Lorsch (1967) on organization and environment. The second section considers Lawrence's adaptation model, which represents an extension of the original O&E work.

Overview and Critique:
The Harvard O&E Program

The original Harvard O&E study clearly represents an important milestone in the conceptual and empirical literature on complex organizations. Its impact has been immense; discussions of the relation between organizational variables and important external factors or conditions have become increasingly pervasive. The importance and impact of environment stand at the core of modern contingency approaches to organizational structure and process. While the theoretical roots or underpinnings for both the role of environment or situation and the key concepts of differentiation and integration may be found in the work of Follet (Metcalf and Urwick, 1942), Barnard (1938), Burns and Stalker (1961), March and Simon (1958), and others, it clearly was the pioneering study of Lawrence and Lorsch (1967) and the work of Thompson (1962) that had the greatest impact on subsequent thinking about the centrality of the environment in modern paradigms of organizational design and behavior.

The O&E study of course was not without its problems; it certainly generated its share of critical comment in the literature. To understand and evaluate better the validity of the criticisms, it is useful to emphasize again the features of the O&E study; as Lawrence stresses, it is imperative to know "what it was and what it was not." After a brief reiteration of the study's features, I shall comment on both the O&E study and other critiques of it.

The O&E study was not an hypothesis or theory-testing study; as Lawrence indicates, it was an exploratory, theory-building effort. Its methods and instruments were not nearly as crude as Paul and his colleagues assert, despite the problematic issues that have subsequently been raised. The O&E study was not longitudinal but was a comparative, cross-sectional analysis. It focused on 10 businesses that were deliberately selected *a priori* to maximize differences in certain critical environmental variables. It was not "just another" intensive Harvard case study, nor was it a "statistical study with a cast of hundreds," as Lawrence states. The O&E study was exploratory—a complex, multimethod work seeking new and exciting, though preliminary, insights. In my estimation, it is necessary to position subsequent critiques against this backdrop to fully evaluate their merit.

Environmental Uncertainty Questionnaire. Along these lines, consider the criticisms of the questionnaire Lawrence and Lorsch (1967) used in their O&E study. Articles by Tosi et al. (1973), Downey et al. (1975), and Pennings (1975) emphasize various problems with the instrument employed to measure uncertainty. The questionnaire, however, was only one of three ways Lawrence and Lorsch measured environmental uncertainty. Use of the instrument must be considered in the light of: (a) the intention of the initial selection of industries to maximize differences in uncertainty, and (b) economic indicators that lent some credence to the choice of industries, as did interviews with some of the managers involved in the research. While the instrument clearly has faults, it was not intended to be the sole measuring device for the critical variable of uncertainty.

Additional criticisms can be levied against these critiques. Tosi et al. (1973), for example, equate uncertainty and volatility. They argue that, while volatility may be different than uncertainty, the two should be correlated. Sufficient reasoning for this assertion, however, is not provided. It may very well be that stability of sales and income (lack of volatility) *reflects* a successful ability to cope with uncertainty. It may be that uncertainty and volatility are not the same thing at all, but that the latter represents an outcome or result of treating or coping with the former. Similarly, Pennings' (1975) attempt to identify differences in environment among 40 units of a *single* organization in the *same* business appears problematic and inconsistent with the intent of the O&E study.

Reactive Nature of Organizations. Another critique of the O&E study is that it represents the organization in a purely reactive mode. Discussions of the effects of uncertainty and the use of such terms as the degree of "requisite integration," it is argued, imply unilateral causality, as the organization responds to the demands and forces of externalities. Similarly, adaptation may be construed to denote only reaction to environmental conditions, with little or no ability to determine, change, or otherwise influence those conditions as they unilaterally affect the organization.

I think that even this criticism may be too sharp and unwarranted, although I agree somewhat with those who argue for the predominantly reactive stance of the organization in the O&E study. It is clear to me that there is a mutual adaptation or bilateral interdependence between organization and environment. Organizations often place themselves strategically by choosing certain market niches over others, thereby "enacting" or choosing a domain (Weick, 1969). I see the O&E study, however, as a "snapshot," a cross-sectional study that chose *a priori* differences in environmental conditions to determine if the organizations subject to those conditions varied on such important dimensions as differentiation and integration. My reading of *Organization and Environment* suggests that the authors surely believe that the organization can have an impact on its domain, but that in many industries the relative influence favors the environmental forces or external stake holders.

The O&E paradigm is far less reactive than the natural selection or population ecology model (Hannan and Freeman, 1978; Aldrich, 1979). The basic propositions in the population ecology model are that: (1) a natural selection process goes on in the environment that affects the structural forms of organizations: and (2) organizational forms must either fit their environmental niches or they fail. The process of natural selection means that existing organizations are survivors that were "selected" by the environment because they had features that the casualties did not. Clearly the emphasis is on environmental determinism; strategic choice and top-management decisions have less impact on organizational change or survival than they do in other paradigms of change and adaptation.

Viewed against this perspective, it becomes increasingly difficult to see work in the Harvard O&E program as only reactive. While the 1967 study emphasized reaction over proaction or strategic choice, other work in the O&E genre stresses the impact of organization on environment (e.g., Lane et al., in press) including of course the chapter by Lawrence in this volume.

Fit. The concept of "fit" still gives me fits. While intuitively pleasing and appealing, this central concept in the O&E model remains elusive and undefined. The problem is exacerbated by the different interpretations and meanings of fit implied by the O&E model and discussed by other contingency theorists (e.g., Van de Ven, 1979).

One could argue, for example, that fit refers to a broad gestalt—a particular configuration of organization and environment that is whole and complete (e.g., a picture). No causality is indicated; both environment and organization are needed to complete the picture. Neither element alone has meaning without the other.

A second meaning of "fit" posits an interaction effect of organization and environment. In the O&E model, it is often stated or implied that an organization's achieving fit with its environment results in increased performance. The covariance of two independent variables, under this interpretation, has an impact on a third, dependent variable; organizational effectiveness is thus heightened or maximized when the fit is achieved.

A third plausible interpretation of "fit" in the O&E model complicates things further. The use of such terms as "requisite" differentiation and integration implies causality. The implication is that the environment defines the structure and related conditions that the organization must develop to remain viable. Fit, then, represents a response to peremptory organizational forces; it represents the way the organization must look and operate to satisfy environmental demands.

The use of fit in the extension of the O&E model by Lawrence in this volume does not clarify the concept. It remains a central, pervasive, and intuitively pleasing concept, but it is still a problematic one, especially with the introduction of terms like "misfit" and "calibration" of fit in the expanded model. Clearly the concept is important. Accordingly, considerations such as the definition of fit and the notion of "equifinality," or the possibility of different, equally effective fits, will provide a fertile field for future research on O&E relations.

Other points could be mentioned, but they are not sufficiently interesting or important to dwell on presently. Suffice it to say that the O&E program of research has been critical to an enrichment of the definition of the organization as an open system. The original O&E study has generated a flood of research and is richly deserving of the label "Program" with a capital P. It appears that the expanded O&E model presented by Lawrence is just as rich, and provides some interesting ideas and hypotheses for future testing.

The Expanded O&E Model

There are two important aspects of the expanded O&E model—the adaptation model—that deserve special attention: (1) refinement and expansion of the concept of environmental uncertainty; and (2) the application of the model to other findings, one result of which is the generation of hypotheses for future testing.

Environmental Uncertainty. The first predominant feature of the adaptation model is the refinement of the concept of uncertainty. While often referred to just as "uncertainty" in the literature on organizations, the concept clearly is not homogeneous (Hrebiniak and Snow, 1980). Environmental uncertainty is heterogeneous, implying a host of factors that affect organizational structure and process.

The adaptation model attempts to cope with this heterogeneity. According to Lawrence, it "positions the familiar environmental dimension of uncertainty against the environmental dimension of resource scarcity. It thus makes a rough distinction between a focal institution's transactions with a domain of information and a domain of tangible resources—physical, human, and energy" (Figure 7-2).

There is one important point in need of clarification before the interplay of the two dimensions is considered. The presentation of the "familiar environmental dimension of uncertainty" and "resource tensions" as the major variables in the adaptation model implies that "uncertainty" and "resource scarcity" are orthogonal—two independent dimensions that affect organizational and managerial behavior. In my estimation, such an inference would be faulty, despite the ease with which it might be drawn upon reading Lawrence's comments.

My interpretation of Figure 7-2 is that "Resource Tensions" and "Strategic Uncertainty" are two dimensions of one overriding or predominant construct—*environmental uncertainty*. The resource domain is clearly related to the information domain; information regarding customers' or competitors' impact on resource availability (two aspects of "Resource Tensions") surely can be expected to vary as a function of factors such as market structure, volatility of the economy, and extent of vertical integration. Similarly, information regarding sources of and needs for "human resources" will vary by industry and degree of people- or machine-intensity.

The point is that Lawrence has expanded upon and increased the specificity of the dimensions of uncertainty. The separation chosen—information and resource domains—seems to be a useful and timely one. The amount of information needed and available for decision making is an often-employed comparison in defining uncertainty (Galbraith, 1973). The organizational and economic literature (e.g., Pfeffer and Salancik, 1978), as well as recent economic and financial conditions, stress the importance of control over resources as a critical element affecting organizational power and performance.

The basis of the adaptation model, then, seems important and timely. The revision or expansion of the term "uncertainty" by Lawrence is a definite contribution of his offering to this volume. Environmental uncertainty surely is a heterogeneous construct composed of different sources of uncertainty or problematic dependencies whose salience for the decision maker can vary over time. Thinking of uncertainty in homogeneous terms will not help us in learning more about the external causes and correlates of organizational behavior. These important lessons are at least implied by the choice of dimensions in Lawrence's adaptation model.

In effect, Figures 7-3 to 7-11 in Lawrence's paper attempt to put into operation the model by using it to: (1) explain and integrate previous research findings, and (2) offer hypotheses for future testing of aspects of organization-environment relations. Figure 7-12 represents my attempt to summarize many of those findings or hypotheses. An analysis of Figure 7-12 reveals a number of points that should be emphasized regarding the adaptation model.

The first is that the adaptation model clearly attempts to explain and integrate a host of material, and the resultant integration and explanation often makes much sense. The placement of organic and mechanistic structures, for example, is consistent with the work of Burns and Stalker (1961). The position of prospectors, reactors, and defenders is wholly consistent with another independent research effort (Snow and Hrebiniak, 1980) that would place those strategic types in the same locations on the adaptation model. The placement of firms based on market structure also seems consistent with the research in economics. It seems logical to assume, using the markets versus hierarchies criteria, that

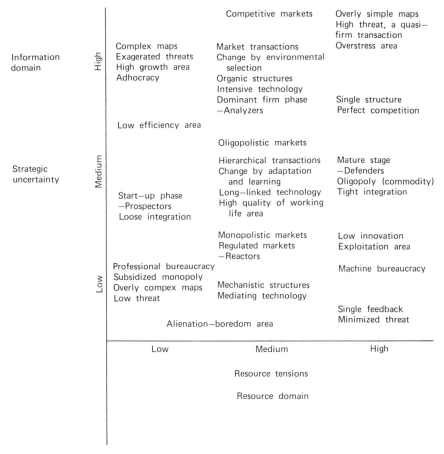

Figure 7-12 Mapping of select dimensions related to the adaptation model.

market transactions tend to dominate in the northern tier of Figure 7-12, while hierarchical transactions are found primarily in the southern tier. Other examples may be mentioned, but the dimensions of uncertainty in the adaptation model, referring to both the information and resource domains, appear to have some utility in explaining and integrating previous work in economics, organization theory, and strategic management.

It also must be stressed, however, that Figure 7-12 does present some issues or problems that are difficult to explain or resolve. For example, it seems logical to me that the area of alienation-boredom is associated with low strategic uncertainty and such correlates as mechanistic structure; I have more difficulty with its association with low to medium levels of resource tension. The placement of and justification for overly simple and complex cognitive maps are somewhat problematic. While I agree that individuals do not perceive things that are not salient to them, and tend to simplify and focus their perceptions when faced with threatening stimuli, I'm not at all convinced that the environmental-enactment process translates into the maps as nicely as Figure 7-12 indicates. Similarly, I'm not certain that I would agree with the assessments regarding the quality of working life areas. But then again, it must be remembered that my opinions reflect my biases and perceptions, a caveat also presented by Lawrence.

A final point, related to the first two, is that Figure 7-12 shows that full measure of the worth of the adaptation model will take more than a modicum of time and effort. Clearly Lawrence is attempting to explain and integrate a multitude of data; evaluation of that Herculean effort will not be construed as a criticism of the adaptation model but as a statement of fact. Indeed a strength of Lawrence's paper is that he has provided us with a host of interesting research directions. Proposed relations between environmental factors and variables such as perceived threat, leader orientation, innovation, and quality of work life offer fertile ground for the proposal and testing of new hypotheses. By making operational uncertainty on the two dimensions, his model adds needed specificity to the external factors that effect organizational design and performance.

One intended purpose of the papers in this volume is for the major authors to provoke ideas for future work on organization design. In my estimation, Paul Lawrence's paper meets these criteria. It expands the concept of uncertainty by focusing on two important aspects or components of that perceived environmental characteristic. His discussion and placement of other studies in relation to the two dimensions, coupled with the generation of hypotheses for future testing, provides direction for an expanded O&E research program. I look forward to hearing more from Paul and others involved with the organization-environment program of research.

REFERENCES

Aldrich, H. E. (1979). *Organizations and Environments,* Englewood Cliffs, NJ: Prentice-Hall.

Barnard, C. (1938). *The Functions of the Executive,* Cambridge, MA: Harvard University Press.

Downey, K., D. Hellriegel, and J. Slocum, Jr. (1975). "Environmental Uncertainty: The Construct and Its Application," *Administrative Science Quarterly* 20:623–629.

Galbraith, J. (1973). *Designing Complex Organizations,* Reading, MA: Addison-Wesley.

Hannan, M. T., and J. H. Freeman (1977). "The Population Ecology of Organizations," *American Journal of Sociology* 82:929–964.

Hrebiniak, L. G., and C. Snow (1980). "Industry Differences in Environmental Uncertainty and Structural Characteristics Related to Uncertainty," *Academy of Management Journal,* December, in press.

Lane, H., R. Beddows, and P. Lawrence (1981). *Managing Large Research and Development Programs,* Albany: State University of New York Press.

Lawrence, P., and J. Lorsch (1967). *Organization and Environment,* Cambridge, MA: Harvard Business School.

March, J., and J. Olsen (1976). *Ambiguity and Choice in Organizations,* Bergen: Universitetsforlaget.

March, J., and H. Simon (1958). *Organizations,* New York: Wiley.

Metcalf, H. C., and L. Urwick, Eds. (1942). *Dynamic Administration: The Collected Papers of Mary Parker Follett,* New York: Harper and Row.

Mintzberg, H. (1979). *The Structuring of Organizations,* Englewood Cliffs, NJ: Prentice-Hall.

Pennings, J. (1975). "The Relevance of the Structural Contingency Model for Organizational Effectiveness," *Administrative Science Quarterly* 20:383–410.

Pfeffer, J., and G. Salancik (1978). *The External Control of Organizations: A Resource Dependence Perspective,* New York: Harper and Row.

Snow, C., and L. Hrebiniak (1980). "Strategy, Distinctive Competence, and Organizational Performance," *Administrative Science Quarterly* 25:317–336.

Thompson, J. (1967). *Organizations in Action,* New York: McGraw-Hill.

Tosi, H., R. Aldag, and R. Storey (1973). "On the Management of the Environment: An Assessment of the Lawrence and Lorsch Environmental Uncertainty Questionnaire," *Administrative Science Quarterly* 18:27–36.

Van de Ven, A. H. (1979). Review of H. E. Aldrich, *Organizations and Environments,* Englewood Cliffs, NJ: Prentice-Hall, in *Administrative Science Quarterly* 24:320–326.

Weick, K. (1969). *The Social Psychology of Organizing,* Reading, MA: Addison-Wesley.

CHAPTER EIGHT

The Markets and Hierarchies and Visible Hand Perspectives

**The Markets and Hierarchies
Program of Research:
Origins, Implications, Prospects**

OLIVER E. WILLIAMSON
University of Pennsylvania
and
WILLIAM G. OUCHI
University of California, Los Angeles

Although organization theory has its origins in sociology and is principally identified with that field, the subject matter is interdisciplinary to
an unusual degree, and is incompletely informed by exclusive reliance
on any single social science. We contend that organization theory is seriously underdeveloped with respect to its economic content, and argue
that it needs greater appeal to economics, although economics of a nontraditional kind. Specifically, we suggest that organization theory in general and organizational design and assessment in particular need to be
more sensitive to transaction costs and to the importance of economizing
on those.

But economics and organization theory have a reciprocal relation
(Ouchi and Van de Ven, 1980). Economics stands to benefit by drawing
upon organization theory. This applies both to the refurbishing of its
behavioral assumptions, which tend to be stark and sometimes implau-
sible, and to the level of analysis, which in economics tends to be rather
aggregative. The Markets and Hierarchies (M&H) program of research

is based precisely on such a strategy. Thus it draws on organization theory to enrich its behavioral assumptions, and it regards the transaction, rather than the firm or market, as the basic unit of analysis.* Joining these behavioral assumptions and microanalytic focus with the economizing concepts and systems orientation characteristic of economics yields new and deeper insights into economic and social organization. This chapter reviews the origins and applications of the Markets and Hierarchies approach with special emphasis on its organization theory aspects. It develops the ramifications for organizational design, and addresses research agenda issues of special interest to organization theory specialists.

ORIGINS

It is rarely possible to do justice to earlier work on which subsequent research relies; nevertheless the following brief statement indicates the origins and background of our research.

Where to begin is somewhat arbitrary, but one decisive contribution to the evolution of the M&H approach was the interdisciplinary program of research and teaching at Carnegie Tech (now Carnegie-Mellon) in the early 1960s. The central figures at Carnegie were Richard Cyert, James March, and Herbert Simon. Williamson was a student in the economics program at Carnegie during this period and was greatly influenced by the prevailing interdisciplinary research atmosphere. The strategy of using organization theory to inform economics in the study of firm and market structures is evident in his work on managerial discretion and in other early papers (see Williamson, 1964, 1965, 1967).

It was not until later that the possibility of accomplishing a genuine synthesis between economics** and organization theory became evident. Two papers were of special significance. The first of these was "The Vertical Integration of Production: Transaction Cost Considerations" (Williamson, 1971), which was an effort to assess the question of make-or-buy in a fully symmetrical way. Ronald Coase, in a remarkably insightful paper, had posed this issue in 1937 and recognized that transaction costs were central to its resolution. Coase observed that vertical integration permitted the firm to economize on the "cost of negotiating and conclud-

---

*J. R. Commons (1934) had urged such an approach much earlier, but both his efforts and those of other institutionalists were outside the mainstream of economic analysis and, except as they are dealt with in the study of economic thought, have been neglected.

**This was economics of a nontraditional kind. An efficiency orientation was maintained, but attention shifted from neoclassical production function issues to the study of transaction costs, in the spirit of J. R. Commons (1934), R. H. Coase (1937), and K. J. Arrow (1969).

ing" many separate intermediate product market contracts by substituting a flexible employment agreement (Coase, 1952: 336). But because the factors that were responsible for differential transaction costs in the intermediate product market were not identified, the argument lacked testable implications. Why not use a flexible employment agreement to organize all transactions rather than just some? Until such time as the transaction cost argument was able to explain the organization of transactions in a discriminating way, it remained rather tautological (Alchian and Demsetz, 1972). Coase's observation, some 35 years later, that his 1937 article was "much cited and little used" (Coase, 1972) is presumably explained by the failure to make the issues operational over that interval.

If, as Coase asserted, differential transaction costs were responsible for decisions to organize some activities one way and some another, a level of analysis that was sensitive to transaction cost differences was evidently needed. Williamson accomplished this by (1) making the transaction the basic unit of analysis, (2) expressly identifying alternative market and internal modes of "contracting," (3) identifying the critical dimensions with respect to which transactions differed, (4) tracing out the transaction cost ramifications, and (5) matching modes to transactions in a discriminating way. Once the vertical integration problem had been made operational in this way, a variety of related applications followed. In this sense, the puzzle of vertical integration was a paradigm problem that, once solved, provided a research strategy that could be repeated. Any problem that could be posed, directly or indirectly, as a contracting problem could be assessed in terms of the identical conceptual apparatus.

These paradigm features were not entirely evident, however, until the paper "Markets and Hierarchies: Some Elementary Considerations" took shape (Williamson, 1973). This paper had its origins in a class discussion of market failures, with special emphasis on Arrow's classic statement of the problem (Arrow, 1969). For each type of market failure that was identified (public goods problem, appropriability problem, information asymmetry, small numbers exchange, etc.), the object was to move the explanation for the condition back to a statement of primitives. The same basic human and environmental conditions that arose in assessing vertical integration kept reappearing. *Bounded rationality* and *opportunism* were the recurring human factors. The environmental factors were *un-*

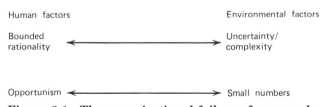

Figure 8-1   The organizational failures framework.

certainty-complexity and *small numbers exchange*. The patterned way in which these human and environmental factors were paired is shown in Figure 8-1.

CONCEPTUAL FRAMEWORK

The rudiments of the conceptual framework upon which the Markets and Hierarchies program of research relies have now been identified. What follows is an elaboration on these.

Behavioral Assumptions

Bounded rationality and *opportunism* are the key behavioral assumptions. These assumptions about the characteristics of human actors are joined with the assertion that viable modes of organization (market, quasi market, or internal) are ones that serve to *economize* on transaction costs. While organization theory specialists relate easily to the concept of bounded rationality, many economists resist it. By contrast, economizing is a much more congenial notion to economists than it is to organization theorists. Opportunism is a concept of which both are wary.

Arrow has characterized an economist as one who "by training thinks of himself as the guardian of rationality, the ascriber of rationality to others, and the prescriber of rationality to the social world" (Arrow, 1974: 16). Given this commitment, any assumption that appears to be at variance with rationality is apt to be dismissed out of hand. If it is not rational, it must be nonrational or irrational, and these are matters for other social sciences to grapple with.

As Herbert Simon has pointed out, however, economists exaggerate the extent to which nonrationality is emphasized by other social sciences. Although economists are the only social scientists who invoke hyperrationality assumptions, rationality is nevertheless a common theme throughout all of the social sciences (Simon, 1978: 2–4). The issue thus is not whether human agents are rational or not. Rather the question is whether the assumption of hyperrationality is needed or if weaker rationality assumptions will suffice.

Partly this is a matter of taste in choosing between strong and weak assumptions where both yield the same implications (Simon, 1978: 8). But there is more to it than tastes. Conceptualizing a problem one way rather than another can have a profound effect on the follow-up research agenda. Thus organization structure is of little import and hence can be disregarded if hyperrationality assumptions are maintained, which explains why the neoclassical theory of the firm describes the organization as a production function rather than a complex hierarchy. The opposite assumption, that human agents are so overwhelmed by complexity that they are incapable of planning, likewise reduces the study of organizational design to insignificance. This appears to be close to the view of March and Olsen (1976) and Mintzberg (1973).

The Markets and Hierarchies approach avoids both of these extremes. An intermediate degree of bounded rationality is attributed to human agents. Organizational design takes on economic significance precisely because the productive utilization of this intermediate capability is of crucial importance. But there is more to organizational design than economizing on bounded rationality. Issues of opportunism also arise and need to be addressed.

Opportunism extends the usual motivational assumption of self-interest seeking to include self-interest seeking with guile. Thus, whereas bounded rationality suggests decision making less complex than the usual assumption of hyperrationality, opportunism suggests calculating behavior more sophisticated than the usual assumption of simple self-interest. Opportunism refers to "making false or empty, that is, self-disbelieved threats or promises," cutting corners for undisclosed personal advantage, covering up tracks, and the like. Although it is a central behavioral assumption, it is not essential that all economic agents behave this way. What is crucial is that *some* agents behave in this fashion and that it is costly to sort out those who are opportunistic from those who are not.

Faced with bounded rationality on the one hand and the proclivity for some human agents to behave opportunistically on the other, the basic organizational design issue essentially reduces to this: organize transactions in such a way as to economize on bounded rationality while simultaneously safeguarding those transactions against the hazards of opportunism.

The Governance of Contractual Relations

The governance of contractual relations warrants careful attention in the degree to which economic agents are subject to bounded rationality *and* are given to opportunism. In the absence of either, the ubiquitous contracting model goes through.

Thus suppose the absence of bounded rationality among opportunistic agents. Mind-boggling though it is to contemplate, such agents will engage in "a single gigantic once-for-all forward 'higgle-haggle' in which all contingent goods and services (i.e., all goods and services at each possible time-cum-environmental condition) are bought and sold once and for all now for money payments made now" (Meade, 1971: 166). Propensities to behave opportunistically will simply be of no account.

Suppose alternatively that agents are subject to bounded rationality but are free of opportunism. Autonomous contracting again applies, though the reasons here are different. Since each party can depend on his or her opposite to honor the spirit as well as the letter of an agreement, successive adaptations can and will be implemented as contingencies unfold. Bridges are thus crossed when they arise, whereas the unbounded rationality model stipulates bridge crossings exhaustively in advance. Adaptive, sequential decision making by nonopportunistic parties will nevertheless reach the same joint profit optimizing result.

The fact is, however, that human agents are neither unboundedly rational nor reliably free of opportunism. Interesting transaction cost issues thereby arise, and organizational design is a relevant concern precisely for this reason. But a predictive theory of efficient organizational structure requires more than an acknowledgment that human actors are subject to bounded rationality and given to opportunism. A schema for framing the dimensions of transactions is needed and must be joined with a description of alternative modes for organizing transactions. In addition, a strategy for matching organizing modes (governance structures) to transactions needs to be devised.

The rudiments of such an approach have been set out elsewhere (Williamson, 1979b). The critical dimensions for describing transactions are (1) uncertainty, (2) the frequency with which transactions recur, and (3) the degree to which durable transaction-specific investments are required to realize least-cost supply. The main governance modes to which transactions need to be matched are: (1) markets (with varying degrees of adjudicatory support); (2) internal organization; and (3) an intermediate form of bilateral exchange referred to as "obligational market contracting."

Our principal interest here is internal organization. Internal organization is well-suited to transactions that involve recurrent exchange in the face of a nontrivial degree of uncertainty and that incur transaction-specific investments. Since internal organization requires the development of specialized governance structure, the cost of which must be amortized across the transactions assigned to it, it is rarely economical to organize occasional transactions internally. Likewise, transactions for which uncertainty is low require little adaptation, hence little governance, and thus can be organized by market contracting. Except, however, as transaction-specific investments are involved, neither frequency nor uncertainty—individually or in combination—justifies the creation of internal organization (with its associated transaction-specific governance structure).

Considering the importance that we attach to transaction-specific investments, some explication is needed. The crucial issue is the degree to which durable, nonmarketable expenses are incurred. Items that are unspecialized among users pose few hazards, since buyers in these circumstances can easily turn to alternative sources, and suppliers can sell output intended for one buyer to other buyers without difficulty. (The argument also turns on the degree to which inputs can be diverted from one use to another without loss of productivity.) Nonmarketability problems arise when the *specific identity* of the parties has important cost-bearing consequences. Transactions of this kind will be referred to as idiosyncratic.

Occasionally the identity of the parties is important from the outset, as when a buyer induces a supplier to invest in specialized physical capital of a transaction-specific kind. Inasmuch as the value of this capital in other uses is by definition much smaller than the specialized use for which it has been intended, the supplier is effectively "locked into" the transaction to a significant degree. This is symmetrical, moreover, in that the buyer cannot turn to alternative sources of supply and obtain the item on favorable terms, since the cost of supply from unspecialized capital is presumably great.* The buyer is thus committed to the transaction as well.

Ordinarily, however, there is more to idiosyncratic exchange than specialized physical capital. Human-capital investments that are transaction-specific commonly occur as well. Specialized training and learning-by-doing economies in production operations are illustrations. Except when these investments are transferable to alternative suppliers at low cost, which is rare, the benefits of the set-up costs can be realized only so long as the relationship between the buyer and seller of the intermediate product is maintained.

Additional transaction-specific savings can accrue at the interface between supplier and buyer as contracts are successively adapted to unfolding events, and as periodic contract-renewal agreements are reached. Familiarity here permits communication economies to be realized: specialized language develops as experience accumulates and nuances are signaled and received in a sensitive way. Both institutional and personal trust relations evolve.

In consideration of the value placed upon economies of these kinds, agents who engage in recurring, uncertain, idiosyncratic transactions have a strong interest in preserving the exchange relation. Autonomous contracting modes give way to internal organization as the value associated with exchange continuity increases. The continuity advantages of internal organization over markets in these circumstances are attributable to its more sensitive governance characteristics and its stronger joint profit maximizing features.

APPLICATIONS

A theory is judged to be more fruitful the "more precise the prediction, the wider the area within which the theory yields predictions, and the more additional lines of future research it suggests" (Friedman, 1953:

---

*This assumes that it is costly for the incumbent supplier to transfer specialized physical assets to new suppliers. On this, see Williamson (1976).

10). The basic exchange paradigm that was originally worked up to address the issue of vertical integration across successive manufacturing stages has proved to be remarkably robust. Although this was not evident at the outset, it quickly became apparent that any organizational relation that can be reformulated as a contracting problem can be addressed in substantially identical terms. Applications of the exchange paradigm include: assessments of the employment relation (Williamson, Wachter, and Harris, 1975; Hashimoto and Yu, 1979); franchise bidding for natural monopolies (Williamson, 1976); the efficacy of capital markets (Williamson, 1975: Chapter 9); oligopoly (Posner, 1969; Williamson, 1975: Chapter 12); vertical market restrictions (Williamson, 1979a); and aspects of inflation (Wachter and Williamson, 1978).

Other applications include: a restatement of contract law in transaction cost terms (Williamson, 1979b: 235–254); the uses of transaction cost reasoning by marketing specialists (Carman, 1978); possible applications to the study of comparative economic systems (Campbell, 1978); and uses of the exchange paradigm to examine noneconomic phenomena—family law being an example (Williamson, 1979b: 258). Of special interest here are the applications of the Markets and Hierarchies approach to matters of internal organization. These design issues are developed in the following section.

Empirical tests of three kinds have been used to assess predictions of the Markets and Hierarchies approach: cross-sectional studies, experimental studies, and case studies. The cross-sectional studies that have been performed test what is referred to as the multidivisional form hypothesis (Williamson, 1975: 150):

> The organization and operation of the large enterprise along the lines of the M-form favors goal pursuit and least-cost behavior more nearly associated with the neoclassical profit maximization hypothesis than does the U-form organizational alternative.

Three studies have been done in which organization form is used as an explanatory variable in studies of business performance. The studies by Peter Steer and John Cable (1978) of British firms and by Henry Armour and David Teece (1978) of U.S. petroleum corporations both confirm the importance of organization form. Teece has since extended the analysis from petroleum firms to assess the ramifications of organization form differences among the principal firms in 15 industries and obtains results that confirm the hypothesis (Teece, 1979).

Richard Burton and Borge Obel (1980) have tested the M-form hypothesis by examining the ramifications of organizational design for profitability in the context of a linear programming model of the firm in which the Danzig-Wolf decomposition algorithm was used. Two different technologies, one more decomposable than the other, were studied. The M-form hypothesis is confirmed for both technologies, the profit difference being greater for the more decomposable technology—which is also an implication of the theory.

Case studies of several kinds have been performed. The most complete of these involves an assessment of franchise bidding for natural monopolies. Demsetz (1968), Posner (1972), and Stigler (1968: 18–19) have argued that franchise bidding is an attractive alternative to rate-of-return regulation in dealing with natural monopolies. An abstract assessment of the contracting ramifications of franchise bidding discloses, however, that the purported benefits of franchise bidding are suspect where market and technological uncertainty are great and incumbent suppliers invest in specialized, long-lived equipment and acquire idiosyncratic skills (Williamson, 1976). A case study of franchise bidding for CATV in Oakland, California, confirmed this. Not only were general ramifications of the contracting approach borne out by the study, but the study corroborated contracting details as well.

ORGANIZATIONAL DESIGN

Consistent with the general thrust of the Markets and Hierarchies approach, organization design is addressed as a transaction cost issue, and economizing purposes are emphasized. The general argument is this: except when there are perversities associated with the funding process, or when strategically situated members of an organization are unable to participate in the prospective gains, unrealized efficiency opportunities always offer an incentive to reorganize.

Inasmuch as these perversities are more common in noncommercial than in commercial enterprises, the argument has stronger predictive force for the latter. Indeed our attention in this section is restricted entirely to the commercial sector. We nevertheless believe that the spirit of the analysis carries over to nonprofit enterprises and government bureaus, which we include in our discussion of the research agenda.

Although the main organizational design "action" entails economizing on transaction costs, this is not to say that technology is irrelevant. But technology by itself rarely has determinative organizational consequences for more than a small group of highly interdependent workers. Indeed, except when the transaction costs of adapting interfaces between technologically separable work stations are great, markets will be the governance mode by which the exchange of intermediate product is accomplished. Internal organization not only has little to offer in these circumstances but incurs unneeded costs.

However, in circumstances in which autonomous contracting is costly and hazardous, governance structures of an internal organizational kind arise. Three applications of this general argument follow, after which we summarize the implications and go on briefly to consider other organizational design traditions and contrast them with the approach favored here.

Vertical Integration*

The recent monograph by Alfred Chandler, Jr. (1977), describing marketing developments during the late nineteenth century provides strong support for the proposition that transaction costs are sufficiently significant to affect the structure of industries, sometimes motivating firms to integrate forward from manufacturing into the distribution stage.

Chandler's Findings. Chandler's description of forward integration into distribution by American manufacturers distinguishes between the developments of infrastructure and the induced distributional response. The appearance of the railroads and the telegraph and telephone systems in the latter part of the nineteenth century permitted wider geographic areas to be served in a reliable and timely way. The "reliability and speed of the new transportation and communication" permitted greater economies of scale to be realized in factory organization (Chandler, 1977: 245). These economies of scale at the factory level were latent, in the sense that the technology was there waiting to be exploited. Because it is not manufacturing cost but delivered cost that matters, however, it became profitable to realize these scale economies only when a low-cost distribution system appeared. That is, so long as transportation expenses were great, the most efficient way to serve markets was by dispersing factories.

Once the new transportation and communication infrastructure was in place, the stage was set for the distributional response. A crucial question was how to devise a coordinated manufacturing-distribution response. In principle, both stages could have remained autonomous: manufacturers could have remained specialized and built larger-scale plants while specialized distributors could have responded simultaneously, either on their own initiative or by contract, by assembling the requisite distribution network. In many industries, however, "existing marketers were unable to sell and distribute products in the volume they were produced. . . . Once the inadequacies of existing marketers became clear, manufacturers integrated forward into marketing" (Chandler, 1977: 287). An administrative override was evidently needed.

Not all industries integrated forward, however, and when they did it was not to the same extent. Some industries linked manufacturing only with advertising and wholesaling; retail integration was not attempted. Nondurable industries that had recently adopted continuous process machinery—cigarettes, matches, cereals, and canned goods are examples;- were in this category (Chandler, 1977: 287). More ambitious and in-

---

*The argument here follows Williamson (1979a, pp. 968–972).

teresting were producer and consumer durables that required "specialized marketing services—demonstration, installation, consumer credit, after-sales service and repair," services that existing middlemen "had neither the interest nor facilities to provide" (Chandler, 1977: 288). Examples here included sewing machines, farm machinery, office machines, and heavy electrical equipment.

A Transaction Cost Interpretation. The new transportation and communication infrastructure permitted manufacturers to serve larger markets in a low-cost way. The effects of these infrastructural developments on plant size are displayed in Figure 8-2. (On the motivation for this, see Scherer, Beckenstein, Kaufer, and Murphy, 1975.)

The *APC* curve shows the average cost of production as plant size increases. These average costs decrease over a wide range due to assumed economies of scale. The curve ADC_1 shows the original average distribution cost of delivering products from a plant. This curve increases throughout because greater sales require marketing to a larger geographic region. The curve ADC_2 shows the average distribution cost after the new infrastructure is put in place. It is consistently lower than ADC_1 but also rises throughout. ATC_1 and ATC_2 are average total cost curves that are given by the vertical summation of *APC* with ADC_1 and ADC_2, respectively. Average total costs reach a minimum at Q_1^* and Q_2^*, where Q_2^* is necessarily larger than Q_1^*, given the stipulated shift in average distribution costs. An increase in plant scale and the extension of service to larger geographic markets are thus indicated.

Problems of implementation, however, are not addressed by this cost curve apparatus. How are the linkages between manufacturing and dis-

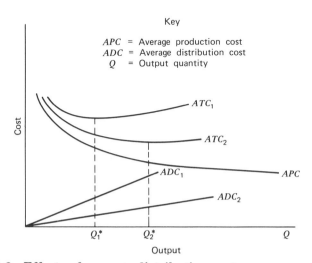

Figure 8-2 Effects of average distribution cost on average total cost.

tribution to be forged? They are not created automatically. If existing middlemen respond in a slow and faltering way to the opportunities that the new transportation and communication infrastructures afford, the stage is set for someone, in this instance the manufacturers, to experiment with new organizational structures.

The issues here are of a transaction cost rather than of a production cost kind. Although a definitive analysis of the "inadequacies of existing marketers" reported by Chandler (1977: 287) would require further research, we conjecture that these distributional difficulties are due to goal incongruence coupled with the hazards posed by small numbers supply relations between autonomous parties. It was difficult for marketers who were accustomed to operating in a local market regime to perceive the opportunities that awaited them. And there was no obvious way to signal these opportunities by relying upon decentralized pricing (Malmgren, 1961). Moreover, even if manufacturers and distributors both perceived the opportunities that the new transportation and communication infrastructure afforded, and if each responded independently in reliance upon the other, problems of divergence would arise if each recorded or interpreted the data differently. Such goal incongruence would exist, moreover, at both an aggregate and a disaggregate level.

In principle, manufactuers could have taken the initiative and effected goal congruence by contract. Coordination by contract is costly, however, where the two parties are bargaining in an unfamiliar situation and the hazards of contracting are great. The hazards to which we refer have been discussed elsewhere in the context of idiosyncratic exchange. Such problems arise when investments in specialized human or physical assets are required in order to complete the transaction in an economical way. With respect to the issues of concern to Chandler, the problems were especially severe when the mass production and sale of consumer or producer durables was contemplated. Distributors here would have to be induced to make specialized (product-and-brand-specific) investments and, once these investments were made, manufacturers and distributors would thereafter often be dealing with each other in what essentially was a bilateral exchange arrangement. Given the hazards of opportunism that arise in such circumstances, both parties were reluctant to rely on autonomous contracting.

Note in this connection that Chandler did not observe vertical integration occurring in uniform degree in all industries. This is precisely what one would anticipate when vertical integration is assessed in transaction cost terms. Thus vertical integration into distribution was negligible in some industries—standardized nuts and bolts being an example. In others, integration involved advertising and wholesaling but not retailing—branded consumer nondurables being in this category. In still others, integration included retailing and related support services—certain branded nondurables being among these. This progression is marked by the degree of transaction-specific investment, which is an implication of transaction cost theory. Other theories of vertical integration, by contrast, are silent on these matters.

This substitution of bureaucratic for market governance occurred in response to profit opportunities. But social cost savings also resulted. In the absence of other factors, net social as well as net private gains accrue when such organizational innovations appear.

Becoming Multidivisional. The transformation of the modern corporation from a functional to a multidivisional structure has been documented by Chandler.* This transformation is treated prominently in the *Markets and Hierarchies* volume (Williamson, 1975: Chapters 8–9). Only a few comments are offered here.

Chandler characterizes the reasons for the success of the multidivision structure thus:

> The basic reasons for its success was simply that it clearly removed the executives responsible for the destiny of the entire enterprise from the more routine operational activities, and so gave them the time, information, and even psychological commitment for long-term planning and appraisal. . . .
>
> [The] new structure left the broad strategic decisions as to the allocation of existing resources and the acquisition of new ones in the hands of a top team of generalists. Relieved of operating duties and tactical decisions, a general executive was less likely to reflect the position of just one part of the whole. (Chandler, 1966: 382–383)

If Chandler is correct, this organizational change from a functional to a multidivisional structure served both to economize on bounded rationality, by relieving top executives of the more routine operational activities, and simultaneously to reduce subgoal pursuit, which is a manifestation of opportunism. Inasmuch as most institutional choices involve trade-offs rather than Pareto-superior moves, this is surely quite remarkable. How was this accomplished?

The difficulties that the functionally organized firm encountered as it grew in size and diversity were attributable to diseconomies of agglomeration. The centralization of what are effectively decomposable parts has adverse operating consequences of three kinds. First, attempts to achieve unneeded coordination generate overhead costs. Second, forced interdependencies give rise to congestion and other spillover costs. Third, opportunistic subgoal pursuit is more difficult to detect and control as the degree of interconnectedness increases. Operating cost increases thus arise out of a failure to recognize essential decomposability. But the deficiencies of the functional structure went beyond these operating cost

*The path-breaking book here is Chandler's *Strategy and Structure* (1966). Williamson's shift of emphasis from the factors that were responsible for managerial discretion to the factors, including especially internal organization, that served to attenuate managerial discretion was much influenced by this book.

features. The functional form also served to confuse organizational purpose by failure to separate strategic from operating decision making.

Although becoming multidivisional would not have been feasible without decomposability, the benefits of reorganization required more than
an assignment of semiautonomous standing to natural subunits within
the firm. Becoming multidivisional further required the development of
a strategic decision-making capability in the central office—indeed would
have been hazardous to implement without this capability. The assignment of investment resources to high yield uses could be reliably accomplished only as the general office (1) had a sense of direction, (2) was able
to evaluate the merits of investment proposals originated by the operating
divisions, and (3) had the capacity to audit and assess operating division
performance.

Removing top management from the operating affairs of the enterprise
meant that, whereas bureaucratic control processes had governed previously, operating divisions were now governed in a quasi-market fashion.
Thus divisions were assigned the status of quasi firms, and the central
office assumed functions of review and resource allocation ordinarily associated with the capital market. As a consequence of these changes the
goal confusion (or incongruence) that had previously reigned was supplanted by subgoal clarity that was meaningfully related to enterprise
objectives. The self-interest seeking that, when coupled with goal incongruence, had once drained the energies of the enterprise was now turned
to productive purposes.

It is noteworthy that the transformation of the functional to the multidivisional form had little if any relation to technology. Organizational
structure was altered, but the underlying technology remained the same
in most instances. Thus although efficiency purposes were served, the
economies driving the change and the economies that were realized were
of a transaction cost rather than technological kind.

Bureaucracies and Clans

The shift from functional to divisional structure has for the most part
been completed in large U.S. corporations (Teece, 1979) and has been
proceeding rapidly in Europe (Franko, 1972). But a further question is
what management "style" ought to be practiced in the large multidivisional enterprise. Issues relating to the "economics of atmosphere" (Williamson, 1975: 37–39) arise in this connection. Ouchi has addressed the
merits of bureaucratic versus clan-type management styles in a series of
recent papers on this subject (Ouchi, 1978, 1979, 1980).

To put the issue one way: What form of contracting ought to prevail
within an organization? As with market modes of contracting, there are
two general options, which we designate as "hard" and "soft" contracting,

respectively. Under hard contracting, the parties remain relatively autonomous, each is expected to press his or her interests vigorously, and contracting is relatively complete. Soft contracting, by contrast, presumes much closer identity of interests between the parties, and formal contracts are much less complete. This is the clan-type management style.

Although contract law specialists, sociologists, and others have long recognized soft contracting practices, the study of soft contracting has only recently come under scrutiny. Ian Macneil's (1974, 1978) work on "relational contracting" is especially instructive. While it is beyond the scope of this paper to review the literature here, we nonetheless think it important to elaborate on the special problems that soft contracting encounters if it is introduced in an alien culture.

The basic argument is this: Soft contracting, to be viable, needs to be supported by a more elaborate informal governance apparatus than is associated with hard contracting. Thus, whereas the latter relies heavily on legal and economic sanctions, the former rests much more on social controls. As compared with hard contracting, soft contracting appeals more to the spirit than to the letter of the agreement.

Four points are relevant in this regard. First, not all transactions need the additional supports afforded by soft contracting. Economizing considerations would dictate that a distinction be made between those that do and that do not, and that each be organized appropriately. Second, the immediate parties to soft contracts are the ones who stand most to benefit from preserving the exchange. Accordingly, they have incentives to develop a bilateral (transaction-specific) trust relation. Third, the institutional infrastructure within which soft contracts are embedded also influences the viability of this type of exchange. And fourth, the design of transactions is a decision variable: depending on their confidence in the trading relation, parties will vary the degree to which trading hazards are introduced.

Trading hazards differ with the degree of transaction-specific investment and with uncertainty. The first of these hazards is obvious: Where investments are of a transaction-specific kind, parties will be unable to divert these assets to alternative uses of an equally productive kind. Accordingly, as the degree of asset specificity increases, additional governance supports are needed. The same applies as uncertainty is increased. The argument here is that the occasions to adapt the transaction to new circumstances increase as the degree of uncertainty increases. Since the incentive to defect from the spirit of the agreement increases as the frequency and magnitude of the indicated adaptations are increased, greater hazards are thereby posed.

Although the degree of uncertainty is commonly beyond the control of the parties, the degree of asset specificity is often theirs to determine. Thus, assume that a particular transaction is subject to an intermediate degree of uncertainty and the parties are attempting to optimize with respect to its transaction-specific features. Specifically, assume the following:

1. The transaction in question involves an employment relation.

2. Two different job designs are under consideration, one of a hard contracting and the other of a soft contracting kind.

3. Human capital skill acquisitions are involved for each job design: Under hard contracting the skills acquired are of a general purpose kind, while under soft contracting they are of a special kind.

4. Physical capital expenditures are identical whichever job design is adopted.

5. Assuming contractual continuity, the more productive job design is the one that involves special-purpose skill acquisition.

Whether this more productive job design is adopted, however, is problematical. In contrast to employees with general-purpose skills, employees who have acquired task-specific skills will be able to move to alternative employment only by experiencing a nontrivial productivity sacrifice in the process. In consideration of these added hazards, employers will be successful in inducing employees to acquire specialized skills only when the workers are either adequately compensated in advance for the hazards or when the job is adequately protected against opportunism during the course of task execution.

Holding governance structures constant, the wage premium needed to compensate workers against the added hazards may easily render the task-specific job design competitively nonviable, especially if workers are risk averse. The question then is whether this potentially more productive job design can be salvaged by surrounding it with transactional safeguards. This brings us back to the matter of bilateral trading relations and the institutional matrix within which trading takes place.

The "special problems" of soft contracting to which we referred earlier are particularly great when soft contracting is introduced into an alien culture. The reason for this is that the entire burden of providing contractual safeguards falls entirely on the immediate parties to the transaction if background cultural supports are missing. Should one of the parties choose to defect, there is no further support for sustaining the transaction to which either can appeal. In contrast, where individual soft contracts are embedded in a soft contracting trading culture, defection is subject to added sanctions. The incentives to defect are accordingly reduced.

To some extent, the parties to the transaction may be able to devise procedural safeguards themselves. One example is the development of "internal labor markets" whereby wages are assigned to jobs rather than to individuals, promotion ladders are defined, a sensitive grievance structure is devised, and so on (Doeringer and Piore, 1971; Williamson, Wachter, and Harris, 1975). But societal safeguards may provide additional security. This varies among economic systems. The "clan" form of organization that Ouchi (1978, 1979) has studied is much more viable in some cultures (e.g., Japanese) than in others (e.g., American).

The limitations of hard contracting are nevertheless great as the need progressively increases for successive adaptations to be made in response to uncertainty. Contracts simply fail to provide adequately for the appropriate responses in advance, and employees may engage in strategic bargaining. The more cooperative work relations associated with soft contracting have a clear advantage in these circumstances. The problem then is how to bring this off. This is a matter for which future research is plainly needed.

Other Organizational Design Traditions

The literature on organizational design is vast, and we address only a small part of it here. Jeffrey Pfeffer's (1978) recent book on this subject distinguishes between longitudinal studies, managerial studies, and the power approach. He observes that most of the longitudinal studies have been preoccupied with measurement to the exclusion of theory (Pfeffer, 1978: xiv). The work of Jay Galbraith (1973) and of Paul Lawrence and Jay Lorsch (1967) is in the managerial tradition. Pfeffer contends that this work is preoccupied with efficiency and effectiveness and neglects power and influence (Pfeffer, 1978: xv). Pfeffer's preferred approach is to regard organizations "as coalitions with ill-defined and inconsistent preferences" (Pfeffer, 1978: xvi), a tradition that he associates with Cyert and March (1963), Karl Weick (1969), and March and Olsen (1976). Organizational design issues are then addressed in terms of control, influence, and power.

Other organizational design approaches that go unmentioned by Pfeffer are the organizational ecology approach (Hannan and Freeman, 1977; Aldrich, 1979) and the theory of organizational structures advanced by Kenneth Mackenzie (1978). Inasmuch as efficiency figures prominently in both of these last two approaches, both are complementary to the Markets and Hierarchies approach. The power approach to organizational design, by contrast, is a very different tradition.

The neglect of power by the M&H approach is not to suggest that power is either uninteresting or unimportant. We submit, however, that power considerations will usually give way to efficiency—at least in profit-making enterprises, if observations are taken at sufficiently long intervals, say a decade. Thus the powers of heads of functional divisions and of their subordinates were vastly altered when functionally organized firms shifted to a multidivisional structure. Were power the only or the main organizational design factor, it is difficult to believe that large American and subsequently European businesses would have undergone such a vast organizational transformation over the past thirty years. From transaction cost and ecological points of view, however, the transformation, once started, was predictable.

Or consider Pfeffer's assertion that if "the chief executive in a corporation always comes from marketing . . . there is a clue about power in the organization" (Pfeffer, 1978: 23). Viewed from a power perspective, the argument evidently is that the marketing people in this corporation have "possession of control over critical resources," have preferential access to information, and are strategically located to cope with "critical organizational uncertainty" (Pfeffer, 1978: 17–28). We do not disagree with any of this but would make the more straightforward argument that the marketing function in this organization is especially critical to competitive viability.

Thus our position is that those parts of the enterprise that are most critical to organizational viability will be *assigned* possession of control over critical resources, will *have* preferential access to information, and will be *dealing* with critical organizational uncertainties. In some organizations this may be marketing, in others it may be R&D, and in still others it may be production. Failure to assign control to that part of the enterprise on which viability turns would contradict the efficiency hypothesis but would presumably be explained as a power outcome.*

Inasmuch as power is very vague and has resisted successive efforts to make it operational, whereas efficiency is much more clearly specified and the plausibility of an efficiency hypothesis is buttressed by ecological survival tests, we urge that efficiency analysis be made the center piece of the study of organizational design. This does not imply that power has no role to play, but we think it invites confusion to explain organizational results that are predicted by the efficiency hypothesis in terms of power. Rather power explains results when the organization sacrifices efficiency to serve special interests. We concede that this occurs. But we do not believe that major organizational changes in the commercial sector are explained in these terms. The evidence is all to the contrary.

---

*Thus suppose that, from a competitive effectiveness viewpoint, marketing is the most important functional area. Suppose further that the founder and his progeny are engineers, and that each has worked his way up through manufacturing. Inasmuch as they have an ownership lock (power) on the system, the chief executive and his principal aides are appointed from these ranks. Although this has the efficiency benefit of coupling ownership and control, the firm may be vulnerable to market developments in relation to its rivals. Power explains the inefficiency (vulnerability) condition.

THE RESEARCH AGENDA

The Markets and Hierarchies approach to the study of organizational issues is relatively new as compared with other research traditions. Neither its power nor its limits have been fully established. Applications to date, however, have been numerous and mainly encouraging. Our discussion here merely suggests additional theoretical, empirical, and public policy applications.

General

As noted earlier, any problem that arises as a contracting problem or can be recast as one can usefully be examined in Markets and Hierarchies terms. This is not to suggest that the contracting paradigm should be applied to the exclusion of other research traditions. We nevertheless believe that insights not easily derived from alternative approaches can often be obtained by assessing transaction cost features. While sometimes these insights may be of a fragmentary kind, often they relate to core issues.

Inasmuch as transaction costs have reference to the costs of running the economic system, the useful comparisons are between alternative modes rather than between a proposed mode and a frictionless ideal. Given that an explicit or implicit exchange is to be accomplished or a coordinated adaptation is to be affected, how should the transaction be organized? For many purposes, the analysis can be thought of as interface management. This applies within and between markets and firms.

Some Specifics

Business History: Markets to Hierarchies.   Transaction cost economics can be applied advantageously to the study of changing organizational structures through time. This is true both of organizational changes since the industrial revolution (Chandler, 1966, 1977) and also preindustrial changes (North, 1978). A richer understanding of the economics of institutions is sure to emerge as business historians, industrial organization specialists, economic theorists, and organization theorists apply their collective talents to the systematic study of institutional issues. Transaction cost economizing is, we submit, the driving force that is responsible for the main institutional changes (for an interpretation of Chandler's recent book in transaction cost terms, see Williamson, 1980). Applications will include product market organization and also changing labor and capital market forms of organization through time.

Bureaucracies.   Applications of Markets and Hierarchies to commercial bureaucracies will be concerned with interface governance. Specific organizational design applications (possibly with special reference to particular functions such as research and development) as well as general applications (again, the matrix form is in need of interpretation) should be possible. Additional empirical tests of the M-form of other hypotheses can also be anticipated. Perhaps most important, the limits of internal organization are poorly understood in relation to the limits of markets. The transaction cost approach appears to have much to offer for such an assessment. The ramifications are of interest both to worker-managed and to capitalist enterprises (Fitzroy and Mueller, 1978). Whether recent developments involving employee participation in Europe constitute a contradiction to the efficiency hypothesis also warrants scrutiny.

Clans. The organization of economic activity by greater reliance on clan-type structures requires study. Both the limitations of clans as well as the discriminating application of clan forms of organization deserve attention. As between alternative forms of *internal* organization, the clan appears to realize greater advantage in circumstances in which uncertainty is great. The argument needs to be elaborated and specific applications attempted, to service industries, high technology industries, and others characterized by extreme performance ambiguity.

The proposition that clan forms join high productivity with emotional well-being (low levels of alienation) deserves further scrutiny. As with other organizational panaceas, we believe that this is too simplistic. Rather the argument needs to be made in a more discriminating way that recognizes transaction cost distinctions. The proposition that defection hazards are greater for clan forms, and that such forms are viable only when accompanied by additional governance supports, also warrants further study. Comparative international studies, in which hard versus soft contracting cultures are scrutinized, may be useful.

Public Policy toward Business. Public policy applications will also continue. This includes both antitrust and regulation. In the antitrust area, issues of strategic behavior and fairness will come under special scrutiny. What has been referred to as the Decision Process Approach, which makes operational "procedural rationality" (Simon, 1978), would appear to hold promise for the microanalytic study of regulatory issues (Williamson, 1979c).

Nonprofit Organizations. The organization of nonprofit enterprises, which are growing in economic importance (Weisbord, 1979), is intriguing and has hitherto evaded explanation of more than a partial or ad hoc kind. Whether the transaction cost approach will be illuminating remains to be seen. One of the problems, with transactions in many nonprofit organizations, as in service businesses, is that they are amorphous. Also the viability tests for nonprofit organizations are often much weaker—partly because product market competition is weak, but also because an effective capital market displacement mechanism (takeover) is missing.

The study of government bureaus suffers from many of these same limitations. Once progress is made in studying nonprofit organizations from a transaction cost (or any other) point of view, follow-up applications to government bureaus should be easy.

CONCLUSION

The Markets and Hierarchies program of research is relatively young in comparison with other research traditions in organization theory. Being young, it has its skeptics. We would not have it otherwise.

For one thing, we are inclined to be eclectic. No single approach applies equally well to all problems, and some issues are usefully addressed from several points of view. For another, we believe that most of the challenges can be met. Sometimes this may require extending the theory to apply to new circumstances. Sometimes it will require sharpening or qualifying parts of the argument. Formalizing aspects of the argument may some- times be needed and appears to be feasible. (See the recent paper by Hashimoto and Yu, 1979, for developments of this last kind.)

The distinctive powers of the approach are attributable to its reliance on transaction cost reasoning and its unremitting emphasis on efficiency. While the particulars differ, the same approach to the study of transac- tions applies quite generally. The core methodological properties are these:

1. The transaction is the basic unit of analysis.

2. Human agents are subject to bounded rationality and self-interest.

3. The critical dimensions for describing transactions are frequency, uncertainty, and transaction-specific investments.

4. Economizing on transaction costs is the principal factor that ex- plains viable modes of contracting; it is the main issue with which organizational design ought to be concerned.

5. Assessing transaction cost differences is a comparative institu- tional exercise.

The approach is able to deal symmetrically with market and nonmarket modes of organization and has successfully addressed a wide variety of organizational issues in a coherent way.

Those who prefer methodology and those who are averse to efficiency analysis will insist, with cause, that there is more to organization theory than economizing on transaction costs. We agree. We submit, however, that efficiency analysis is important to the study of all forms of organization and is absolutely crucial to the study of commercial organizations. And we furthermore contend that the main test of a theory is its implications. So long as alternative theories are evaluated on this standard, we are confident that the Markets and Hierarchies approach will fare well in the comparison.

REFERENCES

Alchian, A. A., and H. Demsetz (1972). "Production, Information Costs, and Economic Organization," *American Economic Review* **62,**12:777–795.

Aldrich, H. E. (1979). *Organizations and Environments,* Englewood Cliffs, NJ: Prentice-Hall.

Armour, H. O., and D. J. Teece (1978). "Organization Structure and Economic Performance: A Test of the Multidivisional Hypothesis," *Bell Journal of Economics* **9:**106–122.

Arrow, K. J. (1969). "The Organization of Economic Activity," *The Analysis and Evaluation Public Expenditure: The PPB System,* Joint Economic Committee, 91st Cong., 1st Session, pp. 59–73.

Arrow, K. J. (1974). *Limits of Organization,* New York: Norton.

Burton, R., and B. Obel (1981). "Analysis of the M-Form Hypothesis for Contracting Technologies," *Administrative Science Quarterly* (in press).

Campbell, R. W. (1978). "New Concepts in the Study of Economic Systems," unpublished manuscript.

Carman, J. M. (1979). "Paradigms for Marketing Theory," in *Research in Marketing,* Greenwich, CT: JAI Press.

Chandler, A. D., Jr. (1966). *Strategy and Structure,* Cambridge, MA: MIT Press.

Chandler, A. D., Jr. (1978). *The Visible Hand: The Managerial Revolution in American Business,* Cambridge, MA: Harvard University Press.

Coase, R. H. (1952). "The Nature of the Firm," *Economica N.S.,* 1937 **4:**386–405, reprinted in G. J. Stigler and K. E. Boulding, Eds., *Readings in Price Theory,* Homewood, IL: R. D. Irwin.

Coase, R. H. (1972). "Industrial Organization: A Proposal for Research," in V. R. Fuchs, Ed., *Policy Issues and Research Opportunities in Industrial Organization,* New York: Columbia University Press.

Commons, J. R. (1934). *Institutional Economics,* Madison: University of Wisconsin Press.

Cyert, R. M., and J. G. March (1963). *A Behavioral Theory of the Firm,* Englewood Cliffs, NJ: Prentice-Hall.

Demsetz, H. (1968). "The Cost of Transacting," *Quarterly Journal of Economics* **82,**2:33–53.

Doeringer, P., and M. Piore (1971). *Internal Labor Markets and Manpower Analysis,* Lexington, MA: D. C. Heath.

Fitzroy, F. R., and D. C. Mueller (1977). "Contract and the Economics of Organization," Discussion Paper 77–25, International Institute of Management, Berlin.

Franko, L. G. (1972). "The Growth, Organizational Efficiency of European Multinational Firms: Some Emerging Hypotheses," *Colloques International Aux C.N.R.S.* **549,**335–366.

Friedman, M. (1953). *Essays in Positive Economics,* Chicago: University of Chicago Press.

Galbraith, J. (1973). *Designing Complex Organizations,* Reading, MA: Addison-Wesley.

Goffman, I. (1969). *Strategic Interaction,* Philadelphia: University of Pennsylvania Press.

Hannan, M., and J. Freeman (1977). "The Population Ecology of Organizations," *American Journal of Sociology* **82,**3:929–964.

Hashimoto, M., and B. T. Yu (1981). "Specific Capital, Employment Contracts and Wage Rigidity," *Bell Journal of Economics* (in press).

Lawrence, D., and J. Lorsch (1967). *Organization and Environment,* Homewood, IL: R. D. Irwin.

Mackenzie, K. D. (1978). *Organizational Structures,* Arlington Heights, IL: AHM Publishing.

Macneil, I. R. (1974). "The Many Futures of Contract," *Southern California Law Review* **47,**5:691–816.

Macneil, I. R. (1978). "Contracts: Adjustment of Long-Term Economic Relations under Classical, Neoclassical, and Relational Contract Law," *Northwestern University Law Review* **72,**1:854–905.

Malmgren, H. (1961). "Information, Expectations and the Theory of the Firm," *Quarterly Journal of Economics* **75**:399–421.

March, J. G., and J. P. Olsen (1976). *Ambiguity and Choice in Organizations,* Bergen: Universitetsforlaget.

Meade, J. E. (1971). *The Controlled Economy,* Albany: State University of New York Press.

Mintzberg, H. (1973). *The Nature of Managerial Work,* New York: Harper and Row.

North, D. C. (1978). "Structures and Performance: The Task of Economic History," *Journal of Economic Literature* **16**:963–978.

Ouchi, W. G. (1977). "The Relationship between Organizational Structure and Organizational Control," *Administrative Science Quarterly* **22**:95–113.

Ouchi, W. G. (1978). "The Transmission of Control through Organizational Hierarchy," *Academy of Management Journal* **21**:248–263.

Ouchi, W. G. (1981). "A Conceptual Framework for the Design of Organizational Control Mechanisms," *Management Science* (in press).

Ouchi, W. G., and A. H. Van de Ven (1980). "Antitrust and Organization Theory," in O. E. Williamson, Ed., *Antitrust Law and Economics,* Houston: Dame Publications.

Pfeffer, J. (1978). *Organizational Design,* Arlington Heights, IL: AHM Publishing.

Posner, R. A. (1969). "Natural Monopoly and its Regulation," *Stanford Law Review* **21,** 548–564.

Posner, R. A. (1972). "The Appropriate Scope of Regulation in the Cable Television Industry," *Bell Journal of Economics* **3**:98–129.

Scherer, F. M., A. Beckenstein, E. Kaufer, and R. Murphy (1975). *The Economics of Multiplant Operation: An International Comparison Study,* Cambridge, MA: Harvard University Press.

Simon, H. A. (1978). "Rationality and Process and Product of Thought," *American Economic Review* **68**:1–16.

Steer, P., and J. Cable (1978). "Internal Organization and Profit: An Empirical Analysis of Large U. K. Companies," *Journal of Industrial Economics* **27**:13–30.

Stigler, G. J. (1968). *The Organization of Industry,* Homewood, IL: R. D. Irwin.

Teece, D. J. (1979). "Internal Organization and Economic Performance," unpublished manuscript, Stanford, CA.

Wachter, M., and O. E. Williamson (1978). "Obligational Markets and the Mechanics of Inflation," *Bell Journal of Economics* **9**:549–571.

Weick, K. E. (1969). *The Social Psychology of Organizing,* Reading, MA: Addison-Wesley.

Weisbrod, B. (1979). "Economics of Institutional Choice," unpublished manuscript.

Williamson, O. E. (1964). *The Economics of Discretionary Behavior: Managerial Objectives in a Theory of the Firm,* Englewood Cliffs, NJ: Prentice-Hall.

Williamson, O. E. (1965). "A Dynamic Theory of Interfirm Behavior," *Quarterly Journal of Economics,* November.

Williamson, O. E. (1967). "Hierarchical Control and Optimum Firm Size," *Journal of Political Economy* **75**:123–138.

Williamson, O. E. (1971). "The Vertical Integration of Production: Market Failure Considerations," *American Economic Review* **61**:112–123.

Williamson, O. E. (1973). "Markets and Hierarchies: Some Elementary Considerations," *American Economic Review* **63**:316–325.

Williamson, O. E. (1975). *Markets and Hierarchies: Analysis and Antitrust Implications,* New York: Free Press.

Williamson, O. E. (1976). "Francise Bidding for Natural Monopolies–in General and with Respect to CATV," *Bell Journal of Economics* **7**:73–104.

Williamson, O. E. (1979a). "Assessing Vertical Market Restrictions: Antitrust Ramifications of the Transaction Cost Approach," *University of Pennsylvania Law Review* **127**:953–993.

Williamson, O. E. (1979b). "Transaction-Cost Economics: The Governance of Contractual Relations," *Journal of Law and Economics* **22**:233–262.

Williamson, O. E. (1979c). "Public Policy on Saccharin: The Decision Process Approach and Its Alternatives," unpublished manuscript.

Williamson, O. E. (1980). "Emergence of the Visible Hand: Implications for Industrial Organization," in A. D. Chandler, Jr., Ed., *Managerial Hierarchies,* Cambridge, MA: Harvard University Press, pp. 182–202.

MARKETS, HIERARCHIES AND HEGEMONY

CHARLES PERROW
State University of New York
Stony Brook

The preceding chapter conveniently summarizes the argument William-son put forth in his 1975 book, *Markets and Hierarchies,* and which he has been elaborating since then in a number of publications that are cited in the Williamson and Ouchi paper. I would like to address the general issues raised by this approach rather than this particular paper. Since the approach has a marked similarity to that of Alfred Chandler's work, brought to a culmination in *The Visible Hand* (1977), I will also discuss his formulation. I will make three general criticisms: (1) the consistency of the argument found in Williamson's *Markets and Hierarchy;* (2) empirical examples that run counter to Williamson and the inadequacy of the empirical support for one of Chandler's key points; and (3) the normative presuppositions underlying their perspective.

Chandler's work is of enormous importance. He completely dominates the interpretation of the rise of industrialism and modern bureaucracy and the spread of the multidivisional form of organizing private economic activity. The work of a variety of less conservative theorists, such as Braverman, Marglin, Edwards, Clawson, and Dawley, stands in the sha-dows, and does not even challenge Chandler's interpretations directly, though they contradict him. Such eminence deserves more critical scru-tiny than Chandler has had so far. Later I will critically examine one part of his argument, that part that fits well with Williamson.

Williamson's theory (and Chandler's) is that hierarchies replaced mar-kets because they were more efficient. Williamson focuses on transaction costs (Chandler on coordination) as a neglected aspect of efficiency, and makes it the primary reason for organizing economic activity within one large organization rather than having several independent organizations that coordinate through buying and selling and lending. Williamson's theory is important for at least two reasons. First, it is one of the few instances of bringing concepts from the field of organizational behavior to bear upon problems formulated by economists. That I find the results unfortunate has nothing to do with the value of such attempts. Second, the theory deals with a basic problem of social structure, that of autonomy

I would like to thank Mitchel Abolafia, Avner Ben-Ner, Mark Granovetter, Egon Neuberger, and Andrew Van de Ven for helpful comments.

and control. Williamson sees the shift from a world of many producers coordinating their work through the market mechanism to a world of few producers who exercise control through the hierarchy of the large corporation as the result of a concern for efficiency in production and distribution.

I will emphasize the control of markets, the control of labor, and the social cost of undesirable sources of private profit. Any efficiencies that obtain through the reduction of the costs of transacting business (Williamson) or coordination (Chandler) are, I argue, minor consequences. They neither motivate entrepreneurs nor make a substantial contribution to profits. Profits come from control of markets and competition, control of labor, and the ability to externalize many other costs that are largely social in nature, that is, to force communities and workers to bear them and not have them reflected in the price of the goods and services.

To a large degree the differences between Williamson and Chandler on the one hand, and myself on the other, do not really depend upon the empirical data nor the logic of the arguments, though my critique will be couched in those terms. Instead they depend upon differences in normative presuppositions or values. I am sure that in some little ways and in a few examples their view is supported, but in most respects it is not. They would no doubt return the favor, and argue that I might be correct about this or that example, and acknowledge various dangers that must be guarded against, but say on balance that the ends of efficiency have been served—at reasonable profit rates—and society is the benefactor. The difference cannot be solved by counting cases; that kind of counting we do not know how to do, and the haggling over the majority of cases, even if we got agreement over the extremes, would be endless. I am sorry that I cannot demolish the efficiency argument in this or any other paper. There is something to be said for it. But I think it is extremely important not to let it go unchallenged. I am sorry that I am not likely to persuade them (and many others) to change their presuppositions, but it is extremely important to firmly state alternative presuppositions. This paper is less firm on that score than I would wish; I hope to present a more detailed statement in a lengthy work in progress. But it is a beginning, and as far as I know, the first direct criticism of these two enormously influential scholars.

Consistency of Williamson's Argument

When I read through *Markets and Hierarchies* for the first time a few years ago I covered the first 116 pages with crabbed and crabby marginal notes to the effect that most of the transactional costs, first mover problems, opportunism, uncertainties, bounded rationality problems, and information impactedness are reproduced in the firm, and sometimes are even greater than those found in markets. Then I read Chapter 7 and found my comments unnecessary, because here Williamson himself notes the existence of these problems within the firm.

In doing so, he would appear to undercut his argument sorely and merely attest to the ubiquity of problems in organized activity, whether it is organized by markets or hierarchies. But he made no note of this, nor has he in his subsequent writings. (And to my surprise, his reviewers have not noted it either.) Chapters 8 and 9 go on to describe some ways of mitigating transaction costs in the firm, but quite inconclusively. There are no additional chapters that describe ways of mitigating the transaction costs of *markets*. Instead the remaining chapters go on to other matters as if the crucial Chapter 7, which was first published in 1973 but fortunately included in the 1975 volume, had not existed.

What do we find in Chapter 7? Virtually all the advantages of hierarchy for reducing transaction costs and opportunism are repealed. Within organizations fixed costs for internal procurement may be "easily" overstated; "fundamentally nonviable internal capability may be uncritically preserved"; managers are "notably reluctant to abolish their own jobs"; group subgoals "are easily given greater weight in relation to objective profitability considerations" (p. 119); cheating, or "exceptions from a system's rationality procurement standards," and logrolling are much easier than in market transactions, and system damaging reciprocities "are simply more extensive internally (I buy from your division, you support my project proposal or job promotion, and so forth) than in the market"—note that here we explicitly find that one of the key elements of transaction costs, group optimization and opportunism, is worse in the firm than in the market.

Fiat, acclaimed heretofore as the dispute settler par excellence, is "efficient for reconciling instrumental differences," that is, presumably telling workers where to get off. But, he continues, fiat "is poorly suited for mediating disputes that have internal power consequences." But presumably this would include all management disputes, and indeed all union-management disputes as well. Instead of fiat we get "compromise," which is close to a market mechanism for the crucial conflicts within the firm. Furthermore, "internal organization," that is, hierarchy, "specifically favors the extension of the compliance machinery," which of course is not a cost-free frictionless device at all, and "the firm might consciously resist the internalizing of incremental transactions for this reason as well." But we have been told, in the paper in this volume and in many others (and in the preceeding six chapters of the Williamson book), that it is the costs of compliance in market transactions that are so high, and here we find the costs may be higher within hierarchies.

This covers just two pages of this remarkable 14-page chapter. But let me go on. The next page reveals that the appearance of hierarchy is attended by sunk costs, information impactedness, unreasonable costs of distinguishing faulty from meritorious performance, partisan appeals from internal subgroups, and the lack of market discipline! On the next page we find that contracts within the firm lack tough-minded and calculative assessments, in contrast to contracts in the market. Furthermore, one of the inevitable developments of market relations that in turn leads people to turn to hierarchy, small numbers bargaining, appears within firms too. On the next page we find again that distortion and opportunism are particularly important in hierarchical relations (p. 123). And here Williamson comes close to saying that integrated firms are less adaptable to changing environments than specialized ones, which contradicts his general thesis. This reminds one of the curious dilemma that he makes for himself earlier, where he would forego the advantages of long-range planning provided by market contracts in favor of allowing events to simply unfold, a surprising virtue of the hierarchy (pp. 9, 25). Elsewhere it is hierarchy that allows long-term planning (e.g., p. 10). Long-term contracts bind the firm and raise transactions costs, he says, but he generally neglects the possibility that they actually allow long-term planning, rational investments, promote market stability, and so on.

Internal opportunism is elaborated on the next page, where we find: "Indeed, the typical internal transaction is really a small-numbers exchange relation writ large," which should make it considerably more serious than those faced in the market (p. 124). The next page tells us that performance assessment is only potentially better in the firm than in the market, and the potential is lost as the firm grows more complex, which it can only do by integrating functions and adding hierarchy. Complexity also limits its power to do internal auditing—and of course increases its need for it (p. 125).

Moving on, we learn that it is all even worse, for in contrast to the market, the costs of opportunism will not show up immediately, but will be delayed and lie hidden (p. 126).

A number of points are mentioned about the disadvantages of large size and complexity that are quite familiar to all of us—impersonality, narrow calculative commitment, lack of stockholder control, rip-off mentality, sabotage, alienation, and so on (pp. 127–129). There are even problems with the promotion ladder, a resource supposedly unavailable in market contracting (p. 129), and serious problems with wage distortions in large firms (p. 130). He says in a footnote that the discussion does not pretend to be exhaustive, but it is extensive enough to have undercut and in places even reversed all the previous arguments for the superior efficiency of hierarchy when we have recurring transactions, uncertainty, and specialized needs.

The next chapter attempts to argue that some of these problems would be mitigated in the M (multidivisional) form of firm. Perhaps, but his examples are not that persuasive to me. In one long example, he says the external capital market cannot get the information about choices of investment decisions that bosses of firms can get from their own divisions.

Internally generated capital, though limited, can be placed where the promise is the greatest and doled out in increments with full disclosure of information from the part receiving it. It is trading breadth for depth (p. 148). But he is comparing the market's ability to assess a multidivisional firm, which is correctly seen as very limited, with management's ability. Obviously management will know more than the market about its divisions. The true comparison is the market's ability to assess the capital needs of *several* nonintegrated firms versus management's ability to assess the needs of several of its own divisions. Here the superiority of the M form is quite unclear, because the market may be much more efficient in assessing several moderate-sized firms than in assessing two giant ones in which vertical integration has already taken place.

In fact, one of the criticisms of multidivisional firms is that their divisions are not subject to the so-called discipline of the marketplace, and they should be; management, while having internal information, may lack comparative information and tends to be too concerned with sunk costs, preoccupied with growth, and so on. Furthermore, the cost of information may be as high internally as in the market, where price signaling, profit statements, and prospectuses are efficient and cheap. This is the real implication of his example of Ford and the spark plugs: The market quickly told Ford what its own internal analysis could not determine (p. 93). Thus, contrary to Williamson's position, my position would be that when there are several firms competing in the capital market, investors can distribute their capital better and more efficiently than when they are confronted with two giant firms that have absorbed the several small ones. This is but one example of the way in which the material from Chapter 7 can be used to question the conclusions of the other chapters.

Another problem with the logic and consistency of the argument is the failure to define transaction costs. He says that this was Coase's problem—a lack of operational utility—and it made Coase's argument circular. But Williamson has a similar problem: Any competing analysis can be reinterpreted by saying that X or Y is really a transaction cost. He moves from quite plausible examples such as negotiating contracts, hiring lawyers, checking on delivery dates and quality, and other terms of specific contracts, to much more general and sweeping references such as the coordination and integration of the flow of goods and services. The latter examples might be seen as a transaction, in that goods move from one station to another, and every time they do a "transaction" has taken place if only to the extent that a worker has noticed it. But if we include such a wide variety of activities under the term "transactions," there is nothing distinctive about Williamson's assertions; everything has its costs, and if you wish to label a great many of these as transactions, then transaction costs will certainly predominate. For a theory that makes such a claim to distinctiveness, the failure to define the key term is both surprising and annoying.

Soon I will criticize Alfred Chandler along with Williamson, since they share a basic perspective, but at this point let me note the superiority of Chandler's analysis in this respect. Chandler is quite careful to distinguish transaction costs from other costs, or to distinguish transactions from other activities, principally coordination (Chandler, 1977: 7). In a paragraph in which he is laying out his basic propositions, he explicitly notes that improved coordination was far more important than reduced transaction costs in the history of industrialization. Unless Williamson broadens his notion of transaction costs to include coordination, Chandler and Williamson are in considerable disagreement. If he does broaden it, he loses the support that discussions of opportunism and bounded rationality give him, since these do not apply well to coordination but only to transactions.

Chandler distinguishes three elements: transactions between units which carry a cost; information costs on markets and sources of supply; and the coordination of the flow of goods from one unit to another, which he says is "of much greater significance" than the other two. Savings in coordination, he notes in another passage, "were much greater than those resulting from lower information and transaction costs" (Chandler, 1977: 7). For Chandler, the superiority of the M (multidivisional) form over the U (unitary) form of organization rests in administrative coordination, or what Max Weber more accurately described as "imperative coordination." This is true for Williamson also, in the end, but it is not consistent with a claim that a "distinctive worldview" is being offered (Williamson, 1975: xii) in that the "transaction is the ultimate unit of microeconomic analysis" (p. xi).

So far I have dealt with the logic and consistency of the argument. I conclude that the elements of his market failures approach—principally transaction costs and opportunism—are at least as significant and sometimes more significant in hierarchical firms of modest or larger size as they are in markets composed of modest-sized firms. This may even be true of the less appropriate comparison of markets and firms, where the firms are very large and the markets thereby incapacitated. This conclusion is based upon assertions and citations provided by Williamson himself, and I could add generously to these assertions and citations to make the case even stronger. Finally, the lack of definition of the key concept, transactions, and its occasional tendency to embrace other aspects of organization that are normally treated separately, reduces the distinctiveness of the theory.

Empirical Evidence— Williamson

But this is not my main criticism of the perspective. That there has been a shift from markets to hierarchies cannot be denied, and it is an extremely important development. My central criticism is that both

Williamson and Chandler offer incorrect explanations for the shift. To illustrate though hardly demonstrate my point, I will discuss one contemporary and several historical examples. The contemporary illustration concerns changes in the popular music industry since the appearance of long-playing records and cheap radios, particularly FM. I have analyzed it in detail elsewhere (Perrow, 1979: 206–215), drawing extensively upon the work of Paul Hirsch, Richard Peterson, and David Berger, so I will be brief here. To summarize first, I argue that initially hierarchy and vertical integration were designed to obtain market control and oligopolistic advantages, rather than the advantages of efficiency. Once you have these goodies, you can realize certain kinds of efficiencies, though others are foregone. Then hierarchy and vertical integration were rendered inefficient by technological changes, which disrupted market hegemony. A less hierarchical form was quickly adapted, because it had other efficiencies. Gradually, however, the dominant firms have moved back to a more oligopolistic position, because control, rather than efficiency, is the key issue. With growing control, they can afford to revert to vertical integration, and vertical integration limits entry and increases market control. Here is the case:

From Tin Pan Alley days until the 1950s the market was dominated by four giants who gradually gained control, on the basis of long-term contracts, of the artists (song writers, singers, bands), the key marketing vehicles (movie studios, record stores, radio programs), the producers, and the manufacturing process. Presumably large economies of scale were available and, by Williamson's reasoning, few transaction costs and little opportunism. The industry was profitable and growing at a respectable rate. What it did not recognize was a demand for more varied forms of music; this might have increased sales. The industry learned of this demand when four technological changes took place: the appearance of TV, which made radio stations very cheap, since it took away their advertising revenues; the appearance of FM, which increased the number of (cheap) stations; cheap transistor radios; and long-playing records. The majors, with their vertical integration and multidivisions, could not capitalize on the changes. They were bound by long-term employment contracts and sunk costs in production, manufacturing, and distribution. Entry costs were suddenly lowered. New firms appeared and experimented with new types of music that had always been performed in local areas but never recorded by the giants. Transaction costs for the small firms were apparently minimal; artists prepared their own productions and brought them to the small firms daily. Contracts were short-term and negotiated on the spot. Sunk costs were minimal as recording studios, stamping plants, and marketing groups sprang up, all ready to service a large number of record companies. A vast new market opened up, and a very variegated one. Hits no longer hung on for months but only for weeks, though they sold many more copies than had been true of the Doris Day, Frank Sinatra types marketed through Makebelieve Ballroom and movie musicals. The market dominance of the big four plummeted and disappeared, even though the expanded market meant that they too increased their sales and profits. The majors then dropped their vertical integration and copied the upstart firms by utilizing weekly contracts for producers and single-item contracts for artists, and by contracting out for studios and stamping plants and promotion. It was cheaper, more efficient and more profitable (though Williamson would presumably be aghast at the number of spot contracts negotiated). The risks were externalized to groups in the market rather than internalized and thus were spread around. But so were the opportunities. Sales, groups, hits, labels, and profits skyrocketed, as did the number of radio stations.

Why was not everyone happy with this profitable state of affairs? My guess is that it had nothing to do with the supposed inefficiencies of the market form of organizing economic activity, but a great deal to do with the insecurity that the new competition brought about and the sizeable profits that small and moderate sized firms were making. The giants feared they would lose their dominant positions, and thus their opportunity to participate at least proportionally in the rising volume of business and the rising rates of profits. In addition, they probably wanted to participate disproportionally—they coveted the profits of their small neighbors. Transaction costs would be trivial in the face of these matters.

In any event, here is what they did—though one of the majors ended up as a minor, and a small upstart firm emerged as a major. First, they increased their transaction costs by substituting expensive, risky, complicated long-term contracts with a few groups for the short, simple, low-risk spot contracts with many groups. To protect this investment they had to intervene in the market and forego the almost costless device of letting listeners decide which contracts made money and should be renewed, and for how long, and instead take the expensive and dangerous route of bribing the disc jockeys and others with money and then drugs to make sure that the few groups they had chosen received air time. Reportedly, they entered into sub rosa contracts with organized crime to this effect. Their smaller competitors had to match this effort, further distorting the market and increasing the cost of entry. When this was not enough for the majors, they had to go to the cost of buying up whole radio stations. While stations are profitable, they are not nearly as profitable as the production and sale of records. Then the majors moved into buying up retail outlets, again restricting the selection of records. In all this, they were attempting to restore the hegemony that existed prior to 1955. I think all these expensive, "inefficient" efforts might fairly be billed as transaction costs, because the service received was selective exposure of their product.

The consequences for the industry are worth noting. While too much has changed for the industry to return to the happy pre-1955 days of 80 percent four-firm concentration ratios, the concentration ratio is approaching that level; cost of entry has increased; the price of records has increased beyond the raw materials price, I suspect; sales rate of growth has declined: and the variety being offered the consumer is being restricted. I expect that innovations such as digital recording are now more difficult because of the large sunk costs to be protected; I also expect that linkage with organized crime will grow. Offhand, it is hard to see the superiority of hierarchy over markets in this case, unless market control and concentration of profits is the criterion.

But is the case merely an exception? Williamson would probably say that it is. In Chapters 11 and 12 of his book he discusses undesirable distortions due to oligopoly, but he plainly considers them to be few in number; oligopoly itself is seen as an efficient and desirable form of organization, as is the conglomerate firm, though there might be some abuses. In contrast, I would consider the socially unredeeming aspects of oligopoly to be extensive and the motives assigned in the music case to be the typical ones. The only way in which this case might be considered an exception is that we rarely find examples of rapid and significant environmental changes that dislodge oligopolistic control; furthermore, after these environmental changes we are able to see oligopoly slowly and deliberately being reestablished.

Chandler's Argument

The music case might also be read as a significant exception to Chandler's position. Chandler argues that the visible hand replaces the invisible one when the technology is capital intensive and the market is not fragmented. This technology was certainly capital intensive, but changes in it fragmented the market. The visible hand, or what Chandler calls administrative coordination, was not a result of market concentration but was rather a means to bring about market concentration. The visible hands are eliminating market "fragmentation." (I prefer the word "diversity.") The difference is important; we should not interpret the effect as the cause. I think that Chandler tends to do this, and I will now examine some examples from the nineteenth century. But first, let's set the stage.

Chandler's book is remarkable in that he can intentionally treat the history of industrialization in the United States without dealing with the labor force or the impact of business upon "existing political and social arrangements" (Chandler, 1978: 6). This may not be Hamlet without the Prince, but it certainly excludes Rosenkrantz and Guildenstern and the rest of the citizens of Denmark. He downplays profits, preferring to speak of efficiencies. Technological innovations are treated with detail and awe, and an almost worshipful tone pervades the endless citations of increases in production. But working conditions are ignored entirely. The notion of externalities, or social costs, was widespread in the nineteenth century, but it has disappeared here. Within these limits, it is a brilliant achievement, but the limits are very grave.

Chandler argues that vertical integration was possible where the technology was capital intensive, and where markets were not fragmented. Where these two conditions obtained, vertical integration was adopted because of the efficiency that it offered, primarily in the area of coordination.

Several issues are raised by the logic of this argument. The first is the familiar but important one of "efficiency for whom." Chandler gives two answers: efficiency for the firm, which means for the capitalists, and efficiency for society in terms of the volume, variety, and low price of goods. As noted, he does not deal with the social costs or externalities involved. What is good for the capitalist is assumed to be good for the worker, the local community, and the nation. Consumption per se is the other measure of efficiency. Alternative methods of production, alternative returns to labor, internalizing social costs into the prices, and so on are not dealt with.

The second issue is the inevitability of the process, the logic of industrialization, which meant that steel firms had to integrate backwards into coal and ore and refineries into marketing. But the process was fairly disorderly. Vertical integration did not take place in all cases where his explanation—capital intensity and fragmented markets—predicted that it would, nor has it in the period from 1920 on. For example, automobile firms still do a great deal of contracting out, and since Ford and GM contract out for quite different things, the decision hardly seems to be governed by transaction, information, or coordinating costs. Chandler's logic suggests they would also own the two biggest rental car agencies, but they don't. In addition, why is there not a Boeing Air Line or a TWA bomber? Why are there can companies, when either canners or food chains could easily integrate forward or backward into can production? And so on.

I suspect that a different explanation for the pattern of vertical integration would run something like this: Firms moved into areas to which their information and contacts led them. That is, up through the first third of this century, they went into related products or related stages of production. Steel firms did not acquire flour mills or telegraph companies, because they did not have much to do with them. (Having investment capital and seeking the diversification allowed by a far more mature industrial economy would be the explanation, after the 1930s, for unrelated acquisitions.) But steel did learn about ore mining, coal companies, railroads, and heavy machinery.

To move into an adjacent area, the acquiring firm had to have capital, or access to it, and this generally meant it had to be quite profitable, though political advantages could substitute for capital. If it is profitable it integrates backward or forward for at least three reasons. First, a firm might find an adjacent area to be highly profitable, but composed of small firms that could not match the capital of the acquiring firm. Second, they might see that the firms could be made profitable, because the acquiring firm could rig the market. In neither of these cases can any efficiencies cited by Williamson and Chandler be demonstrated. Third, acquiring related firms or setting up their own divisions might bring labor problems under control. For example, it could promote more capital-intensive production to reduce labor's power; it could tap a docile or cheap source of labor that is traditionally tied to the adjacent sector but not to its own; it could tap a source that is geographically different and is more docile or cheap. These labor-related reasons for vertical integration might seem to speak of efficiencies, since a dependent, dominated labor force is presumably more efficiently exploited, but these are not the efficiencies Williamson and Chandler would like us to have in mind.

I feel that these reasons for vertical integration are more powerful than reducing coordination or transaction costs. This source of efficiency could well come with the integration, but is likely to be a quite secondary inducement, perhaps one not even contemplated. The explanations I have offered deal with power, or control, not the efficiencies cited by Williamson and Chandler. And these probably provide the best explanation for the failure of some firms to acquire others or build competing units. The target firm or the groups of producers is itself too powerful to be taken over or invaded. Thus, while steel firms moved into ore and coal, at least one of them tried to integrate even further into railroads, was blocked, and had to settle for some limited lines. It also moved forward into fabricating rolling stock, but got out when the business was not profitable. I do not know why they did not move into heavy machinery, but it would be worth exploring from this point of view.

The third issue raised is whether capitalists were sufficiently aware of the potential efficiencies of vertical integration or sufficiently impressed by them so as to constitute a substantial motivating factor. To explore this, let us also include acquiring identical facilities rather than just those of suppliers or distributors, that is, buying a competitive steel mill rather than just a coal company. Awareness is a difficult problem since the available data rarely speaks to this. In addition, a statement such as "I gained a monopoly position or joined the oligopoly in this market because I wanted to avoid transaction and coordinating costs, not because I wanted even higher profits or secure control over the market" is likely to be what Williamson calls "self-disbelieving."

We can only impute motives (perhaps I impugn them), and the case will have to rest on circumstantial evidence and basic presuppositions. Motives may be less a problem with Williamson's work, since he is quite willing to discuss "opportunism"—self-interest seeking with possible guile. But when I attribute to owners and managers the motives of gaining control over the market and over employees regardless of the social costs and even the production efficiencies, I have something more vigorous in mind than Williamson's opportunism. This is not the place for a full statement of the argument, but a few paragraphs will indicate what I mean by control and social cost allocation and how it differs from opportunism and mere profits.

Self-interest with guile is certainly present in economic activity, and the economic system of industrialized nations, East and West, presumably encourages it in all participants. Opportunism may be less marked among those with few opportunities and few resources to use as guileful leverage, and it may be more developed among those with many opportunities and resources. But even if that is true (the greedy capitalist viewpoint), it is not the point. The point is to understand how, in the nineteenth century, a social system could be created that had unprecedented abundance but managed to spread it so niggardly and wastefully, and how in the twentieth century this system could be continually reproduced. It is not greed nor guile nor profits that is at issue, but the concentration of wealth and power.

Market control means greater profits, to be sure. But more is at stake. It also means the power to reproduce the system. Using hierarchies, new entrants to the economic elite can be screened to ensure proper values. Market control means more security for elites. It provides prestigious employment for relatives and members of one's social set. It facilitates access to government and thus influences all social policies. It tolerates waste.

Control over labor also contributes to profits immensely, but again more is at stake. It stabilizes the system, making dissent more difficult and socialization into supporting values easier. It works against changes in the social structure and against changes in forms of social control. It promotes legitimization of the system by making alternatives seem impossible or inconceivable. As sociologists say, control over labor maintains the class structure of power, regardless of what happens to the structure of income or the occupational structure. Finally, both market control and employee control allow social costs to be externalized, in part because the vast majority of employees are dependent solely upon wages for survival.

Thus a major indicator of power and control is indeed profits, but it is not the only one. More important, the best single indicator is profits garnered at the expense of employees and the community. (Obviously it is not an easy indicator to derive, but it hardly follows that it would be a meaningless one.)

In a so-called socialist system, such as Russia or the communist countries of Eastern Europe, we must substitute for profits the preferments that profits could buy in a capitalist society (including enterprise growth) but which are awarded by the state instead. No claim is made that these systems are all that different. Both rely upon wage-dependent labor. In both, the form of employee control and externalization of social costs developed first in the industrial bureaucracies, then spread rapidly to all organizational sectors of society. This form of bureaucracy, based upon widespread wage dependency and legitimated by some rise in living standards for all, was superior to all previous forms of social control.

Thus self-seeking with guile is an organizational and market problem, of course, but hardly commensurate with control over markets, employees, and the allocation of social costs. Further, high profits with indications of large income disparities and indications of social costs is an important measure of this control. It is this, and not narrow efficiencies in production or distribution, that I suggest lay behind the shift from markets to hierarchies, or the emergence of the visible hand.

Empirical Evidence—Chandler

One of the most famous cases of vertical integration in the nineteenth century concerned the growth of the Carnegie Steel Corporation as it moved into transportation, coal, coke, and iron ore. How did it happen? Andrew Carnegie was known as a fanatic on cost cutting, at least in the areas of production, and this may have motivated him to integrate vertically. However, his associate, James Howard Bridges, gives a quite different account, explicitly stating, as if he were reviewing Williamson and Chandler in 1903, that "it was other considerations than increased efficiency and economy that promoted the first and perfect combination of the Carnegie properties" (Bridges, 1903: 135; see also page 168 where he says there was no plan to the acquisitions). The other considerations are interesting. Bridges emphasizes and details coveting the profits of another corporation, maneuvering to get rid of an officer, and accidental events and happenstances, all of which led to acquisitions. Like most observers of that time, he holds that there is a natural evolutionary law that eventually guides it all. (He is an apologist for capitalism and quite antilabor, and the evolutionary theory of the time was used in this fashion.) But it is clear from his detailed account that economy and efficiency were consequences rather than prime movers. When Carnegie found out how much the Pennsylvania railroad was grossing, he decided to build his own to Philadelphia, and we still drive through tunnels on the Pennsylvania Turnpike that were started by Carnegie. The railroad then gave him reduced rates. When a competing, nearby plant turned out to be astoundingly profitable and well laid out, he got the railroad pool to cut it out of the good business until he was able to buy it at distressed prices. He was paying dividends of about 40 percent at the time, so he probably would have bought it at high prices if he had to. Why should we impose a logic of history driven by the efficiency of hierarchical coordination upon this particular chapter in domestic imperialism? Buying and building profitable enterprises meant increased control, and this increased profits—they were fantastical at the end for Carnegie. It had little to do with a bookkeeper's mentality.

I think that integration forward into marketing in a number of other industries may well have had similar motives and dynamics. Williamson devotes considerable space to this, quoting Chandler directly, so let us examine the argument. According to Chandler, those firms that developed high volume mass production as a result of technological changes found that they could not market these goods sufficiently "because existing marketers were unable to sell and distribute products in the volume they were produced. . . . Once the inadequacies of existing marketers became clear, manufacturers integrated forward into marketing" (p. 287).

Two types of mass producers integrated vertically to the market, but for one type Chandler's thesis is hardly needed, because there were no existing marketers to fail—that is, these were new, complex, high-priced, specialized machines that required after-sale contracts for instruction and maintenance by the producer, or they were producers of goods shipped by the new refrigeration techniques. The other type is the one Williamson emphasizes; it seems to fit Chandler's argument—low cost, high-volume consumer nondurables. But when we look closely at Chandler's discussion of these, not a single example provides unambiguous support for his argument, and most absolutely contradict it in at least one respect.

James Duke did not find marketers "unreliable" when he set up his national advertising and sales organization; in fact, he had not yet shifted to high volume production of cigarettes. He integrated forward before he put in the machines to produce the product he was already prepared to absorb. Why? Because he knew that with increasing returns to scale and a very elastic demand curve, the profits would come through distribution and volume sales, not production. This is hardly a case for transaction costs, à la Williamson, or the failure of marketers, à la Chandler. In the case of the match industry, Chandler presents no evidence of the inadequacies of existing marketers; instead, when production was concentrated in one giant plant, a sales organization had *already* been built by the monopoly (p. 293). In the case of flour mills, the new continuous process methods of production had *little* effect upon the market for flour; millers still sold in bulk to wholesalers, thus contravening the thesis. Chandler says that the thesis is supported in the case of oatmeal, however, because one of the giants packaged and advertised a branded breakfast cereal, Quaker Oats, and set up a sales office to work with jobbers. But this hardly supports the argument, because what we have is an entirely new product—as Chandler says, "a product that was even newer to American tastes than the cigarette," so there could hardly be sleepy marketers standing in the way, for Chandler, or large transaction costs for Williamson. Eventually the flour companies moved towards vertical integration, not because of the new output—that happened a decade before—but because demand for roller mill flour leveled off and prices fell.

The problem then was to provide brand identification so that people would want Gold Medal or Pillsbury rather than just any flour. So the firms spent a lot of money on the nonproduction activity of promoting brand identification and creating selling and buying networks. But this was a new activity that had nothing to do with the argument that "existing marketers were unable to sell and distribute products in the volume they were produced" (p. 287); quite the contrary—the existing outlets sold all brands of flour, whereas the emerging giants wanted only their flour sold. It was a socially wasteful expenditure. The examples of canned soups, meats, and condensed milk also provide no evidence for Chandler's thesis, and crucial detail regarding Ivory soap is lacking in the account. Chandler's next example is the Kodak camera with film, but here Eastman created a worldwide marketing network as he was creating his revolutionary new product—no support here.

What these cases have in common is neither a concern with transaction costs nor inefficient marketers. (Indeed why should Chandler believe that wholesalers, distributors, and retailers were systematically possessed of less acumen than producers and would thus fail to seize the chance to make all this money?) Instead, as Chandler notes in passing, they had pioneered low-cost, high-volume production techniques and depended upon stimulating demand rather than efficiency. Demand was inelastic, because the price was too low to increase demand by lowering prices; profits were enormous from the start, so entrepreneurs did not have to go to the capital market and could thus hold close control of the firms. These conditions yielded a classic first-entry advantage, and except for flour, immediate oligopolistic positions that continue to the present. All these swamp the marketing and transaction costs analysts and relegate internal efficiencies to a minor role. These firms used their economic power to stamp out competition or form trusts, buy up or control suppliers, and create new consumer wants by bypassing the market. I suspect, though I have not examined these industries individually, that this achievement also gave them more than normal power over their work force, as it did conspicuously in the case of Carnegie. Recall that after integrating forward and backward, he was in a position to break the union, lower the wages, maintain a 12-hour day, seven-day week for much of the work force and reap extravagant profits. These were some of the socially unredeeming aspects of hierarchy, until unions were allowed to survive and legislation took off some of what Williamson calls the "rough edges of hierarchy."

Normative Presupposition

This brings me to my last point. Recall that I have challenged the consistency of Williamson's argument, saying that the costs of bounded rationality and opportunism are present within as well as between firms;

thus his argument is not distinctive and does not explain the appearance of hierarchy. I challenged the empirical evidence for his and Chandler's position (noting in passing that as to the cause of hierarchy and integration, Williamson and Chandler disagree on the particulars). I suggested that the reasons for hierarchy and integration may have much less to do with efficiency than with the quite different matter of profits and economic power in an increasingly disabled market. Let me insert that I follow Polanyi (1957) in believing that markets are not natural to human society, that so-called free markets have never really existed, that there have been historically better ways of organizing economic activity, and that markets were largely rigged in the nineteenth century. So I would not necessarily favor market transactions; it is just that they appear to be better for people than hierarchical transactions.

There are at least three ways of organizing economic activity—through communal efforts with norms of other-regarding behavior; through markets, where there is more concern with opportunism; and through hierarchies, which are predicated upon the fear of autonomy. Markets substitute bargaining and negotiations for cooperative effort, survey the outputs, and adjust the next contract accordingly. But hierarchies substitute commands, surveillance of behavior, multiple control devices, and authority for bargaining and negotiation. Obey, don't bargain, they say. For Williamson—and Chandler too, I suspect, though he is less explicit in this regard—it is quite obvious that settling disputes through fiat is better than through negotiations and bargaining. If I am the one to be commanded, controlled, or "fiated," I would prefer bargaining and negotiations, written guarantees, legal statements of rights and obligations, and in general the ability to act as an autonomous agent, no matter what the transaction costs. I doubt that I am alone in this preference. Since hierarchy necessarily gives power to the few, I think the many would agree.

The novelist E. M. Forster gave only two cheers for democracy, a special case of the market we might say. He reserved three for love, the beloved republic, the closest to a community. I agree, and while I have no cheers for chaos, I have but one for hierarchies.

REFERENCES

Bridges, J. H. (1903). *The Inside History of the Carnegie Steel Company,* New York: Aldine.

Chandler, A. D. (1978). *The Visible Hand,* Cambridge, MA: Harvard University Press.

Perrow, C. (1979). *Complex Organizations: A Critical Essay,* 2nd ed., Glenview, IL: Scott, Foresman.

Polanyi, K. (1957). *The Great Transformation,* Boston: Beacon Press.

Williamson, O. (1975). *Markets and Hierarchies,* New York: The Free Press.

A REJOINDER

OLIVER E. WILLIAMSON
and
WILLIAM G. OUCHI

Charles Perrow's comment on our paper is curious in several respects. For one thing, although the paper was sent to him well in advance of the publication deadline, he never specifically refers to it. Instead he focuses principally on *Markets and Hierarchies* and aspects of Alfred Chandler's important work. Evidently he had numerous "crabbed and crabby" marginal notes that he wanted to salvage. Whether that is a worthwhile enterprise is for others to judge.

Second, Perrow discloses an incapacity to contemplate trade-offs. Evidently, he would prefer that the issue be put markets *or* hierarchies. That the two should coexist is the source of considerable strain.

Third, we discover that Perrow is a romantic: He tells us that both markets and hierarchies should be supplanted by "communal efforts with norms of other-regarding behavior." We also like cooperative modes of organization. But we further recognize that peer groups have severe limits (of a transaction cost kind), and we have a deep respect for the lessons of history on the limited viability of utopian societies and producer cooperatives.

So much for an overview. Consider a few specifics:

1.   Perrow makes much of the fact that Williamson identifies a number of limitations to internal organization in Chapter 7 of *Markets and Hierarchies*. He further contends that these limits of internal organization are fatal: If internal organization is subject to these disabilities, markets must be better.

This is incorrect. The limitations of internal organization explain why only *some but not all* transactions are shifted out of markets and organized internally. The predictive power of the analysis is that we are able to identify those transactions for which markets have greatest difficulty, as compared with internal organization, and those where markets work comparatively well. Had Perrow read the paper published in this volume, he might have understood this better.

2.   Perrow complains that transaction costs are not defined. This is correct and partially an oversight. Numerous examples of transaction costs are offered, however. For the most part, production costs are recognized in the same way—by illustration rather than by definition.

In any case, costs can be split into two basic groups: production costs and transaction costs. In a very general way, transaction costs are the costs of running the economic system. If one adopts the fiction that in the beginning there were markets, then transaction costs will be recognized as frictions that impede and in particular cases block the formation of markets. If instead one begins with the view that in the beginning there was central planning, transactions costs will be recognized as the frictions that impede and otherwise cause bureaucratic organization to malfunction.

More generally, the analysis of transaction costs focuses attention on *alternative means of contracting*. A preoccupation with technology and steady-state production expenses gives way to the study of the *comparative costs of planning, adapting, and monitoring task completion.*

Given the prominence attached to uncertainty, so that comprehensive contracting is infeasible and sequential adaptation needs arise, it is difficult to understand Perrow's failure to recognize that coordination is an important transaction cost issue. Even if time were a free good, which it is not, coordination problems necessarily arise.

Sometimes the requisite coordination can be effected through spot markets; in other circumstances alternative governance structures are favored. The key task is to (1) identify the relevant dimensions for describing transactions, (2) identify alternative governance structures and the relative strengths of each, and (3) match governance structures to transactions in a discriminating way. Our paper does precisely this, though we concede that considerable work remains before this job is completed.

Others who recognize this as central to the study of organizations and would like to participate are invited to join us. We caution, however, that transaction costs and economizing are central to such an enterprise. Unless others acknowledge this and furthermore understand transaction cost economizing, such participation may be difficult.

3.   Perrow will evidently decline the invitation because he believes that vertical integration, conglomerate organization, and other manifestations of large size are explained by power. If a firm uses steel, make it. If a firm buys paper clips, make them. If a firm uses paper, buy a forest and start a pulp mill. By contrast, the transaction cost approach distinguishes between those transactions that require considerable transaction-specific investment and those where such investments are negligible. The former are candidates for vertical integration; the latter are not.

The problem with the power approach is that vertical integration knows no limits. In the quest for power, integrate everything. This is of course a refutable implication. It is furthermore an implication that is contradicted by the data.

Selective rather than comprehensive vertical integration is predicted by the transaction cost approach. To be sure, this does not rule out the possibility that there will be mistakes. Not all business executives, Andrew Carnegie included, accurately perceive their business opportunities and faultlessly respond. Over time, however, those integration moves that have better rationality properties (in transaction cost and scale economy terms) tend to have better survival properties. The transaction cost approach permits these to be identified in advance. Numerous refutable implications thus are derived, whereas, to repeat, only one refuted implication arises from Perrow's reliance on power.

4. Trade-offs are part of the economist's stock in trade. As noted earlier, Perrow appears to be reluctant to concede trade-offs, but insists instead that pure solutions, as a pure heart, are the answer. His refusal to confront trade-offs results in repeated error in his commentary:

1. His contention that "the crucial Chapter 7" undercuts the argument reflects his misconception that the problem of organization is usefully addressed as market *or* hierarchies *or* peer groups. The fact is that each mode has its distinctive strengths *and* weaknesses, and these need to be matched to transactions in a discriminating way.

2. Perrow observes that if integrated firms are less adaptable to changing environments than are specialized firms, then the general thesis is contradicted. He appears not to recognize that there are intertemporal trade-offs. Vertical integration may have some very attractive features at one point in time, for example, early in an industry's history, but these may be offset by later disabilities. The transaction cost analysis discloses the circumstances under which immediate advantages may arise and also addresses later life cycle hazards. An atemporal analysis would recognize only one class of costs, which may seem to simplify matters. But while simplicity is a virtue, relevance must also be taken into account. The readiness with which Perrow would sacrifice relevance for simplicity discloses an implicit trade-off that others should recognize and, we would counsel, should be unwilling to make.

3. Perrow seems to have difficulty with the notion that firms and capital markets can divide resource allocation functions in an efficient way. Either firms must allocate resources or markets must do it, but not both. Again Perrow's polarity preferences are showing.

4. Perrow's difficulties with oligopoly also disclose his aversion to trade-offs. The fact is, however, that natural monopoly is a condition that we can recognize and furthermore characterize in terms

of an economies versus market power trade-off. The same can be done for an industry that will support only a few firms of efficient size (natural oligopoly). Although Perrow may be prepared to sacrifice economies whenever these give rise to market power, society evidently understands that the elimination of modest market power at the expense of large cost savings is often a bad bargain.

5. To be sure, not all oligopoly outcomes should be accepted with equanimity. Some should be challenged and upset by the courts. The troublesome ones are those that arise out of strategic behavior on the part of dominant firms (or among collusive oligopolists). The issues here are also of a transaction cost kind and have been addressed elsewhere.

Conclusion

Perrow's commentary is testimony to an earlier research tradition in which transaction costs and economizing were treated haphazardly, if at all. Although we understand his reluctance to abandon an old and familiar friend, the time has nevertheless come to recognize that the sweeping version of the power theory on which he relies is bankrupt. Until a more discriminating version of the power theory emerges that does not implicitly rely on efficiency considerations, we cast our vote for efficiency analysis.

REFERENCES

Arrow, K. J. (1969). "The Organization of Economic Activity," *The Analysis and Evaluation of Public Expenditure: The PPB System,* Joint Economic Committee, 91st Congress, 1st Session.

Kanter, R. M. (1972). *Commitment and Community,* Cambridge, MA: Harvard University Press.

Manuel, F. E., and F. P. Manuel (1979). *Utopian Thought in the Western World,* Cambridge, MA: Harvard University Press.

Williamson, O. E. (1968). "Economies as an Antitrust Defense," *American Economic Review* **58:**18–36.

Williamson, O. E. (1979). "Assessing Vertical Market Restrictions," *University of Pennsylvania Law Review* **127:**953–993.

HISTORICAL DETERMINANTS OF MANAGERIAL HIERARCHIES: A RESPONSE TO PERROW

ALFRED D. CHANDLER, JR.
Harvard University

Perrow offers two major criticisms of *The Visible Hand*. The first is that I "treat the history of industrialism in the United States without dealing with the labor force or the impact of business upon 'existing political and social arrangements.' " The second criticism concerns the inadequacies of the concept of administrative coordination to account for the growth of the large enterprise through vertical integration.

As to the first, my aim was to write a history of an institution, the modern large scale multiunit business enterprise. My purpose was to analyze this one, but only one, aspect of the multifaceted history of industrialization in the United States. The basic questions on which I focused were when, where, how, and why did the large multiunit enterprise with its extensive managerial hierarchy initially come into being and continue to grow. If I was to accomplish this task in a reasonable period of time, say a period of five or six years, and to present the findings in a reasonably sized book, say 500 pages of text, the focus had to be sharp. The book therefore has little to say on financial markets, political and legislative action, demographic changes, or the laboring force and labor organizations. This is because I came to believe that these factors were less significant than changing technology and markets in providing answers to the questions with which I was concerned. I certainly hope that scholars will take up the challenge and point out why and how the changing nature of the labor force and labor organization were more significant than markets and technology in explaining why the large business enterprise came when it did and in the sectors and industries that it did. I urge them to develop data about the labor force that would help to explain why hierarchies came to dominate some (but not all) food industries and machinery, chemical and metal industries, while continuing to play an insignificant role in textiles, furniture, fabricated metals, printing and publishing, and other industries. Even more valuable would be to have a labor historian write an institutional history of American labor organizations. The changing membership, organizational structures, operating methods, and goals of the railroad brotherhoods, the Knights, the A.F. of L., the I.W.W., and the C.I.O. would provide an essential counterpart to my study of the growth of the large-scale business enterprise.

Such a comparison would add a critical dimension to the understanding of both sets of institutions. And surely a serious study of the impact of large-scale business enterprise on political and social arrangements calls for still another volume.

More relevant to the themes of this present volume is the concept of administrative coordination. I do feel that Perrow has misunderstood my use of the term, a term central to the argument developed in *The Visible Hand*. I do not argue that "the visible hand replaces the invisible one where technology is capital intensive and the market not fragmented." My position is more limited. I argue that the visible hand of the managers took over when unit costs were lowered through administrative coordination, and that this situation occurred in manufacturing when the technology of production permitted the volume output of standardized products to national and international markets. The best way, then, to respond to his critique may be to summarize briefly how I defined the concept of administrative coordination and related it to the rise of modern, multiunit business enterprise. However, I will make no attempt here to tie my views of administrative coordination to Williamson's more sweeping concept of transaction costs. As Perrow points out, my definition of transaction costs is narrow and more specific, and therefore probably quite different from Williamson's. I will focus only on administrative coordination as it is used in *The Visible Hand*.

The first of the several propositions outlined in the introduction of that book state that modern business enterprise came into being and continued to grow when units that could operate as independent business enterprises were internalized within a single enterprise.

> Such an internalization gave the enlarged enterprise many advantages by routinizing transactions between units. The costs of these transactions were lower. By linking the administration of producing units with buying and distributing units, costs for information on markets and sources of supply were reduced. Of much greater significance the internalization of many units permitted the flow of goods from one unit to another to be administratively coordinated. More effective scheduling of flows achieved a more intense use of facilities and personnel employed in the processes of production and distribution and so increased productivity and reduced costs. In addition, administrative coordination provided a more certain cash flow and more rapid payment for services rendered. The savings resulting from such coordination were greater than those resulting from lower information and transaction costs.

The key word here is *scheduling*—scheduling of both the flows through the processes of production and the payments back to the central office.

In addition, administrative coordination allowed product specifications and market services to be adjusted more quickly and more satisfactorily to customer needs; in this way steadier flows of goods were permitted and customer satisfaction increased.

Therefore administrative coordination, as it is used in *The Visible Hand,* means that schedules (including those for shipments), specifications, and services between a set of geographically separated units involved in production, distribution, transportation, and communication were determined by the decisions of administrators within a managerial hierarchy that controlled these units rather than by a negotiated transaction between operators of independent units, as was the case before the creation of such a managerial hierarchy. As the managers administratively coordinated, they also monitored, planned for, and allocated resources to the units controlled. Thus the visible hand of management replaced what Adam Smith called the invisible hand of price and market mechanism in coordinating, monitoring, and allocation; but it did so, as I argue, only in certain sectors of modern economies.

In *The Visible Hand* I trace how such coordination came, first in transportation and communication and then in distribution and production. Thus by the 1880s the traffic departments of railroads were coordinating the flow of goods across several lines from one distant city or town to another. Where there had been at least seven transshipments and transactions in moving goods overland from Philadelphia to Chicago before the building of the railroads, there was now only one. The revolution in communications was completed even earlier. By the 1870s messages could be sent almost instantaneously over Western Union's telegraph network to almost any point in the settled regions of the nation. Once the railroad and the telegraph permitted the movement of a historically unprecedented volume of goods and messages, modern mass marketers immediately appeared, who coordinated the flow of goods from the manufacturers to the retailers and then directly to the ultimate consumer. Here the coordinator was the buyer for each of the product lines carried by the wholesaler or the new mass retailers—the department stores, the mail order houses, and the chain stores. The buyers set the prices, volume, and specification of the goods in their product line and, with the assistance of the firm's traffic department, scheduled the flows from the manufacturing and processing enterprises to the single unit retailers (if they were wholesalers) or to their own counters or the mailing addresses of their customers (if they were the new mass retailers). Because these retailers reduced the number of transactions and transshipments by eliminating one set of intermediaries, they soon began to replace the wholesaler. This displacement is documented by Figure 8-3, which is based on U.S. Census data as well as on Harold Barger's findings listed on page 224 of *The Visible Hand.* The success of such administrative coordination in reducing costs and prices can also be documented by the outcries of competing Wholesalers and small retailers, whose protests soon reached state capitals and Congress. Such protests, however, were always that the prices of their competitors were too low and not too high. Even at these low prices, the profits from administrative coordination quickly made the

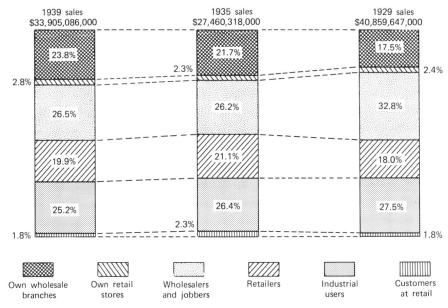

Figure 8-3 Distribution of manufacturers' sales by primary channels: 1939, 1935, and 1929 (from twentieth census of The United States: 1940, Census of Business, Vol. 5. Distribution of Manufacturers' Sales 1939, p. 5).

founders of these retailing enterprises as wealthy as any families in the land.

Shortly after the mass retailers had their start, manufacturers in some industries began to move forward into wholesaling and backwards into the purchasing of materials and so administratively coordinated the flow of goods from the producers and processors of those materials through the processes of production to the retailer. Very rarely did they move into retailing itself. My argument here, as Perrow points out, is that the initial move into distribution came when "the existing marketers were unable to sell and distribute products in the volume produced. ... Once the inadequacies of the existing marketers became clear manufacturers integrated into marketing." To assure the continuing flow of goods into the volume-producing factories and processing plants, the manufacturers also began to purchase their supplies directly from farmers, from mining and lumbering enterprises, and from other manufacturers. In those industries in which such administrative coordination of flows lowered unit costs, the large firm came to dominate the industry, which in turn became oligopolistic in its structure. Where such administrative coordination did not bring these efficiencies, small manufacturing firms continued to thrive. Their industries did not become concentrated.

Before reviewing the reasons for the initial move of manufacturers into marketing, and therefore for the creation of the first managerial hierarchies in American industry, let me emphasize that there is nothing in the logic of the argument just presented to suggest, as Perrow claims it does, that the advantages of administrative coordination would cause automobile companies to own rental car agencies, or aircraft makers to own airlines, or airlines to make bombers. In fact, the logic is exactly the reverse, for there could be little cost reduction in the scheduling of flows between these manufacturing and service industries. Indeed I would argue that in the U.S. administrative coordination and the advantages accrued from it set limits to the long-term profitable growth of the firm through vertical integration. An underlying reason why metal makers in the United States almost never moved into the manufacturing of machines and only rarely into the fabricating of complex metal products—and why the makers of machinery and even fabricated metals have rarely integrated backwards into the production of metals themselves—is that the flow of goods between units using very different processes of production were not large or steady enough to reduce unit costs through administrative coordination. As long as manufacturers were assured of continuing flows into and through the processes of production, they were under little economic pressure to make the heavy investment needed to own their own sources of supplies or markets. This is why Chrysler and General Motors refused to follow Ford's moves into the making of their own steel and glass works, a move that proved to be commercially disastrous. In those years between 1924 and World War II when the company was not running at full capacity, Ford was saddled with much higher fixed costs than its competitors.

It is for this same reason that very few manufacturing firms have moved into retailing. As Figure 8-3 indicates, in 1929 only 2.4 percent of all goods manufactured was sold through retail outlets owned by the manufacturer. The manufacturers instead preferred to rely on the much less expensive method of selling through franchise dealers. This way they coordinated the flows but were spared the cost of an expensive retailer network. For much the same reasons, the mass retailers have preferred to stay out of manufacturing. According to the same census the value of goods manufactured by the retailers themselves was only one-half of one percent of the total value of goods produced. Even the largest mass retailers, such as Sears Roebuck, rarely manufactured as much as 10 percent of the goods they sold in factories that they controlled. When they did move into manufacturing, they did so for the same defensive reasons that caused manufacturers to move backwards into the production of raw and semifinished materials. They wanted to assure a continuing flow of goods at what the manufacturer or marketer thought to be a reasonable price and quality. There were, as Perrow points out, other reasons for backward integration besides cost reduction from administrative coordination, and defensive reasons to assure a continuance of that coordination, but there is little evidence that such integration reduced costs. Where cost reductions did not occur, the properties obtained from these other reasons tended over time to be either spun off or managed as separate enterprises.

The Visible Hand further argues that the manufacturers only began to move into marketing in the 1880s and 1890s, after the filling out of the national railroad network and the perfection of operating procedures that permitted transportation of a massive daily flow of materials into and finished goods out of manufacturing establishments. Even then they appeared only in those industries in which the existing marketers were inadequate, or in some cases no longer even necessary, to sell and distribute the goods in the volume in which they could be produced. The move forward occurred in four types of industries within which manufacturers produced for national and international markets—those making packaged, branded products; those mass-producing perishable products; those making mass-produced light machinery for tens of thousands of customers; and those making standardized volume-produced machines for numerous industrial consumers.

Because this move of manufacturers into mass distribution marked the inception of managerial hierarchies in American industry, I would like to review the reasons for it in all four sets of industries in which this occurred. I will consider the three where Perrow appears to accept my arguments, saying only that "there were no existing marketers to fail," before taking up the fourth, where he challenges my analysis. Such a review is particularly important to understanding the nature of managerial hierarchies, because the large industrial enterprises in the United States have, for almost a century, continued to cluster in much the same types of industries in which they first appeared in the 1880s.

In all four sets of industries, scheduling was essential to maintain the high volume of production. Yet in all four there were other important reasons for the move into wholesaling. The scheduling of flows was of course critical to the makers of the new machines both for household and industrial markets. By the 1880s Singer was producing 10,000 sewing machines a week in each of its major factories. By 1895, two years after its formation, General Electric was processing over 100,000 orders a year. At first companies like Singer, McCormick Harvester, and the predecessors of General Electric tried to sell through independent wholesalers. They soon found that these agents were inadequate. They rarely attempted inventory control, that is, they would wait until the stocks were about to run out and then wire frantically for large replacements. They did not have the skills or facilities to provide after-sales service and repair, nor did they have the capital to issue the necessary consumer credit. Often they were slow in returning the revenues received from sales and so interrupted the cash flows that were essential to the manufacturer to pay suppliers and workers. These manufacturers therefore turned to setting up their own branch of sales networks. Except for Singer and those few firms that relied heavily on direct canvassing of customers, they did not go into retailing, depending instead on franchised dealers. The makers of volume-produced goods for industrial markets, particularly those involved in complex technologies such as the electrical manufacturers, quickly found that for the installation, servicing, and often even for the design of their products, they needed a sales force trained in electrical or mechanical engineering. In these enterprises coordination between the sales, production, and purchasing departments soon involved more than the scheduling of flows. It called for sales personnel, equipment designers, and manufacturing executives to be in constant touch to coordinate rapidly changing technology to the needs of their industrial customers. The same was soon to be true for chemical firms that were developing new and complex substances to be used in manufacturing processes. In addition, the chemical manufacturers often required specialized storage facilities and tank cars to distribute their volatile and often toxic products.

For the makers of perishable products careful scheduling was essential in the movement of large quantities of meat, bananas, and to a much lesser extent, beer. *The Visible Hand* describes the scheduling techniques developed by Armour and Swift that permitted each to butcher six to seven million animals annually and distribute their products to all parts of the nation and even to the urban centers of Europe. These high-volume flows were only possible after the creation of a nationwide network of refrigerated cars and warehouses. It was the refusal of the eastern trunk line railroads to develop, build, and after they had been built, to even carry the new refrigerated cars that forced Swift to build his distribution network and Armour and four others to quickly follow Swift's example. Until the networks were built and the railroads finally surrendered, the wholesale butcher, who was still being supplied live cattle by rail, had little incentive to invest in extensive refrigerated facilities.

In these three sets of industries the existing marketers rarely had the facilities, skills, or capital they needed to distribute the manufacturer's products in the quantity that they could be produced. In the case of the fourth type, the makers of the new packaged and branded goods, the new technology not only permitted the manufacturers to mass produce their products, but to package, can, or bottle them in units small enough to be placed directly on the retailer's shelf for sale to the final customer. Traditionally the wholesaler's task was to take bulk shipments, break them down into small lots, and distribute them to the multitude of retailers. In the years following the Civil War, wholesalers had begun to brand and to advertise the products they thus repackaged, and their salespeople began to take orders for these branded products locally and regionally. Once the new processes had eliminated the need for repackaging, the one service the wholesaler could still provide was to assist in physically distributing the goods. As *The Visible Hand* points out, this is precisely how these manufacturers continued to use wholesalers. However, as time passed many came to rely more on their own depots and warehouses when such an investment permitted a more exact scheduling of flows. Because they now did the packaging—James B. Duke considered his new packaging machines as important as the Bonsack machine itself—they also did the branding and advertising. They sent their salespeople from their branch offices directly to the retailers for orders, and their central office scheduled volume flow through the wholesaler to the retailers. Because they produced in a volume large enough to satisfy national and world markets, they advertised and had their salespeople sell on a national basis. It would have made no commercial sense for wholesale grocers—who, in addition to marketing breakfast cereals and flour, sold condiments, tea, coffee, sugar, fresh and seasonally canned fruits and vegetables, and a variety of other foodstuffs—to put the same amount of marketing effort into one of the many products they sold as the manufacturers put into the single line that they produced for the national market. Thus, when an enterprise manufactured packaged goods that could be sold directly to the retailers, the central office of the manufacturing enterprise, assisted by its traffic department, took over the function of administratively coordinating the flows from the buyers in the wholesaling enterprise.

Where high-volume production required careful scheduling of flows into the processing plant, as well as out to the retailer—and this was the case for the processors of perishable foodstuffs (e.g., Campbell, Heinz, and Borden) and cured tobacco (e.g., Duke)—the manufacturers also built large purchasing networks. Even the makers of flour, oats, biscuits, and canned meat reduced their costs by buying in volume at grain exchanges, stockyards, and from the farmers themselves. Since the farmers were able to supply their materials in the quantity needed, they almost never went into the actual production of food, and since hundreds of thousands of retailers existed, there was little incentive to buy retail outlets.

There is nothing in this argument to suggest that the intermediaries were lazy, sleepy, or had little business acumen. These words are Perrow's, not mine. To repeat, it would have made little business sense for a profit-oriented wholesaler to concentrate on marketing a single line of products when the wholesaler's work force, facilities, and own skills were involved in marketing a wide range of groceries or dry goods or apparel or hardware or furniture or druggists' products in one specific local or regional market.

These, then, are the arguments as to why large integrated enterprises with their managerial hierarchies first appeared in some industries and not in others. In those industries in which products were not mass-produced, in which careful scheduling did not greatly reduce costs by helping to assure steady use of production facilities, in which packaging and branding were not part of the production process, and in which marketing did not require specialized facilities and technical skills—there the large integrated firm appears to have no long-run special advantage. In these industries small manufacturers and intermediaries, both wholesalers and independent manufacturing agents, continued to operate. In consumer goods this was true for manufacturers and processors of a variety of foods, wines, apparel, dry goods, hardware, drugs, and furniture. In producers' goods this was true in the making of lumber products, building supplies, many fabricated metal products, and nonstandardized machine tools and instruments. In iron and steel and other metals that did not require a technically trained sales force, managerial hierarchies remained small. The Carnegie Company, the first to build a sales organization, did so in the mid-1890s. This was after specifications began to be tailored to the specific needs of a variety of customers, causing scheduling to become complicated due to orders with varied specifications being processed in the same works. *The Visible Hand* points out that the iron and steel industry in 1917 still had the largest number of nonintegrated companies of any industry in which the large firm clustered. There the independent wholesaler continued to play an effective role.

Nevertheless, integration forward by the mass producer and backward by the mass retailer increasingly squeezed out the wholesaler. As the census figures reported in Figure 8-3 indicate, the challenge to intermediary marketing producers' goods came both from manufacturers selling directly or through their own branch establishments to their industrial customers. Direct sales usually involved either specialized, made-to-order products for local and national markets, or more standardized products for local markets. Where more standardized, volume-produced goods were sold to many scattered customers in national markets, such as those in the building and construction trades and the mining industries, the manufacturers sold through either independent agents or their own branches. The decision on which to use depended on the complexity of the product and the nature of the market. In the consumer goods industries, in which the large firm had no specialized advantages or needs, the challenge came from the mass retailers. The latter not only had the advantages of eliminating one set of transactions and transshipments, but unlike the wholesaler, retailers could beam advertising directly to the final consumer who came into the store or used their catalogues. Not surprisingly, mass retailers had large advertising budgets from the start, often much larger than those of the mass manufacturers. By 1929, as Figure 8-3 indicates, the independent intermediary still handled almost a third (32.8%) of the goods that went from manufacturers to consumers. Manufacturers' branches (of which only 2.4% retailed) and retailers accounted for 37.9%, with the manufacturers and retailers each taking about half that share. All but 1.8% of the remaining 29.3% went directly from the manufacturers to industrial users. Ten years later, manufacturers' branches and retailers had increased their share to 46.5%, while the wholesalers' share had dropped to a little over a quarter (26.5%) of all goods produced.

Because the mass producers carried out more and differing activities than the mass marketers, and so developed larger and more diversified managerial hierarchies, I argue in *The Visible Hand* that they had a greater potential for growth. So they and not the mass retailers became the great transnational enterprises of today. (One of my introductory propositions was that "Once a managerial hierarchy had been formed and had successfully carried out the function of administrative coordination, the hierarchy itself became a source of permanence, power and continued growth.") In 1973 at least 402 industrial firms (in the world, not just in the United States) had over 20,000 employees. These relatively few enterprises employed a substantial working force, one that totaled 25 million persons. In 1973 close to 90 percent of these enterprises were transnational in their activities, and of those that were not, a majority were in iron, steel, and other metal-working industries. Of the 402 companies, over two-thirds were primarily involved in the production and distribution of food, chemicals, machinery, and metals. Another 23 percent were in industries with similar mass-production, mass distribution characteristics—rubber, petroleum, glass, and paper. Less than 10 percent came out of the remaining nine of the census' two-digit SIC categories—textiles, apparel, lumber, furniture, printing and publishing, leather, fabricated metals, instruments, and miscellaneous. The pattern is strikingly similar to the list given in *The Visible Hand* of the 236 largest manufacturing firms in the United States in 1917. In fact, this pattern appeared as soon as modern transportation made possible high-volume production and distribution, and it has continued relatively unchanged during the past century of rapid industrialization. An understanding of this pattern demands serious scholarly attention.

Let me conclude by agreeing with Perrow that there were many motives for vertical integration, as indeed there were for horizontal combination. The desire to control competition, the hopes of cutting off markets and supplies for competitors, the advantages of picking up profitable property, the hope to maintain or obtain a more tractable working force, the desire to manipulate securities, all played a part in the great merger movement at the turn of the century and continued to do so through the formative years of the modern, large, industrial, multiunit enterprise. But these motives for merger and acquisition were present in all types of industries. They provided incentives to integrate in textiles, lumber, furniture, leather, publishing and printing, and fabricated metals, as well as in metal-making, food, machinery, petroleum, and chemicals. Such motives do not help to explain the questions on which I have focused. They do not help to find answers to why the large managerial enterprise came when it did, where it did, and in the way it did. They are of little help in understanding why in some industries almost the first persons to try created transnational enterprises, where in others no one has yet succeeded in building huge enterprises that dominated their industry.

What the historical record does show is that, although mergers and acquisitions were carried out in a wide variety of industries for a wide variety of reasons, these combinations remained profitable and powerful over the long haul only if they rationalized the facilities acquired or merged, completed the process of integrating production with distribution, and most important of all, created an extensive managerial hierarchy to coordinate, monitor, and allocate resources to the operating units acquired or merged. Even when this course was followed, an enterprise was rarely able to dominate, to become part of an oligopoly, unless it could benefit from lower unit costs achieved through administrative coordination—that is, unless the technology of that industry permitted the volume production of standardized products for national and international markets. I believe that these and other data presented in *The Visible Hand* document the position that, in the United States, technology and market have been the basic determinants of the size of firms and of concentration in industry.

I need hardly add that technology and markets are dynamic. As they change, so do the advantages of existing administrative coordination and the industrial arrangements based on those advantages. The replacement of railroads by long-haul trucks and the coming of the supermarket greatly altered the structure of the meat-packing industry. Perrow has provided a striking example of the impact of technological change on the music, phonograph, and trades industries. Similar cases can be cited for every decade of this century. In fact, such technological and market changes account for nearly all of the turnover—except that which was the result of mergers—on the lists of the largest 200 American industrials since World War II. Nevertheless, the new firms on these lists continued to administratively coordinate production with distribution, and they appeared in the same types of industries as those firms they displaced.

Finally, I would like to stress the need to dig out empirical data if we are to understand the development and continued growth of managerial hierarchies. One cannot base broad generalizations or theoretical concepts on a few or even a hundred case studies. The cases must be placed in the context of a specific process of production and distribution involved, and they need to include those in the whole broad range of industries listed in the Census' Standard Industrial Classification. Nor can many useful generalizations be derived from statistical data unless they are disaggregated according to SIC classifications.

In addition, national as well as industrial characteristics must be understood if we are to generalize about managerial hierarchies. In all modern, technologically advanced economies the giant industrials are congregated in much the same industries. Nevertheless, the timing and the circumstances in which the firms have appeared differ sharply from one country to another. Germany had almost no large firms making consumer branded products until after World War II, but from the 1880s on the Germans were developing powerful managerial enterprises in chemicals and machinery. In Britain the majority of the large firms originally appeared and continued, for most of the twentieth century, to be in the production of branded packaged consumer foods and chemicals. Their enterprises in producers' goods long remained smaller in size and number than those in Germany and the United States. The patterns for France and Japan are different in other ways. Obviously differing resource endowments, markets, uses of technology, educational systems, and labor sources and skills play a part in bringing about these national differences. The more that is known about the similarities and differences between industries and similarities and differences between nations, the firmer the base for generalizations about the growth of large-scale enterprises and the hierarchies that manage them. If such studies of the industrial enterprise and its managers could be correlated with comparable ones on the changing labor force and labor organization, we might begin to understand the processes and the implications of the rapid industrialization that distinguishes the past century and a half from any other period of history.

POSTSCRIPT

CHARLES PERROW

Chandler's important restatement of his views makes it possible to move the argument a bit further by clarifying a large ambiguity in my own position. I have asked Chandler if he would give me the liberty of making a short reply, and he has graciously agreed to this unorthodox procedure. In brief, then, Chandler says that my view fails to account for the variations in integration found in the economy; if power were the motive, it should produce integration everywhere. He is correct; I only tentatively dealt with variations, under the plausible but hardly sufficient explanation of contacts that disclose opportunities, and resistance from powerful targets, such as the Pennsylvania Railroad in the case of Carnegie.

Let me make a more considered argument by contrasting our two views. For Chandler, the *motive* of integration is predominantly cost reduction (only occasionally is simple profitability mentioned, but we might include that too). The *means* for cost reduction are largely administrative coordination. And the *conditions* under which these means can be used are capital intensity and market fragmentation.

For *motives,* I would not consider cost reduction as significant, nor even short-run "profits," but rather maximum long-range profits, which could, for example, require foregoing some cost reduction efficiencies or even short-run profits; preservation of a privileged class position; reproduction of a disciplined and tractable labor force; and maintaining a government that is sympathetic to a number of class-related values such as uneven income distributions, tariffs, and so on. The *means* to achieve these motives would be control over markets, labor, and government (not complete control; competitors, employees, and citizens struggle against integration at times).

The *conditions* under which these means will satisfy the set of motives that produce multidivisional firms would include those cited by Chandler and some additional ones. For Chandler's capital intensity I would prefer high entry costs or other barriers to entry—a broader and more dynamic concept than capital intensity. For a fragmented market, I would substitute the conditions that make it possible to create or increase demand for branded goods·through advertising—a much more restrictive, though dynamic, concept. I would add a structural condition, legislative advantages, which can afford barriers to entry and especially enable social costs to be displaced on to employees and the community. I think we both would agree that in addition there should be the possibility of large-volume production and attendant standardization, and sufficient transportation and communication to reach a large market. When these conditions are met we are likely to get vertical integration; where they are not, it will be difficult. That the economy is being shaped to create these conditions seems apparent; both Williamson and Chandler attest to the rapid growth of the multidivisional form. It would appear that more conditions than recurring transactions, uncertainty and specialized needs (Williamson), and capital intensity and fragmented markets (Chandler) appear to be at work.

A FINAL RESPONSE

ALFRED D. CHANDLER, JR.

The postscript must beget another rejoinder, for Perrow still does not fully understand my concept of administrative coordination, a concept so central to the main arguments in *The Visible Hand.*

First, I certainly agree that long-term profit was the underlying motive for the growth of the firm. Again, as I emphasized in *The Visible Hand* and in the preceding comments, more specific motives were involved in achieving that goal. The most important motivation for forward integration was to assure a more certain outlet for the new high-volume technologies of production. Where existing intermediaries failed to provide the necessary scheduling, advertising, and market services, the manufacturers moved into distribution. Where such scheduling and services were less necessary to distribution, the manufacturers rarely integrated forward. Backward integration was more defensive. That is, it was carried out to assure a continuous supply of raw and semifinished materials into the volume-producing factories. The motives for horizontal combination were of course to control price and production. However, as the data presented in *The Visible Hand* emphasized, few mergers were successful unless their organizers shifted from a horizontal to vertical strategy and so integrated production with distribution, and unless they created a managerial hierarchy to coordinate flows and provide services. Finally, these moves rarely gave them an advantage unless they were in industries in which the techniques of production permitted high-volume throughput of relatively standardized products for national and international markets. Normally such industries have been capital intensive.

The means used to achieve size and dominance historically has been through administrative coordination carried out by managerial hierarchies, which scheduled the flows and provided the services. Indeed a basic theme of *The Visible Hand* is that *such administrative coordination has been the central engine of market power.* Reduced costs and effective marketing services are powerful competitive weapons. Not only did they provide the most certain means of driving out small competitors that were unable to achieve the volume needed to reduce costs, but they created formidable barriers to entry. New competitors had to reach a high level of output and develop comparable services before they were able to compete effectively. In addition, the low unit costs provided funds for massive advertising in consumer goods industries and for intensive research and development in producers goods industries. Such margins further permitted the payment of higher wages and more benefits to the workers, and so helped to assure a more tractable working force.

Thus in all major advanced market economies and in all periods of time since the 1880s, the large firm has clustered in those industries in which high-volume production reduced costs, and scheduling and marketing services assisted in high-volume distribution. In such labor-intensive industries as apparel, leather, lumber, furniture, publishing, and printing—even textiles and simple fabricated metals—the large firm had rarely achieved dominance. In these normally labor intensive industries, administrative coordination could not bring the lowering of costs that made possible lower prices, and could not provide the ample funds for advertising, R&D, and higher wages. So the large firm had much less advantage over the small one.

For example, after Rockefeller and his associates had formed the Standard Oil Trust in 1882 to provide the legal and administrative instruments necessary to reorganize their production facilities, they concentrated what was close to two-fifths of the world's output of refined petroleum in three refineries. Imagine the effect on unit costs if two-fifths of the world's production of shoes were placed in three factories! No amount of effective administrative coordination could have lowered unit cost.

In the consumer sectors of these labor intensive, competitive industries the mass retailer has increasingly taken over the administrative coordination of the flow of goods from the manufacturer to the consumer. The integration backward by the retailers that paralleled the integration forward by the manufacturers meant that the wholesaler whom Harold Barger records as handling over 60 percent of the flow of goods in 1880 handled less than 30 percent by the 1930s.

PART TWO

IMPLICATIONS OF
THE PERSPECTIVES

CHAPTER NINE

Four Laws of Organizational Research

JEFFREY PFEFFER
Graduate School of Business
Stanford University

Instead of summarizing a range of research programs covering the spectrum from action research to traditional sociological research to economics, I have distilled four laws that represent my reactions to the presentations and commentaries.

THE LAW OF UNRESOLVABLE IGNORANCE

The first law, the Law of Unresolvable Ignorance, was prompted initially by my consideration of the Quality of Working Life program of research as summarized by Stan Seashore. The program provides in stark detail a problem that is present in almost all of the programs reviewed, namely, that a great deal of information is gathered in a highly reactive process, and to gather the data, there must be access to corporations or other organizations. Such access is scarcely automatic, given the tremendously comprehensive and detailed information sought, and given the fact that such information and its collection can itself have an important impact on organizations (e.g., Salancik and Pfeffer, 1978). Indeed this is the very point of the survey-research-feedback methodology (Mann, 1957), and is the explicit objective of the sociotechnical, quality of work life, and organization assessment programs of research. Asking the kinds of questions in depth represented by most of the programs can scarcely be seen as a neutral or unimportant intervention into the organizations. Nor are managers oblivious to the reactive effects of such data collection. Thus access in many circumstances will be problematic.

The population ecology perspective of Hannan and Freeman (1977) takes organization theory to task for studying only surviving organizations. They argue that selection on the dependent variable, in this case, survival, diminishes what we can learn about organizations. Rather what is needed are studies that incorporate both organizations that survive as well as those that fail, to understand what determines survival or failure. Their critique of the limitations of the samples employed in most research is minor compared to the problems of access faced by the researchers represented by many of these programs. Not only are we studying only surviving organizations, we are developing a theory of organizations that survive and are willing to be studied. It is reasonable to argue that such organizations are scarcely likely to be a random sample of the population of organizations.

Thus we are confronted with the problem of unresolvable ignorance, given the present research proclivities—we can only gather data on those organizations that will permit access, and these may be atypical of the general organizational population. But what is worse, we can not even determine their representativeness, for in order to do that, we would need information on those other organizations that did not permit access. In a very real sense, the field of organizational behavior knows what it is allowed to know, by those organizations that are willing to provide the data needed for the development and testing of theory.

The problem is analogous to trying to understand the causes and correlates of criminal behavior by collecting behavior on the residents of jails. What one develops is a nice theory of the unsuccessful criminal. The successful criminal, the one not caught and hence not in jail—and these are in the vast majority—is not available for study and data collection. Thus not only do we fail to understand the full range of criminality, we don't even know the dimensions of our ignorance.

The problem of unresolvable ignorance is exacerbated by the field's enchantment with questionnaire or interview techniques, which are among the most reactive ways of gathering data, and with its relative neglect of documentary analysis, the use of archival data, the use of field stimulation methods (Salancik, 1979), and the use of the various trace measures or other indicators that organizations may provide (e.g., Webb et al., 1966). This methodological narrowness is reflected in many if not most of the programs represented at this conference. It is my fond hope that a similar conference held 20 years from now will have more diversity of measures and methods represented. Unless it does, we will not have made a great deal of progress in developing organization theory that is applicable and accurate for most organizations, not just those who are able to be snared in our research nets. The Law of Unresolvable Ignorance threatens to diminish our ability to advance organization theory, unless some steps are taken to overcome it.

THE LAW OF REQUISITE SIMPLICITY

This law reflects the disjunction between the descriptions of people and organizations I have heard at this conference and read in the literature and the nature of the theories produced to explain people and organizations. The first are relatively simple; the latter are quite complicated, convoluted, and complex. If people are boundedly rational, constrained by rules and procedures, prone to act according to habit or custom, with unclear preferences, and subject to various forms of social influence, why do we think it is necessary to develop such intricate models and such complex variables to describe them individually and in interaction?

As others have noted, the phrase complex organizations may refer more to the organization theorists' portrayal of organizations than to the entities themselves (Weick, 1969: 1). Weick's use of Ashby's (1956) Law of Requisite Variety can be turned around to get another view of organizational analysis. Weick argued that to understand equivocal or uncertain systems, equivocal or uncertain processes are required. Daft and Wiginton (1979) have expanded this line of reasoning to suggest that since organizations are complex and uncertain systems, we should use processes for studying them that match their equivocality, for instance, using the more flexible and uncertain natural language rather than mathematical language with its greater certainty and precision.

One might ask how one knows what is or is not uncertain or complex in the first place. If we take Weick's (1969) enacted environment notion seriously, it is clear that in this case particularly, we create the environment to which we then respond. If we use complex, equivocal models and measurement, we will register and perceive a complex, equivocal world. Conversely, if we use relatively simpler processes and models, the world will appear to be simpler and more certain. Which view is in fact correct? The answer to that question is, if one accepts the underlying premises of the concepts of enacted environments and social construction of reality, both unknown and inevitably unknowable.

It is clear that if the boundedly rational managers (March and Simon, 1958) of some of our theories really had to cope with worlds as complex as implied by the numerous measures and models applied to understand those worlds, they would face an impossible task. Yet somehow managers function, organizations operate, and work gets done. In our fascination with change, we overlook the tremendous regularities in activity that occur in social systems. In our fascination with complexity, we overlook the potential for finding simpler models to describe the world—a world that our various theories argue is populated with relatively simple people.

If the process of building theory can be said to be analogous to growing a tree, in which shoots are sent up and branches grow off the shoots and twigs off the branches, then the state of the field can be perhaps described as a bramble bush. We have been too busy growing and fertilizing and have neglected the task of pruning—of rejecting and discarding incorrect, useless, or incomplete notions and concepts. The field has lost sight of Occam's razor and the rule of parsimony. The Law of Requisite Simplicity suggests that the premises underlying many of our theories are correct, and that some relatively straightforward concepts properly applied can account for much of what occurs in organizations. We need to look for a small set of powerful concepts that are relatively simple in their application and measurement. The complexity of our models and measures has well exceeded the complexity of the phenomena we study.

THE LAW OF UNREQUITED EFFORT

One reason why the previous law is so frequently overlooked is because of the operation of the Law of Unrequited Effort. Research on commitment processes (Salancik, 1977; Staw, 1976; Staw and Fox, 1977) indicates that when confronted with feedback indicating that chosen courses of action are not working out, persons are likely to *escalate* their commitments to the previously chosen course of action. In investment decision contexts, more resources may be given to the division that is not performing as well; in wars, more troops may be sent to bolster a failing effort. Staw and Ross (1980) account for this escalation in terms of justification processes. To justify the initial decision, more resources and more effort are expended when that decision appears to be unsuccessful. Much as in the case of Festinger's study of an evangelical group whose predictions of the end of the world failed to materialize (Festinger et al., 1956), individuals are prone to intensify their efforts and increase their commitments when confronted with problems or difficulties.

This process occurs in the area of theory building as well. Indeed it is probably an important reason for the production of contingency theories of various sorts. Two examples can make the point clearer. The early literature on job design (e.g., Herzberg et al., 1959; Turner and Lawrence, 1965) assumed that the more complex and involving the job, the more positive would be the attitudes of those who worked on such jobs. Jobs that provided the opportunity for people to exercise and demonstrate skill, that called for discretion and planning, and that provided feedback were presumed to be more involving and more satisfying. The basic argument was that jobs had properties, people had certain needs or preferences, and that jobs that fulfilled these needs were more satisfying and more motivating (Salancik and Pfeffer, 1977). As studies of actual job attribute-job attitude relationships failed to find consistent evidence for the theory, various modifiers were introduced. The argument was made that the relationship between job attitudes and job attributes was a contingent one, contingent on things such as personal growth need strength (Hackman and Lawler, 1971); living in an urban or rural environment (Turner and Lawrence, 1965; Blood and Hulin, 1967); the strength of various needs (O'Reilly, 1977); and so on for a host of other factors (White, 1978). White (1978) has reviewed this research and found that it has produced remarkably few consistent results, though it has grown to be quite voluminous.

The point is to note that when prophecy failed—when the predictions failed to hold up—the response was not to abandon the underlying theory but rather to intensify the search for moderators, or a series of moderators, that could somehow account for the observed pattern of data. Instead of negative evidence being taken as a reason to begin to think of alternative perspectives, negative evidence was seen often as a reason to intensify the search and redouble the effort to find the real contingencies moderating the job attribute-job attitude relationship (O'Connor et al., 1980).

A similar history can be seen in the structure-context research. The earliest research studies attempted to account for organizational structural dimensions, defined in relatively simple terms, using factors such as size, technology, or the environment. Growing evidence that such formulations did not work well—as in Mohr's (1971) test of the technology argument advanced by Woodward (1965); Pennings' (1975) test of the structural contingency argument derived from Lawrence and Lorsch (1967); and the generally small amount of explained variance found in most such studies—led to the development of new theories incorporating even more factors, such as strategic choice (Child, 1972) and the various factors included in Lawrence's chapter of this book. Furthermore, the measurement of both structure and the context dimensions were refined and examined, as in the research of the Aston group, and controversy over the measurement of environmental uncertainty reviewed by Lawrence. If simple structural relationships were not to be found, it must be because of measurement difficulties and errors, or because various critical factors were not included. As in the case of the job characteristics research, the possibility that the wrong variables, the wrong contextual factors, or an incorrect theoretical formulation was being employed were and are seldom seriously considered.

What the Law of Unrequited Effort suggests is that the way we have gone about developing and testing theory has frequently violated principles of parsimony, and on occasion has taken liberties with the evidence, as Nehrbass (1979) argues in his articulation of the role of ideology in organizational behavior theorizing. Kuhn (1970) has suggested that persistence of theories in the face of contradictory evidence serves useful functions for the development of a science. Certainly one would not want to overthrow theoretical structures carefully built because of an occasional inconsistent datum. By the same token, Kuhn has argued that science progresses through the process of paradigmatic revolutions. What I am suggesting is that we have observed more persistence than revolution. Given the state of the theory and data, more revolution may be needed. The Law of Unrequited Effort may help in understanding something about the development of theories in the field and why they persist.

THE LAW OF NO EFFECT

The Law of No Effect, also known as the illusion of control, summarizes two characteristics of many of the research programs represented in this book and in the field generally. The first characteristic is that in organizational research, we find what we look for. Weick's statement that instead of the usual "I'll believe it when I see it," the converse, "I'll see it when I believe it," is more apropos and may help explain the process. The ability to find what we are looking for is certainly enhanced by the use of constructs difficult to define or utilize, such as transactions costs (Williamson, 1975) and fuzzy measures of the constructs that are more precisely defined. In this regard, multiple measures that are themselves only moderately intercorrelated may only serve to make the problem worse rather than better. A construct that is expanded to include a variety of measures and operationalizations only loosely connected to each other (see Starbuck's critique of the Aston research for a demonstration of this idea) is not a construct at all, but some kind of composite that will not be very useful in developing and testing theory.

The Law of No Effect reminds us that to avoid being trapped by our own selective perceptions and selective attention to information, aided by the imprecision of our measures and constructs, we would be well served to adopt research strategies that follow the logic of strong inference (e.g., Mackenzie and House, 1978), and that employ an explicitly comparative point of view. Strong inference as a strategy for building and testing theory suggests that we learn more from disconfirmation than from supporting our preconceived hypotheses. The problem is posed as one of pruning away ideas or arguments that are incorrect, as well as growing and developing new ones from close attention to the data. It is clearly easy to formulate hypotheses in forms that make them almost incapable of disproof; Abell (1975) has a nice demonstration of this with respect to the use of managerial values or beliefs as an intervening construct, a discussion relevant to those enamored with the concept of strategic choice. The point of strong inference is that we learn nothing from such an activity. Rather, as Salancik and Pfeffer (1977) argued with respect to needs theories, we need to ensure that the theories and their utilization are formulated so that disproof is possible and that we systematically try to find disconfirmation rather than support.

By explicitly comparative point of view, the second element necessary for research strategies, I do not mean comparative over sets of organizations but rather comparative across theories. Given the problems of theory construction and theory testing alluded to many times in these comments, research is well served not by testing data against the null hypothesis or random chance but rather against other theories or plausible explanations for the data. Such a suggestion is also consistent with my arguments earlier that we need more pruning and more paradigmatic revolutions. This will require the explicit confrontation of theory with alternative theory, for it is another theory, not data, that ultimately displaces previously held notions.

The Law of No Effect says that we should be searching for disconfirmation, for no effect, in a comparison of theories. The finding of effects is interesting, but does not provide information as to when the theory being tested fails; finding no effect permits the pruning of ideas and concepts no longer seen to be useful. Since all theories ultimately are displaced, this focus can help speed the process of the evolution and development of knowledge.

The second characteristic of research encapsulated by the Law of No Effect is the pervasive tendency for many theories to confuse sentiment with substance, language with results, and attitudes with behavior. One of the issues that recurs in this book is the extent to which activity is rational, that is, goal directed and prospective, or rationalized, that is, given a retrospective inferring of goals or purpose from action that has already occurred. A second issue pervading much of the research is whether choice, action, and discretion really occur in the sense of guiding and directing organizations, or whether organizational phenomena are best described as being the results of external constraint or natural selection processes. It is the person versus situation controversy moved up a level of analysis; are there choices that guide and direct organizations, much as individual characteristics and cognitive properties may guide and direct individual action, or rather is action largely the function of external constraints, reinforcements, and selection mechanisms?

Virtually all of the research represented in this book, with the possible exception of that summarized by March, takes the proactive, rational view of organizational action. Human systems can be changed, designed, and redesigned at various levels of analysis to provide more fulfilling jobs or more efficient organizations or something else. A discussion of the various functions served by such a perspective is beyond the scope of these brief comments, and is a subject that has been taken up elsewhere (Pfeffer, 1981). For the moment, two cautions are in order. First, as Edelman (1964) has suggested, political language is designed to becloud analysis, and it is important in undertaking political analysis to separate the rhetoric from the reality. Many of our theories have been too quick to use indicators of feeling or sentiment, such as attitudes, as substitutes for assessing what is actually occurring in organizations. Indeed my colleague Jerry Salancik and I have often discussed the fact that in the field of organizational behavior, there is frequently very little that is either organizational or behavioral. Rather much of the research is a study of individual attitudes. Though such studies may be carried out in an organizational context, that context is not used to enrich the theory or the predictions.

Second, except for a few primarily nonempirical outcroppings (Weick, 1969; March, 1978), research has not taken the rationalization, externally controlled, or natural selection perspectives very seriously. We search for the best way of doing things, without asking the more fundamental question of whether anything can be done, or if it matters what is done (see, for example, March and March, 1978, for an example of randomness in administrator selection). The Law of No Effect can serve to remind us that rational choice is a problematic process, and that whether strategic action is possible, given selection mechanisms and external constraints, is an issue very much open to question. Managers and other organizational participants may have no or at least limited effect. The administrative task may be better described as getting people to like or want to do what they are going to do or have to do anyway. The effects may be on sentiments and attitudes rather than on substance. The confusion between the two should be avoided.

CONCLUSION

It seems somewhat quixotic to attempt to summarize or comment on such a diverse set of research programs and particularly to argue, in the face of such institutionalized intellectual authority, that there is much evidence for failure as well as success in these programs. Such an activity is important enough to attempt, however. We have all—and I include myself in this—been too interested in building theories and structure of concepts, and not interested enough in pruning away the intellectual dead wood; we have become too committed to our own perspectives, so that disconfirming evidence becomes accommodated through the introduction of branches, contingencies, and moderating variables, rather than looking for some fundamental alternative perspectives that might make such complication unnecessary; we have become insensitive to the extent to which our research methods have governed the sites we can study, and thereby the range of knowledge and information we can acquire; and we have been too busy looking for effects to learn from those instances in which prophecy fails and effects are not found.

All of these problems are remediable, and I am certain they will be remedied sooner or later. We need a critical organizational behavior, just as there has emerged a critical sociology. The sooner it emerges, the better.

REFERENCES

Abell, P. (1975). "Organizations as Technically Constrained Bargaining and Influence Systems," in P. Abell, *Organizations as Bargaining and Influence Systems,* London: Heinemann, pp. 114–128.

Ashby, W. R. (1956). *An Introduction to Cybernetics,* New York: Wiley.

Blood, M. R., and C. L. Hulin (1967). "Alienation, Environmental Characteristics, and Worker Responses," *Journal of Applied Psychology* 51:284–290.

Child, J. (1972). "Organizational Structure, Environment and Performance: The Role of Strategic Choice," *Sociology* 6:1–22.

Daft, R. L., and J. C. Wiginton (1979). "Language and Organization," *Academy of Management Review* 4:179–191.

Edelman, M. (1964). *The Symbolic Uses of Politics,* Urbana: University of Illinois Press.

Festinger, L., H. W. Riecken, and S. Schacter (1956). *When Prophecy Fails,* Minneapolis: University of Minnesota Press.

Hackman, J. R., and E. E. Lawler III (1971). "Employee Reactions to Job Characteristics," *Journal of Applied Psychology* 55:259–286.

Hannan, M. T., and J. H. Freeman (1977). "The Population Ecology of Organizations," *American Journal of Sociology* 82:929–964.

Herzberg, F., B. Mausner, and B. Snyderman (1959). *The Motivation to Work,* 2nd ed., New York: Wiley.

Kuhn, T. S. (1970). *The Structure of Scientific Revolutions,* 2nd ed., Chicago: University of Chicago Press.

Lawrence, P. R., and J. W. Lorsch (1967). *Organization and Environment.* Boston: Graduate School of Business Administration, Harvard University.

Mackenzie, K. D., and R. House (1978). "Paradigm Development in the Social Sciences: A Proposed Research Strategy," *Academy of Management Review* 3:7–23.

Mann, F. C. (1957). "Studying and Creating Change: A Means to Understanding Social Organization," *Research in Industrial Human Relations,* Industrial Relations Research Association 17:146–167.

March, J. G. (1978). "Bounded Rationality, Ambiguity, and the Engineering of Choice," *Bell Journal of Economics* 9:587–608.

March, J. C., and J. G. March (1978). "Performance Sampling in Social Matches," *Administrative Science Quarterly* 23:434–453.

March, J. G., and H. A. Simon (1958). *Organizations,* New York: Wiley.

Mohr, L. (1971). "Organizational Technology and Organizational Structure," *Administrative Science Quarterly* 16:444–459.

Nehrbass, R. G. (1979). "Ideology and the Decline of Management Theory," *Academy of Management Review* 4:427–431.

O'Connor, E. J., C. J. Rudolf, and L. H. Peters (1980). "Individual Differences and Job Design Reconsidered: Where Do We Go From Here?" *Academy of Management Review* 5:249–254.

O'Reilly, C. A. (1977). "Personality-Job Fit: Implications for Individual Attitudes and Performance," *Organizational Behavior and Human Performance* 18:36–46.

Pennings, J. M. (1975). "The Relevance of the Structural-Contingency Model for Organizational Effectiveness," *Administrative Science Quarterly* 20:393–410.

Pfeffer, J. (1981). *Power in Organizations,* Marshfield, MA: Pitman Publishing.

Salancik, G. R. (1977). "Commitment and the Control of Organizational Behavior and Belief," in B. M. Staw and G. R. Salancik, Eds., *New Directions in Organizational Behavior,* Chicago: St. Clair Press, pp. 1–54.

Salancik, G. R. (1979). "Field Stimulations for Organizational Behavior Research," *Administrative Science Quarterly* 24:638–649.

Salancik, G. R., and J. Pfeffer (1977). "An Examination of Need-Satisfaction Models of Job Attitudes," *Administrative Science Quarterly* 22:427–456.

Salancik, G. R., and J. Pfeffer (1978). "A Social Information Processing Approach to Job Attitudes and Task Design," *Administrative Science Quarterly* **23**:224–253.

Staw, B. M. (1976). "Knee-Deep in the Big Muddy: A Study of Escalating Commitment to a Chosen Course of Action," *Organizational Behavior and Human Performance* **16**:27–44.

Staw, B. M., and F. V. Fox (1977). "Escalation: Some Determinants of Commitment to a Previously Chosen Course of Action," *Human Relations* **30**:431–450.

Staw, B. M., and J. Ross (1980). "Commitment in an Experimenting Society: A Study of the Attribution of Leadership from Administrative Scenarios," *Journal of Applied Psychology* **65**:249–260.

Turner, A. N., and P. R. Lawrence (1965). *Industrial Jobs and the Worker: An Investigation of Response to Task Attributes*. Boston: Harvard University.

Webb, E. J., D. T. Campbell, R. D. Schwartz, and L. Sechrest (1966). *Unobtrusive Measures*, Chicago: Rand-McNally.

Weick, K. E. (1969). *The Social Psychology of Organizing*, Reading, MA: Addison-Wesley.

White, J. K. (1978). "Individual Differences and the Job Quality-Worker Response Relationship: Review, Integration, and Comments," *Academy of Management Review* **3**:267–280.

Williamson, O. E. (1975). *Markets and Hierarchies*, New York: Free Press.

Woodward, J. (1965). *Industrial Organization: Theory and Practice*. London: Oxford University Press.

CHAPTER TEN

Appraising Organization Design Theories

JOHN R. KIMBERLY
Yale University

It is indeed a challenge to comment meaningfully on the creations and contributions that have been described earlier in this book, because each of the traditions is distinguished and therefore has already been dissected publicly many times. It is also a challenge because, in spite of the overall theme of organizational design and behavior promised by the book's title, each tradition has unique features, based on different assumptions about people and organizations, about rules of discovery and evidence, and about the relations between research and practice.

There are of course some common themes. Three in particular strike me: an emphasis on enhancing productive efficiency, an interest in describing and understanding *patterns* in organizational activity, and a concern for creating more humane work systems. Not every tradition exhibited each of these themes, but overall they seemed most prevalent. But even more interesting than the common themes was the way in which the traditions, when laid side by side, collectively embodied certain tensions. These tensions deserve some comment, though not in any particular order of priority.

First was the tension between intuition and measurement. The various traditions represented an interesting diversity in conceptions of the sci-

---

I must congratulate the persons who organized the conference on which this book is based. Their sense of how design can influence importantly the quality of an experience is nothing short of exquisite. To hold lunch the first day in the Egyptian Room of the University of Pennsylvania museum, where the participants were surrounded by marvelous artifacts of a previous civilization, was sheer genius. A clear and unambiguous reminder that the creations and contributions of the past shape the present in myriad ways, most of them subtle, and perhaps many of them unexamined.

entific enterprise and hence in approaches to the challenge of research. Some were dominated by measurement concerns, in which the immediate objective appeared to be quantification—not for the sake of quantification but as the necessary and occasionally sufficient condition for understanding. The traditions represented by Pugh, Seashore, and Van de Ven illustrate this approach most clearly. Some others exhibited an interplay between intuition and measurement, with less of an insistence on rigor but somewhat greater insistence on appreciating context and systemic interdependencies. In this group I would place the traditions represented by Lawrence and Trist. The last were those who emphasized theory, perhaps not to the exclusion of empirical research but certainly as the clear priority. Here I would locate the traditions represented by March and Williamson.

My own sense of where the field is heading in the near term leads me to predict that an emphasis on intuition will reassume the eminence it enjoyed 25 years ago. This orientation will successfully reclaim scientific legitimacy, or at least legitimacy within the collegium, and will be in the ascendancy for the next five to seven years. I believe that this will be a relatively short-lived though theoretically enriching shift in the field.

A related tension in the traditions represented in this book is between idiographic and nomothetic efforts to represent organizations, their design, and influences on their performance. To what extent are there general principles that are universally applicable across all organizations? Is each organization sufficiently unique and complex so that the most we should expect from researchers is sophisticated attempts to capture that uniqueness and complexity? Are there perhaps classes of organizations that are sufficiently similar within themselves and dissimilar to others to favor the creation of middle-range theories?

With apologies in advance to those authors whose views of their own work are at variance with mine, I see the traditions represented by March, Pugh, Seashore, Van de Ven, and Williamson as fundamentally nomothetic in orientation and that of Lawrence and Trist as being more idiographic. Not that the author's intentions and the ways in which his work have been represented are always in harmony. For example, Van de Ven has created a measurement package that has been used by researchers in a variety of organizational settings, yet in his writing he seems somewhat ambivalent about whether his own work is creating general theory or a theory of child welfare organizations in a particular region of the country. Trist has tried to develop a set of concepts that are widely applicable, yet when one reads his research carefully, one has the feeling that while the concepts may be general, the understanding is closely tied to the peculiarities of the particular setting. And Pugh, who started out with a general conceptual framework, appears to have been strongly influenced in the development of his view of organizations by empirical uniformities, which may in fact have been a function of the types of organizations he studied.

Thus the tension between idiographic and nomothetic orientations is both between and within traditions. Those researchers who start with general theory often find apparent uniqueness and complexity when they get out into the field (if they ever do), while those who start with a strong sense that every organization is unique often find similarities as they move from one setting to another. Putting aside quibbles about the relationship of the traditions represented in this book to this dimension, the basic questions remains: What is our business? Is it the business of creating theories of particular organizations, of classes of organizations, or of organizations in general? I have no reason to believe that this question will be satisfactorily answered in the next decade, if indeed it is even useful to try to do so.

Another tension among the traditions described earlier centers on the researcher's conception of the underlying basis for order and direction in organizational life. There are two contrasting models here: a "rational" model, which assumes that organizations can be represented as entities that behave in accordance with principles of maximization of goal-related outcomes; and a nonrational model, which assumes that organizations are collections of individual people who are self-interested and who may form coalitions around issues to pursue results of mutual interest. The rational model emphasizes stability and predictability, whereas the nonrational model emphasizes fluidity and change.

These are of course caricatures, and there are those who see elements of both models in their perspectives on organizations. Again at the risk of doing violence to the authors' conceptions, I would classify early March, Pugh, Seashore, and Van de Ven as rationalists and late March and Trist as nonrationalists. Lawrence and Williamson appear to bridge the two groups. Inherent in the rationalists' view of organizational life is the belief that if managers have information, they will use it. The key design problem then is ensuring that structures and procedures are arranged in such a way that the appropriate information is available in timely fashion. The nonrationalists see information as one among several means used to help reconcile multiple goals and interests in ways that permit the needs of individuals to be met while at the same time adequate organizational performance is encouraged.

Were I to predict what the next five to ten years would hold, I would have to say that hybrid models are most likely to appear—models in which the dominant view is that organizational behavior is aggregated individual behavior and that to understand how and why organizations look and act the way they do, one needs to understand the interplay of interests at work within the organizational system as well as those external to it.

Perhaps the most interesting tension observed was that between theory and practice. Here a number of explicit and implicit questions emerged. Does theory lead practice or does practice lead theory? Should researchers be concerned with the applicability of their work? Whose responsibility is it to find applications? Is applied research atheoretical?

These are not new questions. Nor are they unique to research on organizational design and performance. But they were exquisitely illustrated by the variability in approaches and values represented by the seven research programs. The Harvard, Michigan, and sociotechnical programs in my view have the most immediately applied focus, while the work of March, Pugh, Van de Ven, and Williamson has a less applied focus. More will be said about this point later, but for the moment the question that needs to be addressed squarely has to do with the effects of the relationship between researchers and the system(s) they are observing on what is observed and how it is interpreted. How does a consultative relationship, for example, affect the knowledge generation process? Is research quality inevitably compromised? Is depth of understanding inevitably increased? On the other hand, how seriously is a "pure" researcher likely to be taken in the field research setting? Is access to significant data likely to be more open or more closed and under what circumstances? These are all important questions, which would certainly benefit from self-conscious exploration by organizational researchers, no matter what their beliefs about the relative importance of theory and practice.

The various research programs, then, tend to cluster across tensions. Some tend to emphasize measurement as opposed to intuition, nomothetic efforts as opposed to idiographic efforts, rational as opposed to nonrational models, and theory as opposed to practice. Some emphasize just the opposite. Others defy easy classification, and if one wishes to speculate about where the ideas for research on organizational design and performance are likely to come from, it would quite likely be from the off-quadrant programs, those that do not fit easily into classifications of yesterday's and today's research.

If tensions are one theme that pervade the research programs, images are another. From listening to people talk about their work and from reading their work, I was struck by the extent to which the images of organizations are grounded in the kinds of organizations in which they spend most of their time and in which they have had most of their direct experience. It is hardly accidental that a loosely coupled, garbage-can approach comes from people who spend much time thinking seriously about the way in which universities are organized and run. If this is the case, perhaps we need to be a little more conscious of how our thinking about organizations is shaped by our experience. I argue that these experiences inevitably and invariably, although perhaps unconsciously, dominate the images that animate our research. These images in turn embody the kinds of forces that we come to believe drive and shape organizational life. It is therefore crucial that we understand not only our own imagery but that of other researchers as well.

Thinking about all seven programs also made me wonder about the visibility of ideas. I tried to order the seven programs on a time line and examine their historical origins. That exercise was not terribly productive. Instead a question kept emerging: "What forces propel ideas forward at particular points in time?" And its corollary, "What forces explain their demise?" These questions perhaps have more to do with the sociology of knowledge than with organizational research, but they led in some interesting directions. The ideas represented in the earlier chapters of this book really have not enjoyed anything like a linear form of development in their popularity, and as I thought about why this might be the case, it seemed that at least three lines of inquiry might be pursued: the development of individual careers; dialectics in theory and research; and fluctuations in markets for ideas.

There is an interplay between the propulsion of ideas and the metamorphosis of individual careers. Each of the program representatives in this book has had a distinguished career. Yet in some cases, their careers have undergone (as I see it) relatively dramatic changes in the kinds of perspectives they are using, the kinds of paradigms they seem to be operating within, the kinds of variables they think are important, and the kinds of questions they find interesting; the careers of others have been somewhat more stable. That in itself is interesting—the relationship between personal intellectual development and the development of a perspective or a body of ideas—and is eminently researchable. How do we make decisions as individual researchers about how much to invest in a particular perspective, and how much are we willing to question a particular perspective that we have already invested heavily in? Whose careers have changed and whose have remained stable and why? What are the directions of change? What implications, if any, do these directions have?

A second line of inquiry has to do with dialectics in organizational theory and research and their implications. It does appear that there is a dialectic quality to much of what we do. One particularly poignant example is the relatively recent positive value being attached to in-depth field studies of organizations. That orientation fell out of favor in the late 1950s but is currently being rediscovered. For those whose careers in organizational research are just beginning, you may not want to take Bill Starbuck's critique of the Aston program too seriously, because Peter Blau will enjoy a renaissance, I suspect, in about 1985 as we rediscover many of the flaws and problems in case-study analysis.

The third direction has to do with fluctuations in markets for ideas. Most of the intellectual capital represented in this book deals with two quite different markets, an intellectual-academic market on the one hand

and a managerial market on the other hand. Some of this capital has been much more relevant to and appreciated by the academic market, whereas some is much more relevant to and appreciated by a managerial market. In a limited number of cases, researchers have very successfully managed both markets and have developed ways of thinking about their ideas that have been attractive to both scholars and the practicing audience. The demand characteristics of these markets change over time, however, and the visibility of a particular perspective in either market is often influenced by factors outside the control of researchers.

Finally, as I look to the coming decade, there are both concerns and hopes. First a prediction. In the 1980s we are likely to see research on assessment, design, and performance having an increasingly applied focus, a much more applied focus than is represented by the earlier chapters of this book. As resources in universities become ever more scarce, researchers are going to be inevitably and invariably driven for sources of support to applied problems. The managerial market will be predominant. That trend is likely to have some real consequences both for the way in which research problems are conceptualized and the way we think about theory development. There is an interesting potential tension between some of the realities on the resource side, which are going to push us in the direction of being ever more applied, and the simultaneous reawakening of interest in ethnographic methods and case studies. It is not yet clear how that is going to work out.

Three concerns in particular stand out in the context of an increasing emphasis on applied research. First, we have to be very concerned about a tendency to concentrate on relatively narrowly defined measures of performance and narrowly defined conceptions of what organization performances are and should be. Second, there is likely to be an ascendancy of managerial perspectives in our work and the way we think about the questions that we are going to be asking. Not that managerial perspectives are irrelevant or shouldn't be incorporated and appreciated. But we need to maintain a healthy and independent skepticism, and to the extent that we go too far in the applied direction, we are likely to lose the capacity to be skeptical. Third, conservatism will probably come to dominate our research to a greater extent than it does today. There may be less willingness to experiment, less willingness to be playful, and less willingness to explore because of a performance-driven orientation. Alternative metaphors for understanding and describing the phenomena that we are interested in may thus be in short supply, sharply curtailing creativity.

On the positive side, there are a number of engaging and exciting developments. People are beginning to take seriously the proposition that we can learn much about organizations from looking at their evolution through time. Many researchers are actually doing longitudinal research. Serious theoretical attention is being paid to the evolution of organizations and the interplay between organizations and contexts. Methodologically, there has been an increasing appreciation for history and the application of historical methodology for organization research, which promises to enrich our theorizing considerably. As I think ahead, though, the overriding concern is the tension between diminishing resources on the one hand—where we are going to find the support to do our work—and some very positive intellectual and conceptual developments on the other. The challenge is to define new forms of collaboration between organizational researchers and their subjects. Many suggestions no doubt would come from those individuals whose work is described in this volume. I personally would find it distressing, however, to see organizational research in the decade of the 1980s become dominated by the narrowest forms of managerial orientation.

CHAPTER ELEVEN

Mapping the Field to Create a Dynamic Perspective on Organization Design and Behavior

ANDREW H. VAN DE VEN
School of Management
University of Minnesota

W. GRAHAM ASTLEY
The Wharton School
University of Pennsylvania

This book has presented some of the major research programs that have significantly influenced our thinking about organization design and behavior. Indeed most of them have been assimilated into what might be called "mainstream" organization theory. However, as the commentaries, rejoinders, and debates have indicated, each research program has its limitations, and each is far from representing a completed product. Furthermore, the seven programs are not all-inclusive of the eclectic conceptual domain covered by organization theory. A number of additional fresh new perspectives on organization design and behavior are beginning to surface and command attention among organizational analysts. We believe that an appreciation of these new perspectives is fundamental for injecting and redirecting mainstream perspectives on organization design and behavior with an exciting and challenging agenda for the future.

This chapter has two related purposes: to make sense of the varying perspectives on organization design and behavior, and to call for a broader and more dynamic perspective than is provided in any of the seven research programs examined thus far. To achieve these purposes, the chapter is divided into two parts. Part I reviews the different schools of organization thought in the literature, including that in this book, and classifies them into four basic perspectives: *system-structural, strategic choice, natural selection,* and *collective action* views of organizations. These four views represent qualitatively different conceptions of organization structure, behavior, change, and managerial roles. They provide a repertoire of ways to approach and understand many organizational problems. As Poggi said, "A way of seeing is a way of not seeing." Each view by itself is incomplete; the weaknesses of one appear as strengths in another. In Part II a partial integration and reformulation of the four views is therefore made in order to begin the initial steps of developing a more dynamic perspective on organization design and behavior. We believe that an explanation for why and how change occurs in organization structure and behavior should be a major item on the agenda in future theory, research, and practice of organization design. To stimulate work on this agenda, Part II suggests a framework for examining change in structural forms and personnel action at individual and collective levels of analysis. It argues that organizational change is a dialectical process of forces, which originate not only from outside but also from inside the organization in the part-whole relationships between structural forms and personnel actions.

PART I; FOUR VIEWS ON ORGANIZATION DESIGN AND BEHAVIOR

In its relatively short history, organizational literature has become increasingly eclectic and voluminous as a result of the contributions of psychologists, social psychologists, sociologists, economists, political scientists, anthropologists, and management theorists. To make sense of this burgeoning literature, a simplifying scheme is needed to identify the major contrasting views of organization design and behavior. Figure 11-1 proposes such a simplifying scheme by classifying some of the major schools of thought and their contributing authors into a four-cell matrix. By examining the commonalities among the schools of thought within each cell, four unique views of organization design and behavior become evident, which are summarized in Figure 11-2. Two factors underly the scheme: the level of organizational analysis, and the relative emphasis placed on deterministic versus voluntaristic assumptions about human nature.

Level of Analysis

Organizations can be examined at a number of levels of analysis, including that of individual members, groups, individual organizations, populations or networks of organizations, and even larger communities or societies of organizations. To simplify the presentation, Figure 11-1 distinguishes between those perspectives that focus on micro and macro organizational characteristics. Here the micro level includes individual organizations and the people or positions within them, while the macro level examines populations, networks, and communities of organizations. This micro-macro distinction is useful for incorporating a number of macroperspectives of collective behavior that have been ignored traditionally but are becoming increasingly relevant to the current direction of organization theory.

For other problems or questions, the micro-macro distinction might compare individuals in groups, groups in organizations, individuals in organizations, and so on. Whatever the specific units included in a study, the major reason for making the micro-macro distinction is to direct one's focus on the part-whole relations existing in all forms of collective structure and behavior. Unfortunately, as Hannan and Freeman (1977) and Freeman (1980) point out, far too little attention has been given to the proper level of analysis for examining organizational problems. As will be discussed, the choice of level has subtle and far-reaching substantive consequences that go far deeper than the methodological problems of aggregation and disaggregation, which themselves are important and systematically reviewed by Hannan (1970).

Deterministic Versus Voluntaristic Orientations

The second factor for classifying schools of organization thought is the classical duality between social determinism and free will—the view that human beings and their institutions are either determined by exogenous forces or are autonomously chosen and created by human beings. Since human beings and social collectivities are the essential objects of study, an explicit awareness of one's philosophy of human nature is fundamental to understanding organization and management. Although organizational analysts are often not explicit about their assumptions of human nature, it is clear that they take a stand somewhere between the two philosophical poles of determinism and voluntarism, and the stand they take predictably influences the frame of reference of their analysis.

This implication has been clearly developed elsewhere by Weeks (1973) and Burrell and Morgan (1979), and is summarized in Table 11-1. They show that a related set of assumptions and approaches to organizational analysis are associated with, but not necessarily caused by, the deterministic-voluntaristic orientations. Of course the assumptions and approaches summarized in Table 11-1 are polar extreme alternatives, and all the schools of thought listed in Figure 11-1 take more moderate positions. Classification of these schools according to their relative emphasis on determinism versus voluntarism is therefore largely arbitrary. Indeed Burrell and Morgan (1979) classified all the schools listed in Figure 11-1 as being objective and deterministic, with the exception of critical

	Focus on structural configurations	Focus on personnel actions, processes
Macro level (Populations or networks of organizations, industries, communities)	Natural selection view 1. Societal Evolution 2. Scientific Marxism 3. Population Ecology 4. Institutional Economics (current views)	Collective action view 1. Societal Guidance 2. Critical Marxism 3. Social Ecology 4. Pluralism/Collective Bargaining
Micro level (Individual organizations, groups and persons)	System–structural view 1. Structural–Functionalism 2. Human Engineering 3. Social Systems Theory 4. Structural Contingency Theory	Strategic choice view 1. Quality of Working Life 2. Strategic Policy Formulation 3. Decision Theory 4. Interaction Theory

Deterministic . . . . Voluntaristic

Figure 11-1 Classification of major schools of organization design and behavior (from W. G. Astley and A. H. Van de Ven (1981).

Marxism. We see greater differences between schools of thought on the determinism-voluntarism axis than Burrell and Morgan (1979) admit to.

Thus, as Figure 11-1 indicates, two underlying dimensions are used to classify the literature on organization design and behavior: macro-micro levels of analysis and deterministic-voluntaristic orientations. Several other dimensions were considered and rejected in developing the classification scheme, including organismic versus mechanistic analogies, rational versus natural systems, and order or regulation versus conflict or radical change perspectives. Although mechanistic analogies from the natural sciences and organismic analogies from the biological sciences have been used frequently for distinguishing organizational theories, they are more incorrect than correct and have facilitated sloppy thinking about

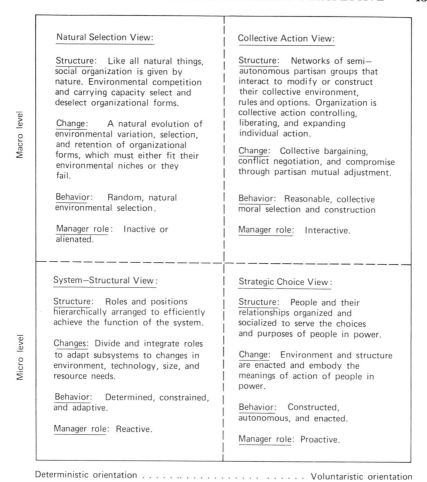

Natural Selection View:

Structure: Like all natural things, social organization is given by nature. Environmental competition and carrying capacity select and deselect organizational forms.

Change: A natural evolution of environmental variation, selection, and retention of organizational forms, which must either fit their environmental niches or they fail.

Behavior: Random, natural environmental selection.

Manager role: Inactive or alienated.

Collective Action View:

Structure: Networks of semi—autonomous partisan groups that interact to modify or construct their collective environment, rules and options. Organization is collective action controlling, liberating, and expanding individual action.

Change: Collective bargaining, conflict negotiation, and compromise through partisan mutual adjustment.

Behavior: Reasonable, collective moral selection and construction

Manager role: Interactive.

System—Structural View:

Structure: Roles and positions hierarchically arranged to efficiently achieve the function of the system.

Changes: Divide and integrate roles to adapt subsystems to changes in environment, technology, size, and resource needs.

Behavior: Determined, constrained, and adaptive.

Manager role: Reactive.

Strategic Choice View:

Structure: People and their relationships organized and socialized to serve the choices and purposes of people in power.

Change: Environment and structure are enacted and embody the meanings of action of people in power.

Behavior: Constructed, autonomous, and enacted.

Manager role: Proactive.

Macro level

Micro level

Deterministic orientation . . . . Voluntaristic orientation

Figure 11-2   Summary of four views of organization and behavior (from W. G. Astley and A. H. Van de Ven 1981).

organizations. As Deutsch (1951) pointed out, to examine an organization as though it were a machine or an animal tends to make the study of an organization something it is not. This is not to say that analogies are not useful for understanding a lesser-known phenomenon from a better-known one. It is to say that these analogies have outgrown their usefulness, and that few significant advances to the understanding of organizations will likely be obtained with these metaphors. Gouldner's (1959) "rational" model relates to the classical theory of bureaucracy, while the "natural system" view is patterned on the organic analogy. Thus the rational versus natural systems dimension is largely subsumed in the

Table 11-1   Assumptions and Approaches Often Associated with
Deterministic-Voluntaristic Views of Human Nature

Assumption/Approach	Deterministic Orientation	Voluntaristic Orientation
Human Nature Assumption *Organization structure and behavior are:*	Determined and constrained by external causal forces.	Autonomously chosen and created by human beings.
Ontological Assumption *The essence of organization structure and behavior is:*	Objective; an external, concrete reality existing in nature.	Subjective; an internal, nominal construction of individuals' consciousness.
	Focus is on the formal structural-functional characteristics of the social system in relation to its environment.	Focus is on the emergent action and act-meanings of individuals and their interactions with one another.
Epistemological Assumption *The nature and origin of knowledge is:*	Positivistic; obtained by verifying and falsifying laws and causal relations existing in nature.	Antipositivistic; obtained by recognizing the internal frames of reference within subjects and observers.
Methodological Approach *Tendencies to:*	Search for universalistic principles and techniques that are generally or widely applicable.	Search for particularistic principles and techniques relevant to a specific problem or condition.
	Deductive and nomothetic methods of study often used, relying on quantitative, comparative, large-scale surveys.	Inductive and idiographic methods of study often used, relying on qualitative, historical case studies.

Adapted from Weeks (1973) and Burrell and Morgan (1979)

already-rejected mechanistic versus organic distinction. Burrell and Morgan (1979) resurrected the conflict versus order debate by classifying schools of organizational thought according to their emphasis on regulation versus radical change. As will be discussed in Part II of this chapter, this classification fails to appreciate forces of order and disorder and regulation and change at either micro or macro levels in any theory of organizations. The reader is forewarned that while the micro-macro and deterministic-voluntaristic dimensions discussed in this section are useful for classifying schools of organization thought, in Part II these dimensions are reconstituted to facilitate the study of change in organization design and behavior.

The classification scheme in Figure 11-1 exaggerates the differences represented by the four views and truncates the contributions of schools of thought listed in each cell of the matrix. In actuality there is a good deal of confusion and boundary overlap between the views. However, the trade-off benefits of the classification scheme are its clarity in reducing complexity to manageable proportions and also its potential for obtaining a broader repertoire of viewpoints for examining organization structure and behavior. Our ultimate aim is analogous to Otto Rank's (1941) call for a "psychology of difference" instead of simply comparing "different psychologies." While we begin by identifying differences in organizational theories with the classification scheme, the scheme itself will be reconstituted in order to develop a theory of difference in organization structure and behavior. As will be discussed in Part II, such a theory of difference is basic to understanding how and why change occurs over time in organizational structure and behavior.

THE SYSTEM-STRUCTURAL VIEW

The notion that the design of an organization inevitably entails the curtailment of individual freedom through the application of rational control procedures has dominated the scientific study of organizations. It had its genesis with Frederick Taylor's belief that industrial organization, like any other part of reality, is permeated by intractable regularities, laws that can be discovered by observation and experiment, and scientific truths that must be applied to regulate activity in the maximization of productivity. The idea was further promoted by administrative management theorists, such as Fayol, who were concerned with the discovery of a set of principles, which, when correctly applied to the particular situation, would prove invaluable guides to the construction of a rational, efficient framework for management. Though his underlying philosophy was quite different from that of these early management theorists, Max Weber too contributed to the theoretical demise of individual freedom and spontaneity by asserting that modern society was becoming increasingly rationalized and bureaucratized through "impersonal, calculable" rules and procedures that eventually take from individuals the capacity to understand their own activities in relation to the organization as a whole.

Even human relations theory may be seen as a sophisticated extension of classical management theory's emphasis on control, since it largely replaces the engineering of physical conditions and external control procedures by the engineering of social and psychological conditions that control behavior less obtrusively. More recent approaches recognize that different forms of control may be appropriate for different situations, but nevertheless explicate essentially the same philosophy and tradition.

Reference here is to the various contingency perspectives on organizations (Woodward, 1965; Thompson, 1967; Lawrence and Lorsch, 1967), on work groups (Zaleznik and Moment, 1964; Van de Ven and Delbecq, 1974) and on individual leadership, motivation, and job design (House and Wigdor, 1969; Hackman and Lawler, 1971; Porter et al., 1975).

In this book the system-structuralist view is exemplified in the Aston research program described by Pugh (in Chapter 4), the organization assessment framework discussed by Van de Ven (in Chapter 6), and the organization and environment contingency theory presented and defended by Lawrence (in Chapter 7).

Although there is considerable diversity and debate among these schools, what is common is a deterministic orientation toward social structure and behavior. It is the kind of determinism that is implicit in structural-functionalist (Parsons, 1951; Skinner, 1972) and systems perspectives (Homans, 1961; von Bertalanffy, 1968; Katz and Kahn, 1978). For purposes of analysis, these schools of thought impersonally focus on positions as the basic elements of an organization. Positions are interrelated and aggregated into departments and larger subsystems in such a way that they instrumentally achieve the function or goal of the overall organizational system. Positions are structured by prescribing the "roles," or behavioral expectations, duties, and responsibilities associated with each organizational position. It is roles, not individuals, that are structured. Individuals occupy these roles and positions and must therefore be carefully selected, trained, and controlled to meet the requirements of their incumbency. Individuals are thereby immersed as component parts of a structured, interlocking system that shapes their behavior.

It is important to understand that system-structuralists impute an underlying logic of effectiveness to the design of the system. Structures are the products of functional imperatives. Given that organizational goals are predetermined, performance constraints and technical principles govern the design of jobs, groups, divisions, and the overall organization. The process approximates an exercise in engineering that must conform to a cost-benefit calculus. The manager must decide what is correct behavior by systematically relating its consequences to objectives. Rational laws supposedly guide the manager in this search for optimal techniques.

Once the structure is functioning, changes or adaptations are largely viewed as the result of exogenous shifts. Thus, as Pugh, Lawrence, and Van de Ven elaborate upon in their chapters, with changes in various characteristics of the organization's environment, technology, size, available resources, and tasks undertaken, the organization and its subunits must respond by redividing or reintegrating its roles and subsystems into new configurations if the overall organization is to survive or remain effective. The "contingent" factors constitute constraints to which the system must adapt its internal structure.

The manager's basic role thus emerges as a *reactive* one. It is a technician's role of fine-tuning the organization according to exigencies it confronts. Managerial behavior is believed to be explainable through information processing and search models (Galbraith, 1977). As Pfeffer and Salancik (1978) state, to manage the organization the manager must perceive, process, and respond to environmental demands and constraints. Since there is no shortage of competing environmental demands, the basic question becomes one of deciding which demands to react to. The focus of managerial decision making, therefore, is not on choice but on gathering correct information about contextual variations and on examining the consequences of responses to alternative demands.

THE STRATEGIC CHOICE VIEW

The notion that organization structure and behavior are imbued with logic and rationality has been so pervasive that it has historically led most theorists to either: (1) presume that choice behavior must also be rational—or at least intendedly so (as March clearly describes in his discussion of theories of choice in Chapter 5); or (2) to relegate individual choice to a separate world of indeterminate practices (as Lindblom does)—the world of the spontaneous, the emergent, the affective, the informal, the nonrational.

Roethlisberger and Dickson (1949) distinguished between the "logic of cost and efficiency" on the one hand and the "logic of sentiment" on the other. They regarded the former as the concern of management when designing formal structure, while the latter explained aberrations from the formal structure by workers. As Gouldner (1959) indicated, such a distinction between "rational" and "natural-system models" has tended to reinforce the status of formal structure and to obscure its nonrational elements. Anything nonrational has simply been explained as anomalous and, by implication, regarded as unimportant to an understanding of the central elements of organizational life. Nonrational individual choice has consequently been banished from the center-stage of organization theory.

The serious emergence of a competing paradigm within management theory was not witnessed until the publication of *Organizational Choice* (Trist, Higgin, Murray, and Pollock, 1963). As Trist elaborates in Chapter 2, the sociotechnical researchers refuted the idea that there was only one way of designing work organizations. The supposed "technological imperative" could apparently be disobeyed with positive results. By combining the desirable social and psychological properties of the shortwall method of coal mining with the superior technological capabilities of the longwall method, Trist and Bamforth (1951) demonstrated that considerable discretion was available in the design of a composite method that was tailored to the enhancement of the quality of working life as well as to the technical demands of machinery. The significance of the sociotechnical concept was the attention it drew to the possibility of incorporating real choices into the formal design of the work system itself.

This idea was given further visibility in 1972 with John Child's call for the notion of "strategic choice," which was prompted by Alfred Chandler's (1962) historical development of the proposition that the structural forms of American industrial enterprises were the result of management strategies. Child criticized structural contingency theory for its deterministic explanation of organizational design as the product of technical demands presented by environment, technology, and size. He argued that decision making about organizational structure is not simply a matter of accommodating to operational exigency; it is equally a strategic event that includes reference to the value positions of the actors involved and the political processes in which they engage.

Child's explanation was based on the fact that large proportions of variance in organizational structure are not attributable to "contingent" factors; performance constraints afford considerable leeway for the exercise of choice in designing organizational structure to suit the preferences of those who hold power. Moreover, as the debate in Chapter 8 indicates, the exercise of this choice turns on one's ideology of management thought—whether organizations are viewed as impartial technical instruments for minimizing costs of executing transactions (Williamson and Ouchi) and administrative coordination (Chandler), or as coalitions of people with vested interests who manipulate the environment to gain greater control and power (Perrow).

Phenomenologists have provided additional impetus for the strategic choice view. They ascribe little merit to technical necessity and suggest that organizational life is largely the product of choice and the way individuals construct their social realities (Mead, in Strauss, 1956; Berger and Luckmann, 1966; Weick, 1979). "Social roles and institutions exist only as an expression of the meanings which men attach to their world" (Silverman, 1970: 134). Here organizational change is not externally induced, as system structuralists argue. It arises from within, through human interactions that modify, change, and transform social meanings, and therefore the structure of organizations. Organizational roles and structure provide a framework for action, but these are constantly susceptible to modification as people succeed in imposing their own definitions of reality upon the situation (Salaman, 1980).

This subjective and arbitrary view of strategic choice was carried several steps farther in Chapter 5 by March and Lindblom. They indicate that decision makers view many strategic organizational activities as being rational and purposive. In fact, however, they often simply occur for indeterminate reasons, be it accident, expedience, habit, or unconscious preference. Actions are observed to precede goals; solutions are invented before problems are found, and strategy formulation and planning occur after these "strategies" and "plans" have been accomplished. Yet in order to make such capricious and arbitrary behavior appear rational and purposeful, a retrospective logic is invented by people to rationalize such behavior. Retrospective consciousness superimposes a quality of logic upon the existing order (Berger and Luckmann, 1966). The reason for this seemingly nonrational sense-making, March explains, is that where strategic choices are made in ambiguous situations (as they usually are, or they would be routine choices), classical assumptions of rational decision behavior collapse, and no satisfactory alternative assumptions have yet been found. As a consequence, Lindblom concludes that decision making in organizations remains an indeterminate practice that cannot be captured as though it were a technology or craft.

To summarize, the strategic choice view draws attention to *individuals,* their *interactions,* and their *perceptions,* as opposed to *positions* and their *interrelations* and *functions* in the system-structural view. Both environment and structure are enacted and embody the meanings of action of people, particularly those in power. Managers are viewed as acting in a *proactive* role, and their choice behavior can be described as being intendedly purposeful, hedonistic, and rational.

THE NATURAL SELECTION VIEW

Focusing specifically upon organization-environment relationships, three macro societal perspectives have recently gained increasing attention in the organizational literature: population ecology, scientific Marxism, and certain institutional economics approaches to organizations. These approaches commonly focus on the structural and demographic characteristics of populations of organizations across communities, industries, or society at large. Relying on biological analogies and social Darwinism, social organization is viewed as deterministically given by nature and its evolution as governed by natural "ecological" laws. Environmental (or economic) competition and carrying capacity (or resource scarcity) are the external forces that select and deselect specific forms of organizations. Populations of organizations survive or fail regardless of the actions taken by particular organizations within them. This is because a natural evolutionary process of variation, selection, and retention is viewed to go on in the environment, and both individual organizations and populations of organizations must either fit their environmental niches or they fail. The macro organizational schools of thought that incorporate this basic theme are here called the natural selection view of organizations.

Population ecology theorists argue that while there are limited degrees of strategic choice or internal control over changes in social systems, most sources of change are intractable to human manipulation; they are the result of "natural" external conditions in the environment (Campbell, 1969; Hannan and Freeman, 1977; Aldrich, 1979; Pennings, 1980;

McKelvey, 1981). They suggest that, in explaining change in organization design, far too much emphasis has been placed on concepts central to the strategic choice view—concepts such as leadership, motivation, decision making and participation, and other "autogenic" forces (McKelvey, 1981). Greater attention needs to be given to demographic and economic factors in the environment, which in the long run select some organizations for extinction and allow others to survive regardless of internal organizational factors and managerial action.

Aldrich (1979) gives three reasons why strategic choice is seldom exercised and is severely constrained by external environmental forces. First, while new environmental niches may be selected occasionally by organizational decision makers, there are significant constraints on this selection because potential niches may be excluded by law, funding restrictions, or other barriers to entry. Second, only a small minority of the large and politically well-connected organizations have sufficient power to strategically influence their environments: the vast majority cannot meaningfully shape their environment. Third, decision makers' perceptions of environmental realities tend to be distorted by social and cultural factors, no matter how much search and information processing goes on. As a result, occasions for making nonroutine or critical decisions often pass by unrecognized, and truly strategic choices are seldom attempted. The argument is not that strategic choice is impossible, but rather that environmental pressures severely constrain the potential for organizational decision makers to either change their environmental niche or their organizational form (Van de Ven, 1979).

Environmental determinism is also embraced by system-structuralists who, as stated above, view organization design as dependent upon "contingency" factors such as environmental uncertainty and resource scarcity. What distinguishes the two deterministic views, however, is that organization change is a product of *internal adaptation* for system-structuralists, while it is the product of *external selection* in the natural selection view (Aldrich and Pfeffer, 1977).

In Chapter 7 Lawrence proposes to expand the "selection" reasoning of population ecologists into the "adaptation by learning" realm. He argues that if an organization survives the early stage of external selection, its niche can grow in size and evolve into a more differential and integrated subsystem. This new position in the environmental niche enables the organization to learn to adapt to subsequent environmental changes that would have been fatal at an earlier stage. Various stages in the life cycle of organizations represent movements between cells or niches in the environmental uncertainty-resource scarcity matrix (see Figure 7-3). With each movement, qualitatively different environmental challenges are confronted. To survive each of these moves, organizations must implement different internal adaptation strategies in terms of altering their technologies, structures for differentiation and integration, learning procedures, and criteria of organizational effectiveness.

Natural selection theorists would make two criticisms of Lawrence's internal adaptation model. First, they would argue that Lawrence overexaggerates the degree to which organizations are flexible enough to make the adaptations needed to survive. Sunk costs, political resistance to change, historical precedent, legal and fiscal constraints, and "group think" induce structural rigidities and inertia. Given that there are limits to structural adaptation, this internal adaptation perspective must be supplemented by a selection orientation. Thus, when niches no longer attract sufficient resources to sustain a particular organizational form, that form becomes obsolete because of structural inertia and is thus selected out. At the same time, resources transfer into new areas, creating niches that are so novel that limited adaptations of existing organizations cannot provide adequate degrees of fitness, and entirely new organizational forms must therefore be selected in.

The second criticism that population ecologists would raise is that it is meaningless to focus on the actions of single organizations to understand change in organizational designs. If the ability of the typical organization to influence its environment or maneuver into new environments is quite limited, then single organizations can improve their performance only by fine tuning to operating contingencies within the confines of their present niches. Since major organizational change is primarily the product of environmental selection, the fine tuning of organizational structure becomes mostly irrelevant to its survival. No amount of fine tuning within present niches is sufficient to ensure survival, since the important factor in the long term is whether the distribution of resources in society will supply the conditions constituting a niche *for that type of organization* in the first place. Thus the focus shifts to entire species of organizations, which come and go in "waves," for example, as whole industries are born and extinguished (Aldrich, 1979). The actions of any particular organization thus have little consequence in the face of social, economic, and historical forces that overwhelm it.

As Hannan and Freeman (1977) and McKelvey (1979) indicate, this argument explains organizational behavior by raising the level of analysis from a consideration of the actions of single organizations to focus on populations of organizations, populations that possess systemic properties of their own. By identifying classes of organizations categorized by virtue of their homogeneous elements, one can begin to understand the common environmental vulnerabilities shared by members of the class, and hence the patterns underlying the distribution of organizations across varying environmental conditions and niches. It is for this reason that organizational existence must be regarded as an attribute of the population, not its constituents.

Population ecologists admit, however, that their model works best for small, powerless organizations operating in environments with dispersed resources. For example, it is easy to see how environmental factors such as market shifts can select and deselect organizations for survival in conditions approximating perfect competition. On the other hand, it is much more difficult to state that organizations operating in concentrated industries under oligopolistic and monopolistic conditions are also at the mercy of their environments. How can the determinist cope with the widespread realities of industry concentration that prevail in modern society?

In an interesting treatment of this question in Chapter 8, Williamson interprets growing industrial concentration as an attempt to prevent opportunistic exploitation from occurring. According to this thesis, the invisible hand of market forces begins to fail when a condition of "information impactedness" occurs. This condition refers to an asymmetrical distribution of information that interferes with the optimal allocation of resources through market exchange transactions. It occurs when uncertainty and bounded rationality combine to inhibit the dissemination of information throughout the market, and when "small numbers" conditions coupled with opportunistic behavior permit the exploitation of this situation. Under these circumstances, internal organization transactions, or hierarchies, will replace "markets." Internal organization possesses superior monitoring and control capabilities and is thus able to curb opportunism and avoid its associated "transaction costs."

A concern for efficiency therefore underlies the growth of industrial concentration, which the shift from markets to hierarchies represents. Internal organization is desirable because it avoids the inefficiencies associated with opportunistic behavior in failing markets. Put differently, internal organization manifests the tendency to reestablish the natural operation of economic rationality when market conditions are no longer able to perform this function. Industrial concentration, in this view, is not a device for manipulating the environment; it is simply the product of neutral economic laws that determine it.

A similar interpretation of industrial concentration and the growth of large-scale organization is given by Chandler. He explains the historical development of vertical integration and multidivisional organization as the pursuit of efficiencies deriving from "administrative coordination."

Williamson's approach is in accord with the natural selection view in the sense that he explains patterns of market structure, ranging from pure competition among many organizations to monopoly by one, from the perspective of economic determinism. He explains the shift from markets to hierarchies as a triumph of the interests of the economic "system" as a whole over the opportunistic tendencies of its constituent members (1975: 27). Optimization of efficiency in allocating resources throughout the total economy is the major criterion. In this respect Williamson follows

Schumpeter, Marx, and Engels, since these theorists also portrayed the natural evolution of the economy and its institutions as subject to deterministic laws. Thus:

> Mankind is not free to choose. . . . Things economic and social move by their own momentum and the ensuing situations compel individuals and groups to behave in certain ways whatever they may wish to do (Schumpeter, 1947).

> Capitalism subjects every individual capitalist to the immanent laws of capitalist production as external coercive laws. Competition forces him continually to extend his capital for the sake of maintaining it, and he can only extend it by means of progressive accumulation (Marx, 1930, Vol. 2: 651).

> Marx's structural perspective sees bourgeoisie and proletariat alike as doing what they *must* rather than what they *will;* men are under constraint to pursue their typically different courses of action by reason of the different positions they occupy within the social structure. For Marx and Engels, structure centers on constraint and constraint is understood as an impersonal property. . . . i.e., a social "position" (Gouldner, 1980: 89).

If, then, historical necessity drives the evolution of society and its organizations down naturally determined paths, the manager's basic role is relegated to being an *inactive* or *symbolic* one in the natural selection view. When shifts occur in the environment, individual managers can do little in the short or intermediate run (Hannan and Freeman, 1977). For example, with rising interest rates the construction industry slows or shuts down, and all one can do is hope the environmental shift is temporary and that one can ride it out. In addition to being inactive, the manager's role also becomes a symbolic one because of the pervasive need by people to believe in personal causation as opposed to a willingness to accept environmental determinism (Pfeffer and Salancik, 1978: 263). As a symbol, managers can be used as scapegoats or visible referents for attributing success or failure to a clearly identifiable "responsible" source by outside observers.

Alternatively, if one adopts a more critical Marxian perspective, the manager's role in the natural selection view is one of *alienation.* Where natural random forces replace rationality, and where organizations survive or fail regardless of what managers do or suffer, individuals are relegated to conditions of powerlessness, meaninglessness, isolation, and self-estrangement—all the conditions that define Marx's theory of alienation (Blauner, 1964).

The natural selection view, then, consists of two major arguments. Population ecologists, focusing mainly on small organizations, argue that environmental forces overwhelm the actions of single organizations, channeling and determining their fate in the long run. Institutional economists and economic historians, on the other hand, argue that intractable economic laws force organizations (large and small) to act in accordance with the constraints of efficiency maximization. The collective action view, which we will now examine, challenges both of these positions. While retaining a population level of analysis, the collective action view reestablishes management on a self-regulating footing by restoring human purposes, choices, and actions to the design of the interorganizational world.

THE COLLECTIVE ACTION VIEW

Organizational ecologists, social planners, political economists, and lawyers tend to take a far more voluntaristic and proactive stance to macrosocial change than that represented by the natural selection view. Witness, for example, the book titles of leading social planning theorists: *Truth, Love, and Social Change*, for *Retracking America, Redesigning the Future*, and for *Man and Society in an Age of Reconstruction* (Warren, 1971; Friedmann, 1973; Ackoff, 1974; and Mannheim, 1940, respectively). So also Etzioni (1968) states that "hope for the future lies in the creation of an active society." Benson characterizes this active society as a political economy whose features are manifested in the dynamics of interorganizational networks. These networks must be analyzed at a population level of analysis, since they possess distinctive properties of their own.

> The interorganizational network is a fundamental unit of analysis in the study of advanced industrial societies. The importance of the interlocking network of organizations has been established at least since publication of Mill's *The Power Elite* (1956). . . . Increasingly, societal problems in advanced industrial or postindustrial societies are framed in organizational and interorganizational terms. . . . The interorganizational network is treated here as an emergent phenomenon, delineating a kind of analysis with distinctive features and concerns. The network, as an emergent entity, has characteristics which are objects of investigation in their own right (Benson, 1977).

The collective action view focuses on this network of semiautonomous organizations and stakeholders who join together as a social action system to construct or modify their collective domain, working rules, and options. As a social system, Van de Ven, Emmett, and Koenig (1974) state that the actions of organizational parties are symbiotically interdependent, and over time network participants take on specialized roles and develop normative expectations of each other regarding their rights and conduct. The social structure of this network is such that it can act as a unit and make decisions to attain collective goals and self-interests of the member organizations. This implies that the network can perform actions similar to an autonomous organization and that it can participate in and adjust to other social collectivities more encompassing than itself, just as individual organizations do by being participants in the network.

Generally collective decisions emerge out of the bargaining, negotiation, compromise, and mutual adjustment among partisan participants. Modifications and changes that are necessary in achieving joint decisions and actions "occur incrementally through the waxing and waning of the resource allocation mechanism, and through changes in legitimation of shifting domains" (Warren, 1967: 413). These actions are based on customs and norms of reasonable value and practice that are the working rules of collective action. Organization is thus viewed as collective action that controls, liberates, and expands individual freedom (Commons, 1950).

The collective action and natural selection views commonly focus on the population level of organizations, and both purport to explain how and why organizational changes occur at the macrosocial level. Yet they differ radically in their explanations; the natural selection view emphasizes environmental determinism, and the collective action view stresses collective purpose and choice in constructing the environment. How and why, then, one might ask, can these two views differ so much in their explanations? The answer turns on the different definitions of population and the nature of interdependence between organizations in this population by the natural selection and collective action views. Consequently their explanations of order and change in social structure are predictably different, as we will now see.

The natural selection view defines a population as an aggregate or agglomeration of organizations that are relatively homogeneous in their structural form and are thereby mutually susceptible to environmental vulnerability (Hannan and Freeman, 1977). All organizations within the population share certain "key elements" that constitute their "common form." As a consequence, the theoretical question addressed by these authors concerns the limitations experienced by different organizational forms in different environments. This explains the occurrence and distribution of different types of organization across differing environmental conditions.

Hannan and Freeman specifically acknowledge that they are using the term population "and the ecological theories implied thereby" in a restricted sense. In so doing they diverge from "conventional treatments of human ecology," which view populations of organizations as "analogous to communities" with "collective means of adapting to environmental situations." Such a conventional treatment of the population by organization ecologists is provided by Amos Hawley (1968).

Like Hannan and Freeman, Hawley emphasizes populations of organizations as the point of reference. However, whereas Hannan and Freeman identify the elements of a population simply by virtue of their *common susceptibility to environmental influence*, Hawley identifies the elements of a population by virtue of their *internal organization*. For Hannan and Freeman, the population is simply an assemblage or agglomeration of elements subject to the same fate at the hands of the environment. For Hawley, the population is not an incoherent agglomeration, but a coherent organization, an "integrated system having some degree of unit character." "Organization," it is contended, is the very attribute that transforms an assemblage of individual elements into a population with properties of its own.

It follows that Hawley would not even accept Hannan and Freeman's single-species "populations" as populations in the proper sense of the term. These single-species "populations," which comprise a homogeneous set of organizations, share an "intraspecific relationship known as *commensalism.*" True populations emerge only when the quality of corporate unity can be attributed to them. Such unity derives from the functional interdependence that develops on the basis of complementary differences in an "interspecific relationship" known as *"symbiosis."* As a population becomes more complex and more organized with the addition of a new species, symbiotic interdependence is extended, and the population tends toward a state of system closure from environmental influences. In a symbiotically interdependent population there are always some units directly involved with the environment, while the others secure access to the environment indirectly through the boundary-spanning units. As a result, organizational members of a population are selectively buffered from the environment by becoming increasingly involved in symbiotic relationships with complementary population members.

The contrasting definitions of populations and interdependence account for the different approaches in the natural selection and collective action views. Natural selection theorists highlight the influence of environment by defining populations in terms of their common vulnerability to environment. The greater this vulnerability, the greater will be the population effect—by definition. And by focusing on populations of homogeneous elements that are commensalistically related (i.e., indirectly related because of common dependence on environment), attention is drawn to the open system condition in which each individual element in the population interacts directly with the environment and is therefore directly influenced by it.

In contrast, the collective action view defines populations in terms of their complementary and symbiotic relationships and their degree of internal organization. Moreover, by focusing on tendencies toward closure, which remove most parts of the population from direct contact with the environment, the effects of environment are automatically played down, while the social constructions of human action are highlighted. The greater the insulation from environmental influence through system closure, the greater the population effect—by definition.

Furthermore, symbiosis stimulates creative *action;* commensalism implies *reaction.*

The symbiotic union enhances the efficiency of production or creative effort; the commensal union, since its parts are homogeneous, can only react and is suited, therefore, only to protective or conservative actions (Hawley, 1968).

Thus the development of symbiotic interdependence tempers the effects of environment through the construction of a human-made world of controlled conditions. Symbiotic community envelops organizations, and eventually populations of organizations, in a protective "social" environment that insulates it from the effects of the "natural" environment:

> As the reliance on exchange advances, the social environment actually displaces the natural environment as the critical set of influences. A population is never emancipated from its dependence on physical and animate matters, but the importance of locale declines with increasing involvement in a network of intersystem relations (Hawley, 1968).

The proactive collective action versus reactive natural selection views is also reflected in the use of the term "domain" by the former, and "niche" by the latter. Niche refers to a predefined location in a given environment to which one must adapt. Domain, as Trist describes in Chapter 2, connotes a sphere of influence or activity in which one can actively exercise sovereignty.

With these differences between collective action and natural selection views, one can more clearly appreciate Perrow's debate with Williamson and Chandler in Chapter 8. The latter argue that the concentration of resources in large multidivisional firms is the product of intractable economic laws or efficiency considerations. A collective action interpretation, on the other hand, for which Perrow could serve as a good spokesman, posits that interorganizational networks and resource concentration result from political agreement and social definition rather than economic fiat.

The notions of network corporation and system closure have immediate implication for the analysis of populations of organizations from a power perspective. This results from the fact that the key units that span network boundaries determine or regulate the conditions essential to the functions of units having only indirect relations with the environment. The role of environment-mediation confers power on such "gatekeeper" organizations. At the same time, power is not confined to boundary mediators; it is held by all other units to a degree that varies inversely with the number of steps removed from direct contact with the gatekeepers. Power is thus an attribute of function, and its asymmetric distribution varies directly with degrees of system closure (Hawley, 1968). This suggests that underlying the move toward industrial concentration through symbiotic devices such as vertical integration are motives beyond those representing an economizing of "transaction costs" (Williamson, 1975) and "administrative coordination" (Chandler, 1977).

This is why Benson (1977) characterizes interorganizational networks in terms of "political economy" rather than in terms of population ecology. The political economy perspective argues that interorganizational behavior must be explained in terms of the process of resource acquisition, and that control of resources is implicitly linked to interorganizational power, since a powerful organization can force others to accept its terms in negotiations of disputes or in cooperative ventures. The political significance of interorganizational relationships is also, we believe, what causes Perrow (1981) to directly challenge the economic-efficiency arguments of Williamson and Chandler. Perrow argues that the monopolization of control that industrial concentration brings is not the consequence of efficiency considerations but the very reason why industrial concentration takes place. Industrial concentration, in this view, represents an attempt to exploit the social environment in the pursuit of "hegemony."

Furthermore, this view of interorganizational networks in terms of power and domination does not imply that organizations throughout the network are completely immobilized by virtue of symbiosis and their domination by key functionaries. Organizations still exercise some degree of choice and display partially autonomous action. This is a point made by Gouldner (1959). Gouldner acknowledges the constraints of interdependence that exist in functional systems, but points out that not all interdependent links are of equal strength and equally binding. Some links are more loosely coupled with others. If, then, there are varying degrees of functional interdependence, so also are there degrees of functional autonomy. The existence of loose coupling indicates the possibility of independent choice and autonomous action. Moreover, the degree of functional autonomy or interdependence that particular organizations experience is also a matter of choice. Thompson and McEwen (1958) make this point by drawing attention to the trade-off that organizations make between, on the one hand, accepting interdependent ties with other organizations in order to stabilize their existence and, on the other hand, refraining from entering such relationships in order to preserve autonomy. Collective action, then, is not a functional imperative. When it does occur, it is merely a preferred mode of survival chosen by the organizations who are participant to it.

The notion of functionally autonomous organizations partially constrained by collective interdependence draws one's attention to the forces of conflict and disruption, as well as cooperation in collective action. It is here that a *pluralistic* approach to the analysis of power and to *incremental* processes of partisan mutual adjustment become increasingly relevant. Collective decision making adds problems—of power, incompatible preferences, and choosing between partisan interests—to the limitations of individual decision makers described by March in Chapter 5.

While the strategic choice view generally takes an elitist approach to power or assumes that a consensus exists among organizational decision makers, in the collective action view many decision situations are characterized by problematic preferences, unclear technologies, and fluid participation among partisan interest groups (Cohen, March, and Olsen, 1972).

Under these conditions a pluralistic model of collective problem solving and choice—as proposed by Trist in Chapter 2 for developing interorganizational domains and by Van de Ven's OA process model in Chapter 6 for assessing collective behavior—replaces the traditional rational model of decision making described by March in Chapter 5. Since a single strategic decision unit seldom commands sufficient competence and information to obtain an overview of such a complex situation, whatever decisions it makes will be arbitrary. Furthermore, since few commonly accepted preferences and technologies exist with respect to a complex problem, whatever decisions are made by a single coalition will be partisan. It is therefore highly doubtful if strategic collective decisions can or should be made solely by an elite decision-making unit. Instead the ambiguity of complex problems and the great potential for decision failures point directly to the need for decentralized, incremental, and partisan decision processes (Dahl and Lindblom, 1976; Lindblom, 1965; Lindblom and Cohen, 1979). Lindblom (1965) has shown that such a strategy imposes on no one the heroic demands for information, intellectual competence, and value judgments that are required of a central decision unit as the strategic choice view assumes. Instead rationality is obtained from the participation of a multiplicity of partisan decision makers pursuing their own interests and values in interaction with others.

> Groups become watchdogs for values they fear will be neglected by other groups: each group consequently develops sensitivity to certain lines of consequences and becomes more competent to explore them than do other groups to whom these consequences are incidental (Lindblom, 1965: 156.).

Multiple decision makers bring the energies, skills, and values that are needed to identify the relevant issues and consequences of alternative approaches to strategic problems that would otherwise be neglected by a central decision unit.

With this kind of decentralized partisan mutual adjustment going on, one might ask, "What is the ultimate criterion for obtaining order and social cohesion in the collective action view?" This question is particularly important, since environmental determinism and economic efficiency laws have been dismissed as explanations for social order and change in the collective action view. As we have seen, the pursuit of self-interest does occur in collective action, but it occurs only to the extent that is permitted within limits defined by a normative order. Thus the collective action view answers the question by pointing to the importance of *norms, customs,* and *laws* as the ultimate working rules for collective action.

As organizations enter symbiotic relationships, these relationships become infused with shared values that turn self orientations into collective orientations. Interactions eventually take place in accordance with prevailing norms, a process that is sometimes called "institutionalization" (Berger and Luckmann, 1966).

Institutionalization occurs through a long process of trial and error as some kinds of collective activities prove to be expedient while others do not. As these beneficial patterns of acting are discovered, they tend to be repeated and in time symbolized and communicated to others. Eventually people who continually interact come to share the idea that "these are the ways things should be done." It is the frequent repetition of acts over time that solidifies them as symbols and customs. Norms are thus symbolic outgrowths reflecting common experiences encountered over time during the collective struggle for existence.

This process of norm formation is not usually a rational or random endeavor, but rather emerges as an evolving set of working rules based on reasonable solutions to everyday transactions among conflicting parties. This norm-formation process represents a core contribution of John R. Commons, recognized as a founder of both institutional economics (Chamberlain, 1963) and industrial relations-collective bargaining (Kochan, 1980). Commons argued that people are not simply adapters to the working rules of collective action. Instead norms, customs, and laws are continuously evolving. In the process of dealing with each other, bargaining, negotiating, transacting, compromising, they bend and mold the customs, modify the judicial gloss on the law, and help to create the very customs that govern their economic relationships. Collective action thus controls the individual; but the individual has some power, especially in concerted effort with others, to modify the nature of collective control (Chamberlain, 1963).

> This may not be ideal, and it is not logical, neither is it revolutionary. It is the discovery, through investigation and negotiation, of what is the best practicable thing to do under the actual circumstances of conflicting economic interests, organized as they are, to impose their collective will on individuals and on each other (Commons, 1950: 25).

In the process of development and evolution, norms become dissociated from the specific situations in which they first arose and are slowly generalized to cover broad areas of collective activity. With this, they take on the character of an "institutionalized thought structure" for directing and regulating social life (Warren, 1971). As such, norms are experienced as self-evident directives, confronting social actors as moral obligations that must be adhered to. Durkheim (1933) emphasized the "moral basis of social contracts" in advanced societies in which functional interdependence among organizational units becomes progressively dominant. Norms derive their ability to direct social life from the fact that they are imbued with a sense of morality rather than sheer pragmatism, so that people feel compelled to abide by them. Moral obligation should not, however, be interpreted as external constraint, since for Durkheim it is a liberating force in social life. By making possible collective organization, it frees us from the need to contrive new patterns of acting in each situation we encounter. Compliance with norms is voluntary rather than coerced. It signifies the adoption of a collective orientation with which one identifies. Actors thus voluntarily choose to act as components of a collectivity rather than as independent agents.

The crucial themes in this collective action view can now be summarized. Interorganizational activity focuses on networks of symbiotically interdependent and yet semiautonomous and partisan individuals and groups, who interact and execute transactions to modify or construct their collective environment, working rules, and options. Organization is thus viewed as collective action that controls, liberates, and expands individual action. Change occurs primarily through collective bargaining, negotiation, compromise, and mutual adjustment among partisan interest groups. Movements toward solutions are based on norms, customs, and laws of reasonable value and practice, which are the working rules of collective action. Norm formation results from collective interaction. In the process of becoming dissociated from their specific origins and transmitted through customs and laws, norms become sources of collective regulation that apply generally. Though they arise from the expedient acts of individuals, they become regulative and take on the character of a social force. Normative cohesion, like functional cohesion, has human origins but is peculiar to collective association at the population level of analysis.

In this view the manager's role is an *interactive* one. Indeed an individual manager or person is viewed only in relation to how that person interacts or transacts activities with others, the basic unit of analysis being a transaction between parties in a network. Working rules of collective action protect the terms for a willful exchange among the parties. In this way the voluntaristic notion of individual freedom is achieved—not as a natural right but as a collective achievement.

CONCLUSION

From a practical standpoint, simple observations of organizational behavior suggest there is a ring of truth to each of the four views of organization design and behavior. Over time, individuals and organizations are confronted with problems and situations requiring them to operate within and switch among the four different views described above. In addition, a given set of organizational problems can be viewed from a number of different perspectives, and the way these problems are defined will significantly influence how they will be addressed. Thus the managerial problem is not only one of diagnosing what view of organization and management is appropriate for a given set of problems, but also one of being sufficiently flexible to switch views from one issue to another over time, and often instantaneously. In this sense, the four different views provide a *repertoire* of ways to quadrangulate on a given set of problems.

The four views also highlight that when investigators focus on different organizational questions, situations, and problems, they tend to adopt different views of structure, behavior, change, and personnel roles. This was illustrated by the comparative ease in making sense of the major research programs described in this book once they were interpreted in terms of the four views. At first the research programs might have appeared to be nonadditive and incompatible. Now, through the lenses of the four views, they appear complementary and additive because the issues and questions various investigators are dealing with have given rise to different views of organization design and behavior.

One is likely to ask, "Which view represents the most appropriate model of organization design and behavior?" This is a misdirected question for three reasons. First, it ignores the fact that each view by itself is incomplete; the weaknesses of one appear as strengths in another. Second, as we will discuss, it does not critically evaluate the validity of the scheme underlying the four views. Particularly troublesome are the operational ambiguities in making the micro-macro and deterministic-voluntaristic distinctions. The static conceptions of organization and management represented by the four views are also troublesome, claims within each view for explaining change notwithstanding. Third, such a question overlooks the reality of dialectical problems, tensions, and directions that are a normal and inherent part of collective behavior, especially in complex organizations and in populations of organizations. While the collective action view admits to some of these contradictions, in the main they do not become evident until one begins to play one view off on another.

A more productive question is, "Should the four views be integrated?" The answer depends upon one's purposes. Many organizational problems and topics of inquiry can be pursued in a more robust way by keeping the four views distinct, and by simply recognizing the existence of the separate views to broaden one's perspective on organizations. However, a partial integration of the four views has clear benefits for developing a theory of change in organization structure and behavior. As we will discuss in the next section, a reconstitution of the four views contains the basic desiderata for developing a theory of change.

PART II:
DEVELOPING A DYNAMIC PERSPECTIVE ON ORGANIZATION DESIGN AND BEHAVIOR

Our purpose in the remainder of this chapter is to call for and outline steps toward a more dynamic perspective on organizations than is available in any one of the views discussed thus far. *"How and why does change occur in organizational structure and behavior over time?"* This question is central to understanding collective behavior. Yet it is one of the major unanswered questions in each of the perspectives covered in this book. Seashore, in Chapter 3, is the most explicit in calling for a more dynamic perspective for assessing and understanding the structure and functioning of organizations:

> The complexity of organizations makes it unlikely that significant insights into causal processes will occur from casual, unguided observation. There is a need for some model or theory of change processes.

Organizations and populations of organizations, after all, are not static entities; they emerge and dissolve, grow and decline, and go through periods of stabilization, transition, and transformation. How and why do these changes come about? While most of the perspectives in this book tend to emphasize strategically planned and managed changes, they often occur without plan, by accident, and for seemingly indeterminate reasons. As Veblen (1967), Schumpeter (1947), and Commons (1950) emphasized long ago, we need a theory of collective action that takes the cumulative change of institutions as its chief concern—one that takes an historical account of the changing interaction between individual and collective behavior, the conflict between new and old forms of social orders, and key aspects of the evolving institutional environment.

Hernes (1976) and Dahrendorf (1959) have suggested that a theory of structural change should meet the following desiderata:

1. Explain both statics and dynamics of organizational functioning by including factors that explain both stability or temporary equilibria (pressures toward unity, consensus, order) and instability or disequilibria (pressures toward conflict, pluralism, and disruption).
2. Identify and explain the sources of change from both within the organization (e.g., from dialectical contradictions and tensions within the structure) and outside the organization (e.g., from exogenous environmental forces).
3. Include macro and microfactors and show reciprocal relations among them. Part-whole relations are basic to any basic understanding of "me-we" or self versus collective orientations and tensions.
4. Include time or an historical accounting system that explains the lead and lag effects of changes in micro and macroorganizational characteristics.

These desiderate can be achieved with a partial integration of the four views. "Integration" here does not mean simply collapsing the four views into one. Instead it means that certain concepts from the four views will be juxtaposed, selected, and revised to create a new theory in terms of these four desiderata. Indeed, as Kaplan (1964: 297) observes:

> A new theory requires its own terms and generates its own laws; the old concepts are not merely reorganized, but reconstituted; the old laws not just corrected, but given new meaning.

Figure 11-3 illustrates the first steps in developing such a theory by proposing a framework for examining change in organization structure and behavior over time. The figure shows that the framework: (1) reconstitutes the deterministic-voluntaristic axis to one that focuses more concretely on *structural design* and *personnel actions* within these structures; (2) replaces the micro-macro distinction with one that examines *part-whole* or "me-we" frames of reference at various levels of organizational analysis; and (3) outlines selective concepts central to each view for examining *structure, behavior,* and *performance.* Another basic dimension to the framework is *time,* which is illustrated by the arrows connecting blocks of concepts and levels of analysis. A theory of change would articulate these arrows by explaining movement in part-whole concepts of structure and personnel actions over time. This will not be possible to accomplish here, and represents a major agenda for further work. Only preliminary steps to an explanation of change in structure and behavior can be made here by discussing the implications of the dimensions underlying the overall framework.

STRUCTURAL FORMS AND PERSONNEL ACTIONS

The deterministic-voluntaristic distinction in the four views has been reconstituted to focus more concretely on whether the object of study is the structural designs of jobs, groups, organizations, and populations, or the actions of people within these structures. This was done because it is clear from the above description that the four views are more concerned with addressing different questions and aspects of organizations than they are with focusing on the same questions and phenomena from different viewpoints. While the questions are formulated differently, the central and common focus of the two deterministic views is the structural forms or designs of organizations. So also, while the assumptions differ somewhat, the two voluntaristic views commonly focus on the actions or processes of individuals or groups within structures. Indeed, apropos to our initial statement that one's degree of voluntarism-determinism predictably influences the frame of reference taken to the study of organizations, one must equally admit the possibility that the subject matter predictably influences the relative emphasis one places on voluntaristic versus deterministic approaches of investigation.

Questions about the objective structural configurations of organizations and populations and how they are selected or adapted to exogenous forces are facilitated by taking a deterministic frame of reference and a positivistic method to the subject matter. Social structure is a configuration of parts (positions and subsystems), and a structural description is a characterization of the way the components are interrelated in the overall system or population. Thus a standard procedure for schools of thought in the deterministic views is to describe the size, structural differentiation, interdependence, and integration of jobs, groups, organiza-

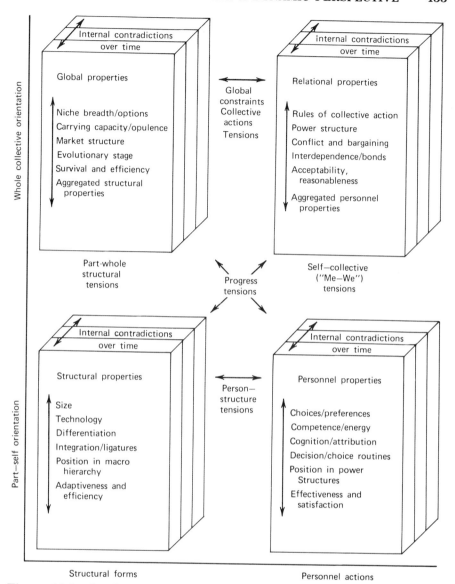

Figure 11-3 A scheme for examining change in organization structure and behavior.

tions, and populations, and then to construct models that explain this resulting output structure (Hernes, 1976: 519). The natural selection view places greater emphasis on external factors in the environment or economy that select and determine the structural forms of organizations, while the system-structuralist view emphasizes how structures are adapted internally to fit external shifts. Neither the natural selection or the system-structuralist views pay much attention to the actions of individuals within or outside of these structures.

An understanding of the values, aspirations, and actions of individuals is less amenable to a deterministic analysis. This is because people often do not behave in accordance with the laws of nature or machines as assumed with the biological or mechanical analogies relied upon in the deterministic approach. Indeed Parsons (1949: 119) clearly admits that questions dealing with values, partisan utopias, and phenomenology are very difficult to approach from a positivistic framework, and these same problems are also difficult to deal with when one tries to reduce them to either a problem of natural selection or of mechanistic determinism. If one repudiates these solutions, Parsons (1949: 114) states that there is no recourse but to abandon the positivistic approach.

A voluntaristic approach facilitates the study of personnel actions and behavior because it admits to the idiosyncratic, subjective, and crescive nature of human beings. The strategic choice view commonly focuses on the proactive but limitedly rational actions and choices of individuals in power, and it seeks to explain how these individuals construct their social orders. A similar question is pursued in the collective action view, but it is modified by the assumption that there are problematic preferences among multiple conflicting and partisan interest groups, which must be reconciled by some degree of collective regulation. As a result, the problem is not simply one of learning and overcoming the cognitive limits of a powerful set of homogeneous decision makers (in the strategic choice view), but also one of questioning and reconciling whose values and preferences are being served by the collectivity.

Thus it turns out that one reason why the deterministic-voluntaristic axis appeared useful for classifying the literature in the previous section is because these philosophical assumptions either influenced or were the consequence of questions about structural designs and the actions of people within these structures. However, the deterministic-voluntaristic dimension camouflages the essence of the subject matter being investigated. *Structural forms* and *personnel actions* are the central questions of interest to organization and management, not objective determinism or subjective voluntarism. As Dahrendorf (1959: 147) admonishes in relation to the study of social classes:

> Many of the classifiers formulate triumphantly what they call "subjective-objective" concepts of class. . . . Theirs is a cheap triumph, for it consists no more than the solution of a self-made task. They could have saved themselves, and us, many words by simply stating . . . that they proposed to deal with their subject matter both in its structure and in the personnel of this structure.

This criticism of our initial classification scheme is appropriate in the sense that it misdirects the inquiry by claiming that deterministic views of organization structure and voluntaristic views of personnel action are mutually exclusive and require one to decide in favor of one over the other approach. There are sound pragmatic, philosophical, and methodological grounds for arguing that the two approaches are not only compatible but jointly necessary for developing a dynamic appreciation of organizations.

Pragmatically, other than the purists, few will deny that organizations exhibit objective structural characteristics and that people exist within these structures who perceive what's going on, have preferences and expectations, and act in predictable and unpredictable ways. The interesting questions and problems, then, turn on how structural forms and personnel actions interrelate and produce tensions that stimulate changes over time.

For example, at the job level are the problems of selecting, socializing, and rewarding individuals for structural positions and examining how their actions over time restructure these positions. Also over the years there are the growing tensions of misfits between the changing personal aspirations, needs, and growth of individuals with changing career options for promotion and mobility among positions in the organization structure. At the group level there is the interesting question of how the structural division and integration of labor and resources among subunits both influence and are influenced by the social-psychological emergence of different norms, interaction patterns, conflict, and power relations within and between groups. At the organizational level is the question of how organization structure both influences and reflects environmental shifts and strategic choices of powerful individuals within and outside the organization over time. Finally, at the population or community level are questions about how organizational niches or market structures are both the product and constraint of collective working rules arrived at through a long series of political contests and bargains among partisan interest groups.

These questions are interesting because they: (1) admit to both deterministic and voluntaristic views of organizational life; (2) juxtapose these views by reciprocally relating structural forms and personnel actions at comparable levels of analysis; and (3) focus on how these relationships unfold over time in complementary and contradictory ways.

Unfortunately, the interesting aspects of these questions are often destroyed when attempts are made to reconstitute these observable patterns and events into theoretical models. Because of training, socialization, and cognitive limitations, most theorists reduce the observed complexity by: (1) constructing a unidirectional causal model among a limited set of factors, over a narrow slice of time, which is assumed to be in equilibrium; and (2) grounding and justifying their models in one of two metatheoretical approaches of inquiry, determinism or voluntarism.

The problem with most unidirectional causal models of organizations is that they are conceptually vacuous and empirically incorrect. As Weick (1979) states, "When any two events are related interdependently, designating one of those two *cause* and the other *effect* is an arbitrary designation" (p. 77). Most theorists and "managers get into trouble because they forget to think in circles. . . . Problems persist because managers (and theorists) continue to believe that there are such things as unidirectional causation, independent and dependent variables, origins, and terminations" (p. 86).

Examples are pervasive: job satisfaction predicts performance (Brayfield and Crockett, 1955); efficiency annihilates power (Williamson, 1978); structure follows strategy (Chandler, 1962); environment, technology, and size determine structure (Aldrich, 1979; Woodward, 1965; Blau and Schoenherr, 1971); ends determine means (Galbraith, 1977); and the past determines the present (Simon, 1947). These assertions are wrong because each relationship also operates in the reverse direction: performance affects satisfaction (Lawler and Porter, 1967); power dominates efficiency (Perrow, Chapter 8); strategy making is retrospective justification of an organization's structure (Staw, 1977); structure predicts technology and size, and when aggregated defines the environment (Van de Ven, 1977, 1979); means determine ends (March, Chapter 5); and the future predicts the present (Commons, 1950).

In each of these examples causation is circular, not linear. Moreover, in efforts to identify ultimate causes and effects, the most interesting parts of these examples have been ignored, namely, an investigation of the process over time by which the loops in these circular relationships unfold. To say that A causes B and B causes A is predictive, but it is conceptually vacuous until one can explain the process by which this reciprocal relationship unfolds over time.

One explanation for the unidirectional logic in many models of organization is found in the deterministic versus voluntaristic assumptions and methods that theorists use to ground and justify their models. Because determinism and voluntarism have historically been viewed as antithetical, it is commonly believed that if one adopts a deterministic approach it is necessary to negate and oppose the voluntaristic view and vice versa. Philosophically and methodologically, this belief is not correct.

Over the centuries, the voluntarism-determinism debate among philosophers has centered on the following two statements.

The deterministic argument is: (A) Every physical event has a cause; (B) all human actions are physical events; therefore (C) all human actions are caused. The voluntaristic argument is: (A) all responsible acts are free acts; (B) but some acts are responsible; therefore (C) some acts are free. These two statements represent a paradox; taken singly, each seems incontestably true, but taken together they are logically inconsistent. Over the centuries philosophers have attempted to resolve the paradox in one of two ways: (1) by showing one of the arguments to be false by attacking the validity of premises A or B in either statement; or (2) by showing that each does not in reality entail the contrary of the other. Unable to convincingly deny the validity of premises in either statement, no satisfactory conclusion to the debate has been reached to date in terms of the first approach (O'Connor, 1971).

With regard to the second approach, a consistency hypothesis has been widely hailed among recent philosophers as a solution to the paradox; arguing that determinism and free will are compatible, indeed, some claim that free action is impossible without a degree of determinism.

> To say that my conduct is free is to say it is under my own control—i.e., guided by my own intentions, motives, and desires. To say this is not to say that my conduct is in any way uncaused (meaning a description of regularities, not a prescription for compulsory regularity). Thus, it is not paradoxical to say the same action is both caused and free (O'Connor, 1971: 74).

This exercise in logic provides a method for integrating the deterministic and voluntaristic approaches to organizational analysis. The method turns on whether each approach is presented as the *negation* or the *contrary* of the others. For example, a determinist might *negate* the voluntaristic view by stating that "autonomous choice and enactment are not all-powerful determinants of organization structure," whereas another might assert the *contrary* by stating, "Organization structure is not enacted or autonomously chosen; instead, human choice and perceptions are determined by external environmental forces." As Gouldner (1980: 82–88) notes, the negation simply states what is not, not what is; it leaves open the question of what is being affirmed. The contrary, however, opposes or negates a statement *and* adds the alternative to the statement. While the contrary is a dramaturgically stronger and more positive statement, it argues for replacing one view for another and for polarizing positions into mutually exclusive views. Negation is a weaker and more ambiguous statement that presents no positive alternative to what it opposes, but simply rejects. However, the negation permits an integration of seemingly divergent views because it leaves the question open to a number of plausible alternative explanations, including the possibility of the contrary. For to say that choice and enactment are not all-powerful is not necessarily to say that they are weak; to say choice is not autonomous is not necessarily to say that choice and enactment are dependent. Thus, by considering the deterministic and voluntaristic approaches as simply the negation (not the contrary) of each other, it is not inconsistent to integrate findings obtained from the two approaches. However, an integration based on an ambiguous negation of one view by another threatens the identity and dissolves the boundaries of each view.

Part-Whole Relations

The micro-macro distinction in the four views has been reconstituted in Figure 11-3 to focus on part-whole or self versus collective ("me-we") frames of reference for examining change in structural forms and personnel actions. On the surface, this was done to avoid the semantic ambiguity and the arbitrary classifications that the terms "micro" and "macro" organization have come to take on over the years. It turns out, however, that these semantic and arbitrary designations have significant substantive consequences.

Unfortunately, very few attempts have been made to examine organizational problems and topics across levels of analysis. What is particularly notable in all the research programs included in this book is that they all include several levels of organizations in their investigations. Most organizational analysts, reinforced by the curricula in their schools and disciplines, have tended to carve up the field by levels of analysis (i.e., the individual, the group, the organization, the population) and to establish their distinctive niches by focusing narrowly on selective problems or issues that appear most observable at their chosen level of organizational analysis.

Such a division of scholarship not only inhibits an in-depth understanding of selective topics within a particular level of organization, but it also tends to mask the very problems and issues central to understanding why and how change occurs in organizations. This is because with the present divisions, one tends to overlook that: (1) many theories that purport to be macro organizational are in fact dealing with micro issues, and those that purport to be micro are macro in perspective; (2) many problems apparent at one level of organizational analysis manifest themselves in different and contradictory ways at other levels; and (3) social change is a dialectical process, a major part of which originates from conflicting forces produced by opposing part-whole relationships in collective behavior.

1. *Many studies that purport to investigate macro organizational phenomena rely upon or develop micro organizational theories, and vice versa.* Witness, for example, the following:

Many management "strategy and policy" studies that focus on the firm as a total unit are based on psychological theories of individual cognition, decision behavior, and learning (e.g., Steiner and Miner, 1977; Lorange, 1980).

So-called "micro" studies of choice behavior are becoming increasingly macro as the focus evolves from the bounded rationality of individuals to collective decision-making conditions of problematic preferences, unclear technologies, and fluid participation among multiple participants (March and Olsen, 1976).

Marx's theory of macro social and macro economic change is in essence a social-psychological theory consisting of two levels of social structure and two parties. The parties are two interdependent classes caught in a fatal conflict because of their respective roles in the whole structure. The class in power defends the status quo (system of ownership and relations of production) that it presently controls and has inherited; the subordinate class attacks, not so much out of resentment against its oppression, but in the name of a new technology or future potential for satisfying its wants and needs (Dahrendorf, 1979: 55).

The institutional economics view of collective action by Commons (1950) can be examined productively as a small group sociogram consisting of five parties to a transaction: two buyers, two sellers, and a sovereignty.

The obvious implication is that those investigating macro organizational topics can learn much from psychology and social psychology, just as the micro organizational investigators can significantly broaden their understanding by relying on sociology, political science, and institutional economics.

A less obvious implication is that it is easy to fall into "the fallacy of the wrong level" (Galtung, 1967) when one is not clear as to the level of organization being studied or the disciplinary base used to examine it. Analogous to the ecological and individualistic fallacies in measurement (Hannan, 1970), this fallacy is committed when one projects onto groups special characteristics or properties that are in fact aspects of individuals and vice versa. People, not organizations or environments, make decisions and have goals. The natural selection theorists commit the fallacy of the wrong level in their explanation of social change. In essence, Aldrich (1979) proposes that the environment, not managers, selects the organizational forms that will survive or fail. What does the environment refer to? If it is not an aggregation of many people, then we are at a loss to know who does the selecting and why particular organizational forms were chosen (Weick, 1979: 90). As Berger and Luckmann state, "Man is capable of producing a world that he then experiences as something other than a human product" (1966: 57). One easily loses sight of and mislabels microorganizational characteristics and behavior when they are aggregated to a macrolevel of analysis.

2. *Many problems and solutions apparent at one level of organization manifest themselves in different and contradictory ways at other levels.* As a social structure, an organization consists of patterned social relations within and between its parts and the whole. As Figure 11-3 illustrates, at the micro level one focuses on the analytical structural and personnel properties of the parts in the collective. At the macro level the focus is on the global and relational properties of the whole collective (Lazarsfeld and Menzel, 1969). These global and relational properties can in turn be viewed as the structural and personnel properties of the organization when examined as a member of a population or network of organizations. However, one's compass or frame of reference is substan-

tially altered when the focus is on the relationships between the parts and the whole or between micro and macro levels of analysis.

For example, relying on the concept of requisite variety, Weick (1979), March and Olsen (1976), and Aldrich (1979) have argued that with increasing environmental complexity, uncertainty, and variety, the overall structure of the organization becomes more complex, loosely coupled, decentralized, particularistic, and anarchistic. If this is so, then the structure of the individual parts or groups within the organization will become more simple, tightly coupled, hierarchical, universalistic, and cohesive—all the factors that lead to nonadaptiveness, narrowness, and "group think." Although Weick et al. clearly did not intend or write about this consequence, it is the result of a basic principle of opposite part-whole relations established in 1908 by Georg Simmel. "The elements of differentiated social circles are undifferentiated, those of undifferentiated ones are differentiated" (Blau translation, 1964: 284). Conant and Ashby's (1970) principle of requisite variety at the macrolevel turns out to be a law of requisite simplicity at the micro level.

Burrell and Morgan (1979) classify organization theories in terms of "regulation," those that emphasize an underlying unity, consensus, order, and maintenance of the status quo in organizations, and "radical change," those that focus on conflict, coercion, contradictions, and disruptive forces inherent in organizations. The radical change "paradigm" includes Marxian perspectives, while Burrell and Morgan classify the rest of the extant literature into the regulation "paradigm." This is an unfortunate classification, because it can be shown that any macro theory of conflict and coercion includes a micro theory of order and consensus and vice versa.

In his theory of social change, Marx posits the development of a fatal struggle, conflict, and revolution between proletariat and bourgeoisie classes. However, he fails to give due recognition to the forces of cohesion and unity within the classes. Systems and structural-functional theories of organizations have been attacked by Marxists (Dahrendorf, 1959; Burrell and Morgan, 1959) and action theorists (Silverman, 1970) alike for their inability to explain change because of the emphasis on order, consensus, and unity. While this is true at the macro organizational level, at the micro level it is only possible because of coercion, domination, and control of disruptive tendencies. If this were not so, there would be no need for rules, indoctrination, socialization, and control mechanisms in organizations; these are central concepts in structuralist theories of organization. By classifying organizational theories into separate paradigms of "regulation" and "radical conflict," instead of recognizing that elements of order versus conflict and consensus versus coercion are necessarily present at either micro or macro levels of any theory of organizations, Burrell and Morgan have unwittingly defined away an important source of the very dialectical forces that are central to a theory of change in structural forms and personnel actions.

3. *Change in organizational structure and behavior is a dialectical process of forces that originate not only from outside but also from inside the organization.* Complementarities and contradictions inherent in part-whole relations and between structural constraints and personnel actions are the major internal forces that stimulate change.

With a few notable exceptions, much of the organizational literature has focused on exogenous or external factors that produce change in organizational structure and behavior. Witness, for example, the emphasis on the environment, technology, resource scarcity, and individual differences as the major predictors of organization structure and behavior in the natural selection and system-structuralist views. The notable exceptions include Gomberg (1974), Gouldner (1959), Dahrendorf (1959; 1979), Blau (1964), and Hernes (1976), who emphasize that intrinsic sources of change—particularly those emerging from tensions between part-whole relations—need to be incorporated to explain change in social structure.

Gomberg (1964) points out that the very concept of organization implies the existence of conflict—conflict with other individuals, the environment, other individual organizations, and above all, conflict within the organization. If no conflict were present, there would be no need for organization, as the ends of individuals would be realized without any effort. The mere expression of a desire would be self-actuating. Gomberg goes on to show that the cyclical history of business organizations can be interpreted in terms of the Hegelian dialectic of *thesis, antithesis, and synthesis.*

> The structuring of an organization is identified with the thesis. The resulting hierarchy spawns the seed of its own opposition, the antithesis. The need for revision is generated within the womb of the organization by the activity of the old hierarchy. The need for new and revised functions grow until they challenge the existing hierarchy. This antithesis, when fully developed, challenges the existing structural hierarchy. Out of this clash emerges either decline or a new hierarchy and set of relationships which we identify as the new temporary synthesis. This synthesis now emerges as the thesis in a new cycle of conflict and thus the process repeats itself as innovating organizers or entrepreneurial managers pursue their satisfactions from the continuous building up of tensions in order to savor their subsequent release. The history of management can be interpreted as this kind of dynamic process. (Gomberg, 1964: 52–53)

Through the establishment of working rules, customs, and laws of collective action (Commons, 1950), safeguard mechanisms of due process have been established to prevent these conflicts from becoming a war of mutual extermination between contesting parties. However, the area that remains without a mechanism of due process today is conflict between middle and upper levels of management. As Evan (1960) pointed out, the subordinate member of the managerial hierarchy, in contrast with the unionized manual worker, is at the mercy of the decisions of his or her immediate superior; these superiors, in decisions regarding their subordinates, may function simultaneously as judge, juror, and prosecutor.

From a structural viewpoint, Gouldner (1959) has stressed that varying degrees of both autonomy and interdependence of subunits in an organization are an important source of change in social structures. Centralized direction of an overall organization paradoxically implies a degree of functional autonomy for subunits in order for each to be able to effectively organize its operations to meet the unique task requirements it was delegated. This autonomy of subunits serves as a catalyst for change, because they in effect are "exogenous" social forces contained within the macro structure to which it must continuously adjust.

Blau (1964) further refined Gouldner's concept by noting that the dependence of subunits—not so much on each other as on the larger social structure—directly conflicts with their autonomy. "The conflict is inevitable, since both some centralized coordination and some autonomy of parts are necessary for organized collectivities" (1964: 303). Blau goes on to show that the relations between groups and collectivities are manifest in their interdependence, in the mobility of individuals between them, and in the social interaction between individuals acting as representatives of their groups and in their roles as group members, whether this involves actions in the pursuit of collective or individual ends. Since individuals can simultaneously belong to many groups, Blau's image of part-whole relations is not one of concentric circles with mutually exclusive memberships at each level. Instead it is one of intersecting circles because networks of social relationships that define group structure are interpenetrating and overlapping, and the boundaries between them are neither sharp nor fixed; "groups expand and contract with the mobility of members in and out of them" (Blau, 1964: 284).

These part-whole relations were recently extended by Dahrendorf (1979) to examine change in both social structure and personnel action. He argues that the concept of "life chances"—the structural options from which individuals can choose and the ligatures that enable them to make their choices—should be a key concept for the understanding of social change. *Options* are the objective alternatives, opportunities, or possibilities of action given by a social structure from among which an individual can choose, even if they are often prescribed by a person's role. "Option" and "choice" are the macro structural and the micro personal sides of the same coin. Options are structural opportunities for choice, the directions in which the individual can choose to go. *Ligatures* are allegiances or links with others that are weighted with emotional feelings of bondage. "Ligatures" and "bonds" are the micro structural and the macrointerpersonal relations sides of the same coin. Ligatures give meaning to the structural position or role that the individual occupies, while bonds express the relationship of the individual to others in the collectivity. Ligatures create bonds and thus the foundation of action; structural options require individual choices and are thus open for the future.

With these part-whole dimensions, Dahrendorf (1979) argues that advances and declines in life chances are a product of the dialectics between options, choices, ligatures and bonds. Ligatures without options are oppressive. Feudal caste structures were largely all ligatures and no choice; what people could do depended on their status or role, since there were few alternative options. Modernization and division of labor increased options that extended opportunities for individual choice, and in a sense greater freedom. However, options without bonds are meaningless because the mere opportunity of choice without a defined position represents a social vacuum or desert in which lack of coordinates make any direction equally preferable to any other. The extension of options and choices inevitably imply a disruption of ligatures and a reduction in the intensity of bonds, simply because of human limitations in maintaining the intensity of bonds with increasing numbers of ligatures. Ties are severed and new roles or structural positions are created when people choose and make use of the options offered by a social structure. Dahrendorf (1979) concludes that social progress, or advancements in life chances, occurs when a balance is obtained in the inverse relation between choices or options and bonds or ligatures.

The immediate implication of Dahrendorf's argument for organization design and behavior is that there is an ongoing dialectic among these part-whole dimensions of structure (ligatures and options) and personnel action (choices and bonds) that may explain change and progress in structural forms and personnel action. Macro organizational structural differentiation creates new options from which individuals can choose. Exercise of this choice to enter a new option implies that the individual alters or creates a new position in the micro level of the structure. Associated with this new position will be a revised set of roles that define the new ligatures and bonds of the individual with others in the whole collectivity. Bonds and ligatures are socially constructed, give meanings, and legitimate the new position that the individual occupies. Through time, the individual interacts and establishes more intense bonds with some and less intense bonds with others as he or she becomes involved in relations of power and authority that all collective action implies. Conflict and power struggles in the collectivity emerge over the control and distribution of institutionalized options. However, those in power become weaker the more they try to defend the institutionalized structure of options with antiquated norms, customs, and laws that are no longer considered legitimate mechanisms for regulating conflict. The power struggle reaches a climax when new options are envisioned and become the rallying focus to galvanize disparate interest groups within the collective to join together to do battle with those in power in order to actualize the new options in the social structure. These new options provide new opportunities for individual choice and represent the start of the next cycle of change in structural forms and personnel action.

In summary, a theory of structural change should show how macro variables affect individual choices and behavior and how these micro dynamics in turn change macro structure and behavior. Micro components of a theory of change will often incorporate macro phenomena as constraints or opportunities, and macro structure and behavior are generally the intended and unintended results of aggregates of individual actions and choices (Hernes, 1976).

CONCLUSION

This is as far as we have come. It is clear that we have far to go to develop a perspective sufficiently dynamic to address the question, *"How and why does change occur in organizational structure and behavior over time?"* Since this question is central to understanding collective behavior, it should become a major agenda item for future theory and research.

This chapter reviewed the diverse schools of thought on organization design and behavior, including those in this book, and classified them into four basic perspectives: system-structural, strategic choice, natural selection, and collective action views of organizations. These four views are not independent of each other, having largely emerged historically as a reaction to each other. The four views represent very different conceptions of organizational structure and of individuals—their roles, capabilities, opportunities, and limitations in changing the form and functions of organizations. As a result, each view offers a different account of how organizations are created, change, behave, and dissolve.

However, by itself each perspective constitutes an incomplete description; the weaknesses of one view appear as strengths in another. We therefore attempted to reconstruct the four views, which hopefully may provide a more realistic and broader repertoire for understanding how and why change occurs, not only in organizational structures but also in the roles and behavior of individuals within them. To understand these changes, we argued that there is a need to examine the tensions and contradictions that emerge over time between part-whole or individual and collective levels of organizational analysis and between structural designs and the actions of people at each of these levels. Much further work is needed to develop this framework for explaining how and why change occurs in organizational design and behavior. It represents a challenging and exciting agenda for future theory, research, and practice. As Czeslaw Milosz stated during his Nobel lecture in poetry for 1980:

> In a precarious balance of opposites a certain equilibrium can be achieved thanks to a distance introduced by the flow of time. "To see" means not only to have before one's eyes. It may mean also to preserve in memory. "To see

and describe" may also mean to reconstruct in imagination. A distance achieved thanks to the mystery of time must not change events, landscapes, human figures into a tangle of shadows growing paler and paler. On the contrary, it can show them in full light, so that every event, every date becomes expressive and persists as an eternal reminder of human depravity and human greatness. Those who are alive receive a mandate from those who are silent forever. They can fulfill their duties only by trying to reconstruct precisely things as they were and by wrestling the past from fictions and legends (Milosz, 1981: 14).

REFERENCES

Ackoff, R. (1974). *Redesigning the Future,* New York: Wiley.

Aldrich, H. (1979). *Organizations and Environments,* Englewood Cliffs, NJ: Prentice Hall.

Astley, W. G., and A. H. Van De Ven (1981). "Central Perspectives and Debates in Organization Theory," Philadelphia: Center for the Study of Organizational Innovation, University of Pennsylvania, Discussion Paper 101.

Benson, J. K. (1977). "Organizations: A Dialectical View," *Administrative Science Quarterly* 22:1–21.

Blau, P. M. (1964). *Exchange and Power in Social Life,* New York: Wiley.

Blau, P. M., and R. H. Schoenherr (1971). *The Structure of Organizations,* New York: Basic Books.

Blauner, R. (1964). *Alienation and Freedom,* Chicago: University of Chicago Press.

Brayfield, A. H., and W. Crockett (1955). "Employee Attitudes and Employee Performance," *Psychological Bulletin* 52,5:396–424.

Berger, P. L., and T. Luckmann (1966). *The Social Construction of Reality,* Garden City, NY: Doubleday.

Burrell, G., and G. Morgan (1979). *Sociological Paradigms and Organizational Analysis,* London: Heinemann Educational Books.

Campbell, D. (1969). "Variation and Selective Retention in Socio-Cultural Evolution," *General Systems* 16:69–85. Reprinted in H. Aldrich, Ed., *Organizations and Environments,* Englewood Cliffs, NJ: Prentice Hall.

Chamberlain, N. (1963). "The Institutional Economics of John R. Commons," in *Institutional Economics,* Berkeley: University of California Press.

Chandler, A. (1962). *Strategy and Structure,* Garden City, NY: Anchor Books.

Chandler, A., (1977). *The Visible Hand,* Cambridge: Harvard University Press.

Cohen, M. D., J. G. March, and J. Olsen (1972). "A Garbage Can Model of Organizational Choice," *Administrative Science Quarterly* 1,17:1–25.

Commons, J. R. (1950). *The Economics of Collective Action,* Madison: University of Wisconsin Press.

Conant, R. C., and R. W. Ashby (1970). "Every Good Regulator of a System Must Be a Model of That System," *International Journal of Systems Science* 1,2:89–97.

Dahl, R., and C. Lindblom (1976). *Politics, Economics and Welfare,* Chicago: University of Chicago Press.

Dahrendorf, R. (1959). *Class and Class Conflict in Industrial Society,* Stanford, CA: Stanford University Press.

Dahrendorf, R. (1979). *Life Chances: Approaches to Social and Political Theory,* Chicago: University of Chicago Press.

Deutsch, K. W. (1951). "Mechanism, Organism and Society: Some Models in Natural and Social Sciences," *Philosophy of Science* **18**:230–252.

Durkheim, E. (1933). *The Division of Labor in Society,* trans. by G. Simpson, New York: Free Press.

Etzioni, A. (1968). *The Active Society,* New York: Free Press.

Evan, W. (1960). *The Organization Man and the Due Process of Law,* New York: Bell Telephone Laboratory, mimeograph.

Freeman, J. (1980). "The Unit Problem in Organizational Research," in W. M. Evan, Ed., *Frontiers in Organization and Management,* New York: Praeger.

Freidman, J. (1973). *Retracking America,* Garden City, NY: Doubleday.

Galbraith, J. R. (1977). *Organization Design,* Reading, MA: Addison-Wesley.

Galtung, J. (1967). *Theory and Methods of Social Research,* New York: Columbia University Press.

Gomberg, W. (1964). "Entrepreneurial Psychology of facing Conflict in Organizations," in G. Fisk, Ed., *The Frontiers of Management Psychology,* New York: Harper and Row.

Gouldner, A. (1959). "Organizational Analysis," in R. Merton, R. Broom, and L. Cottrell, Eds., *Sociology Today,* New York: Harper and Row.

Gouldner, A. (1980). *The Two Marxisms: Contradictions and Anomolies in the Development of Theory,* New York: Seabury Press.

Hackman, J. R., and E. E. Lawler (1971). "Employee Reactions to Job Characteristics," *Journal of Applied Psychology,* Monograph, **55**:259–286.

Hannan, M. T. (1970). "Problems of Aggregation and Disaggregation in Sociological Research," *Working Papers in Methodology,* No. 4, Chapel Hill, NC: Institute for Research in Social Science.

Hannan, M. T., and J. Freeman (1977). "Obstacles to Comparative Studies," in P. S. Goodman, J. M. Pennings, and Associates, Eds., *New Perspectives on Organizational Effectiveness,* San Francisco: Jossey-Bass.

Hawley, A. H. (1968). "Human Ecology," in D. L. Sills, Ed., *The International Encyclopedia of the Social Sciences,* New York: Crowell-Collier-Macmillan.

Hernes, G. (1976). "Structural Change in Social Processes," *American Journal of Sociology* **82**,3:513–545.

Homans, G. C. (1961). *Social Behavior: Its Elementary Forms,* New York: Harcourt, Brace and World.

House, R., and L. Wigdor (1969). "The Effects of Performance on Job-Satisfaction," in L. L. Cummings and W. E. Scott, Eds., *Readings in Organizational Behavior,* Homewood, IL: Richard Irwin.

Kaplan, A. (1964). *The Conduct of Inquiry: Methodology for Behavioral Science,* New York: Chandler.

Katz, D., and R. L. Kahn (1978). *The Social Psychology of Organizations,* 2nd ed., New York: Wiley.

Kochan, T. A. (1980). *Collective Bargaining and Industrial Relations,* Homewood, IL: Richard Irwin.

Kuhn, T. S. (1962). *The Structure of Scientific Revolutions,* Chicago: University of Chicago Press.

Lawrence, P. R., and J. W. Lorsch (1967). *Organizations and Environments,* Cambridge: Harvard Business School.

Lazarsfeld, P. F., and H. Menzel (1969). "On the Relation between Individual and Collective Properties," in A. Etzioni, Ed., *A Sociological Reader in Complex Organizations,* New York: Holt, Rinehart and Winston.

Lawler, E. E., and L. W. Porter (1967). "The Effect of Performance on Job Satisfaction," *Industrial Relations* **7**,1:20–28.

Lindblom, C. (1965). *The Intelligence of Democracy*, New York: Free Press.

Lindblom, C., and D. K. Cohen (1979). *Usable Knowledge: Social Science and Social Problem Solving*, New Haven: Yale University Press.

Lorange, P. (1980). *Corporate Planning: An Executive Viewpoint*, Englewood Cliffs, NJ: Prentice-Hall.

Mannheim, K. (1940). *Man and Society in an Age of Reconstruction*, New York: Harcourt, Brace and World.

March, J. G., and J. Olsen (1976). *Ambiguity and Choice in Organizations*, Oslo, Norway: Universitetsforlaget.

Marx, K. (1930). *Capital*, Vol. 2, New York: International Publishers.

McKelvey, W. (1979). "Comment on the Biological Analog in Organizational Science, on the Occasion of Van de Ven's Review of Aldrich," *Administrative Science Quarterly* **24**,3:488–493.

McKelvey, W. (1981). *Organizational Systematics: Taxonomy, Evolution, Classification*, in press.

Mead, G. H. (1956). *On Social Psychology*, A. Strauss, Ed., Chicago: University of Chicago Press.

Milosz, C. (1981). "The Nobel Lecture," *New York Review of Books* **28**,3:11–14.

O'Connor, D. J. (1971). *Free Will*, Garden City, NY: Anchor Books.

Parsons, T. (1949). *The Structure of Social Action*, 2 vols., New York: Free Press.

Parsons, T. (1951). *The Social System*, New York: Free Press.

Pennings, J. M. (1980). "Strategically Interdependent Organizations," in P. Nystrom and W. Starbuck, Eds., *Handbook of Organization Design*, New York: Oxford University Press.

Pfeffer, J., and G. R. Salancik (1978). *The External Control of Organizations: A Resource Dependence Perspective*, New York: Harper and Row.

Porter, L. W., E. E. Lawler III, and J. R. Hackman (1975). *Behavior in Organizations*, New York: McGraw-Hill.

Rank, O. (1941). *Beyond Psychology*, New York: Dover Publications.

Roethlisberger, F., and W. Dickson (1949). *Management and the Worker*, Cambridge: Harvard University Press.

Salaman, G. (1980). "Roles and Rules" in G. Salaman and K. Thompson, Eds., *Control and Ideology in Organizations*, Cambridge: MIT Press.

Schumpeter, J. (1947). *Can Capitalism Survive?*, New York: Harper and Row.

Silverman, D. (1970). *The Theory of Organizations*, New York: Basic Books.

Simmel, G. (1955). *Conflict and the Web of Group Affiliations*, New York: Free Press.

Simon, H. A. (1947). *Administrative Behavior*, New York: Free Press.

Skinner, B. F. (1972). *Beyond Freedom and Dignity*, New York: Knopf.

Staw, B. M. (1977). "Motivation in Organizations: Toward Synthesis and Redirection," Chapter 2 in B. M. Staw and G. R. Salancik, *New Directions in Organizational Behavior*, Chicago: St. Clair Press.

Steiner, G. A., and J. B. Miner (1977). *Management Policy and Strategy: Text, Readings, and Cases*, New York: Macmillan.

Thompson, J. D. (1967). *Organizations in Action*, New York: McGraw-Hill.

Thompson, J. D., and W. J. McEwen (1958). "Organizational Goals and Environment: Goal-Setting as an Interaction Process," *American Sociological Review* **23**:23–31.

Trist, E. L., and K. Bamforth (1951). "Some Social and Psychological Consequences of the Longwall Method of Coal Getting," *Human Relations* **4**:3–38.

Trist, E. L., G. W. Higgin, H. Murray, and A. B. Pollock (1963). *Organizational Choice,* London: Tavistock.

Van de Ven, A. H. (1977). "A Panel Study on the Effects of Task Uncertainty, Interdependence, and Size on Unit Decision Making," *Organization and Administrative Sciences* **8,**2:237–253.

Van de Ven, A. H. (1979). "Review of Aldrich's *Organizations and Environments,*" *Administrative Science Quarterly* **24,**2:320–326.

Van de Ven, A. H., and A. L. Delbecq (1974). "A Task Contingent Model of Work-Unit Structure," *Administrative Science Quarterly* **19,**2:183–197.

Van de Ven, A. H., D. Emmett, and R. Koenig, Jr. (1974). "Frameworks for Inter-organizational Analysis," *Organization and Administrative Sciences Journal* **5,**1:113–129.

Veblen, T. (1967). *The Theory of the Leisure Class,* New York: Penguin Books.

Von Bertalanffy, L. (1968). *General System Theory,* New York: George Braziller.

Warren, R. (1967). "The Interorganizational Field as a Focus for Investigation," *Administrative Science Quarterly* **12**:396–419.

Warren, R. (1971). *Truth, Love and Social Change,* Chicago: Rand-McNally.

Weeks, D. R. (1973). "Organisation Theory—Some Themes and Distinctions," in G. Salaman and K. Thompson, Eds., *People and Organizations,* London: Longmans.

Weick, K. (1979). *The Social Psychology of Organizing,* 2nd ed., Reading, MA: Addison-Wesley.

Williamson, O. E. (1975). *Markets and Hierarchies,* New York: Free Press.

Williamson, O. E. (1978). "Efficiency Annihilates Power," given as a lecture at the *Center for the Study of Organizational Innovation Colloquium Series*, Philadelphia.

Woodward, J. (1965). *Industrial Organization: Theory and Practice,* London: Oxford University Press.

Zaleznik, A., and D. Moment (1964). *The Dynamics of Interpersonal Behavior,* New York: Wiley.

Author Index

Subject Index